Lecture Notes in Artificial Intelligence   3690

Edited by J. G. Carbonell and J. Siekmann

Subseries of Lecture Notes in Computer Science

Michael Pěchouček   Paolo Petta
László Zsolt Varga (Eds.)

Multi-Agent Systems and Applications IV

4th International
Central and Eastern European Conference
on Multi-Agent Systems, CEEMAS 2005
Budapest, Hungary, September 15 – 17, 2005
Proceedings

 Springer

Series Editors

Jaime G. Carbonell, Carnegie Mellon University, Pittsburgh, PA, USA
Jörg Siekmann, University of Saarland, Saarbrücken, Germany

Volume Editors

Michael Pěchouček
Czech Technical University in Prague
Department of Cybernetics
Czech Republic
E-mail: pechouc@labe.felk.cvut.cz

Paolo Petta
Medical University of Vienna
Institute of Medical Cybernetics and Artificial Intelligence
Centre for Brain Research
Austria
E-mail: Paolo.Petta@MedUniWien.ac.at

László Zsolt Varga
Computer and Automation Research Institute
of the Hungarian Academy of Sciences
Hungary
E-mail: laszlo.varga@sztaki.hu

Library of Congress Control Number: 2005932125

CR Subject Classification (1998): I.2.11, I.2, C.2.4, D.2, H.5.3

ISSN   0302-9743
ISBN-10   3-540-29046-X Springer Berlin Heidelberg New York
ISBN-13   978-3-540-29046-9 Springer Berlin Heidelberg New York

Springer is a part of Springer Science+Business Media

springeronline.com

© Springer-Verlag Berlin Heidelberg 2005
Printed in Germany

Typesetting: Camera-ready by author, data conversion by Scientific Publishing Services, Chennai, India
Printed on acid-free paper   SPIN: 11559221   06/3142   5 4 3 2 1 0

Preface

The aim of the CEEMAS conference series is to provide a biennial forum for the presentation of multi-agent research and development results. With its particular geographical orientation towards Central and Eastern Europe, CEEMAS has become an internationally recognised event with participants from all over the world. After the successful CEEMAS conferences in St. Petersburg (1999), Cracow (2001) and Prague (2003), the 2005 CEEMAS conference takes place in Budapest. The programme committee of the conference series consists of established researchers from the region and renowned international colleagues, showing the prominent rank of CEEMAS among the leading events in multi-agent systems.

In the very competitive field of agent oriented conferences and workshops nowadays (such as AAMAS, WI/IAT, EUMAS, CIA, MATES) the special profile of CEEMAS is that it is trying to bridge the gap between applied research achievements and theoretical research activities. Our ambition is to provide a forum for presenting theoretical research with an evident application potential, implemented application prototypes and their properties, as well as industrial case studies of successful (but also unsuccessful) agent technology deployments. This is why the CEEMAS proceedings volume provides a collection of research and application papers. The technical research paper section of the proceedings (see pages 11–499) contains pure research papers as well as research results in application settings while the application papers section (see pages 500–530) contains papers focused on application aspects. The goal is to demonstrate the real life value and commercial reality of multi-agent systems as well as to foster communication between academia and industry in this field.

CEEMAS is also very special and unique in the fact that it is constantly contributing to building an agent research community. The programme committee has decided to create a special collection of short papers to provide an opportunity to present ongoing research work with the potential of achieving mature and higher-impact research results in the near future. This allows researchers to expose their work for constructive criticism and discuss their projects with other experts in an early phase of their research. On the other hand this also provides the audience with fresh, innovative and highly motivating ideas that may deserve further investigation. Short papers have been also divided into research (see pages 531–631) and application (see pages 632–664) tracks.

The topics of the CEEMAS proceedings cover an enormously wide range of areas such as: abstract and specific agent architectures, methods and modelling approaches for agent oriented software engineering, agent communication and protocols, and also classical problem domains such as learning, planning, trust and reputation. Besides formal domains such as logical modelling and game-theoretical approaches to agency, substantial attention has been paid to scalability, robustness and performance issues as well as methods for coordination and teamwork. CEEMAS also features papers about applications from the field of manufacturing, utility distributions, Internet trading, virtual enterprises or defence.

We received 113 submissions, and each paper was reviewed by at least two independent reviewers. Of the submitted papers, 48 were accepted as full research papers and 3 as full application papers. In addition, 8 short application and 25 short research papers were accepted.

Many individuals and institutions have supported the organisation of this conference and made CEEMAS 2005 a high-quality event. Our special thanks go first to the authors and invited speakers for their invaluable and strenuous work. Also, the work of the Programme Committee members who accepted the heavy load of the two-phase review of a large number of contributions is gratefully acknowledged. We are especially thankful to the conference department of the Computer and Automation Research Institute of the Hungarian Academy of Sciences, and in particular to Magdolna Zsivnovszki, for their excellent organisational activities and the computer work related to the preparation of the electronic versions of this volume.

Separate thanks go to AgentLink, the European Coordination Action for Agent-based Computing, for the continual support of the CEEMAS conferences from their very initiation in 1999 in St. Petersburg, and to AITIA Inc., for supporting CEEMAS 2005.

As a result, the present collection of papers provides a valuable resource for researchers in the field of multi-agent systems and open distributed systems in general.

July 2005   Michal Pěchouček
                                                                   Paolo Petta
                                                                   László Z. Varga

Organisation

CEEMAS Steering Committee

Barbara Dunin-Keplicz, Poland
Michael Luck, UK
Jörg Müller, Germany
Michal Pěchouček, Czech Republic
László Z. Varga, Hungary
Vladimir Gorodetski, Russia
Vladimír Mařík, Czech Republic
Edward Nawarecki, Poland
Paolo Petta, Austria

CEEMAS 2005 General Co-chairs

General Chair: László Z. Varga, Hungary
Programme Co-chair: Michal Pěchouček, Czech Republic
Programme Co-chair: Paolo Petta, Austria
Tutorials Chair: Andrea Omicini, Italy
Industrial, Demonstrations Track Chair: Gábor Tatai, Hungary
Posters Chair: Katalin Bognár, Hungary

CEEMAS 2005 Programme Committee

Stanislaw Ambroszkiewicz, Poland
Magnus Boman, Sweden
Luís Botelho, Portugal
Monique Calisti, Switzerland
Cristiano Castelfranchi, Italy
Krzysztof Cetnarowicz, Poland
Helder Coelho, Portugal
Ulises Cortés, Spain
Frank Dignum, The Netherlands
Grzegorz Dobrowolski, Poland
Danail Dochev, Bulgaria
Edmund H. Durfee, USA
Shaheen Fatima, UK
Stephan Flake, Germany
Martyn Fletcher, UK

Roberto A. Flores, Italy
Matjaz Gams, Slovenia
Marie-Pierre Gleizes, France
Piotr Gmytrasiewicz, USA
Chihab Hanachi, France
Karin Hummel, Austria
Toru Ishida, Japan
Catholijn Jonker, The Netherlands
Matthias Klusch, Germany
Jiří Lazansky, Czech Republic
John-Jules Meyer, The Netherlands
László Monostori, Hungary
Luc Moreau, UK
Eugenio Oliveira, Portugal
Andrea Omicini, Italy

Mihaela Oprea, Romania
Sascha Ossowski, Spain
Marek Paralie, Slovakia
Radoslav Pavlov, Bulgaria
Jeremy Pitt, UK
Agostino Poggi, Italy
Stefan Poslad, UK
Omer Rana, UK
Alex Rogers, UK
Robert Schaefer, Poland
Onn Shehory, Israel
Carles Sierra, Spain
Alexander Smirnov, Russia

Olga Stipánková, Czech Republic
Niranjan Suri, USA
Simon Thompson, UK
Robert Tolksdorf, Germany
Chris van Aarts, The Netherlands
Wiebe van der Hoek, The Netherlands
József Váncza, Hungary
Rineke Verbrugge, The Netherlands
Filip Verhaeghe, Belgium
Herbert Wiklicky, UK
Steven Willmott, Spain
Franco Zambonelli, Italy

Additional Reviewers

Alexander Adrowitzer
Eric Andonoff
Holger Billhardt
Tibor Bosse
Henrique Lopes Cardoso
Mehdi Dastani
Alberto Fernández
Pierre Glize
Mark Hoogendoorn
Bernhard Klein
Francesca Marzo
Simon Miles
Nicoleta Neagu
Brendan Neville

Luis Nunes
Fabio Paglieri
Daniel Ramirez-Cano
Luis Paulo Reis
Giovanni Rimassa
Ana Paula Rocha
Alexei Sharpanskykh
Victor Tan
Ivan Trencansky
Peter-Paul van Maanen
Giosue Vitaglione
Pavel Vrba
Joachim Zottl

CEEMAS 2005 Local Organisers

Local arrangements chair: Gusztáv Hencsey, Hungary
Secretariat: Magdolna Zsivnovszki, Hungary

Table of Contents

Invited Paper

Research Papers

Agent Communication, Interaction Protocols and Mechanisms

Agent Models and Architectures

Agent Oriented Software Engineering, Modelling and Methodologies

Coordination, Teamwork, Social Knowledge and Social Reasoning

Formal Methods and Logic in MAS

Learning and Evolution of MAS

Personal Agents and Agent-Based User Interfaces

Planning and Scheduling in MAS

Scalability, Robustness and Performance Issues

Self-organising Systems in Emergent Organisations

Trust, Reputation, Reliability, Security and Intrusion Detection

Application Papers

Short Research Papers

Agent Communication, Interaction Protocols and Mechanisms

Agent Models and Architectures

Coordination, Teamwork, Social Knowledge and Social Reasoning

Learning and Evolution of MAS

Personal Agents and Agent-Based User Interfaces

Planning and Scheduling in MAS

Scalability, Robustness and Performance Issues

Self-organising Systems in Emergent Organisations

Trust, Reputation, Reliability, Security and Intrusion Detection

Short Application Papers

Palpable Computing and the Role
of Agent Technology

Giovanni Rimassa, Dominic Greenwood, and Monique Calisti

Whitestein Technologies AG, Pestalozzistrasse 24, 8032 Zürich, Switzerland
{gri, dgr, mca}@whitestein.com

Abstract. This paper presents a computing approach, called *Palpable Computing*, complementing and extending Ambient Computing notions and techniques. The main contribution of this paper lies in defining and discussing what role Agent Technology can play in Palpable Computing, and which of its ideas and technical approaches are (or are not) well suited to be adopted as a support for the Palpable Computing vision.

1 Introduction

Ambient computing has been associated with various trends and definitions. Regardless of which perspective is taken, the common and central focus is on a new paradigm for user centric computing and interaction. In the near future, people will have access to distributed networks of intelligent devices populating their daily environments and providing them with information, communication and diverse services at any time and in any location. These networked systems are expected to adapt themselves to user requirements and even anticipate their needs. The ability to appropriately engineer such systems has generated and is continuously triggering challenging questions in several areas of computer science, engineering and networking.

Palpable computing aims to provide some concrete answers by extending and complementing the ambient computing vision, concepts and techniques. The key idea, as detailed in the following sections, is to define systems that users can intuitively notice, understand, use and control in the most appropriate way according to the specific context/situation. Software that adapts to changes in the environment, minimizing human intervention and service interruption, is the central foundation of such an approach. Our proposition is that *Agent Technology* offers powerful concepts and consolidated techniques to specify, design and build palpable software systems [1] - as discussed in the second part of this paper.

2 The PalCom Project

Defining and investigating Palpable Computing is the overall goal of the PalCom project [4]. PalCom is an integrated project in EU's 6th Framework Programme

M. Pěchouček, P. Petta, and L.Z. Varga (Eds.): CEEMAS 2005, LNAI 3690, pp. 1–10, 2005.

under the initiative *"The Disappearing Computer"* in the *Future and Emerging Technologies (FET)*, part of the *Information Society Technologies*. The project started in January 2004 and will last four years.

The project consortium is composed by twelve partners, mostly academics, with a very diverse set of skills and interests. A significant percentage consists of Computer Science departments and IT companies, but other partners deal with Architecture, Interaction Design, and Ethnography. The chosen approach to effectively leverage this broad set of know-how and expertise was to act simultaneously in a technology-driven and a user-driven fashion.

The term "palpable" is meant to denote systems that can be noticed and mentally apprehended. Palpable systems should support people in understanding and controlling their operation, letting the users choose the level of information provision and automation they see most fit for a specific situation. While a precise definition of "palpable system" and "palpability" will be built throughout the project duration, a first step was to set up a dialectic relationship between Palpable Computing and Ambient Computing. This was achieved with the definition of six pairs of *palpable qualities*:

1. **Invisibility** complemented by **Visibility**
2. **Scalability** complemented by **Understandability**
3. **Construction** complemented by **De-construction**
4. **Heterogeneity** complemented by **Coherence**
5. **Change** complemented by **Stability**
6. **Sense-making** complemented by **User control**

The first element of each pair in the list above is generally a cornerstone of Ambient Computing, whereas the second element opposes it and represents the new focus added by Palpable Computing. In true dialectic fashion, the advancement is expected to be made by overcoming the conflict and finding an innovative, better, balance.

The PalCom project is expected to provide two major results. On the one hand, the technology-driven activity and the user-centered prototyping and scenario evaluation will yield an *Open Architecture* to drive design and implementation of software system that can exhibit palpability. On the other hand, the overall effort in characterizing what palpability is and which systems and use circumstances are palpable, will result in the production of a *Conceptual Framework* serving as guidance to conceive, understand, and assess palpable systems in the broadest perspective.

2.1   The PalCom Open Architecture

The Open Architecture is the technical nexus of the PalCom project. Its goal is to serve as the means of transcribing the palpable qualities discussed in Section 2 into a set of interrelated, computationally realised concepts drawn into a coherent and encompassing structure. This implies that it must capture the essence of how human actors interact with, and within, their everyday environments through distributed populations of palpable and non-palpable resources.

To some degree, the existing architectural specification builds upon established concepts in relevant fields of software engineering expertise. But it also specialises this know-how to weave a consistent computational fabric that, as the sum of its parts, delivers the means to pragmatically enable aspects of palpability in genuine and useful ways.

Realised as a set of documents, the scope of the architecture includes:

- **PalCom Runtime environment (PRE).** An optional infrastructual element, the PRE allows PalCom Software Components to execute across multiple hardware devices and operating systems. It defines a virtual machine that has a common object format and common binary standard, and is designed to be language independent. In use, it enables strong portability, mobility and dynamic updating of software components.
- **PalCom Communication Model.** Connectivity is a fundamental aspect of the PalCom Architecture as it empowers devices and services to collaborate. PalCom devices are required to be network enabled, but not bound to any particular media or protocol. The basic model supports announcement and discovery of deployed services via publish/subscribe. Peer to peer messaging is also supported.
- **PalCom Component Model.** This model defines the common unit of software functionality, deployment, and composition in PalCom. As a unit of functionality, a PalCom Component represents both infrastructure and domain-specific software building-blocks. Components can be composed to form aggregated behaviours and are instantiated as PalCom Runtime Components.
- **PalCom Resource Model.** Resources are those elements of the Architecture that can be manipulated and reasoned about. This spans from available memory on a device, to a human user in terms of their role and associated actions. The Resource Model defines the relationships between these resources and how they may be manipulated to realise palpable applications.
- **PalCom Contingency Model.** Closely associated with the Resource Model, this addresses a core quality of palpability - resilience. It defines how contingent plans can be devised to ensure continued, seamless operation of active systems whilst providing visibility over the reasons why a problem has occurred.
- **PalCom Assembly Model.** A PalCom Assembly defines the scope of an application in terms of the resource interrelationships required for its delivery. At the highest level assemblies consist of a set of interacting devices.

The relationship between these models is described by an Architecture Overview document that consolidates the major concepts, qualities and usage guidelines to provide an abstract specification to guide system designers in the creation of concrete palpable applications.

The key concepts identified by the PalCom Architecture are illustrated in Figure 1. As can be seen, the notion of *resource* is envisioned as a central concept, encompassing both low-level device-based resources such as memory, and high-level resources such as components, services, devices and actors.

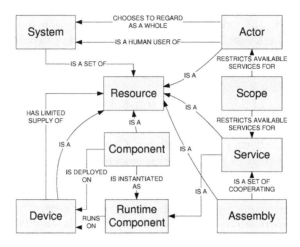

Fig. 1. Key concepts of the PalCom Open Architecture

Actors interact with a PalCom system through *assemblies*, which realize the notion of a task whose execution is adaptable toward actor-specific needs. To execute their tasks, assemblies orchestrate appropriate domain-specific and infrastructure services available within the PalCom System and configure them according to the tasks quality of service requirements. When orchestrated into a specific assembly, *services* must interact cooperatively with one another to fulfil their respective and collaborative tasks. This requires a *runtime infrastructure* that allows PalCom assemblies and services to execute and communicate with one another in, what is, an inherently distributed computing environment. This runtime infrastructure must also support the concurrent execution of multiple assemblies, which may compete with one another for available resources. The PalCom Open Architecture follows a strict component-based approach. This helps in the realization of services in a strictly modular fashion and will typically employ a shared repository to promote reusabability.

2.2   The PalCom Conceptual Framework

As shown in Section 2.1, the PalCom Open Architecture, albeit covering many aspects, is basically a high-level specification for the design of software that can run on a variety of devices with strong networking capabilities. However, PalCom features both the ambitious goal to go beyond Ambient Computing and a diverse expertise set in the project consortium. In engineering-driven efforts the most general conceptual document is the system architecture: the Conceptual Framework is both wider in scope and more general in abstraction than the PalCom Open Architecture. It generalizes some concepts and ideas from it, but also adds an entirely new dimension.

The added dimension relates to *use*. While the Open Architecture guides the designers of palpable systems and applications, the Conceptual Framework is supposed to allow both users and designers to understand and organize knowl-

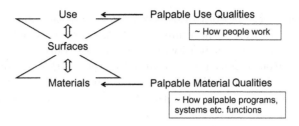

Fig. 2. The basic metaphor of PalCom Conceptual Framework

edge about palpable systems. The *use* dimension stems from the multidisciplinary approach adopted in PalCom, one of the main staples of which is *participatory design* [7].

The PalCom Conceptual Framework is still a work in progress. So far, a first metaphor has proven to be useful in relating technology-centered and use-centered aspects of PalCom. Three items compose the metaphor:

1. *Materials.* This item represents how palpable systems function.
2. *Use.* This item represents how people work/interact with palpable systems.
3. *Surfaces*, representing the boundary between palpable systems and the people using them.

The elements of the metaphor and their relationships are depicted in Figure 2.

The *material* concept aims at suggesting that a computational system, due to the way it has been built, has some properties of its own (akin to the physical and chemical properties of a "real" material). Properties of the materials in this metaphor are some of the familiar non-functional software qualities: *flexibility, resilience, security, scalability.*

Such properties affect what can and cannot be done with the system, but they are by no means sufficient to predict how the system will be used once made available to real people. The *use* concepts, instead, consider exactly what happens in that case. Most of the qualities that concern the use are then relating to how people perform their tasks. Some examples of PalCom use properties are:

- **Indexicality.** This property is also named *situatedness.* It refers to the property that people's action and sentences have, of receiving (part of) their meaning through the context in which they are performed.
- **Intersubjectivity.** This property relates to the fact that people usually assume that their own actions and language will be understood by others in a way that will facilitate interaction.
- **Reciprocity of Perspective.** This property signifies that people generally assume that, if they put themselves into someone else's shoes, they would see the situation in the same way.

As the list above shows, key properties belonging to the *use* dimension are strongly dependent upon a context that is extremely volatile and hard to capture, being linked to social and behavioral traits of users and of their operating environment.

The Conceptual Framework bridges *materials* and *use* dimensions with the concept of *surfaces*. Physical materials lend themselves to use only through their surfaces; likewise, palpable systems will have to expose only a part of themselves to the outside. Surfaces must not be reduced merely to the idea of interfaces in a software engineering sense. What is exactly a surface still depends on the use dimension: two different users could form two equally effective models of the same system. In the PalCom metaphor, the two are using the same material through two different surfaces. Most of the concepts pertaining to the *surfaces* dimension show an external view on some technical entities in a computing system. As an example, the definition of *Connection*, in the context of the *surfaces* part of the PalCom metaphor, is not what a network engineer would give, but rather what a person that is proficient with using wireless devices, though potentially unaware of the technical details of their working, would.

3   Agent Technology and Palpability

Previous sections described the PalCom project goals. The main question is now whether, and how, can Agent Technology provide conceptual and practical contributions to this effort. Quite a few hints suggest a positive answer: ideas and requirements emerged in the initial phases of work are pretty much in line with essential features of the Agent Technology approach.

At the Open Architecture level, a loosely coupled and very dynamic component model is advocated. It is also stated that, in order to support the emergence of effective usage from human actors, palpable systems will have to follow a *task-oriented* model (as opposed to a more standard, application-oriented one), focussing on implementing user goals. The communication model fosters asynchronicity, relying on publish-subscribe discovery and communication protocols, while resorting to direct message passing between mutually aware components.

All the above prescriptions nicely match multi-agent systems (autonomous software components, perceiving from and acting on their environment, managing their own resources, communicating asyncronously with one another either through direct messaging or through a shared environment).

At the Conceptual Framework level, the *materials* dimension is a more abstract rendering of the Open Architecture and matches Agent Technology the same way. Slightly more surprising, instead, is that the *use* dimension also has many agent-friendly concepts. Indexicality immediately recalls agent situatedness, while intersubjectivity and reciprocity of perspective can readily point to behavioral implicit communication [2] or mutual agent modeling.

This is not due to chance at all, but follows from the multi-agent systems approach, where researchers have since long drawn inspiration from the social sciences. However, social sciences concepts and theories must be distinguished from their versions adopted and implemented in software multi-agent systems. When taking *agency* in its broadest meaning, it is true that agent situatedness is exactly indexicality. However, when considering a software agent, the situatedness it can exhibit is just a stripped down version of what a human can do.

While situatedness is effective in improving its behavior, it by no means make a software agent comparable to a human.

Thus, software agents should be left out of the *use* dimension. Actually, their exhibiting lesser versions of most use properties suggests a critical Agent Technology contribution in the *materials* and *surfaces* dimensions.

Much work is still needed to bring about the overall Palpable Computing vision and to precisely define the role of Agent Technology into it. The next subsections consider the two first research directions the authors are presently following.

3.1 User-Aware Surfaces

Applying Agent Technology at the *surfaces* level naturally recalls *user agents*. Surfaces in PalCom Conceptual Framework are the contact point between human users and a software system, where user agents reside. The more or less common design is to select one specific software agent and attach it to a human user.

Often, system designers follow the presentation approach of giving that software agent an antropomorphic or zoomorphic semblance. The user is then invited to think of the software system as being somehow inhabited by a kind of synthetic creature, helping with the user tasks. Other times, a more standard GUI or VUI is used. Anyway, from the point of view of the system, the human user is wrapped and shielded by her own user agent. The resulting situation is thus:

– Human users are invited to see interacting with the software system as *being like* interacting with another human.
– The software system is designed to consider interacting with human users as *being like* interacting with another autonomous software entity (agent).

A very interesting critique of this approach, from a sociological perspective, is made in [5], and partly in [6]. With no completeness ambition, some relevant points made there are:

– User agents foster the idea of a perfect, almost invisible infrastructure at the service of the user, abstracting away the human labor that is still involved in performing most high-tech tasks.
– While trying to keep the previous promise, the software models humans as autonomous, rational entities. It then engineers the human-machine interaction as between equals (i.e. both parties are autonomous and rational).
– However, it is generally the case that agency doesn't lie in the qualities of the human or of the machine. Instead, agency is a relational capacity that is enacted when a (specific) human and a (specific) machine come together and interact within a context that is made by the whole history of both.

Willing to accept this critique, an antropomorphic user presentation risks being counterproductive for an user agent. The level of agency in an interaction depends on the unique human-machine shared context. Inducing the human user to think of the software agent as another human would generate behaviors and expectations that are unsuited to actual system capabilites.

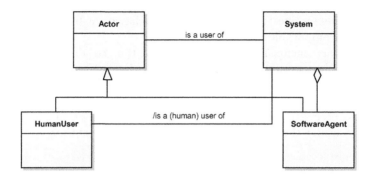

Fig. 3. An UML model of Actor-System interaction structure

Even more important, though, is the converse: having the software agent modeling its user as *just* another software agent ends up unduly restricting the interaction. The system must be aware of when it is interacting with a human user. Some interaction properties will stay the same whether the user is a human or not, but in order to obtain a palpable system, other interaction traits will drastically change. A possible UML diagram describing this awareness is depicted in Figure 3.

As Figure 3 shows, a software agent can both be a part of a system and also act as the external user (named Actor in the Conceptual Framework). The association *"is a user of"* connects an actor and the system it uses, and regardless whether the actor is a human or a software agent. However, the derived[1] association *"is a (human) user of"* captures the fact that just knowing that the actor is a human adds valuable information for the system.

The following list presents the features that a software agent needs to have in order to be able to effectively exploit that valuable information. An agent:

- Needs to know whether a perceived event was sent to it by a human or not (thus enabling human-to-machine behavioral implicit communication).
- Needs to model which effects of the actions it can perform can be perceived by the humans it is interacting with (thus enabling a machine-to-human behavioral implicit communication).
- Must know or infer the effect that its modification of the environment can have on the humans it is aware of.

The authors believe that, if software agents acting at the system boundary have these features, Agent Technology can provide a significant push towards realizing the vision of Palpable Computing, improving user experience with the system while leaving the interaction space open for emergence of new uses. In the terms of the PalCom Conceptual Framework metaphor, such software agents can be the key to engineer *user-aware surfaces*.

---

[1] In UML, a *derived association* is an association whose pairs can be computed from the association it derives from. In this case, each (HumanUser; System) pair in the *is a (human) user of* association is also an (Actor; System) pair in the *is user of* association.

3.2   Autonomic Materials

The PalCom Conceptual Framework chose to use the *materials* element of its metaphor to suggest that human users can perceive software systems as having some basic properties, which can be leveraged to flexibly create usages. In order to discuss a possible role of Agent Technology at the *materials* level, a first step is to initially consider physical materials and see how some consideration can be transferred to computational systems.

Some properties of physical materials, though natural, can be described by the same *feedback loop* idea that is commonly used in engineering (e.g., an elastic material is subject to a feedback force proportional to its displacement from the equilibrium position). It is also well known that the *sense-compute-act* loop of a software agent configures it as a kind of feedback controller with respect to its environment.

Recently, the IBM-fueled vision of *Autonomic Computing* [3] has added yet another perspective on feedback loops and software, claiming that software systems should be *self-regulating, self-configuring* and *self-protecting*. The overall emphasis here is on *automation* through *all-in-software feedback control of computational systems.*

Within this perspective we see that Palpable Computing arises from the *situated and contextual use* of some *computational materials* within the fabric of an application. A material is perceived as a resource that projects a tangible, yet often transient, presence into the feedback field persisting between the user surface and the computational infrastructure enacting a palpable application.

As such, a resource, whether it be e.g. memory, a physical device or human user[2], automatically reflects its functional and embodied properties to both its human and computational consumers. By positioning an agent with deliberative capabilities within this field we can tune the use of resources to the changing context of an extant application while maintaining a coherent understanding of the effect on human engagement. This balance between the management of potentially complex and dynamically fluxing task structures, and the reflective condition of participating human users is one that requires the agent be embodied with decisiveness and thus the ability to take initiative in determining solutions within a changing resource landscape.

Another aspect of the agent role is to effect contingent reasoning in resolving problem conditions arising from within the computational environment. If a device fails, for example, the agent will use its comprehension of that device's influence both on the environment and its human users to assess the impact and take contingent actions to enact a repair or other resolution. Contingency is essentially the capability of adapting to both predictable and unpredictable events, the former resolveable with contingent planning, but the latter requiring a degree of reasoning to determine courses of action. This positions the agent as a means to regulate stability through causal adaptation.

---

[2] A human user can be treated as a resource in terms of their role and the operational characteristics associated with that role.

4   Conclusions

Today, there is a significant amount of work that is attempting to understand how we, as humans, will continue to explore and experience interaction with computing machinery throughout our everyday lives. Palpable Computing aims at extending and complementing the Ambient Computing vision by focusing on the definition of *palpable* systems as systems that can be noticed and mentally apprehended by users.

This paper has proposed two main research directions the authors are currently pursuing to understand and propose how Agent Technology concepts and mechanisms can contribute to ground and consolidate the definition of palpability and the implementation of palpable systems.

Acknowledgements. The authors would like to thank Thomas Lozza for his valuable contribution and all PalCom partners for their collaboration. Part of the research work described in this paper has been funded thanks to the Swiss State Secretariat for Education and Research (SER) 03.0495-2 Grant.

References

1. Calisti, M., Greenwood, D., (2003) "On the Road to Ambient Intelligence", European Workshop on Multi-Agent Systems, Oxford, U.K.
2. Castelfranchi, C. "SILENT AGENTS: From Observation to Tacit Communication". In Proc. of First Int'l Workshop on Modeling Other Agents from Observations (MOO 2004), pages 25-32.
3. IBM Research. "Autonomic Computing Manifesto".
   Available at http://www.research.ibm.com/autonomic/manifesto/
4. The PalCom project Home Page.
   http://www.ist-palcom.org/
5. Suchman, L. "Figuring Service in Discourses of ICT: The case of software agents". In Wynn, E. et al (Eds.) Global and Organizational Discourses about Information Technology . Dordrecht, The Netherlands: Kluwer, pp. 15-32.
6. Suchman, L. "Figuring Personhood in the Sciences of the Artificial". Available at http://www.lancs.ac.uk/fss/sociology/papers/suchman-figuring-personhood.pdf
7. Winograd, T. "Bringing Design to Software". Addison-Wesley, 1996

A Dynamic Joint Protocols Selection Method to Perform Collaborative Tasks

José Ghislain Quenum and Samir Aknine

Laboratoire d'Informatique de Paris6,
8 rue du Capitaine Scott, 75015 Paris, France
{jose.quenum, samir.aknine}@lip6.fr

Abstract. The work achieved in multi-agent interactions design mostly relates to protocols definition, specification, etc. In this paper we tackle a new problem, *the dynamic selection of interaction protocols*. Generally the protocols and the roles agents play in protocol based interactions are imposed upon the system at design time. This static selection severely limits the openness, the dynamic behaviours agents are expected to exhibit, the integration of new protocols, etc. To address this issue, we developed a method which enables agents to select protocols themselves at runtime when they need to interact with one another. We define the concepts and the mechanisms which enable agents to perform this dynamic selection.

1 Introduction

Generally, the interaction protocols which support the execution of agents collaborative tasks are imposed upon multi-agent systems (MAS) at design time. This *static* protocols selection severely limits MASs in the openness and dynamic integration of new protocols perspectives. As an illustration of this problem, consider a goods transportation multi-agent system composed of *trader agents* (T_i) and three kinds of *carrier agents*: *air carrier agents* (AC_i), *land carrier agents* (LC_i) and *rail carrier agents* (RC_i). Let's consider that two independent designers, A and B, modelled the agents of the system. A *trader agent* T_1 from designer A expects an *air carrier agent* AC_0 from designer B to transport a good g. To carry out this collaborative task, both agents need to execute an interaction which we assume is based on a protocol. Consider that A has chosen the FIPA Request Protocol [FIP01] for this interaction while B has chosen the FIPA Contract Net Protocol (CNP) for the same interaction. At runtime, when T_1 sends the (request[1]) message to AC_0, the latter will reply a not-understood message and the desired interaction won't take place. Hence, because the protocols A and B statically selected are different the needed interaction can't take place thus cancelling the execution of the related collaborative task. To address this drawback agents should be enabled to select their coordination mechanisms in order to execute collaborative tasks.

As yet, there have been some efforts [BETJ00, Dur99] to enable agents to dynamically select the roles they play during interactions using Markov Decision Processes, planning or even probabilistic approaches. However, these efforts don't suit protocol

---

[1] We designate messages by the performative they contain.

M. Pěchouček, P. Petta, and L.Z. Varga (Eds.): CEEMAS 2005, LNAI 3690, pp. 11–20, 2005.

based coordination mechanisms. Indeed, as protocols are partially sorted exchange sequences of pre-formatted messages, selecting them to execute a task requires that their descriptions match that of the collaborative task. The solutions proposed so far do not explicitly focus on protocols and do not check such compliance either. To address this void, we developed a method which enables agents to dynamically select protocols and roles in order to interact. Our method puts the usual assumptions about multi-agent interactions a step further. First, some interaction protocols may appear at runtime. Thus, starting from a minimal version, agents interaction models can grow-up by integrating these protocols from safe and authenticated libraries of interaction protocols when needed. Second, there may be different designers in the system, therefore several protocols specification formalisms may coexist.

Rather than explicitly indicating the protocols and the roles to use for all the agents which will execute the underlying interaction, we suggest that agents designers simply describe collaborative tasks in the model of the agents which should start their execution. As soon as an *agent* locates such a description, it looks for a set of protocols which may help execute the collaborative task. Switching from collaborative tasks models to protocols requires the agents to analyse both models and detect their adequacy. In this paper, we focus on the selection mechanism and assume that agents are able to perform conversions from tasks descriptions to protocols. Two important questions greatly impact the dynamic protocols selection method: (1) are the agents able to interpret all the protocols specification formalisms currently in use in the MAS? (2) do they rely on one another during the protocol selection? We identified two possible responses to these questions and therefore two possible ways to dynamically select protocols in order to execute collaborative tasks: a joint protocol selection where all the agents decide together which protocol to use and an individual protocol selection where each agent individually makes its decision which it may adjust depending on the exchange sequence. In this paper, we only describe the joint protocol selection mechanism.

We argue that our method suits MASs openness and introduces more flexibility in protocols execution since it copes with the dynamic integration of protocols. In this paper we detail the principles, concepts and algorithms of our method. We exemplify it using the goods transportation MAS briefly described above.

The paper is organised as follows. Section 2 formally defines the protocol selection problem and sheds some light on the solution we propose. Section 3 details the joint selection variant we developed. Section 4 discusses some related work and section 5 draws some conclusions.

2   The Dynamic Protocol Selection Problem

We formally define a protocol as a triple $\{\mathbf{R}, \mathbf{M}, \Omega\}$ where $\mathbf{R}$ is a set of interacting roles which can be of two types: *initiator* and *participant*, $\mathbf{M}$ is the set of messages exchanged during the protocol execution and Ω the sequence of messages exchange. An *initiator* role is the unique role in charge of starting the protocol whereas a *participant* role is any role taking part in the protocol. We assume that each agent is provided with an *interaction model*, $\mathcal{I} = \{r_1, r_2, \ldots r_n\}$, which contains the configured roles this agent can play during interactions [QSA03]. We also define a collaborative task as a set of automata which execute independently but coordinate their inter-related activities by exchanging some messages. Moreover, we classified the protocols used in MASs in three categories: (1) *1-1 protocols*, which are protocols made of two roles (initiator and participant) both of them having only one instance (e.g. Request protocol); (2) *1-1^N protocols*, again protocols made of two roles with several instances of the participant (e.g. CNP); (3) *1-N protocols*, which are protocols with several distinct participant roles each of them having only one instance (e.g. an auction protocol with one buyer, one seller and one auctioneer).

The dynamic protocol selection problem consists in enabling agents to map protocols to collaborative tasks instead of leaving the designer to decide. Concretely, given a collaborative task t_j which a set $\mathcal{A} = \{a_1, a_2, \ldots a_k\}$ of agents can execute, we state the selection problem as *how can any of these agents select a protocol and a role inside this protocol to execute t_j?* The solution to this problem is triple $(\mathcal{A}, p_j, m)$ where $\mathcal{A}$ is the set of participant agents, p_j the protocol to use and m an associative array which maps each agent to the role(s) it will play in p_j. To find out this solution, we developed two variants of a dynamic selection method. First, all the agents which will execute the task collectively select a protocol and assign roles to each agent in this protocol. This is the *joint protocol selection* which assumes that agents trust one another and that they don't dread publishing their knowledge and preferences during the selection. Second, each agent individually selects its role and execute the interaction adjusting its choice to the messages exchange sequence. This variant is called the *individual protocol selection*. It is carried out concomitantly to the targeted interaction. This variant assumes that agents do not trust one another and/or the system is heterogeneous and several agents systems with different protocols specification formalisms are plugged together. In the remainder of this paper we only describe the joint protocol selection.

3 Joint Protocol Selection

In the joint protocol selection all the agents which will perform the collaborative task validate together the protocol they'll use to interact. In order to contrast the messages exchanged during the joint selection and those of typical interactions, we introduced five new performatives which we define as follows.

call-for-collaboration the sender of this performative invites the receiver to take part in an interaction based on the protocol described in the content field. The related task is also described in this field.

unable-to-select the sender of this performative informs the receiver that it cannot play a participant role in the referenced protocol. An agent may reply this performative, though identified as a potential participant for the protocol, because of its autonomy or some errors occurred in some fields.

stop-selection the sender of this performative asks the receiver to stop the selection process the message is associated with.

ready-to-select the sender of this performative notifies the receiver of the participant roles, listed by order of preference, it can enact regarding the protocol and task it received. To avoid going back and forth about protocols sharing the same background we extended the list to compatible roles. Roles of protocols are compatible when they can execute safe interactions albeit the difference in their respective specifications. As an example the initiator role of CNP can interact with either the participant role of CNP or that of Iterated CNP (ICNP [FIP01]); while the initiator of ICNP can't interact with the participant of CNP because of the probable iterations.

notify-assignment the sender of this performative informs the receiver about the role the latter has been assigned to in the jointly selected protocol.

As outlined earlier, once the initiator agent finds the description of a collaborative task it identifies some protocols and for each protocol a set of potential participants. Both steps provide the initiator agent with a sparse matrix: potential participants linked to protocols. The initiator agent may direct the matrix exploration near protocols or agents or the both of them. Whatever exploration direction the initiator adopts, it can overcome the matrix sparsity by selecting as next element (protocol or agent) the one holding the least sparse vector. This strategy can be refined by adding some knowledge whether about protocols or agents. And coupling this knowledge to the description of the task the initiator agent will prefer selecting an agent for a given protocol because it better suits the collaborative task to perform, or find out a protocol for a given agent because of its efficacy in performing such a task.

Once the initiator has constructed its matrix and identified an exploration strategy, it invites one or several potential participants sending a call-for-collaboration wherein it encapsulates the descriptions of a protocol and a task. Each of the contacted participants may decline the invitation replying an unable-to-select. They may also accept the invitation sending a ready-to-select. When the initiator agent receives some proposals, it tries to select one of the protocols. If it succeeds, it notifies the participant(s) through a notify-assignment. The initiator may also reject all the proposals sending a stop-selection. The latter message is also sent in reply to an unable-to-select. When no protocol has been selected after an iteration, the initiator agent will take the process again until a solution is found or no more exploration is possible.

3.1 *1-1* Protocols

Since the *1-1 protocols* only contain one participant role played by only one agent, the solution to the dynamic selection problem can be refined to a couple (a_i, p_j) where p_j is the selected protocol and a_i the agent which will play the participant role. For this class of protocol, the potential participant agents are contacted one after the other.

Consider, by way of illustration, a *trader agent* T_1 which needs the air transportation of a delicate good g_2 in such a quantity that at least one *air carrier agent* can achieve it. This collaborative task, of course, requires an interaction based on a *1-1 protocol*. Let's consider that T_1 identified two *1-1 protocols*: FIPA Request and Incremental Problem Solving (IPS); IPS protocol allows an initiator and a participant to incrementally come up with a solution to a given problem. The sequence diagrams of both protocols are given in Figures 1(a) and 1(b). If only one *air carrier agent* has been identified, the selection process is performed in one iteration and if it fails the related collaborative task

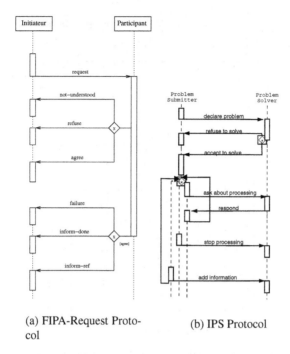

(a) FIPA-Request Protocol   (b) IPS Protocol

Fig. 1. Request and IPS protocols sequence diagrams

Table 1. Matrix for task t_1

	AC_0	AC_1	AC_2	AC_3	AC_4	AC_5	AC_6
IPS	x	x		x	x		x
Request			x	x	x		x

fails. If several *air carrier agents* have been identified, let's consider that the matrix in Table 1 is the one T_1 constructed for this task. Consider T_1 explores the matrix visiting protocols and exploits some knowledge about protocols. If the task is described so that T_1 should provide the participant agent with richer information during transportation (e.g. the air route to follow), T_1 will prefer the IPS protocol and contact agents from the set $\{AC_0, AC_1, AC_3, AC_4, AC_6\}$.

When the selection fails with the current agent and as long as there are still unexplored potential participant agents for IPS, T_1 will continue contacting them. In absence of solution when the potential participants set has been thoroughly explored for a protocol, the same process is taken again upon another protocol if there is any. In case no solution has been found and no more protocol or participant can be explored, the dynamic protocol selection fails and the subsequent task remains not executed.

3.2 $1\text{-}1^N$ Protocols

Because $1\text{-}1^N$ protocols are like $1\text{-}1$ with several instances of the unique participant role, we can also refine the solution to the dynamic selection to a couple $(\mathcal{A}, p_j)$ where

	AC$_0$	AC$_1$	AC$_2$	AC$_3$	AC$_4$	AC$_5$	AC$_6$	AC$_7$	AC$_8$	AC$_9$	AC$_{10}$
IPS_{1-1^N}	x	x	x	x	x	x	x	x	x	x	x
CNP	x	x	x	x		x		x	x	x	
$Request_{1-1^N}$	x	x	x	x	x	x	x	x	x	x	x

(a) Matrix for task t_2

	IPS_{1-1^N}	CNP	$Request_{1-1^N}$
AC$_0$		2	1
AC$_1$	3	1	2
AC$_2$	1	2	
AC$_3$			1
AC$_4$	2		1
AC$_5$	1		2
AC$_6$	1	3	2
AC$_7$	2	1	
AC$_8$	2	1	3
AC$_9$	1		
AC$_{10}$			1

(b) Agents preferences

Fig. 2. Matrix and agents preferences for task t_2

$\mathcal{A}$ is the set of participant agents and p_j the protocol to use. For this category of proto-cols the matrix is explored only in a protocol-oriented way since all the identified agents for a protocol should be contacted at the same time. Once all the contacted agents have replied, the initiator agent selects a common protocol for the agents which replied a `ready-to-select`. We devised several strategies to perform this selection but here we only describe one, *the largest set strategy*, which looks for the role the highest num-ber of agents selected. If there exists a role r_i that all the agents pointed out, then this one is selected. Otherwise, we look for a role that involves the largest set of agents. Therefore, we consider the protocols that the highest number of agents mentioned in their `ready-to-select`. If there are several such protocols, we look among them for one that the highest number of agents prefer. If there are still several such protocols, for each role r_i, we compute the difference dif_i between the set of agents e_i which pointed out r_i and the union of such sets for all the other most preferred roles except e_i: $dif_i = (e_i - \bigcup_j \{e_j\}, j \neq i)$. Then, we select the largest dif_i which corresponds to the role selected by agents which didn't much vary in their choices. Finally, if there are still several protocols we perform a random selection among the remainders.

As an example, let's consider that T_1 needs an air transportation of g_2 in such a quantity that no *air carrier agent* is able to transport it and that time and other resources constraints prevent any *air carrier agent* from performing more than one transportation turn. Thus T_1 needs to make several *air carrier agents* transport some quantity of g_2. This collaborative task should then be performed by means of a *1-1^N protocol*. In sake of illustration we introduce variants to Request and IPS protocols which we call respectively $Request_{1-1^N}$ and IPS_{1-1^N}. In $Request_{1-1^N}$ there are several instances of the unique participant role. Such a protocol better suits situations where there is a need to split the task in smaller parts and make participants execute them in parallel. In IPS_{1-1^N} there are also several instances of the unique participant role and the initiator discusses with each of them. The protocols T_1 identified as well as the agents which can enact participant roles in these protocols are given Figure 2.

Using the default strategy (the least sparse vector) with protocols, T_1 sent a call-for-collaboration to all the agents identified for IPS_{1-1^N}. The preferences of the agents are given in Figure 2(b). We use digits 1, 2 and 3 to express the degree of these preferences (1 is the highest and 3 is the lowest). Figure 2(b) reveals that IPS_{1-1^N} and $Request_{1-1^N}$ are the protocols the highest number of agents mentioned but IPS_{1-1^N} is the most preferred protocol. So T_1 selects this protocol and interacts with AC_1, AC_2, AC_4, AC_5, AC_6, AC_7, AC_8 and AC_9. AC_0, AC_3 and AC_{10} will be sent a stop-selection message.

3.3 1-N Protocols

Here again, the matrix is explored only in a protocol-oriented way. The initiator agent a_i waits for all the participants it contacted to reply and gathers the ready-to-select messages. The roles are clustered following the protocols they belong to and the protocols which have not been identified by the initiator agent are eliminated. For each protocol p, a_i maps each role r_j to a set of agents which mentioned it in their ready-to-select: $candidates(r_j) = \bigcup_k \{a_k\}$. If $candidates(r_j) = \emptyset$, the protocol r_j belongs to is no more considered in the selection process. Moreover, as there exists several participant roles in *1-N* protocols, some of them may receive their first message from other participant roles. Thus, we introduce a new relation, *father*, which we define as follows: given two roles r_1 and r_2 of a *1-N* protocol, if r_1 is the sender of the first message r_2 receives then r_1 is the father of r_2 and we note $r_1 = father(r_2)$. For each protocol the initiator agent constructs a tree t from the candidates set it constructed. The nodes of this tree are the roles of the protocol. A node r_m is child of another node r_n if $r_n = father(r_m)$. t is explored in a breadth-first way and for each node r_j of t an agent a_j (actually as many as the cardinality of the role imposes) is assigned to r_j from $candidates(r_j)$. Assigning a role to an agent can be performed by any well known resource allocation algorithm (e.g. election algorithm). An improvement during the roles assignment is to avoid situations where the same agent plays several roles in a protocol. Thus, when candidates is a singleton, its only one agent is removed from all other candidates sets it appears in when these are not singletons. As well, while exploring t, once a role has been assigned to an agent we should remove this agent from all the candidates sets it appears in provided these are not singletons.

As an example consider that the *trader agent* T_1 needs the transportation of a good g_3 stored in a particular warehouse which can only be reached by a *land carrier agent*. But, time constraints prevent us from performing this transportation only by land. Hence T_1 should coordinate different types of *carrier agents* so that g_3 gets transported on time. Concretely, a *land carrier agent* will move g_3 from the warehouse to the nearest railway station and a *rail carrier agent* will move it to the nearest airport and finally an

Table 2. Agents preferences

	r_1	r_2	r_3	r_4	r_5	r_6
AC_0			1			2
AC_1			1			2
AC_2			1			
LC_3	2			1		
LC_4	2			1		
RC_5		1				
RC_7		1				
LC_{10}	2			1		

air carrier agent will bring it to the location T_1 mentioned. Such a collaborative tasks requires a *1-N* protocol wherein the *carrier agents* play different participant roles.

Here again, we introduce new variants of Request and IPS which we call $Request_{1-3}$[2] and IPS_{1-3} respectively. In $Request_{1-3}$ an initiator requests a participant r' to perform some processing. As soon as r' agrees in performing the task it requests another participant r'' which will later request a third participant r'''. Finally, when r''' completes its processing it sends the resulting information to r'' which encapsulates it in its own result and sends it to r' which eventually sends the whole result to the initiator. In IPS_{1-3} we organised the three participants in quite a similar way adding the discussion between roles. In this example we designate by r_1, r_2 and r_3 the participant roles of $Request_{1-3}$ and r_4, r_5 and r_6 the participant roles of IPS_{1-3}. T_1 contacted agents $\{AC_0, AC_1, AC_2, LC_3, LC_4, RC_5, RC_7, RC_8, AC_9, LC_{10}\}$ for the protocol $Request_{1-3}$ and the preferences of these agents are given in Table 2. This table reveals that RC_8 and AC_9 replied unable-to-select and that no agent mentioned r_5 thus excluding the IPS_{1-3} from the selection process. Finally, T_1 constructs the candidates tree following the *father* relation and assigns each role to an agent (LC_{10} for r_1, RC_5 for r_2 and AC_2 for r_3). All the other agents receive a stop-selection message.

4   Related Work

Protocols selection in agents interactions design is something generally done at design time. Indeed, most of the agent-oriented design methodologies (*Gaia* [WJK00] and *MaSE* [DW00] to quote a few) all make designers decide which role agents should play for each single interaction. However dynamic behaviours and openness in MAS demand greater flexibility.

To date, there have been some efforts to overcome this limitation. [Dur99] introduces more flexibility in agents coordination but it only applies to planning mechanisms of the individual agents. [Bou99] also proposes a framework based on multi-agent Markov decision processes. Rather than identifying a coordination mechanism which suits best for a situation, this work deals with optimal reasoning within the context of a given coordination mechanism. [BETJ00] proposed a framework that enables

---

[2] Since we only need three participants for the task at hand.

autonomous agents to dynamically select the mechanism they employ in order to coordinate their inter-related activities. Using this framework, agents select their coordination mechanisms reasoning about the rewards they can obtain from collaborative tasks execution as well as the probability for these tasks to succeed. The main requirement the selection process faces in protocol based coordination mechanisms is whether or not there exists in the agent interaction model roles capable of supporting the desired interaction. To fill this void, we proposed a method to enable agents to dynamically select protocols basing on their interaction capacities.

5   Conclusion

Designing agents for open and dynamic environments is still a challenging task, especially in regard to protocol based interactions. Two main concerns arise from interactions modelling and design in such systems. First, how to configure interactions which are based on generic protocols so that consistent messages exchange will take place? Second, does it sound that designers always decide which protocols and roles to use every time an interaction is asked for? We address both issues by developing several methods. In this paper we focus on the second concern. We argued that due to openness and dynamic behaviours more flexibility is needed in protocols selection. Furthermore, in the context of complex applications demanding multi-protocols agents, moving from static to dynamic protocol selection greatly increases the efficiency of the system and properly handles situations closer to openness where all the protocols are not known at design time. Thus, we enabled agents to dynamically select protocols upon the prevailing circumstances.

One outcome of the dynamic protocol selection is that the protocols to use are no more hard-coded in all agents model. Rather, designers mention collaborative tasks descriptions in the *initiator agent* model making the latter in charge of initiating the interaction. Then, using the dynamic selection method we developed, they will select the adequate protocols and execute the underlying interactions. Alongside this method are three other components: the task model, the protocol model and the mechanisms to match both models. Currently these components depend on each agent designer/programmer and we aim at unifying all these components in a whole.

References

[BETJ00]   R. Bourne, C. B. Excelente-Toledo, and N. R. Jennings. Run-time selection of coordination mechanisms in multi-agent systems. In *Proceedings of the 14th European Conference on Artificial Intelligence*, pages 348–352, Berlin, Germany, August 2000.

[Bou99]   C. Boutilier. Sequential optimality and coordination in multiagent systems. In *Proceedins of the Sixteenth International Joint Conference on Artificial Intelligence (IJCAI-99)*, pages 478–485, 1999.

[Dur99]   E. H. Durfee. Practically coordinating. *AI Magazine*, 20(1):99–116, 1999.

[DW00]   S. Deloach and M. Wood.   An overview of the multiagent systems engineering methodology.   In P. Ciancarini and M. Wooldridge, editors, *Proceedings of the 1st Interational Workshop on Agent Oriented Software Engineering*, volume 1957. Springer Verlag, June 2000.

[FIP01]   FIPA. Fipa interaction protocol library specification. Technical report, Foundation for Intelligent Physical Agents, 2001.

[QSA03]   J. G. Quenum, A. Slodzian, and S. Aknine. Automatic derivation of agent interaction model from generic interaction protocols. In P. Giorgini, J. P. Muller, and J. Odell, editors, *Proceedings of the Fourth International Workshop on Agent-Oriented Software Engineering*. Springer Verlag, 2003.

[WJK00]   M. Wooldridge, N. Jennings, and D. Kinny. The gaia methodology for agent-oriented analysis and design. *Autonomous Agents and Multi-Agent Systems*, 3:285–312, 2000.

A Formal Framework for Interaction Protocol Engineering

Fernando Alonso, Sonia Frutos, Genoveva López, and Javier Soriano

Facultad de Informática, Universidad Politécnica de Madrid,
28660 Boadilla del Monte, Madrid, Spain
{falonso, sfrutos, glopez, jsoriano}@fi.upm.es

Abstract. This paper presents a formal framework devised to support interaction protocol (IP) engineering. The proposed framework is organized into three views that consider all the stages of a protocol engineering process, i.e. the design, specification, validation, implementation and management of IPs. The *modeling view* allows visual IP design. The *specification view* automatically outputs, from the design, the syntactic specification of the IPs in a declarative-type language called ACSL, which improves IP publication, localization and machine learning by agents. Finally, the *implementation view* provides a formal operational semantics for the ACSL language. This semantics allows protocol property verification and eases automatic code generation from the ACSL specification for the purpose of simulating code execution at design time, as well as improving and assuring correct IP compliance at run time.

1 Introduction

In the context of multi-agent systems (MASs), the approach to interaction based on *Speech Act Theory* [6] is one of the most widely used mechanisms for supporting activities such as information, task and resource sharing, action coordination and distribution, conflict resolution and agreement management. This approach assumes that agents carry out *communicative actions* in the same manner as other actions, i.e. to further their intentions, in an attempt to appropriately influence the mental state and behavior of other agents. On the basis of these premises, several *Agent Communication Languages* (ACLs) have been conceived that model communicative actions, also referred to as *speech acts*, as typed messages that constitute the building blocks for communication. KSF's KQML [7] and FIPA-ACL [8] are the two most significant examples of ACLs.

However, agents do not participate in isolated message exchanges, they enter into *conversations*, i.e. coherent message sequences designed to perform specific tasks that require coordination, such as negotiations or agreements. This exchange sequence may emerge spontaneously [12] or have been agreed upon beforehand and specified by means of an *interaction protocol* (IP) [11]. A priori specification of IPs and agreement on the particular protocol to be used in a given conversation eases the design of agents capable of entering into coherent conversations with other agents in open environments. The importance of IPs in

M. Pěchouček, P. Petta, and L.Z. Varga (Eds.): CEEMAS 2005, LNAI 3690, pp. 21–30, 2005.

the design of an agent society is evident not only from their fitness for structuring behavior, but also as an organizational factor [1].

This *a priori* approach necessarily depends on the provision of a *framework* to support the modeling of interactions between agents that considers all the stages of a *protocol engineering* process, i.e. the design, specification, validation, implementation and management of IPs, considered as resources. Some aspects to be taken into account when building such a framework are:

– The ease of modeling the communicative agent behavior, mainly, the behavior of agents that obey complex interaction patterns, especially open (in terms of number of roles and/or agents) and concurrent patterns.
– Protocol maintainability and ease of reuse at both the design and specification level.
– Reliability, from the viewpoint of design validation and property verification and as regards assuring proper protocol compliance by participant agents.
– Availability and accessibility of both the protocols (i.e. designs and specifications) and ongoing conversations (i.e. protocol instances, protocol state and participant agents). This aspect is related to agent interoperability in terms of interaction.
– Scalability of both the designs and specifications (ease of composition) and the ongoing conversations for adaptation to large MAS.

This paper presents a formal framework, organized into three views, which deals with all these aspects at the IPs architectural design, formal specification and implementation level. The qualities of the developed framework have been extensively tested as part of research project *TIC2001-3451*[1], the purpose of which was to develop an architecture, based on the cooperative and strongly distributed paradigm, to manage telecommunications infrastructures holonically by means of autonomous agent societies.

The remainder of the paper is organized around the three views of the proposed framework as follows. Section 2 presents an overview of the framework. We then describe the fundamental elements of first the *modeling view* (section 3) and then the *specification view* (section 4) in detail. Section 5 deals with the *implementation view*. Finally, section 6 compares our approach with other related work.

2   Overview of the Proposed Framework

The problem of IP specification is not new to MAS developers, and a wide range of solutions have been proposed (cf. [5]). We find, however, that there is a huge void between the existing proposals based on formal techniques, whose design is extremely complex (e.g. colored Petri nets [9]), and the graphic notation-based techniques (e.g. AUML [10]), which are devoid of precise semantics and rule out automatic specification exchange and interpretation for the purpose of specification simulation, validation and execution. The proposed framework intends to fill this gap by means of three interrelated views:

---

[1] Work on this project has been partially funded by the Spanish Ministry of Science and Technology.

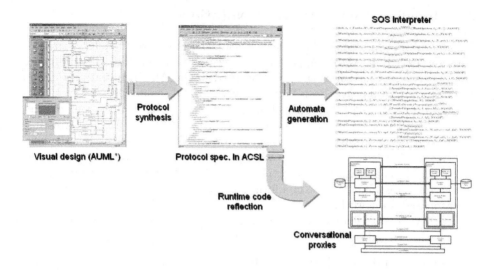

Fig. 1. Tools and products of the proposed framework

– The *modeling view* eases the visual design of IP architecture by means of an AUML-based graphic notation. The proposed notation extends existing AUML and furnishes this notation with formal semantics. This is essential for developing the *specification view*.

– The *specification view* automatically outputs the syntactic specification of an IP from its architectural design in a declarative-type language, developed by the authors, called ACSL [2]. This improves IP publication, localization and machine learning by agents. ACSL is an abstract syntax for which an XML grammar has been developed by means of the XML Schema formalism, in order to be able to validate the specifications syntactically, and to make easier their use in Internet environments.

– The *implementation view* is based on the provision of an structural operational semantics (SOS) for the ACSL language. The developed formalism allows us to verify the properties of the designed IPs, such as their termination in finite time, conversational state reachability or the absence of deadlocks or starvations. On the other hand, the developed formalism automatically outputs code from the ACSL specification for the purpose of (1) simulating protocol execution at design time and (2) improving and assuring correct IP compliance at run time.

Figure 1 shows the products of the IP engineering process and the tools of the proposed framework. These tools allow: (1) the visual composition of IPs in $AUML^*$ notation, (2) automatic ACSL specifications generation(using an XML grammar) for models built in $AUML^*$, (3) the output of a semantic interpreter associated with these specifications, and (4) the generation, by means of code reflection techniques, of conversational proxies that improve IP compliance at run time.

3   Modeling View: $AUML^*$ Notation

To support the modeling phase, the developed framework includes a graphic notation, called $AUML*$, supported by a visual modeling tool. The proposed notation is an extension of the notation used in the AUML initiative *Protocol Diagrams*, which has also been furnished with formal semantics.

The *Protocol Diagrams* proposed by the AUML initiative are extremely helpful for designing IPs. Nevertheless, while AUML notation is fine for providing a simple representation of the designer's view of an IP, it is a basic and semi-formal notation (just consider the widespread use of informal annotations). It is, therefore, inadequate as a starting point for automatically outputting the syntactic expression of the IP in a formal specification language as developed in the proposed framework.

First, we had to extend AUML notation to include other important aspects that need to be taken in account in complex interactions:

Correlation and causality Generally, agents participate in more than one dialogue at the same time. Therefore, relationships of correlation and causality between messages need to be specified so that each message can be associated with the specific IP instance to which it belongs, and messages from different IPs involved in the interaction can be related.

The time factor The time factor needs to be considered in IP design. It should be possible to specify a pause between exchanges for a finite time and establish deadlines for both an exchange sequence and for the global interaction.

Protocol exceptions Apart from describing the basic message exchange pattern, a protocol diagram should also consider the interaction flow triggered by the occurrence of a protocol exception as a result of out-of-sequence message reception, message loss, time-outs, etc.

Event management An IP should consider the occurrence of given events as triggers of a given exchange pattern.

Compensation protocols It should also be possible to express *transactional contexts* within the main exchange pattern and associate compensation protocols (cancellations, renegotiations, etc.) with such contexts.

Figure 2 shows a screenshot of the $AUML^*2ACSL$ tool which has been developed as part of the proposed framework. It illustrates the Iterated Contract Net protocol design, proposed by FIPA [11], in $AUML^*$ notation. The *symbol palette* shows the new constructs. Section 4 explains what they are used for in more detail.

Apart from the AUML extension, this notation had to be formalized semantically as a provision for formalizing the other views of the proposed framework, principally the *specification view*. To be able to output an ACSL specification, we needed a lot of information not covered in the notation proposed by AUML or, alternatively, expressed informally by annotations, apart from additional constructs not included in AUML notation. Figure 2 also shows a dialogue including some semantic elements associated with an ACL *counterPropose* exchange. The meaning of these elements is described in section 4.

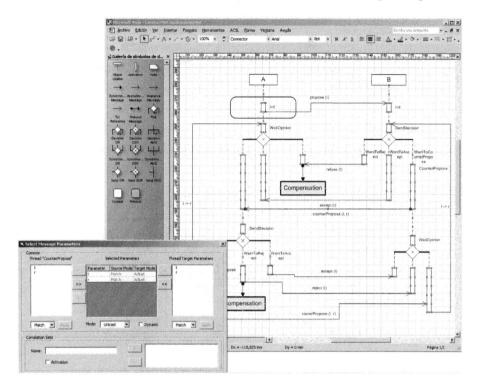

Fig. 2. $AUML^*2ACSL$ tool screenshot

4   Specification View: ACSL Language

ACSL defines an abstract syntax that establishes a vocabulary that provides
a standard formal description of the contractual aspects of IPs modeled using
$AUML^*$ for use by design, implementation and execution monitoring libraries
and tools. ACSL separates internal agent IP implementation from its external
description. This is a key point for improving communication interoperability
between heterogeneous agent groups and/or agents that run in heterogeneous
agencies (platforms). It is based on ACL messages specifying the message flow
that represents an IP between two or more agents and requires no special-purpose
implementation mechanism. The following sections describe briefly the structure
of ACSL. See [2] for a more detailed description of the language.

Figure 3 illustrates the overall structure of a protocol specification in ACSL.

It shows how the specification is composed of a *name*, a *header* and a *body*, all
defined in the context of a block element *protocol*. The *name* element identifies
the protocol for the purpose of referencing from other specifications in which
it is to be embedded or with which it is to be interlinked. The *header* element
declares the correlation sets (*cSetDecl*) and the properties (*paramSetDecl*) used
in the message exchanges for correlation and dynamic linking and to specify
the semantic elements, respectively. The body of the protocol contains the spe-

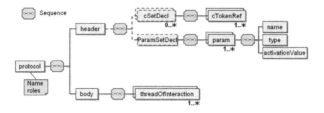

Fig. 3. Syntactic organization of a *protocol* specification

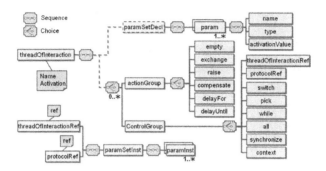

Fig. 4. Language constructs for specifying a *thread of interaction*

cification of the basic exchange pattern(*body* block). This item is formed by the composition of many *threadOfInteraction* elements that fork and regroup to describe the communicative behavior of the agent. The *threadOfInteraction* element is used to directly specify an exchange pattern or reference a protocol definition included in another specification by means of a qualified name. A *threadOfInteraction* (Figure 4) combines zero or more basic actions, references to subprotocols, conditional and iterative constructs and other *threadOfInteraction* that are interpreted sequentially, in the same order in which they are referenced.

Message exchanges (*exchange* element) are the fundamental atomic actions in agent interaction. ACSL includes only the exchange properties that are part of the protocol specification.

A *threadOfInteraction* eases the composition of an exchange pattern by means of a set of control constructs (*ControlGroup* in figure 4) that express conditional, concurrent and iterative interaction flows.

Switch: A *switch* expresses a conditional behavior equivalent to the XOR connector in AUML notation. The Boolean *multiChoice* attribute allows the *switch* to also express conditional behavior equivalent to the OR connector in AUML notation.

While: The *while* construct repeats the exchange pattern determined by a thread of Interaction an undefined number of times. The specified beha-

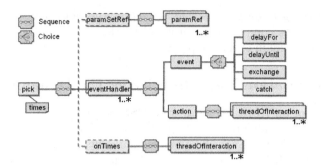

Fig. 5. Language constructs for the *pick* element

vior is executed until the given (*condition*) is no longer true. The condition is opaque, as discussed earlier.

All: The *all* construct expresses the concurrent execution of a set of interaction flows that is not subject to any time order. *All* expresses the semantics of the AND connector in AUML notation.

Pick: The *pick* construct (figure 5) expresses precondition waits. It waits for the reception of an event (or set of events) and then executes an exchange pattern associated with this event. The possible events are message reception and end of a *delay* action. If the *times* modifier is specified, *pick* will be repeated a predefined number of times (for example, to specify wait for n messages) before finally executing the exchange pattern associated with the construction *onTimes*.

Repeat: The *repeat* construct repeats the exchange pattern given by a thread of interaction a pre-established number of times. The actual number of times it is repeated is opaque, i.e. is not part of the ACSL specification.

Synchronize: The *Synchronize* construct establishes the set of threads of interaction that should be synchronized after an *All*, a multiple-choice *Switch* or an *Or*.

The atomic action *raise* in Figure 4 represents the firing of an exception related to the IP and can model real situations that call for cancellation or abnormal or unexpected termination of the protocol in question. The *raise* action causes the invocation of the IP that allows the agents to recover from abnormal situations or finish if recovery is not possible. This protocol is specified by means of an *exception* block element declared after defining the flow pattern (*threadOfInteraction* block) of the *context* with which the exception is to be associated.

In the event of an error occurring during a complex interaction that involves one or more protocols, the agent involved should be given the chance to start up a conversation characterized by one or more appropriate IPs that *compensate*, as far as possible, for this error, taking the system back to a state similar to what it was at the start of the interaction. This conversation is called *compensation protocol*. Figure 4 showed the language constructs that participate in the description of this behavior. A compensation protocol is defined in a context by means of a named *compensation* block. A *compensation* block is explicitly invoked by means of the *compensate* process that references the block name. Accordingly, the initiation of the compensation protocol by this agent can be asynchronous with respect to its main exchange pattern.

5   Implementation View: Specifying the Dynamics of IPs

The definition of an XML grammar for ACSL by means of the *XML Schema* formalism can only validate the IP specifications syntactically. To be able to validate and evaluate these specifications semantically, the ACSL language needs to be furnished with formal and operational semantics that can unambiguously describe the dynamic meaning of its syntactic constructs.

The features of ACSL have led to the use of the concept of *Structural Operational Semantics* (SOS) [4] as an approach for specifying the dynamic meaning of IPs. The *dynamic meaning* of a protocol is obtained from the dynamic meaning of the different syntactic constructs that appear in its specification. It covers the execution of the specification, including expression evaluation, message sending and reception and the execution of other non-communicative actions.

The SOS denotes a formalism that can specify the meaning of a language by means of syntactic transformations of the programs or specifications written in this language. Some special points had to be taken into account to apply the SOS formalism, designed for programming languages, to a specification language such as ACSL. The definition of operational semantics suited for ACSL represents a three-step process:

1. Definition of a terminal and labeled transitional term-rewriting system based on the operational semantics described in [3],
2. Definition of the interpreter I for this system, as proposed in [4], whose behavior is specified by a set of production rules. I is modeled as a function whose argument is a protocol P specified in ACSL in an environment ω, and describes the behavior of $\langle P, \omega \rangle$ as an (in)finite series of productions like $\langle P, \omega \rangle \rightarrow \langle P_1, \omega_1 \rangle \rightarrow \langle P_2, \omega_2 \rangle \rightarrow \ldots$ If P ends, then the result is $\langle END, \omega_n \rangle$.
3. Process of outputting the interpreter for each ACSL construct.

The provision of formal semantics for ACSL means that the IP specification can be analyzed to find out whether the IP has certain properties, such as termination in finite time, conversational state reachability or no deadlocks and starvations. On the other hand, the provision of operational semantics makes it possible to automatically derive IP implementation from protocol specification, easing its simulation and the automatic generation of proxies that assure that each participant effectively complies with the protocol rules and provides assistance for protocol machine learning. The details of this view are left for a later paper.

6   Related Work and Conclusions

Other work has been completed along the lines presented in this paper. Thus, [13] presents a coordination language called COOL, which is founded on speech act-based communication and a structured conversational framework that captures the coordination mechanisms used by agents. COOL has been used to design and validate coordination protocols for multiagent systems. The coordination activity is modeled as a conversation between two or more agents and is specified by means of a declarative language whose syntax is intrinsically linked to the finite state machine model, which is an impediment to its use in concurrent coordination environments. More recently, [14] explored the conversion of COOL policies to Petri Nets to enable their analysis. The language provides support for conversation embedding, error recovery and conversation continuation, but it does not cover aspects like message correlation and obscures specification. [15] presents the Z specification language, which is applied to contract-net protocol formalization as a goal-directed system. The *Agentis* framework presented later in [16] also specifies the IPs in Z. [17] presents the AgenTalk coordination language, which adds the notion of inheritance to conversation specification. [18] introduces the notion of a conversation suite as a collection of widely used conversations known by many agents and [19] uses definite clause grammars to specify conversations. Finally, [1] proposes a coordination model for specifying IPs, possibly open and concurrent. The model is supported by a high-level Petri Net-based Object-Oriented language called CoOperative Objects (COO) that covers all the steps of protocol engineering, enabling it to express concurrency or validate and simulate the specified protocol. But this is at the cost of obscuring their interpretation, because the model does not have a graphic representation close to the designer's view of the protocol. Although each of these approaches contributes in one way or another to our general understanding of the concept of framework, more work is needed to improve the design, sharing and use of IPs by agents. This paper has attempted to contribute to this effort by presenting a formal framework organized as three viewpoints which improves IP modeling, publication, localization, exchange and machine learning by agents. It also allows protocol property verification and eases automatic code generation (protocol synthesis) for the purpose of simulating code execution at design time, as well as improving and assuring correct IP compliance at run time.

References

1. Hanachi, C., Sibertin-blanc, C.: Protocol Moderators as Active Middle-Agents in Multi-Agent Systems. In Autonomous Agents and Multi-Agent Systems, Vol. 8. Kluwer Academic Publishers, The Netherlands (2004) 131-164
2. Soriano, J., Alonso, F. and López, G.: A Formal Specification Language for Agent Conversations. In: Marik, V., Mller, J.P. and Pechoucek, M. (eds.): Multi-Agent Systems and Applications III. LNCS 2691, Springer-Verlag, Berlin (2003) 214-225
3. Eijk, R., Boer, F., Hoek, W. and Meyer, J-Ch.: Operational Semantics for Agent Communication Languages. In Dignum, F and Greaves, M. (eds.): Issues in Agent Communication, LNCS 1916, Springer-Verlag, Heidelberg (2000) 80–95
4. Plotkin, G.D.: A structural approach to operational semantics. Technical Report DAIMI FN-19. Aarhus University, Computer Science Department, Denmark (1981)
5. Dignum, F., Greaves, M. (eds.): Issues in Agent Communication. LNCS 1916, Springer-Verlag, Heidelberg (2000)

6. Searle, J.R., Vanderveken, D.: Foundations of Illocutionary Logic. Cambridge University Press, Cambridge (1985)
7. Finin, T. et al. Specification of the KQML agent-communication language. ARPA Knowledge Sharing Initiative, External Interfaces Working Group (1993)
8. FIPA-Foundation for Intelligent Physical Agents: FIPA ACL Message Structure Specification. http://www.fipa.org/specs/fipa00061, FIPA (2002)
9. Cost, R.S. et al. Modeling agent conversations with CPN. In Bradshaw, J. (ed.): Workshop on Specifying and Implementing Conversation Policies (1999) 59–66
10. Odell J. et al. Representing agent interaction protocols in UML. In Ciancarini, P. and Wooldridge, M. (eds.): Agent Oriented Software Engineering (AOSE'00) Workshop, Limerick, Ireland (2000) 121–140
11. FIPA-Foundation for Intelligent Physical Agents. FIPA Interaction protocol Library Specification. http://www.fipa.org/specs/fipa00025, FIPA (2003)
12. Dignum, F.: From Messages to Protocols. In Dignum, F. and Sierra, C. (eds.): European Perspective on Agent Mediated Electronic Commerce. Springer-Verlag, Heidelberg (2000)
13. Barbuceanu, M and Fox M.S.: COOL: A Language for Describing Coordination in Multiagent Systems. In Proceedings of the First International Conference on Multi-Agent Systems (ICMAS'95). AAAI Press, San Francisco, USA (1995) 17–24
14. Galan, A. and Baker, A.: Multi-agent communications in JAFMAS. Workshop on Specifying and Implementing Conversation Policies, Washington (1999)
15. d'Inverno, M. and Luck, M.: Formalising the Contract Net as a Goal-Directed System. In W. V. de Velde and J. Perram (eds.): Agent Breaking Away. LNAI 1038. Springer-Verlag, Heidelberg (1996) 72–85
16. d'Inverno, M., Kinny, D. and Luck, M.: Interaction Protocols in Agentis. In Proceedings of the International Conference on Multi-Agent Systems ICMAS'98 (1998)
17. Kuwabara, K. et al.: AgenTalk: Describing multiagent coordination protocols with inheritance. In Proceedings of the Seventh IEEE International Conference on Tools with Artificial Intelligence (ICTAI'95), Herndon, Virginia (1995)
18. Bradshaw, J.M. et al.: Kaos: Toward an industrial-strength open agent architecture. In Bradshaw, J.M. (ed.): Software Agents. AAAI/MIT Press, Cambridge (1997) 375–418
19. Labrou, Y. and Finin, T.: Semantics and conversations for an agent communication language. In Huhns, M. et al. (eds.): Readings in Agents. Morgan Kaufmann (1997) 584–591

Towards a Conversational Language for Artificial Agents in Mixed Community

Alexandra Berger[1,2] and Sylvie Pesty[1]

[1] Laboratoire Leibniz-IMAG - Equipe MAGMA,
46, avenue Félix Viallet 38031 Grenoble Cedex
[2] Département de Philosophie, Université du Québec à Trois-Rivières,
3351, Boul. des Forges, CP 500 Trois-Rivières, Québec, Canada G9A 5H7
{Alexandra.Berger, Sylvie.Pesty}@imag.fr

Abstract. Present agent and interaction (agent communication language: ACL) models have been conceived for pure artificial agent communities, most often strongly linked with knowledge exchange. But these models are not adapted to conversational interactions, and particularly to mixed community melting artificial and human agents. We first underline these model limitations. We propose a first step towards a *conversational* agent language fitting with a BDI agent model in respect with Speech Acts Theory and integrating essential elements of the conversational background. This proposition is a continuation of Chaib-draa and Vanderveken's work [1] on a recursive semantics for ACL according to the situation calculus.

1 Introduction

Artificial agent models like BDI (Belief, Desire, Intention) agents [2,3] and models of interaction between agents like KQML (*Knowledge Query Manipulation Language*) [4] and FIPA ACL (*Foundation for Intelligent Physical Agent*) [5], have always been conceived for precised application tasks, and mostly for information exchange. These communication languages are only dedicated to artificial agents systems. However, we are meeting a new step in the evolution of computing systems in which these models are not enough efficient, the task being not yet the exclusive issue for multi-agent systems. Because we now need to count with human agents in agent communication, we also need to ensure more common conversations between artificial and human agents evolving into mixed community.

Considering these mixed communities, usual pure artificial agent communication languages are no more adapted. Usual ACLs are too task-linked and do not take the background parameters into account, and as far as we are concerned the conversational background ones. We then propose a first step towards a *Conversational Language* between artificial agents of mixed community fitting as close as possible with Speech Acts theory [6,7,8], a valid theory of human interaction.

So as to build this language, we propose to lean our research on Vanderveken's work [8] on speech act theory and those in recursive semantics for an agent communication language [1]. We carry on and complete this research by a formal definition of the set of speech acts and take into account the conversational background essential for speech acts comprehension.

M. Pěchouček, P. Petta, and L.Z. Varga (Eds.): CEEMAS 2005, LNAI 3690, pp. 31–40, 2005.

Our aims in this article is to consider the current interaction languages, then to introduce a formalization of speech acts theory and finally to propose, in accordance with the theory, a possible capture of the conversational background for an efficient agent *Conversational* language between human and artificial agents.

2   BDI Agents and Agent Communication Languages Nowadays

2.1   BDI Agents

BDI agent model roots in Bratman's [9] research on intentions integration into action theory, taking future directed actions and consequently partial planning into account. Cohen and Levesque [2] have formalized this philosophical research on which the BDI intelligent agents of Rao and Georgeff [3] was constructed. These BDI agents have mental states : beliefs (B), desires (D), and intentions (I) which permit them to act *rationally*. These are parts of the field of cognitive agents which aims to create agents not only intelligent, but also rational because they can *reason* before acting. BDI models are nowadays a crucial paradigm for human like agent actions modeling [10]. But, if action theory is surely adapted for *basic* actions, we believe that conversational actions need a particular management such as the contextualization that could be captured by means of speech act theory.

2.2   Agent Communication Languages

Agent Communication Language, like KQML and FIPA ACL have the same seminal idea from ordinary language philosophy [11,6] that each utterance is an act – *i.e., an action* – which aims to accomplish, to do something. So that FIPA ACL and KQML messages, like speech acts, express an illocution value – *i.e. an action specification* – applied to a propositional content. The essential difference between these two languages stands in theoretical considerations, more precisely in the language semantics which roots in different agent theory. For FIPA ACL, the theoretical aspects dealing with the formal semantics of interaction languages were largely developed by Sadek [12]. Although these languages were founded on Speech Act theory [6,8], they do not define language primitives in each act categories, but only in assertive and directive primitives – *i.e., respectively, Inform and Request and their derived acts.* So that agent communication capabilities are sharply restricted : agents cannot produce commissive or expressive acts, such as: *promise, felicitate,* or *apologize.* Primitives are essentially task-oriented which seems to be justified because FIPAs project was to propose specifications for an interaction langage so as to maximize agent-based applications interoperability, and only for artificial agents.

As Singh [13] noticed, these languages are neither conceived nor usable for exchanges such as dialog ones. Recent Phd Thesis of Guerin [14] also supports this idea. Singh argues also that acts should not be defined anymore exclusively on agent mental states, because this provide an unique model of agency which reduces the set of realizable agent models. Interactions are over-controlled and sometime counter-intuitives, *e.g.* an agent cannot repeat so as to confirm a proposition. According to Singh, it is necessary to take account of social aspects in order to evolve from *mental agency* to *social agency* to consider current situation, and in particular the agents social context which needs to be apprehended, according to us, by the consideration of the conversational background. Then, so as to permit artificial agents to ensure dialog with other agents, humans included, with a larger autonomy of interpretation and expression, we propose to keep the use of speech act theory but to exploit it deeper, consequently we could make use of the overall set of existing performative verbs.

In the next section, we expose speech act theory and its advantages for the definition of a conversation language between agents (Conversational-ACL).

3   Speech Acts Theory

3.1   Theory Presentation

According to the ordinary language philosophy initiated by Austin [11], primary units of meaning in the natural language use and comprehension are illocutionary acts with felicity conditions (success and satisfaction conditions), despite of *simple* truth conditions of propositions as in the *classical* logical trend. By attempting to perform illocutionary acts that the speaker expresses and communicates his minds by means of discourse. The speaker expresses propositions with diverse defined forces, he refers to objects under concepts, makes predication acts and expresses a propositional content with certain conditions. So that, elementary illocutionary acts are like $F(P)$: they are composed by an illocutionary force F and a propositional content P. We can then express a proposition P with some constraints with the help of the illocutionary force applied on this proposition. By studying the illocutionary force and the propositional content, illocutionary logics appears to be an efficient tool for formal semantics to analyse the meaning of every type of sentences which expresses every type of illocutionary acts. Illocutionary logics, for speech acts theory, is essential and complete for discourse analysis and synthesis. Speech acts theory, considering each utterance as a whole action, is entirely enrolled in action theory's domain. So that, it looks relevant to practically make use of it, by defining a Conversational-ACL, inside a BDI agent model which roots in a compatible theory of action.

3.2   Speech Acts Theory Taxonomy

As we have mentioned it, elementary speech acts are formally traduced by $F(P)$, where F stands for the illocutionary force with which the act is performed on P, the propositional content. The illocutionary force components define conditions which must be observed for the speech act to be performed with success and satisfaction. The six illocutionary force components are: the **illocutionary point**, the **mode of achievement**, the **degree of strength**, the **propositional content conditions**, the **preparatory conditions**, the **sincerity conditions**. There is five primitive illocutionary forces which have respectively an illocutionary point, no particular mode of achievement, a neutral degree of strength, and propositional content, preparatory and sincerity conditions determined by the illocutionary point. The five primitive illocutionary forces are: **assertive** to describe states of the world, **directive** to attempt to make someone do something by telling him, **commissive** to commit yourself to do something, **declarative** to do something only by performing the corresponding illocutionary act, **expressive** to express feelings and attitudes. These five forces are expressed through five verb classes named *performative verbs*. The set of performative verbs of each class is obtained by varying the different primitive forces components applying the following operations: addition of propositional content, preparatory or sincerity conditions, restriction of the mode of achievement or modulation of the degree of strength.

3.3   Success and Satisfaction Conditions

Like all human actions, illocutionary acts have success conditions considering that they can succeed or not (*e.g.* when I order something to someone on which I have no authority). Illocutionary acts have also satisfaction conditions because they are directed to some states of affairs on which the speaker has no control (*e.g.* if someone who has authority on me orders me something and I do not obey). **Success conditions** are those that must be observed in the context of utterance for the speaker to perform the speech act.An illocutionary act $F(P)$ is performed with success if and only if the speaker: (i) has achieved the illocutionary point of the force F on the propositional content P with the correct mode of achievement, and P respects all the propositional content conditions of F in this context; (ii)presupposes all the propositions determined by the preparatory conditions of F; (iii) expresses, with the right degree of strength, mental states noted $m(P)$ having the psychological modes m deduced from the sincerity conditions of F (joy, sadness, compassion,...).

The **satisfaction conditions** must be met in the world of an utterance context for an illocutionary act to be satisfied. An illocutionary act $F(P)$ is satisfied in a context of utterance if and only if P is true considering the right direction of fit of the illocutionary point F. As a conclusion, giving a complete set of practical tools for utterance analysis [7], illocutionnary logics allows to complete a cognitive approach of BDI agents. Moreover, the *"catalogue"* of performable speech acts for conversation is multiplied by the great combinatory possibility of the illocutionary forces components of speech acts theory; we can then go through the carency of slight differences and types of performative verbs in ACL as a response to Singh [13].

4   Towards an ACL for Conversational Agents

In Chaib-draa and Vanderveken [1], the authors propose a recursive semantics based on success and satisfaction conditions for agent communication langages. This work roots in Vanderveken's general semantics [8] and in illocutionnary logics [7], in accordance with speech acts theory. This work constitutes a semantical base for an ACL which seems to us particularly relevant to evolve towards an efficient Conversational-ACL. As a conclusion, giving a complete set of practical tools for utterance analysis [7], illocutionary logics allows to complete a cognitive approach of BDI agents. Moreover, the *catalogue* of performable speech acts for conversation is multiplied by the great combinatory possibility of the illocutionary forces components of speech acts theory; we can then go through the deficiency of slight differences and types of performative verbs in ACL as a response to Singh [13].

In order to clarify this presentation, we expose briefly, in the next section, the proposition of Chaib-draa and Vanderveken [1]. Then, we introduce our proposition to complete this semantics and illustrate it through two essential primitive illocutionnary acts (as in FIPA ACL): *Inform* and *Request*, we then propose a formal definition of the performative verb *Promise* which may expand the capabilities of expression of artificial agents in mixt community. The entire set of available speech acts in not described here.

4.1   The Recursive Semantics of Chaib-draa and Vanderveken

Chaib-draa and Vanderveken [1] proposed the use of the situation calculus as to formalize an adequate reasoning about action (language or not) and its effects in the world. The situation calculus is originally a first order formalism for action modelization. In the case of actions to communicate, the situation calculus enables the representation of the preconditions and the consequences of each action. As far as FIPA ACL is concerned, we should talk about *FP – i.e., feasibility preconditions –* and *RE – i.e., rational effects*. The most important point, according to us, in the situation calculus is that it allows to formalize strong context dependent utterances, because it takes the current situation (conversational background included) and the immediate next one into account. So that, the situation calculus appears to be an efficient tool for action formalization in multi-agent systems, and, particularly, for conversation between agents. According to this point of view, Chaib-draa and Vanderveken [1] have proposed a semantics based on the situation calculus integrating intensional logics' and illocutionary logics' semantics.

In the situation calculus, terms represent complete states of the world – *i.e. situations*. To perform – *i.e. to accomplish with success and satisfaction –* an action α in a situation s will be noted by $do(\alpha,s)$. The possibility to perform α in a situation s will be formalized by $Poss(\alpha,s)$. The initial situation will be noted S_0 and the situations will be arranged by the relation $\succ$, where $s'\succ s$ means *s' can be achieved from s by performing one or more actions*. The authors [1] have introduced a set of binary accessibility relations on situations for an adequation with speech acts theory. These operators are the following : **belief** $(bel(i,p))$, **desire** $(wish(i,p))$, **goal** $(goal(i,p))$ (non-primitive operator contrary to Cohen and Levesque [2]), **capability** $(can(i,a,p))$, **commitment** $(cmt(i,p))$, **has.plan** (planning) $(has.plan(i,\pi,p))$, **intention** $(int(i,p))$ defined on the base of *commitment* and *has.plan*, and **obligation** $(oblig(i,j,p))$ in connection with a norm. The definition of these operators allows the expression of the **success** $(success(ACT))$ and **satisfaction** $(satis(direction\ of\ fit)(ACT))$ **conditions** of each act type also formalized by the enunciation of six propositions permitting to express all the possible nuances of the illocutionary force components of an act, and then, all the performable illocutionary acts.

As a result, the situation calculus enables to express the different states of affairs encountered in speech acts theory in agreement with a rational BDI modeled agent. Moreover, as we will illustrate it, mental attitudes can be embedded in a background, in this case conversational, and we think this is the power of this semantics to evolve from *mental agency* to *social agency* [13]. Actually, Chaib-draa and Vanderveken have suggested that it is possible to take into account some elements of the background necessary for the definition of the success and satisfaction conditions of an act, such as the degree of strength or the role of an agent. We then propose a solution to include them, considering the fundamental role of the context -*i.e., conversational background*. Moreover, by considering the conversational background, we reach a higher level of interpretation -*i.e., a pragmatical level-* and not only a semantical or syntactical level of meaning without any context.

Remark 1. This formalization is a compromise between theory and computation in order to allow the use of speech acts theory into artificial agents so as to permit them to converse as adequately as possible in natural language with human agents. As a result, it is not a formalization of human-human interaction but of a possible human-agent interaction.

4.2 A Conversation Language Between Agents: Conversational-ACL

Among all elements of the conversational background that an agent must take into account when he analyses and interprets speech acts, the degree of strength and the role of agents are certainly the most important ones [15]. Actually, they are necessary for the contextualization of an act: the degree of strength to quantify the emphasis with which the act was performed, and the role to interpret acts where the hierarchy is needed for comprehension and for production too. These variables were not included in the proposition of Chaib-draa and Vanderveken [1], we then make a proposition of inclusion: to evolve from $do(says.to(i,j,\langle f,p\rangle),s))$ to $do(says.to(i,j,\langle f,p\rangle),s), degree, role)$. The degree of strength and the role are expressed by relative integer number (positive or negative) clearly pointing out the power more or less important of the illocutionary act. The role is expressed by a relative integer number too interpretable from a given semantics. We can then think over to precise some elements (*e.g.* the sex or the age of agents) or to take other elements into account, like variables denoting emotional aspects involved in a rational contextualized reasoning.

Remark 2. The force f is a primitive one (assertive, directive,...) and the degree of strength is rejected outside its scope for more visibility and flexibility.

The possibility of verifying the success and satisfaction conditions of illocutionary acts is essential, in particular for a conversational agent because we cannot perform adequately an illocutionary act if these conditions are not encountered. These constraints also allow to form attempts on the subsequent situations since the situation of utterance only by placing some clues of comprehension in the linking of actions. For example, in the case of a command which is satisfied only when it is obeyed, we then emit the attempt for the performance of an action satisfying the illocutionary act, in other words the illustration of obedience. For an act of promising that should be successful only if the speaker commit himself to accomplish a given action, we should then construct a list of commitments – *i.e., commitment stores* – of the conversation members noticeable with the consideration of the subsequent situations. The formalization of the natural language utterance into speech acts can permit to extract commitments and then use them into dialog games for a dynamical management of interaction [16]. Finally the ability to manage a large variety of parameters into the same communication language allows a dynamical management of acts sequencing, whereas classical interaction protocols define *a priori* and consequently fix series of actions. So that we should organize conversations between agents in function of a dialog taxonomy like the one of Walton and Krabbe [17], or in function of the agent capability coming from its role, or else in function of dialog strategies in accordance with game theory [18].

So as to illustrate our proposition, we propose a re-definition of two of the primitive communicative acts of FIPA ACL *Inform* and *Request* using the recursive semantics to carry out interesting aspects. We then give the formal definition of the performative verb *Promise* to show the possibility to allow artificial agents to interact with human agents as close as it is permitted by speech acts theory.

Inform. In speech acts theory, the performative verb *Inform* is not a primitive but an assertive verb of degree of strength 2 (+2) in reference to the assertive primitive *assert*, because *informing of a proposition p* is not only *asserting a proposition p*, but it means *believing the proposition* (having reason(s) for the truth of proposition p) and also *believing that the hearer do not already believe it* and then *having the intention of causing him to believe it*. We consider here that the agents role is neutral (0 value) and not relevant for the example. The speech act *Inform* in a given situation s is formalized by:

$$s = do(says.to(i, j, \langle inform, p \rangle), s_u, 2, 0) \tag{1}$$
$$\text{with} \quad (\forall s')(s' \succ s)$$
$$s_u = bel(i, p)[s] \wedge bel(i, (\neg bel(j, p)))[s] \wedge int(i, bel(j, p))[s'] \tag{2}$$
$$\text{and } s' = bel(j, p)[s'] \tag{3}$$

The speech act depends on the preconditions defined in the situation of utterance s_u and has effects on the following situation s' – *i.e. the next complete state of the world* –, in other words, a *perlocutionary* effect which might be verified by the agent in the following conversation. The satisfaction conditions will then be:

$$success(says.to(i, j, \langle inform, p \rangle), s) \equiv cond.success(\langle inform, p \rangle)[s] \tag{4}$$
$$satis_{wd}^{wl}(says.to(i, j, \langle inform, p \rangle), s) \equiv p[s] \wedge p[s_u] \wedge bel(j, p)[s'] \tag{5}$$

The success conditions (4) of this speech act must then be verified in the *cognitive* state of the agent. The speech act *do(says.to(i,j,$\langle inform, p \rangle$),$s_u$,2,0)* will be performed *successfully* if and only if: (i)The speaker i has achieved the illocutionary point of *informing* on the propositional content p; (ii) without any particular mode of achievement; (iii) with the propositional content condition that p is true in the given context; (iv) i presupposes the preparatory condition that the hearer j does not know p; (v) i expresses this speech act that he believes p with the degree of strength 2, and his mental state is *bel(i,p)*; (vi) and the speaker i is sincere.

Finally, the satisfaction conditions (5) of this illocutionary act should be verified considering the following situation, next complete state of the world resulting from the speech act. The illocutionary act *do(says.to(i,j,$\langle inform, p \rangle$),$s_u$,2,0)* will then be *satisfied* if and only if: (i) p is in fact true in situation s and (ii) if j believes p because of i's performance of the *Inform* speech act.

Request. Among the communicative acts of FIPA ACL, *Request* is the directive primitive. According to speech acts theory, it is not the directive primitive which is the performative verb *question*, although *request* has a neutral degree of strength. *Request* has the particular mode of achievement that the hearer has an option to refuse the request. Moreover, the directive verbs class has the particular preparatory condition that the speaker believes his hearer is able to perform the action expressed by the conditional content. This action could be a simple demand of information. The verb *request* has also the sincerity condition that the speaker desires that proposition p becomes true because of the action performance of his hearer. *Request* definition will then be:

$$s = do(says.to(i, j, \langle request, p \rangle), s_u, 0, 0) \tag{6}$$

$$\text{with} \quad (\forall p')(\forall a)(p \Rightarrow a)(\forall s')(s' \succ s)$$

$$s_u = bel(i, can(j, a, p'))[s] \wedge bel(i, Poss(j, a))$$

$$\wedge wish(i, p)[s] \wedge int(i, do(j, a))[s'] \wedge \neg oblig(j, i, a) \tag{7}$$

$$\text{and } s' = a[s'] \wedge p[s'] \tag{8}$$

Success and satisfaction conditions will be:

$$success(says.to(i, j, \langle request, p \rangle), s) \equiv cond.success(\langle request, p \rangle)[s] \tag{9}$$

$$satis_{wl}^{wd}(says.to(i, j, \langle request, p \rangle), s) \equiv (\exists s', s'')(s'' \succ s' \succ s)$$

$$Poss(a, s'), ..., Poss(a, s'') \wedge success(says.to(i, j, \langle request, p \rangle), s'')$$

$$\supset p[do(a, do(a, do(a, s'')))] \tag{10}$$

do(says.to(i,j,⟨request, p⟩),s_u,0,0) will be *successfully* (9) performed if and only if: (i)the speaker i has achieved the illocutionary point of *requesting* on the propositional content p; (ii) with the particular mode of achievement that the hearer has the option to refuse the request; (iii) with the propositional content condition that p becomes true in a subsequent situation because of performance of j of the action a expressed by the propositional content; (iv) the speaker i presupposes the preparory condition that his hearer j is able to perform the action expressed by the propositional content p; (v)i performed this act with the neutral degree of strength; and (vi) with the sincerity condition that i has sincerely the desire that p becomes true.

Finally, the satisfaction conditions (10) of this act will be verified from the cognitive state of the agent, in function of its conditions of success and of the situation resulting from the speech act. *do(says.to(i,j,⟨request, p⟩),s_u,0,0)* will be *satisfied* if and only if: (i) action a implied by p is in fact possible in the following situation(s) (future action(s)); (ii) the speech act is successfully performed in s; and (iii) j makes p becoming true because of his action(s) in the following situation(s).

We have presented here two examples of illocutionary acts used in FIPA ACL in an other format and with other specifications. As we have seen before, from the five primitive speech acts based on recursive semantics we can derive all the possible speech acts, in all categories, by varying the illocutionary forces components. And oppositely to FIPA ACL and KQML, it is possible to define the entire set of illocutionary acts including speech acts like promising, congratulating, confirming and apologizing...

Promise. So as to illustrate the possibility for agents to express the act of promising, here comes the formal definition of the performative verb *Promise* from which derive all the comissive performative verbs. This permitting to express commitments and then to list *commitment stores* and to verify them. The formal definition of *Promise* will then be:

$$s = do(says.to(i, j, \langle promise, p \rangle), s_u, 0, 0) \tag{11}$$

$$\text{with} \quad (\forall p')(\forall a)(p \Rightarrow a)(\forall s')(s' \succ s)$$

$$s_u = bel(i, can(i, a, p')[s] \wedge bel(i, Poss(i, a))$$

$$\wedge wish(j, p)[s] \wedge int(i, do(i, a))[s'] \tag{12}$$

$$\text{and } s' = a[s'] \wedge p[s'] \tag{13}$$

The success and satisfaction will be defined as:

$$success(says.to(i, j, \langle promise, p \rangle), s) \equiv cond.success(\langle promise, p \rangle)[s] \tag{14}$$

$$satis_{wl}^{wd}(says.to(i, j, \langle promise, p \rangle), s) \equiv (\exists s', s'')(s'' \succ s' \succ s)$$

$$Poss(a, s'), ..., Poss(a, s'') \wedge success(says.to(i, j, \langle promise, p \rangle), s'')$$

$$\supset p[do(a, do(a, do(a, s'')))] \tag{15}$$

The performance of the speech act depends on given preconditions in the situation of utterance s_u and has effects on the next situation s' – *i.e., the next complete world state* –, in other words, the act has a *perlocutionary* effect which is expected and which could be verified in the dialog continuation.

The success conditions (14) of this act will be verified from the cognitive state of the agent. The speech act $do(says.to(i,j, \langle promise, p \rangle), s_u, 2, 0)$ will then be *successful* if and only if: (i) The speaker i has achieved the illocutionary point of *promising* on the propositional content p; (ii) without any particular mode of achievement; (iii) with the propositional content condition that p becomes true in a subsequent context because of i's performance of action a implied by the propositional content p; (iv) i presupposes the preparatory condition that he is himself able to perform action a and that the hearer j has an interest for it; (v) i express this act with the neutral degree of strength ; and (vi) the particular sincerity condition is that i sincerely desires that p becomes true because of his performance of the action a.

Finally, the satisfaction conditions (15) will be verified from the cognitive state of the agent, in function of its conditions of success and of the situation resulting from the speech act. $do(says.to(i,j, \langle promise, p \rangle), s_u, 0, 0)$ will be *satisfied* if and only if: (i) the action a implied by the propositional content p is actually possible in one of the subsequent situations, in other words, if a is a future action; (ii) the speech act is successfully performed in s; (iii) and if i makes p becoming true because of his performance of the action a in the subsequent situation(s).

These three examples pointed out the possibilities offered by the use of this formalism for an adequate application of speech acts theory and open real perspectives for a Conversational-ACL between agents in mixed communities. In order to evaluate agents in which this ACL can be used, we are now defining both the whole *catalogue* of agent speech acts and specifying a real application of web services in which human agents could converse with multiple artificial agents in order to construct complex plans, such as a trip planning.

5   Conclusion

The recursive semantics of Chaib-draa and Vanderveken [1] using the situation calculus appears to be an efficient tool to formalize communication between artificial and human agents in mixed community. It adequately takes the advantages of speech acts theory, insufficiently exploited in current ACL, like FIPA ACL or KQML. We can then achieve an essential *computational* dimension of speech act theory implementation for artificial agents.

We have proposed to carry on Chaib-draa and Vanderveken's work to reach a formal definition of agent speech acts strongly linked with the conversational background (situation, degree of strength, role,...) and to conform it with a rational BDI agent model. Moreover, this proposition takes mental attitudes into account like other communication languages semantics, but also the social clues which are fundamental for conversation in *context*.

References

1. Chaib-draa, B., Vanderveken, D.: Agent communication language: A semantics based on the success, satisfaction and recursion. In: Proceedings of ATAL'98. (1998)
2. Cohen, P., Levesque, H.: Intention is choice with commitment. AI **42** (1990) 213–261
3. Rao, A.S., Georgeff, M.P.: Bdi agents: From theory to practice. In: Proceedings of IC-MAS'95, MIT Press (1995) 312–319
4. Finin, T., Labrou, Y., Mayfield, J.: KQML as an agent communication language. Software Agents (1997)
5. FIPA: Agent communication language. http://drogo.cselt.stet.it/fipa (1997)
6. Searle, J.: Speech Acts. Cambridge U. P. (1969)
7. Searle, J.R., Vanderveken, D.: Foundation of Illocutionary Logic. Cambridge U. P. (1985)
8. Vanderveken, D.: Meaning and Speech Acts. Volume 1 & 2. Cambridge U. P. (1990)
9. Bratman, M.E.: Intention, Plans, and Practical Reason. Harvard University Press (1987)
10. Wooldridge, M.: Reasonning about Rational Agents: Intelligent Robots and Autonomous Agents. MIT Press (2000)
11. Austin, J.: How To Do Things With Words. Oxford University Press (1962)
12. Sadek, M.D.: Attitudes mentales et interaction rationnelle: Vers une thorie formelle de la communication. PhD thesis, Universit de Rennes 1, France (1991)
13. Singh, M.: Agent communication languages: Rethinking the principles. IEEE Computer **31** (1998) 40–47
14. Guerin, F.: Specifying Agent Communication Language. PhD thesis, Dept. of Electrical and Electronic Engineering, Imperial College, University of Aberdeen (2002)
15. Fasli, M.: From social agents to multi-agent systems : Preliminary report. In et al., V.M., ed.: Proceedings of CEEMAS 2003, Springer Verlag (2003) 111–121
16. Flores, R.A., Pasquier, P., Chaib-draa, B.: Conversational semantics with social commitments. In Boissier, O., Z.Guessoum, eds.: Proceedings of AAMAS-04 Workshop on Agent Communication (AC'2004). (2004)
17. Walton, D., Krabbe, E.: Commitments in Dialogue. State University of New York (1995)
18. Maudet, N., Chaib-draa, B.: Commitment-based and dialogue-game based protocols: new trends in agent communication languages. Knowledge Engineering Review **17(2)** (2002)

Adaptive Mobile Multi-agent Systems

Alexandru Suna and Amal El Fallah Seghrouchni

LIP6, University of Paris 6
{Alexandru.Suna, Amal.Elfallah}@lip6.fr

Abstract. This paper presents a framework called HIMALAYA enabling to design and implement adaptive and distributed mobile multi-agent systems (MMAS). A distributed MMAS in our framework is a set of hierarchies of intelligent and mobile agents connected with respect to a topology. An MMAS is adaptive if its topology is flexible (agents are created or removed, the links between agents change in a dynamic manner) and if the internal structure of the agents may dynamically change, by acquiring new knowledge or capabilities. The features of HIMALAYA favor a dynamic adaptability and reconfiguring of systems.

1 Adaptive MMAS

This paper presents a framework called HIMALAYA, dedicated to the design of mobile multi-agent systems (MMAS) to be deployed on a network of computers. Our main objective is to meet the requirements of mobile computation and to ensure the adaptability of distributed MMAS faced to both cognitive and computational challenges.

The mobile computation is often required to improve the systems' performances, since it provides powerful programming constructs for designing distributed and mobile applications. Thanks to the mobile agents paradigm, it becomes easy to design *active entities* that move through the network and perform tasks on *hosts* (*sites* or *computers*), thus reducing the network traffic and increasing the scalability and the flexibility of such applications.

Despite the plethora of approaches and platforms for mobile agents, the main focus remains on the development of mobile objects and processes. Mainly implemented using object-oriented frameworks, these platforms provide a collection of extensible classes modelling simple concepts of agent that are specified rather at the implementation level.

The adaptability usually deals with open and dynamic environments in order to overcome the increasing complexity and dynamics of distributed and cooperative applications. Nevertheless, the adaptability feature remains *the quest for the Holy Grail* in the multi-agent systems (MAS) field. Indeed, the numerous existing approaches often tackle the adaptability issue from the cognitive point of view, *i.e.* the agents' behavior (represented by mental states, plans, reasoning mechanisms, etc.) is adapted according to some changes, usually concerning the environment, including other agents.

M. Pěchouček, P. Petta, and L.Z. Varga (Eds.): CEEMAS 2005, LNAI 3690, pp. 41–50, 2005.

In HIMALAYA framework, mobility and adaptability are introduced for the following reasons:

1. From a cognitive point of view, we are interested to design intelligent agents as basic building blocs of MMAS rather than simple mobile objects. Indeed, the agents in HIMALAYA are mobile but are also endowed with "intelligent skills" leading to more autonomy at the agent level and also at the MAS level as a whole. Thanks to the mobility and to some specific features we developed, our agents and consequently the MAS are able to reconfigure themselves autonomously, to acquire new knowledge and capabilities and to dynamically adapt their structure according to the changes in the environment and the demands of target applications. Hence, two levels of adaptability can be distinguished in HIMALAYA:

- an MMAS can adapt its structure (*e.g.* number of agents, topology, the location of its components, etc.) and consequently can improve the services it offers, *i.e.* since new skills (*capabilities*) can be created dynamically from other elementary or composite skills.
- an adaptive agent can exchange with other agents more than usual messages: an agent can transfer his capabilities, acquire new ones, move from an execution environment to another one, etc.

2. From the computational point of view, mobility and adaptability allow the MMAS reconfiguring and consequently the optimization of distributed executions of MMAS deployed on a network of computers.

Mobility and adaptability raise at least two questions: which structure is flexible enough to enable this dynamics and which kind of operations can make easy and effective the improvements we propose at the agent and MAS levels? To answer these questions, HIMALAYA is based on three fundamental concepts: mobility, hierarchical representation of agents and mechanisms for inheritance as allowed by the underlying representation. HIMALAYA is composed of two elements: CLAIM, an agent oriented programming language and SyMPA, a platform supporting the deployment and the execution of agents written in CLAIM.

The HIMALAYA environment is functional and has been used for developing several complex applications that proved the expressiveness of the language and the robustness of the platform: an e-commerce application [6], research of information in a network [7], a network of distributed cooperative digital libraries [12], an application for load balancing and resource sharing [19] using mobile agents or the modelling of the coffee market in Veracruz, Mexico [20].

The rest of this paper is organized as follows. The next section summarizes the related work, section 3 emphasizes the features of our framework, section 4 illustrates the adaptability mechanism through an example and section 5 concludes this paper and outlines our future work.

2   Related Work

The work presented in this paper is situated at the intersection of three domains: agent-oriented programming, concurrent languages and mobile agent platforms.

On one hand, agent-oriented programming (AOP) languages, such as *AGENT-0* [17], *AgentSpeak* [21], or *3APL* [10] allow representing mental states of agents, containing beliefs, goals, intentions or abilities, offer reasoning capabilities and communication primitives, but do not support agents' mobility. On the other hand, concurrent languages such as the *ambient calculus* [4], the *safe ambients* [13] or *Klaim* [5] have been proposed to formalize concurrent processes, that can communicate and migrate in a distributed environment. They have well defined operational semantics, but in none of these languages it is possible to represent intelligent agents, with explicit believes, plans, goals or reasoning. A detailed presentation of all these languages can be found in [6]. *Quantum* [15] or *CyberOrgs* [11] use a hierarchical model, with primitives similar to those in our framework, including mobility. However, these approaches focus on resource consumption and do not treat intelligent aspects of agents.

CLAIM is a high-level programming language combining in a heterogenous framework elements from AOP languages and from concurrent languages. Agents are hierarchically represented and use mobility primitives inspired by the ambient calculus. In addition an agent contains cognitive elements, explicitly programmed within agents, enabling powerful reasoning mechanisms, while the mobility primitives have been adapted for reconfiguring intelligent agents. To our knowledge, this feature is a novelty in the field of ambient based formalisms.

Several platforms supporting MMAS exist nowadays [18], such as *Aglets* [1], *D'Agents* [9] or *Grasshopper* [2]. All of them offer mechanisms for agents' creation, communication, migration and management, while insuring a high level of security. However, the supported agents are actually mobile objects while a higher level of abstraction is required. *MobileSpaces* [16] is a platform that uses a hierarchical representation of agents, allowing adaptability, similar to our approach. However, the agents are Java objects.

SyMPA is a distributed platform offering all the necessary mechanisms for a secure execution of MMAS written in CLAIM (an agent oriented language, not object oriented as in other platforms). In addition, the platform supports the implementation of all the reconfiguring operations that will be presented below.

Agents concepts have been often used to bring adaptability to distributed systems and application, but the implementation of these concepts is never done (to our knowledge) using an agent oriented approach, as presented in this paper, where not only knowledge can be exchanged between agents but also capabilities.

Considering all these existing approaches, we noticed the necessity for a unified framework allowing to design and implement intelligent and mobile adaptive multi-agent systems and HIMALAYA tries to fill this gap.

3 Supporting Adaptive MMAS: The Himalaya Framework

The HIMALAYA framework (figure 1) is composed of two elements already presented in previous articles. This paper focuses on adaptability issues.

CLAIM [6] is a high-level agent-oriented programming language that allows to design MMAS, to define agents or classes of agents. It combines cognitive and computational elements, allowing to deal with a hierarchical representation of agents and with dynamic gathering of intelligent elements. The language has an operational semantics [8] useful for the verification of the built MMAS.

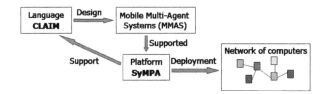

Fig. 1. HIMALAYA Framework

The second component of our framework is SyMPA [18], a distributed platform implemented in Java, compliant with the specifications of the MASIF [14] proposition from the OMG, that supports MMAS written in CLAIM and offers all the necessary mechanisms for agents' management, communication, mobility, security and fault-tolerance. It also provides a CLAIM interpret and graphical interfaces for monitoring agents' execution and behavior.

3.1   An MMAS in Himalaya

An MMAS in HIMALAYA is a set of hierarchies of agents deployed on several computers connected via a network. An agent is a node in a hierarchy, an autonomous, intelligent and mobile entity which contains sub-agents, running processes and cognitive elements.

The agents in HIMALAYA are implemented using CLAIM [6]. The main components of an agent, presented below using a simplified notation, are:

The knowledge base. (denoted by K_α for an agent named α) contains pieces of information about the other agents' classes and capabilities or user-defined propositions about the environment he is acting in.

The goals (denoted by G_α). An agent has goals given *a priori* or goals generated (his own or requested by other agents) during his execution.

The capabilities. (denoted by C_α) are the main elements of an agent. A capability allows to execute a process if a certain message is received and if an (optional) condition is verified, having possible effects (post-conditions).

The processes. Once a capability activated, the corresponding process is executed, in parallel with the already running processes of the agent. Therefore, an agent α contains a set of concurrent running processes, $P_\alpha = p_i \mid p_j \mid ... \mid p_k$. An agent can execute several types of processes, but their description is outside the scope of this paper (see [6] for details). In the next section we present only the processes related to dynamic adaptability of an MMAS.

The sub-agents. Because of the hierarchical representation, an agent may have several sub-agents. This structure evolves during the execution, *i.e.* the set of sub-agents changes when they migrate or are eliminated.

An agent, *e.g.* α, is denoted by $\alpha(G_\alpha, K_\alpha, C_\alpha, P_\alpha)$, representing his goals, knowledge base, capabilities and his concurrent running processes.

The previous elements concurrently allow for HIMALAYA agents a *reactive behavior* (an agent activates capabilities when the corresponding messages arrive and the conditions are verified) and a *goal-driven behavior* (an agent executes capabilities in order to achieve goals).

3.2 Adaptability Operations

HIMALAYA framework enables a dynamic reconfiguring of MMAS. With respect to the hierarchical representation of agents, the adaptability operations allow a dynamic evolution of the topology and of the cognitive components of agents. We distinguish three types of primitives: for mobility, for inheritance and for dynamic creation and removal of agents. They are briefly described below and represented in a graphical manner. The hierarchies' modifications will be obvious on the figures and the agents' components that change will be explicitly represented. For readability reasons, an agent *e.g.* written α will be read as $\alpha(G_\alpha, K_\alpha, C_\alpha, P_\alpha)$. For a detailed presentation, in particular concerning the operational semantics of these primitives, the reader is invited to see [8].

The mobility primitives. are inspired by the ambient calculus [4]. Thus, an agent moves as a whole, with all his components (intelligent elements, running processes and sub-agents). Using *in* (figure 2), an agent can enter another agent from the same level in the hierarchy (*i.e.* having the same parent) and using *out*, an agent can exit his parent (figure 3). For security reasons, these operations are controlled by an asking/granting permission mechanism. The *move* mobility operation is a direct migration into another agent, anywhere in the MMAS (figure 4). Nevertheless, the *move* operation is subject to permissions using a specific protocol (see [6]).

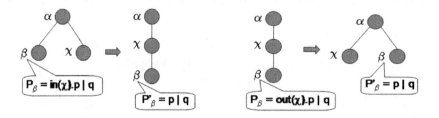

Fig. 2. In operation   **Fig. 3. Out** operation

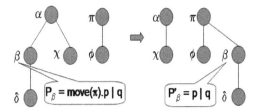

Fig. 4. Move operation

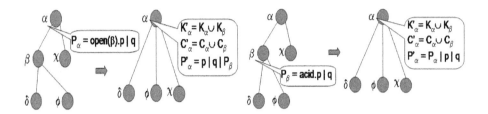

Fig. 5. Open operation (absorption)   **Fig. 6. Acid** operation (dissolution)

The inheritance primitives. are inspired by the ambient calculus, but they have been adapted to suit our goal: dynamic reconfiguring of intelligent MMAS. Taking full advantage of the hierarchical representation of agents and using the *open* primitive, an agent can open the boundaries of one of his sub-agents, thus inheriting the latter's running processes and sub-agents, as in the ambient calculus, but also the knowledge base and capabilities (figure 5). In this case, we say that the sub-agent is **absorbed** by his parent. The *acid* primitive (figure 6) is similar to *open*, but it is an agent who decides to open his own boundaries, and as a consequence, his components are inherited by his parent. In this case, we say that the sub-agent **dissolves** himself into his parent.

Thence, both in absorption and in dissolution situations, an agent dynamically gathers new capabilities and enriches his knowledge base; it is what we call inheritance in our framework (quite different from the inheritance concept in the object-oriented programming). Both operations are controlled by permissions.

Dynamic creation and removal of agents. Another important element towards the system's adaptability is the possibility to create and remove agents

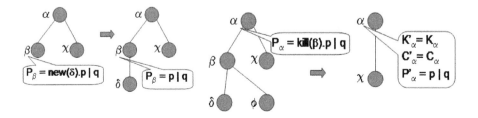

Fig. 7. New Agent operation   **Fig. 8. Kill** operation

dynamically. New agents are created using the *newAgent* primitive (figure 7) and an agent can completely remove (without inheriting his computational or cognitive components) one of his sub-agents using the *kill* primitive (figure 8).

4   Case Study: Adaptive MMAS

In order to illustrate the dynamic adaptability of MMAS in HIMALAYA and to show that the framework is operational, we implemented an application inspired by a strategy games, *Age of Empires*. A village of people in a prehistoric era tries to survive by gathering resources. There are sites of resources distributed on computers of a network. Each site can contain three types of resources: wood, stone and food. The population is represented by a *Creator* agent that can create *Seeker* agents and resource gatherer agents, one type for each type of resource: *WoodCutter*, *Miner* and *Hunter*. Each type of agent has capabilities for gathering only his corresponding resource. The goal is to gather all the resources. We implemented two scenarios for gathering resources, one where agents do not use the dynamic gathering of cognitive elements and the second where they are using inheritance primitives.

4.1   Using Specialized Agents

In the first scenario (figure 9), the *Creator* creates (using **newAgent**, (9.1.) in the figure) a *Seeker* agent which finds the list of sites and migrates to them (using **move**, (9.2.)). Arriving on a site, he finds the available resources and requests specialized agents from the *Creator*, who will create (using **newAgent**, (9.3.)) one specialized agent for each type of resource, agents that migrate (9.4.) to specific resource agents on the site. After gathering the resources, they return to the village (9.5.) with the resources, give them to the *Creator* and wait for other requests. Meanwhile, the *Seeker* moves to other sites (9.6.), searches for resources and asks for specialized agents. If there is no specialized agent available when a new request arrives, a new one is created.

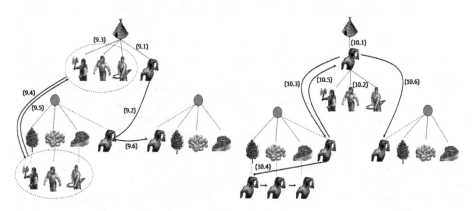

Fig. 9. First Scenario   **Fig. 10.** Second Scenario

4.2 Using Absorption

In the second scenario (figure 10), we are using the inheritance features of our framework. The *Seeker* is first created (using ***newAgent***, (10.1.) in the figure), then the specialized agents are also created, they enter the *Seeker* (using ***in***, (10.2.)) and are absorbed by him (using ***open***). In this way, the *Seeker* will acquire their capabilities and will be able to gather the three types of resources. Thus, he dynamically readapts himself in order to be able to execute tasks not possible before. He migrates next to the known sites (using ***move***, (10.3.)), enters each resource agent (10.4.), gathers resources, returns to the *Creator* with the resources (10.5.) and goes on with the gathering process to other sites (10.6.).

4.3 Test and Results

In order to test our application, we implemented the agents in the two scenarios using CLAIM and we deployed the platform on ten computers connected via a local network. We started 10 sites of resources on these computers, with identical resources (20 units of wood, 20 of stone and 30 of food). There is one population and a *Creator* was started, having initially 50 units of wood, 50 of stone and 50 of food. Resources are consumed when creating new agents.

In the first scenario, a *Seeker* was created, he went to the first known site and requested help for the resources he found. Consequently, three specialized agents were created by the *Creator*, one for each resource, they went to the site, gathered resources and returned to the *Creator*. Meanwhile, the *Seeker* went to other sites. At site 3, a new *Hunter* was created because the first one had not arrived yet at the *Creator*, and at site 5 a new *Miner* was created. Next, there were always available specialized agents.

The second scenario followed the behavior presented in section 4.2. One *Seeker* having all the capabilities for gathering the three types of resources (after absorbing the three specialized agents) travelled through all the sites and gathered the resources.

The results show that the time for gathering all the resources is shorter when there are specialized agents for each type of resources (figure 11*a*, representing the time for gathering resources growing progressively with the sites' discovering), because they can gather resources in parallel. Nevertheless, using the inheritance primitives, only one dynamically reconfigured agent able to gather all types of resources will gather all the resources in an almost similar time as 6 agents (1 Seeker and 5 specialized agents). Figure 11*b* represents the evolution of number of agents in the course of time. Also, the final amount of resource is bigger in the second scenario (as we can see in the figure 11*c*, for the food's evolution in time; the evolution of the other resources is similar), because resources were spent for creating additional specialized agents. The implemented scenarios shows the expressiveness of our framework. We do not state that one of the scenarios is better: one is faster; the other allows to have more resources at the end. The scenarios were started from identical configurations and we just provided the system's behavior in both cases.

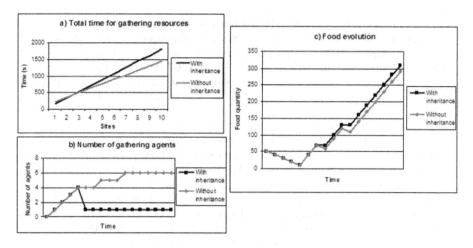

Fig. 11. Results

5   Conclusion and Future Work

In this paper we proposed a framework for building distributed and adaptive MMAS, based on a flexible hierarchical topology of the multi-agent system and on dynamic mental states of agents that can continuously evolve in an autonomous manner, thanks to the adaptability operations. Thus, the number of agents and the links between them change; the agents can also gather, during their execution, computational elements (processes, sub-agents) and cognitive elements (knowledge, capabilities), allowing a dynamic reconfiguring of an MMAS, giving the system a full scope to adapt its structure in order to meet the requirements of target applications.

Our short term future work is two-folds. First, we would like to experiment our framework in more open environments, and on a bigger number of computers connected through the Internet. Secondly, we would like to apply the emphasized concepts to real systems. We intend to develop a planner for systems' reconfiguring. The designer should specify the initial configuration of his application/system and the target configuration that fulfills his requirements; the system should be able to reconfigure itself even if the execution environment changes, by adapting its structure and by transferring intelligent elements. As target applications, we would like to tackle the domain of ambient intelligence.

References

1. Aglets workbench on-line: http://www.trl.ibm.co.jp/aglets.
2. Grasshopper on-line: http://www.grasshopper.de.
3. Bordini R.H., Hübner J.F., Vieira R.: Jason and the Golden Fleece of Agent-oriented Programming. In Multi-agent Programming. Kluwer (to appear) 3-38
4. Cardelli L., Gordon A.D.: Mobile ambients. In Foundations of Software Science and Computational Structures. LNAI **1378** (1998) 140-155

5. de Nicola R., Ferrari G., Pugliese R.: Klaim: a kernel language for agents interaction and mobility. In IEEE Transactions on Software Engineering (1998) 315-330
6. El Fallah Seghrouchni A, Suna A.: Claim: A computational language for autonomous, intelligent and mobile agents. LNAI **3067** (2004) 90-110
7. El Fallah Seghrouchni A, Suna A.: An unified framework for programming autonomous, intelligent and mobile agents. LNAI **2691** (2003) 353-362
8. El Fallah Seghrouchni A, Suna A.: Programming mobile intelligent agents: an operational semantics. In Proceedings of IAT'04, Beijing, China. IEEE Press (2004)
9. Gray R., Kotz D., Cybenko G., Rus D.: D'agents: Security in a multiple-language, mobile-agent system. In Mobile Agents and Security, LNCS, **1419** (1998) 154–187
10. Hindriks K., deBoer F.S., der Hoek W., Meyer J.J.Ch.: Agent programming in 3APL. In Intelligent Agents and Multi-Agent Systems, **2** (1999) 357-401
11. Jamali N, Agha G.: Cyberorgs: A model for decentralized resource control in multi-agent systems. In Proceedigd of Workshop on Representations and Approaches for Time-Critical Decentralized Resource/Role/Task Allocation of AAMAS (2003)
12. Klein G., Suna A, El Fallah Seghrouchni A.: A methodology for building mobile multi-agent systems. In Proceedings of SYNACS (2004)
13. Levi F., Sangiori D.: Controlling interference in ambients. In Proceedings of the 27th ACM SIGPLAN-SIGACT symposium (2000) 352-364
14. Milojicic D., Breugst M., Busse I, Campbell J., Covaci S, Friedman B., Kosaka K, Lange D., Ono K, Oshima M., Tham C., Virdhagriswaran S., White J.: MASIF, the OMG mobile agent system interoperability facility. In Mobile Agents (1998) 50-67
15. Moreau L., Queinnec C.: Design and semantics of Quantum: a language to control resource consumption in distributed computing. In Usenix Conference on Domain-Specific Languages (DSL) (1997) 183-197
16. Satoh I.: Mobilespaces: A framework for building adaptive distributed applications using a hierarchical mobile agent system. In IEEE International Conference on Distributed Computing Systems (2000) 161-168
17. Shoham Y.: Agent oriented programming. Artificial Intelligence **60** (1993) 51-92
18. Suna A, El Fallah Seghrouchni A.: A mobile agents platform: architecture, mobility and security elements. In Proceedings of ProMAS'04, LNAI **3346** (2005) 126-146
19. Suna A., Klein G., El Fallah Seghrouchni A.: Using mobile agents for resource sharing. In Proceedings of IAT'04, Beijing, China. IEEE Press (2004)
20. Suna A., Lemaitre C., El Fallah Seghrouchni A.: E-commerce using an agent oriented approach. In Proceedings of the Iberagents Workshop, Puebla, Mexico (2004)
21. Weerasooriya D., Rao A., Ramamohanarao K.: Design of a concurrent agent-oriented language. In ATAL '95. LNAI **890** (1995) 386-402

Agent Encapsulation in a Cognitive Vision MAS

Bernhard Jung[1] and Paolo Petta[1,2]

[1] Austrian Research Institute for Artificial Intelligence (OFAI),
A-1010 Vienna, Freyung 6/6, Austria
[2] Dept. of Med. Cybernetics and AI, Centre for Brain Research, Med. Univ. of Vienna,
A-1010 Vienna, Freyung 6/2, Austria
{bernhard.jung, paolo.petta}@ofai.at

Abstract. We cast a baseline cognitive vision design into a multi-agent framework and therein address the questions how and to what extent explicit consideration of coordination may affect the design and performance of such systems. In an
analysis of our decomposition into task-dependent entities using both, functional
and physical approaches to encapsulation, we show that different kinds of algorithms with different notions of architecture and representation become possible.
We describe the evolution of our implementation out of a traditional monolithic
design. Functionalities akin to notions of conventional tracking and reasoning
now emerge out of the distributed interaction between component agents, with a
performance at least on par with the baseline system.

1 Introduction

This work was carried out in the context of an Austrian Joint Research Project (JRP)
"Cognitive Vision" (see Sect. 6). The domain of Cognitive Vision emerged out of traditional Computer Vision, as "an attempt to achieve more robust, resilient, and adaptable computer vision systems by endowing them with a cognitive faculty: the ability to learn, adapt, weigh alternative solutions, and even the ability to develop new
strategies for analysis and interpretation" [ECVision Roadmap V4.2, p.2]. The scientific foundations for Cognitive Vision include visual sensing; architecture; representation; memory; learning; recognition; deliberation & reasoning; planning; communication; and action: issues not independent of each other. Furthermore, the definitions
of architecture (a "minimal set of information processing modules and their network
of inter-relationships") and representation ("any stable state of a cognitive systems")
[ibid. p.11] reflect a classical view. In our interaction with project partners from traditional Computer Vision, we challenge the view that a vision architecture can be seen
as a functionally (in the sense of processing or transformation functions) reduced set of
processing modules when the system should be goal-directed and purposive; that representations are stable when visual input is noisy, imprecise, or ambiguous; and that vision
algorithms necessarily deliver valid results at all times (i.e., are perfect functions).

We show how a traditional vision architecture was recast into a multi-agent design
that does not follow the typical functional decomposition into detector, tracker, and
reasoner, but employs a combination of the functional and physical approaches to encapsulation [Shen & Norrie 1999, Parunak et al. 2001]. Consequently, within this new

M. Pěchouček, P. Petta, and L.Z. Varga (Eds.): CEEMAS 2005, LNAI 3690, pp. 51–61, 2005.
© Springer-Verlag Berlin Heidelberg 2005

solution, representation is not a stable state of the system and cannot be pinned down to specific data in some components, but is distributed among agents and their interaction patterns. Following an agent-based design process, we switched from a design perspective that regards vision as a transformation process to one in which cognitive vision is realised as interaction of task- and purpose-dependent agents.

Section 2 describes our point of departure in terms of the scenario and the classical vision solution used to derive and evaluate our approach. In Sect. 3 our MAS-based solution is presented in detail; Sect. 4 reports results; Sect. 5 discusses related work on agent-based systems in computer vision; and Sect. 6 concludes with a discussion and future perspectives.

2   The Point of Departure

The starting point of our work was an implementation of the classical functional transformation approach to solve the Hide&Seek M6 (aka "shell game") scenario of the Austrian JRP "Cognitive Vision". It consists of a stationary camera, two black cups and an orange ball on a table, and a single human hand moving and lifting the cups in turn to hide and unhide the ball (see Fig. 1).[1] Questions to be answered by the system include: "Where is the ball?"; "What is hiding the ball?"; and "What was the trajectory of a cup, the ball, or the hand?". To this end, beyond detection and tracking of objects, capability to reason about occlusion is also required.

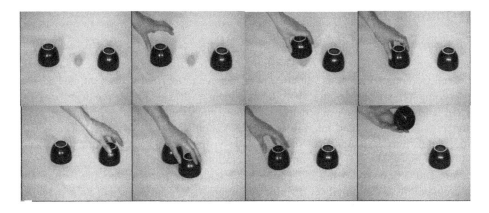

Fig. 1. A sequence from the JRP Hide&Seek M6 scenario (covering only part of the activity)

A MatLab-based implementation follows the transformational approach to derive trajectories and occlusion relations of objects in the scene.[2] It comprises three object detectors that perform colour-based segmentation and calculate different properties for the blobs (=contiguous regions) derived, including area; centre of gravity; bounding

[1] To be available at <URL:http://www.acin.tuwien.ac.at/groups/robtec/fsp/fsp.htm>

[2] Provided by A. Opelt, G. Schweighofer, A. Pinz & R. Tomasi from the Institute of Electrical Measurement & Measurement Signal Processing (EMT), Graz University of Technology.

box; and solidity. *Object detection* is then based upon these properties. These detectors are used by *trackers* that consider objects detected in subsequent frames to be the same as long as the distance between their centres of gravity remains below a given threshold. The trackers can thus detect *new* objects as well as the *loss* of previously detected and tracked ones. This information is used by a reasoner to maintain an *occlusion tree* registering which object is currently hidden by which other one. For each lost object, a hiding object is looked for: if successful, the lost object is assigned to its hider and hereafter assumed to move together with it. New objects are first assumed to have been *unhidden* and a match is attempted to hidden object entries in the occlusion tree. If a match is found, the hitherto hidden object is unlinked from its hider and updated with the information about the newly detected object. The new object is thus *unified* with the old one. In this manner, stable reasoning about occlusion of the ball and temporary occlusions by the hand hiding the cups is achieved.

To obtain an efficient baseline system[3], this solution (referred to as "EMT solution") was cast into the JRP's common framework by modularising the monolithic MatLab-based architecture into specialised detectors and associated trackers for balls, cups, and skin; and an occlusion tree reasoner. This application was used subsequently to assess and compare correctness, performance, and architectural features of our new design.

3   Tracking and Reasoning by Agent Coordination

MAS *coordination* [Lesser 1998] aims at ensuring coherent behaviour of a system consisting of multiple autonomous agents pursuing interdependent activities—e.g. intending to work on the same or overlapping subproblems; disposing of alternative methods or data to generate a solution; or producing results of one subproblem that also contributes to the solution of another. Coordination typically requires the *detection* of interdependencies; a *decision* which coordination action to apply; and *coordination mechanisms* (for an overview of available techniques, see e.g. [Omicini & Ossowski 2003]) that shape the way the agents perform these tasks. In our architecture, each task-relevant object in the scene is represented by a dedicated agent. These *object agents* are supported by a limited number of specialised *detector agents*, that provide an anchoring to entities detected in the current image. In this design, tracking and reasoning functionalities *emerge* out of the interactions among object agents, and between object and detector agents (see Fig. 2). Roles with responsibilities and authorities are assigned to agent types at design-time (see Sect. 3.1 and 3.2). This leads to organisational restrictions: e.g. each object agent is associated to a specific detector agent. At run-time, agent coordination is guided by creation and termination of agents; auctioning; contracting; and matchmaking. This is implemented via agent communication following a predefined conversation policy [Greaves et al. 1999].

Even though the design of this conversation policy was guided by the ideas of tracking and (occlusion tree) reasoning, and it does include specific "tracking" and "reasoning" phases (see Sect. 3.3), the overall tracking and reasoning capabilities expressed by the system cannot be pinned down to particular component agents, but come

---

[3] The MatLab code was found to be an order of magnitude slower than its C/C++ equivalent.

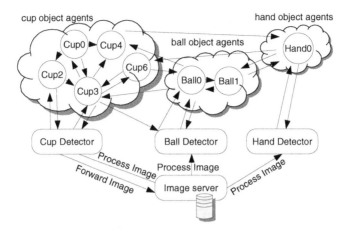

Fig. 2. The architecture, consisting of an image server agent and detector agents interacting with object agents (Cup1 and Cup5 are supposed to have come and gone in the observed scene). Unlabelled arrows indicate communication paths.

about in a distributed fashion, relying also on properties (e.g. continuity) of the environment. In the following, we first describe the responsibilities of detector and object agents and then discuss the conversation policy governing agent interaction in more detail.

3.1 Detector Agents

A *detector agent* is responsible for the detection of object blobs of a given type in the images provided by an image server agent (connected to a live camera or accessing an image sequence store). It distributes the information about these blobs to interested object agents of the same type (see Sect. 3.2). The interest of an object agent is expressed in terms of multiple regions of interest in the image and is specified on demand.[4] A detector agent is further responsible for mediating among multiple object agents claiming a blob, by holding an *auction* and awarding the blob to the object agent that submitted the bid expressing the highest confidence in this blob representing itself (=the particular object) in the current image (see Sect. 3.3). A detector agent will spawn *new object agents* for unmatched blobs (i.e., not claimed by the existing object agent population), and serves as a *matchmaker agent* [Wong & Sycara 2000] distributing requests to object agents to identify hider objects for objects that disappeared with the current frame. Furthermore, it is the joint responsibility of the set of all detector agent instances to coordinate the tracking and reasoning phases in the conversation policy (see Sect. 3.3).

3.2 Object Agents

An *object agent* represents an object detected in the scene and is associated to the detector agent that spawned it. Object agents are responsible for the matching of blobs

---

[4] The specification of more than one area is required to handle reappearance after occlusion correctly, as explained in the following.

offered by their detector agents to the data maintained locally about the most recent blob of their scene objects and thereby for coherent tracking of objects. The distance between centres of gravity of blobs serves as coherence measure and must lie below a given threshold. This presupposes a certain coherence of information across subsequent frames (cf. end of introduction to Sect. 3). They further handle disappearance and reappearance events in the scene by linking and unlinking themselves to hider objects. Once linked, a *contract* is established [Jennings 1996] between the agents representing the hider and the hidden objects, and the "hider object" agent subsequently propagates position changes to the "hidden object" agents. Object agents also send updates of their areas of interest to their detector agent. These areas are usually extended bounding boxes around currently assumed object positions (and, in the case of hidden objects, also the locations of their disappearance).

By these means, detector agents automatically offer blobs also to object agents representing hidden objects; reappearance can be detected, and no "object merging"— unification of newly instantiated re-appearances of objects with representations of their earlier occurrences—as in the original EMT approach is necessary. If the object referred to by an object agent goes undetected for some time without identification of an appropriate hider, the object agent will eventually assume its object disappeared from the scene for good, and die.

3.3   Conversation Policy

Coordination among agent instances is governed by an encompassing conversation policy, articulated into a tracking and a reasoning phase. A simplified diagram of the policy is shown in Fig. 3. The *tracking phase* of the policy is started by the image server agent that sends ProcessImage messages to the (three) detector agents available. In case a detector agent fails to identify any blobs of its kind in the current image within the regions of interest of its object agents, it sends them NoBlobFound messages, to be confirmed by a BlobConfirmed return message. Otherwise, the detector agents try to assign each of the blobs detected to one of their existing object agents, based on the location of the blob and the areas of interest of the object agents being managed: a blob may be offered to multiple object agents, and an object agent may have multiple blobs offered by its detector agent. To this end, detector agents send DetectedBlobs messages to their object agents. Each of these returns a BlobSelection message, with the index of the blob assessed the most likely reference to the object it represents and a confidence measure[5], or an index value of -1 to report that no blob of interest was identified. The detector agent waits for all BlobSelection messages to be returned and resolves ambiguous selections by sending a ConfirmBlob message to the object agent that expressed the highest confidence. In subsequent iterations, blobs remaining are offered to object agents not yet awarded a blob, and the sub-policy ends with a (possibly empty) remainder set of not assignable blobs for which the detector agent spawn new object agents. The *tracking phase* thus ends with receipt of the messages confirming

---

[5] Calculated over the centre of gravity of the blob offered and the last known object position or location of disappearance.

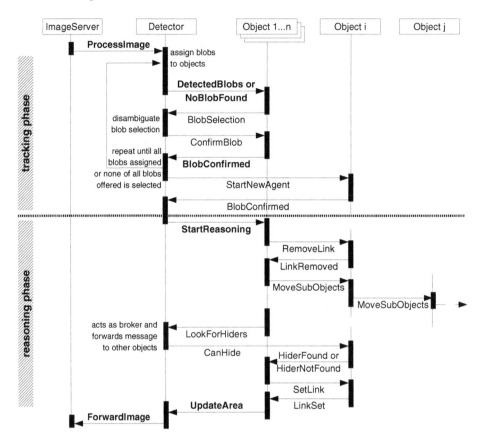

Fig. 3. Schematic sequence diagram for the conversation policy. Mandatory messages are set in bold font. Parallel messages, conditions for messages, and synchronisation between detector agents, are omitted for clarity. See main text (Sect. 3.3) for details.

creation of new agents (if any). Before starting the reasoning phase, *all* detector agents must have finished the tracking phase.

In the *reasoning phase*, detector agents act as matchmakers. We adopted this as approach of choice, given that detector agents know about all object agents they have spawned and message broadcasts are not necessarily desirable, as detector agents have information about the area an object is located in and can thus perform a kind of targeted multi-casting for CanHide messages (see below). This phase is initiated by the detector agents sending StartReasoning messages to all known object agents. These determine whether they have reappeared, in which case they send RemoveLink requests to their hider object agents, which confirm link removal (LinkRemoved). Next, every hider object agent remaining sends a MoveSubObjects message to the hidden object agents linked to it, thus propagating the relative movement of its own object. This message is forwarded recursively to further hidden objects. Acknowledge messages for MoveSubObjects are not sent because no explicit synchronisation before further policy steps is required, and we also assume reliable communication.

Table 1. Timing results of the baseline and the MAS-based systems

Framework components	time (s)
None (image server only)	6.0
Baseline detector	37.5
Baseline detector+tracker	41.7
All three baseline components	46.6
MAS-based solution	40.5

approximate tracking & reasoning times (s)	
Baseline solution	9.1
MAS-based solution	3.0

The next policy step is to identify hider objects for all disappeared objects. Disappeared object agents broadcast LookForHiders messages to *all* detector agents; these forward these requests as CanHide messages to all objects they know to be in the neighbourhood of the disappeared objects. Potential hiders determine confidence values for them being the cause of specific occlusions and accordingly return HiderFound or HiderNotFound messages to the disappeared object agent. In the case of multiple possible hiders, the disappeared object agent selects the one with the highest confidence and sends a SetLink request to it. This request is confirmed by a LinkSet message from the hider object agent. Object agents end their participation in the policy by adjusting their area of interest via an UpdateArea message to their detector agent. Upon receipt of all UpdateArea messages from their object agents by the different detector agents, the reasoning phase ends, and the image server is asked by means of a ForwardImage message to proceed to the next image.

4   Results

Performance measurements were obtained for the baseline system (Sect. 2) and our MAS solution (Sect. 3) on a Pentium M 1.6 GHz notebook under Gentoo Linux.[6] Both cases processed 100 frames of the scenario (with all objects visible and one occlusion of the ball); the time of the whole process was measured. To assess relative processing times of the three sub-components in the baseline solution, we added one component after the other. The results summarised in Table 1 clearly identify the detector algorithms as the major bottlenecks. As the same detector algorithms are used in all configurations, the difference of about six seconds between the baseline and the MAS solutions can be attributed to tracking and reasoning. MatLab-generated code seems to be inherently slower than hand-written C/C++ code, so these results cannot be interpreted as the agentified solution being three times faster at tracking and reasoning. However, it does indicate the agentified solution to be no worse. Correctness of both approaches was assessed merely by visual inspection of bounding boxes and names of tracked objects with links to bounding boxes and names of hidden objects overlayed on the image sequence. The approaches show slight differences in the times of object reappearance during phases of occlusion, but all objects are tracked and labelled correctly at the end of the occlusion episode. Concerning architectural features, our approach is easier to

---

[6] Working memory requirements appear to be secondary, on the order of 40MB resident and 160MB virtual size of a multi-threaded process.

maintain due to the modularisation and decoupling of processing steps (a prerequisite for further work on asynchronous operation in decelerated real-time, Sect. 6), and to extend by adding new detector agents and more complex object interaction models. Scalability can be achieved by distribution of agents over multiple machines.

5   Related Work

The modularisation of the EMT solution was guided by the structure of the available MatLab code, resulting in detector, tracker, and reasoner components. Out of these, our final solution uses detector and object agents only. The modules of neither solution correspond directly to what [Boissier & Demazeau 1992] termed *basic agents*, i.e., cells of a two-dimensional matrix of focus (contours, highlights, range data, stereo-vision, ...) and representation (image, image features, scene features, ...) dimensions, following the traditional decomposition of [Marr 1982]. [Bianchi & Rillo 1996] follow up on the work of Boissier & Demazeau and present a distributed control architecture applied to purposive computer vision tasks. The system is specified in terms of a set of behaviours which are decomposed into tasks and delegated by autonomous agents to basic agents. In contrast, our agents follow more or less a functional decomposition (EMT, Sect. 2) or represent task- and purpose-dependent entities (object-agents, Sect. 3). [Graf & Knoll 2000] propose a MAS architecture with a greater degree of flexibility than Boissier & Demazeau and Bianchi & Rillo. Their agents accomplish specific vision tasks by a goal-driven communication process. Master agents with complex planning and interpretation capabilities are distinguished from slave agents encapsulating image processing algorithms. The papers of a special issue of Pattern Recognition on agent-based computer vision [Rosin & Rana 2004] provide a recent snapshot of the state of the art in the area. They demonstrate how MAS technology can be applied to a variety of vision tasks while underscoring that the full potential of the agent and multi-agent paradigm is still to be uncovered. The editorial addresses also the criticism of agent-based systems that *"they are just an elaborate and unnecessary metaphor, and often do not actually provide better results than traditional techniques"* [ibid.], suggesting that agent-based systems should be considered as an alternative approach to computer vision, and that *"it would be useful for the vision community to consider the full potential of the "agent" and multi-agent paradigm"* [ibid.] The history of MAS in vision reflects to some extent the evolution from strict control to increasingly flexible coordination; from decomposition according to [Marr 1982] (transformation functions) to increasingly more flexible run-time behaviours (online service realisation). In our approach, we try to go a step further and provide a different perspective by moving from functional, transformational decompositions that can be aggregated to service realisation to task- and purpose-dependent agents (cf. [Shen & Norrie 1999, Parunak et al. 2001]).

Relating the idea of representation as a stable state of a cognitive system as defined in [ECVision Roadmap V4.2, p. 11] to our approach reveals that representation cannot be pinned down to particular data in specific agents. The concept of occlusion for instance is "represented" in the contracts between the hider and the hidden objects: it evolves dynamically over time. We cannot look at the system's state at a certain time and derive occlusion relations from it. A contract might be setup by momentary failure of a detector leading to the illusion of an occlusion; this fact is nothing but a distraction when the task is to interpret the scene, and this bad contract is soon resolved as the object is detected again. An occlusion relation requires some stability of information in the agents and interaction patterns between them to arise. It cannot be found in the micro-states of an agent or the states of a conversation, nor is it modelled explicitly as a reified macro-state. Even so, this dynamic and active form of representation allows for the system's interpretation of occlusion.

Due to our research focus on architectures for building computer vision systems rather than modelling cognitive behaviour, our approach is not directly comparable to typical cognitive architectures like ACT-R or SOAR. At this early stage, we also do not yet have entities comparable to short/long-term memory or explicit knowledge. Decentralisation and decoupling in our solution may remind of distributed blackboard based interpretations [Lesser & Erman 1980] or blackboard architectures in general (e.g. [Hayes-Roth 1995]). There are important differences between HEARSAY and our approach concerning both the domain and the processing: Relations between utterances occur over time only; in the visual domain relations occur over both time and space and are mediated via two-dimensional image sequences. Hypothesis processing in HEARSAY is transformational, based on grammar hypotheses, and not interpretational; while HEARSAY focuses on constraining the search space of a given problem, we focus on permanent (re-)interpretation of continuous input, that is driven not by internal state but by events in the scene.

6   Discussion and Outlook

We have shown that taking the agent perspective on computer vision can lead to algorithms with different decompositions (reflected in the scope and responsibilities of agents) and to solutions that are inherently distributed. Even so, the solution presented is still a far cry from exploiting the full potential of MAS. In the following, we discuss selected aspects, some limitations, and conclude with an outlook of how to try overcome them.

The conversation policy of our current design has two major synchronisation points[7], one after the tracking phase, and the other after the reasoning phase. Both are necessary to perform consistent tracking and reasoning and to keep in sync with the image data. Whether and how this explicit synchronisation can be removed—e.g., by another conversation policy or intelligent scheduling—is subject of future work. Implementation of conversation policies can be facilitated by framework support for hierarchical finite state machines. As this support is currently not available in our framework, the actual implementation is not well structured, and the description of the conversation policy was assembled from existing code and design fragments that guided the implementation. The autonomy of agents in our system is not yet an absolute necessity for the kind of coordination we investigate, as various timing issues have been ignored for the

---

[7] There are also some minor ones, e.g. after link removal for a disappeared object, right before the MoveSubObject messages.

time being. In particular, all agent behaviour is synchronised with the video frame rate and not real-time. Nevertheless, the agent paradigm already is of value in the design of the overall system and of the interactions to be coordinated.

As an alternative to the agentified solution, one could come up with two functions corresponding to the tracking and reasoning phases that perform the same kind of tracking and reasoning our system does. Arguably, these could be easier to implement, not requiring an agent framework nor mechanisms for explicit synchronisation with the image stream. We propose, however, that a main feature of our approach lies in the change of viewpoint on the problem of tracking and reasoning it affords. Although the design of appropriate conversation policies requires more (or at least different) skills and leads to a complex system, it does simplify the integration of heterogeneous detectors and coverage of specific objects (e.g., objects not capable of hiding or being hidden). Even so, we grant that thinking and designing locally from an agent's viewpoint as well as locally in space (in terms of regions of interest), requires non-local dependencies to be captured explicitly (e.g., the impact of changes in lighting or cast shadows) and may lead to unpredictable (for better or worse) system behaviour (a typical problem of complex systems). But while these properties of such a MAS may be seen as disadvantages when building industrial systems, they may in fact be an important advantage when it comes to grasping the complexity of vision. As the current results show, the presented agentified solution does not differ significantly from the original design in terms of correctness or speed while introducing a new perspective on decomposition of vision systems.

Acknowledgements

The authors would like to acknowledge the discussions and interactions within the Cognitive Vision JRP, that all formed valuable contributions to this work. The original EMT solution was provided by A.Pinz (FWF S9103-N04) and R.Tomasi. JRP partner ACIN provided zwork as the common framework of the JRP. This research was carried out in the context of the projects S9103-N04, S9106-N04 and S9107-N04 of the FWF Austrian Science Fund. The Austrian Research Institute for Artificial Intelligence is supported by the Austrian Federal Ministry for Education, Science and Culture and by the Austrian Ministry for Transport, Innovation and Technology.

References

[Bianchi & Rillo 1996] Bianchi R.A.C., Rillo A.H.R.C.: A Distributed Control Architecture for a Purposive Computer Vision System, *Proc. IEEE Intl. Joint Symposia on Intelligence and Systems (IJSIS'96)*, 288–294, 1996.

[Boissier & Demazeau 1992] Boissier O., Demazeau Y.: A Distributed Artificial Intelligence View on General Purpose Vision Systems, in Werner E., Demazeau Y., Decentralized AI 3, North-Holland Amsterdam/New York, 311–330, 1992.

[ECVision Roadmap V4.2] A Research Roadmap of Cognitive Vision. ECVision: The European Research Network for Cognitive Computer Vision Systems. IST–2001–35454. 4.2 11–2–05, 2005. <URL:http://www.ecvision.org/research_planning/ECVisionRoadmapv4.2.pdf>

[Graf & Knoll 2000] Graf T., Knoll A.: A Multi-Agent System Architecture for Distributed Computer Vision, *International Journal of Artificial Intelligence Tools*, 9(2):305–319, 2000.

[Greaves et al. 1999] Greaves M., Holback H., Bradshaw J.: What Is a Conversation Policy?, in Bradshaw J. et al. (eds.), Workshop Notes, "Specifying and Implementing Conversation Policies", Third Intl. Conf. on Autonomous Agents (Agents '99), Seattle WA, 1999.

[Hayes-Roth 1995] Hayes-Roth B.: An Architecture for Adaptive Intelligent Systems. Artificial Intelligence **72**:329–365, 1995.

[Jennings 1996] Jennings N.R.: Coordination Techniques for Distributed Artificial Intelligence, in O'Hare G.M.P., Jennings N.R. (eds.), Foundations of Distributed Artificial Intelligence, Wiley Chichester/London/New York, 187–210, 1996.

[Lesser 1998] Lesser V.: Reflections on the Nature of Multi-Agent Coordination and Its Implications for an Agent Architecture. *AAMAS*, **1**(1):89–111, Kluwer Academic Publishers, 1998.

[Lesser & Erman 1980] Lesser V., Erman L.D.: Distributed Interpretation: A Model and Experiment, *IEEE Transactions on Computers*, **29**(12):1144–1163, 1980.

[Marr 1982] Marr D.: Vision, Freeman and Company, New York, 1982.

[Omicini & Ossowski 2003] Omicini A., Ossowski S.: Objective versus Subjective Coordination in the Engineering of Agent Systems, in Klusch M. et al.(eds.): *Intelligent Information Agents: The AgentLink Perspective*. LNAI 2586. Springer Berlin Heidelberg, 179–202, 2003.

[Parunak et al. 2001] Parunak H.Van Dyke, Baker A.D., Clark S.J.: The AARIA Agent Architecture: From Manufacturing Requirements to Agent-Based System Design. *Integrated Computer-Aided Engineering*. **8**(1):45–58, IOS Press Amsterdam, 2001.

[Rosin & Rana 2004] Rosin P.L., Rana O.F. (eds.): *Pattern Recognition*, Special Issue on Agent Based Computer Vision, **37**(4):627–855, 2004.

[Shen & Norrie 1999] Shen W., Norrie D.H.: Agent-Based Systems for Intelligent Manufacturing: A State-of-the-Art Survey, *Knowledge and Information Systems*, **1**(2):129–156, Springer Berlin Heidelberg, 1999.

[Wong & Sycara 2000] Wong H., Sycara K.: A Taxonomy of Middle-Agents for the Internet, in Durfee E. et al. (eds.), Proc. 4th Intl. Conf. on MultiAgent Systems (ICMAS-2000), July 10–12, 2000, Boston, MA, IEEE Press, New York, NY, 465–466, 2000.

A Model of Multi-agent System Based on Policies and Contracts[*]

Beishui Liao and Ji Gao

Institute of Artificial Intelligence,
Zhejiang University, Hangzhou 310027, China
Beishui@126.com, gaoji@mail.hz.zj.cn

Abstract. Due to the dynamic nature of virtual organizations (VOs), it is necessary that the multi-agent system for VO formation and cooperation should be
aware of the mutable business requirements or user's preferences within VO
environments and integrate these dynamic business requirements into its decision making process. We present a model of multi-agent system based on policies and contracts, in which the requirements for both the system and the individual agents can be defined dynamically by means of policies. On the one
hand, at the system level, the duties and rights of roles can be specified or modified in terms of policies presented by the VO administrators. And on the other
hand, role enacting agents are guided by policies defined by their owners. The
policy and contract extended agent model (BGI$_{PDC}$) is the core of the system,
which is formally specified in this paper.

1 Introduction

Currently, a large number of research efforts have been made to cope with the challenges about service integration under the context of virtual organization (VO), including web services, grid computing, policy-based management, and multi-agent
technology, etc. Among them, agent technology is an ideal candidate. In order to
make explicit, predictable and stable the interactions between participating agents of
multi-agent system, much recent research such as [1,2,3,4] extended the traditional
BDI-based agent model with some social mechanisms, including norms and contracts.
However, these methods can't reflect the dynamic requirements of the VO. When
norm-based multi-agent systems are developed, the system's objectives (requirements) usually should be pre-determined, so they can't fully support those VO applications whose objectives (high-level business requirements) should be modified frequently at run time. Fortunately, the ideas of policy-based management (PBM) are
useful to treat this problem. According to [5,6], policies are a means to dynamically
regulate the behavior of system components. While sharing much in common with
norm-based approaches, policy-based perspectives differ in subtle ways. Feltovich
pointed out that norms are designed offline, while policy-based approaches support
dynamic runtime policy changes, and not merely static configurations determined
in advance [7].

---

[*] This work is supported by the National Grand Fundamental Research 973 Program of China
under Grant No.2003CB317000.

So, in this paper, we introduce the idea of policy-based management into traditional multi-agent system model. On the one hand, we propose a structure of multi-agent system based on policies, roles and contracts. There are three characteristics of this structure. First, the duties and rights of each role are specified in terms of policies that may be modified frequently before the role enactment, then the objectives of the role are indirectly fulfilled by role enacting agent (REA), thus the system is able to timely response to the variation of high-level business requirements. Second, the cooperation of individual agents of a multi-agent system is associated by means of contracts that are signed by REAs and VO management agent. Third, the owner (stakeholder) of each individual agent in the system can specify policies to influence the agent's behavior so that the agent's decision making is made as consistent as possible with its owner's objectives. On the other hand, as to individual agent, its motivations include both internal ones (its own desires) and external ones, therefore the traditional BDI agent is not feasible in that it only considers the internal motivations. We extend the traditional BDI agent model with obligations arose from guidance policies (P-Obligations for short) and obligations from contracts (C-Obligations for short), called BGI_{PDC} agent model.

This paper focuses on the policy-driven multi-agent model, while the details of the representation and deployment of policies are not involved, the reader is referred to [5,6]. The structure of this paper is organizes as follows. In section 2, we propose the architecture of multi-agent system based on policies and contracts. In section 3, the policy and contract extended BDI agent (BGI_{PDC}) formal model is presented, which is the core of the multi-agent system. Then in section 4, a case is put forward to show how the proposed system works. And finally, section 5 is related work and conclusions.

2   The Architecture of Multi-agent System Based on Policies and Contracts

The focus of the approach proposed here is the idea that the multi-agent system and the individual agents are driven by the requirements that can be specified dynamically in terms of policies, rather than those only defined statically in advance. We propose a policies and contracts based multi-agent system (P-MAS for short) as shown in Figure1. Corresponding to this figure, P-MAS model is defined formally as a tuple: P-MAS = ⟨P-OM, P-REA, CRE⟩ where P-OM denotes policy-based organization model, P-REA denotes a set of policy-driven role enacting agents, and CRE denotes a set of contracts signed by the role enacting agents and the VO manager. Now, we describe in details the definition of *policy*, *P-OM*, *CRE* and *P-REA* respectively as follows.

Firstly, *policy* is the driven element of the system. There are two dimensions of policy: the role-based VO policy (RVP for short) and the individual agent policy, called guidance policy (GP for short). The former is defined by VO administrator (VO Admin in figure 1) the rights and the duties of a role, while the latter is specified by specific agent's owner (Owner or VO Admin in figure 1) to express the local objectives or preferences. Formally, a policy can be defined in the form of EBNF as follows.

```
Policy ::= RVP| GP
RVP    ::='Obl('Role1 [Role2] Pred1 [Pred2] ')' |
           'Pms('Role1 [Role2] Pred1 [Pred2] ')' |
           'Prh('Role1 [Role2] Pred1 [Pred2] ')'
GP     ::='Obl('Owner Agent1 [Agent2]Pred1 [Pred2]')'|
           'Pms('Owner Agent1 [Agent2] Pred1 [Pred2]')'|
           'Prh('Owner Agent1 [Agent2] Pred1 [Pred2]')'
```

In this definition, *Role1* and *Role2* are a role identity as the subject and target of the policy respectively, *Pred1* and *Pred2* are a predicate expression as the policy objective and policy precondition respectively, *Owner* is the owner (stakeholder) of individual agent, and Agent1 and Agent2 are policy subject and target respectively. There are three modalities of RVP, i.e., obligations, permissions and prohibition. We use $Obl(r1, r2, \phi|\psi)$, $Pms(r1, r2, \phi|\psi)$, and $Prh(r1, r2, \phi|\psi)$ to denote them respectively. The GP is denoted by $Obl_Y(i, j, \phi|\psi)$, $Pms_Y(i, j, \phi|\psi)$, or $Prh_Y(i, j, \phi|\psi)$, in which Y is the owner of the agent i.

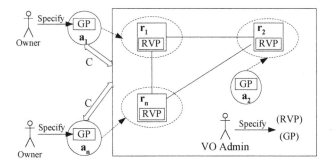

Fig. 1. The Architecture of Multi-agent system based on policies and contracts

Secondly, policy-based Organization Model (*P-OM*) is the abstract level of a multi-agent system. The formal definition of P-OM is a tuple ⟨P-Roles, P-IR⟩ where P-Roles is a set of policy-based roles and P-IR is a set of interaction relations between roles.

The policy-based role (r_1, r_2, r_n in figure 1) is different from the traditional ones in that here the duties and rights of a role are specified by the policies that can be specified at run time. Formally, a policy-based role (P-Role) is defined in the form of EBNF as follows.

```
P-Role::= 'Rol(' Role-ID Objective Right Duty ')'
Right ::={RVP}      Duty  ::={RVP}
```

In this definition, *Role-ID* is a role identity, Objective is a set of objectives required by the role, and RVP is defined as the above definition. On the other hand, the P-IR illustrates the interaction scenes of roles, and P-IR ⊆ P-Roles × P-Role.

Thirdly, *CRE* is a set of contracts. A contract ("C" in figure 1) is signed when a role enacting agent reaches an agreement with VO management agent. The contract clauses (C-Clauses) include rights and duties defined in a role and other clauses arose during negotiation. A contract is defined in the form of EBNF as follows.

```
Contract   ::='Contract(' N Ag VMA {C-Clause} ')'
C-Clause   ::='Obl('N subject Object Pred-1 [Pred-2]')'|
                'Pms('N subject Object Pred-1 [Pred-2]')'|
                'Prh('N subject Object Pred-1 [Pred-2] ')'
Subject  ::= VMA|Ag
Object   ::=VMA|Ag|Other-Role|Other-Agent
```

In this definition, N is a specific authority, which monitors the contract enforcement and carries out the sanctions when some violations arise. Ag and VMA are role enacting agent and VO management agent respectively. The *Subject* of a contract can be VMA or Ag, while the *Object* of a contract can be VMA, Ag, other role, or other agent. *Pre-1* and Pred-2 are the objective and the condition of a contract respectively. We use $Obl_N(i, j, \phi|\psi)$, $Pms_N(i, j, \phi|\psi)$, and $Prh_N(i, j, \phi|\psi)$ to denote the three classes of contract clause respectively.

Finally, *P-REA* is a set of policy-driven role enacting agents. During the formation of a VO, the VO management agent (VMA) will recruit prospecting agents to take up the roles. Each agent may negotiate with the VMA about the duties and rights of the specific roles that are defined in terms of policies. When they reach an agreement, a contract will be signed by the two parties. Then, the agent will take up the role. We call this type of agent policy-driven role enacting agent (P-REA, for example, a1, a2, an in figure1). From the perspective of a P-REA, its owner (stakeholder) can also specify guidance policies to guide or constrain its behavior to meet the high-level business requirements. So, the motivation sources of P-REA include its owner desires, P-Obligations and C-Obligations. Obviously, the traditional BDI agent is not feasible in policies and contracts based multi-agent system. In this paper, we propose an extended BDI agent model, call BGI_{PDC} agent model, which is formulated in details in the next section.

3 BGI_{PDC} Agent Model

3.1 Syntax

The logical language (BGI_{PDC}) for policy-driven agent representation is based on the BDI logic presented in [8] which is in turn an extension of CTL* logic, a propositional branching-time logic. The temporal operators A (universal path quantifier, or inevitable), X (next), and U (until) express properties over time. The operators E (existential path quantifier, or optional), F (sometimes), and G (always) are defined in terms of the primitive temporal operators as $E(\phi) \equiv \neg A(\neg\phi)$, $F(\phi) \equiv trueU\phi$ and $G(\phi) \equiv \neg F(\neg\phi)$. We distinguish agent's internal motivations, desires (DES), from its external motivations, the obligations produced by contracts ($CObl_N$) and guidance policies (PObl), while agent's goals are the outputs of the decision making on these motivation inputs, as shown in the decision process of BGI_{PDC} agent (figure 2). In addition, operators

$\mathrm{CPms_N}$, $\mathrm{CPrh_N}$, PPms and PPrh are defined as $\mathrm{CPms_N(\phi)} \equiv \neg\mathrm{CObl_N}(\neg\phi), \mathrm{CPrh_N(\phi)} \equiv \mathrm{CObl_N}(\neg\phi)$, $\mathrm{PPms(\phi)} \equiv \neg\mathrm{PObl}(\neg\phi)$ and $\mathrm{PPrh(\phi)} \equiv \mathrm{PObl}(\neg\phi)$ respectively.

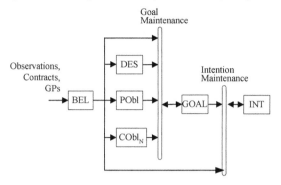

Fig. 2. The Decision Process of $\mathrm{BGI_{PDC}}$ Agent

The state formula and path formula of $\mathrm{BGI_{PDC}}$ are defined as follows:

- any primitive proposition is a state formula;
- if $\phi1$ and $\phi2$ are state formulas and x is an individual or event variable, then $\neg\phi1$, $\phi1\vee\phi2$, and $\exists x\phi1(x)$ are state formulas;
- if ϕ is a state formula and i, j are agents then $\mathrm{BEL}(i, \phi)$, $\mathrm{GOAL}(i, \phi)$, $\mathrm{INT}(i, \phi)$, $\mathrm{PObl}(i, \phi)$, $\mathrm{CObl_N}(i, j, \phi)$ and $\mathrm{DES}(i, \phi)$ are state formulas;
- if ψ is a path formula, the $\mathrm{E}(\psi)$, $\mathrm{A}(\psi)$ is a state formula;
- any state formula is also a path formula; and
- if $\psi1$ and $\psi2$ are path formulas, then $\neg\psi1$, $\psi1\vee\psi2$, $\psi1U\psi2$, $X\psi1$ are path formulas.

3.2 Formal Semantics of $\mathrm{BGI_{PDC}}$

A model for $\mathrm{BGI_{PDC}}$ is a tuple $M = \langle W, E, T, \prec, \mathcal{U}, \mathcal{B}, \mathcal{G}, \mathcal{I}, \mathcal{D}, \mathcal{O}^P, \mathcal{O}^C, \pi\rangle$ where W is a set of worlds, E is a set of primitive event types, T is a set of time points, $\prec$ is a binary relation on time points, $\mathcal{U}$ is the universe of discourse which is a tuple itself $\mathcal{U} = \langle \mathcal{U}_{P\text{-}REA}, \mathcal{U}_{P\text{-}Roles}, \mathcal{U}_{CRE}, \mathcal{U}_{GP}, \mathcal{U}_{others}\rangle$, $\mathcal{B}$ is belief accessibility relation, $\mathcal{B}: \mathcal{U}_{P\text{-}REA} \to \wp(W\times T\times W)$, and $\mathcal{G}, \mathcal{I}, \mathcal{D}, \mathcal{O}^P$ and $\mathcal{O}^C$ similarly for goals, intentions, desires, P-Obligations and C-Obligations respectively, and finally π interprets the atomic formulas of the language.

In the following, we give the semantics of beliefs, goals, intentions, desires, and two kinds of obligations, while the semantics of the other state and path formulas are similar to those defined in [8,9] and not presented here.

Beliefs, Goals, and Intentions. A belief ϕ of an agent i is represented as $\mathrm{BEL}(i, \phi)$. There are three classes information as inputs of belief component, including observations about the environments, contracts signed with other agent and guidance policies for individual agents (GPs) specified by its owner. The semantics for the state formulas BEL(i, ϕ) is as follows:

$$M_{V,w_t} \vDash \text{BEL}(i,\phi) \text{ iff } \forall w_t' \text{ s.t. } \mathcal{B}_i(w_t, w_t'), M_{V,w_t'} \vDash \phi$$

For the beliefs of agents we use a KD45 axiomatization relative to each agent.

A goal of an agent i is represented as GOAL(i, ϕ). We assume a KD axiomatization to ensure the consistency of the goals. A goal of BGI$_{PDC}$ agent is the production of three motivations, i.e., desires, P-Obligations and C-Obligations. The semantics of GOAL(i, ϕ) is defined in the standard way in the Kripke model.

$$M_{V,w_t} \vDash \text{GOAL}(i,\phi) \text{ iff } \forall w_t' \text{ s.t. } \mathcal{G}_i(w_t, w_t'), M_{V,w_t'} \vDash \phi$$

An intention of an agent i is represented as INT(i, ϕ). Just like goals, intentions have a KD axiomatization and its semantics is as follows.

$$M_{V,w_t} \vDash \text{INT}(i,\phi) \text{ iff } \forall w_t' \text{ s.t. } \mathcal{I}_i(w_t, w_t'), M_{V,w_t'} \vDash \phi$$

Desires, P-Obligations and C-Obligations. A desire ϕ of an agent i is represented in the logics as DES(i, ϕ). For the desires, the inconsistencies are allowed, so the D axiom is not satisfied. In order to decide the preference order of different desires, we adopt the methodology proposed by F.Dignum et al [10] that related to the set of desires there is a preference ordering on the set of possible worlds indicating their relative desirability.

The formal semantics of the obligations are based on the standard deontic logic (SDL) as presented in [11]. We extend SDL to allow for multiple modalities to denote P-Obligations and C-Obligations from different motivation sources. So, in BGI$_{PDC}$ logic, there are two kinds of obligations, i.e., P-obligations PObl(i, j, ϕ) and C-obligations CObl$_N$(i, j, ϕ), where i and j can be the same entity. When i = j, PObl(i, j, ϕ) and CObl$_N$(i, j, ϕ) are written as PObl(i, ϕ) and CObl$_N$(i, ϕ) respectively. The accessibility relation $\mathcal{O}^P$ and $\mathcal{O}^C$ for PObl(i, j, ϕ) and CObl$_N$(i, j, ϕ) respectively yield the deontically ideal worlds relative to a world w at time point t. The $\mathcal{O}^P$ and $\mathcal{O}^C$ are formed according to the preference ordering of obligations. As for obligations CObl$_N$(i, j, ϕ) arose from sanction-based contract clause Obl$_N$(i, j, $\phi|\psi$), the preference ordering of them is based on the sanctions (s) for their violations. For each situation w_t there is a value of that world for agent i, with respect to its relation to agent j and VO authority N: CS(w_t, i, j, N). This value can be seen as the cost of the sanction (CS) in case i does not fulfill its obligation towards j and defines the preference ordering for the operator CObl$_N$(i, j, ϕ). On the other hand, as far as obligations PObl(i, j, ϕ) created by the individual agent policies are concerned, the preference ordering of them is based on the utility losses and utility gains when the agent violates and fulfills the obligations, similar to the utilitarian semantics proposed by Lang et al [12]. For each situation w_t, there is a value of utility u(w_t) which defines the preference ordering of the operator PObl(i, j, ϕ).

So the accessibility relation $\mathcal{O}^P$ and $\mathcal{O}^C$ can be defined as $\mathcal{O}^P(w_t, w_t')$ iff $u(w_t) \leq u(w_t')$, and $\mathcal{O}^C(w_t, w_t')$ iff $CS(w_t', i, j, N) \leq CS(w_t, i, j, N)$, respectively. Thus, we define the semantics of these two kinds of obligations as follows.

$$M_{v,w_t} \vDash \text{PObl}(i, j, \phi) \ \textit{iff} \ \forall w_t' \ s.t. \ \mathcal{O}_{i,j}^P(w_t, w_t'), M_{v,w_t'} \vDash \phi$$

$$M_{v,w_t} \vDash \text{CObl}_N(i, j, \phi) \ \textit{iff} \ \forall w_t' \ s.t. \ \mathcal{O}_{i,j}^C(w_t, w_t'), M_{v,w_t'} \vDash \phi$$

We adopt D system for P-Obligations and C-Obligations. This ensures that there may not be deontic conflicts.

3.3 Other Basic Axioms

In BGI$_{PDC}$ logic, we adopt the strong realism, so there are the following axioms:

(A1) $\text{DES}(i, \phi) \Rightarrow \text{BEL}(i, \phi)$
(A2) $\text{PObl}(i, j, \phi) \Rightarrow \text{BEL}(i, \text{PObl}(i, j, \phi))$
(A3) $\text{CObl}_N(i, j, \phi) \Rightarrow \text{BEL}(i, \text{CObl}_N(i, j, \phi))$
(A4) $\text{INT}(i, \phi) \Rightarrow \text{GOAL}(i, \phi)$

As for BGI$_{PDC}$ agent, goals are chosen from three sources: desires, C-Obligations, and P-Obligations. Due to the requirement that in policies and contracts based multi-agent system, each participating agent should do its best to fulfill the enacted role so that the system's objectives can be achieved as well as possible, and then it should comply with its owner's guidance policies to carry out the dynamic requirements of the stakeholder, we have the following rule:

Rule1: If a BGI$_{PDC}$ agent has to make a choice for a goal between mutual exclusive situations, then it should choose an alternative preferred by its C-Obligations first, one preferred by its P-Obligations second, and one preferred by its own desires third.

According to the Rule1, we have the following axioms stating the compatibility between desires, C-Obligations, and P-Obligations of BGI$_{PDC}$ agent respectively.

(A5) $\text{DES}(i, \phi) \Rightarrow \neg\text{CObl}_N(i, j, \neg\phi)$
(A6) $\text{DES}(i, \phi) \Rightarrow \neg\text{PObl}(i, j, \neg\phi)$
(A7) $\text{PObl}(i, j, \phi) \Rightarrow \neg\text{CObl}_N(i, j, \neg\phi)$

In addition, C-Obligations and P-Obligations are arisen from the Contracts and guidance policies respectively. We have the following axioms:

(A8) $\text{Obl}_N(i, j, \phi|\psi) \Leftrightarrow A(E(\psi) \Rightarrow X\text{CObl}_N(i, j, \phi))$
(A9) $\text{Obl}_Y(i, j, \phi|\psi) \Leftrightarrow A(\text{BEL}(i, Y) \wedge E(\psi) \Rightarrow X\text{PObl}(i, j, \phi))$

Finally, violation of C-Obligation will give rise to sanctions by the VO authority. Then there is a following axiom (We suppose proposition $s(N, i)$ denotes that agent i is sanctioned by N):

(A10) $\text{CObl}_N(i, j, F\phi) \wedge A \Diamond (\neg\phi) \Rightarrow A \Diamond \text{INT}(N, s(N, j))$

4 A Case Study

Suppose that there is a souvenir production VO (SP for short). A souvenir is composed of several accessories from different accessory providers (AP_1, AP_2 ..., AP_n). When the accessories for a specific souvenir are prepared, they will be assembled by a souvenir assembler (SA) to produce a souvenir product. Roles AP_1, Ap_2, ..., AP_n and SA can be enacted by specific agents at run time by means of negotiations and signing contracts. In this VO, a management agent (called m) take charge of the negotiations with role enacting agents, signing contracts with them, and treating other VO affairs. Now, a user u1 signs a contract (C1) with m as follows (We suppose that the souvenirs' type is "A" which is composed of two accessories A1 and A2):

C1:$\{Obl_N(m, u1, \phi1), Obl_N(u1, m, \phi2|\phi1), Obl_N(m, u1, \phi3|\neg\phi1), Obl_N(u1, m, \phi4|\neg\phi2)\}$ in which

$Obl_N(m, u1, \phi1)$ — Agent m is obliged to provide 200 pieces of type A souvenirs before 2005-3-17 ($\phi1$) to user u1;

$Obl_N(u1, m, \phi2|\phi1)$ — User u1 is obliged to send 5000$ within 2 days ($\phi2$) to m if m has done $\phi1$ before the deadline;

$Obl_N(m, u1, \phi3|\neg\phi1)$ — If m hasn't done $\phi1$ before the deadline, agent m is obliged to provide 50$ within two days ($\phi3$) to user u1;

$Obl_N(u1, m, \phi4|\neg\phi2)$ — If u1 hasn't done $\phi2$ before the deadline, it is obliged to send 5100$ within 2 days ($\phi4$) to m.

With this contract, the administrator of SP specifies the policies $Obl(AP_1, SA, \phi5)$, $Obl(AP_2, SA, \phi6)$, $Obl(SA, m, \phi7)$ and for role AP_1, AP_2 and SA respectively, in which

$Obl(AP_1, SA, \phi5)$—Role AP_1 is obliged to submit the accessory A1 before 2005-3-12 ($\phi5$) to SA;

$Obl(AP_2, SA, \phi6)$—Role AP_2 is obliged to submit the accessory A2 before 2005-3-12 ($\phi6$) to SA;

$Obl(SA, m, \phi7)$—Role SA is obliged to submit the souvenir A before 2005-3-15 ($\phi7$) to m.

Based on these policies, the three roles are represented as follows:

AP_1: $\{$produce (A1), $Obl(AP_1, SA, \phi5)\}$; AP_2: $\{$produce (A2), $Obl(AP_2, SA, \phi6)\}$; SA: $\{$assemble (A), $Obl(SA, m, \phi7)\}$.

Then, agents who are able to take up these roles join the VO and enact the roles respectively by contracts. Now, take the agent who enacts the role AP_1 for example to show how the decision of an individual agent is influence by three motivations: internal desires, P-Obligations, and C-Obligations. Suppose that the agent a1 signs a contract C2 with the VO management agent m as follows:

C2: $\{$ $Obl_N(a1, SA, \phi5)$, $Obl_N(m, a1, \phi8|\phi5)$, $Pms_N(m, a1, \phi9|\neg\phi5)$, $Obl_N(m, a1, \phi10|\neg\phi8)\}$ in which

$Obl_N(a1, SA, \phi5)$— Agent a1 is obliged to submit the accessory A1 before 2005-3-12 ($\phi5$) to SA;

$Obl_N(m, a1, \phi8|\phi5)$ — Agent m is obliged to send 4000$ within 4 days ($\phi8$) to a1 if a1 has done $\phi5$ before the deadline;

$Pms_N(m, a1, \phi9\vdash\neg\phi5)$ — If a1 hasn't done $\phi5$ before the deadline, Agent m is permitted to set a bad reputation ($\phi9$) to a1;

$Obl_N(m, a1, \phi10\vdash\neg\phi8)$ — If m hasn't done $\phi8$ before the deadline, it is obliged to send 4200\$ within 2 days ($\phi10$) to m.

Meanwhile, agent a1 has a belief $BEL(a1, \phi11)$ which gives rise to a desire D1: $DES(a1, \phi11)$, in which

$\phi11$— The accessory A3 is more profitable than A1, so it is desirable to take A3 ($\phi11$) as a goal (a1 believe that producing A3 means giving up producing A1 (B1)).

In additional, the owner of a1 (owner1) may define a policy G1: $Obl_{owner1}(a1, \phi12)$ in which

$Obl_{owner1}(a1, \phi12)$ — Agent a1 is obliged to prefer reputation to the profit ($\phi12$).

According to C2, D1, G1 and the Axiom A8 and A9, a1 has the following three motivation sources for selection: $CObl_N(a1, SA, \phi5)$, $PObl(a1, \phi12)$ and $DES(a1, \phi11)$. Based on the beliefs $BEL(a1, \phi5\rightarrow \neg\phi11)$ (B1), $BEL(a1, \phi12\rightarrow\phi5)$ and the Rule1, a1 forms its goal $GOAL(a1, \phi5)$.

On the other hand, if a new user u2 submits another request and signs contract C3, the VO administrator can specify new policies to define roles, while the owners of role enacting agents can specify different policies to guide the behavior of corresponding agents. So, in this way, the formation and operation of multi-agent system are driven by dynamic policies.

5 Related Work and Conclusions

Recently, a great amount of research efforts have been made on the multi-agent modeling based on norms, contracts and roles [1,13,14]. While our work presented in this paper sharing much in common with these approaches in that we also adopted roles and contracts for multi-agent organizing, our work was focused on introducing policy management idea to multi-agent system to let the multi-agent system be aware of the dynamic business requirements and integrating these dynamic business requirements into its decision making process. On the other hand, there were also a lot of researches focused on the extended BDI logic based on the obligations and norms [10,15,16]. By comparison, the BGI_{PDC} logic concentrated on how to accommodate the desires, P-Obligations and C-Obligations into the extended BDI logic.

In conclusion, the multi-agent system and the BGI_{PDC} logic proposed in this paper formulated a logic framework that is feasible to be applied in the open and dynamic VO environment in which the requirements of both systems and individuals are mutable. Compared to the traditional multi-agent system, the main novelties of this paper are two-fold. First, duties and rights of a role are defined by policies. In this way, the VO administrators have the approaches to specify high-level business requirements to the system from the perspective of a VO. On the other hand, owners of individual agents are able to direct the behavior of the agents by defining guidance policies. Second, by extending traditional BDI agent model with obligations that arise from policies and contracts, we introduce the BGI_{PDC} agent that is capable of treating both the internal and external motivations and forming consistent goals when it works in the policies and contracts based multi-agent system.

However, there is a great deal of further work required to make the policies and contracts based multi-agent system and BGI$_{PDC}$ logic more comprehensive, including an automatic policy refinement mechanism for translating high-level policies (reflecting the business goals and human's preferences) into low-level ones (understandable and enforceable by agents), a belief revision model that is able to cope with conflict policies, a more flexible approach for goal choosing from three sources (desires, C-Obligations, and P-Obligations) rather than only in terms of Rule 1 specified in Section 3.3, etc.

References

1. Vazquez-Salceda, V.Dignum, and F.Dignum 2005. Organizing Multiagent Systems. JAAMAS, Kluwer. Forthcoming.
2. V. Dignum, et al 2002. Formal Specification of Interaction in Agent Societies. In Proceedings of FAAB 2002, 37-52. Springer-Verlag..
3. Boella and van der Torre 2004. Contracts as legal institutions in organizations of autonomous agents. In Proceedings of AAMAS'04,948-955, IEEE, Inc.
4. F.Dignum 1999.Autonomous Agents with Norms. Artificial Intelligence and Law,Vol7:69-79.
5. G. Tonti, J.M. Bradshaw, et al.Semantic Web Languages for Policy Representation and Reasoning: A Comparison of KAoS, Rei, and Ponder. Proc. Second International Semantic Web Conference (ISWC2003). October,2003.
6. Beishui Liao, et al. Ontology-Based Conceptual Modeling of Policy-Driven Control Framework: Oriented to Multi-agent System for Web Services Management. In Proceedings of AWCC 2004, 346-356, Springer-Verlag, 2004.
7. Feltovich,et al 2003. Order and KAoS: Using policy to represent agent cultures. In Proceedings of the AAMAS 03 Workshop on Humans and Multi-Agent Systems. Melbourne, Australia.
8. Rao and Georgeff 1991. Modeling rational agents within a BDI architecture. In Proceedings of the KR'91, 473-484. Morgan Kaufmann Publishers.
9. Fasli 2003a. Interrelations between the BDI primitives: Towards heterogeneous agents. Cognitive Systems Research 4(2003): 1-22.
10. 10.F.Dignum, Kinny and Sonenberg 2001. Motivational Attitudes of Agents: On Desires Obligations and Norms. In Proceedings of the CEEMAS 2001, 61-70. Spring-Verlag.
11. Wright 1951. Deontic logic. Mind, 60:1–15, 1951.
12. Lang, van der Torre and Weydert 2002, Utilitarian Desires. Autonomous Agents and Multi-Agent Systems, 5:3, 329-363.
13. Fasli 2003b. From Social Agents to Multi-agent Systems: Preliminary Report. In Proceedings of CEEMAS 2003, 111-121. Spring-Verlag.
14. Dastani, V. Dignum, and F. Dignum 2002, Organizations and Normative Agents. In Proceedings of EurAsia ICT2002, 982-989. Spring-Verlag.
15. Broersen, Dastani, and van der Torre 2003. BDIO-CTL: Obligations and the Specification of Agent Behavior, In Proceedings of IJCAI2003, 1389—1390.
16. Fasli 2002. On Commitments, Roles, and Obligations.In Proceedings of CEEMAS 2001, 93-102. Spring-Verlag.

Case-Based Student Modeling in Multi-agent Learning Environment

Carolina González[1,2], Juan C. Burguillo[1], and Martin Llamas[1]

[1] Departamento de Ingeniería Telemática, Universidad de Vigo, Vigo 36200, Spain
{cgonzals, jrial, martin}@det.uvigo.es
[2] Departamento de Sistemas. Universidad del Cauca, Popayán, Colombia
cgonzals@unicauca.edu.co

Abstract. The student modeling (SM) is a core component in the development of Intelligent Learning Environments (ILEs). In this paper we describe how a Multi-agent Intelligent Learning Environment can provide adaptive tutoring based in Case-Based Student Modeling (CBSM). We propose a SM structured as a multi-agent system composed by four types of agents. These are: the Case Learner Agent (CLA), Tutor Agent (TA), Adaptation Agent (AA), and Orientator Agent (OA). Each student model has a corresponding CLA. The TA Agent selects the adequate teaching strategy. The AA Agent organizes the learning resources and the OA Agent personalizes the learning considering the psychological characteristics of the student. To illustrate the process of student modeling an algorithm will also be presented. To validate the Student Model, we present a case study based an Intelligent Tutoring System for learning in Public Health domain.

1 Introduction

Many developers of educational systems consider Intelligent Tutoring Systems (ITS) and Learning Environments as different and even contradictory ways of using computers in education. The recent success of such well-known Intelligent Learning Environments [1] showed that these ways are not contradictory, but rather complementary. ITS are able to control learning adaptively at various levels, but generally do not provide tools to support free exploration. Learning environments support exploratory learning [2], but they lack the control of an intelligent tutor. Without such control the student often works inefficiently and may never discover important features of the subject.

ILEs can monitor students, help them to perform their tasks and provide them with feedback in a manner that contributes to their learning process. For the students to learn effectively and efficiently, ILEs should provide teaching strategies according to the specific domain knowledge and objectives.

The Student Model is the main component within the Intelligent Learning Environment and, contains information about the student knowledge. It obtains the information by dinamically observing and recording the student's behaviour, answers, problem-solving strategies, and analyzing them in order to deduct their

M. Pěchouček, P. Petta, and L.Z. Varga (Eds.): CEEMAS 2005, LNAI 3690, pp. 72–81, 2005.

level of understanding about the domain. This information is processed and used to individually adapt the system to each student.

Intelligent agents have been quite successful at observing student's behaviour and, therefore, they have been widely used in learning environments in order to capture the characteristics of the student and perform student modeling tasks [3].

Building a student model involves defining; the "who", is modelled; the "what", or the goals, plans, attitudes, capabilities, knowledge, and beliefs of the student; the "how" the model is to be acquired and maintained; and the "why" , including student's information to give assistance, to provide feedback, or to interpret the student behaviour [4]. The need for simplicity and ease of understanding in Student Models is very high. It derives from the fact that distance education is addressed to students who vary greatly in their educational background. Due to the lack of physical tutor-student contact, sometimes the distance student has the feeling that the teacher is unreachable when needed. This is the reason why Student Models should provide bi-directional benefit to both instructors and students, by enabling students to monitor their own progress and utilise the feedback provided by the model on a continuous basis.

There are many techniques for generating student models; however most of these techniques are computationally complex and time consuming for example: Bayesian Networks [5], Fuzzy student modeling approach [6], the Dempster-Shafer theory [7]. Other techniques can only record what a student knows and not the students' behaviour and features. Examples are: overlay model [8], stereotype and combination model [9]. A comparison of Case-Based Reasoning and Bayesian Networks for student modeling is realized in [10]. This study shows that CBR is the best and easiest approach for constructing a student modeling.

We propose a multi-agent approach to student modeling in which each student model has a corresponding Case Learner Agent. This agent uses the CBR paradigm [11] to generate the student profile. The CBR paradigm is simple and do not require complex inference algorithms, moreover offers well-founded methodologies and experiences with respect to both mathematic and algorithmic aspects. In our approach, we included an Orientator Agent to customize the learning considering the psychological characteristics of the student. In order to constructing the knowledge of the students, we used CaseML [12] a semantic enriched markup language.

In our approach the student model is improved because: it is easy to handle and to maintain beneficiating to both the tutor and the student; to promote student reflection because reporting the student's misconceptions and the reasons why they have happened; and to facilitate the supervision of the students by enabling the tutor to have a solid and continuous view of the student performance.

The outline of this paper is as follows: Section 2 describes an overview on Student Models. Section 3 presents the Student Modeling Process. In Section 4, the construction of the Student Model by Case-based Reasoning is described.

Section 5 presents the modeling algorithm. Section 6 exposes a case of study: An Intelligent Tutor System for learning in Public Health. Finally in the Section 7 some conclusions are presented.

2   An Overview on Student Models

Many researchers have tried to classify and formalize the student model in a unified framework. VanhLehn [13] uses three dimensions (bandwidth, knowledge type and differences between student and expert) to construct the student model. Ragnemalm [14] regards the student modeling problem as a process to connect the student's input in the ILE, the conception of the system and the representation of the correct knowledge. Self [15] tries to provide a theorical computational basis for student modeling, which is psychologically neutral and independent from the applications.

Generally the student models are classified into three traditional model types according to the assumptions about the student's knowledge: (1) overlay, (2) analytical, and (3) predictive models [16]. Most ITS use the overlay model. It considers the student's knowledge as a part of the expert's knowledge and use a set of concept-value pairs to represent the student's knowledge. The analytical model makes a distinction between the student's knowledge and the expert's knowledge. The system determines whether students have knowledge or not by checking how the student uses the knowledge that the system defines. An experience using this model is WEST [17]. The predictive model takes into account that the student's knowledge can be extended beyond the expert knowledge. This model provides more flexibility as new perturbations can be added into an existing model when needed, while the overlay and differential models always consider the student's knowledge as a subset of the expert knowledge. However, the perturbation model brings more difficulty. This model was implemented in DEBUGGY and IDEBUGGY systems [18].

These traditional models have some disadvantages (1) the student may follow different problem solving approaches; (2) cannot predict what student knows; (3) may hold different beliefs that are not a subset of the domain knowledge; and (4) most models represent knowledge with procedural net increasing the complexity model. Case-based paradigm is another approach to student modeling, which has been used by some authors to conceive and develop a student model for Intelligent Tutoring Systems. We propose a case-based student modeling (CBSM) structured as a multi-agent system that takes into account several components that are essential for efficient adaptive teaching process. They are: (1) knowledge level, (2) learning style, (3) learning goals, and (6) psychological characteristics.

3   Student Modeling Process

In order to construct the Student Model, information about student should be acquired.

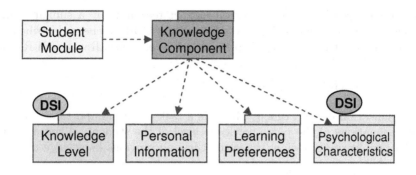

Fig. 1. Content of the Student Model

3.1   Content of the Student Model (SM)

A comprehensive student model should contain information about the previous student's knowledge, the student's progress, preferences, interests, goals, personal information and any other information related to the student. Based on the dependence upon the subject domain, the content held in student models consists of two parts: domain specific information and domain independent information.

- **Domain specific information (DSI):** it is also named student knowledge model (SKM) which represents a reflection of the student's state and level of knowledge in term of a particular subject domain.
- **Domain independent information (DII):** it is slightly different from system to system. The domain-independent information about a student may include learning goals, cognitive aptitudes, measures for motivation state, preferences about the presentation method, factual and historic data, etc.

We propose a student model that includes individual and cognitive characteristics grouped in a component named Knowledge Component. This component contains information related to the (1) knowledge level of the student, (2) personal information, (3) learning preferences, and (4) psychological characteristics. Figure 1 shows the content of the student model.

4   Constructing the Student Model by Case-Based Reasoning

The student modeling has been recognized as a complex and difficult but important task by researchers. The method of student modeling includes a representation of the knowledge and reasoning of the student, and the way how the student acquires new knowledge in order to perform intelligent learning.

Case-Based Reasoning (CBR) is a problem-solving paradigm that is able to utilize the specific knowledge gained from previous experiences in similar situations (cases) to solve a new problem. Instead of relying on exact reasoning in

a well ordered world, CBR focuses on inexact reasoning by a similarity measurement among objects. The process involved in CBR has been described as a
cyclic process that integrates four phases: Retrieve, Reuse, Revise and Retain.

4.1   Student Model Initialization

The initialization of the Student Model is a task of great importance to makes
initial estimations of the new knowledge level of the student. When a student
starts a new learning session, the system has no previous knowledge about his
learning skill.

In this study, the information about the students is regarded as cases. When
the student starts learning, the information about the students is extracted from
the student model and is converted into a new case. When there is a new student,
he is asked to take some tests, then the system analyses his tests results to gather
information and initialize the student model. For representing cases, we have
revised several types of methods from unstructured cases to structured problem
solving episodes and we had selected CaseML because it is a semantic enriched
markup language.

Additionally, CaseML solves the problems presented in traditional case representation as: (1) needs a human interpreter, (2) fails to describe complex objects,
and (3) needs of approaches for similarity assessment that allow to compare two differently structured objects. Basically CaseML define a Case Ontology for describing cases, it defines a set of classes and properties between classes. The

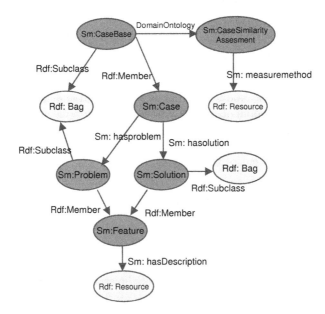

Fig. 2. CaseML Scheme

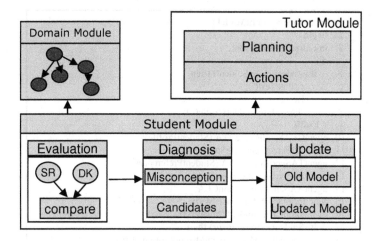

Fig. 3. Student Model Stages

figure 2 shows a scheme for representing cases that include the classes and their relationships. The student model presented here is structured as a multi-agent system integrated by: (1) Case Learner Agent (CLA), (2) Tutor Agent (TA), (3) Adaptation Agent (AA), and (4) Orientator Agent (AO). The student modeling process by these agents taking account the student model stages presented in Figure 3.

Case Learner Agent (CLA): It is an CBR-Agent. It is responsible for retrieve the information about the student and identifies his profile. In the retrieval process, the CLA agent evaluates cases and uses the k-nearest algorithm [19] to determine the matching grade. After the evaluation, the most similar cases are selected (if there is more than one case, the case with the highest rank is selected and prepared for adaptation). After the process is completed, the CLA agent storages the new case in the casebase. Additionally, this agent keeps communication with the Tutor Agent and updates the student model.

Tutor Agent (TA): It selects a specific teaching strategy for the different students profiles, personalizing the learning process. It interacts with the CLA to get information about the students and to produce changes in the teaching paradigm.

Adaptation Agent (AA): It organizes the learning resources according to the teaching strategy implemented by the TA. It takes into account the student profile to present the contents and information, making a customized learning.

Orientator Agent (ACG): It gives an emotional guide to the student when he/she fails in the learning process due to pshychological problems as: memory, motivation, personality, and learning ability.

5   The Modeling Algorithm

Let us illustrate a modeling algorithm. Below we explain the process referencing every line in the pseudo-code. Figure 4 shows the modeling algorithm. Line 3.

```
1.  Procedure StudentModel ( )
2.  begin
3.  initialize studentmodel;
4.  do
5.     if (student=NewStudent) then
6.         realizeTest( );
7.     else
8.         ProcedureStudentProfile( );
9.     EndIf
10. agentCLASendRequestTA (StudentProfile);
11. agentTASelectTeachingStrategy;
12. agentTASendRequestAA (StudentPreferences);
13. agentAAOrganizeLearningResources;
14. agentAASendInformationCLA;
15. monitoringCLA(StudentTasks);
16. evaluationCLA(StudentsAnswers);
17.    if (StudentAswers=Error) then
18.        procedure ManagementMisconceptions(Error);
19.        begin
20.           if (error=notAdequateTeachingStrategy) then
21.               agentCLASendRequestTA (error);
22.               agentTAModifyTeachingStrategy;
23.           else  if (error=personalityProblems) then
24.               agentCLASendRequestAO (error);
25.               procedureEmotionalGuideAO (StudentInformation);
26.               agentCLAUpdatedStudentModel( );
27.               EndIf
28.           EndIf
29.        end
30.    else
31.        endSession( );
32.    EndIf
33. EndDo
34. end
35.
36. ProcedureStudentProfile (attributes : features)
37. begin
38.    if  (retrieveCase) then
39.       search (attribute=tempatt);
40.           evaluation(attributes: features );
41.           ProcedureMatching (features);
42.           adaptation ( );
43.           indexing ( ) ;
44.    EndIf
45. end
46.
47. ProcedureMatching (features)
48. begin
49.    reviseFeatureCaseBase ( );
50.    computeDegreeSimilarity ( );
51.    computeDegreeMatch( );
52.    rankingCases( );
53. end
```

Fig. 4. Pseudo-code for the Student Modeling Process

Initialize the student model: When the student interacts with the system for the first time, the information is acquired.

Line 8. The ProcedureStudenProfile generates the student profile. First the CLAAgent evaluates and filters the cases. This agent combines searching and matching techniques. In line 36, the new case is analyzed, and evaluated (e.g. cases with the same goals than the current case).

Line 47. The ProcedureMatching is implemented to check the corresponding features in the cases stored using the k-nearest neighbour algorithm. Based on the result of the matches, CLA identify those that best address the requirements of the new situation, ranking the cases from highest to lowest, getting the student profile.

Line 10. The CLAAgent sends a request to the TAAgent with the student profile. Then the TAAgent selects the teaching strategy in line 11.

Line 12. The TAAgent sends a request to AAAgent in order to organize the learning resources according to the student preferences. This information is returned to the students through the CLAAgent in line 14.

Line 15 and 16. The CLAAgent monitorizes the students' tasks and evaluates the students' answers.

Line 17. If the students' answers corresponding to misconceptions or fails, the ProcedureMisconceptions will be called. If the fail is related with an inadequate teaching strategy, the CLAAgent sends a request to the TAAgent in order to modify the teaching strategy in line 22. If the fail is due to personality problems the ProcedureEmotionalGuide is called in line 25.

Line 31. If the students' answers are correct, the session finished and the CLAAgent updates the student model in line 26.

6   Intelligent Tutoring System for Learning in Public Health

The ITS was developed within the SINCO project [20] considering the MAS-CommonKads methodology [21]. The system is developed under a multi-agent approach compatible with the FIPA standards [22]. In the development Java, JavaScript and XML are used. The ITS modules are distributed and divided in smaller parts called agents. These agents work like autonomous entities, and act rationally in accordance with their environment perceptions and knowledge status.

The principal purpose of the Intelligent Tutoring System in Public Health was the learning improvement and the decisions making process, by means of the use of personalized tutoring, letting adaptation to new teaching strategies according to the student profile. For this purpose, the system used an Evaluator Agent (EA) that was responsible for evaluating the student behaviour.

We have considered necessary to redesign the student model to improve the student performance. For this, we structured the student model as a multi-agent system that uses the CBR paradigm to obtain the student profile.

The kernel of the new student model contains student individual characteristics together with psychological aspects like level of concentration, intelligence, motivation, etc.

7   Conclusions

The aim of this paper is to show the use of case-based reasoning with multiagent systems in student modeling within a Intelligent Learning Environment. With our approach is possible to categorize students according to their knowledge level and learning preferences, to motivate them to learn in user friendly environments that suits with their learning style. The multiagent system integrates a set of agents that realizes continuous student assistance and tutoring during the learning sessions. The use of an Orientator Agent is very important to give an emotional guide to the students when misconceptions or fails are reported.

Acknowledgments

We want to thank "Ministerio de Educación y Ciencia" for its partial support to this work under grant "MetaLearn: methodologies, architectures and languages for E-learning adaptive services" (TIN2004-08367-C02-01).

References

1. Moundridoud, M., Virvou, M.: Authoring intelligent tutoring system over the world wide web. Proceedings IEEE First International Symposium in Intelligent Systems **1** (2002) 160–165
2. Kashihara, A., Kinshuk, O.R., Rashev, R., Simm, H.: A cognitive load reduction approach to exploratory learnig and its application to an interactive simulation-based learning system. Journal of Educational Multimedia and Hypermedia **9(3)** (2000) 253–276
3. Crews, T.R., Jr: Intelligent learning environments: using educational technology to assist complex problem solving. Frontiers in Education Conference. 27th Annual Conference. 'Teaching and Learning in an Era of Change'.Proceedings. **2** (1997) 911–916
4. Khuwaja, R.A., Evens, M.W., A, R.A., Michael, J.A.: Architecture of circsim-tutor: a smart cardiovascular physiology tutor. Proceedings IEEE Seventh Symposium on Computer-Based Medical Systems **3** (1994) 158–163
5. Petrushin, V.A., Sinista, K.M.: Using probabilistic reasoning techniques for learner modelling. World Conference on AI in Education (1993) 418–425
6. Hawkes, L.W., J, D.S., A, R.E.: Individualized tutoring using an intelligent fuzzy temporal relational database. International Journal of Man-Machine Studies **33** (1990) 409–429
7. Bauer, M.: A dempster-shafer apporach to modeling agent references for plan recognition. User modelling and User-Adapted Interaction **5** (1996) 317–348
8. F, S.A., Kinshuk: Model for distance education system in maldives. Proceedings of E-Learn **ISBN 1-880094-9** (2003) 2435–2438

9. Jeremic, Z., V, D.: Desing pattern its: Student model implementation. Proceedings of the IEEE International Conference on Advanced Learning Technologies **ISBN 0-7695-2181** (2004) 864–865

10. González, C., Burguillo, J., Llamas, M.: A comparison of case-based reasoning and bayesian networks for student modeling in intelligent learning environments. 16th European Conference on Machine Learning (ECML) and the 9th European Conference on Principles and Practices of Knowledge Discovery in Databases (PKDD). (2005) Espera de publicación.

11. Craw, S., Jarmulak, J., Rowe, R.: Learning and applying case-based adapatation knowledge. Lecture Notes in Computer Science **2080** (2001) 131

12. Huajun, C., Zhaohui, W.: On case-based knowledge sharing in semantic web. Proceedikngs of the The 15th IEEE International Conference on Tools with Artificial Intelligence **ISSN 1082-3409** (2003) 200–207

13. VahLehn, K.: Student modelling. Foundations of Intelligent Tutoring Systems **Lawrence Erlabum Associates Publishers** (1988) 55–78

14. Ragnemlam, E.L.: Student diagnosis in practice:bridging a gap user modelling and user-adapted interaction. **5(2)** (1995) 93–116

15. Self, J.: Grounded in reality: the infiltration of ai into practical educational systems. IEEE Colloquium on Artificial Intelligence in Educational Software **313** (1988) 1–4

16. Yazdani, K.: Intelligent tutoring system: An overview. Artificial Intelligence and Education **1** (1987) 183–201

17. Yang, A., Kinshuk, A, P.: A plug-able web-based intelligent tutoring system. Proceedings of the Xth European Conference on Information Systems **ISBN 83-7326-077-3** (2002) 1422–1429

18. R, B.R.: Diagnosing bugs in a simple procedural. Intelligent Tutoring System **Academic Press** (1982) 116–125

19. Joussellin, A., Dubuisson, B.: A link between k-nearest neighbord rules and knowledge based systems by sequence analysis. Pattern Recognitizion Letters **6** (1987) 287–295

20. González, C., Burguillo, J.C., Vidal, J.C., Llamas, M.: Sinco: Intelligent system in disease prevention and control. an architectural approach. Lecture Notes in Computer Science **3337** (2004) 129–140

21. Sánchez, A., Medina, M., Castellanos, N.: Ontological agents model based on mas-commonkads methodology. Proceedings of the 14th International Conference on Electronics Communications and Computers (2004) 19–23

22. Nicol, R., O'brien: Fipa-towards a standard for software agents. In http://www.bt.com/publications/bttj/ **16** (2003)

Intelligent Virtual Environments for Training: An Agent-Based Approach

Angélica de Antonio, Jaime Ramírez, Ricardo Imbert, and Gonzalo Méndez

Technical University of Madrid, Madrid, Spain
{jramirez, angelica, rimbert}@fi.upm.es, gonzalo@gordini.ls.fi.upm.es
http://decoroso.ls.fi.upm.es

Abstract. In this paper we propose an architecture for the development of Intelligent Virtual Environments for Training, which is based on a collection of cooperative software agents. The first level of the architecture is an extension of the classical Intelligent Tutoring System architecture that adds to the expert, student, tutoring and communication modules a new module which is called World Module. Several software agents compose each module. Moreover, the proposed architecture includes agents able to simulate the behavior of human students and tutors, as well as agents able to plan the procedures to be taught (given an initial state and a desired final state) prior to the tutoring process.

1 Introduction

Training is a promising application area of three dimensional virtual environments. These environments allow the students to navigate through and interact with a virtual representation of a real environment in which they have to learn to carry out a certain task. They are especially useful in situations where the real environment is not available for training, or it is very costly or risky. An Intelligent Virtual Environment for Training (IVET) results from the combination of a Virtual Environment (VE) and an Intelligent Tutoring System (ITS). IVETs are able to supervise the actions of the students and provide tutoring feedback. Let's consider as an example training the operators of a nuclear power plant in the execution of maintenance interventions. In the real environment, the trainees would be subject to radiation, which is of course unacceptable for their health, and additionally it would be impossible to reproduce some maintenance interventions without interfering with the normal operation of the plant. In VEs for training, the supervision of the learning process can be performed by human tutors or it can be performed by intelligent software tutors, also known as pedagogical agents (in this case we will refer to the system as an IVET). Those pedagogical agents, in turn, can be embodied and inhabit the virtual environment together with the students or they can be just a piece of software that interacts with the student via voice, text or a graphical user interface. Some pedagogical agents have been developed to date, in some cases with quite advanced tutoring capabilities. One of the best known is STEVE, developed in the Center for Advanced Research in Technology for Education (CARTE) of

M. Pěchouček, P. Petta, and L.Z. Varga (Eds.): CEEMAS 2005, LNAI 3690, pp. 82–91, 2005.

the University of Southern California (USC) [1]. In the remaining of this paper, we will describe the architecture of the system (sections 2 and 3) and the agents that are endowed with human features (section 4). Then, we will explain how the system works (section 5). Finally, some conclusions and future work are shown (section 6).

2 An Extension to the Architecture of Intelligent Tutoring Systems

The development of three dimensional Virtual Environments (VEs) has a quite short history, dating from the beginning of the 90s. The youth of the field, together with the complexity and variety of the technologies involved, have led to a situation in which neither the architectures nor the development processes have been standardized yet. Therefore, almost every new system is developed from scratch, in an *ad-hoc* way, with very particular solutions and monolithic architectures, and in many cases forgetting the principles and techniques of the Software Engineering discipline [2]. Some of the proposed architectures deal only partially with the problem, since they are centered on a specific aspect like the visualization of the VE [3] [4] or the interaction devices and hardware [5]. When we get to IVETs, the situation is even worse. Our approach to the definition of an architecture for IVETs is based on the agent paradigm. The rationale behind this choice is our belief that the design of highly interactive IVETs populated by intelligent and autonomous or semiautonomous entities, in addition to one or more avatars controlled by users, requires higher level software abstractions. Objects and components (CORBA or COM-like components) are passive software entities which are not able to exhibit the kind of proactivity and reactivity that is required in highly interactive environments. Agents, moreover, are less dependent on other components than objects. An agent that provides a given service can be replaced by any other agent providing the same service, or they can even coexist, without having to recompile or even to reinitiate the system. New agents can be added dynamically providing new functionalities. Extensibility is one of the most powerful features of agent-based systems. The way in which agents are designed make them also easier to be reused than objects. Starting from the idea that an IVET can be seen as a special kind of ITS, and the pedagogical agent in an IVET can be seen as an embodiment of the tutoring module of an ITS, our first approach towards defining an standard architecture for IVETs was to define an agent for each of the four modules of the generic architecture of an ITS: Student Model, Expert Model, Tutoring Model and Communication Model.

The ITS architecture, however, does not fit well with the requirements of IVETs in several respects. IVETs are usually populated by more than one student, and they are frequently used for team training. An ITS is intended to adapt the teaching and learning process to the needs of every individual student, but they are supposed to interact with the system one at a time. However, in a multi-student IVET, the system would have to adapt both to the characteristics of each individual student and to the characteristics of the team. Consequently, the student module should model the knowledge of each individual student but also the collective knowledge of the team. The student is not really out of the limits of the ITS, but immersed in it. The student interacts with the IVET by manipulating an avatar within the IVET, possibly using very complex virtual reality devices such as HMDs (head mounted displays), data gloves or motion tracking systems. Furthermore, each student has a different view of the VE depending on their location within it. The communication module in an ITS is usually realized by means of a GUI or a natural language interface that allows the student to communicate with the system. It would be quite intuitive to consider that the 3D graphical model is the communication module of an IVET. However, there is a fundamental difference among them. In an IVET some of the learning goals may be directly related to the manipulation and interaction with the 3D environment, while the communication module of a classical ITS is just a means, not an end. For instance, a nuclear power plant operator in an IVET may have to learn that in order to open a valve he has to walk to the control panel, which is located in the control room, and press a certain button. Therefore, the ITS needs to have explicit knowledge about the 3D VE, its state, and the possibilities of interaction within it.

As a first step we decided to modify and extend the ITS architecture by considering some additional modules. First of all, we split the communication module into a set of different views for all the students with a particular communication thread for each student, and a centralized communication module to integrate the different communication threads. Then we added a World Module, which contains geometrical and semantic information about the 3D graphical representation of the VE and its inhabitants, as well as information about the interaction possibilities. The tutoring module is unique to be able to make decisions that affect all the students as well as specific tutoring decisions for a certain student. The expert module will contain all the necessary data and inference rules to maintain a simulation of the behavior of the system that is represented through the VE (e.g. the behavior of a nuclear power plant). The student module, finally, will contain an individual model for each student as well as a model of the team.

3   An Agent-Based Architecture for IVETs

Taking the extended architecture described in the previous section as a starting point, the next step was to decide which software agents would be necessary to transform this component-oriented architecture into an agent-oriented architecture. In an agent-oriented architecture, each agent is capable of performing a certain set of tasks, and is capable of communicating with other agents to cooperate with them in the execution of those tasks. Figure 1 shows how the extended ITS architecture is transformed, from a modular point of view, into an agent-based architecture. Our agent-based architecture has five agents corresponding to the five key modules of the extended ITS architecture: a Communication Agent, a Student Modeling Agent, a World Agent, an Expert Agent, and a Tu-

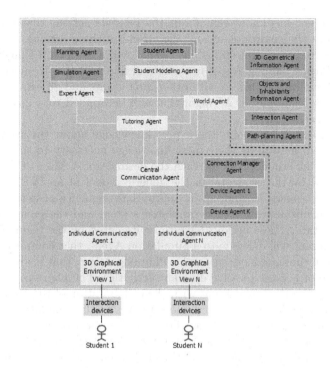

Fig. 1. Agent-based architecture for IVETs

toring Agent. Each of these principal agents may relate to, communicate with and delegate some tasks to other subordinate agents, giving rise to multi-level agent architecture.

The Communication Agent will delegate part of its responsibilities to a set of Individual Communication Agents dedicated to each student. There is also a Connection Manager Agent which is responsible for coordinating the connections of the students to the distributed system.

The Student Modeling Agent is in charge of maintaining a model of each student, including personal information, their actions in training sessions, and a model of the students' knowledge. The model of each student will take the form of an agent, a Student Agent, which will reflect, as faithfully as possible, all that is known or inferred about the student. A more detailed description of the Student Agents will be presented in section 4.

The World Agent is related to the 3D Geometrical Information Agent; the Objects and Inhabitants Information Agent; the Interaction Agent; and the Path Planning Agent. The 3D Geometrical Information Agent has geometrical information on the objects and the inhabitants of the world. This agent, for instance, will be able to answer questions about the location of the objects. The Objects and Inhabitants Information Agent has semantic knowledge about the objects and the inhabitants of the world. This agent will be able to answer questions about the utility of the objects or the objects being carried by a student. The

Interaction Agent has knowledge about the possible actions that the students can perform in the environment and the effects of these actions. For instance, it will be able to answer questions like "What will it happen if I push this button?". The Path Planning Agent is capable of finding paths to move along the environment avoiding collisions with other inhabitants and objects. For the purpose of finding these paths, A* algorithm will be applied to a graph model of the environment.

The expert agents contains the expert knowledge about the system that is being simulated, as well as the expert knowledge necessary to solve the problems posed to the student and to reach the desired goals. Most of the activities to be executed by the students, in the generic model of an IVET that is being considered, consist of finding an appropriate sequence of actions, or plan, to go from an initial state of the simulated system and the environment to a desired final state. These actions have to be executed by the team of students. The Expert Agent will delegate to a Simulation Agent, that contains the knowledge about the simulated system, and a Planning Agent, that is able to find the best sequence of actions to solve different activities. The plan for an activity is worked out by the Planning Agent with the collaboration of three other agents: the Path-Planning Agent, the Interaction Agent and the Simulation Agent. The Path-Planning Agent can determine whether there is a trajectory from a certain point of the world to another one. The Interaction Agent provides information about the actions that a student can directly execute in the environment. The Simulation Agent provides information about some high-level actions that can be executed over the simulated system (e.g., a nuclear power plant). One of these high-level actions will typically require the execution of one or more student' actions, therefore a hierarchical planning will be performed. In the nuclear power plant domain, an example of a high-level action may be to *raise the reactor's temperature.* This high-level action would be decomposed into two student actions, *go to the control panel* and *press the button that closes the input water valve.*

The Tutoring Agent is responsible for proposing activities to the students, monitoring their actions in the virtual environment, checking if they are valid or not with respect to the plan worked out by the Expert Agent, and making tutoring decisions. The activities that can be proposed by the Tutoring Agent are dependent on the particular environment that is being simulated in the IVET, and they can be defined by means of an authoring tool. Some XML files will define the activities in the IVET, the characters that should take part on them and the role to be performed by each character. In section 4, a more detailed description of the Tutoring Agent will be given.

4   Modeling Human Tutors and Students

One of the key assets of ITSs, against other "non intelligent" computer based instructional approaches, is their suitability to adapt themselves to any student's particular skills, knowledge and personal characteristics. This adaptability can be only reached through a proper student modeling by every Student Agent.

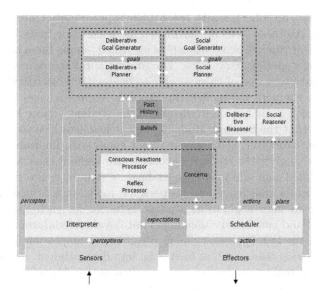

Fig. 2. Architecture for agents with behavior influenced by personality and emotions

Figuring out the student's abilities and beliefs/knowledge is usually not a trivial issue. To better individualize its training and appropriately understand the student's behavior, a representation of some of its personal features (personality traits, mood, attitudes) should be defined and maintained. With this aim, the Student Agent has been designed following a three-layered agent architecture able to manage emotional-driven behaviors (this architecture is described in detail in [6]). All three layers (viz, a reactive layer, a deliberative layer and a social one, showed interwoven in figure 2), share a common knowledge structure called personal model, which is part of the agent's beliefs.

The personal model manages beliefs about Defining Characteristics (DCs) of the student, all the traits that mark out its general behavior, including its personality traits and physical characteristics. By inferring an approximate value for each student DC, the Student Agent will be able to provide the rest of the IVET agents with better predictions about the student's behavior. That may be crucial to adapt the training to the specific student.

In addition, the personal model maintains beliefs about the student's Transient States (TSs), characteristics whose values represent the current state of the student. The most interesting TSs of the *personal model*, in order to understand the student's behavior, are emotions and physical states. Emotions are of paramount importance for the Student Agent, because students' behaviors are rarely only guided by rational, logical decisions, but also by emotional motivations.

The designed architecture identifies the appropriate influential relationships among these components of the personal model, along with similar relationships among them and other agent components, such as attitudes and concerns. That way, the values of the inferred variable elements (namely, TSs, attitudes and concerns) will always be coherent with the student's personality traits and physical characteristics. All these elements have been modeled using fuzzy logic, in order to deal with uncertainty. The relationships identified among them have been represented through special fuzzy rules. The architectural components have been designed so that every one of them is able to deal with those fuzzy values.

Apart from the personal model, the Student Agent manages all the beliefs that the system has -or has inferred- about the student. Those beliefs include the knowledge that the Student Modeling Agent has identified as learnt by the human student. Moreover, the Student Agent copes with information useful to reconstruct and analyze the student's evolution throughout the training process, information stored into the agent's past history structure. So, from the data about the student's knowledge and its personal model, the Student Agent will always be able to infer a plausible student behavior for each situation, based on both logical and emotional reasoning. That is valuable information for some other agents in the IVET, since it makes possible the adaptation of the training strategy considering issues such as having an impulsive student, or a clumsy one handling virtual reality devices, or one in a bad mood. Modeling each specific student by means of the architecture of figure 2 is only one face of the coin. The other one is modeling the trainer, i.e. the Tutoring Agent.

The adaptation of the tutoring strategy to every particular student may also encompass how the virtual tutor will behave: a student may need a tutor with a particular character (e.g., training children may require a funny, enthusiastic tutor, while for training nuclear plant operators a more serious one will be more convenient), or with a specific mood (e.g., if a student does not pay much attention to the procedure for long, a disgusted tutor may be effective). The reason is that students, despite having a virtual representation in the IVET, are human, and humans expect to identify human-like behaviors in the rest of the IVET characters, including the tutor. Poor or upsetting tutor behaviors will lead to a lack of believability, possibly reducing the student's feeling of presence and therefore the effectiveness of the training. As a consequence, the same architecture for agents with behavior influenced by personality and emotions used in the Student Agent has also been used for modeling the Tutoring Agent.

5   Walkthrough of the Agent-Based Architecture

In this section, a walkthrough of the behavior of the IVET during a learning session will be presented. The activities to be taught must be previously specified by using an authoring tool, and the IVET must be correctly configured for the kind of activity at hand. During the training, when an activity is posed to the student, the agents system, based on the planning capacity of the Expert Agent, will compute the plan or sequence of actions associated with the activity, given the initial state and the desired final state of the world. Moreover, during the planning process, the Path Planning Agent will compute the ideal trajectories that the students must follow to accomplish the plan. We situate ourselves in the domain of the dams and reservoirs, and we suppose that the activity to be taught is related to avoiding the destruction of a dam when the amount of stored water is too high. In order to avoid this catastrophe, an operator must open the dam to allow a certain amount of water to go out the reservoir. For performing that action, the operator will have to use a key that will activate the opening mechanism after introducing a certain code in the control panel of the dam. In order to learn this activity, the student must perform it in the virtual environment. Thus, at a certain moment, the student, using proper interaction devices, tries to carry out the action *use the key*. When this happens, the Individual Communication Agent associated with the student informs about this action to the Central Communication Agent, and eventually the message is delivered to the Tutoring Agent.

5.1   Action Verification and Execution

Now, the Tutoring Agent needs to find out whether the action can be executed under the current conditions in the virtual world, that is, if the preconditions of the action hold. For that, the Tutoring Agent resorts to the Interaction Agent via the World Agent. The Interaction Agent determines that he needs to check whether the student (his virtual representation in the virtual world) is carrying the key, and whether he is close enough to the control panel of the dam to *use the key*. In order to check these preconditions, the Interaction Agent will deposit them in a blackboard, and it will ask the 3D Geometrical Information Agent and the Objects and Inhabitants Information Agent to check the preconditions that are related to each one. A blackboard is used so that the Interaction Agent does not need to know which Agent can check each precondition. In this example, each precondition corresponds to one and only one of the aforementioned Agents.

If all the preconditions of the action hold, the Interaction Agent must guarantee the execution of the consequences of the action. For that, sometimes it needs to delegate on other agents, such as the World Agent (in particular, some of its subordinate agents) and the Simulation Agent, using again a blackboard communication mechanism. One of the consequences, managed by the Interaction Agent itself, will be launching the 3D animation in the virtual world that represents the student using the key. The command is sent via the Communication Agents (for all the students, since all the students should observe the animation). Another consequence of the *use the key* action, this time managed by the Simulation Agent, will be opening the dam, only if the student has introduced the correct code previously; otherwise, using the key will not have any effect on the dam. In order to distinguish between these two situations, the Simulation Agent must know whether the student has introduced the correct code.

5.2   Tutoring Actions

When the Tutoring Agent receives the result of verifying the preconditions of the action from the Interaction Agent, it asks the Student Agent to register the action and the result of the verification, and it checks whether the executed action is valid with respect to the plan associated with the activity. If this action is the next correct action according to the plan, the Tutoring Agent asks the Student Agent to register that the student has carried out the correct action at this moment. Otherwise, at this point, different tutoring strategies may be applied. One of them may be to allow the student to go on in spite of having just executed an incorrect action, whenever the state resulting from the execution of the action can still be transformed into the desired final state of the activity. This strategy poses a new problem, since the Tutoring Agent needs to know whether the desired final state is reachable from the current state of the world. For the purpose of finding this out, the Planning Agent must be endowed with the capacity of re-planning. Another more strict tutoring strategy may decide to explain the student the mistake, and to give the student another opportunity to accomplish the activity.

5.3 Dealing with Movements

The movements of the student in the virtual world are considered as a special kind of action that is managed in a different manner to the one explained above. As the student moves through the environment, the Central Communication Agent informs the 3D Geometrical Information Agent of the new student's positions. At the same time, the Tutoring Agent asks the 3D Geometrical Information Agent for these positions, in order to compare them with the ideal trajectory provided by the Path Planning Agent for the current activity, and in order to inform the Student Agent so that it can store the trajectory followed by the student during the training session. As a result of the comparison between the ideal trajectory and the student's trajectory, the Tutoring Agent computes a quality measure of the student's trajectory, and this measure is stored by the Student Agent.

6   Conclusions and Future Work

An agent-based architecture is proposed in this paper for the design of Intelligent Virtual Environments for Training. The roots of this architecture are in the generic architecture of an Intelligent Tutoring System, which has been firstly extended to be applicable to IVETs, and has been then transformed into an agent-based architecture by the identification of the set of generic agents that would be necessary to accomplish the tasks of each module. One of the advantages of the proposed architecture is that it is possible to build a basic infrastructure of agents that work as a runtime engine. In order to develop a new IVET, the author's task will consist of: selecting the desired agents among the available ones (e.g. selecting the Tutoring Agent that implements the desired tutoring strategy); configuring the parameters that govern the behavior of those agents (e.g. the duration of the session, the number of mistakes that will be allowed before the Tutoring Agent tells the student the correct answer, etc.); providing the data specific to the new IVET and subject matter (e.g. the geometrical model of the VE, the curriculum, the actions that are possible in the new VE and their effects on the simulation, etc.); and in the worst case creating new agents and registering them in the platform. The proposed architecture, and its realization in a platform of generic and configurable agents, will facilitate the design and implementation of new IVETs, maximizing the reuse of existing components and the extensibility of the system to add new functionalities. One of the drawbacks of the proposed architecture in its current state is that it can only be used with collective activities where students do not need to perform actions at the same time, that is, concurrent actions are not permitted. In order to allow this kind of actions, the architecture must be extended so that it can deal with the planning, verification and execution of concurrent actions (the verification and the execution of an action was explained by means of a simple example in section 5). In this sense, cooperative actions, that is, actions that require the intervention of more than one student at the same time, will deserve a special treatment. In a first approach to the problem of planning without concurrent actions, STRIPS and A* algorithms have been employed. However, currently, we are replacing STRIPS with a temporal planner able to deal with concurrent actions. Two temporal planners, SHOP2[1], a hierarchical task network planner, and LPG[2], a domain-independent planner, are being compared. In addition, in order to allow for efficient re-planning, the chosen planner will be modified to take advantage of an already known plan to reach the desired final state in the world.

References

1. Rickel, J., Johnson, W.: Task-Oriented Collaboration with Embodied Agents in Virtual Worlds. In: Embodied Conversational Agents. Eds. Boston: MIT Press (2000)
2. Munro, A., Surmon, D., Johnson, M., Pizzini, Q., Walker, J.: An open architecture for simulation-centered tutors. In: Artificial Intelligence in Education. Open Learning Environments: New Compu-tational Technologies to Support Learning, Exploration and Collaboration. (Proceedings of AIED99: 9th Con-ference on Artificial Intelligence in Education), Le Mans, France (1999) 360–67
3. Alpdemir, M., Zobel, R.: A component-based animation framework for devs-based simulation environments. In: Simulation: Past, Present and Future. 12th European Simulation Multiconference. (1998)
4. Demyunck, K., Broeckhove, J., Arickx, F.: Real-time visualization of complex simulations using veplatform software. In: Simulation in Industry'99. 11th European Simulation Symposium (ESS'99). (1999) 329–33
5. Darken, R., Tonessen, C., Passarella, J.: The bridge between developers and virtual environments: a robust virtual environment system architecture. In: Proceedings of the SPIE - The International Society for Optical Engineering. Volume 2409. (1995) 234–40
6. Herrero, P., Imbert, R.: Design of Believable Intelligent Virtual Agents. In: Developing Future Interactive Systems. Idea Group Publishing (2005) 177–211

---

[1] http://www.cs.umd.edu/projects/shop/
[2] http://zeus.ing.unibs.it/lpg/

Patient Driven Mobile Platform to Enhance Conventional Wheelchair, with Multiagent System Supervisory Control

A.B. Martínez[1], J.Escoda[1], T.Benedico[1], U.Cortés[1], R. Annicchiarico[2],
C.Barrué[1], and C. Caltagirone[2]

[1] Universitat Politècnica de Catalunya,
C/ Jordi Girona 1-3. 08034 Barcelona, Spain
{antonio.b.martinez, josep.escoda,toni.benedico}@upc.edu
{cbarrue, ia}@lsi.upc.edu
[2] IRCCS Fondazione Santa Lucia,
Via Ardeatina 306. 00179 Roma, Italy
{r.annicchiarico, c.caltagiorone}@hsantalucia.it

Abstract. This paper presents a group of intelligent mobile platforms, which can transport conventional wheelchair over them. Theses platform are supervisory controlled by a multiagent system, that support senior citizens or persons with disabilities situated in a given context (such as a Hospital) This system makes a main contribution enhancing the autonomy and mobility of the target population in the selected context and also serve as a stimuli in the rehabilitation phase.

1 Introduction

In this paper, we present an assistive framework for disabled persons who are no longer able to independently provide to his own self-care, and needs support for a basic activities of daily living (ADL). The principal aim of this work is the integration of autonomous agent technology with a robotic platform and sensor technologies to build specific *e*-Tools [7].

Automated guided vehicles lately are getting out of the industrial bounds and expanding into other context interacting closer to humans. Some examples are: mail delivering in offices [5], guidance in museums [6] or dispensing pills in hospitals. In our case the robotic platform uses the agent-based services to enhance the autonomy and mobility of senior citizen or persons with disabilities situated in hospitals.

We present a platform for disabled people in the lowest level of a multi agent system structure [7]. The idea of using mobile platform comes from the great number of conventional wheelchair (CWCH) stock used for many purposes at hospitals, and the aim of having an AI environment that supports an intelligent wheelchair. So, it makes sense, that instead of changing the manual driving wheelchair for an automatic one, to build a platform that can carry the wheelchair as an intermediate approach. In such situations the patient will drive the platform according to her capabilities. More over a reduced number of mobile platform will permits sharing it among many patients and CWCHs and then optimize the resources.

M. Pĕchouček, P. Petta, and L.Z. Varga (Eds.): CEEMAS 2005, LNAI 3690, pp. 92–101, 2005.

A mixed manual/automatic control of the platform acts as stimuli to the patients that have reduced physical and/or cognitive capabilities. The MAS must then supervise and control the platform according to the patient's profile and manage the whole set of platforms.

2 Previous Work

Figure 1 shows an inside view of a wheelchair prototype with spherical wheels that was developed previously [1], [4].

This prototype has been the inspiration for the development of the mobile platform that will be explained in this communication. The main advantage of using spherical wheels is the increase of manoeuvrability. Also, it can be noticed that the small radius of the wheel makes it possible to build a flat platform allowing the idea that CWCH gets over the platform and can be transported A more detailed explanation about omnidirectional wheels can be found in [1].

Fig. 1. Wheelchair with omni-directional wheels that inspires the developing of the platform

2.1 The e-Tools Project

Our target population is characterized by the presence of some degree of functional disability. The occurrence of one of more different pathologies (e.g., Cerebrovascular, Parkinson, Alzheimer disease) results in different patterns of physical and/or mental disability. These features are better defined by so called profiles of disability. Each patient can be then classified according to a well defined profile characterized by different needs.

That means that mobile platform should be flexible to the needs of different patients; at the same time, the mobile platform has to be flexible to the needs of the same patient in different times: patients go a pathway of changing (dys) functionality-possibly improving - during their illness.

The typical environment considered is a hospital for the neuro-motor rehabilitation, referring to a real institution represented by IRCCS S. Lucia Foundation, located in Rome. Rehabilitation hospitals are in some way different from primary care hospitals; in this case the goal is help the patients to recover enough self-dependency in order to independently perform - at as a high level as possible - their basic ADL. During their recovering, patients are trained to make progress in the necessary skills to make their discharge to home possible.

In our approach to the problem the CWCH will be driven by the robotic platform, supporting the mobility. The platform, supported by the MAS has to show complete autonomy in tasks such as path planning and location in the environment, and at the same time pay attention to the user's needs and requests. Although the robotic platform will be functioning in a well-known environment, structural elements like corridors, rooms, or halls may differ. The scenario depicted in this section is based on a daily problem and applies solutions related to multiagent systems, machine learning and other AI techniques, affective computing, wireless devices and robotics.

The system will combine the mobile platform hardware with a MAS that controls the behaviour of the chair, monitors the patient's status and interacts with him/her through a flexible interface that provides more or less assistance in navigation, depending on the patient's individual capabilities. Navigation should be autonomously controlled by the MAS most of the times, to relieve the user from tedious low-level decision-making tasks. To make this possible, the platform will be wirelessly connected to the environment, where an agent-based coordination layer will provide extra information to the robotic platform Multi-Agent System. To support the agent-based coordination layer and to connect it with the robotic platform Multi-Agent System, active landmarks will be placed. These active landmarks are small wireless machines installed in some strategic places of an area to transmit local information to the mobile entity. Similar initiatives and ideas can be found in the design of intelligent buildings for disabled and elderly people (see for example [8]) and in the last generation of road traffic support systems. In order to filter all the information received from the sensors and send only relevant information to a given platform, each room must be monitored and controlled by a MAS. This agent-based controller can proactively make decisions about room conditioning, or process sensor signals in order to extract meaningful information (e.g. to track a given person in the room).

These elements can be structured in the architecture as it was introduced in [7]. It consists of the following levels:

The *lowest level* contains all the physical devices that are connected to the environment. This level includes the cameras and sensors attached to the walls, patient monitoring systems, PDA's or other portable devices and intelligent mobile platform.

The *second level* comprises the hardware controllers that operate the physical devices and send information to the next level. In the case of complex devices such as mobile platform or cameras, this level should also perform tasks that might need immediate actions to be taken: *e.g.*, in the case of the camera, a behaviour to follow a person that is being tracked; or in the case of the robotic platform, effective obstacle detection and avoidance (*reactive navigation*) to ensure a high user´s safety [9].

The *third level* is composed of agent-based controllers that receive information from the hardware controllers and combine it with the knowledge they have about the state of the system, to infer *what* information they need to improve their knowledge, *where* to obtain it, and *how* to obtain it. The MAS has been described with more details in [13]

These MAS can also reason about the *relevance* of the information they receive, and distribute it to other agents or controllers that may need it. In order to integrate the information from the different agents in the environment and to coordinate activities and actors (patients, doctors, caregivers), the total population of agents composes the agent-based coordination layer (see §4). As part of this coordination, agents have to reason about the laws, norms and protocols that rule the environment where they interact [10]. A *wireless network* provides connections among the previous layers. Since not only the patient's wheelchairs but also the environment and other people's portable devices have agent-based controllers connected to the network, interaction and coordination issues should be solved by the software agents.

3   The Mobile Platform

Figure 2 presents an augmented reality view of the platform carrying a CWCH. The platform design takes into account its dimensions in such a way that CWCH could surpass the 15mm border to climb onto the platform.

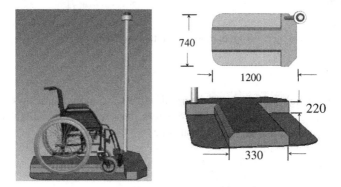

Fig. 2. Mobile platform views (units in mm) with laser positioning system

The platform system architecture is based on a distributed system, where all the elements are linked through a CAN bus network. At the heart of system there is a control unit, based on industrial PC that connects itself through a wireless link with the MAS. The user interface for interacting with the patient can be, for instance, a PDA, link via USB with industrial PC.

The control unit sends control orders to three power motor control units to move the platform, following the MAS decisions. The platform has two rechargeable standard batteries with little dimensions and autonomy in continuous work of 4 – 5h.

For navigation and obstacle avoidance a positioning sensor (camera, laser based goniometer [2], [3], or range finder [6]) are necessary. Own platform is equipped with a range finder laser (Leuze Rotoscan RS4) for detection obstacles and a laser-based goniometer for positioning the platform, non for reactive navigation, see figure 4, but its planned to replace it for a cheaper one in future versions, e.g. omni-directional camera. The actual positioning algorithm is explained in [2].

Finally, the platform is equipped with a developed joystick, explained in the next sections. This is the principal interface with the patients and is easily usable for them.

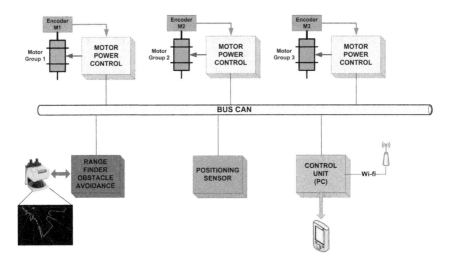

Fig. 3. Platform system architecture

3.1 Kinematics

As we can see in figure 3, the way spherical wheels are mounted allows two kind of movements: the steering rotation, that transfers movement to the platform, and the free rotation, perpendicular to the previous one.

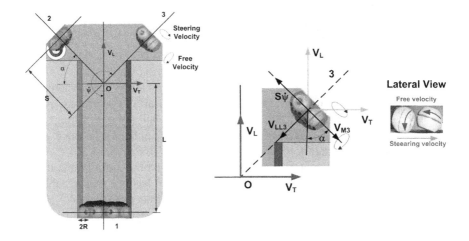

Fig. 4. Platform coordinate systems used to obtain wheel velocities

In order to obtain the kinematics equations [1] to control the platform, the free rotation is worthless. We must focus on steering velocity, expressing it in terms of world-coordinate velocities, as shown in equation (1).

$$V_{M3} = R\dot{\theta}_3 = -V_L \cos\alpha + V_T \sin\alpha - S\dot{\psi} \tag{1}$$

Once the equations for each steering velocity are developed, they can be joined in a common expression, in the form of jacobian matrix as shown in equation (2).

$$\begin{bmatrix} \dot{\theta}_1 \\ \dot{\theta}_2 \\ \dot{\theta}_3 \end{bmatrix} = \frac{1}{R} \begin{bmatrix} 0 & -1 & -L \\ \cos\alpha & \sin\alpha & -S \\ -\cos\alpha & \sin\alpha & -S \end{bmatrix} \cdot \begin{bmatrix} V_L \\ V_T \\ \dot{\psi} \end{bmatrix} \equiv [J] \cdot \begin{bmatrix} V_L \\ V_T \\ \dot{\psi} \end{bmatrix} \tag{2}$$

3.2 Maneuverability

One of the main benefits of the omnidirectional platform presented in this work is its maneuverability. We may sum up all its moving capability in three basic maneuvers, as shown in figure 3. The reason for this is that typical user interfaces are provided with a joystick to control the wheelchair. However, the kinematics of our platform, needs three velocity values, longitudinal velocity (V_L), translation velocity (V_T) and rotation velocity ($\dot{\psi}$). As the standard joystick is capable of commanding only two of these values, not the three at the same time, we end up clustering maneouvers in three different basic moves.

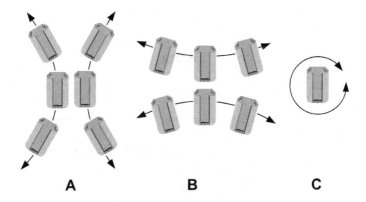

Fig. 5. Basic allowable manoeuvres

Figure 5.A shows the typical traveling maneuver, where V_T is fixed to 0. The user takes control over V_L and $\dot{\psi}$. This can easily be done by mapping the y-axis of an enhanced joystick into V_L, and the x-axis into $\dot{\psi}$. Sometimes, when lateral path correction must be done within little space, the maneuver presented in figure 5.B may be used. In this case, V_L is fixed to 0. The enhanced joystick x-axis is mapped into V_T, and the y-axis into $\dot{\psi}$. At last, but not least, figure 5.C shows the simple turning-maneouver, where V_L and V_T are both 0. This enhanced joystick must somehow allow the user to choose the rotation direction. This maneuver shows to be very efficient in small spaces as a bathroom.

3.3 Enhanced Joystick

The driving of the platform will be done either by the user, when he has enough cognitive capabilities or by the MAS when it detects deviation from a scheduled pattern, or the platform is heading towards forbidden areas or risky situations. It is clear that there is a potential conflict that has to be solved by the MAS in such a way that it preserves patient's integrity but trying to accomplish her desires and also her ADL in as much as possible.

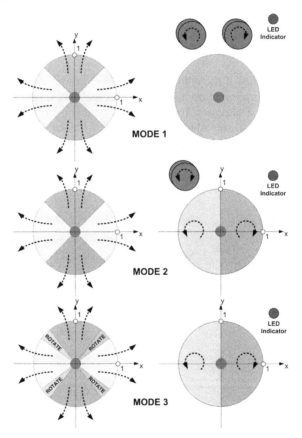

Fig. 6. Schematic representation of enhanced joystick operational modes

From the point of view of designing a control interface with a joystick, some basic guidelines have been presented in the last section. However, several issues need to be solved yet: how may users select which kind of maneuver they want to perform? How the turning direction should be specified? Some possible answers are presented in Figure 5, which shows three possible control interfaces in order of growing complexity that can be implemented depending on the physical and cognitive user profile.

In order to design the control interface, we must take into account the degree of utilization of the three available maneuvers. In ordinary driving, actions shown in figure 5.A and figure 5.B will be the most used ones. Thus, in order to begin one of these maneuvers the user only needs to move the joystick out of its center along with the main direction of the desired maneuver. Once inside the chosen one, the joystick behaviour is as described above. When finished with the maneuver, user must leave joystick in the relaxed central position.

The main difficulty in the control interface design is defining the way user may perform a turning maneuver. This refinement arises in the definition of several user interfaces that allow the user to choose turning maneuver in three different ways.

In the first one, shown as mode 1 in figure 6, the interface is provided with two buttons, each of them representing one rotating direction. As long as the user pushes one of the buttons, the platform will turn in the corresponding direction.

In mode 2, there is only one button in the interface. It is used by the user to indicate the willing of performing a turning maneuver. Once pushed and released, the x-axis of the enhanced joystick is used to indicate direction of turning and magnitude of rotation velocity.

Mode 3 is the most complex one, from the cognitive and physical user requirements point of view. The enhanced joystick is also used to enter into turning maneuver. To do this, the joystick is moved out of its center along with a diagonal direction. Once inside turning maneuver, joystick x-axis is used the same way as in mode 2.

4   Designing the *e*-Tools Agent Based Coordination Layer

In our plan to deploy e-Tools in a real, complex environment such as the IRCCS Santa Lucia, the design and implementation of the agents in the agent-based coordination layer should be made taking into account not only the organizational structures and internal regulations of the IRCCS itself, but also any external requirement defined by the context of IRCCS. In order to introduce all these factors in the design of the multi-agent architecture, we will use the *HARMONIA* approach, introduced in [10]. The idea is to define the agent-based coordination layer as an electronic institution, where not only coordination between the patients, the medical staff and the *e*-Tools is provided but also safety mechanisms are included to ensure that the behaviour of the system as a whole and of each individual agent is both *legal* and *acceptable* from the institutional perspective.

Our MAS has the following basic agents. First, we have the Patient Agent (PA), that could be integrated into the platform or connected to it using a PDA. This agent should provide all the available and permitted services to the patient and it should take care of his/hers personal security. Each PA provides a personalized way of interaction with the patient and therefore patients could use it to ask for help or to ask the platform to drive her/him to a given place into the permitted space or to ask the system to show a possible path to the destination. Also, the PA takes under its responsibility the audit of the patient's biometric signals and it acts in consequence.

The Caregiver Agents (CA) will be situated in the PCs belonging to the medical and healthcare personnel as well as in their individual PDA. The CA will be in charge of managing all the patient's help request messages and will notify them to the healthcare staff, so they can be attended properly. Also, it will notify any anomaly in the patient's biometric signals and it will generate a request for help, if needed.

We also consider the necessity of having an agent that undertakes responsibility for the network of sensors. Its basic target is to distribute the information from all available sensors to all the agents that maybe interested. The list of actual sensors for this space include: movement, landmarks, cameras, presence, etc. Finally, we have a Main Agent (MA) that represents the hospital entity. Among its objectives are to maintain the monitorisation of all patients, to manage their daily living activities and to provide them all with the mobility plans that may need to achieve them.

5 Conclusions and Future Work

At this point we can conclude that the goals have been covered, that is to implement the basis of the multi-agent system that gives support to the *e*-tools project. Agents PA, CA and MA have been successfully implemented and tested. Full integration between the MAS and the physical platform still to be completed and fully tested. In [13] we presented already some experiments including a group of 13 neurological patients to show the benefits of the enhanced joystick as control interface.

The tools envisaged here are applicable to support a wide range of disability levels and needs, and can be used by a wide range of users – from elders with moderate physical impairment and mild cognitive limitations to people with severe impairments (cognitive and/or physical) and disabilities, caregivers, etc. These MAS are devised to support the execution of ADL and of healthcare maintenance tasks – including standardized behavioural assessments useful in medical monitoring. In addition, they connect patients to the outside world.

The role of the MAS is to support/act in the following actions: Go to relative a position and orientation; Go forward while avoiding obstacles; Go down the hallway following wall(s); Navigate through a doorway; Navigate avoiding forbidden and/or dangerous areas and. Make turns while avoiding obstacles.

Agent-based cognitive systems, as e-Tools, will enable aging adults to stay at a well-know environment, as their home, longer and to take care of themselves.

Our future work is directed in two different directions. First, we aim to fully deploy the system in a real environment as Sta Lucia. Second, we are interested in pursuing feedback from potential users and working toward the next design of the platform.

References

1. Agulló Batlle, J. Les rodes omnidireccionals, el darer pas evolutiu de la roda. In Memorias de la Real Academia de Ciencias y Artes de Barcelona. Vol. LXI, Num. 7 (2004)
2. Agulló Batlle, J., Font, J.M., Escoda, J. : Dynamic positioning of a mobile robot using a laser-based goniometer. In IEEE IFAC Symposium on Intelligent Autonomous Vehicles. ISBN: 008 044237 4. Lisboa (2004)

3. Alenyà, G., Escoda, J., Martínez, A.B., Torras, C. : Using laser and vision to locate a robot in an industrial environment: A practical experience. In ICRA05 submitted. Barcelona (2005)
4. Agulló, Batlle, J., Font, J.M., Escoda, J. : Guiado de un robot móvil con cinemática de triciclo. In Anales de Ingeniería Mecánica. No. 15, Vol. 4, pp. 2981-2986 ISBN/ISSN: 1698-5990. Leon (2004)
5. Prassler, E., Stroulia, E., Strobel, M. , Kämpke, T.: Mobile robots in office logistics. In 27th International Symposium on Industrial Robots, 153 – 159. Milan (1996)
6. Fox, D., Burgard, W., Thrun, S. : Markov localization for mobile robots in dynamic environments. In Journal of Artificial Intelligence Research, 11: 391-427 (1999)
7. Cortés, U., Annicchiarico, R., Vázquez-Salceda, J., Urdiales, C., Cañamero, L., López, M., Sànchez-Marrè, M., Caltagirone, C.: Assistive technologies for the disabled and for the new generation of senior citizens: the e-Tools architecture. In AI Communications, 16: 193–207 (2003)
8. ARIADNE, Access, Information and Navigation Support in the Labyrinth of Large Buildings, http://www.cyber.rdg.ac.uk/DSRG/ariadne/ariadne.htm
9. Urdiales, C., Poncela, A., Annicchiarico, R., Rizzi, F., Sandoval, F., Caltagirone, C.: A topological map for scheduled navigation in a hospital environment. In e-Health: Application of Computing Science in Medicine and Health Care, pages 228–243 (2003)
10. Vázquez-Salceda, J. The Role of Norms and Electronic Institutions in Multi-Agent Systems: The HARMONIA Frameworks. Whitestein Series in Software In Agent Technologies (2004)
11. Regolamento Organico dell'IRCCS Fondazione Santa Lucia. htttp://www.hsantalucia.it , (2004)
12. 12.V. Dignum, J.-J.Ch. Meyer, H. Wiegand, and F. Dignum, F.: An organisational-oriented model for agent societies. In G. Lindemann, D. Moldt, M. Paolucci, and B. Yu, editors, Proceedings of the International Workshop on Regulated Agent-Based Social Systems: Theories and Applications (RASTA '02), Bologna, volume 318 of Mitteilung, pages 31–50, Hamburg (2002). Fachbereich Informatik, Universität Hamburg.
13. Barrué C.,Cortés U.,Martínez A.B.,Vázquez-Salceda J., Annicchiarico R., Caltagirone C. An e-institution framework for the deployment of e-Tools to support persons with disabilities. 3rd Workshop on Agents Applied in Health Care 19th International Joint Conference on Artificial Intelligence – IJCAI 2005 pp1-10

SECMAP: A Secure Mobile Agent Platform

Suat Ugurlu and Nadia Erdogan

Istanbul Technical University, Computer Engineering Department,
Ayazaga, 34390, Istanbul, Turkey
suat@suatugurlu.com, erdogan@cs.itu.edu.tr

Abstract. This paper describes a mobile agent platform, Secure Mobile Agent Platform (SECMAP), and its security infrastructure. Unlike other agent systems, SECMAP proposes a new agent model, *the shielded agent model*, to meet security requirements and provides functionalities which ensure the implementation of the the shielded agent model. It provides secure agent communication and migration facilities, and maintains security policy information to examine agent actions and to prevent undesired/unauthorized activity, while employing cryptographic techniques to meet security constraints.

1 Introduction

A mobile agent is a program that has the autonomy to travel around a network to accomplish its tasks [1][2]. Mobility involves the movement of executable code and associated execution state between different hosts on the network. A mobile agent is executed in an environment called a mobile agent platform which is a distributed abstraction layer that provides mechanisms for both communication and mobility support.

Any piece of code which is run on a computer system can potentially threaten the security, privacy, and integrity of the system and its users [3]. Security issues have gained new importance with the extensive use of mobile code systems. Any mobile code platform suffers from four basic categories of potential security threats[4]:

Leakage: unauthorized attempts to obtain information belonging to or intended for someone else
Tampering: unauthorized changing (including deleting) of information
Resource stealing: unauthorized use of resources (e.g., memory, disk space)
Antagonism: interactions not resulting in a gain for the intruder but annoying for the attacked party.

Meeting security requirements is fundamental to mobile agent systems and an inability to provide a feasible agent security model seriously hinders a wider adoption of mobile code based applications. An acceptible mobile agent based system requires secure techniques for agent migration and communication, and also mechanisms for higher level security management and maintenance.

This paper describes a new mobile agent platform, SECMAP, that especially focuses on security issues present in agent systems. Unlike other agent systems,

M. Pěchouček, P. Petta, and L.Z. Varga (Eds.): CEEMAS 2005, pp. 102–111, 2005.

SECMAP proposes a new agent model, the *shielded agent model*, for security purposes. A shielded agent is a highly encapsulated software component that ensures complete isolation against unauthorized access of any type. SECMAP provides secure agent communication and migration facilities, and maintains security policy information to examine agent actions and to prevent undesired/unauthorized activity. Additionally, SECMAP continuously monitors and reports on the execution of an agent from its creation to its completion.

2   Security Model of SECMAP

In a mobile agent system, agents cannot be reliably associated with end users without taking certain precautions. The approach taken by SECMAP is to treat every agent as a distinct principal and to provide protection mechanisms that isolate agents. SECMAP differs from other mobile agents systems in the abstractions it provides to address issues of agent isolation. SECMAP provides a light-weight implementation of agents; they are implemented as threads instead of processes. Each agent is an autonomous object with a unique name.

A Secure Mobile Agent Server (SMAS) resident on each node presents a secure execution environment on which new agents may be created or to which agents may be dispatched. SMAS provides functionalities that meet security requirements and allow the implementation of the *shielded agent model*. A shielded agent is a highly encapsulated software component that ensures complete isolation against unauthorized access of any type. On a request to create a new agent, SMAS instantiates a *private object* of its own, an instance of predefined object *AgentShield*, and uses it as a wrapper around the newly created agent by declaring the agent to be a *private object* of *AgentShield* object. This type of encapsulation ensures complete isolation, preventing other agents to access the agent state directly. An agent is only allowed to communicate with its environment over the SMAS engine through the methods defined in a predefined interface object, *AgentInterface*, which is made the private object of the agent during the creation process. The interface provides limited yet sufficient functions for the agent to communicate with SMAS. All variables of agents are declared as private and they have corresponding accessor methods.

SECMAP allows the concurrent execution of several agents on the same host and each agent runs as a separate thread in the same memory area of the host. In this mode of operation, the shielded agent model suffices to guarantee inter agent isolation and protection. Figure 1 depicts the layered structure of a shielded agent. SECMAP employs cryptographic techniques to meet security constraints. Each SMAS owns a certificate which is used to identify its identity and to encrypt and decrypt data. A requests from a SMAS is not processed before the validity of the SMAS identitiy is verified. A SECMAP agent's code and state information are kept encrypted during its life time using Data Encryption Standard (DES) algorithm. They are decrypted only when the agent is in *running state* on the host's memory. Thus, an agent is identified as a black box on a host, except while in memory. To protect agents during migration over the network, agent code and state data are encrypted as well while in transfer and can only be decrypted on the target host after retrieving the appropriate DES key from the security manager.

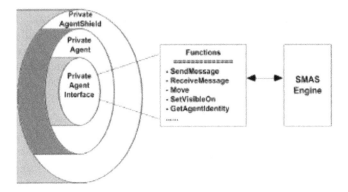

Fig.1. The shielded agent model

SECMAP employs a policy based authorization mechanism to permit or restrict agents to carry out certain classes of actions. Agent communication, migration, disk I/O, access to system resources are some of the events that require enforcement of security policies. SECMAP allows for policies to be dynamically defined and be enforced by intercepting agent service requests. It monitors, time stamps and logs all agent activity in a file, in order to be later analyzed to determine the actions an agent carried out on the host. In case an unexpected result is recognized, the route of the agent can be traced and how the agent was executed on each host can be found. In addition, in case of a threat, SMAS has the privilege hinder the activites of an agent. This is accomplished by purging all agent-related variables known to the SMAS such as Agent policy, Agent Identity, Agent message queues, etc. Under this condition, the agent can no longer be effective as any attempt to communicate or to carry out actions monitored by the security manager will lead to exceptions. However, if the agent includes a piece of code such as *"while (true) { }"*, it will continue its execution and consume CPU time. SECMAP can not prevent this kind of an attack.

3   SECMAP Architecture

Figure 2 shows the SECMAP architecture. The main component of the architecture is a Secure Mobile Agent Server (SMAS) which provides a platform in which agents exist and interact with other agents. In order to execute agents, each computer node must host a SMAS. SMAS is responsible of agent management tasks such as creation or activation, agent communication, agent migration, and policy management, each contributing to the implementation of the *shielded agent* model. Furthermore, having full control over agent activities, SMAS can identify what an agent attempts to do and if it has the rights. A second component of the architecture is an API which works as the interface between an agent and its SMAS platform. An agent can request communication or migration via this interface. The interface has limited functions and is the only way for the agent to interact with its environment.

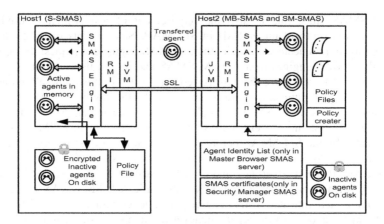

Fig. 2. SECMAP Architecture

3.1 SMAS Modes of Operation

A SMAS may operate in three modes according to the functionality it exhibits. It can be configured to execute in any of the three modes on a host through a user interface.

Standard Mode (S-SMAS): S-SMAS provides standard agent services such as agent creation, activation, inactivation, removal, communication, and migration. It also includes a policy engine that checks agent activity and resource utilization according to the rules that are present in a policy file, which has been received from a Security Manager SMAS. In addition, S-SMAS maintains a list of all active agents resident on the host and notifies the Master Browser SMAS anytime an agent changes state. Keeping logs of all agent activities is another important task S-SMAS carries out. Log content may be useful in the detection of attacks which are difficult to catch instantly.

Master Browser Mode (MB-SMAS): When agents are mobile, location mappings change over time, therefore agent communication first requires a reference to the recipient agent to be obtained. In addition to supporting all functionalities of S-SMAS, MB-SMAS also maintains a name-location directory of all currently active agents in the system. This list consists of information that identifes the host where an agent runs and is kept up to date as information on the identities and status (active/inactive) of agents from other SMAS is received.

Security Manager Mode (SM-SMAS): In addition to supporting all functionalities of S-SMAS, SM-SMAS performs authentication of all SMAS engines, handles policy management, and maintains security information such as DES keys and certificates.

Every SMAS engine has a module to create its self signed certificate. The private key that the SMAS has created for itself is kept in its secure place and the public key is sent to the SM-SMAS. The programmer managing the SM-SMAS can import this public key into the key store of SM-SMAS so that SM-SMAS can trust the SMAS engine. SMAS also should import the SM-SMAS public key into its key store as well to recognize the SM-SMAS as a trusted communication party. No SMAS engine whose public key is not imported into the SM-SMAS key store can communicate with the SM-SMAS since this is also the requirement of SSL which is used as the communication protocol under RMI in SECMAP. Since agents of different SMAS will need to communicate with each other, a SMAS engine can request the certificates of all other SMAS engines from the SM-SMAS and import them into its key store in order to be able to recognize them as trusted parties. Up to this point, all requirements for encrypted communication are provided but still there is a strong need to distinguish who is who. SM-SMAS also creates authentication keys for each of SMAS in the system.   After establishing a SSL session, any SMAS should be authenticated by the SM-SMAS before it can start up as a trusted server. SM-SMAS holds an IP address and key pair for each of SMAS engine that wants to be authenticated. If the supplied key and the IP address of the requesting SMAS engine are correct then it is authenticated. Once authenticated, SM-SMAS recognizes the SMAS. Every authenticated SMAS engine gets a ticket with a specified life time from the SM-SMAS, and uses this ticket whenever it attempts to start communication with other SMAS engines. The target SMAS engine first refers to SM-SMAS to verify the validity of the ticket before proceeding with the necessary actions to fulfill the communication request. This mode of operation prevents any untrusted entity in the network to masquerade as a valid SMAS.

The system is managed with a decentralized control; several MB-SMAS and SM-SMAS may be active and cooperate for a smooth execution. They share their data and keep it coherent. When initializing a S-SMAS on a node, the programmer specifies the addresses of the MB-SMAS and the SM-SMAS it should register to. S-SMAS sends its agent list to MB-SMAS and, in return, receives the identities of all other agents active on the system. We call those S-SMAS that a MB-SMAS or a SM-SMAS cooperates with as its *partners*. When a MB-SMAS gets a request to return an agent identity, it cooperates with its partners to obtain the current agent identities. A similar mode of processing is true for SM-SMAS. If a SM-SMAS can not authenticate the request, directs it to its partners for possible authentication. Additionally, when a S-SMAS communicates its MB and SM-SMAS, it obtains the addresses of their partners and saves them, in order to use as a contact address in case its communication to its MB-SMAS or SM-SMAS fails. This approach adds robustness against network or node failures.

An important component of SM-SMAS is the policy creator. Policy creator can create different sets of policies and install them on different SMAS engines.

Agent activities related to resource usage such as disk I/O or creation of network connections directly by using socket objects are first checked by the SMAS engine and blocked if not coherent with its security policy. SMAS engine achieves this by creating a *custom java security manager* monitoring all resource accesses. SMAS also enforces security policies to permit or restrict other agent activities such as messaging and migration.

3.2 Security Policies

SECMAP guarantees that an agent performs only the activities that it is permitted by verifying each action request by the agent against a set of policy rules. Security policies are created by SM-SMAS and sent to other SMAS. Policy rules can be defined for the following purposes:

– An agent can be restricted to communicate with only certain agents, with only agents on a certain SMAS or can be totally restricted to send and receive messages. Restrictions can be applied to sending or receiving separately.
– An agent may be restricted to migrate to only certain hosts or a host may be restricted to not accepting any agent from certain other hosts.
– An agent may be restricted to not performing disk I/O on the host it is running on or only specific agents may be allowed to carry out specific disk operations.
– An agent can be restricted to not creating or accepting socket based connections to other applications on the network. A host's socket factory may be totally prohibited to be used by any agent.
– An agent's access to system variables of the host may be restricted .

Imposing time-based restrictions for all types of rules is also possible. Furthermore, there are other security settings that are configured on SM-SMAS, however not in the form of a security policy. For example, an agent's size can be restricted to an upper limit in order to prevent an agent to use a host's memory and cause a memory leak.

The use of policies results in a more dynamic execution environment. Restrictions on agent activities may be altered at any point in time during execution with an appropriate modification of the agent policy, requiring no change in the agent code. With this approach, a higher level of security and also of flexibility is attained.

4 SECMAP Agents

SECMAP requires agents to conform to a software architectural style, which is identified by a basic agent template shown in Figure. 3. The agent programmer is provided a flexible development environment with an interface for writing mobile agent applications. He determines agent behavior according to the agent template given and is expected to write code that reflects the agent's behavior for each of the public methods. For example, code for the *OnCreate()* method should specify initial actions to be carried out, or code for the *OnMessageArrive()* method should define agent reaction to message arrival. In accordance with this style, an agent may be in one of different states throughout its existence and exhibits the following behavior:

```
public class Main extends Agent{
    public void OnMessageArrive(){... }
    public void OnCreate(){ ... }
    public void OnActivate(){... }
    public void OnInactivate(){... }
    public void OnTransfer(){... }
    public void OnEnd(){... }}
```

Fig. 3. Agent Template

State on_create: On an initial creation, a unique identity, an instance of class AgentIdentity is defined for the agent. An agent is referenced through its identity, which consists of three parts. The first part, a random string of 128 bytes length, is unique identification number and, once assigned, never changes throughout the life time of the agent. The second part is the name which the agent has announced and wishes to be recognized with. While the first two parts are static, the third part of the identity has a dynamic nature: it carries location information, that is, the address of the SMAS on which the agent is currently resident, and varies as the agent moves among different nodes. This approach facilitates efficient message passing.

State on_activate: An agent becomes active and starts executing while in this state. An agent should be active in order to be able to communicate with other agents. A programmer may prefer not to specify any code for this state, if just activating the agent meets his goals. He can then program the *OnMessageArrive* method of the agent to send and receive messages.

State on_inactivate: When an agent enters this state, its execution is stopped and its context (data, variables and code) is saved in the SMAS agent directory. The agent can not send or receive messages while in this state.

State on_transfer: An agent may request to migrate to another host anytime while it is active. SMAS inactivates the agent before the transfer begins, interacts with the remote SMAS to transfer its code and state data, and if the transfer operation completes successfully, deletes the agent from the local SMAS agent directory. Meanwhile, the remote SMAS re-creates the agent in its last state and activates it so that it starts execution.

State on_end: The agent is removed from the local SMAS on successful migration. The agent template prevents agents from sharing information through static variables, consequently eliminating the possibility of backdoor communication.

4.1 Agent Communication

SECMAP agents communicate via messages. SMAS supports asynchronous message exchange primitives through methods of *AgentInterface.* Agent communication is secured by transferring encrypted message content through SSL. Agents are provided with a flexible communication environment where they can question the results of message send requests, wait for responses for a specified period of time, and receive messages or replies when it is convenient for them. Figure 4 shows the communication framework and how a request to send a message proceeds. During agent creation, SMAS, while instantiating a shield object for the agent, also creates three queues: one for outgoing messages, one for incoming messages and one for reply messages. The input and output queues are monitored by two threads which are spawned on agent activation. The thread monitoring the input queue alerts the agent if a message arrives, while the thread monitoring the output queue alerts the SMAS engine to route messages to their destination.

Communication is asynchronous. When an agent issues a send message call through the *AgentInterface,* the message is placed into the output queue by the agent shield and the call returns. From then on, the agent may continue with its operations. It may question the result of the send request, or, if it expects a response, it may retrieve the reply message at any point suitable in its execution path. The thread monitoring the output queue alerts the SMAS engine to route the message. After the SMAS on the recipient host places the message into the input queue of the target

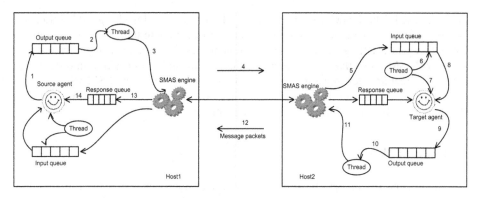

Fig. 4. Agent Communication Framework

agent, the input queue thread alerts the agent of the arrival of a new message. Subsequent to being alerted, the agent can issue a call to receive the message at any time. Reply messages are also routed as regular messages are. The only difference is that the SMAS engine sending the reply sets the acknowledgement field at the end of the message packet object so that the message can be placed in the reply queue of the agent to which the call returns a result. The reply can be retrieved at any time.

Before an agent can send a message to another agent, it needs to learn the name of the receiver agent. An agent learns the identity of the target agent via a call to the SMAS, which cooperates with MB-SMAS to return the required information, an object of type is AgentIdentity. Messages are created as instances of the *Message* class and consist of two parts. The first part is the name of the message, while the second consists of a parameters. Parameters can be of any type that can be serialized.

4.2 Agent Migration

SECMAP supports weak migration of agents between remote hosts on a call to the *Move* method of *AgentInterface*. The agent issues a *Move(address)* call to migrate to another host. The call returns a result object through which the agent can question the result of the transfer request. The *address* field of the call specifies the remote SMAS, IP address of the host remote SMAS is running on and the name of the remote SMAS The SMAS engines involved in the migration process carry out the following steps:

–   The agent is inactivated on local SMAS and an inactivation information message is sent to MB-SMAS.
–   Agent code and state information are saved in the local SMAS agent directory. All class files belonging to the agent are zipped into a single file in order to reduce agent transfer time. Agent state is written into another file. Once agent code and state is written into the disk, they are encrypted and no one can decrypt them since only SM-SMAS has the correct key. Local SMAS gets the key from the SM-SMAS.
–   The agent code and state are transferred to the remote SMAS. The remote SMAS re-creates the agent, loads its code, state and identity from the transferred files after decrypting them and activates the agent. As agent code and state are held in an encrypted and zipped file, a customized class loader rather than the system class

loader is used. The loadClass() method of the newly developed AgentClassLoader has been enhanced with new capabilities in order to complete this phase of migration. Once the agent is activated, an acknowledgement message of activation information is sent to MB-SMAS so that it can update the agent's location information in order to be able to redirect any new message destined to this agent to the correct SMAS.

–   The agent is deleted from the source SMAS if the transfer is successful. If any of the steps described above fails, SMAS cancels the transfer.

5 Related Work

Developers and researchers have taken a variety of approaches to security of mobile agent environments. Hohl [5] proposes what he refers to as Blackbox security to scramble an agent's code in such a way that no one is able to gain a complete understanding of its function. Proof carrying code [6] requires the author of an agent to formally prove that the agent conforms to a certain security policy. By digitally signing an agent, its authenticity, origin, and integrity can be verified by the recipient. The idea behind path histories [7] is to let a host know where a mobile agent has been executed previously. State appraisal [8] attempts to ensure that an agent's state has not been tampered with through a state appraisal function which becomes part of the agent code. In general, there does not seem to be a single solution to the security problems introduced and most of the solutions are inadequate in protecting agent and host data, while others that provide adequate protection cause an unacceptable overhead to the programmer. However, work is still going on, and new system are being developed [9] [10].

6 Conclusions and Future Work

This paper describes a mobile agent platform, SECMAP, and its security infrastructure. The system has been especially developed against security threats that both agents and hosts may be exposed to. Security features are inserted into the system core at design time. The system has an open and flexible architecture that can further be enhanced in the future to meet additional requirements.

SECMAP allows for completely isolated lightweight agents through a new shielded agent model which protects the agent from its environment, while, at the same time, providing secure, flexible and efficient communication facilities. SECMAP introduces trusted nodes into the infrastructure, to which mobile agents can migrate when required, so that sensitive information can be prevented from being sent to untrusted hosts. Sources of requests are authenticated before they are processed to verify that they really come from their stated, trusted sources. This approach does not appear to be fully explored elsewhere. The built in support to secure agent communication and migration relieves the programmer of extra coding, providing a transparent execution environment. SECMAP employs cryptographic techniques to meet security constraints. An agent's code and state information are kept encrypted during its life time, being decrypted only when the agent is in *running state* on the host memory. Thus, an agent is identified as a black box on a host, except while in memory. Unlike several agent systems, SECMAP employs policy rules to protect not only hosts but also agents. An agent's capabilities such as, communication, migration, I/O, socket communication can be totally or partially restricted. Policies can be changed after agent deployment as well. SECMAP monitors and records all agent activities. These traces can be used not only for debugging purposes but also for security purposes. An intelligent analysis of these records may provide additional security benefits and can help to detect certain kinds of attacks which are normally very difficult to detect.

Currently, work is in progress on detection and resolution of policy conflicts and enforcement of security policies. Our future work also includes the addition of dynamic policy creation capability to the architecture with the help of log analysis.

References

1. S. Franklin and A. Graesser "Is it an Agent, or just a program? A taxonomy for Autonous Agents" Proc. Third International Workshop on Agent Theories, Architecures,and Languages, Springer -Verlag,1996.
2. Karnik, N.M., Tripathi, A.R., 1998. Design issues in mobile-agent programming systems. IEEE Concurrency 6 (3), 52–61.
3. M. Hauswirth, C. Kerer, and R. Kurmanowytsch, "A flexible and extensible security framework for Java code", Technical Report TUV-1841-99-14, Technical Univ. of Vienna.
4. G. Coulouris, J. Dollimore, and T. Kindberg. Security. In *Distributed systems - concepts and design*, International Computer Science Series, pages 477-516, 2nd edition. Addison-Wesley, Reading, Mass. and London, 1994.
5. F. Hohl. "Protecting mobile agents with blackbox security" Proc. 1997 Wksp. Mobile Agents and Security , Univ. of Maryland , Oct 1997
6. G. C. Necula and P. Lee. "Safe, untrusted agents using proofcarrying Code" In Giovanni Vigna, editor, Mobile Agents and Security, Number 1419 in LNCS, pages 61-91. Springer-Verlag, Berlin, 1998.
7. D. Chess, B. Grosof, C. Harrison, D. Levine, C. Parris, and G. Tsudik, "Itinerant agents for mobile computing", In M. N. Huhns and M. P. Singh, editors, Readings in Agents, pages 267-282. Morgan Kaufmann, San Francisco, CA, 1997.
8. W. Farmer, J. Guttmann, and V. Swarup, "Security for mobile agents: Authentication and state appraisal", In E. Bertino, H. Kurth, G. Martella, and E. Montolivo, editors, Proc. of ESORICS 96, Number 1146 in LNCS, pages 118-130. Springer-Verlag, Berlin, 1996
9. C. Bryce, J.Vitek, "The JavaSeal Mobile Agent Kernel", Autonomous Agents and Multi-Agent Systems, 4, 359-384,2001
10. V.Varadharan and D.Foster, "A Security Architecture for Mobile Agent Based Applications" World Wide Web:Internet and Web Information System, 6,93-122, 2003

What Is Context and How Can an Agent Learn to Find and Use it When Making Decisions?

Oana Bucur, Philippe Beaune, and Olivier Boissier

Centre G2I/SMA, ENS des Mines de Saint-Etienne,
158 Cours Fauriel, Saint-Etienne Cedex 2, F-42023, France
{bucur, beaune, boissier}@emse.fr

Abstract. Developing context-aware applications needs facilities for recognizing context, reasoning on it and adapting accordingly. In this paper, we propose a context-based multi-agent architecture consisting of context aware agents able to learn how to distinguish relevant from non relevant context and to make appropriate decisions based on it. This multi-agent system interacts with a context manager layer, based on an ontological representation of context, which is able to answer context-related queries. The use of this architecture is illustrated on a test MAS for agenda management, using the JADE-LEAP platform on PCs and PDAs.

1 Introduction

The rise of pervasive computing has stressed the importance of *context*. As defined in [5], this concept consists in "any information that can be used to characterize the situation of an entity". This definition does not indicate how to choose among all the available context information the one that is relevant or how to deal with it to make contextualized decisions. Existing works handle this problem in an explicit or implicit manner. In this paper, our goal is to draw a common base for context-aware reasoning. We propose a layered architecture made of a Context Manager (CM) layer, on which a context-based multi-agent layer is defined. Since pervasive applications are inherently open, they may be contain several "societies" of heterogeneous and situated agents. Thus, agents must be able to sense and manage context but also to communicate it. We propose an ontology-based representation for contextual information. The defined agents can learn how to discern relevant from non-relevant context and how to make appropriate decisions based on it.

In this paper, we demonstrate our proposal with a case study of an open and interoperable context-aware agenda management, implemented using Multi-Agent System (MAS). Our MAS is made of several meeting scheduler agents called mySAM (my Smart Agenda Manager). A mySAM agent assists its user in fixing meetings by negotiating them with other mySAM agents and by using context knowledge to decide to accept or reject a meeting proposal made by another agent. Knowledge about how to seslect relevant context and how to use it to deal with a meeting proposal is acquired through individual and multi-agent learning (knowledge sharing).

M. Pěchouček, P. Petta, and L.Z. Varga (Eds.): CEEMAS 2005, pp. 112–121, 2005.

Before describing the proposed architecture and the way agents are able to learn context for decision-making (section 3), we will present the ontology-based context representation (section 2). We then exemplify our work in the agenda management application (section 4). Before concluding, we will situate our approach in related work.

2 "Context" in MAS

In this section, we define "context" and describe how we represent it to design and implement our context-based MAS.

2.1 What Is "Context" - Definition and Classification

From Dey's definition, context may be further described as a set of attributes and a finality. The *finality*, **f**, is the goal for which the context is used at a given moment (e.g. to decide whether a proposal for an appointment should be accepted or not, to see whether the current situation is similar to another one or not, to understand a conversation, etc.). Let's note F the set of finalities.

A *context attribute* (*a*) designates the information defining context, e.g. "ActivityLocation", "NamePerson", "ActivityDuration". We consider a context attribute as a function, with one or more parameters, returning a value. For instance, context attribute "NamePerson" is a function defined on the set of Persons, returning a String value corresponding to the name of a person. We name V_a the definition domain of *a*, the set of possible values that *a* may take (example: V_{time} =[0,24[ ). We define *valueOf* as an application from A x P_a to $P(V_a)$, where A is the set of all attributes, $P(V_a)$ is the power set of V_a, and P_a is the set of parameters needed to compute the value of *a*. Not all attributes are relevant for a finality. We define *isRelevant(a,f)*, a predicate stating that attribute *a* is relevant for the finality *f*. Let's call $RAS(f)$ the *Relevant Attribute Set* for the finality *f*: $RAS(f)$ = { $a \in A$ | *isRelevant(a,f)*=true }.

We call an *instantiation of context attribute* $a \in A$ as a pair (a,v) where *v* is the set of values $v \in P(V_a)$ of *a* at a given moment. For instance, (Day, {14}), (roleOfPersonInGroup, {Team Manager}), (PersonIsMemberOf, {MAS Group, Center_X, University_Y}) are instantiation of respective context attributes *Day*, *roleOfPersonInGroup, PersonIsMemberOf*. Let's note I the set of instantiated context attributes as I = {(a,v) | $a \in A$ ∧ *valueOf(a)=v*}. We call *Instantiated Relevant Attribute Set* of a finality *f* - *IRAS*(**f**), the set of instantiated context attributes relevant for a finality *f*: $IRAS(f)$ = {(a,v) | $a \in RAS(f)$ ∧ $(a,v) \in I$}.

Let's notice that in related work ([13], [18], [19]), the notion of "context" is often understood as being what we defined as the IRAS. To explain the difference between RAS and IRAS let's consider the following example. Given finality f = "deciding whether to accept or not a meeting", RAS(f)={"RoleOfPersonInGroup", "ActivityScheduledInSlot"} is considered, i.e. role played by the person who made the proposal and if the receiver has something already planned for the proposed time slot. The resulting IRAS for a student may be $IRAS_{student}(f)$={(RoleOfPersonInGroup, {teacher}), (ActivityScheduledInSlot, {Activity001})} and for a teacher

IRAS$_{teacher}$(f) = { (RoleOfPersonInGroup, {student}), (ActivityScheduledInSlot, {Activity255)}. As we can see, the difference between IRAS of student and teacher may lead to different rational decisions. Usually RAS used is almost the same for different users when needed to make decisions for the same finality, but the decision itself is IRAS-dependent. Taking into account the definitions that we proposed so far we now describe the representation that we defined.

2.2 Representing Context Attributes

Our aim is to represent context in a general and suitable manner for all applications that need to represent and reason about it. Several representations of context exist: contextual graphs ([1]), XML (used to define ConteXtML [17]), or object oriented models ([7]). All these representations have strengths and weaknesses. As stated in [8], lack of generality is the most frequent weakness: usually, each representation is suited for a specific type of application and expresses a particular vision on context. There is also a lack of formal bases necessary to capture context in a consistent manner and to support reasoning on its different properties. A tentative answer in [8] was the entity-association-attribute model, is an extension of the "attribute-value" representation, contextual information being structured around an entity. An entity represents a physical or conceptual object. We based our proposal on this idea.

To take into account the need for generality, and also considering the fact that we aim at having several MAS, each dealing with different contexts (that we will need to correlate in some way), an ontology-based representation seems reasonable. This is not a novel idea, Chen *et al.* ([3]) defined context ontologies using OWL. In their model, each context attribute is represented as an OWL property (DataTypeProperty or ObjectProperty, depending on the range of values). We extended this representation due to the limitations it imposes when we need to represent more complex context attributes (like role, activities already planned, etc.).

Table 1. The description of the class #ContextAttribute

Property Name	Property Type	Domain	Range	Multiple values
name	Datatype	#ContextAttribute	String	No
noEntities	Datatype	#ContextAttribute	Integer	No
entitiesList	Object	#ContextAttribute	#Entity	Yes
valueType	Object	#ContextAttribute	#Entity	No
multipleValue	DataType	#ContextAttribute	Boolean	No

What we did was to add to the ontology the class "#ContextAttribute" (see table 1.) corresponding to our definition of a context attribute as defined in section 2.1. This class is composed of the following properties: name, number and list of entities (parameters) it connects to, type of its value. Instances of that class will be the context attributes that are known and used in that system by the CM . In our domain ontology, the class "#Entity" is the super class of all concepts, e.g. in MySAM, #Person, #Group, #Room, #Activity, etc. are subclasses of #Entity. In Table 2. we give some examples of context attributes that we defined for the MySAM application. For instance, the context attribute `RoleOfPersonInGroup` is described with the following instance of class #ContextAttribute:

- Name = roleOfPersonInGroup
- NoEntities = 2 (we need to connect this attribute to a person and a group)
- valueType = #Role (value for this attribute is an instance of the class #Role)
- multipleValues = "false" (a person can only play one role in a group)
- entitiesList = { #Person; #Group} (connected entities are instances of class #Person and of class #Group)

Table 2. Some examples of context attributes defined in MySAM ontology

Person – related	Time-related
InterestsPerson :(Person)-> String	TimeZone : (Time) -> Integer
StatusPerson :(Person) -> String	DayOfWeek : (Date) -> String
Supervises : (Person) -> Person*	TimeOfDay : (Time) -> String
RoleOfPersonInGroup :(Person,Group)-> Role	
Location - related	**Activity – related**
PersonIsInRoom : (Person, Room) -> Boolean	ActivityStartsAt:(Activity)->Time
PersonIsAtFloor : (Person, Floor) -> Boolean	ActivityEndsAt :(Activity)-> Time
PersonIsInBuilding:(Person,Building)-> Boolean	AcivityGoal : (Activity) ->String
	ActivityParticipants: (Activity) -> Person*
Agenda - related	**Environment – related**
BusyMorning : (Agenda) -> Boolean	DevicesAvailableInBuilding : (Building) -> Device*
BusyAfternoon : (Agenda) -> Boolean	DevicesAvailableInRoom:(Room)->Device*
BusyEvening : (Agenda) -> Boolean	DevicesAvailableAtFloor : (Floor) -> Device*

3   Architecture for a Context-Based Learning MAS

The proposed layered architecture is composed of mySAM agents (Fig. 2), that assist a user. Agents interact with each other and with a context management layer composed of context managers (CM – Fig. 1). Being connected to the current state of the environment, a CM provides agents with context. The CM and not the agents have the responsibility to compute the values of context attributes in the environment. Agents learn how to recognize relevant context and how to act accordingly. We start by describing the CM and continue by the details of the dedicated learning part of the agent's architecture.

3.1   Context Manager (CM)

The main functionalities of CM are to let the agents know which is the context attributes set (defined in the ontology) that it manages and to compute IRAS corresponding to RAS given by the agents at some point of processing. When entering a society, an agent asks the corresponding CM to provide it with the context attributes that it manages. Acting as intermediary between agents and the environment, CM is able to answer requests regarding its managed context attributes. This way, if, for instance, CM answers "Date" and "ActivityLocation" to an agent querying it about context attributes for managing rendez vous, even if the agent knows that other context attributes exist – e.g., "roleOfPersonInGroup"– it knows that it cannot ask CM for the value of this attribute since this latter is not able to compute it.

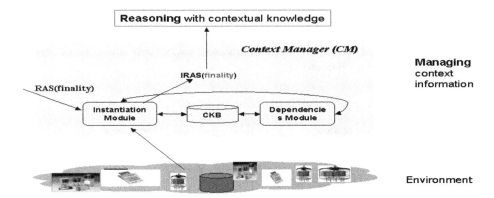

Fig. 1. Context manager architecture

The Context Knowledge Base contains the ontology of the domain, defined as a hierarchy with #Entity as root, and all instances of class #ContextAttribute that will be managed by the CM. The *instantiation* module computes the IRAS(f) for a given RAS(f). The *dependencies* module computes the values for derived attributes by considering possible relations between context attributes concerning their relevance: if one attribute is relevant for a situation and it has a certain value, then another attribute could also be relevant for that situation.

3.2 Context-Based Learning Agent

Although a mySAM agent has some negotiation modules (in order to establish meetings), we focus here on its management and reasoning on context modules. The context-based agent architecture that is the core of a MySAM agent is general and it is not restrained to the kind of application considered to illustrate our approach. It has two main modules (see Fig. 2): *selection* of relevant attributes for a certain finality f (RAS(f)) and *decision* based on instantiated attributes (IRAS(f)) provided by CM.

For example, for a finality relative to deciding whether accepting or not a "2 participants" meeting, the RAS built by the selection module could be {"ActivityScheduledInSlot", "roleOfPersonInGroup"}; or, for a finality relative to a "several participants" type of meeting, the RAS could be {"ActivityParticipants", "ActivityDescription", "PersonInterests", etc}. The decision module knows how to accept a meeting if we have nothing planned for that period of time and if the person that demands this meeting is our chief, for instance.

Several approaches have been proposed [20], [26] recently concerning multi-agent learning. Since the specific mono-agent learning method that is used for learning modules attached to the decision-making based on IRAS is application dependent, we will not detail it here. We just highlight the necessity to add a multi-agent learning perspective and to point out what are the consequences.

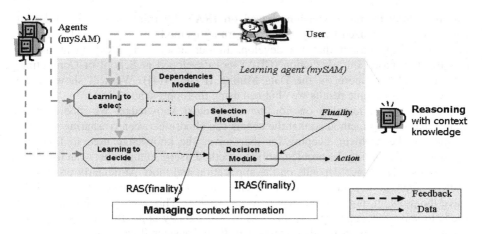

Fig. 2. Context-based agent architecture

Learning how to select RAS(f). Learning how to choose the relevant context attributes is important in our targeted applications since the amount of available context information is too large and the effort needed to compute the values for all those attributes rise efficiency problems. From an individual learning perspective, agents use the user's feedback to learn *how to choose* among context attributes those that are relevant for a given situation. In our application, mySAM memorizes the attributes chosen by the user as being relevant for that situation before making a decision. Next time the agent will have to deal with the same type of situation, it will be able to propose to the user all known relevant attributes, so that the user adds or deletes attributes or uses them such as they are.

Using the context ontology defined in section 2.2, agents are able to share a common understanding of the manner of using context attributes and knowledge. To improve the method used in individual learning of *how to choose* relevant context attributes, we made agents able to share knowledge, focusing on attributes that other agents in the system have already learnt as relevant in that situation. When an agent does not know which attributes are relevant for the considered situation f, it can ask other agents what are the attributes which they already know as being relevant in that situation (their RAS(f)). In the same way, if an agent needs more feedback on attributes in a specific situation, it can again try to improve its set of relevant attributes, by asking for others' opinion. The resulting RAS(f) is the union of the ancient RAS with the new relevant attributes proposed by other agents. Next time the agent will be in the situation f, it will propose the new obtained RAS to the user, so he can choose to keep the new attributes, to add some more or to delete some of them that seem not relevant for him. For example, when deciding about a meeting with a friend, the agent's RAS is {ActivityStartsAt, ActivityDuration}. The agent asks others what their RAS is and, at the end of the sharing session, its RAS will become {ActivityStartsAt, ActivityDuration, dayOfWeek, BusyEvening}. The user can then choose to keep the attribute "dayOfWeek" as relevant and to remove "BusyEvening" from the list of relevant attributes for this finality.

Learning how to make decisions based on IRAS. Learning *how to use* relevant context may be realized by any machine learning method developed in AI, suited to the type of application that we develop. In our case, a mySAM agent uses a classification based on association (CBA) tool developed at School of Computing, University of Singapore, in the Data Mining II suite ([4]). We will show in the following section some results we obtained using this approach.

For multi-agent learning on *how to use* context knowledge, we modified the knowledge sharing method so that the agents can choose between (i) sharing only the solution to the problem, keeping for themselves the knowledge used to find that solution, or (ii) sharing the problem-solving method itself, so that others can use it for themselves. The choice depends on the application and more particularly on privacy matters. The second solution is more efficient in that it gives an agent the method to solve the problem, not just the answer to its problem. This way, next time the agent needs to solve the same type of situation, it will directly apply the method, without asking again for help from other agents. But if, as considered in mySAM, the agents should not share all their criteria for accepting or rejecting a meeting, then sharing just the solution (an "accept/reject" decision) should be preferable. We implemented the latter solution in our agenda management case study. For more details on learning methods, see [2].

4   Implementation and Results

In order to validate our proposal, we developed the system proposed as a case study in section 1, a multi-agent system containing several mySAM agents and one CM . Agents were deployed with the JADE/LEAP platform ([9]) to run on handheld devices. Each mySAM agent is a JADE agent with a graphical interface that allows a user to manage her agenda. This graphical interface has been simplified to deploy mySAM agents on a HP iPAQ 5550 Pocket PC.

For learning *how to use* relevant context (for acceptance or refusal of meeting proposals), mySAM agents use CBA (Classification Based on Association) algorithm. CBA gives better results than C4.5 [4] and it generates rules comprehensive for both agents and humans. The rules have been used with Jess ([11]) inference engine.

In order to provide examples for learning algorithm, the system has been used (for meeting negotiations) by several members in our department for several weeks. Here is an example of the rules we obtained using CBA on the examples generated by using mySAM: *IF ActivityDuration = 120 AND BusyMorning = true AND BusyEvening = true   THEN class = no* ("class" specifies whether the agent should accept or refuse the proposed meeting). When no rule matches the specific context, mySAM is constrained to use *a multi-agent knowledge-sharing* session on how to use this specific context (IRAS) to find the solution. It asks all known agents in the system for their opinion on the situation, and counts each opinion as a vote for "accept", "reject" or "unknown". The agent then proposes to its user the decision that has the most votes. Agents consider an "unknown" result as a "reject" (by default, an agent will reject all meeting proposals that neither it, nor other agents know how to handle). We choose to use this "voting" procedure because not all agents will want to share their decision-making techniques, but an "accept/reject/unknown" answer is reasonable.

The CM is also implemented as a JADE agent. It is a special agent in the system that has access to the domain ontology that defines the context attributes that it will manage. It answers to context-related queries from all agents that are in the system. The ontology was created using Protégé 2000 ([16]) and CM accesses the ontology using Jena ([10]), a Java library designed for ontology management.

Agents interactions in the system are as follows: mySAM agents can query the CM using a REQUEST/INFORM protocol, negotiations between mySAMs being done using a PROPOSE/ACCEPT/REJECT protocol.

When testing mySAM we were able to draw several conclusions. Using a selection step to choose the RAS for a situation helps in having smaller and more significant rules. Using all attributes to describe a situation is not only difficult to deal with, but also unnecessary. We tested our hypothesis on a set of 100 examples. For 15 context attributes used, we obtained an overall classification error of 29.11% and more than 40 rules. When we split the example set on several finalities ("meeting_with_family", "meeting_with_friends", "work_meeting"), and for each situation we take into account a limited number of context attributes (7 for a meeting with family, 11 for others), the error becomes 7.59% and the number of obtained rules drops to an average of 15.

Sharing with other agents just the decision (accept/reject) is preferable, because the agent that received the answer will then add this situation to its examples list, from where it will then learn the appropriate rule. Even if it will be slower than just sharing the specific rule, the privacy problem is this way addressed, because the agent shares just the answer to a specific situation, and not the reasoning that produced the answer.

5 Related Work

In this section we'll present a brief state of the art in context definition, context-aware MAS and context-aware architectures, in order to position our work relative to what has been done in this domain. We don't position our work relative to the learning domain, because our goal was not to propose a learning algorithm, but to use some already proposed methods for the specific goal of dealing with context [26].

Our definition of context is quite similar to definitions proposed by Persson [15], Brezillon [1], Edmonds [6], or Thevenin and Coutaz ([22]) in the sense that it is based on: (i) elements that structure context and (ii) its use, i.e. the finality when using it. The definition we proposed takes into account those two dimensions of context; it also explains how to manage them when designing context-based MAS.

In MAS, the notion of context is used to describe the factors that influence a certain decision. In applications similar to our agenda management application, there are several works that adapt to context: Calendar Apprentice [14], Personal Calendar Agent [13], Distributed Meeting Scheduler [19], Electric elves [18], etc. Most of these works don't mention the idea of "context" but they all use the "circumstances" or "environmental factors" that affect the decision to be made. In making Calendar Agent ([12]), Lashkari et al. use the notion of context, but they assume that the relevant context is known in advance, so that every context element that they have access to is considered relevant for the decision to be made. These approaches are not application-independent when handling context, because they do not provide neither a general representation of context knowledge nor methods to choose relevant context elements for a specific decision. This is the main difference and contribution of our work in the sense that we propose a MAS architecture based on an ontological representation of context and that can permit an individual and multi-agent learning of how to choose and use context. MySAM is just a case study to validate our approach.

Mostly, context is used in an ad-hoc manner, without trying to propose an approach suitable for other kind of applications. However, there is some research in proposing a general architecture on context-aware applications, like CoBrA, proposed by Chen et al.[3] or Socam, by Gu et al [21]. We based our architecture on CoBrA and Socam, but we added the learning modules for choosing relevant context and using it. The context broker and interpreter are similar to our CM, with the difference that our concern was not how to retrieve information from sources, but mostly how to represent it and how to reason on context knowledge based on this representation.

6 Conclusions

In this article, we have presented a definition of context, notion that is used in almost all applications, without consistently and explicitly taking it into account. We have proposed an ontology-based representation for context and a context-based architecture for a learning MAS that uses this representation. We then validated our approach by implementing a meeting scheduling MAS that uses this architecture and manages and learns context based on the definitions and representation we proposed.

As future work, we will extend this framework for context-based MAS to be used for any kind of application that considers context to adapt. The CM will be able to deal with all context-related tasks (including the calculation of context attributes values) and to share all this context-related knowledge. In order to make this possible, our future work will focus on representing and managing how to calculate the values for context attributes, and the importance of different attributes in different situation (making a more refined difference between relevant and non relevant attributes).

In what concerns learning agents, the framework will provide agents with several individual learning algorithm and all that is needed to communicate and share contextual knowledge (how to choose, compute and use context to make decisions).

References

1. Brezillon, P. – "Context Dynamic and Explanation in Contextual Graphs", In: Modeling and Using Context (CONTEXT-03), LNAI 2680, Springer Verlag p. 94-106, 2003.
2. Bucur O, Boissier O, Beaune P – "Knowledge Sharing on How to Recognize and Use Context to Make Decisions", to appear in Proc. of Workshop "Context Modeling for Decision Support", Vth International and Interdisciplinary Conference "Context 05".
3. Chen H., Finin T., Anupam J.   – "An Ontology for Context-Aware Pervasive Computing Environments", The Knowledge Engineering Review, p. 197–207, 2003.
4. Data Mining II – CBA - http://www.comp.nus.edu.sg/ ~dm2/
5. Dey A., Abowd, G.– "Towards a better understanding of Context and Context-Awareness", GVU Technical Report GIT-GVU-00-18, GIT, 1999.

6. Edmonds B. – "Learning and exploiting context in agents", in proc. of AAMAS 2002, Bologna, Italy, p. 1231-1238.
7. Gonzalez A., Ahlers R. – "Context based representation of intelligent behavior in training simulations", Transactions of the Society for Computer Simulation International, Vol. 15, No. 4, p. 153-166, 1999.
8. Henricksen K., Indulska J., Rakotonirainy A – "Modeling Context Information in Pervasive Computing Systems", Proc. First International Conference on Pervasive Computing 2002, p. 167-180.
9. JADE (Java Agent Development framework) : http://jade.cselt.it/
10. Jena Semantic Web Framework - http://jena. sourceforge.net/
11. Jess: http://herzberg.ca.sandia.gov/jess/index.shtml
12. Lashkari Y., Metral M., Maes P – "Collaborative Interface Agents", Proc. of CIKM'94, ACM Press.
13. Lin S., J.Y.Hsu – "Learning User's Scheduling Criteria in a Personal Calendar Agent", Proc. of TAAI2000, Taipei.
14. Mitchell T., Caruana R., Freitag D., McDermott J., Zabowski D.– "Experience with a learning personal assistant", Communications of the ACM, 1994.
15. Persson P.– "Social Ubiquitous computing", Position paper to the workshop on 'Building the Ubiquitous Computing User Experience' at ACM/SIGCHI'01, Seattle.
16. Protégé 2000 - http://protege.stanford.edu/.
17. Ryan N.– "ConteXtML: Exchanging contextual information between a Mobile Client and the FieldNote Server", http://www.cs.kent.ac.uk/projects/mobicomp/fnc/ConteXtML.html.
18. Scerri, P., Pynadath D., Tambe M.– "Why the elf acted autonomously: Towards a theory of adjustable autonomy " , AAMAS 02, p. 857-964, 2002.
19. Sen S., E.H. Durfee – "On the design of an adaptive meeting scheduler", in Proc. of the Tenth IEEE Conference on AI Applications, p. 40-46, 1994.
20. Sian S. S. – "Adaptation Based on Cooperative Learning in Multi-Agent Systems", Descentralized AI, Yves Demazeau & J.P. Muller, p. 257-272, 1991.
21. Tao Gu, Xiao Hang W., Hung K.P., Da Quing Z – "An Ontology-based Context Model in Intelligent Environments", Proc. of Communication Networks and Distributed Systems Modeling and Simulation Conference, 2004.
22. Thevenin D., J. Coutaz. – "Plasticity of User Interfaces: Framework and Research Agenda". In Proceedings of INTERACT'99, 1999, pp. 110-117.
23. Turney,P. – "The identification of Context-Sensitive Features: A Formal Definition of context for Concept Learning", 13th International Conference on Machine Learning (ICML96), Workshop on Learning in Context-Sensitive Domains, p. 53-59.
24. Turner, R. – "Context-Mediated Behaviour for Intelligent Agents", International Journal of Human-Computer Studies, vol. 48 no.3, March 1998, p. 307-330.
25. Widmer G.– "Tracking context changes through meta-learning", Machine Learning, 27(3):259-286, Kluwer Academic Publisher.
26. Weiss G., Dillenbourg P.– "What is "multi" in multi-agent learning?", P. Dillenbourg (Ed) Collaborative-learning: Cognitive, and computational approaches, p. 64-80, 1999.

A Formal Modelling Framework for Developing Multi-agent Systems with Dynamic Structure and Behaviour

Petros Kefalas[1], Ioanna Stamatopoulou[2], and Marian Gheorghe[3]

[1] Department of Computer Science,
CITY College, Thessaloniki, Greece
kefalas@city.academic.gr
[2] South-East European Research Centre, Thessaloniki, Greece
istamatopoulou@seerc.info
[3] Department of Computer Science, University of Sheffield, UK
M.Gheorghe@dcs.shef.ac.uk

Abstract. Multi-agent systems exhibit highly dynamic behaviour within dynamic environments. Modelling of individual agents within such systems demands considering both evolving data structures and the control over their internal changing states. In addition, modelling of the overall system implies modelling of the agents' configuration, including their ability to exchange messages as well as the ability to re-structure their formation over time. This paper presents a formal modelling framework based on Communicating X-machines, allowing the specification of multi-agent software systems with a dynamic structure and behaviour. A case study illustrates the proposed modelling approach.

1 Introduction

Multi-agent system complexity is due to substantial differences in attributes between their individuals, high computational power required for the processes within agents, non-trivial type or volume of data manipulated by these processes and considerable amount of communication in order to achieve coordination and collaboration. The use of a computational framework that is capable of modelling both the dynamic aspect (change) and the static aspect (data and knowledge), will facilitate modelling and simulation of such complex systems.

The majority of models created for biological or biology-inspired multi-agent systems are based on an assumed, fixed system structure that is not realistic. Our contribution is to show how most of the modelling requirements are captured through the use of a distributed state-based formal method, namely Communicating X-machines. In particular, we propose an extension of Communicating X-machine Systems, which includes the rules under and operations with which a multi-agent system changes its configuration over time.

Our motivating example is given in Sect. 2 of this paper. In Sect. 3, we briefly discuss the use of formal methods in agent-oriented software engineering and we

M. Pěchouček, P. Petta, and L.Z. Varga (Eds.): CEEMAS 2005, LNAI 3690, pp. 122–131, 2005.

informally present X-machines. Formal definitions are given in Sect. 4 and a model for our motivating example in Sect. 5. Finally, we discuss various issues arising from the use of X-machines in multi-agent system development as well as existing tools.

2   Motivation

Our research is motivated by the implications of using formal methods in modelling biological systems. As in any software system, formal specification and modelling can lead towards a better understanding of the system under development, verification of important properties and application of complete test strategies. In biological processes bio-entities can be conceived as simple agents that act autonomously in a dynamic and complex environment but also communicate in order to achieve a desired emergent behaviour. Such a behaviour is apparent in swarms or colonies of social insects as well as in epithelial tissues formed out of individual cells [1, 2].

For example, consider the following scenario: a number of identical agents A are located in a plane and move freely (randomly) in space (Fig. 1.a). When two identical agents A collide (Fig. 1.b), a new type of agent L is generated (Fig. 1.c). When any agent A comes close (within a threshold distance) to any agent L, agent A follows the movement of L from then on, as a satellite, staying at the threshold distance (Fig. 1.d). Agents L can have up to a certain number of satellite agents—if this number is reached then a complete assembly is formed (Fig. 1.e). A complete assembly has the ability to immobilise or destroy any agent A, which enters the virtual cycle of the assembly (Fig. 1.f). This kind of scenario resembles a number of situations, which appear in abundance in chemistry, biology, swarms, robotics, artificial life systems, self-assembly etc.

Systems like the above consist of agents with common characteristics; they sense their local environment through stimuli and have an internal state which is determined by a set of values that characterise a particular instance of their life time as well as what they know or believe about themselves, other agents and the environment. They also possess a set of behaviours, triggered by stimuli and their internal state. Finally, agents are able to communicate information with other agents under specific circumstances. In the previous example, agents know their position in space and sense free space or other agents of type A or L. When an agent A becomes a satellite of an agent L, then the former behaves as a blind follower by receiving the new direction of the latter through communication. Communication is established between an agent L and all its satellites.

In addition, these multi-agent systems are highly dynamic in structure. The configuration of the system (overall system state), is implied by the number of agents that are present at any given time as well as the way these agents interact. Evolution of the system may imply that some new agents come into play, others cease to exist, some change roles, while the communication channels between agents are re-configured over time.In the previous example, a new type of agent L is born when two agents A collide and disappear from the system. The same

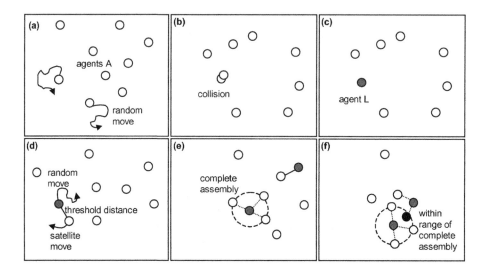

Fig. 1. Six system instances showing the agents' behaviour

happens when an agent A enters the virtual cycle of a complete assembly. Finally, new communication channels are configured when agents becomes satellites.

3   Formal Methods for Multi-agent Systems

In an attempt to formally model each individual agent as well as the dynamic behaviour of the overall system, we need a formal method that is capable of rigorously describing all the essential attributes, i.e. change, behaviour, communication and dynamics. It is also important that the level of abstraction imposed by a formal method is appropriate enough to lead towards the implementation of a system. The most widely used formal methods are accompanied by toolkits, which make their adoption wider by researchers and industry. A plethora of formal methods are available to use. Some of them have the means to efficiently define the data structures of a system and the operations employed to modify the values in these structures (Z, VDM). Some others describe well the control over a system's states (FSM, Petri Nets). Also, there are formal methods that put emphasis on the concurrency and communication of processes (CCS, CSP). Finally, new computation approaches as well as programming paradigms inspired by biological processes in living cells, introduce concurrency as well as neatly tackle the dynamic structure of multi-component systems (P Systems, Brane Calculus, Gamma, Cham, MGS) [3, 4, 5].

In agent-oriented software engineering, there have been several attempts to use formal methods, each one focusing on different aspects of agent systems development, in order to: move to the implementation through refinement of the specification and to be able to develop proof theories for the architecture [6], capture the dynamics of an agent system [7], focus on the specification of the dynamics of the reasoning and acting behaviour of multi-agent systems [8], etc. Other attempts were made in order to verify properties of agent models, based on model checking, or to focus on program generation of reactive systems through a formal transformation process [9, 10]. Wider approaches formally specify multi-agent systems and then directly execute the specification while verifying important temporal properties [11]. Finally, less formal approaches, which accommodate the distinctive requirements of agents, have been proposed [12]. An interesting comparison of various formal methods for the verification of emergent behaviours in swarm-based systems is reported in [13].

X-machines are a formal method that was firstly introduced by Eilenberg [14] but was later considered suitable as a specification language [15]. A particular class of X-machines, the stream X-machines, was found to be well-suited for modelling of reactive systems. Since then valuable findings using the X-machines as a formal notation for specification, modelling, communication, verification and testing purposes have been reported [16, 17, 18].

The X-machine (XM) models possess characteristics that make them useful for specifying software systems. XM models consist of a number of states, just as a Finite State Machine (FSM) does. But in contrast to FSM, an XM model has a memory, which accommodates mathematically defined data structures, pretty much as Z does. The transitions between states are labelled by functions. The functions are not applied only to inputs but also to memory values and produce outputs and new memory values. The XM models consume a stream of inputs and produce a stream of outputs, through a number of computation steps (a computation step being the application of one function).

An XM with no initial state and memory is called an *X-machine type*. Types can be used to create instances of XM that can all be part of a larger system. XM instances are able to communicate between them. A number of approaches have been proposed for asynchronous and synchronous communication [16]. In principle, a function of a machine can produce an output, which can be directed to an input stream of another machine.

4 Dynamic Communicating X-Machine Systems

Definition 1. The 8-tuple $XM = (\Sigma, \Gamma, Q, M, \Phi, F, q_0, m_0)$ defines a *stream X-machine* [18] where:

- Σ and Γ are the input and output alphabets respectively;
- Q is the finite set of states;
- M is the (possibly) infinite set called memory;
- Φ is a set of partial functions φ that map an input and a memory state to an output and a possibly different memory state, $\varphi : \Sigma \times M \to \Gamma \times M$;
- F is the next state partial function, $F : Q \times \Phi \to Q$, which given a state and a function from the type Φ determines the next state. F is often described as a state transition diagram;
- q_0 and m_0 are the initial state and initial memory respectively.

For the modelling of systems where more than one agents need to co-exist, the XM model needed to be extended by new features, such as hierarchical decomposition and communication. A Communicating X-machine (CXM) model consists of several XM that are able to exchange messages. This involves modelling the participating agents and defining the rules of their communication.

Definition 2. A *Dynamic Communicating X-machine System* Z is defined as $Z = ((C_i)_{i=1,\ldots,n}, CR, R, GC)$ where:

- C_i is the i-th CXM component i.e. an XM whose functions $\varphi \in \Phi$ are able to either receive input from other communicating components or send outputs to be received as input by other components' functions or both;
- CR is a relation defining the communication among the components, $CR \subseteq C \times C$ and $C = \{C_1, \ldots, C_n\}$. A tuple $(C_i, C_k) \in CR$ denotes that the CXM component C_i can output a message to a corresponding input stream of CXM component C_k for any $i, k \in \{1, \ldots, n\}$, $i \neq k$;
- R is the set of rules that refer to the configuration of the system, i.e. they define how the operators that will be affecting the structure of the communicating system are to be applied;
- GC is the set of definitions of all components that exist or may be added to the system. These definitions act as genetic codes for the system, i.e. GC is the set of XM types.

Definition 3. The *state* SZ of a Communicating X-machine System is defined as $SZ : \mathbb{P}(S)$ where S is a set of 3-tuples $S = \{(q_c, m_c, \varphi_c)_i \mid \forall C_i, 1 \leq i \leq n, q_c \in Q_i, m_i \in M_i, \varphi_c \in \Phi_i\}$ (q_c is the state in which C_i is in, m_c is the memory value of C_i and φ_c is the last function that has been applied in C_i) such that each tuple represents the current computation state that an XM is in.

The rules that drive the evolution of the system structure are generally of the form *condition* $\rightarrow$ *action* whereby, if the condition allows, an appropriate action which includes one or more reconfiguration operations is being performed. The reconfiguration operators involved have been inspired by Population P Systems [19], which are by definition capable of changing their structure while evolving. In the descriptive definitions that follow $\mathcal{XM}$ is the set of all XM types, $\mathcal{C}$ is the set of all CXM components and $\mathcal{Z}$ the set of all CXM Systems (the complete definitions may be found in [20]):

Definition 4. The *Attachment operator* **ATT** : $\mathcal{C} \times \mathcal{C} \times \mathcal{Z} \rightarrow \mathcal{Z}$ is responsible for establishing communication between two existing CXM components. It takes as arguments two CXM components C_i, C_k and the current CXM System Z (to which they belong) and outputs the system Z' according to which C_i and C_k are able to communicate.

Definition 5. The *Detachment operator* **DET** : $\mathcal{C} \times \mathcal{Z} \rightarrow \mathcal{Z}$ removes communication channels between an existing CXM component and the set of other existing components with which it currently communicates.

Definition 6. The *Generation operator* **GEN** : $\mathcal{XM} \times \mathcal{Z} \rightarrow \mathcal{Z}$ creates and introduces a new CXM component of type XM into the system.

Definition 7. The *Destruction operator* **DES** : $\mathcal{C} \times \mathcal{Z} \rightarrow \mathcal{Z}$ is used for the removal of an existing CXM component from the system along with all the channels that allow its communication with other components.

Because of the memory structure that is inherent to XM models, a temporal logic such as the Computational Tree Logic (CTL) [21], is not by itself adequate for the purposes of model checking. In order to overcome the lack of expressiveness and to avoid the refinement of X-machines, $\mathcal{X}m$CTL , an extension of CTL, has been defined [17], that can handle the processing of the memory structure for the model checking of an X-machine. This is accomplished with the use of two extra memory quantifier operators, besides the temporal operators and the path quantifiers, that quantify memory instances within a single state: $\mathbf{m_x}$, meaning "there exists a memory value", and $\mathbf{M_x}$, meaning "for all memory values". Additionally, an appropriate algorithm has been devised [17] that can model check systems expressed as X-machines with the properties to be checked expressed in $\mathcal{X}m$CTL .

5   Modelling Agents with X-Machines

The two types of agents, A and L, presented in the example of the introduction can be modelled as X-machines, whose state transition diagrams F_A and F_L are shown in Fig. 2. $Q_A = \{moving\ freely, collided, following\ L, dead\}$. The memory of agent A holds its current position, the identifier of the agent L that is being followed (or noL if none is followed) and the threshold distance, under which a bond is made with an agent L so $M_A = (Z \times Z) \times (\mathcal{L} \cup \{noL\}) \times R$, where $\mathcal{L}$ is the set of all possible identifiers of agents of type L. The input set $\Sigma_A = (\mathcal{L} \cup \mathcal{A} \cup \{space\}) \times (Z \times Z)$, where $\mathcal{A}$ is the set of all possible identifiers of agents of type A. The output set Γ_A is a set of messages.

Accordingly, for the agent L, $Q_L = \{moving\ freely\}$, $\Sigma_L = (\mathcal{A} \cup \{space\}) \times (Z \times Z)$, and Γ_L is a set of messages. The memory $M_L = (Z \times Z) \times \mathbb{P}(\mathcal{A}) \times N$, where the second memory position holds the set of satellite agents of type A and the third position holds the number of agents A that are needed for a complete assembly. Indicatively, some of the functions in the two Φ sets are:

$move((space, (x, y)), ((cx, cy), noL, d)) =$
    $(movingFreely, ((x, y), noL, d))$, if $neighbours((x, y), (cx, cy))$

$follow((myL, (x, y)), ((cx, cy), myL, d)) =$
    $(followL, ((cx', cy'), myL, d))$,
    where $(cx', cy') = calculate\_coord(d, (x, y), (cx, cy))$

$meet\_A((agentA, (cx, cy)), ((cx, cy), myL, d)) =$
    $(collidedWithA, ((cx, cy), noL, d))$

$move((space, (x, y)), ((cx, cy), setA, maxA)) =$
    $(movingFreely, ((x, y), setA, maxA))$, if $neighbours((x, y), (cx, cy))$

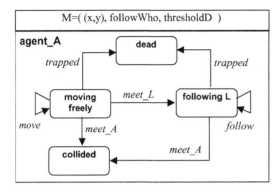 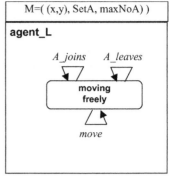

Fig. 2. The two X-machine types used in the example

$$A\_joins((agentA, (x, y)), ((cx, cy), setA, maxA)) =$$
$$(agentAJoins, ((cx, cy), setA \cup agentA, maxA)),$$
$$\text{if } |setA| < maxA \wedge agentA \notin setA$$

The CXM model consists of all agent models that are instantiated with an initial state and an initial memory. So, initially the system of Fig. 1.a is $Z = (C, \emptyset, R, GC)$ where $C = \{A_1, A_2, ..., A_9\}$, R contains the rules of dynamically configuring the system structure and GC contains the two XM types of agents that exist in the system, i.e. A and L.

SZ, the overall current system state, may for example look like $SZ = \{(moving\ freely, ((3, 15), noL, 4.5), \varepsilon)_{A_1}, ...\}$.

The rules in R for dynamic configuration describe the situations which, if present in the system state SZ, change the configuration of the system. All rules imply application of one or more reconfiguration operators **ATT**, **DET**, **GEN**, and **DES**. For example, the rule that is applicable when two agents of type A collide is the following:

$$((moving\ freely, ((X, Y), noL, d), \varphi_i)_{A_i} \in SZ$$
$$\vee (following\ L, ((X, Y), anL, d), \varphi_i)_{A_i} \in SZ)$$
$$\wedge ((moving\ freely, ((X, Y), noL, d), \varphi_j)_{A_j} \in SZ$$
$$\vee (following\ L, ((X, Y), anL, d), \varphi_j)_{A_j} \in SZ)$$
$$\wedge A_i \neq A_j$$
$$\rightarrow Z' = \mathbf{GEN}(L_k, \mathbf{DES}(A_j, \mathbf{DES}(A_i, Z))), \text{where } k = |C| + 1$$

Also the rule that creates a satellite agent A of an agent of type L is:

$$(moving\ freely, ((X1, Y1), noL, d), \varphi_i)_{A_i} \in SZ$$
$$\wedge (moving\ freely, ((X2, Y2), setA, m), \varphi_k)_{L_k} \in SZ$$
$$\wedge d \leq distance((X1, Y1), (X2, Y2))$$
$$\rightarrow Z' = \mathbf{ATT}(A_i, L_k, Z)$$

Figure 3 shows a formation consisting of one agent instance of type L (L_{10}) and two agents instances of type A (A_1 and A_2). While moving, L_{10} sends its new coordinates to A_1 and A_2 which use them as inputs to follow L_{10}. The

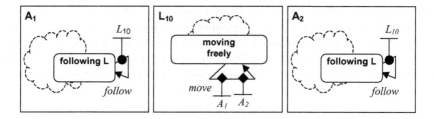

Fig. 3. Communication between an agent A with its two satellite agents. A solid circle denotes the acceptance of input from another component whereas the solid diamond the direction of output to another component

corresponding function of L_{10} is transformed so that the its output is transformed into the format that is understandable by the *follow* function of the A agents.

Finally, $\mathcal{X}m$CTL may be used to verify properties of the individual models. In this example, we may need to verify that "under no circumstances will an agent of type L have more than the maximum allowed number of satellites". The temporal logic formula that expresses this property is $\mathbf{AGM_x}(|M(2)| \leq M(3))$ where $\mathbf{A}$ is the path quantifier "for all paths" and $\mathbf{G}$ is the temporal logic operator "for all states" respectively, and the syntax $M(n)$ refers to the n-th element of the memory structure, in this case the set of satellite agents ($M(2)$) and the maximum allowed number of satellites ($M(3)$). Currently, further work is being done towards the verification of CXM Systems' properties that would allow us to answer questions such as, for example, "does the system always reach a state when all the agents of type A are extinct?", i.e. it would allow us to model check for certain properties featured by the entire collection that the components constitute.

6   Discussion

X-machines can be thought to apply in similar cases where StateCharts and other similar notations, such as SDL, do. In principle, XM are considered a generalization of models written in similar formalisms since concepts devised and findings proven for XM form a solid theoretical framework, which can be adapted to other, more tool-oriented methods. XM have other significant advantages.

Firstly, XM provide a mathematical modelling formalism for a system. Consequently, a model checking method for X-machines is devised that facilitates the verification of safety properties of a model. The $\mathcal{X}m$CTL language apart from the usual CTL operators, includes operators that deal with memory values (properties) of the machines [17]. Though up to know, only individual XM models may be verified, ongoing research is being conducted towards finding ways for model checking CXM Systems. This would facilitate the verification of properties that a collection of individuals exhibits as a whole.

In addition, XM offer a strategy to test the implementation against the model, which is a generalization of W-method for FSM testing. The testing strategy generates all test cases for a given model and therefore it is guaranteed to determine correctness if certain assumptions in the implementation hold [18].

A modelling language, called XMDL, is devised, which is a tagged language with appropriate syntax and semantics in order to develop XM models and CXM systems. The process of doing this is incremental, without loss of any description developed at an earlier stage. That is, if the aim is to develop a communicating system, the individual types of models are build first, they are validated and tested, and then the instances of those types as well as their communication interface are added on top later on. This is a disciplined approach that leads towards a specific methodology of developing XM models, and resembles existing bottom-up methodologies used to develop multi-agent systems [22].

Finally, a number of tools around XMDL have also been developed [23], with most prominent the one that compiles XMDL to Prolog and animates the model through a sequence of inputs. This was proven particularly useful to understand the computation of models and informally validate whether the right model for a particular system was developed.

7   Conclusions

We have presented an extension of communicating X-machines that is able to facilitate formal modelling of multi-agent systems through the use of rules that invoke operators that change the system structure and behaviour. We are currently working on implementing those features on top of existing tools and develop alternative hybrid formal models, inspired by membrane computing. We have also been experimenting with the compilation of a particular class of XM to NetLogo [24], which will give a clearer picture of the animation in terms of a two-dimensional movement and interaction of simple agents.

References

[1] Kefalas, P., Holcombe, M., Eleftherakis, G., Gheorge, M.: A formal method for the development of agent-based systems. In Plekhanova, V., ed.: Intelligent Agent Software Engineering. Idea Publishing Group Co. (2003) 68–98

[2] Holcombe, M.: Computational models of cells and tissues: Machines, agents and fungal infection. Briefings in Bioinformatics **2** (2001) 271–278

[3] Păun, G.: Computing with membranes. Journal of Computer and System Sciences **61** (2000) 108–143 Also circulated as a TUCS report since 1998.

[4] Banatre, J., Le Metayer, D.: The gamma model and its discipline of programming. Science of Computer Programming **15** (1990) 55–77

[5] Berry, G., Boudol, G.: The chemical abstract machine. Journal of Theoretical Computer Science **96** (1992) 217–248

[6] d'Inverno, M., Kinny, D., Luck, M., Wooldridge, M.: A formal specification of dMARS. In Singh, M.P., Rao, A., Wooldridge, M.J., eds.: Intelligent Agents IV. Volume 1365 of Lecture Notes in AI. Springer-Verlag (1998) 155–176

[7] Rosenschein, S.R., Kaebling, L.P.: A situated view of representation and control. Artificial Intelligence **73** (1995) 149–173

 [8] Brazier, F., Dunin-Keplicz, B., Jennings, N., Treur, J.: Formal specification of multiagent systems: a real-world case. In: Proceedings of International Conference on Multi-Agent Systems (ICMAS'95), MIT Press (1995) 25–32
 [9] Benerecetti, M., Giunchiglia, F., Serafini, L.: A model-checking algorithm for multi-agent systems. In Muller, J.P., Singh, M.P., Rao, A.S., eds.: Intelligent Agents V. Lecture Notes in Artificial Intelligence. Springer-Verlag (1999) 163–176
[10] Attoui, A., Hasbani, A.: Reactive systems developing by formal specification transformations. In: Proceedings of the 8th International Workshop on Database and Expert Systems Applications (DEXA 97). (1997) 339 – 344
[11] Fisher, M., Wooldridge, M.: On the formal specification and verification of multi-agent systems. Intern. Journal of Cooperating Information Systems 6 (1997) 37–65
[12] Odell, J., Parunak, H.V.D., Bauer, B.: Extending UML for agents. In: Proceedings of the Agent-Oriented Information Systems Workshop at the 17th National conference on Artificial Intelligence. (2000) 3–17
[13] Rouf, C., Vanderbilt, A., Truszkowski, W., Rash, J., Hinchey, M.: Verification of NASA emergent systems. In: Proceedings of the 9th IEEE International Conference on Engineering Complex Computer Systems (ICECCS'04). (2004) 231–238
[14] Eilenberg, S.: Automata, Languages and Machines. Academic Press (1974)
[15] Holcombe, M.: X-machines as a basis for dynamic system configuration. Software Engineering Journal 3 (1988) 69–76
[16] Kefalas, P., Eleftherakis, G., Kehris, E.: Communicating X-machines: A practical approach for formal and modular specification of large systems. Journal of Information and Software Technology 45 (2003) 269–280
[17] Eleftherakis, G.: Formal Verification of X-machine Models: Towards Formal Development of Computer-based Systems. PhD thesis, Department of Computer Science, University of Sheffield (2003)
[18] Holcombe, M., Ipate, F.: Correct Systems: Building a Business Process Solution. Springer-Verlag, London (1998)
[19] Bernandini, F., Gheorghe, M.: Population P Systems. Journal of Universal Computer Science 10 (2004) 509–539
[20] Kefalas, P., Eleftherakis, G., Holcombe, M., Stamatopoulou, I.: Formal modelling of the dynamic behaviour of biology-inspired agent-based systems. In Gheorghe, M., ed.: Molecular Computational Models: Unconventional Approaches. Idea Publishing Inc. (2005) 243–276
[21] Emerson, E.A., Clarke, E.M.: Characterising correctness properties of parallel programs as fixpoints. In: Proceedings of the 7th International Colloquium on Automata, Languages and Programming. Volume 85 of Lecture Notes in Computer Science. Springer-Verlag, New York (1981) 169–181
[22] Collinot, A., Drogul, A., Benhamou, P.: Agent oriented design of a soccer robot team. In: Proceedings of the 2nd Intern. Conf. on Multi-Agent Systems. (1996) 41–47
[23] Kefalas, P., Eleftherakis, G., Sotiriadou, A.: Developing tools for formal methods. In: Proceedings of the 9th Panhellenic Conference in Informatics. (2003) 625–639
[24] Wilensky, U.: Netlogo. http://ccl.northwestern.edu/netlogo. Center for Connected Learning and Computer-based Modeling. Northwestern University, Evanston, IL. (1999)

Discovery of Crises via Agent-Based Simulation of a Transportation System*

Edward Nawarecki, Jarosław Koźlak,
Grzegorz Dobrowolski, and Marek Kisiel-Dorohinicki

Institute of Computer Science,
AGH University of Science and Technology, Kraków, Poland
{nawar, kozlak, grzela, doroh}@agh.edu.pl

Abstract. The contribution deals with a class of intelligent decentralized systems that are marked by the possibility of arising critical situations. The work starts from the elaboration of an overall methodology dedicated to the discovery of crises and support of anti-crisis activities. Then the case of transportation enterprise support system is discussed in detail. A simulation study of anti-crisis management in such a system concludes the work.

1 Introduction

As it has been repeatedly discussed and confirmed, a paradigm of multi-agent systems is especially powerful when looking for the representation of existing, designed or foreseen systems of hybrid technical-human nature. Notions of autonomy and decentralization, granularity and distribution, proactiveness and environment dependency are distinctive for such systems. Acceptance of the agent-based approach opens possibility for solving many problems that until now has been tractable only with respect to tightly coupled centralized systems. Some of these problems are risk and critical situations (states) analysis [10,1].

The systems under consideration may both be designed from scratch as multi-agent ones (operating in the virtual world, e.g. network information services, virtual enterprises), as well as function in the reality as a set of cooperating autonomous subsystems of whatever origin (e.g. transportation systems, industrial complexes). Such systems (virtual as well as real) are marked by the possibility of arising critical situations that can be caused by both outer (e.g. undesirable interference or the forces of nature) and inner (e.g. resource deficit, local damages) factors. Generally, a crisis is interpreted here as a threat of loss (partial or complete) of the system functionality.

As it will be shown, crisis identification, evaluation of possible effects and application of prevention (anti-crisis) actions occur to be much more difficult tasks in the case of such (multi-agent) systems. The mentioned above features (mainly: autonomy of the agent's decisions, lack of global information and hardly predictable behaviour) stems for quite different solutions.

---

* This work was partially sponsored by State Committee for Scientific Research (KBN) grant no. 3 T11C 025 27.

M. Pěchouček, P. Petta, and L.Z. Varga (Eds.): CEEMAS 2005, LNAI 3690, pp. 132–141, 2005.

The paper tries to solve, at least partially, the three specified tasks. A function schema and appropriate information structure are proposed that can serve as a basis for analysing and managing critical situations. They specify how the system can be monitored and a simulation model of its behaviour created in the face of a particular crisis. The results of simulation studies are the scenarios of the crisis progress. The investigation of the scenarios may lead to finding a strategy of avoiding the crisis or, at least, reducing its effects. The simulation model is also in the shape of a multi-agent system [8].

General considerations are illustrated and verified with the case of a real transportation enterprise, which is represented by an agent-based model. A particular organization of the enterprise including an originally proposed anti-crisis policy is modelled together with its field of operation.

The paper is organized as follows. Section 2 describes the idea of monitoring and foreseeing critical situations in multi-agent systems. Section 3 is devoted to the description of an agent-based model of a transportation enterprise together with specific solutions of monitoring and management tasks. The considered critical situations arise as traffic jams and impassable roads. At the end (section 4) the chosen results of simulation studies illustrating the applied anti-crisis policy are presented.

2   Management of Critical Situations in MAS

A critical situation is recognized as a particular state or sequence of states that violate or lead to the violation of global as well as local (the agents') goals of the system. Thus critical situations can be local (concerning a single agent) and global (involving not only all but also a group of agents). Arising of a local crisis may entail a global one in the future, but functional abilities of the system very often allow avoiding consequences at the global level. On the contrary, the threat of a global crisis usually requires especially invented mechanisms.

Two kinds of critical situations can be distinguished: *direct* and *indirect*. The direct one means the threat of loosing operability of the system in consequence of unavailability of the some agents' actions. The primary cause of an indirect critical situation is the lack of resources that, in turn, gives deficit of functionality. The detection of both kinds can be realised by a monitoring sub-system based on individual evaluations pointed out the loss of functionality, or observations of the distribution of some resources crucial to the agent's or system activity.

Let us discuss shortly the conditions for the case of local critical situations. In the obvious way an agent monitors his state as well as evaluates it on his own. Significant reduction of the set of possible strategies of further operation in a particular state can be the indication of a crisis. Analysis with respect to global critical situations is a bit harder. This is because of the problem of determining the multi-agent system state. The state can be easily defined as composition of the agents' states but its calculation is usually operationally impossible because of the following features of MAS.

– There are no strong enough synchronization mechanisms to determine the simultaneity of agents' states.

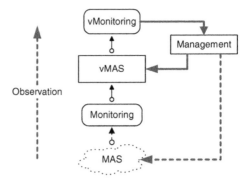

Fig. 1. Management structure for the case of *real* system

- The system state is highly multi-dimensional so that the high cost of information acquisition should be taken into account.
- Agents are autonomous. They usually intend to disclose only as much information as it is necessary for the system operation.

Putting all descriptions of the agents' states together, possibly in a single place, and regarding them as simultaneous is the only way to construct the description of the whole system state.

It seems obvious that it is hard or even pointless to search for any universal manner of management of critical situations in MAS. However, the principal assumptions of MAS operation allow for specification of an architecture, which seems to be general enough to be used as a reference one for describing crises management activities [7].

The architecture is a four-layer one as presented in figure 1. The bottom layer (MAS) constitutes the system under consideration. The directly higher layer (Monitoring) consists of agents that are assigned to gathering information about the subject system by inquiring and observing done according to the agent paradigm [4]. An agent-based model of the reality is situated as the next layer (vMAS): its agents try to reconstruct future states of the system using the monitoring data. Here scenario-based studies of the model are carried out aiming at critical situations detection and search for an anti-crisis policy. The main purpose of the upper monitoring layer is the evaluation of situations (states) arising in the course of simulations carried out using vMAS. The elaboration of a reach enough bunch of scenarios leads to finding the strategy of avoiding crises in the real system or, at least, reducing their effects. The agents of the upper layer may be equipped with the ability of decision making and, in turn, have an effect on the real system – selected strategies may be applied in the reality as a direct management or influence on mechanisms (e.g. organization) of the system. This may create a loop of semi-automatic prevention of crises in the proposed architecture.

The approach may be formally described in terms of the organizational model of a multi-agent system using some elements of M-Agent architecture [2]. Assuming that the state of MAS is observed only in certain moments of time $t_0, t_1, \ldots, t_{k-1}, t_k$ its dynamics in k-th step of operation may be illustrated by the following diagram:

$$\dots \xrightarrow{\text{org}(t_{k-2},t_{k-1})} \text{mas}(t_{k-1}) \xrightarrow{\text{org}(t_{k-1},t_k)} \text{mas}(t_k) \xrightarrow{\text{org}(t_k,t_{k+1})} \dots$$

$$\Big\downarrow \varUpsilon \qquad\qquad \Big\downarrow \varUpsilon$$

$$\dots \qquad \omega(t_{k-1}) \qquad\qquad \omega(t_k) \qquad \dots$$

$$\Big\downarrow \qquad\qquad \Big\downarrow \tag{1}$$

$$\dots \xrightarrow{\text{vorg}(t_{k-2},t_{k-1})} \text{vmas}(t_{k-1}) \xrightarrow{\text{vorg}(t_{k-1},t_k)} \text{vmas}(t_k) \xrightarrow{\text{vorg}(t_k,t_{k+1})} \dots$$

$$\Big\downarrow \widetilde{\varUpsilon} \qquad\qquad \Big\downarrow \widetilde{\varUpsilon}$$

$$\dots \qquad \widetilde{\omega}(t_{k-1}) \qquad\qquad \widetilde{\omega}(t_k) \qquad \dots$$

where:

$\text{mas}(t_k), \text{vmas}(t_k)$ – states of MAS and vMAS respectively, encompassing the states of all agents $\text{ag} \in \text{Ag}$ and the environment env:

$$\text{mas} \equiv \langle \text{Ag}, \text{env} \rangle \tag{2}$$

consecutively each agent is described in terms of actions $\text{act} \in \text{Act}$ it is able to perform depending on its state stat:

$$\text{ag} \equiv \langle \text{Act}, \text{stat} \rangle \tag{3}$$

$\text{org}(t_{k-1},t_k), \text{vorg}(t_{k-1},t_k)$ – organisations emerged in MAS and vMAS respectively, which manifests in actions performed by agents:

$$\text{org}(t_{k-1},t_k) \equiv \{(\text{ag},\text{act},t) : \text{ag} \in \text{Ag}, \text{act} \in \text{Act}, t \in (t_{k-1},t_k)\} \tag{4}$$

$\varUpsilon, \widetilde{\varUpsilon}$ – observation heuristics for MAS and vMAS respectively,
$\omega, \widetilde{\omega}$ – representation of some global effects of the emerged organisations in MAS and vMAS respectively, acquired via observation heuristics:

$$\varUpsilon : \text{mas} \to \omega \tag{5}$$

For the sake of simplicity obvious variants of equations (2)-(5) for vMAS were skipped in the above definitions.

3   Crises in Transportation Systems

Plenty of various transportation system models can be found in literature (e.g. [6,9]). Their exact shape (also their complexity) depends on their general purpose or formal approach applied. Here a rather simple model is proposed oriented mainly towards the illustration of the information aspects of the proposed architecture. Solutions to the objective transportation problem introduced here are of the second importance.

It is assumed that a transportation system is modelled as a multi-agent system, so that agents represent vehicles moving around in a graph-like environment, where edges represent roads and vertices represent intersections:

$$\varGamma = (V,Y) \quad v_i \in V \quad y_{ij} \in Y \tag{6}$$

It is also assumed that the information about the cost of using a road is available for the agents in terms of *weights* of edges:

$$\lambda : Y \rightarrow \mathbb{R}^+ \tag{7}$$

This measure may represent the length, or more generally the throughput of a road. It describes the environment of MAS and thus it does not directly depend on (the states of) agents (i.e. the actual traffic).

The traffic is generated due to orders realised for the agent customer defined according to (3) as:

$$\mathsf{ag}^c = \langle \{\xi\}, \Theta \rangle \tag{8}$$

where ξ denotes the action of negotiating and making contracts with selected vehicles, and Θ is the set of orders to be distributed among them:

$$\Theta = \{(u, v_i, v_j, \tau) : u \in \mathbb{N}, \; v_i, v_j \in V, \; \tau \in \mathbb{R}^+ \times \mathbb{R}^+\} \tag{9}$$

Each order is described by requested load u, route from source vertex v_i to destination vertex v_j, and finally time window τ the order has to be realised within.

A vehicle agent may be similarly defined as:

$$\mathsf{ag}^v{}_k = \langle \{\xi, \chi\}, \langle \Theta_k, \Theta_k^*, \Gamma_k \rangle \rangle \tag{10}$$

where ξ is the action of making contract that is performed together with the agent customer, and χ encompasses all tasks that may be executed by a vehicle moving around a graph and realising orders. The state of a vehicle agent is defined in terms of allocated orders Θ_k, orders being realised Θ_k^*, and planned route Γ_k.

The action of making contract ξ means that selected orders of the customer Θ^* are allocated to a vehicle:

$$\xi : \Theta \rightarrow \Theta \setminus \Theta^* \text{ and } \Theta_k \rightarrow \Theta_k \cup \Theta^* \tag{11}$$

It is assumed that negotiations denoted by ξ are conducted by agents so as to maximize their *utility* (subjective measure of profit) of realising order(s). For each vehicle agent this may be defined as:

$$c_k(\Theta_k \cup \Theta^*, \Gamma_k) \tag{12}$$

and for the customer agent it is:

$$\sum_{\mathsf{ag}^v{}_k} c(\Theta_k \cup \Theta^*, \Gamma_k) \tag{13}$$

which means that the utility in both cases depends on the set of all orders $\Theta_k \cup \Theta^*$ to be realised by vehicle $\mathsf{ag}^v{}_k$ that takes part in the negotiations and its planned route Γ_k (e.g. how long it would take to realise the orders). Nevertheless it should be emphasised that utility functions of a vehicle c_k and of a customer c need not (in practice even *must not*) give the same values for the same orders and vehicles (the goals of a vehicle and a customer may differ).

Action χ is executed when a vehicle agent crosses a vertex and may result in starting some orders (loading) if the vertex is the source one for them, or finishing some orders (unloading) if their destination is reached, and finally updating the planned route:

$$\chi: \Theta_k \rightarrow \Theta_k \setminus \Theta^+ \text{ and } \Theta_k^* \rightarrow \Theta_k^* \cup \Theta^+ \setminus \Theta^- \text{ and } \Gamma_k \rightarrow \Gamma_k' \qquad (14)$$

where Θ^+ denotes the set of orders just started (loaded), Θ^- denotes the set of just finished (unloaded) orders, and Γ_k' is the new (updated) planned route.

To recapitulate, a transportation system modelled as a multi-agent system consists of two kinds of agents and a graph-like environment, which according to (2) may be formulated as:

$$\text{mas} = \langle \{\text{ag}^c\} \cup \{\text{ag}^v_k : k = 1, 2, \ldots\}, \langle \Gamma, \lambda \rangle \rangle \qquad (15)$$

The transportation system dynamics (the observed effect of the emerged organisation) is described by momentary values of vehicle flows in its edges:

$$0 \leq x_{ij} \leq x_{ij}^{max} \qquad (16)$$

where $x_{ij} = x_{ij}(t_k)$ is the number of vehicles going through edge $y_{ij} \in Y$ in some time t_k and x_{ij}^{max} is the maximum flow allowed in the given edge. Also for each vertex (intersection) the balance equation for the flows coming in and out holds:

$$\sum_{y_{ij} \in Y_j^+} \delta_{ij} = \sum_{y_{ij} \in Y_j^+} x_{ij}^+ - \sum_{y_{jk} \in Y_j^-} x_{jk}^- \qquad (17)$$

where $Y_j^+ = \{y_{ij} : v_j \in V\}$ and x_{ij}^+ is the number of vehicles coming into vertex v_j, similarly $Y_j^- = \{y_{ij} : v_i \in V\}$ and x_{jk}^- is the number of vehicles coming out of vertex v_j. This equation introduces a convention that allows to reflect a situation when it occurs impossible for all incoming vehicles to leave the vertex—its left side represents a queue of vehicles remaining in traffic jams (inversely, relieving the jams restores the balance). In such a situation it is possible that $x_{ij}^- \neq x_{ij}^+$ for some edge $y_{ij} \in Y$.

Having the transportation system defined, concrete tasks can be assigned to the layers of the proposed architecture. As monitoring of the transportation system is now the goal, appropriate deployment of monitoring spots can be related to the graph and parameters of the flows. Another decisive factor of the deployment comes from the higher level purpose of the monitoring. If the purpose is to supervise the whole transportation system in the sense of foreseeing its transportation capacities the spots can be located in the chosen vertices of the graph straightforwardly. Then flows coming in and out of such vertices are monitored according to the formula:

$$\omega = \{\omega_j = \sum_{y_{ij} \in Y_j^+} x_{ij} : v_j \in V\} \qquad (18)$$

The goal of vMAS is to predict the future load of roads based on the observations of local vehicle flows (fig. 2), so that the monitoring data may be used for the prediction of future traffic by i-th vMAS agent:

$$\Omega_i^*(t) = \{\omega_{ij}^*(t_k) : t_k > t\} \qquad (19)$$

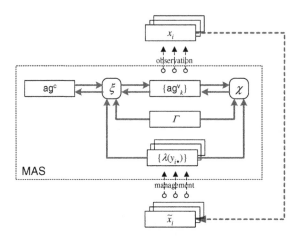

Fig. 2. Anti-crisis management in transportation MAS

And then the overall prediction may be obtained via cooperation of vMAS agents:

$$\tilde{\omega}(t) = \{\omega_j^*(t_k) = \prod_{\mathrm{ag}_i} \omega_{ij}^*(t_k) : t_k > t\} \tag{20}$$

and some anti-crisis policy may be defined e.g. in terms of traffic rerouting via changing the weights of particular roads in mapping λ—see eq. (7).

4   Crises Management at Work

The aim of the experiments reported below was to show, how the consequences of the crisis situations, that are, in that case, traffic jams and impassable roads, could be minimised, using the proposed management scheme. The orders were allocated according to the dynamic PDPTW as described in [5].

The transportation network (the graph Γ) and its changes is presented in fig. 3. The numbers next to the vertices are their identifiers and the numbers next to the edges are their weights. During the experiments 80 vehicles were used. The generation of transport requests was performed as presented in [3]. In central nodes (marked on the graph as black points) the request frequency was 5 times higher than in normal nodes.

There were four network configurations being examined:

- basic configuration Ψ_1 – the graph of 100 nodes and 272 arcs, composed of four subgraphs 0-24,5-49, 50-74 and 75-99, which are connected by unique arcs;
- configuration Ψ_2 – after removing an arc which connects nodes 64 and 85 (marked as a dotted line);
- configuration Ψ_3 – after adding a new arc (marked as a dash line) connecting nodes 24 and 45 with weight equal to 2000;
- configuration Ψ_4 – change in the weight of the new arc from 2000 to 5000.

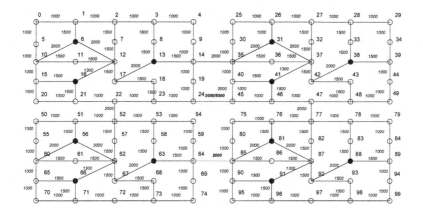

Fig. 3. Transport network and its modifications

The goal of such configuration choice was to show the system working without perturbations (configuration Ψ_1), the system after a crisis, which caused cutting of one arc (configuration Ψ_2), the results of attempting to limit the consequences of the crisis, introducing two different by-pass arcs: one of good quality (configuration Ψ_3) and the second of bad quality, i.e. increasing the travel time (configuration Ψ_4).

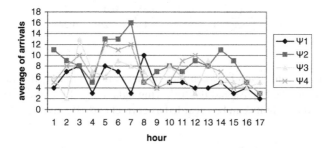

Fig. 4. Vehicles arriving at node 14

Figures 4 and 5 present the numbers of arrivals to the selected nodes 14 and 24, and the table 1 contains the average numbers of vehicles arriving in selected nodes for each examined configuration. The numbers of arrivals at nodes 14 or 24 increase after removing arc 64-85 (configuration Ψ_2) in comparison to the basic configuration Ψ_1). This is because there is only one travel path between sub-graphs 50-74, 0-24 and 25-49, 75-99, which must contain node 14. Adding a new connection between 24 and 45 brings an even distribution of traffic between arcs 24-45 and 14-35 (configuration Ψ_3). The number of vehicles arriving at node 24 increases, because previously they arrived to node 14 through nodes 9 or 13. The modification of a new arc in configuration Ψ_4 results in connection 14-35 being used more often by the vehicles.

The obtained results are highly intuitive and confirm the proper definition and realization of the model. The traffic balance of configuration Ψ_2 stems from the fact that the

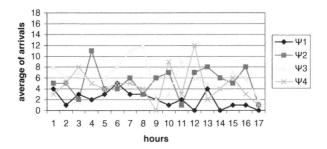

Fig. 5. Vehicles arriving at node 24

Table 1. Average of vehicles arrivals at selected nodes counted in time

configuration	$-\Psi_1-$	$-\Psi_2-$	$-\Psi_3-$	$-\Psi_4-$
Node 14	5.06	8.65	6.29	7.29
Node 24	2.06	5.24	6.29	4.65
Node 35	5.12	8.41	5.94	6.88
Node 45	1.76	3.82	5.35	5.47
Node 22	4.12	6.59	6.94	5.88
Node 47	4.94	6.18	6.70	7.41
Node 77	5.29	6.47	7.29	6.82
Node 64	4.94	1.06	0.65	0.76
Node 85	5.12	0.65	0.88	0.94
Node 99	0.12	0.41	0.29	0.24

edges belong to the only path between the sub-networks—the transit. The reaction of the traffic to adding the bypass and the following balancing of the alternative bypasses via changing of the weights can be regarded as correct and effective.

5   Concluding Remarks

The article is concerned with the application of agent approach to the problem of management of critical situations. Design assumptions and the proposal of the overall architecture of a (sub-)system dedicated to the discovery of crises and the support of anti-crisis activities are described.

One of possible applications is the management support for a transportation enterprise that operates in highly dynamic and uncertain environment of a road network that is a kind of the generator of critical situations. Considerations are carried out on the basis of the model of the network that plays here a role of a real system. Some parameters of the model are, in turn, subjects of monitoring in the designed layered architecture, other form a means for management. The particular organization of the enterprise including an originally proposed anti-crisis policy is modelled also. A conclusion that can be formulated at the point is that the implemented policy allows for the achievement of balanced traffic in the network also in the face of critical situations.

Simulation experiments partially presented in the paper confirm the main ideas of the approach. Future work will concentrate on its application to the transportation enterprises of different organization in order to justify and deepen solutions and conclusions elaborated so far.

References

1. J. Collins, M. Tsvetovas, R. Sundareswara, J. van Tonder, M. Gini, and B. Mobasher. Evaluating risk: flexibility and feasibility in multi-agent contracting. In O. Etzioni, J.-P. Müller, and J. M. Bradshaw, editors, *Proceedings of the Third International Conference on Autonomous Agents (Agents'99)*, pages 350–351. ACM Press, 1999.
2. G. Dobrowolski, M. Kisiel-Dorohinicki, and E. Nawarecki. Dual nature of mass multi-agent systems. *Systems Science*, 27(3):77–96, 2002.
3. A. Gendreau, F. Guertin, J. Potvin, and R. Sguin. Neighborhood search heuristics for a dynamic vehicle dispatching problem with pick-ups and deliveries. Technical report CRT-98-1, University of Montreal, 1998.
4. M. Kisiel-Dorohinicki. Monitoring in multi-agent systems: Two perspectives. In B. Dunin-Keplicz, A. Jankowski, A. Skowron, and M. Szczuka, editors, *Monitoring, Security, and Rescue Techniques in Multi-Agent Systems*, Adv. in Soft Computing. Springer-Verlag, 2005.
5. J. Kozlak, J.-C. Creput, V. Hilaire, and A. Koukam. Muti-agent environment for dynamic transport planning and scheduling. In M. Bubak, G. van Albada, P. Sloot, and J. Dongara, editors, *Computational Science – ICCS 2004, Part III*, Lecture Notes in Computer Science 3038. Springer-Verlag, 2004.
6. H. K. Lee, H.-W. Lee, and D. Kim. Macroscopic traffic models from microscopic car-following models. *Physical Review E*, 64(5):056126, Nov. 2001.
7. E. Nawarecki, M. Kisiel-Dorohinicki, and G. Dobrowolski. Architecture for discovery of crises in MAS. *Fundamenta Informaticae*. Accepted for publication.
8. A. M. Uhrmacher and K. Gugler. Distributed, parallel simulation of multiple, deliberative agents. In D. Bruce, L. Donatiello, and S. Turner, editors, *Procedings of the 14th Workshop on Parallel and Distributed Simulation (PADS00)*, pages 101–110. IEEE Press, 2000.
9. J. Wahle, L. Neubert, and M. Schreckenberg. Modeling and simulation of traffic flow. *Computer Physics Communications*, 121/122:402–405, Nov. 1999.
10. S. Wu and V. Soo. Risk control in multi-agent coordination by negotiation with a trusted third party. In D. Thomas, editor, *Proceedings of the 16th International Joint Conference on Artificial Intelligence (IJCAI-99-Vol1)*, pages 500–505. Morgan Kaufmann Publishers, 1999.

Evaluating the Feasibility of Method Engineering for the Creation of Agent-Oriented Methodologies

Brian Henderson-Sellers

Faculty of Information Technology,
University of Technology, Sydney,
PO Box 123, Broadway,
NSW 2007, Australia
brian@it.uts.edu.au

Abstract. In the context of agent-oriented methodologies, previous work has created a number of specific method fragments for use with the OPF metamodel and repository. These have been derived from an analysis of a large number of stand-alone agent-oriented methodologies. In order to evaluate the feasibility of this method engineering approach, a different AOSE methodology has been selected so that a scientific experiment could be undertaken. The hypothesis that the agent-enhanced OPF repository could be used without change to engineer any other AOSE methodology was proved false since two tasks for the creation of agents based on role modelling needed to be added to the repository.

1 Introduction

Method engineering requires the provision of a repository of method fragments from which industry strength methodologies can be created. For this to be successful, the repository contents need to be comprehensive in their support of a particular paradigm. Over the last two years, studies have been undertaken of what method fragments are needed to fully support agent-oriented software engineering (AOSE) methodologies. These were added to a repository that was originally not agent-oriented – the OPF repository based on an underpinning metamodel [1].

The fragments currently in the agent-enhanced OPF repository were gleaned from a number of AOSE methods. It is thus reasonable to anticipate that the fragments in the repository are sufficient for the support of these methods. As in a scientific experiment where a theory or numerical model is created by using data from n sources and then a set of data from an $n+1$th source is used for validation, here we propose the null hypothesis that the OPF repository is now comprehensive with respect to current AO methodological thinking and test this assumption by an evaluation of the mappings to the methodology proposed in [2], a methodology not in the original data set used to construct the repository enhancements.

2 A Method Engineering Framework – Based on OPF

Methodologies for industry may be a single, comprehensive and inter-related set of work units, work products and actors to perform the embedded software development

M. Pěchouček, P. Petta, and L.Z. Varga (Eds.): CEEMAS 2005, pp. 142–152, 2005.

process. Since it is generally recognized (e.g. [3]) that one size doesn't fit all, many researchers have sought for alternative approaches and frameworks. One of the most promising is that of method engineering (ME) [4,5]. In this approach, a "personalized" method is created for a specific organization, a specific division or a specific project by bottom-up construction from a number of method fragments [6]. These fragments have been pre-constructed and placed in a repository from which they can be selected by the organization's method engineer. Method fragments may describe a particular Task, such as AND/OR decomposition, or a particular Work Product, such as an Agent structure diagram etc., each of which is defined in terms of a clearly specified and standardized interface. The creation of these fragments may follow one of several paths [7,8] and ideally should be based upon an underlying conceptual model as embodied in a methodology metamodel [9].

While ME has been used in traditional and object-oriented (OO) methodologies for some years, it is only recently that the approach has been applied to the fragmentization of agent-oriented methodologies. In a precursor to the FAME (Framework for Agent-oriented Method Engineering) project, we have utilized the OPEN Process Framework (OPF) [1] – in particular, its underpinning metamodel and initially OO-based repository (Figure 1) – as a proof of concept. For later work in FAME (a funded three-year project: 2004-2006/7), we will use the OPF-based work for guidance and inspiration as we identify not only appropriate metamodel for agent-oriented modelling languages (see preliminary work in [10,11]) but also the process standard of AS4651 [12] and, subsequently, its ISO incarnation. Here, we report on the final test of the OPF-based research project.

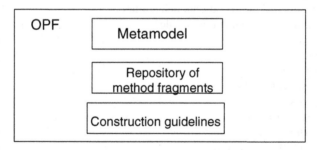

Fig. 1. The OPEN Process Framework consists of a metamodel from which is generated a large number of method fragments stored in repository. The OPF also includes a set of construction guidelines (not discussed here).

In the OPF pilot, we have augmented the OPF repository of method fragments by those derived from a large number of stand-alone agent-oriented methodologies, namely MaSE, Prometheus, Gaia, Cassiopeia, Agent Factory, MAS-Common-KADS, Tropos, PASSI and CAMLE. These span the various kinds of MAS identified in [14] – those based on object technology, either role-based or non-role-based, and those based on Knowledge Engineering (for details see summary in [13] – also Table 1).

Each of these fragments corresponds to one of the classes in the OPF metamodel. There are five major, top-level classes: Work Unit, Work Product, Producer, Stage and Language (Figure 2). There are also three important subtypes of Work Unit. These are Activity, Task and Technique. It was found, when undertaking the

Table 1. Summary of OPF method fragments previously gleaned from a number of AO methodologies. Listed are (a) new Tasks, (b) new Techniques and (c) new Work Products. Source documents referred to are [15-24] (after [25]).

(a) New Tasks and (indented) associated subtasks	Refs
Construct agent conversations	[15]
Construct the agent model	[15-18]
Define ontologies	[19]
Design agent internal structure	[16,19,20]
Define actuator module	[19]
Design perceptor module	[19]
Determine agent communication protocol	[21]
Determine agent interaction protocol	[21]
Determine control architecture	[21]
Determine delegation strategy	[21]
Determine reasoning strategies for agents	[21]
Determine security policy for agents	[21]
Determine system operation	[21]
Gather performance knowledge	[21]
Identify emergent behaviour	[21]
Identify system behaviours	[18]
Identify system organization	[21]
Define organizational rules	[17]
Define organizational structures	[17]
Determine agents' organizational behaviours	[18]
Determine agents' organizational roles	[18]
Identify sub-organizations	[17]
Model actors	[22]
Model agent knowledge	[20]
Model agent relationships	[20]
Model agents' roles	[21]
Model responsibilities	[17]
Model permissions	[17]
Model capabilities for actors	[22]
Model dependencies for actors and goals	[22]
Model goals	[22]
Model plans	[22]
Model the agent's environment	[21]
Model environmental resources	[17]
Model events	[16]
Model percepts	[16]
Specify shared data objects	[16]
Undertake agent personalization	[21]
Subtask to Create a System Architecture:	[19,20]
Determine MAS infrastructure facilities	

(b) New Techniques	Ref	New Techniques	Ref
Activity scheduling	[21]	Environmental evaluation	[23]
Agent delegation strategies	[21]	Environmental resources modelling	[17]
Agent internal design	[15,16]	FIPA KIF compliant language	[23]
AND/OR decomposition	[22]	Learning strategies for agents	[21]
Belief revision of agents	[21]	Market mechanisms	[21]
Capabilities identification	[22]	Means-end analysis	[22]
& analysis		Organizational rules specification	[17]
Commitment management	[21]	Organizational structure	[17]
Contract nets	[21]	specification	
Contributions analysis	[22]	Performance evaluation	[21]
Control architecture	[21]	Reactive reasoning: ECA rules	[21]
Deliberative reasoning:	[21]	Task selection by agents	[21]
Plans		3-layer BDI model	[23]

(c) New Work Products	Ref	New Work Products	Ref
Agent acquaintance diagram	[16,17]	Network design model	[20]
Agent class card	[20]	Platform design model	[20]
Agent design model	[20]	Protocol schema	[16,17]
Agent overview diagram	[16]	PSM specification	[20]
Agent structure diagram	[16]	Role diagram	[15]
CAMLE behaviour diagram	[24]	Role schema	[17]
CAMLE scenario diagram	[24]	Service table	[17]
Caste collaboration diagram	[24]	Task hierarchy diagram	[20]
Caste diagram	[24]	Task knowledge specification	[20]
Coupling Graph	[18]	Task textual description	[20]
Domain knowledge ontology	[20]	(Tropos) Actor Diagram	[22]
Functionality descriptor	[16]	(Tropos) Capability Diagram	[22]
Goal hierarchy diagram	[15]	(Tropos) Goal Diagram	[22]
Inference diagram	[20]	(Tropos) Plan Diagram	[22]

augmentation of OPF's repository with AO-focussed fragments, only a small number of Activities were needed and that most of the fragments were instances of the metaclasses Task, Technique and WorkProduct.

Additions to the repository were undertaken incrementally so that for each successive AO methodology analysis, fewer and fewer new fragments were identified. In the penultimate analysis (that of PASSI [26]), only one new task was identified – although as with all other methodologies a significant number of (potentially overlapping) work products were proffered. Now, in this paper, as a check for closure we test the hypothesis that the OPF repository is now replete and capable of modelling and representing the process aspects any other AO methodology (the suites of diagrams used are still too varied between AO methodologies – they require separate, special treatment). To do this, we take the role-focussed methodological work of Kendall and colleagues [1,27-30], identifying the appropriate fragments contained in this approach and then evaluating whether the enhanced OPF repository can adequately model these.

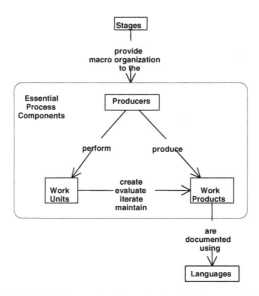

Fig. 2. The five major classes in the OPF metamodel

3   Evaluation Test – The Role-Based Methodology of Zhang *et al.*

A standard research methodology in science in the context of model building and model validation is to create a (often numerical) model, exemplifying some hypothesis, by incorporating a number of data sets. The model is then checked and modified until it is in accord with these data sets. However, this only provides an internal validity and consistency check. What then happens is that a "validation" experiment is conducted in which an objective assessment is undertaken against a new data set i.e. one that did NOT contribute to the model building and internal validation.

This is precisely the methodology used here. We have created an agent-oriented method engineering framework by using a large number of data sets. Here, each data set corresponds to our analysis of a single AO methodology as indicated in the references to Table 1. Having accomplished this creation stage, we now seek an external validation by identifying an AOSE methodology that has not yet been used in the creation of the agent-enhanced OPF repository. One such methodology is that of Zhang et al. [2] (referred to henceforth as the ZKJ methodology). This is a role-based methodology that falls clearly within the range of AO methodologies already analysed (as discussed in Section 2)[1].

The ZKJ methodology focusses on the identification of goals and roles. It represents the process by a set of ten "activities", each having an input, an output, a control and a mechanism. Four of these activities are grouped as "object-oriented analysis activities", the rest being focussed on agent goals and roles.

---

[1] Another possible choice, Adelfe [31], addresses adaptive MASs and is thus deemed out of scope for the present study.

The four object-oriented activities are Identify Actors, Identify Use Cases, Identify Objects and Determine Business Objects. These are said to be derived from [32]. There are six activities focussed on roles and goals. These are named, in this approach, Identify Goals, Develop Goal Cases and Identify Beliefs, Identify Roles, Assign Goals to Responsibilities, Assign and Compose Roles, and Identify Composite Roles.

Use cases, once identified, are used as input to the activity of Identify Goals. A goal in ZKJ is said to be a desired state that identifies what is to be done whereas an activity is viewed as a process that says how things are to be done. Identification of goals from use cases follows an iterative goal decomposition strategy as described in [30]. A variation on the use case is used to describe the interactions of the agents in the context of a specific goal – this is called a "goal case" and seen as central to agent identification describing as they do the set of plans that an agent will finally execute to achieve a particular goal. Here a single activity is used to develop these goal cases and, at the same time, identify the agent's beliefs, said to represent the knowledge that an agent possesses. Although coupled, the granularity of such a linking of two essentially different activities causes a potential clash with the atomic nature of the OPF repository-held method fragments (see Section 4).

Role identification is an important activity in the ZKJ methodology. Roles are seen as able to execute a set of activities in order to fulfil one or more responsibilities. Roles have access to resources and are identified from patterns of interaction and collaboration. The resultant set of roles is documented using a variant of the well-known CRC card [33], here called the Role, Responsibility and Collaboration (RRC) card. Roles are then linked to goals with the activity named Assign Goals to Responsibilities. This uses a goal hierarchy diagram and results in a set of RGC (Responsibility, Goal, Collaborator) cards – another CRC variant. The next activity, Assign and Compose Roles takes the results of the previous two activities to create specifications for agents in terms of their goals, goal cases, collaborators and beliefs. This is expressed with a GCB card (Goals, Goal Cases, Collaborators and Beliefs) used in the subsequent implementation stages. The last ZKJ activity, Identify Composite Roles, is not separately described and would appear to have serious overlaps with the activity of Assign and Compose Roles. With this lack of definitive information in [32], we remove it from the "test data" suite for this evaluation.

4 Test Results

To evaluate whether the agent-enhanced OPF repository provides all the method fragments needed for a method engineer to construct the ZKJ methodology, we need to ensure that all the method fragments described in Section 3 exist in the enhanced OPF repository (Table 1) and to provide a clear mapping from the OPF-based fragments to the new methodology. As noted earlier, we focus on the process-focussed method elements, primarily Activity, Task and Technique. In broad terms, a ZKJ activity maps to a Task in the OPF. However, since, according to [2], a ZKJ activity defines *how* things are to be done, there would appear to be a convolution of both an OPF Task and its corresponding Technique(s) into the ZKJ activity. Nevertheless, the descriptions and examples in [2] tend to focus on the task-like aspects rather than the technique-like aspects (using the OPF style of terminology).

This mapping is provided in Table 2. Here we see that the object-oriented activities of the ZKJ methodology map directly to method fragments (tasks) in the OPE repository. Of more interest here are the agent-focussed fragment mappings. Of the five activities from [2] only two are well supported, one in a many to one case and two are not. Thus the hypothesis is negated, indicating that a further iteration is required in adding method fragments to the OPF repository. Although we have shown previously [15-24] that there are sufficient fragments to recreate those particular methodologies i.e. those used in enhancing the OPF repository, our current study has highlighted areas of deficiency that must be remedied. We thus undertake further analysis in order to recommend yet further enhancements to the OPF repository.

Table 2. Mapping from fragments existing in the enhanced OPF repository to fragments described in the paper of Zhang *et al.* [2]

OPF repository fragment	Zhang et al. fragment
Model actors	Identify actors
Construct the object model with Technique: Scenario development	Identify use cases
Identify CIRTs	Identify objects
Develop business object model (BOM)	Identify business objects
Model goals	Identify goals
Model plans Model agent knowledge Technique: Scenario development	Develop goal cases and identify beliefs
Model agent roles	Identify roles
	Assign goals to responsibilities
	Assign and compose roles
Notes: CIRT stands for Class, Instance, Object, Type and is the generic "classifier" advocated in the OPF.	

In particular, we note that the ZKJ methodology's strong emphasis on roles identifies some AOSE-focussed tasks that none of the other methodologies either undertake or stress. The existing support in the agent-enhanced repository in the area of roles follows one standard viewpoint i.e. that agents are identified, followed by identification plus allocation of appropriate roles. This is a very object-oriented viewpoint where the entity (class, object or agent) is the main concept being modelled and roles are typically seen as incidental. In agent-oriented approaches there is a strong conviction by many AOSE methodologists that roles are really the predominant concept that is to be modelled [35-37]. In this viewpoint, roles come first and, having identified roles and perhaps associated goals and responsibilities (as here), then roles are composed into agents. Without entering into a debate about the pros and cons of such a viewpoint, it is certainly necessary to add new method fragments that permit such a viewpoint to be supported. Using the standard OPF interface description style, we thus propose the addition of the following two tasks:

TASK NAME: Assign goals to responsibilities

Typical supportive techniques: Agent internal design, responsibility identification, role assignment, 3-layer BDI model

Explanation: Using a goal hierarchy diagram as input and beginning at the leaves, each goal is assigned to a particular responsibility and collaborations between roles identified. The output is a RGC (Responsibility, Goal, Collaboration) card showing relationships between responsibilities, goals and the role's collaborators.

TASK NAME: Assign and compose roles

Typical supportive techniques: Agent internal design, composition structures, responsibility identification, role assignment, 3-layer BDI model

Explanation: Using the RGC cards, responsibilities and roles can now be composed together to identify agents, along with the agent's goals and collaborator. The steps to be undertaken involve

- Assigning roles for the design of the agent, composing them as needed
- Assigning roles to create agents, bearing in mind coupling and cohesion
- Possibly splitting and/or merging, based on the insight that the goals form the basic expertise of the agents.

In respect of the many-to-one mapping in Table 2, it is worth noting that a goal case is a specific form of a use case attached to a goal describing a set of plans. There is some support for this via the Task: Model plans as well as Technique: Scenario development. The notion of a goal case, per se, is, however, novel.

Finally, although we have stated that the work products are out of scope for this study, it is interesting to note the extensive use made of some variant of the CRC card in the ZKJ methodology. In the original OPF repository, Role Responsibility Collaborator cards were used [34] and goals were added in the Agent Class Card work product introduced in [23].

5   Future Extensions – Replacement of OPF by SMSDM

Since this study has highlighted deficiencies in the comprehensiveness of the method fragments in the enhanced OPF repository, further evaluative studies are needed. Another AOSE methodology, outside of the set so far used, will be identified and the above experiment repeated – iteratively until closure is reached. However, as the FAME project takes over from this prototype project using OPF, we intend to undertake a major replacement of the OPF metamodel and repository contents by a new, standard metamodel (SMSDM), as documented in [12]. Since this has a different conceptual architecture than OPF, some revision of both the conceptual basis and the generated fragments will ensue. One issue for future research is that of the appropriate granularity. For instance, as seen here, using a single activity/task, here the Develop Goal Cases and Identify Beliefs activity in ZKJ which needs three tasks to support it in OPF, indicates some problems with consistent granularity levels. This will also be investigated in an upcoming paper [in preparation].

Acknowledgements

I wish to acknowledge financial support from the University of Technology, Sydney under their Research Excellence Grants Scheme and from the Australian Research Council (grant number DP0451213). Thanks also to Cesar Gonzalez-Perez for his useful comments on an earlier draft. This is Contribution number 05/08 of the Centre for Object Technology Applications and Research.

References

1. Firesmith, D.G. and Henderson-Sellers, B., 2002, *The OPEN Process Framework. AN Introduction*, Addison-Wesley, Harlow, Herts, UK
2. Zhang, T.I., Kendall, E. and Jiang, H., 2002, An agent-oriented software engineering methodology with applications of information gather systems for LLC, *Procs AOIS-2002*, Toronto, May 2002, 32-46
3. Cockburn, A., 2000, Selecting a project's methodology, *IEEE Software*, **17(4)**, 64-71
4. Kumar, K. and Welke, R.J., 1992, Methodology engineering: a proposal for situation-specific methodology construction, in *Challenges and Strategies for Research in Systems Development* (eds. W.W. Cotterman and J.A. Senn), J. Wiley, Chichester, 257-269
5. Brinkkemper, S., 1996, Method engineering: engineering of information systems development methods and tools, *Inf. Software Technol.*, **38(4)**, 275-280.
6. Ralyté, J., Rolland, C. and Deneckère, R., 2004, Towards a meta-tool for change-centric method engineering: a typology of generic operators, *Procs. CAiSE 2004*, LNCS 3084, Springer, 202-218
7. Ralyté, J. and Rolland, C., 2001, An assembly process model for method engineering, *Advanced Information Systems Engineering*), LNCS2068, Springer, 267-283.
8. Ralyté, J., 2004, Towards situational methods for information systems development: engineering reusable method chunks, *Procs. 13th Int. Conf. on Information Systems Development. Advances in Theory, Practice and Education* Vilnius Gediminas Technical University, Vilnius, Lithuania, 271-282
9. Henderson-Sellers, B., 2003, Method engineering for OO system development, *Comm. ACM*, **46(10)**, 73-78
10. Beydoun, G., Gonzalez-Perez, C., Low, G. and Henderson-Sellers, B., 2005, Synthesis of a generic MAS metamodel, *Procs. SELMAS2005* (eds. A. Garcia, R. Choren, C. Lucena, A. Romanovsky, T. Holvoet and P. Giorgini), IEEE Digital Library, IEEE, Los Alamitos, CA, USA, 27-31
11. Beydoun, G., Gonzalez-Perez, C., Low, G. and Henderson-Sellers, B., 2005, Towards method engineering for multi-agent systems: a preliminary validation of a generic MAS metamodel, *Procs. AOSDM'2005 at SEKE'05*, Taipei, 14-16 July 2005
12. Standards Australia, 2004, Australian Standard 4651-2004: Standard metamodel for software development methodologies, 72pp
13. Henderson-Sellers, B., 2005, Creating a comprehensive agent-oriented methodology - using method engineering and the OPEN metamodel, Chapter 13 in *Agent-Oriented Methodologies* (eds. B. Henderson-Sellers and P. Giorgini), Idea Group, Hershey, PA, USA
14. Tran, Q.-N.N., Low, G.C. and Williams, M.-A., 2005, A preliminary comparative feature analysis of multi-agent systems development methodologies, *Agent-Oriented Information Systems II*, LNAI 3508, Springer, 157-168

15. Tran, Q.-N.N., Henderson-Sellers, B. and Debenham, J. 2004, Incorporating the elements of the MASE methodology into Agent OPEN, *Procs. ICEIS2004 - Sixth International Conference on Enterprise Information Systems,* INSTICC Press, **Volume 4**, 380-388

16. Henderson-Sellers, B., Tran, Q.-N.N. and Debenham, J., 2004, Incorporating elements from the Prometheus agent-oriented methodology in the OPEN Process Framework, *Procs. AOIS@CAiSE2004,* Riga Technical University, Latvia, 370-385

17. Henderson-Sellers, B., Debenham, J. and Tran, Q.-N.N., 2004, Adding agent-oriented concepts derived from GAIA to Agent OPEN, *Procs. 16th International Conference, CAiSE 2004,* LNCS 3084, Springer, 98-111

18. Henderson-Sellers, B., Tran, Q.-N.N. and Debenham, J., 2004, Method engineering, the OPEN Process Framework and Cassiopeia, *The Symposium on Professional Practice in AI* (eds. E. Mercier-Laurent and J. Debenham), IFIP, 263-272

19. Henderson-Sellers, B., Tran, Q.-N.N., Debenham, J. and Gonzalez-Perez, C., 2005, Agent-oriented information systems development using OPEN and the Agent Factory, *Procs. ISD 2004,* Vilnius, 9-11 September 2004, Kluwer, 149-160

20. Tran, Q.-N.N., Henderson-Sellers, B., Debenham, J. and Gonzalez-Perez, C., 2004, MAS-CommonKADS and the OPEN method engineering approach, *Procs. ICITA,* Sydney, July 4-7 2005, IEEE Computer Society Press

21. Debenham, J. and Henderson-Sellers, B., 2003, Designing agent-based process systems - extending the OPEN Process Framework, Chapter VIII in *Intelligent Agent Software Engineering* (ed. V. Plekhanova), Idea Group Inc., Hershey, PA, USA, 160-190

22. Henderson-Sellers, B., Giorgini, P. and Bresciani, P., 2004, Enhancing Agent OPEN with concepts used in the Tropos methodology, *Engineering Societies in the Agents World IV. 4th International Workshop, ESAW' 2003,* LNAI 3071, Springer, 328-345

23. Henderson-Sellers, B. and Debenham, J., 2003, Towards OPEN methodological support for agent-oriented systems development, *Procs. First International Conference on Agent-Based Technologies and Systems,* University of Calgary, Canada, 14-24

24. Gonzalez-Perez, C., Henderson-Sellers, B., Debenham, J., Low, G.C. and Tran, Q.-N.N., 2004, Incorporating elements from CAMLE in the OPEN repository, *Intelligent Information Process II,* Springer, 55-64

25. Henderson-Sellers, B., 2005, From object-oriented to agent-oriented software engineering methodologies, *Software Engineering for Multi-Agent Systems - Volume III Research issues and practical applications,* LNCS 3390, Springer, 1-18

26. Henderson-Sellers, B., Debenham, J., Tran, N., Cossentino, M. and Low, G., 2005, Identification of reusable method fragments from the PASSI agent-oriented methodology, *Procs. AOIS@AAMAS2005,* 26 July 2005, 89-96

27. Kendall, E.A., Malkoun, M. and Jiang, C., 1995, A methodology for developing agent based systems for enterprise integration, *EI'95. IFIP TC5 SIG Working Conf. on Modeling and Methodologies for Enterprise Integration,* Heron Island, Queensland, Australia

28. Kendall, E.A., Malkoun, M.T. and Jiang, C., 1997, Multiagent system design based on object-oriented patterns, *J. Obj.-Oriented Prog. (ROAD),* **10(3),** 41-47

29. Kendall, E.A., 1998, Agent roles and role models: new abstractions for multi-agent system analysis and design, *Int. Workshop on Intelligent Agents in Information and Process Management, German Conference on AI,* Bremen, Germany, September 1998

30. Kendall, E.A., Krishna, M., Pathak, C.V. and Suresh, C.B., 1998, Patterns of intelligent and mobile agents, *Agents '98,* May 1998.

31. Bernon, C., Gleizes, M.-P., Picard, G. And Glize, P., 2002, The ADELFE methodology for an intranet system design, *Procs. AOIS2002,* Univ. Toronto, 27-28 May 2002, 1-15

32. Jacobson, I., Christerson, M., Jonsonn, P. and Overgaard, J., 1992, *Object-Oriented Software Engineering – A Use Case Driven Approach*, Addison Wesley
33. Beck, K. and Cunningham, W., 1989, A laboratory for teaching object-oriented thinking, *Procs. 1989 OOPSLA Conference, ACM SIGPLAN Notices*, **24(10),** 1-6
34. Firesmith, D.G., Henderson-Sellers, B. and Graham, I., 1997, *OPEN Modeling Language (OML) Reference Manual*, SIGS Books, New York, NY, USA, 271pp
35. Odell, J.J., Parunak, H.V.D. and Fleischer, M., 2003, The role of roles in designing effective agent organizations, *Software Engineering for Large-Scale Multi-Agent Systems. Research Issues and Practical Applications*, LNCS 2603, Springer, 27-38
36. Koning, J.-L. and Hernandez, I.R., 2004, Limitations in AUML's roles specification, *Intelligent Information Processing II*, Springer, 79-82
37. Odell, J., Nodine, M. and Levy, R., 2004, A metamodel for agents, roles, and groups, *Agent-Oriented Software Engineering V. 5th International Workshop. AOSE 2004*, LNCS 3382, Springer, 78-92

Formalizing Compatibility and Substitutability of Rolebased Interactions Components in Multi-agent Systems

Nabil Hameurlain

LIUPPA Laboratory, Avenue de l'Université, BP 1155, 64013 Pau, France
`nabil.hameurlain@univ-pau.fr`
`http://www.univ-pau.fr/~hameur`

Abstract. This paper focus on compatibility and substitutability of roles in MAS. We propose a formal specification of role-based interactions components together with their composition. We investigate compatibility of roles, and propose two compatibility relations, characterised to their degree of change by property (safety and liveness) preservation. Our approach is enhanced with the definition of behavioural subtyping relations, related to the principle of substitutability. We show the existing link between compatibility and substitutability concepts, and namely their combination, which seems to be necessary when we deal with incremental design of role-based complex interactions. The suitability of our approach is shown by its application to an interaction protocol example.

1 Introduction

Roles are basic buildings blocks for defining the organization of multi-agent systems, together with the behavior of agents and the requirements on their interactions [5]. Modeling interactions by roles allows a separation of concerns by distinguishing the agent-level and system-level concerns with regard to interaction. An important characteristic of real-world agent systems is that an agent may have to change the role it plays over time. If some flexibility constraints require some variety of these roles, agents have to adapt their architecture and functionality as they adopt new roles. These additional capabilities must be dynamically acquired because only a few roles can be hard-coded into an agent. Besides, while designing the overall organization of a system, it is valuable to reuse roles previously defined for similar applications, especially when the structure of interaction is complex. To this end, roles must be specified in an appropriate way, since the composition of independently developed roles can lead to the emergence of unexpected interaction among the agents.

Component Based Development (CBD) [11] promises to facilitate the construction of large-scale applications by supporting the composition of simple building blocks into complex applications. In CBD, software systems are built by assembling components already developed and prepared for integration. Therefore, the specification of components is useful to both components users and components developers. The specification provides a definition of the component's interface and it must be precise and complete for users; for developers, the specification of a component also provides

M. Pĕchouček, P. Petta, and L.Z. Varga (Eds.): CEEMAS 2005, LNAI 3690, pp. 153–162, 2005.

an abstract definition of its internal structure. The verification of such a well-established specification is needed for a safe composition of systems from components, enabling the effective development of reliable component-based software systems.

It appears that the facilities brought by the CBD approach fit well the issues raised by the use of roles in MASs. Although the concept of role has been exploited in several approaches [1, 2, 3, 4, 5, 13] in the development of agent-based applications, no consensus has been reached about what is a role and how it should be specified and implemented. In our previous work, we have presented RICO [6] (Role-based Interactions COmponents) model for specifying complex interactions based on roles in open MAS. It proposes a specific definition of role, which is not in contrast with the approaches mentioned above, but is quite simple and can be exploited in specifications and implementations. In RICO, when an agent intends to take a role, it creates a new component (i.e. an instance of the component type corresponding to this role) and this role-component is linked to its base-agent. Then, the role is enacted by the role-component and it interacts with the role-components of the other agents.

In this paper, we focus on Petri nets-based specification of role components together with their compatibility and substitutability. We show the existing link between compatibility and substitutability concepts, and namely their combination, which seems to be necessary when we deal with incremental design of complex interactions.

The structure of the paper is as follows. Section 2 presents the basic definitions of labelled Petri nets together with Components-nets formalism and their main properties. Section 3 gives a formal semantics for role-based interactions components and their composition. In section 4 we provide two compatibility relations and their characterisation by property preservation. In this section, we also propose two subtyping relations and study the preservation of roles components compatibility to their degree of change by the principle of substitutability [7]. An example of interaction protocol is studied to illustrate our approach. In section 5 we present conclusion and related approaches.

2   Component-Nets Formalism (C-Nets)

Backgrounds on Labelled Petri nets. A marked Petri net $N = (P, T, W, M_N)$ consists of a finite set P of places, a finite set T of transitions where $P \cap T = \varnothing$, a weighting function $W : P \times T \cup T \times P \rightarrow \mathbb{N}$, and $M_N : P \longrightarrow \mathbb{N}$ is an initial marking. The preset of a node $x \in P \cup T$ is defined as $^\bullet x = \{y \in P \cup T, W(y, x) \neq 0\}$, and the postset of $x \in P \cup T$ is defined as $x^\bullet = \{y \in P \cup T, W(x, y) \neq 0\}$. We denote as $LN = (P, T, W, M_N, l)$ the (marked, labelled) Petri net in which the events represent actions, which can be observable. It consists of a marked Petri net $N = (P, T, W, M_N)$ with a labelling function $l : T \longrightarrow A \cup \{\lambda\}$, where A is the set of services, that is the alphabet of observable actions, and $\{\lambda\}$ denotes the special unobservable action, which plays the usual role of an internal action. A transition $t \in T$ is enabled under a marking M, noted M (t >, if $W(p, t) \leq M(p)$ for each place p. In this case t may occur, and its occurrence yields the follower marking M', where $M'(p) = M(p) - W(p, t) + W(t, p)$, noted $M(t > M'$. A sequence of actions $w \in A^* \cup \{\lambda\}$ is enabled under the marking M and its occurrence yields a marking M', noted $M(w >> M'$, iff either $M = M'$ and $w = \lambda$ or there exists some sequence $\sigma \in T^*$ such that $l(\sigma) = w$ and $M(\sigma > M'$. The first condition accounts for the fact that λ is the label image of the empty sequence of transitions. A marking is stable if no unobservable action λ is enabled: M stable if not $(M(\lambda >>)$. For a marking M, Reach $(N, M) = \{ M'; \exists \sigma \in T^*; M(\sigma > M'\}$ is the set of reachable markings of the net N from the marking M.

In this paper, among the very numerous semantics, which may be used to compare behaviour of roles, only failure and bisimulation semantics will deal with (see [9] for a comparative study of these relations). The failure semantics involve linear case dealing with the safety property (e.g. deadlock-freeness), whereas bisimulation semantics are the finest and involve the branching case dealing with the liveness property (e.g. the success termination).

Definition 2.1 (Failures) Let $N = (P, T, W, M_N, l)$ be a labelled net. Then the failures of the net N on T' is $F(N, T') = \{(\sigma, S); \sigma \in T^*, S \subseteq T'$, and there exists some marking M such that $M_N(\sigma > M$, and $\forall t \in S$, not $(M(t >)\}$. The label image of the failures of N is $F(N) = l(F(N, T)) = \{(l(\sigma), X); X \subseteq A$, and $\forall a \in X$, not $(M(a>>)$, for all M stable such that $M_N(\sigma > M\}$.

Definition 2.2 (Bisimulation) Let $N = (P, T, W, M_N, l)$ and $N' = (P', T', W', M_{N'}, l')$ be two labelled nets. We say that N and N' are bisimilar, noted $N \approx_{BiSim} N'$, iff there exists a bisimulation relation $R \subseteq$ Reach (N, M_N) x Reach $(N', M_{N'})$ such that :
1. $(M_N, M_{N'}) \in R$,
2. $\forall (M_1, M'_1) \in R, \forall a \in A \cup \{\lambda\}, \forall M_2, M_1(a>> M_2 \Rightarrow \exists M'_2, M'_1(a>> M'_2$ and $(M_2, M'_2) \in R$,
3. and vice versa: $\forall a \in A \cup \{\lambda\}, \forall M'_2, M'_1(a>> M'_2 \Rightarrow \exists M_2, M_1(a>> M_2$ and $(M_2, M'_2) \in R$.

Components nets (C-nets). Component-nets formalism [12] combines Petri nets with the component-based approach. Semantically, a Component-net involves two special places: the first one is the input place for instance creation of the component, and the second one is the output place for instance completion of the component. A C-net (as a server) makes some services available to the nets and is capable of rendering these services. Each offered service is associated to one or several transitions, which may be requested by C-nets, and the service is available when one of these transitions, called *accept-transitions*, is enabled. On the other hand it can request (as a client) services from other C-net transitions, called *request-transitions*, and needs these requests to be fulfilled. For the simplicity, and in order to make our approach more general, we will specify C-nets by labelled classical Petri nets instead of high level (e.g. Coloured) Petri nets.

Definition 2.3 (C-net) Let $CN = (P \cup \{I, O\}, T, W, M_N, l_{Prov}, l_{Req})$ be a labelled Petri net. CN is a *Component-net* (C-net) if and only if:

1. The labelling of transitions consists of: $l_{Prov} : T \longrightarrow Prov \cup \{\lambda\}$, where $Prov \subseteq A$ is the set of provided services, and $l_{Req} : T \longrightarrow Req \cup \{\lambda\}$, where $Req \subseteq A$ is the set of required services.

2. *Instance creation*: the set of places contains a specific *Input* (source) place I, such that $^\bullet I = \varnothing$,

3. *Instance completion*: the set of places contains a specific *Output* place O, such that $O^\bullet = \varnothing$.

4. *Visibility*: for any $t \in T$ such that $t \in \{I^\bullet \cup {}^\bullet O\}$: $l(t) \in A$.

The first requirement allows to focusing either upon the server side of a C-net or its client side. The last requirement states that all the transitions related to the Input place I, and to the Output place O, are necessarily observable actions. They give input (parameters) and output (results) of the performed net.

Notation. We denote by [I] and [O], which are considered as bags, the markings of the Input and the Output place of CN, and by Reach (CN, [I]), the set of reachable markings of the component-net CN obtained from its initial marking M_N within one token in its Input place I.

Definition 2.4 (completion + reliability = soundness) Let $CN = (P \cup \{I, O\}, T, W, M_N, l)$ be a *Component-net* (C-net). CN is said to be *sound* if and only if the following conditions are satisfied:

1. *Completion option*: for any reachable marking $M \in Reach(CN, [I])$, $[O] \in Reach(CN, M)$.

2. *Reliability option*: for any reachable marking $M \in Reach(CN, [I])$, $M \geq [O]$ implies $M = [O]$.

Completion option states that, if starting from the initial state, i.e. activation of the C-net , it is always possible to reach the marking with one token in the output place O. *Reliability* option states that the moment a token is put in the output place O corresponds to the *termination* of a C-net without leaving dangling references.

Operations on C-nets. To define our compatibility and subtyping relations, we need two basic operations on the C-nets: abstraction of services, and asynchronous composition, used for testing type substitutability together with compatibility.

- The *abstraction* operator λ labels as not observable and internal actions, some transitions of a Labelled C-net. It introduces new non-stable states, from which the refusal sets are not taken into account for the failure semantics. Formally, given a C-net N = (P, T, W, M_N, l), for each $H \subseteq A$, $\lambda_H(N) = N' = (P, T, W, M_N, l')$ such that $l'(t) = l(t) = a$, if $t \in T$ and $a \in A \setminus H$, $l'(t) = \lambda$ else.

- The *parallel composition* operator $\oplus$: C-net $\times$ C-net $\longrightarrow$ C-net computes the set of parallel compositions of traces, interleaving actions. The composition $\oplus$ is made by communication places allowing interaction through observable services in *asynchronous* way. Given a client C-net and a server C-net, it consists in connecting, through the communication places, the request and accept transitions having the same service names: each accept-transition of the server is provided with an *entry-place* for receiving the requests/replies. Then, the client C-net is connected with the server C-net through these communication places by an arc from each request-transition towards the suitable entry-place and an arc from the suitable entry-place towards each accept-transition.

3   Specification of Role-Based Interactions as Components

Formal Specification of Role-based Interactions Components. In our RICO model [6], a role component is considered as a component providing a set of interface elements (either attributes or operations, which are provided or required features necessary to accomplish the role's tasks), a behavior (interface elements semantics), and properties (proved to be satisfied by the behavior). Role components allow a proper means for modelling and specifying complex interactions. For instance considering role-based interactions components as the active members of protocols facilitates the modeling of complex interaction protocols, especially open and concurrent ones. Thus, an agent can play one or more roles at the same time in different conversations (protocols occurrences), and each participation is managed by a specific component.

Definition 3.1 (Role Component) A Role Component RC for a role $\Re$ is a four-tuple RC = (Behav, Var, Serv, Prop), where,

- Behav is a C-net describing the life-cycle of RC.
- Var is a set of variables, a list of role components identities in the system that RC knows and with which it may interact, together with attributes referenced by the properties defined in Prop.
- Serv is an interface through which RC interacts with other role components, for instance messaging interface. It is a pair (Req, Prov), where Req is a set of required services, and Prov is the set of provided services by RC, and more precisely by Behav.
- Prop is a set of safety and liveness properties [8] that are defined on Serv and Var, and have been verified on Behav. Safety properties are invariants that state: "nothing bad happens". In contrast, liveness properties state "something good happens". A property is included in Prop only when it is verified.

Definition 3.2 (Role Components composition) A Role (Component), RC = (Behav, Var, Serv, Prop), can be composed from a set of primitive Role-Components, RC_i = (Behav$_i$, Var$_i$, Serv$_i$, Prop$_i$), i = 1, ..., n, noted RC = $RC_1 \otimes ... \otimes RC_n$, as follows:

- Behav = Behav$_1 \oplus ... \oplus$ Behav$_n$.
- Var $\subseteq \cup$Var$_i$, i = 1, ..., n. A variable in $\cup$Var$_i$ is included in Var if and only if this variable is a role components identity or referenced by the properties defined in Prop.
- Serv = (Req, Prov) such that Req (or Prov, respectively) $\subseteq \cup$Req$_i$ (or $\cup$Prov$_i$), i = 1, ..., n. A service in $\cup$Req$_i$, (or $\cup$ Prov$_i$) i = 1, ..., n is included in Req (or Prov) if and only if this service may be used by RC, when RC interacts with other Role-Components.

- Prop is a set of safety and liveness properties defined on Serv and Var, and have been verified on Behav. When incremental verification is possible, the properties in Prop may be verified by utilizing the properties in $Prop_1, ..., Prop_n$.

```
Role-Component fm_Vendor;
attributes
            //list of bidder agents
bidders: list of agent*;
            //the creator agent
vendor: agent*;
current-price: Currency;
services
            // service provided
to_bid(); //receive a bid
            //receive a payment
to_pay(p: Currency): Status;
            // services required
//send the new price
to_announce(newp: Currency);
to_attribute();
to_give(f: fish);
Behavior
```

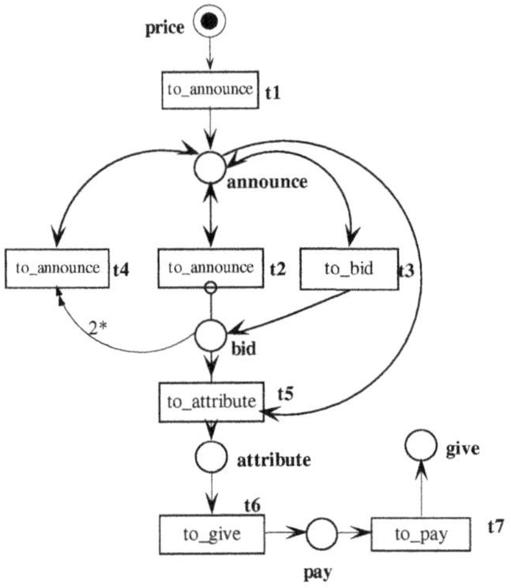

```
Role-Component fm_Buyer;
attributes
            //the creator agent
bidder: agent*;
            //the vendor agent
vendor: agent*;
portfolio: Currency;
current-price: Currency;
services
            // service required
to_bid();

to_pay(p: Currency): Status;
            // services provided
to_announce(newp: Currency);
to_attribute();
to_give(f: fish);
Behavior
```

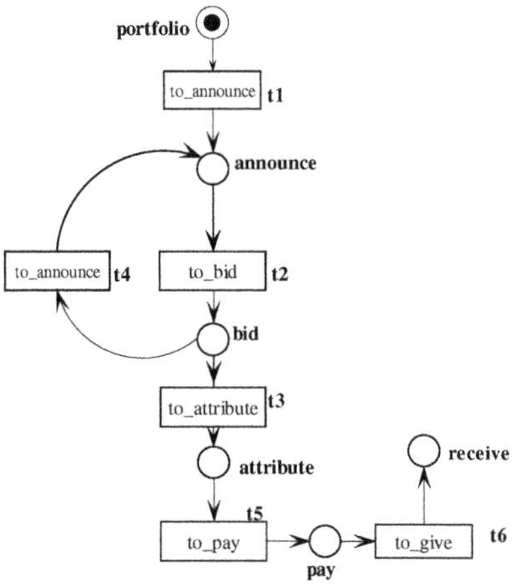

Fig. 1. The Vendor (resp. Buyer) in the fish-market protocol as a role-component, fm_Vendor (resp. fm_Buyer)

An Example: The Fish-market Auction Protocol. To illustrate our specification of role-based interactions components, we will study an example of interaction protocols, the fish-market auction protocol. In any *conversation* following the rules of this protocol, we have a single vendor, and a number of potential buyers, the bidders. The vendor have a bucket of fish to sell for an initial price and announces (to_announce()) this price. A buyer can make a bid (to_bid()) to signal its interest. If no (or more than one) buyer is interested, the vendor announces (`to_announce()`) a new lower (or higher) price. When one and only one buyer is interested, the vendor attributes (`to_attribute()`) fish to that bidder. Once the bucket of fish is attributed, the vendor gives (`to_give()`) the fish and receives the payment, while the buyer pays (`to_pay()`) the price and receives the fish. The specifications of the Vendor and the Buyer as role components are given in figure 1. For the simplicity, the behaviour parts (Behav) are specified by classical Petri nets instead of high-level Petri nets (see [6] for complete specification by means of high-level (Objects) Petri nets, and the verification of some safety and liveness properties using Petri nets tools).

4   Compatibility and Substitutability of Roles

Compatibility of Roles. Compatibility deals with composition of roles and property preservation. The first compatibility relation is named weak compatibility. It is a very powerful way to guaranty the correctness of the role when reasoning about the dead-lock-freeness. Sometimes this is not enough, and we want to claim that some liveness properties are preserved by the role's composition like the proper (or successful) termination, that is the soundness of the role's behaviour. This is the aim of strong compatibility relation. These two proposed compatibility relations are symmetric.

Definition 4.1 (Weak and Strong compatibility) Let RC_1 = (Behav$_1$, Var$_1$, Serv$_1$, Prop$_1$) and RC_2 = (Behav$_2$, Var$_2$, Serv$_2$, Prop$_2$) be two Role Components. Let RC = $RC_1 \otimes RC_2$ = (Behav, Var, Serv, Prop).
1. RC_1 and RC_2 are *weakly* compatible, noted $RC_1 \approx_{WC} RC_2$, iff Behav satisfy completion option.
2. RC_1 and RC_2 are *strongly* compatible, noted $RC_1 \approx_{SC} RC_2$, iff Behav is sound.

Example 1: As an example, let us take RC_1 = fm_Vendor and RC_2 = fm_Buyer shown in figure 1. The behaviours of these two components are sound. Let $RC = RC_1 \otimes RC_2$; we can check that RC_1 and RC_2 are weakly and strongly compatible. Further, for instance RC and RC_2 are also related by the weak and the strong compatibility relation.

Property 4.1 (Hierarchy of compatibility relations) The compatibility relations form a hierarchy: $\approx_{SC} \Rightarrow \approx_{WC}$.

Substitutability of Roles. Our main interest is to define behavioural subtyping relations (reflexive and transitive) capturing the principle of substitutability [7], that is the capacity to replace one role by another one without losing (agent) behaviours. The first proposed subtyping relation, called weak subtyping, deals with refusals (failures) services by the role component. Instead, the second one, called strong subtyping, which is more restrictive than weak subtyping, is based on bisimulation semantics dealing with the branching case. In our context, we use abstraction operation (operator λ) to treat old and new services.

Definition 4.2 (Weak and Strong subtyping) Let RC_1 = (Behav$_1$, Var$_1$, Serv$_1$, Prop$_1$), RC_2 = (Behav$_2$, Var$_2$, Serv$_2$, Prop$_2$), and Serv$_i$ = (Req$_i$, Prov$_i$), i=1,2, such that: Prov$_1$ $\subseteq$ Prov$_2$, Req$_2$ $\subseteq$ Req$_1$, Var$_1$ $\subseteq$ Var$_2$, and Prop$_1$ $\subseteq$ Prop$_2$.
Let G =Prov$_2$ \ Prov$_1$ and H = Req$_1$ \ Req$_2$.

1. RC_2 is *weak* subtype RC_1, denoted $RC_2 \leq_{WS} RC_1$, iff,

   $F(\lambda_G(\text{Behav}_2)) = F(\lambda_H(\text{Behav}_1))$.

2. RC_2 is *strong* subtype RC_1, denoted $RC_2 \leq_{SS} RC_1$, iff,

   $\lambda_G(\text{Behav}_2) \approx_{\text{BiSim}} \lambda_H(\text{Behav}_1)$.

In both *weak and strong* subtyping relations, the (super-) role component RC_1 can be substituted by a (sub-) role component RC_2 and the agent (component) will not be able to notice the difference since : (a) the sub-role has a smaller set of required services (Req$_2$ $\subseteq$ Req$_1$) and a larger set of provided services (Prov$_1$ $\subseteq$ Prov$_2$) than the super-role, and (b) the attributes (variables) and the properties of the super-role are preserved in the sub-role (Var$_1$ $\subseteq$ Var$_2$ and Prop$_1$ $\subseteq$ Prop$_2$), (c) the new provided services added in the sub-role component RC_2 as well as possible old required services of RC_1 are considered unobservable, through the abstraction operation, w.r.t. the failure equivalence (resp. bisimulation) when we deal with weak (resp. strong) subtyping.

Example 2: As an example, let us take again RC_1 = fm_Vendor, RC_2 = fm_Buyer shown in figure 1, and let RC = $RC_1 \otimes RC_2$ be a Vendor's Component implementation, that is Prov = Prov$_1$ and Req = Req$_1$. Let RC' = RC $\otimes$ RC_2 be a Vendor/Buyer Component, such that Prov' = Prov $\cup$ Prov$_2$ = Prov$_1$ $\cup$ Prov$_2$ and Req' = Req = Req$_1$, where Prov' and Req' are respectively the provided and the required services of RC'. So, we can check that RC' $\leq_{SS}$ RC.

Property 4.2 (Hierarchy of subtyping relations) Let $\mathfrak{R}C$ = {RC_1, ..., RC_n} be the set of role components in the system. The subtyping relations $\leq_{SS}$ and $\leq_{WS}$ are reflexive and transitive on $\mathfrak{R}C$, and form a hierarchy: $\leq_{SS}$ $\Rightarrow$ $\leq_{WS}$.

As expected, the $\leq_H$ subtyping relations, where H$\in$ {WS, SS}, are compositional for the composition operator $\otimes$; for instance, extending (resp. reducing) the provided (resp. required) services of a role component also extends (resp. reduces) the provided (resp. required) services of its composition with any role component.

Property 4.3 (Subtyping are compositional)
$RC_2 \leq_H RC_1$ where H $\in$ {WS, SS} $\Rightarrow$ $\forall$RC, RC $\otimes$ RC_2 $\leq_H$ RC $\otimes$ RC_1.

Compatibility and Substitutability of Roles. Substitutability guarantees the transparency of changes of roles to agents. Namely, the compatibility between components should not be affected by these changes. The following theorem study the preservation of compatibility by substitutability, dealing with the two compatibility relations together with the two subtyping relations given in this paper.

Theorem 4.1 (Compatibility preservation by substitutability)
1. $RC_2 \leq_{ws} RC_1 \Rightarrow (\forall Ag, Ag \approx_{wc} RC_1 \Rightarrow Ag \approx_{wc} RC_2)$;
2. $RC_2 \leq_{ss} RC_1 \Rightarrow (\forall Ag, Ag \approx_{sc} RC_1 \Rightarrow Ag \approx_{sc} RC_2)$.

5 Conclusion and Related Work

The aim of this paper is to integrate specification and verification methods into the Component Based Development of roles together with their compatibility and substitutability. The specification of roles is based on C-nets, a formalism combining Petri nets with the component-based approach. Each role component has an interface and an internal process, specified by a C-net, describing its life cycle together with it properties. Two notions of compatibility and substitutability (weak and strong) between roles are investigated together with role's property preservation by composition. We furthermore studied the interconnection between compatibility and substitutability of roles, and investigated the characterisation of compatibility by behavioural substitutability, which seems necessary when we deal with incremental design of complex interactions. Our behavioural subtyping relations take into account the non-determinism, and the composition mechanism of roles, and determine automatically the compatibility, which is preserved.

The next step for this work is to explore the notion of parametric contracts [10] in the definition of role's compatibility and substitutability. Our aim is to define flexible compatibility and substitutability relations between roles, depending on their context of use. So, parametric contracts link the provided and required interfaces of the same role component, and when the required interfaces are not fully meet, the component can still offer part of its provided interface.

Related Work. There are many approaches and methodologies for the specification of roles (-based interactions) in multi-agents system. In recent years, roles formation, configuration among roles, and static semantics of roles have been proposed [1, 2, 5]. [5] proposes a meta-model to define models of organizations, based on three concepts: agent, group, and role. Our approach is in the same line, since interactions are based on roles, and the agents that hold a role in the same conversation of a protocol constitute a group. However, our approach gives a formal and precise definition of the interaction patterns – protocols and roles – and groups are defined on the basis of conversations, i.e. occurrences of protocols. In [1], authors study the conditions under which an agent can enact a role and what it means for an agent to enact a role. They define possible relations between roles and agents, and discuss functional changes that an agent must undergo when it enters an open agent system. This work completes our approach, and one can use the proposed relations as constraints interaction requirements that the agents that take up the role must meet. In [2], they argue for the importance of enactment/deactement of roles by agents in multiagent programming, in particular when dealing with open systems. This work study the dynamics of roles in terms of operations performed by agents; their formalization is conceptually based on the notion of cognitive agents, and therefore, we claim that it can be easily exploited in our specification of role components. In [13], Gaia methodology adopts an abstract, semiformal description to express the capabilities and expected behaviors of roles involved in protocols. This work is close to ours, since it is based on the organizational abstractions for analysis and design of complex and open interactions, but one possible limitation, is the formal specification, validation and namely the implementation of roles. This is due to the fact that, the life-cycle of roles in Gaia is only expressed by safety and liveness properties, and this methodology does not directly deals with formal analysis and implementation issues. [3] develops a role concept for a modeling approach based on the UML and graph transformation systems. They also provide a run-time semantics for roles on concepts from the theory of graph transformation. This approach allows a convenient model for the concurrency, reactivity, and the autonomy of agents. Nevertheless, engineering issues raised related to the use of roles such as the validation and the verification of agent's behavior.

References

1. M. Dastani, V. Dignum, F. Dignum. "Role Assignment in Open Agent Societies", AAMAS'03, ACM 2003.
2. M. Dastani, M. B. van Riemsdijk, J.Huslstijn, F. Dignum, J-J. Meyer. "Enacting and Deacting Roles in Agent Programming". Proceedings of AOSE'04, LNCS, 2004.
3. R. Depke, R.Heckel, J.M.Kuster. "Roles in Agent-Oriented Modeling", International Journal of Software engineering and Knowledge engineering, vol 11, No. 3 (2001) 281-302.
4. G. Cabri, L. Leonardi, F. Zambonelli. "BRAIN: a Framework for Flexible Role-based Interactions in Multi-agent Systems". Proceedings of CoopIS 2003, 2003.
5. J. Ferber, O. Gutknecht, "Aalaadin. A Meta-model for the Analysis and Design of Organizations in Multiagent system", ICMAS'98, 1998.
6. N. Hameurlain, C. Sibertin-Blanc. "Specification of Role-based Interactions Components in MAS". In Software Engineering for Multi-Agent Systems III: Research Issues and Applications, LNAI/LNCS, pp 180-197, Vol. 3390, Springer-Verlag, 2005.
7. B. H. Liskov, J. M. Wing. "A Behavioral Notion of Subtyping". In ACM Trans. on Programming Languages and Systems, Vol 16, n° 6, Nov. 1994.
8. Z. Manna, A. Pnueli. "Temporal Verification of Reactive Systems-Safety", LNCS, Springer-Verlag, 1995.
9. L. Pomello, G. Rozenberg, C. Simone. "A Survey of Equivalence Notions for Net Based System". In Advances in Petri Nets. G. Rozenberg Ed., LNCS 609, Springer-Verlag 1992.
10. R.H. Reussner, J. Happe, A. Habel. "Modelling Parametric Component Contracts and the State Space of Composite Components by Graph Grammars", FASE/ETAPS 2005, LNCS Vol. 3442, pp 80-95, Springer-Verlag, 2005.
11. C. Szyperski. "Component Software-Beyond Object-Oriented Programming", Addison-Wesley, 2002.
12. W.M.P. Van der Aalst, k.M. van Hee, R.A. van der Toorn. "Component-Based Software Architectures: A framework Based on inheritance of Behaviour". Beta Working Paper Series 45, Eindhoven University of Technology, 2000.
13. F. Zambonelli, N. Jennings, M. Wooldridge. "Developing Multiagent Systems: The Gaia Methodology", ACM TSEM, Vol 12, N° 3, July 2003, pp317-370.

MAS Meta-models on Test:
UML vs. OPM in the SODA Case Study

Ambra Molesini[1], Enrico Denti[1], and Andrea Omicini[2]

[1] DEIS, Alma Mater Studiorum, Università di Bologna,
Viale Risorgimento 2, 40136 Bologna, Italy
amolesini@deis.unibo.it, enrico.denti@unibo.it
[2] DEIS, Alma Mater Studiorum, Università di Bologna a Cesena,
Via Venezia 52, 47023 Cesena, Italy
andrea.omicini@unibo.it

Abstract. In the AOSE (Agent-Oriented Software Engineering) area, several research efforts are underway to develop appropriate meta-models for agent-oriented methodologies. Meta-models are meant to check and verify the completeness and expressiveness of methodologies.

In this paper, we put to test the well-established standard Unified Modelling Language (UML), and the emergent Object Process Methodology (OPM), and compare their meta-modelling power. Both UML and OPM are used to express the meta-model of SODA, an agent-oriented methodology which stresses interaction and social aspects of MASs (multi-agent systems). Meta-modelling SODA allows us to evaluate the effectiveness of the two approaches over both the structural and dynamics parts. Furthermore, this allow us to find out some desirable features that any effective approach to meta-modelling MAS methodologies should exhibit.

1 Meta-models for MAS

The definition of a methodology is an interactive process, in which a core is defined and then extended to include all the needed concepts. Meta-modelling enables checking and verifying the completeness and expressiveness of a methodology by understanding its deep semantics, as well as the relationships among concepts in different languages or methods [1]. According to [2],

> the process of designing a system (object or agent-oriented) consists of instantiating the system meta-model that the designers have in their mind in order to fulfil the specific problem requirements. In the agent world this means that the meta-model is the critical element(...) because of the variety of methodology meta-models.

In the context of MASs, a meta-model should be a structural representation of the elements (agents, roles, behaviour, ontology, ...) that constitute the actual system, along with their composing relationships. Several meta-models of AOSE methodologies can be found in the literature—for instance, GAIA [2], PASSI [2], ADELFE [2], Tropos [3], MESSAGE [4], IGENIAS [5]. Although a number of

M. Pěchouček, P. Petta, and L.Z. Varga (Eds.): CEEMAS 2005, LNAI 3690, pp. 163–172, 2005.
© Springer-Verlag Berlin Heidelberg 2005

these (PASSI, MESSAGE, ADELFE) adopt some kind of UML extensions to express system models, while others (GAIA, TROPOS, IGENIAS) adopt some ad-hoc symbology for the same purpose, the meta-models of all such methodologies are still expressed in UML.

1.1 Why UML for Meta-models

The Unified Modeling Language (UML)[6] is the industry-standard language for specifying, visualising, constructing, and documenting the artifacts of software systems. Like other methods, UML is based on the *decomposition principle*, here in the form of *aspect decomposition*. A system is then expressed as a multiplicity of different models, each representing a specific system aspect: actually, UML defines 12 types of diagrams, whose 4 represent the static application structure, 5 are devoted to capture the system's dynamic behaviour, and 3 are related to the organisation and management of application modules. Altogether, all these models are expected to convey a complete system specification.

However, although the availability of so many models constitutes a richness from the expressiveness viewpoint, each model introduces its own set of symbols and concepts, thus leading to an unnatural complexity in terms of vocabulary, model multiplicity and model integration [7]. This is a problem both for maintaining consistency among the different system models and views, and for the mental integration of such views, since integrating several models within one's mind an is a very difficult process. That is why the need to concurrently refer to different models in order to understand a system and the way it operates and changes over time is a critical issue, known as the *multiplicity problem* [8]. Despite this issue, however, the general adoption of UML as a world standard for system modelling makes it the first natural choice for representing meta-models.

Adopting UML to express *meta-models of methodologies* endorses some specific issues, since representing a methodology is inherently different from representing a system at the object level. In particular, when meta-modelling methodologies, UML leads to emphasise objects and object relations, leaving aside the procedural aspects, which can be revealed only indirectly, by object operations and message exchanges. Moreover, the five behavioural diagrams provided by UML to capture the dynamic behaviour of a system at the object level become of little use at the meta-level, as they were defined to express which and how interaction occurs, rather than what interaction is and what role it plays—which is what is needed when representing a methodology. So, UML-based meta-models usually exploit only package diagrams, class diagrams, and associations.

1.2 Why OPM for Meta-models

In order to better address the issues of representing the dynamics at the meta-level, and possibly reduce the risk of inconsistency related to the multiplicity problem, it is natural to "look outside" the UML world, looking for some alternative approach. The *Object Process Methodology* (OPM henceforth) [9] is an integrated approach to the study and development of systems in general, and of software systems in particular. OPM is also a reflective methodology, i.e. a methodology that can model itself without requiring any auxiliary means or external tools. OPM unifies the system's life-cycle stages (specification, design and implementation) within one single frame of reference, using a single diagramming tool—Object-Process Diagrams (OPDs)—and a corresponding subset of English, called Object-Process Language (OPL).

The basic assumption of OPM is that not only objects, but *objects and processes* constitute two equally-important classes of things, which together describe the functioning, structure and behaviour of a system in a single framework (i.e., without multiplying diagrams) in virtually any domain. Indeed, OPM's basic principle is that structure and behaviour in a system are so intertwined that effectively separating them is extremely harmful, if not impossible. Therefore, unlike the object-oriented approach, behaviour in OPM is not necessarily encapsulated within a particular object class construct: using stand-alone processes, one can model a behaviour that involves several object classes and is integrated into the system structure. Processes can be connected to the involved object classes through *procedural links*, which are divided, according to their functionality, into three groups: *enabling* links, *transformation* links, and *control* links.

Opposite to UML's aspect-based decomposition, which intrinsically violates the OPM's goal of a single all-describing model, OPM adopts *detail decomposition*: rather then decomposing a system according to its various aspects, decomposition proceeds by exploring the system's *abstraction levels*. This is done via three *refinement/abstraction mechanisms*: *unfolding/folding*, which refines/abstracts from the structural parts of a thing (mainly an object), *in-zooming/out-zooming*, which exposes/hides the inner details of a thing (mainly a process) within its enclosing frame, and state *expressing/suppressing*, which exposes/hides the states of an object.

1.3 Why Meta-modelling SODA

Interaction is a major source of complexity in software systems. This is particular true in multi-agent systems, where interaction can take different forms: for instance, *social interaction* is concerned with agents interacting with each other, while *environmental interaction* regards the agents' interaction with their environment. Although most methodologies still focus on *intra-agent* issues, more recently, methodologies like GAIA [10] and Hermes [11] have begun emphasising the role of interaction, shifting their focus toward social interaction.

So, since our purpose here is to exploit an agent-oriented methodology as a reference for stressing the pros and cons of different meta-modelling approaches, a methodology addressing only intra-agent issues would not fit: we need a methodology that widely deals with *inter-agent* issues, so that the social aspects of multi-agent systems are in the front line. SODA [12] is a methodology which explicitly focuses on suitably modelling the social aspects of a MAS. As such, it assumes interaction to be the key aspect of its modelling process: a system entity appears in a SODA model only in that it is involved in some interactions. So, designing a multi-agent system in SODA amounts to defining agents in terms

of their required observable behaviour, i.e., of the interactions in which agents
are involved, and of the agents' roles in the MAS. In addition, taking interaction
into account implies to consider relevant coordination issues, addressed by
SODA in the design phase. Therefore, in the following we first define the SODA
meta-model in UML (Section 2.1) and in OPM (Section 2.2), then comparatively
discuss the pros and cons of such meta-models and, by doing so, of the
two approaches in general (Section 3).

2   SODA Meta-models

SODA (Societies in Open and Distributed Agent spaces) [12] is an agent-oriented
methodology for the analysis and design of agent-based systems. SODA focuses
on inter-agent issues, like the engineering of societies and infrastructures for
multi-agent systems. Since this conceptually covers all the interaction within an
agent system, the design phase deeply relies on the notion of *coordination model*
[13]. In particular, coordination models and languages are taken as a source of
the abstractions and mechanisms required to engineer agent societies: social rules
are designed as coordination laws and embedded into coordination artifacts, and
the social infrastructure is built upon coordination system.

The analysis phase is characterised by three models: the *role model*, the
resource model and the *interaction model*. The *design* phase is based on three
strictly-related models, deriving from the models defined in the analysis phase; in
particular, the analysis' role model maps on the design's *agent model* and *society
model*, while the analysis' resource model maps on the design's *environment
model*. The analysis' interaction model, in its turn, generates the interaction
protocols and coordination rules referenced by the design's models (see [12] for
more details).

2.1   SODA Meta-model in UML

The UML meta-model of SODA (Figure 1) reflects the SODA distinction between
the analysis phase (top) and the design phase (bottom). In the analysis phase,
the *boundaries* between the resource model, the interaction model, and the role
model are well defined; in the design phase, instead, no such boundaries are
shown, because the entities of the analysis sub-models do not map one-to-one
onto analogous entities of the design model. It is worth noting that this UML
model clearly emphasise the *centrality of interaction* which is typical of the
SODA approach: in fact, if the interaction model were deleted, along with the
corresponding classes in the design phase, concepts such as roles and resources
would turn out to be separate and unrelated from one another.

Although this model captures the SODA concepts and associations as far as
UML's (large yet somehow limited) graphical vocabulary makes it possible, the
result is not completely satisfactory, for several reasons. First, UML provides
basically a unique type of concept/symbol (the class) to represent entities which
are conceptually distinct in the meta-model. More precisely, while using the

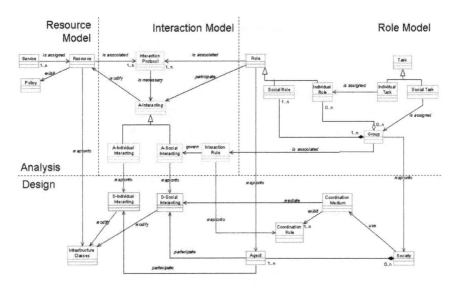

Fig. 1. SODA Meta-model in UML

UML class notion to capture the SODA *organisational structure*—i.e., entities such as roles, tasks, groups, society, agents, resources, infrastructure classes— leads to a satisfactory representation of these aspects, the same cannot be said for *interaction*, whose classes are qualitatively different from the others (both in the analysis and in the design phase), as they try to model an intrinsically dynamic dimension by means of an intrinsically static abstraction.

The model entities are connected to each other by different relations— inheritance, composition, aggregation, and generic association. In particular, the relations between Group and (respectively) Individual role / Social role empha- sise that a Social role may either coincide with an already defined Individual role (aggregation), or be defined *ex-novo* (composition). Moreover, the relations between the structural entities and the "interaction entities" are critical from the modelling viewpoint, since such entities are qualitatively different; this is why they are expressed by a generic (tagged) association.

Another key aspect concerns the connections from the analysis phase to the design phase. The label "map onto" is somehow vague, yet underlines the in- trinsic difficulty in expressing the complex mapping from the analysis to the design phase via a single association link. For instance, when mapping Role onto Agent, the association itself is unable to express that Agent *inherits* task, per- missions and interaction protocols from Role: so, a suitable label is the only (yet unsatisfactory) way to express this fact.

2.2   SODA Meta-model in OPM

Figure 2 shows the SODA meta-model in OPM. Of course, many aspects discus- sed above—the distinction between the two phases, the analysis sub-models, the

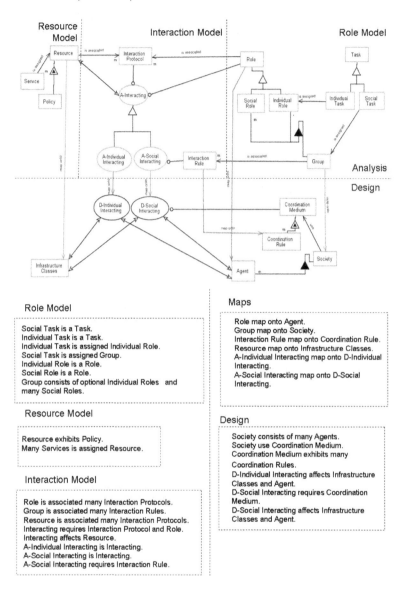

Fig. 2. SODA Metamodel in OPM: OPD (top) and OPL (down)

centrality of interaction, the association "map onto",—still hold: so, the overall model structure is basically the same as in Figure 1.

However, the richer expressiveness of OPM's graphical vocabulary with respect to UML makes it possible to model the key aspect of interaction as an OPM *process*, rather than as a class, thus expressing the dynamic aspects that the (static) class notion alone could not capture. By doing so, the OPM metamodel of SODA captures the transient nature of interaction in much a better way

than its UML counterpart. Furthermore, the richness of the OPM graphical vocabulary offers a better alternative to replace UML generic (tagged) associations
with a new, semantically-clear symbology. For instance, the relation between Resource and Policy (and between Coordination Medium and Coordination Rule)
now adopts a specific symbol to express that Policy not only has a structural
relation with Resource, but is also an attribute of Resource.

On the other hand, since OPM introduces just one symbol (the solid black
triangle) to represent both composition and aggregation, distinguishing between
different relations (e.g Group/Individual Role, Group/Social Role) now requires
a careful reading of the *participation constraint* of the relation (where * means
"optional", *m* means "many", etc.). However, this aspect can be easily faced by
using OPM's textual counterpart, OPL, that provides a human-readable description of the Object Process Diagram; the OPL of SODA meta-model is shown
in Figure 2 (bottom). Despite the richness of OPM's vocabulary, some meta-
modelling relations are still difficult to express: this is particularly true for the
relations between structural entities and "*X*-Interacting" processes, that even
the (several) object/process link types provided by OPM are unable to capture
at a semantically-satisfactory level (more details in Section 3.2).

3   Discussion

In this Section, we discuss and compare the SODA meta-models in UML and
OPM, outlining the respective pros and cons. Generally speaking, both meta-
models fall short in modelling the SODA concept of interaction and the relations
between the structural parts and dynamic parts; in particular, this applies to
the relation of "participation", as we outline below.

3.1   Pros and Cons of SODA Meta-model in UML

The structural parts of the SODA methodology are well modelled. Due to its
graphical vocabulary, UML is forced to model the SODA concept of interaction
via its class notion, thus giving a static view of interaction, as if it were always
present in the system—which is obviously misleading, since interaction has intrinsically a transient nature; indeed, capturing the transient aspects through a
class diagram can be difficult.

On the other hand, UML enables the concept of "participation" to interaction to be expressed better than in OPM, thanks to the a generic tagged
association: interestingly, this is possible just because interaction is represented
as a class. However, distinguishing the semantic peculiarities of such associations based just on the label is not easy. For instance, although we used the same
generic association for modelling the participation both in the analysis and in
the design phases, in the first case the semantics is that Role participates to
Interaction, while in the latter we mean that not only Agent plays an active
part in interaction, but its internal state is changed by interaction, too.

3.2   Pros and Cons of SODA Meta-model in OPM

As mentioned above, the main advantage of OPM with respect to UML concerns interaction modelling, which exploits OPM's notion of process to represent the dynamic aspects. During the construction of the meta-model, however, we perceived the lack of a sort of *"tagged instrument link"* to connect objects and processes: currently, OPM's instrument link is only untagged. Such a link would have been appreciable, for instance, to express that Role *participates* to the A-Interacting process—not just that it is necessary, as expressed by the standard instrument link. In fact, necessity is a static concept, while playing an active part in interaction, as Role does, implies dynamics. A similar problem emerged in the relation between the A-Social Interacting process and the Interaction Rule object, where we could not express that Interaction Rule *governs* the social interaction—again, a more specific concept than just "being necessary".

Analogously, in the design phase, we used an *Effect link* to represent the relations between the Agent object and the *X*-Interacting processes; this is semantically correct because the internal state of Agent is modified by interaction, but does not express the crucial fact that Agent takes an active part to interaction, while the Effect link just expresses that its internal state is modified as a consequence of interaction. As a last issue, in the relation between the D-Social Interacting process and the Coordination Medium object, we could not express that the Coordination Medium *mediates* the social interaction by enacting the Coordination Rule—which, again, is more than just a mere "necessity".

3.3   Summing Up

Both UML and OPM proved expressive enough to capture in their meta-model the structural parts of the SODA methodology: so, for instance, the role model and the resource model are expressed in a clear way, with a specific semantics. At the same time, as partially mentioned above, both approaches present some problems, the main being that they fall short when asked to appropriately model the concept of interaction. In particular, the relation of participation, even though existing in both approaches, seems unable to capture the general concept of "participating to interaction" in a satisfactory way. This seems to indicate that while both UML and OPM methodologies are suitable to model the dynamic behaviour of *systems*, this ability is not conserved if they are used to build *meta-models*—actually, quite a different usage—although OPM expressiveness under this viewpoint is a little better than UML's.

So, we feel that neither OPM nor UML are fully adequate to capture the real essence of MAS methodologies, where interaction, in all its nuances—from a simple message exchange to mediated interaction via coordination media—is a key issue. In fact, suitably meta-modelling MAS methodologies seems to call for a specific approach, which is able to model both the structural and the dynamic parts of a methodology, and to explicitly express the idea of participating to interaction.

4   Conclusions

Several research efforts are being devoted to developing meta-models for MAS methodologies, however standardisations of methodologies for develop meta-models are not going still along way off. Although UML is often used for that purpose, meta-modelling methodologies (and in particular agent-oriented methodologies) presents several peculiarities. In this paper, we put to the test two meta-modelling approaches—UML and OPM—in order to check their expressiveness and suitability to the meta-modelling of MAS methodologies. While UML was an obvious reference for its widespread adoption, OPM was selected because even though it is an emergent methodology, it is stable and exhibits several interesting features—in particular, the explicit notion of process, and the capability of describing in a single framework all the crucial aspects of a system, instead of spreading them onto separate diagrams. Among MAS methodologies, we took SODA as our reference because it is explicitly focused on the MAS social aspects, thus putting interaction in clear evidence: this made it possible to evaluate the effectiveness of the UML and OPM approaches with respect to the issue of suitably representing interaction and, more generally, the dynamic aspects, other than the structural part.

The results of the mutual comparison between the two SODA meta-models indicates that neither approach is actually able to capture all the desired aspects in a satisfactory way. In particular, while the structural part is reasonably well modelled in both cases, the dynamic part is captured only partially—probably because both UML and OPM were introduced to model object-oriented systems, rather than systems in general; so as a consequence, they are not particularly suited to meta-modelling AOSE methodologies, especially because of their limited expressive power in capturing agent-oriented abstractions.

It should be noted that research on meta-models is also active in other field of computer science. Some papers (e.g. [14] and [15]) present meta-models for the construction of methodologies in general: meta-models are used there to "instantiate" a new methodology with the desired characteristics. Instead, our approach to meta-models moves from an existing methodology (SODA) and aims at creating a meta-model that could well capture the methodology concepts and their mutual relationship as well.

Therefore, future work will be mainly devoted to explore how to overcome such modelling weaknesses, and to devise out some meta-modelling approach to AOSE methodologies that couldfully capture the core interaction aspects.

References

1. van Hillegersberg, J., Kumar, K., Welke, R.J.: Using metamodeling to analyze the fit of object-oriented methods to languages. In: 31st Hawaii International Conference on System Sciences (HICSS 1998). Volume 5:Modeling Technologies and Intelligent Systems., Kohala Coast, HI, USA, IEEE Computer Society (1998) 323–332

2. Bernon, C., Cossentino, M., Gleizes, M.P., Turci, P., Zambonelli, F.: A study of some multi-agent meta-models. In Odell, J., Giorgini, P., Müller, J.P., eds.: Agent-Oriented Software Engineering V. Volume 3382 of LNCS., Springer (2004) 62–77 5th International Workshop, AOSE 2004, New York, NY, USA, July 19, 2004, Revised Selected Papers.
3. Bresciani, P., Giorgini, P., Giunchiglia, F., Mylopoulos, J., Perini, A.: Tropos: An agent-oriented software development methodology. Autonomous Agent and Multi-Agent Systems (8) **3** (2004) 203–236
4. Gòmez-Sanz, J.J., Pavòn, J., Garijo, F.: Meta-models for building multi-agent systems. In: 2002 ACM Symposium on Applied Computing (SAC 2002), New York, NY, USA, ACM Press (2002) 37–41
5. IGENIAS: Home page. (http://grasia.fdi.ucm.es/ingenias/metamodel/)
6. UML: Home page. (http://www.uml.org/)
7. Dori, D., Reinhartz-Berger, I.: An OPM-based metamodel of system development process. In Song, I.Y., Liddle, S.W., Ling, T.W., Scheuermann, P., eds.: ER. Volume 2813 of LNCS., Springer (2003) 105–117
8. Peleg, M., Dori, D.: The model multiplicity problem: Experimenting with real-time specification methods. IEEE Transactions on Software Engineering **26** (2000) 742–759
9. Dori, D.: Object-Process Methodology: A Holistic System Paradigm. Springer (2002)
10. Zambonelli, F., Jennings, N.R., Wooldridge, M.: Developing multiagent systems: The Gaia methodology. ACM Transactions on Software Engineering and Methodology (TOSEM) **12** (2003) 317–370
11. Cheong, C., Winikoff, M.: Hermes: A methodology for goal-oriented agent interactions. (2005) 4th International Conference on Autonomous Agents and MultiAgent Systems (AAMAS05). Poster.
12. Omicini, A.: SODA: Societies and infrastructures in the analysis and design of agent-based systems. In Ciancarini, P., Wooldridge, M.J., eds.: Agent-Oriented Software Engineering. Volume 1957 of LNCS., Springer (2001) 185–193 1st International Workshop (AOSE 2000), Limerick, Ireland, 10 June 2000. Revised Papers.
13. Ciancarini, P., Omicini, A., Zambonelli, F.: Multiagent system engineering: The coordination viewpoint. In Jennings, N.R., Lespérance, Y., eds.: Intelligent Agents VI. Agent Theories, Architectures, and Languages. Volume 1757 of LNAI., Springer (2000) 250–259 6th International Workshop (ATAL'99), Orlando, FL, USA, 15–17 July 1999. Proceedings.
14. Henderson-Sellers, B., Gonzalez-Perez, C.: A comparison of four process metamodels and the creation of a new generic standard. Information & Software Technology **47** (2005) 49–65
15. Gonzalez-Perez, C., McBride, T., Henderson-Sellers, B.: A metamodel for assessable software development methodologies. Software Quality Journal **13** (2005) 195–214

Programming an Agent as Abstract State Machine*

Grzegorz Dobrowolski

Institute of Computer Science,
AGH University of Science and Technology, Kraków, Poland
grzela@agh.edu.pl

Abstract. A software architecture of autonomous agents based on the idea of abstract state machine—ASM is proposed. The architecture establishes links between well-founded notions and recognized mechanisms of multi-agent systems and procedures of their systematic design and implementation as computer-network applications. A pilot version of the related software and its application example are presented shortly.

1 Introduction

It is commonly agreed that notion *agent* occurs to be a useful component, which can facilitate software development by virtue of its high level abstractions for autonomy (decentralization) and interactions. Nevertheless, it is hardly to point at any particular agent technique that stepped down towards engineering practice to become a supplement of the implementator's toolbox. Even often used term *agent architecture* rather means description of algorithms that governs the agent's behaviour then encompasses references to software engineering.

The presented paper is located in a rather narrow stream of publications that can be entitled Searching for an agent-based software engineering paradigm. Articles: [9] (the well), [7] (idea of agent-oriented UML), [1,8] (inter-agent communication layer of the so-called agent platforms), [5] (general approach to agent-based engineering) can serve as significant examples.

The discussed architecture is meant as a bunch of means necessary for realization of autonomous software agents (consequently—multi-agent systems) selected according to a particular model of agency. It can be seen as a skeleton that supports implementation of agent-based software dedicated to various fields of applications. In the presence of several agent platforms that facilitate programming of network aspects (communication and mobility) of multi-agent systems (e.g. [1]), the crucial problem is to find such a general architecture that would be easy for description in terms of software engineering and thus—for approval of programmers.

The architecture based on the idea of *abstract state machine*—ASM [2] is proposed in the article. It generalizes *finite* state machine often used in software solutions. One of the essential differences here is that state transitions are not caused by external signals (input of an automaton) but are the effects of autonomously taken decisions that may be only loose consequences of stimuli from the agent's environment.

---

* This work was partially sponsored by State Committee for Scientific Research (KBN) grant no. 7 T11C 033 21.

M. Pěchouček, P. Petta, and L.Z. Varga (Eds.): CEEMAS 2005, LNAI 3690, pp. 173–182, 2005.

ASM has been chosen as the base for a definition of the agent's architecture for two important purposes. ASM has good theoretical foundation. Both the automaton and its state are defined in terms of abstract algebra. So it can be awaited that the formulated architecture will be justified and easy for theoretical development. On the other hand, the applied algebraic operations (static functions in general sense) are augmented with—so called—dynamic functions that introduce into ASM elements traditionally implemented in programming languages. This way ASM acquire expression power of the languages and can be easily approved by practicing engineers. At the same time, such augmented algebraic structure gains interpretation of (computer) memory and abstract switching from a state to state—its contents changes.

The article consists of: a sketch of the reference model of agency (with premises of an agent modeling), some introduction to ASM and, finally, description of the proposed software architecture. Everything is exemplified with a pilot implementation on the basis of JADE platform and a simple exercise.

2   The Reference Model of an Agent

A presented beneath model of an agent (see also [4]) is constructed according to the *black-box* schema—a part of a domain is taken out and constitutes a system through specification of all interactions observed. In this way the model effectively reflects the agent's ability to interact with his neighborhood and other agents (the features that are a base for a multi-agent system creation) but also defines in general his internal (abstract) architecture.

The approach leads to the adoption of the following assumptions crucial to the model.

1. Excluding physical impact on an agent, the rest of agent–neighborhood interface is fully controlled by the agent himself.
2. An agent operates in a discrete manner. His activity is a finite sequence of actions (elementary) performed by him.
3. An agent decides on the sequence in the sense of both actions to do and time moments of their initiation.
4. The basic mechanism of an agent model is sequential initiation of actions, called further **mechanism of choice**.

The assumptions seem to be enough general to encompass possible algorithms and implementation techniques of artificial agents as well as to describe the presence of human beings in multi-agent systems.

Definition 1. *Agent Λ is a three-tuple of the form:*

$$\Lambda = \{ A, S, F \subset S \times A \times S \} \tag{1}$$

where: A *finite set of actions (elementary) of agent Λ;*
   S *finite set of internal states of agent Λ;*
   F *three-element relation describing permitted succession of states and actions of agent Λ—in the given state the agent can perform an action (the second element) that leads him to a new state (the third element).*

Sustaining cause-effect conjunction requires relation F to have the following feature:

$$(s, a, s_1) \in F \ \wedge \ (s, a, s_2) \in F \ \Rightarrow \ s_1 = s_2 \tag{2}$$

Relation F reflects the possible combinations of states and actions. Each state implies a subset of actions allowed. Assigning and performing a particular action is an effect of the choice mechanism of an agent (an elementary action can be performed several times).

Definition 2. *Let mapping f of the form:*

$$s_{i+1} = f_{a_i}(s_i) \ \equiv \ \exists \, (s_i, a_i, s_{i+1}) \in F \ : \ F \in \Lambda \tag{3}$$

denote performing action $a_i \in A$ and changing the agent's state. To emphasize the cause-effect conjunction, appropriate states are indexed with natural numbers.

Definition 3. *Manifold but finite application of mapping f, represented in the formula beneath by operator $\otimes$, is called activity of agent Λ:*

$$(f_{a_j} \otimes f_{a_{j+1}} \otimes \cdots \otimes f_{a_k}) \ \equiv \ f_{\{a_j, a_{j+1}, \dots, a_k\}} \ : \ a_j, a_{j+1}, \dots, a_k \in A \in \Lambda \tag{4}$$

The agent's activity can be denoted also as a sequence of chosen and performed elementary actions of him.

Constitution of a multi-agent system comes next with an *interaction relation* that links given actions of two (or more) agents. Thus, it describes potential cooperation (interactions) in the system. An interaction is realized when the appropriate actions are chosen and performed by the agents. None of the actions can be performed independently (separately). Consequently, activity of a multi-agent system can be defined as a composition of activities of its members.

Questions with respect to action realisation as well as many others issues of the model can be left beyond the scope of the paper without loss of readability but are available in [6,3].

3   Elements of ASM

Due to practical orientation of the paper, only indispensable for the proposed architecture elements of ASM theory will be reported beneath in a rather general manner. A reader is referred to [2] for details.

ASM can be defined as a finite set of formulas of the shape:

$$\{ \ \text{if } \textit{condition}_i \text{ then } \textit{updates}_i \ \}_{\ i=1,\dots,n} \tag{5}$$

where $\textit{condition}_i$ is the predicate of a logic assumed for the particular ASM, and $\textit{updates}_i$ is a set of assignments:

$$f(t_1, \dots, t_n) := t \tag{6}$$

each of which is understood as a change of value (or definition) of function f for the values of parameters equal to $t_1, \dots, t_n$ to new value t (for the sake of readability indexes which identify a concrete function and, next, ASM are neglected).

Functioning of ASM is done by cyclical performing of the following operations. All $\{condition_i\}_{i=1,...,n}$ are evaluated concurrently and these $updates_i$ for which conditions are true are marked. Next—also concurrently—the marked updates are realized through appropriate calculations of functions and assignments. The end of the longest assignment completes a cycle.

Assignment (6) is performed as a corresponding operator of imperative programming languages. Firstly, the values of parameters (here: $v_1, \ldots, v_n$) are calculated according to their list, next—the value of the function ($v = f(v_1, \ldots, v_n)$). To make the value accessible in the next cycle, its identification—called location—is introduced via the function name and list of its calculated parameters. Location l can be interpreted as a piece of memory (with an address), which stores value v of the function. The whole described operation is an update of the location to that value —(l, v).

Stepping from a cycle to cycle, we have just two kinds of locations: staying untouched or having been just modified.

If for a given ASM we put together all locations possible during its life time, they create the memory of the automaton. Departing from some state (starting one) and performing appropriate location updates in each cycle, the evolution of the automaton state is obtained. For unambiguous determination of a next state it is necessary the bunch of updates in each cycle to be not conflicting, i.e. the following formula to hold for each pair in a cycle

$$(l, v) \wedge (l, v') \Rightarrow v = v' \tag{7}$$

It means that although the functions can use whatever data describing the state, their results must be located in distinct places of the memory.

Functions (updates and locations) as well as conditions can be classified according to their features. So we have *static* functions—not affected during ASM run and *dynamic* ones, which algorithm depends on the automaton state. In turn, dynamic functions fall into four categories: *controlled*, *in* or *monitored*, *out*, and *shared*. *Controlled* functions can be modified only by other updates of the same automaton while *in* functions are modified only by the neighbourhood (reflect its influence) and, in consequence, can occur at right-hand side of assignment (6) only. On the contrary, *out* functions (modelling influence of an automaton) can stay only at left-hand side of (6) but are accessible for the neighbourhood. *Shared* functions combine features of *controlled* and *in* ones. *Static* and *controlled* functions are identified as *internal* ones while the rest are grouped as *external* functions.

The assumption is that *in* functions (updates, locations) are determined in each state as well as synchronization of *shared* functions realization is established.

It is obvious that the functions have different numbers and types of arguments—*signatures*. Signatures of all the functions define the signature of ASM.

4   Software Architecture of an Agent

Although the methodology based on ASM serves with a possibility of working with modules (here: sub-ASM) or procedures, we start our discussion with the agent's modular structure, which is generated by the specificity of his applications and implementation conditions. Next, these modules (especially one of them) will be described in terms of ASM to introduce the proposed architecture.

From the point of view of establishing of a multi-agent system the most important is a sphere which embraces modules of communication and interface. The former is dedicated to interactions with other software agents, the latter—with a human agent. These two modules can be present and utilized in extent depending on tasks allocated to a particular type of agents in the system.

If an agent is mobile, the sphere is embraced by yet another module that realizes mobility of his code and calculations. It can be arranged in this way because mobility influences, in fact, the structure of information flows, not their contents.

All the above modules support multi-direction and multi-aspect interchange of information that, in turn, needs management also with respect to its semantics. A unifying idea here is to use protocols (communication, interaction), which occur to be powerful enough to stimulate and realize even very complicated cooperation patterns among agents. So is a need for a module of protocols management.

The rest of the semantic analysis is carried out in a central module of an agent— *kernel*. Internal structure of the kernel strongly depends on the role of an agent in the system as well as applied algorithms and data structures. As examples can serve here these introduced by the negotiation management module or knowledge base. It is obvious that the kernel is the most important and, usually, the most complicated agent's module. It is also the most specific for agent-based techniques.

Therefore, let us focus our attention on the kernel, remembering that the rest of modules can be represented by ASM also. Moreover, some of them do not need any deeper analysis, e.g. the protocols management module exploits the idea of a finite state machine, the interface module may be built using one of the popular graphic libraries. Similarly, the communication is ready to use, when one of the agent platforms is the basis for implementation.

The point of departure towards the kernel architecture are conclusions of sections 2 and 3. They also dictate the way of describing the agent's features and mechanisms in terms of ASM.

Action ith **of an agent** is represented in ASM by expression $updates_i$ in a formula of shape (5), no matter the action is internal or external. Updates of an action are of either *controlled* or *in* or *out* type depending on the direction of an information flow with respect to a kernel. Respective examples of them are actions of: auto-perception, perception, sending a message.

Expressions $condition_i$ of the all specified agent's actions create in common the **mechanism of choice** of appropriate **actions**. On the assumption that in a single step of an automaton a single action can be chosen at most, the mechanism works sequentially as it was postulated. If more than one condition is true than the cause-effect conjunction is also preserved. It is due to the main assumption of ASM that a set of updates is not contradictory in each step (see eq. (7)). Then all triggered actions can be regarded as a single but compound action.

Now it is very easy to define the **agent's state** as a union of his updates (locations), i.e. the state of ASM that describes an agent.

Having the main elements of the agent's architecture defined, we can illustrate the idea with a diagram in figure 1. Some details are discussed further.

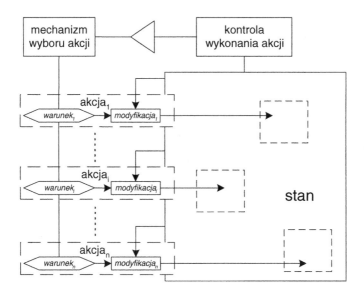

Fig. 1. Software agent architecture based on ASM

Controlled updates model internal actions of a kernel and thus an agent. *In* and *out* updates of a kernel create its interface with outer modules. Some of them can be, in fact, a main part of execution of some external actions of an agent. Let us consider *receiving a message* as an example. The main part of it is an *in* update that modifies the kernel state in the appropriate location. The location stores the message contents and some additional information about communication like progress of an interaction protocol used. Analysis of the contents that can, but has not to, follow (in any period of time) is modelled as independent *controlled* updates with their own locations. Of course, the analysis has access to the location of the actual *receiving a message* action.

In this way the proposed architecture realizes yet another postulate about the (limited) **agent's autonomy**. In the above example the agent must receive a message (it is originally forced by the neighbourhood) but its analysis and possible consequences are decided by him (analysis is an autonomous action).

The necessary condition of receiving a message is its completion by the communication module. It can be done in such a way that the appropriate $condition_i$ is dependent on some flag in the location of receiving action of the kernel.

Actions that are directed outside in their information aspect are realized analogously. A kernel executes *out* updates, which location is available to a dedicated module. In general, execution of some (*external*) actions involves a few modules that cooperate as it is shown above. Cooperation of modules can be designed in both synchronous and asynchronous modes.

Thus applying ASM supports design of a **modular architecture**. It is easy to consider hardware elements in the framework of the architecture also. Then some locations can be realized as device registers that work for an agent as a part of the interface with the real neighbourhood.

5   A Pilot Implementation and an Example

As a primary test of the presented idea, a pilot implementation in the bed of JADE Platform [1] has been decided and done. The following facts can serve here as motivation: JADE is well-known and intensively used for several years and can be regarded as a stabilized programming tool; JADE fully implements communication as well as other mechanisms necessary to build a multi-agent system; the architecture of JADE is open to assimilation of a particular software solution of an agent. Summarizing, JADE provides an environment for a kind of *rapid development* in the subject and allows to concentrate only on the main module of an agent—a kernel.

The implementation has been carried out in two steps:

1. Building JAVA interface *IAMSAgentFormula* in order to give representation of the agent's action (a pair of $condition_i$, $updates_i$ in terms of ASM).
2. Building JAVA classes *AMSAgent* (specialization of JADE class Agent) and *AMSAgentBehaviour* (specialization of JADE class Behaviour) in order to express the agent's functions.

Some details of the implementation are given in figure 2 that show the UML schema of the classes (and interface). A reader is encouraged to inspect components of them, assuming that the names are self-descriptive.

Following ASM, the agent's function is the cyclical performing of the three phases: concurrent evaluation of all $condition_i$ and choice of actions to do; examination if the corresponding $updates_i$ are not contradicted; and at last concurrent realization of the actions. Each phase must be completed before the next one is activated.

Although performing the first and third phases does not cause any specific difficulties to the presented idea, the second phase triggers some doubts. In the case of inconsistency in $updates_i$ ASM can not switch to the next state— the agent fails. The reaction which is suggested in publications about ASM (e.g. [2]) is to unconditionally stop the agent. The adopted solution is to throw an exception with requirement of termination of the agent. The underlying mechanism needs declarations which locations are updated by the given action.

To investigate features of the proposed architecture in practice and check the shortly described above pilot implementation some tests have been carried out. For the sake of simplicity one of them a group of agents that constitute a model of *Slot machine* has been chosen for presentation here. Once again a reader is referred to the UML diagram now presenting classes and methods of the slot machine agents (see fig. 3). Two types of them are programmed.

1. These that model drums of the machine. Each of them works independently but concurrently producing a drawing.

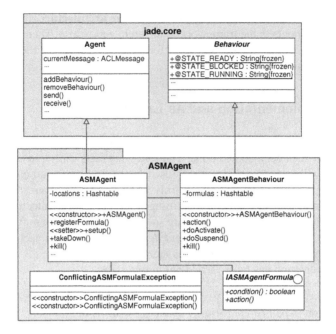

Fig. 2. UML diagram of the JADE implementation of ASM architecture

2. A type that is represented by the single agent coordinating the agents of the former one. The agent built of just five ASM formulas activates the drums, receives information about their positions when stop, and carries out the appropriate user interface. The coordination is done on the FIPA-ACL communication basis.

Nevertheless the example is very simple, some important facts has been confirmed. The proposed architecture can be followed by flexible and intuitive programming tools. Concurrency can be easily achieved that is the main requirement for contemporary applications. The only doubt concerns the problem of a scale in the sense of number of threads of agent-based applications built. But, one ought to remember that a designer can restrict the concurrency as long as efficiency of his application is preserved.

6   Summary

Programming an agent based on the ASM idea is presented in the paper. The proposed architecture establishes links between well founded notions and recognized mechanisms of multi-agent systems and procedures of systematic design and implementation of them as computer-network applications. Moreover, steady development and growing scope of ASM application positively sketch out perspectives of the proposed architecture. In particular, the architecture allows for:

– effective definition of the agent's state, which is one of central notions in the theory of agent and systems of them;

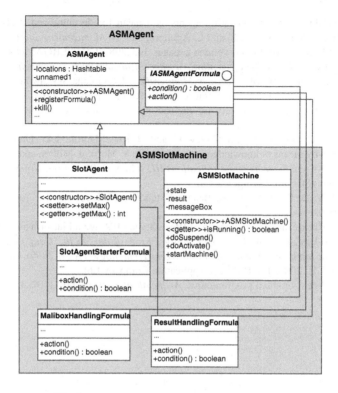

Fig. 3. UML diagram of the slot machine agents

- flexible and intuitive programming of agents of whatever purpose;
- specification and verification of agent-based software done according to the proposed architecture with the range of formal methods as well as practical procedures (light) applied directly in a process of software production;
- independent implementation of the agent's modules and actions, which opens possibility to design learning agents (acquiring abilities to perform new actions).

The above features has been in majority confirmed by the reported both pilot implementation and example.

Further work in the area will concentrate on deeper analysis of the approach based on advanced examples and applications. It is also foreseen a direction aimed at improvement of the related software e.g. by implementation of action conditions evaluation according to fuzzy, or other, logics.

References

1. F. Bellifemine, A. Poggi, and G. Rimassa. JADE — A FIPA-compliant agent framework. In *Proc. of the 4th Int. Conf. on the Practical Applications of Agents and Multi-Agent Systems (PAAM-99)*, pages 97–108, London, UK, 1999.
2. E. Börger and R. Stärk. *Abstract State Machines*. Springer-Verlag, 2003.

3. G. Dobrowolski. Network operating agents as a mean for decentralized decision support systems. In Z. Binder, B. Hirsch, and L. Aguilera, editors, *Management and Control of Production and Logistics MCPL'97*, volume 2, pages 393–398. IFAC/PERGAMON, 1998.

4. G. Dobrowolski. *Technologie agentowe w zdecentralizowanych systemach informacyjno-decyzyjnych*, volume 107 of *Rozprawy Monografie*. Uczelniane Wydawnictwa Naukowo-Dydaktyczne Akademii Gʾrniczo-Hutniczej im. S. Staszica, Krakʾw, 2002.

5. N. Jennings. On agent-based software engineering. *Artificial Intelligence*, (117):277–296, 2000.

6. E. Nawarecki, G. Dobrowolski, S. Ciszewski, and M. Kisiel-Dorohinicki. Ontology of cooperating agents by means of knowledge components. In V. Mařik, J. Müller, and M. Pěchouček, editors, *Multi-Agent Systems and Applications III*, volume 2691 of *Lect. Notes in Artif. Intelligence*, pages 180–190. Springer, 2003.

7. J. Odell, H. V. D. Parunak, and B. Bauer. Extending UML for agents. (opublikowane w WWW), 2000.

8. S. Poslad, P. Buckle, and R. Hadingham. FIPA-OS: the FIPA agent Platform available as Open Source. In J. Bradshaw and G. Arnold, editors, *Proc. of the 5th Int. Conf. on the Practical Application of Intelligent Agents and Multi-Agent Technology (PAAM 2000)*, pages 355–368, Manchester, UK, 2000. The Practical Application Company Ltd.

9. Y. Shoham. Agent-oriented programming. *Artificial Intelligence*, 60:51–92, 1993.

The PASSI and Agile PASSI MAS Meta-models Compared with a Unifying Proposal

Massimo Cossentino[2], Salvatore Gaglio[1,2],
Luca Sabatucci[1], and Valeria Seidita[1]

[1] Dipartimento di Ingegneria Informatica (DINFO),
University of Palermo,
Viale delle Scienze, 90128 -Palermo- Italy
[2] Istituto di Calcolo e Reti ad Alte Prestazioni (ICAR),
Consiglio Nazionale delle Ricerche(CNR),
Viale delle Scienze, 90128 -Palermo- Italy
cossentino@pa.icar.cnr.it, gaglio@unipa.it, sabatucci@csai.unipa.it,
seidita@csai.unipa.it

Abstract. A great number of processes for multi-agent systems design
have been presented in last years to support the different approaches
to agent-oriented design; each process is specific for a particular class
of problems and it instantiates a specific MAS meta-model. These differences produce inconsistences and overlaps: a MAS meta-model may
define a term not referred by another, or the same term can be used with
a different meaning.

We think that the lack of a standardization may cause a significant
delay to the diffusion of the agent paradigm outside research context.
Working for this unification goal, it is also necessary to define in unambiguous way the terms of the agent model and their relationships
thus obtaining a unified MAS meta-model. In this work we propose the
PASSI MAS meta-model, the results of its adaptation to the needs of an
agile process (Agile PASSI), and a comparison with an existing unifying
proposal of MAS meta-model composed by considering three different
processes (ADELFE, Gaia and PASSI).

1 Introduction

In order to approach the design and development of a multi-agent system (MAS)
in a rigorous way, many approaches have been explored; all of these deal the development phases addressing high level terms such as agent, goal, role, task and
collaboration. Hence, the design of a system may be seen as the instantiation
of these elements in order to fulfill some specific problem requirements. The description of the elements involved in the design phases, and their relationships,
can represent one of the fundamental steps in building a new one and specifically
in the definition of its MAS meta-model (MMM hence afterward). The various
agent-oriented design processes, presented in these years, are significantly different: goal-oriented, situation-oriented, requirement-oriented are examples of

M. Pĕchouček, P. Petta, and L.Z. Varga (Eds.): CEEMAS 2005, LNAI 3690, pp. 183–192, 2005.

different philosophical possible approaches [1,2,3,4,5]. Each of these proposes a different way to face modeling; this diversity is caused by observing the system from different perspectives, considering different aspects of the problem and specific theoretical background or a specific application context. Besides each process forces the designer to assign an implicit meaning to each MMM component and that is often not coherent with the choices of other authors.

Even if this variety of design processes may be viewed as a richness, the differences among their meta-model components could create some perplexities when a designer moves from a design process to another, or when two designers try to communicate about a shared solution (pattern for agents).

A first step toward interoperability among different agent oriented design processes was the proposal of a unifying MAS meta-model [6] created starting from three different approaches (Adelfe, Gaia, and PASSI).

The purpose of this work is to present a description of the MAS meta-model of two design processes that use a quite different approach (PASSI[4,7] and Agile PASSI[8,9]). In this analysis we put in evidence two aspects related to the unifying MMM definition: i) we can highlight the differences among elements definition from comparing specific MMMs with the unifying one; ii) we can also show how to derive a specific MMM from the unifying one.

This paper is structured as follows: in section 2 we present the PASSI and Agile PASSI design processes while their meta-models are described in section 3 where we also underline the most relevant differences among them, finally in section 4 we present the unifying MMM resulting from the study in [6] and in 5 we compare the three presented MAS meta-models.

2   The PASSI and Agile PASSI Design Process

PASSI (Process for Agent Societies Specification and Implementation)[4,7] is a step-by-step requirement-to-code design process conceived for developing multi-agent systems. It is characterized by some distinctive features: (i) it is requirement driven, (ii) it is iterative and incremental, (iii) it focus the attention to ontological model of the domain in the design of agents.

PASSI is composed of five models addressing different design levels of abstraction. The **System Requirements Model** represents an anthropomorphic model of the system requirements in terms of agency and purpose. It consists of a functional description of the system: the designer identifies system requirements using use case diagrams, and organizes them in responsibility groups (that will assigned to agents). The next model, the **Agent Society Model**, fully exploits the agent paradigm: now an agent is seen as an autonomous entity capable of pursuing an objective through its autonomous decisions, actions and social relationships. The activities involved in this model aim to depict agent internal plans, knowledge and social abilities in order to model interactions and dependencies among entities of the society. The **Agent Implementation Model** defines the implementing details of the solution in terms of classes, attributes and methods. In this phase the designer uses conventional class diagrams, to describe the static structure of the involved agents, and activity or state chart diagrams, to describe the behavior of individual agents. The **Code Model** is a representation of the solution at the code level while the **Deployment Model** describes the distribution (and their eventual migrations) of sub-systems across available hardware processing units.

Agile PASSI [9,8] derives from PASSI through the reuse of some of its fragments and it has been assembled complying a method engineering approach [10,11,12]. It is a light process created, according to the agile manifesto [13], with the aim to develop, in a short time, small-medium size systems. An agile process is easy to understand and to use because it is principally code oriented; for these reasons Agile PASSI comes to be well suited for those applications where coding is more important than documentation. In order to be compliant with agile modeling principles [13,14], Agile PASSI is an iterative process; it is composed of five steps (a low number) and it strongly oriented to communication among customers and developers during all the development phases (and in particular during the planning one). The fragments (portions of the design process) we have extracted from PASSI are: (i) *Domain Requirements description* (the description of system functionalities through use case diagrams), (ii) *Agent Identification* (the identification of logically related sets of functionalities that are put under an agent's responsibility), (iii) *Domain Ontology description* (the description of the agent knowledge in term of concepts, predicates and actions), (iv) *Code Reuse* (a technique for reuse portion of projects and code using design patterns) and (v) *Testing* (single agent and society test). This selection was done taking in consideration the PASSI philosophy: we have maintained use case diagrams as the base for agents identification and we have not changed the fundamental role of the ontology in the process. From the other side we respected the requirements for an agile process: low importance for the completeness of documentation and rapid code production.

The result of the composition of these fragments is a new process including five steps: **Requirements**, a model of the system requirements that is composed of two activities: Planning and Sub-Domain Requirements Description; **Agent Society**, a view of the agents involved in the solution, their interactions and their knowledge about the world. It is composed of two activities: Domain Ontology Description and Agent Identification; **Test Plan**, the phase of test planning; **Code**, a solution domain model at code level; **Testing**, the performing of the previous planned tests.

3   The PASSI and Agile PASSI MAS Meta-Models

The description of the PASSI MAS meta-model (Figure 1) addresses three logical areas: (i) the problem domain, (ii) the solution domain and (iii) the agency domain; they are introduced in an order that reflects our choice of an agent approach for solution refinement and modeling.

In the problem domain we include components describing the requirements the system is going to accomplish: these are directly related to the requirements

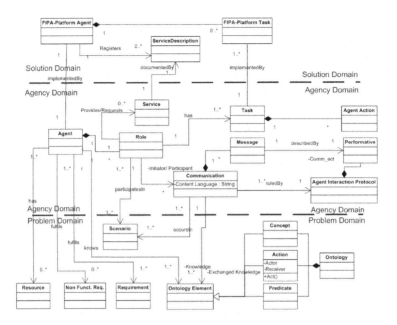

Fig. 1. The PASSI MAS meta-model

analysis phase of the PASSI process. Then we introduce the agency domain components; they are used to define an agent solution for the problem. Finally, in the PASSI MMM solution domain, agency-level components are mapped to the adopted FIPA-compliant implementation platform elements (we suppose the platform supports at least the concepts of agent and task); this represents the code-level part of the solution and the last refinement step.

Going into the details of the model, we can see that (Figure 1), the Problem Domain deals with the user's problem in terms of scenarios, requirements, ontology and resources. Scenarios describe a sequence of interactions among actors and the system to be built; Requirements are represented with conventional UML use case diagrams. The ontological description of the domain is composed of concepts (categories of the domain), actions (performed in the domain and effecting the status of concepts) and predicates (asserting something about a portion of the domain, i.e. the status of concepts). Resources are the last element of the problem domain. They can be accessed/shared/manipulated by agents. A resource could be a repository of data (like a relational database), an image/video file or also a good to be sold/bought. The Agency Domain contains the components of the agent-based solution. In PASSI an agent is responsible for realizing some functionalities descending from one or more functional requirements. It also has to respect some non functional requirement constraints (like for instance performance prescriptions). It lives in an environment from which it receives perceptions (the related knowledge is structured according to the designed domain ontology). Sometimes an agent has also access to available resources and it is capable of actions in order to pursue its own objectives or

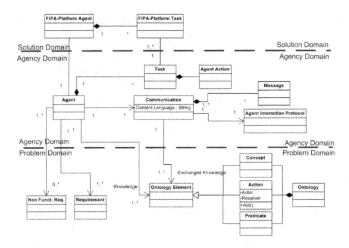

Fig. 2. The Agile PASSI MAS Meta-Model

to offer services to the community. Each agent during its life plays some roles. A role is a peculiarity of the social behavior of an agent. When playing a role, an agent may provide a service to other agents. In PASSI, a task specifies the computation that generates the effects of a specific agent behavioral feature. It is used with the significance of atomic part for defining the overall agent's behavior. This means that an agent's behavior can be composed by assembling its tasks and the list of actions that are executed within each task cannot be influenced by the behavior planning. Tasks are structural internal components of an agent and they contribute to define the agent's abilities; these cannot be directly accessed by other agents (autonomy) unless the agent offers them as a set of services. A communication is an interaction among two agents and it is composed of one or more messages. The information exchanged during a communication is composed of concepts, predicates or actions defined in the ontology. The flow of messages and the semantic of each message are ruled by an agent interaction protocol (AIP). The last Agency Domain element (Service) describes a set of coherent functionalities exported by the agent for the community.

The Implementation Domain describes the structure of the code solution in the chosen FIPA-compliant implementation platform and it is essentially composed of three elements: (i) the FIPA-Platform Agent that is the base class catching the implementation of the Agent entity represented in the Agency domain; (ii) the FIPA-Platform Task that is the implementation of the agent's Task, (iii) the ServiceDescription component that is the implementation-level description (for instance an OWL-S file) of each service specified in the Agent Domain.

Like the previous one, the Agile PASSI MMM (Figure 2) is partitioned in three logical areas: (i) problem domain, (ii) agency domain and (iii) solution domain. Agile PASSI was assembled starting from fragments extracted from PASSI, so the collection of MAS components descends from these fragments following a particular design process [8] also considering the particular applications the agile process was conceived to solve. An agile process principally addresses code production, so in this case MAS meta-model components are mainly centered on the agent element and its related implementation parts. Using Agile PASSI a multi-agent system is conceived following five phases: planning, requirements design, agent society design, coding and testing; during the first two phases the elements present in problem domain area of MMM are instantiated; these elements are: i) functional and non functional requirements (used to describe the user point of view on the problem solution), and ii) domain ontology (composed of concepts, predicates and actions). As regards the Agency Domain, its central component is obviously the agent that is conceived in the same way as it is in conventional PASSI; it is composed of tasks representing significant (but not divisible) parts of its behavior and its capability of pursuing an objective realizing some functionalities, besides it uses communications to interact (communicating or requesting collaborations) with other agents, each communication being composed of messages ruled by an agent interaction protocol (like it is in PASSI). The solution domain is nearly the same of conventional PASSI since it is composed of the *Agent* and *Task* implementation elements.

4   A Unifying MAS Meta Model

An initial proposal of unifying MAS meta-model has been presented by C. Bernon et al. in [6] with the aim of contributing to the interoperability among agent oriented design processes; in their work the authors started with a comparison of some existing process with a specific attention for the differences among their MAS meta-models (MMM) components. The three studied design processes (ADELFE, Gaia and PASSI) are quite generic, in fact none of them refers to a specific agent architecture (like BDI or purely reactive agents).

The study was conducted using the classification of the terms (representing a MAS) accordingly to the following four categories: (1) Agent Structure: agent, role, responsibility, task, goal, plan and service; (2) Agent Interactions: (direct and undirect) communication, protocol, message; (3) Agent Society and organizational structure: social structure and organization rule; (4) Agent Implementation: FIPA-Platform agent and FIPA-Platform Task. The analysis confirmed that in the processes under exam, multiple definitions exist for the same component/concept; some are quite similar (there are small differences in the meaning), while some others are completely different. In order to maintain some level of generality they defined an unifying MMM (in Figure 3) with the aim to be used as a reference point for further comparisons and discussions about different design processes and related components.

5   A Comparison of the Presented Meta-models

It is a common belief that a general process, suitable to solve any kind of problems, does not exist, so it is clear that a MAS meta-model as huge as the one

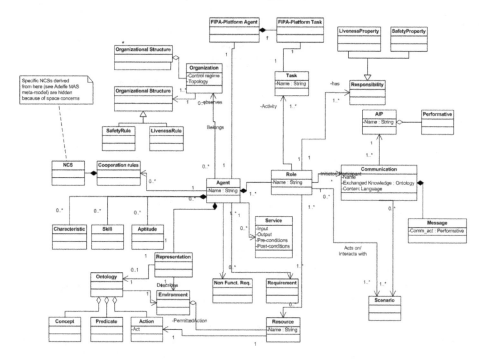

Fig. 3. The Unifying MAS meta-model (from [6])

described in section 4 cannot be used without some level of customization of its structure. Specializing different elements from MMM meets the different design philosophies on which each design process is based; now we will compare the PASSI and Agile PASSI MMMs with the unifying one with the aim of pointing out the differences among various concepts without forgetting that the unifying meta-model elements derives from the unification of three existing design processes already including PASSI.

Our comparison will deal with the four specific aspects of the MMM already discussed in the previous section. In the following we will refer to Figure 4 to show what elements and what relationships from the unifying meta-model we can find in the PASSI one (black drawn elements), what elements and relationships are newly introduced (dark-filled elements) and how the concepts and their definitions are specialized to create the MAS meta-model representing the PASSI design process. Elements from the unifying MMM that are not used in PASSI/Agile PASSI are gray-designed and as it can be seen they are a significant part of the model itself. Besides we will underline that because of slightly different interpretations of meta-model concepts (and philosophical choices that are beyond of each approach) it is possible that meta-models sharing the same elements can lead to significantly different design processes.

Agent Structure: in PASSI an agent is defined as a composition of roles; tasks, specifying a specific computation generating some kind of behavior, are associ-

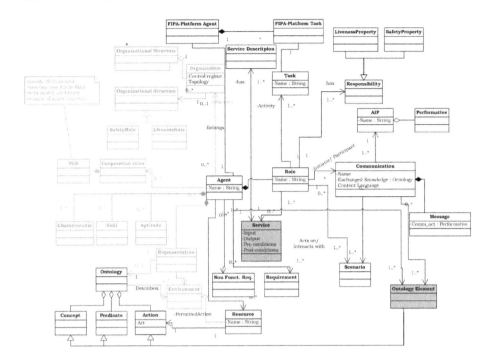

Fig. 4. The PASSI elements in the Unifying MAS meta-model

ated to each role. From all of this descends that a design process based on PASSI is performed through a sequence of steps leading from an early identification of agents to the definition of their roles and the description of their communications, while for instance in Gaia[15], being different the definitions of agent and role, we can see that the process is initially based on roles definition and only in a second time on the agents identification.

Instead in Agile PASSI, an agent is composed only by tasks, the concept of role is not necessary and so it is not present in Agile PASSI meta-model.

Agent Interaction: as regards the agent interaction capability in PASSI (and Agile PASSI) we see it is based on communications; they refer to an agent interaction protocol and the knowledge exchanged during the communication is seen as an instance of the domain ontology; this points out how important it is in PASSI to create a relationship between communications and the ontology through an *ontology element* while it is not necessary to introduce the concept of *environment* of Adelfe[16], where an agent can interact with another agent directly through communications or indirectly through the environment.

Agent Society: social relationships in PASSI are modeled through the definition of services that can be provided or accessed by agents. The service providing imply that agents would play social roles so to participate in scenarios interacting with other through communications; an agent can handle some resources that are relevant for the remaining part of society and accessing them can trigger some kind of interactions. During the design flow in PASSI a static structural representation of the agent society is made through a class diagram where classes (agents) can be grouped in packages representing the social structures (groups, communities,...); differently in Gaia, the agent society is considered more than a collection of interacting agent but it is an entity with a well defined structure. From this structure a designer can identify agent activities, assigning a role for each social one; once all the roles that compose one agent are defined, their activities and responsibilities are converted into a set of services. Agent society is not modeled in Agile PASSI.

Agent Implementation: in PASSI and Agile PASSI a direct mapping exists between the elements of the MAS meta-model and their implementation; each agent is coded using the base agent class of the selected implementation platform and it contains the tasks that are used by roles (that have not a direct code level implementation). No similar mapping is provided by Gaia or Adelfe.

6   Conclusions

A large number of MAS design processes have been developed in the last years and probably others will be created in future; each of these is characterized by specific features characterizing the single approach. In all of these cases, differences among the various design processes (sometimes referred to as *methodologies*) reflect in correspondent differences among the MAS meta-models. In this work we presented the MAS meta-models of the PASSI and Agile PASSI design processes and compared them with a unifying proposal of MAS meta-model resulting from the study of three existing design process MMMs. Our aim was both to evaluate whether from the proposed unifying MMM we could derive a new design process (Agile PASSI) and to speculate about the fact that different processes, although similar in some parts of the MAS meta-models, can have very different approaches to the design of their systems (some examples dealt with the order in which the different elements are instantiated during the design time). We can conclude that the unifying proposal despite of the level of generality that it introduces still sufficiently supports the PASSI/Agile PASSI MAS meta-models and besides, in section 5, we observed that the unique schema representing a MMM is not sufficient to underline some specific design process; conversely, several different solutions can be drawn to instantiate the same meta-model; it still remains to explore the importance that the different definitions of the MMM elements can have in constraining the overall process.

References

1. Capera, D., Georg, J.P., Gleizes, M.P., Glize, P.: The amas theory for complex problem solving based on self-organizing cooperative agents. In: Proc. of the 1st International Workshop on Theory And Practice of Open Computational Systems (TAPOCS03@WETICE 2003), Linz (Austria) (2003)
2. Castro, J., Kolp, M., Mylopoulos, J.: Towards requirements-driven information systems engineering: the tropos project. Inf. Syst. **27** (2002) 365–389

3. Wooldridge, M., Jennings, N.R., Kinny, D.: The gaia methodology for agent-oriented analysis and design. Journal of Autonomous Agents and Multi-Agent Systems **3** (2000) 285–315
4. Cossentino, M., Potts, C.: A case tool supported methodology for the design of multi-agent systems, Las Vegas (NV), USA, The 2002 International Conference on Software Engineering Research and Practice, SERP'02 (2002)
5. DeLoach, S.A., Wood, M.F., Sparkman, C.H.: Multiagent systems engineering. International Journal on Software Engineering and Knowledge Engineering (**11**) 231–258
6. Bernon, C., Cossentino, M., Gleizes, M., Turci, P., Zambonelli, F.: A study of some multi-agent meta-models. Lecture Notes in Computer Science **3382** (Jan 2005) 62 – 77
7. Cossentino, M.: From requirements to code with the passi methodology. In Henderson-Sellers, B., Giorgini, P., eds.: Agent-Oriented Methodologies, Idea Group Inc. (2005 (in printing))
8. Cossentino, M., Seidita, V.: Composition of a new process to meet agile needs using method engineering. In Ed., E., ed.: LNCS Series. (2004) 36–51
9. Chella, A., Cossentino, M., Sabatucci, L., Seidita, V.: From passi to agile passi : tailoring a design process to meet new needs. In: 2004 IEEE/WIC/ACM International Joint Conference on Intelligent Agent Technology (IAT-04), Beijing, China (2004)
10. Brinkkemper, S.: Method engineering: engineering the information systems development methods and tools. Information and Software Technology **37** (1995)
11. Kumar, K., Welke, R.: Methodology engineering: a proposal for situation-specific methodology construction. Challenges and Strategies for Research in Systems Development (1992) 257–269
12. Saeki, M.: Software specification & design methods and method engineering. International Journal of Software Engineering and Knowledge Engineering (1994)
13. Beck, K., al.M. Beedle, van Bennekum, A., Cockburn, A., Cunningham, W., Fowler, M., Grenning, J., Highsmith, J., Hunt, A., Jeffries, R., Kern, J., Marick, B., Martin, R., Mellor, S., Schwaber, K., Sutherland, J., Thomas, D.: (Agile manifesto) http://www.agilemanifesto.org.
14. Alliance, A.: (http://www.agilealliance.org)
15. Zambonelli, F., Jennings, N., Wooldridge, M.: Developing multiagent systems: the gaia methodology. ACM Transactions on Software Engineering and Methodology **12** (2003) 417–470
16. Bergenti, F., Gleizes, M.P., Zambonelli, F.: Methodologies and Software Engineering for Agent Systems. Kluwer (2004)

The Synthesis Stage in the Software Agent Development Process

Fernando Alonso[1], Sonia Frutos[1], Loïc Martínez[1], and F. Javier Soriano[1]

[1] Facultad de Informática, Universidad Politécnica de Madrid,
28660 Boadilla del Monte (Madrid), Spain
{falonso, sfrutos, loic, jsoriano}@fi.upm.es

Abstract. In most existing software agents methodologies, system analysis is dependent on an agent-oriented, object-oriented or knowledge-based design paradigm. This simplifies the complex transformation of the conceptual model produced during analysis into the physical model output at design time. We, like other authors, believe that the conceptual model has to be conceived as independent of the design paradigm and that the physical model should be driven by the solution, both models leading to very different conceptions of the problem. In this paper we present the SONIA agents development methodology that includes a transitional synthesis stage between analysis and architectural design that mends the break between the construction of the two models.

1 Introduction

The software agent development process, and generally any software development process, can be viewed as the application of three transformations [1] (Fig. 1): requirements in the application domain are transformed into a conceptual model of the problem (T1- *Analysis*). The conceptual model is transformed into a physical model that represents the software product properties (T2-*Design*). And the physical model is transformed into a computable model, the program (T3-*Implementation*).

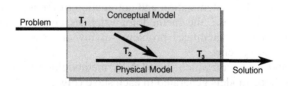

Fig. 1. The essential software process

The conceptual and physical models are two very different ways of looking at the problem, and its implementation involves a drastic change in the use of processes, methods and tools.

Additionally, there is no perfect method for either model [2]. The current trend is, therefore, to integrate different methods, tools and techniques, using whichever is the best in each individual situation. This raises the analysis dilemma: developers have to

M. Pěchouček, P. Petta, and L.Z. Varga (Eds.): CEEMAS 2005, LNAI 3690, pp. 193–202, 2005.
© Springer-Verlag Berlin Heidelberg 2005

choose the best suited techniques for each problem. To make this decision, developers have to analyse the problem and choose a method of analysis before they are really familiar with the problem. If the chosen technique uses design terminology, then the problem-solving paradigm has been preconditioned, and this paradigm could turn out not to be the best suited when the problem has been analysed in detail. In conclusion, a good methodology should not force a given architecture upon developers from the very beginning. It is the outcome of the system specifications analysis that should point developers towards the best suited architecture for solving the problem [3].

By contrast with this idea, most agent methodologies propose design paradigm-dependent analysis to elude these problems and bridge the gap between the implementation of the two models (for example, Tropos [4], Gaia[5], Prometheus [6], MAS-CommonKADS [7]).

In this paper, we briefly describe a methodological approach that defines an architecture-independent generic analysis model, including, as the first design phase stage, a synthesis stage (which is the paper's core), that smoothes the step from the conceptual to the formal model. In Section 2, we describe the structure of the proposed SONIA methodology. Section 3 details the synthesis stage, and Section 4 states the conclusions on the advantage of this approach.

2 SONIA Methodology

Based on research and development efforts in the field of AOSE (Agent Oriented Software Engineering), we think that an agent-oriented development methodology should have the following features [8]: (i) it should not condition the use of the agent paradigm right from analysis; (ii) it should naturally lead to the conclusion of whether or not it is feasible to develop the system as a MAS; (iii) it should systematically identify the components of a MAS, if the problem specifications call for an agent society; (iv) it should naturally lead to this organizational model; (v) it should produce reusable agents; and, (vi) it should be easy to apply and not require too much knowledge of agent technology.

The SONIA (Set of mOdels for a Natural Identification of Agents) methodology [8] basically embraces the previous approaches: the generation of a multi-agent architecture to solve a problem (whose conceptualization is not conditioned by the agent paradigm) and the systemization and automation of the activities of identifying MAS components. Likewise, the methodology defines an agent society model that flexibly and dynamically facilitates problem solving and can be used to integrate indispensable legacy systems.

The phases and stages of which the SONIA methodology is composed are listed below, along with the models generated in each stage (Fig. 2):

– *Conceptualization*: The problem is analyzed using the Set Theory Based Conceptual Model (SETCM) [9,10], an analysis method that was defined to combine a formal foundation with a pragmatic approach. This analysis method is design-independent.

   The result is an *Initial Structural Model*, which describes the overall structure of the domain (concepts, associations, attributes, classifications, etc.) and an *Initial Task Model*, which describes the problems to be solved (tasks) and the task decomposition and control of the resolution of the subtasks (task methods).

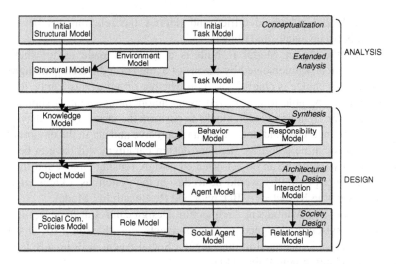

Fig. 2. Phases of the SONIA methodology

- *Extended Analysis*: Having conceptualized the problem, the models built are refined and expanded to capture the system environment and external entities.

    The Extended Analysis Stage produces the following models: an *Environment Model*, which defines the external system entities and system interactions with these entities; a *Structural Model*, which can extend the system knowledge with knowledge that the external entities supply to the system; and a *Task Model*, which can extend the tasks performed by the system with any tasks required to interact with external entities.

- *Synthesis*: This stage provides the building blocks for the component-driven bottom-up identification of agents that is performed during the design. In this process, basic elements are identified first (bottom level) and are used to identify and define agents (top level).

    It produces the following models: a *Knowledge Model*, which identifies the knowledge blocks inherent to the problem by grouping concepts and associations from the Structural Model; a *Behavior Model*, produced by grouping tasks, subtasks and methods from the Task Model; a *Responsibility Model*, output by establishing the relationships between knowledge blocks and behaviors, and a *Goal Model*, which represents the main objectives of the system. This stage bridges domain-dependent analysis and (software) solution-dependent design and is described in detail under point 3.

- *Architectural Design*: The purpose of the second stage of Multiagent Architecture Design is to define the architectural elements by means of the following models: an *Agent Model*, which identifies and defines, from the Knowledge, Behavior, Responsibility and Goal Models, what elements should be designed as autonomous agents; an *Object Model*, which identifies and defines, from the Knowledge and Responsibility Models, what passive elements there are in the environment; and an

Interaction Model, which identifies and defines the relationships between the agents and between agents and objects.

Not until the Agent Model is built is a decision made as to whether the architecture can be implemented by means of agents or a different paradigm needs to be used. This choice is chiefly based on whether or not agents can be identified. For an entity to be able to considered as an autonomous agent, it should have a behavior and the right knowledge blocks to perform the tasks of this behavior, have at least one defined goal and one utility, and perceive and act in the environment.

If no agents can be identified, another design paradigm will have to be chosen. One possibility would be an object-oriented design, reusing Object and Interaction Models. Another possibility would be to design the system as a knowledge-based system, reusing the Knowledge, Behavior and Responsibility Model.

– *Society Design*: The Multiagent Architecture Design can result in an *agent society*, in which the system is designed as a set of agents embedded in a social structure. Several models are generated in this stage: a Social Agent, a Role, a Relationship, and a Social Commitment Policy [11].

3 Synthesis Stage

As mentioned earlier, we consider a design paradigm-independent analysis to be best. In this case, the step from analysis models to architectural design models is usually a traumatic process because they are too far apart. Thus, the transition to design has to be undertaken with special care (Fig. 3).

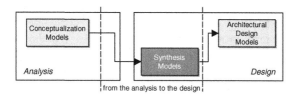

Fig. 3. Transition from analysis models to design models

This approach is based on synthesizing information of the analysis models as higher-level structures related to the reference paradigm, that is, restructuring the analysis information to adapt it to the design tools. Synthesis is the first design phase, whereby the viewpoint switches from the domain (analysis) to the solution (design). Consequently, it should ease the identification and formalization of computable structures that are coherent with agent orientation from the analysis models.

The Synthesis stage produces the models that are used later for the component-driven identification of agents. For this purpose, it re-groups elements of the Structural and Task Models to produce four other models: a Knowledge Model, a Behavior Model, a Responsibility Model, and a Goal Model.

The process of outputting these models and their application to a real case study, ALBOR (Barrier-Free Computer Access)[1], is described in the following sections [10]. ALBOR was conceived as an Internet-based intelligent system designed to provide guidance on the evaluation of disabled people's computer access skills and on the choice of the best suited assistive technologies.

3.1 Knowledge Model

The *Knowledge Model* can identify the knowledge blocks by grouping Structural Model concepts and associations. The knowledge blocks will be used internally or shared by the agents.

These clusters are identified on the basis of the concepts and associations of which they are composed, which meet the following conditions:

- They are strongly related to each other. The clusters are internally highly cohesive.
- They have little relationship to the other concepts and associations (low-coupled grouping).
- They are used to perform the same tasks.

The activities to be performed to output the first version of the Knowledge Model are:

1. Identify clusters of concepts and/or associations
2. Identify relations between knowledge blocks
3. Describe knowledge blocks

A new technique modifying Kelly's Trait Analysis [12] was used to identify concepts and associations. This technique identifies clusters of concepts and associations that have the first two properties of a knowledge block: high cohesion and low coupling.

To systematize the application of this technique, the conceptual diagram of the Structural Model is first transformed into a directed graph, as follows:

- For each concept and association create a graph node.
- For each association, create an arc from each association source concept node to the association node and an arc from the association node to the association target concept node.
- For each classification, create an arc from each subconcepts node to the superconcept node.

Then a 2D table is built that stores the connectivity (number of arcs or connections) between each pair of nodes in the graph. Finally, the Trait Analysis-based technique is applied using the connectivity between two graph clusters as a measure of comparison. The technique will involve iteratively applying the clustering algorithm until no more concepts and/or associations can be clustered.

Fig. 4 shows the conversion of the ALBOR conceptual diagram output during analysis into a directed graph and groupings of concepts/associations (knowledge blocks). In this step, we obtain three knowledge blocks *KB1*, *KB2* and *KB3*.

---

[1] ALBOR is a project funded by the UPM (Technical University of Madrid) and IMSERSO (Spanish Institute of Migrations and Social Services).

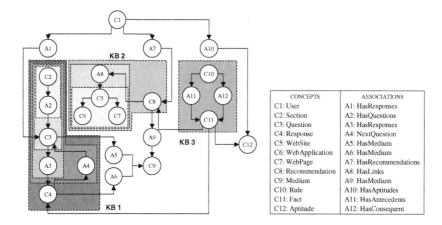

Fig. 4. Clusters of concepts/associations (knowledge blocks)

This technique makes no distinction between concepts and associations when transforming the conceptual diagram into a graph. Therefore, we will have to apply the rules listed in Table 1 to check whether or not the clusters are valid.

Table 1. Rules for dealing with invalid relations (r) between knowledge blocks (k) / concepts (c) / associations (a), siendo s un concepto o una asociación perteneciente al origen de a

Components	Rules for dealing with invalid relations
$r(k, c)$	R1: IsAssociation(r) $\wedge$ IsSource(c, r) $\rightarrow$ Add c to k
	R2: IsAssociation(r) $\wedge$ IsTarget(c, r) $\rightarrow$ Do not add c to k {r will be dealt with at later stages}
	R3: IsClassification(r) $\wedge$ IsSubconcept(c, r) $\rightarrow$ Add c to k {c belongs to knowledge block containing the classification's superconcept}
	R4: IsClassification(r) $\wedge$ IsSuperconcept(c, r) $\rightarrow$ Do not add c to k {r will be dealt with at later stages}
$r(k, a)$	R5: $\neg$HasAttributes(a) $\wedge$ Source(a) = {s} $\wedge$ (Cardinality(s, a) = 0..1 $\vee$ Cardinality(s, a) = 1..1) $\wedge$ $s \in k \rightarrow$ Add a to k
	R6: $\neg$HasAttributes(a) $\wedge$ $\forall s \in$ Source(a) (Cardinality(s, a) = 0..* $\vee$ Cardinality(s,a) = 1..*) $\wedge$ $\forall s \in$ Source(a) $s \in k \rightarrow$ Add a to k
	R7: HasAttributes(a) $\vee$ ($\exists$ $s \in$ Source(a) (Cardinality(s, a) = 0..* $\vee$ Cardinality(s, a) = 1..*)) $\vee$ ($\exists k_1,k_2 \exists s_1,s_2 \in$ Source(a) $k_1 \neq k_2 \wedge s_1 \in k_1 \wedge s_2 \in k_2$) $\rightarrow$ Do not add a to k {r will be dealt with at later stages}

The knowledge blocks identified in Fig. 4 are modified as a result of applying these rules. Associations $A5$ and $A6$ are added to the knowledge block *KB1* applying rule *R5*. *C12* is added to *KB3* applying *R3* and *A9* is added to *KB2* applying *R5*.

The resulting clusters of the first version of the model can only satisfy the conditions of being highly cohesive and fairly unrelated to other clusters. The final version of the model, which is output when the Responsibility Model is completed, will meet all the conditions.

3.2 Behavior Model

The *Behavior Model* is the result of grouping tasks and methods of the Task Model. The behaviors will be part of the agents.

These clusters are characterized because the tasks and subtasks of the grouping:

– Depend on others through task methods.
– Use the same knowledge blocks for problem solving.

The activities to be performed to output the first version of the Behavior Model are:

1. Identify clusters of tasks and/or subtasks
2. Identify time dependences between behaviors
3. Describe behaviors

In this first version of the Behavior Model, one cluster is generated for each first-level task in the task/method diagram of the Task Model, adding its subtasks to the cluster. Fig. 5 shows the cluster of ALBOR tasks/methods (*B1, B2, B3* and *B4*). The time dependences between behaviors are then calculated from the preconditions and postconditions of these clusters. A behavior *B2* depends on a behavior *B1*, if there is a knowledge block (and concepts and/or associations) in the postcondition of *B1* that is also in the precondition of *B2*.

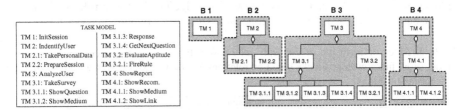

Fig. 5. Clusters of tasks/methods (behaviors)

The resulting clusters for the first version of the model can only satisfy the condition of interdependency through task methods. The final version, which is output when the Responsibility Model is completed, will meet all the conditions.

3.3 Responsibility Model

The *Responsibility Model* is output by relating knowledge blocks to behaviors. This model is essential for identifying agents and environment objects. A basic activity is to refine the Knowledge and Behavior Models to meet all their conditions.

The activities to be performed to output the Responsibility Model and the final versions of the Knowledge and Behavior Models are:

1. Identify the use relations of concepts/associations/knowledge blocks in behaviors
2. Modify the Knowledge Model
3. Modify the Behavior Model
4. Identify responsibilities between knowledge blocks and behaviors
5. Describe responsibilities

The Knowledge and Behavior Models are refined first by identifying the use relations between concepts/associations/knowledge blocks in behaviors and incorporating in a 2D table. A mark will be placed at the intersection between a behavior with a concept/association/knowledge block if they are used to perform a task/subtask belonged to that behavior (that is, if it appears in the precondition or postcondition of the task/subtask) (see Table 2).

Table 2. Relations of use between concepts/associations/knowledge blocks and behaviors

		Behaviors			
		B1	B2	B3	B4
Concepts / Aassociations	C1	X	X	X	X
	A1			X	
	A7			X	
	C9			X	X
	A10			X	
KnowledgeBlocks	KB1			X	
	KB2				X
	KB3			X	

To output the final Knowledge Model, all the concepts/associations will have to be included in one knowledge block. The rules in Table 3 can be used to determine when to add a concept/association to an existing knowledge block or when to cluster a number of concepts/associations as a new knowledge block. These rules of inclusion will be based on the use relations of concepts/associations in output tasks/subtasks.

Table 3. Rules of inclusion of concepts (c) / associations (a) of the unclustered Structural Model (usm) in knowledge blocks based on relations $X{:}Y$ (where X are tasks/subtasks and Y are concepts/associations)

Inclusion Rules
(r = 1:1 ∨ r = 1:N) ∧ (c/a are not related to other elements of usm) ∨ (c/a are related to other elements of usm ∧ the constraints in Table 1 hold) → Cluster c/a in an existing knowledge block
(r = N:M) ∧ (c/a are not related to other elements of usm ∨ (c/a are related to other elements of usm ∧ the constraints in Table 1 hold) → Cluster c/a∈ r to form a new knowledge block

The following actions are taken taking into account the relations of use (Table 2) and inclusion rules (Table 3). Concepts *C1* and *C9* have a N:M relation with more than one behavior, which means that two knowledge blocks (*KB4* that contains the concept *C1* and *KB5* the concept *C9*) are created. On the other hand, concepts *A1*, *A7* and *A10* have a 1:N relations with behavior *B3* and can be added to the knowledge to which they are related (*A1*, *A7* and *A10* are included in *KB4*).

To output the final Behavior Model, the behaviors will have to meet the second of the conditions set out in its definition. This condition demands that the same knowledge block should be used to perform the tasks of a single behavior. The rules in Table 4 can be used to evaluate whether more than one behavior should be clustered as one or divided into more than one behavior on the basis of the use relations of concepts/associations in the output tasks/subtasks.

Table 4. Rules of behavior clustering/division based on relations (r) $X{:}Y$ (where X are behaviors and Y is knowledge block)

Clustering/division rules
r = 1:N → divide behaviors into more than one behavior.
{Algorithm: each behavior will contain a subtask of the next level of decomposition of the main task of the divided behavior. Analyze the relations between the new behaviors and the new knowledge block to check that they are 1:1. If so, stop; otherwise, divide the behaviors again}
r = N:1 → cluster the behaviors into one

As a result of applying these rules, behavior *B3* is divided into two behaviors in ALBOR. On the other hand, there were no behavior clusters.

3.4 Goal Model

The *Goal Model* is composed of the system objectives. The aim of this model is to be able to identify agent goals. The agent will execute behaviors to achieve its goals.

The activities to be performed to output the Goal Model are:

1. Identify goals
2. Describe goals

These goals are logical conditions imposed on the state of knowledge and are identified from Behavior Model task postconditions. The goals are a subset of the union of the postconditions of the behaviors that define the system goals. The designer's task is to decide which subset of postconditions defines the system goals.

In ALBOR, a single goal "new Users.recommendations" has been identified for the EvaluateAptitude behavior (B4), whose meaning is to get new recommendations for a user.

3.5 Transition to Architectural Design Phase

The agents and objects were identified during architectural design from the Responsibility Model. The knowledge shared by several behaviors was chosen as *objects*. Following this criterion, we identified the "Users" and "Media" objects (white box in Fig. 6).

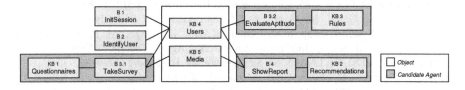

Fig. 6. Identification of objects and candidate agents

A *candidate agent* will be output for each knowledge block that is the responsibility of a sole behavior (relation 1:1). In the case of ALBOR, three candidate agents were identified: 'Survey-Taker' agent (*B3.1* and *KB1*), 'Decision-Maker' agent (*B3.2* and *KB3*) and 'Advisor' agent (*B4* and *KB2*) (grey box in Fig. 6). The *B1* and *B2* were not assigned, because they do not have any proper knowledge.

Not all candidate agents will be converted to agents. This will be confined to agents that meet all the requirements for becoming an *autonomous agent*, i.e. agents that have at least one defined goal and utility, and sense and act in the environment. In ALBOR, the three candidate agents identified earlier meet these two conditions and qualify as autonomous agents.

4   Conclusions

This paper aims to contribute to the methodological issue of agent-based development by defining a new methodology, SONIA, that includes a synthesis stage to smooth the transition between the design paradigm-independent analysis and paradigm-dependent multiagent architectural design. For this purpose, we described the models underlying this synthesis stage (knowledge, behavior, responsibiliy and goal model) and the mechanisms for building them.

References

1. Blum, B. I. Beyond Programming, Oxford University Press, New York (1996)
2. Shapiro, S. Splitting the difference: the historical necessity of synthesis in software engineering. IEEE Annals of the History of Computing, 19(1) (1997) 20-54
3. Alonso, F., de Antonio, A., González, A. L., Fuertes, J. L., Martínez, L.A.: Towards a Unified Methodology for Software Engineering and Knowledge Engineering. Proc. of the IEEE International Conference on Systems, Man and Cybernetics (IEEE SMC'98), San Diego, USA (1998) 4890-4895
4. Bresciani, P, Giorgini, P, Giunchiglia, F and Mylopoulos, J Tropos: An Agent Oriented Software Development Methodology, Int. J. of Autonomous Agent and MultiAgent System, 8(3) (2004) 203-236
5. Zambonelli, F, Jennings, N R, and Wooldridge, M Developing Multiagent Systems: The Gaia Methodology, ACM Transactions on Software Engineering and Methodology, 12(3) (2003) 317-370
6. Padgham, L and Winikoff, M Prometheus: A Methodology for Developing Intelligent Agents, in: Giunchiglia, F, Odell, J, and Weiss, G (eds.): Agent-Oriented Software Engineering III, LNCS 2585, Springer-Verlag, Heidelberg (2003) 174-185
7. Iglesias, C A, Garijo, M, González, J C, and Velasco, J R Analysis and Design of Multiagent Systems using MAS-CommonKADS, in: Singh, M P, Rao A S, and Wooldridge, M (eds.): Intelligent Agents IV: Agent Theories, Architectures, and Languages (ATAL97), LNAI 1365, Springer-Verlag, Heidelberg (1999) 313-326
8. Alonso, F., Frutos, S., Martínez, L.A., Montes, C.: SONIA: A Methodology for Natural Agent Development. In: Gleizes, M. P., Omicini, A., Zambonelli, F. (eds.): Engineering Societies in the Agents World V, LNCS/LNAI 3451, Springer-Verlag, Heidelberg (2005) 245-260
9. Martínez, L.A.: Method for Independent Problem Analysis. PhD Thesis. Universidad Politécnica de Madrid. Spain (2003)
10. Alonso, F., Frutos, S., Fuertes, J. L., Martínez, L. A., Montes, C.: ALBOR. An Internet-Based Advisory KBS with a Multi-Agent Architecture. Int. Conference on Advances in Infrastructure for Electronic Business, Science, And Education on the Internet (SSGRR 2001), L'Aquila, Italy (2001) 1-6
11. Alonso, F., Fernández, F., López, G., Rojas, F., Soriano, J.: Intelligent Virtual Agent Societies on the Internet. In: de Antonio, A., Aylett, R., Ballin, D. (eds.): Intelligent Virtual Agents, LNCS/LNAI 2190, Springer Verlag, Heidelberg, Berlin (2001) 100-111
12. Kelly, G. A.: The Psychology of Personal Constructs. Norton (1995)

Use Case and Actor Driven Requirements Engineering: An Evaluation of Modifications to Prometheus

Mikhail Perepletchikov and Lin Padgham

RMIT University,
School of Computer Science and Information Technology
{mikhailp, linpa}@cs.rmit.edu.au

Abstract. This paper describes modifications to the System Specificaton Phase of the Prometheus agent development methodology. The modifications include introduction of actors, and provision of additional structure to the System Specification Phase of Prometheus. The introduction of actors and additional structure leads to better understanding of the system and its environment, and allows the intended users of the system to be directly involved in the system specification process. Also, the proposed approach is use-case driven, thus conforming to the approach prescribed by Rational Unified Process (RUP). The refined methodology has been evaluated by volunteering RMIT students taking a class on 'Agent-Oriented Programming and Design'. Results indicate that the refined methodology is more systematic, produces a more balanced set of design artifacts and is perceived by users to be less complex.

1 Introduction

For building large, industrial multi-agent systems a solid well developed Agent Oriented Software Engineering methodology is required, to guide developers through the system development lifecycle. Prometheus [1] is one such methodology. Prometheus is quite detailed, providing substantial guidance to the developer regarding various aspects of system design, and how design artefacts should relate to each other. This detailed, structured guidance is important for obtaining well designed systems, particularly when using a new or unfamiliar paradigm. However the initial phase of System Specification is less structured than other parts of the methodology. In particular, the identification of initial scenarios, percepts and actions have not been associated with clear processes.

This work addresses that weakness by introducing actors, and providing greater structure for the first phase of Prometheus. This includes refinements to make it use-case driven, thus conforming to the guidelines specified by Rational Unified Process [2,3]. The approach developed was then empirically compared to the original Prometheus System Specification Phase, using students in an agent programming and design course. The evaluation indicated that the changes led to a more systematic process for the elicitation of the initial system goals, use-case scenarios, percepts and actions. These results were statistically significant using standard statistical analasys.

In the following sections we introduce the Prometheus methodology, and the refinements and modifications we have made to the System Specification phase. Then we describe the evaluation process and present an analysis of the results. In concluding we briefly review related work in agent oriented requirements engineering.

M. Pěchouček, P. Petta, and L.Z. Varga (Eds.): CEEMAS 2005, LNAI 3690, pp. 203–212, 2005.

2   Overview of the Prometheus Methodology

The Prometheus methodology contains three main design phases: (i) System Specification, (ii) Architectural Design, (iii) Detailed Design. Each of these contains a number of structured processes and results in specified design artifacts. We describe them briefly, with particular attention to the System Specification phase.

System Specification System specification in Prometheus consists of a number of interleaving, iterative steps, to define goals, functionalities, scenarios and environmental interface in the form of actions and percepts. An early step is to define a set of initial high-level goals that specify the reasons for building the system. These goals can then be refined by using the informal technique of asking 'how can we achieve this goal?' [4]. The goal refinement process results in a number of sub-goals for every original goal under consideration. Similar subgoals are then grouped together to provide a framework for the specification of functionalities. Another step is the development of scenarios that demonstrate how processes are composed within the system. There is also a step to specify the set of actions and percepts that constitute the system interface with the environment.

The scenarios used in Prometheus are more comprehensive than those used in OO analysis, and the techniques for defining alternative cases are defined. The main part of a scenario consists of a sequence of steps. Possible steps are achieving a Goal, performing an Action, receiving a Percept, or executing a nested Scenario.

Most of the activities of the System Specification Phase of Prometheus are supported by the 'Prometheus Design Tool' (PDT), a freely available prototype software design tool available at: www.cs.rmit.edu.au/agents/pdt

Architectural Design The Architectural Design phase uses artifacts produced in the System Specification Phase to determine what *agents* will be included in the system and the interaction between these agents. The interactions between agents are modelled using *interaction diagrams* and *interaction protocols*. The interaction diagrams are developed by refining scenarios identified in the previous phase. Also, the overall system structure is captured using a system overview diagram. In addition, the *messages* between agents and *shared data* repositories are determined.

Detailed Design The Detailed Design phase uses artifacts produced in the Architectural Design Phase to define the internals of every agent in the system and to specify how agents accomplish their overall tasks. Each agent is refined in terms of its *capabilities*, *internal events*, *plans*, and *data structures*. Each capability has the capability overview diagram that captures design of the plans within this capability and the events that are associated with these plans. The dynamic behavior is described by *process specifications* based on the interaction protocols identified in the previous phase.

3   Modified System Specification Phase

The revised system specification process consists of the following steps: (i) Identification of *actors* and their interactions with the system; (ii) Developing *scenarios* illustrating the system's operation; (iii) Identification of the *system goals* and sub-goals;

(iv) Specifying the interface between the system and its environment in terms of *actions, percepts* and any *external data*; (v) Grouping goals and other items into the basic *functionalities* of the system.

The first modification of the original Prometheus process is the addition of *actors* for which the system has relevance. These actors are any persons or roles which will interact with the system, as well as any other stakeholders whose goals should be considered. Actors may be other software systems, as well as humans. The concept of Actor is not new in the AO development methodologies, for example Tropos methodology also uses actors in its Early and Late Requirements Phases [5].

Use cases are then developed for each actor that will interact with the system, in much the same way as for object oriented analysis. The input from actor to agent system is then identified as a *percept*, while the outputs from system to actors are defined as *actions*. This process results in improved structure for identifying percepts and actions. Each use case identified based on actors becomes an initial scenario.

The second modification is that scenarios are linked to goals in a similar way to that of the Goal-Scenario coupling framework (GSCF) [6] which is based around the notion of a Requirement Chunk (RC) (a pair of <Goal, Scenario>). Since a goal can be described as a contextual property of a scenario, and scenarios show concrete steps for achieving a goal, the correlation between goal-oriented and scenario-driven approaches can bring a number of benefits as described in [6]. The linkage used in the revised Prometheus is not as strict as the one used in GSCF[1]. We use a unidirectional coupling where each scenario necessarily has a goal which is linked to it (where we also use the same name), but the more specific goals may not require a scenario.

Each initially identified scenario is then developed, with a number of detailed steps, where each step is a *goal, scenario, action* or *percept*. A step *other* is also allowed within Prometheus. With the coupling identified above, any nested scenario identified, automatically introduces a goal. Goals introduced as steps may warrant development of a scenario, in which case the goal step is automatically modified to be a scenario step.

Initial goals are identified via the initial use-cases as described above, and also by examining the initial system description. Further goals are then identified by a process of abstraction and refinement [7]. For each goal, we ask the question *how?* and *why?*, thus identifying new goals, and forming a goal hierarchy.

One further modification that is introduced is the notion of two kinds of goal refinement: *AND-refinement* and *OR-refinement* as described by van Lamsweerde [7]. If a goal is AND-refined, we mean that subgoals (or answers to the question *how?*) are steps in achieving the overall goal, and each step must be done. If it is OR-refined, then subgoals are alternative ways of achieving the goal, and doing any one of them is sufficient. Agent systems typically have both these kinds of refinements. OR-refinements allow for choice in the way of achieving goals, while AND-refinements allow for breaking down into smaller pieces. This process supports calculations for scoping as described in [8].

Finally, after goals and scenarios are sufficiently developed, goals are grouped into functionalities, where similar goals are grouped together. Actions and percepts are also allocated to functionalities. Scenarios are then annotated with information about which functionality each step belongs to.

---

[1] In GSCF, every goal must be linked to a scenario, and vice-versa.

4   Evaluation of Revised System Specification

In order to evaluate the revised Prometheus, it was compared to the original methodology in a study using volunteering RMIT students from a class in agent oriented programming and design. Although students are a different group than professional software engineers, we have observed in our work with industry, that as agent oriented programming is a new paradigm, experienced engineers need a similar level of guidance to that required by students. Also, the class contained some graduate students with professional experience. Thus, although there are some limitations to the data, and further analysis would be desirable, we consider there is good reason to believe it to be valid.

The study had eighteen students, randomly assigned to two control and two experimental groups. The control groups used the original Prometheus' system specification process for an assignment, while the experimental groups used the revised process. Both groups also answered a questionnaire.

The experimental groups were provided with a detailed description of the activities used in the revised System Specification phase, similar in level of detail to the description of the original System Specification phase provided to the class as a whole, within the textbook [1]. The experimental groups also had a short face-to-face session to answer any questions regarding the revised methodology. The original System Specification phase was presented at a two-hour lecture to the whole class.

The small assignment that the students were working on, was based on a hypothetical Meeting Scheduler system to assist academics in organising meetings. The students were asked to develop a system specification for this system. This was worked on during two, two-hour, group-based tutorial sessions and was then completed and submitted individually. In addition to final submissions, we collected data at the end of the first two hour tutorial, regarding numbers of goals, functionalities, scenarios, percepts and actions that had been identified.

The questionnaire used to compare the revised with the original approach,was structured using mostly quantitative responses in order to facilitate statistical analysis of the results. The questions were related to the perceived degree of difficulty in identifying scenarios, goals, actions and percepts. The students were also asked to indicate an approximate number of hours spent on the assignment and to rate the overall complexity of the approach used. Steps were taken to ensure that participation in the study in no way affected student grades. Subsequent analysis of marks distribution confirmed that there was no significant difference in marks between the two populations.

In order to explore differences between the two approaches, we counted the numbers of each concept type that were identified and described. The relevant concepts at this stage are: goals, scenarios, percepts, actions and functionalities. Actors are relevant only for the revised approach and so were not counted. We then looked at two issues with regard to this data. The first was any difference between the two groups in terms of average instances of a concept being specified. The second was variation across each population in terms of the number of instances of each concept that were identified. This was an attempt to assess how systematic the process was.

Significance was assessed using the *t-Test* for the difference between the means of two independent groups [9], and the ***F-Test*** for the difference in the variances of two independent groups [9]. A p-value of 0.05 or smaller was considered to be statistically significant, as is standard practice.

Answers to the questionnaire were also analysed for differences in mean values, and for differences in variance between groups, using the same tests as for numbers of concepts specified. Number of hours spent was also analysed similarly.

5   Results of Comparison

We present firstly our results in terms of numbers of concepts identified, both after the initial two hours work, and in the final assignment. Then we present results based on answers to the questionnaire, including analysis of differences in time taken to complete the work.

5.1   Concept Identification

The following analysis discusses results regarding each of the artifacts in turn. Figure 1 shows the average number of system specification artifacts identified by the students during the **first** tutorial. Figure 3 shows the same data for the final assignment. Figures 2 - 4 show variances in numbers of identified artifacts based on the initial and final assignment data for both groups.

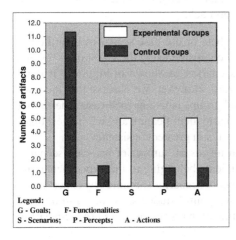
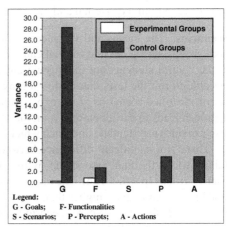

Fig. 1. Means for interim number of each concept type identified

Fig. 2. Variance in interim numbers of each concept type identified

Goals. Both average number and variance of goals showed significant difference after the initial tutorial ($p = 0.00994$ and $p = 0.00247$ respectively), with control students identifying 80% more goals at this stage than experimental students, as shown in figure 1. The larger number of goals identified early on by the control group can be attributed to the difference in the process, as experimental students iterated more over actors, use-case scenarios, goals actions and percepts. The reduced variance for the experimental

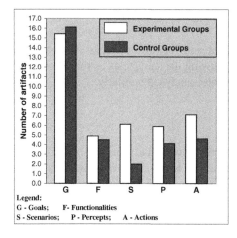

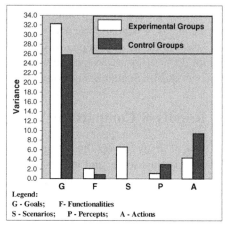

Fig. 3. Means for final number of each concept type identified

Fig. 4. Variance in final numbers of each concept type identified

group (figure 2) can be interpreted as evidence of a more systematic structured process. There are no significant differences in means and variances in numbers of system goals submitted for the final assessment by both groups (figures 3 and 4). Variance in both groups is quite high, possibly indicating that the goal refinement process is quite subjective in both the original and modified approach.

Scenarios. The means and variances of numbers of use-case scenarios identified by both groups during the first tutorial cannot be compared using the t-Test or F-Test due to the control students not identifying any scenarios, as shown in Figure 1. It is not possible to run the tests due to division by zero. However, we observe that the number of identified scenarios of the experimental groups is five in each case. The revised approach leads to earlier emphasis on the scenario identification and we suggest that it also provides a systematic approach which results in greater consistency.

There is a significant difference between means of number of use-case scenarios submitted for the final assessment by the students belonging to the experimental and control groups ($p = 0.00136$). The mean number of scenarios submitted by experimental students is significantly higher than that of the control students, as shown in figure 3. We conclude that the use-case scenario identification process is more productive using the revised methodology.

The variances in number of scenarios submitted for the final assessment are also unable to be compared using the F-Test due to lack of any variance in the control group and subsequent division by zero problems. This lack of variance in the control group can be explained by the fact that the assignment required at least two scenarios to be submitted. The fact that all students in the control group submitted the minimum, whereas those in the experimental groups identified more scenarios than required, provides some evidence that the scenario identification process is easier in the revised approach.

Functionalities. There are no significant differences in the number of identified functionalities during the first tutorial, and in the number of functionalities submitted for the assessment by both groups. Also, the variations between both groups are not significantly different. This is unsurprising as the modified methodology does not introduce any changes to the functionality-related processes.

Percepts and Actions. The experimental group identified significantly more percepts and actions during the initial two hours as shown in figure 1 ($p = 0.00007$). This can be explained, as previously, by the different initial focus in the two methodologies.

Initial variance cannot be compared due to lack of any variance in the experimental group (figure 2). This shows high consistency between the experimental students when identifying percepts/actions. Given the small number of percepts/actions identified by the control students, the associated variance is relatively large (4.67), indicating less structure for identification of percepts/actions in the original approach.

In the final assessment, the only significant difference was for the mean number of percepts, with the experimental group being significantly higher ($p = 0.02929$). For the final assessment, the mean number of actions, and the variances in both actions and percepts, were not significantly different between the two groups at the level of $p \leq 0.05$, however they show the same tendency towards higher average numbers, and less variance in the experimental group. This suggests the possibility of a more productive process for identification of the system interface.

5.2   Questionnaire

The questionnaire covered three areas: difficulty of identifying/specifying instances of the various concepts, complexity of the overall approach, and overall time taken for doing the system specification. We look at each of these in turn.

Time Spent. As all students spent four hours on the assignment within tutorials, we looked at additional time spent outside of class. The mean additional time spent by experimental students is 3.4 hours, while the mean additional time for control students is 4.8 hours. Although the mean time spent on the assignment by the experimental students is lower than that of the control students, the difference is not statistically significant at the level of $p \leq 0.05$ using the t-Test.

Although mean time spent was not significantly different between the two populations, the variance in time did differ significantly, with the experimental group showing significantly less variance ($p = 0.00374$). We suggest that this is evidence that the revised approach is more systematic than the original.

Overall Complexity. There is a significant difference between both means and variances of overall complexity ratings in the two groups (p equals to 0.01795 and 0.00974 respectively). Control students indicated a higher mean complexity(3.75 vs 2.5) and a higher variance in their ratings, as shown in figures 5 and 6.

We also note that **all** experimental students ranked overall complexity of the approach as either fairly low (2) or (3) which is the midpoint and possibly should be interpreted as undecided. Control students were split between high complexity (5) and fairly low (2), with a couple of midpoint scores. Half of the control students ranked complexity as high.

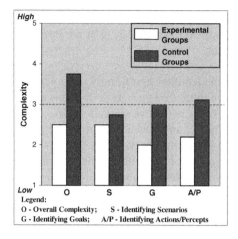
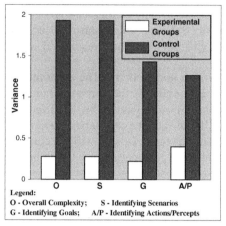

Fig. 5. Means of questionnaire responses regarding complexity

Fig. 6. Variance of questionnaire responses regarding complexity

Difficulty of individual System Specification Activities. There is a significant difference between both means and variances of difficulty ratings in the two groups in regards to goal identification activity (p equals to 0.02696 and 0.01835 respectively). Also, there are significant differences between variances of difficulty ratings in regards to scenario identification activity (p = 0.00974), and between means of difficulty ratings with regard to percept/action identification (p = 0.04199), as shown in figures 5 and 6.

Experimental students specified a lower mean difficulty, and their answers had lower variance for each activity under investigation. Although not every difference was significant at the level of $p \leq 0.05$, the trends towards lower difficulty ratings and lower variance in scores is similar to the statistically significant result with respect to the rating of an overall complexity.

We can also observe that **all** experimental students ranked difficulties of system specification activities as either low (1), fairly low (2) or undecided (3). Ratings of the difficulties of individual activities provided by the control students were, in contrast, scattered between high and low. Forty percent of the control students rated difficulty of the activities as either high (5) or fairly high (4), while another forty percent rated difficulty as fairly low (2) or low (1).

Also, we asked the experimental students to specify whether the introduction of actors helped them in developing the system specification. All ten experimental students said that the introduction of actors benefited them when working on the assignment.

5.3   Results Summary

– Less variance in numbers of initial system specification artifacts identified by experimental students supports the hypothesis that the revised methodology is more systematic. The difference in variances of the two groups is shown to be statistically significant for numbers of identified goals, scenarios, and percepts/actions.

- Higher mean numbers of use-case scenarios and percepts/actions submitted for the assessment by the experimental students supports the hypothesis that the revised methodology provides a more productive, guided approach for identification of use-case scenarios, and system interface components used in the System Specification Phase. The difference was statistically significant for submitted scenarios and percepts. The same trend can be observed for the number of submitted actions though it is not statistically significant.
- Lower complexity/difficulty ratings and lower variance in ratings of the experimental students supports the hypothesis that the revised methodology is easier to apply and understand than the original one, and that it can be used in a systematic, consistent manner. The difference in mean scores was statistically significant for the ratings of Overall Complexity, Identification of goals, and Identification of percepts/actions. The difference in variance was statistically significant for the ratings of Overall Complexity, Identification of goals, and Identification of scenarios.

6   Related Work

The use-case scenario is an important entity used in requirements modelling outside of the agent paradigm [10,3]. One of the main advantages of use-case scenarios is the ability to directly involve users of the system in the specification and analysis of the system. Scenarios demonstrate how processes are composed within the system. As such, developing scenarios can be a very effective way to elicit goals and to help in the discovery of various cases. Arguably, scenarios are easier to elaborate than goals [6], and since scenarios describe concrete steps for reacting to some input from the environment, they capture real-life requirements.

Although various RE approaches have argued a benefit in coupling goals and use cases [6,11], they usually do not describe any concrete steps for enforcing such coupling.

6.1   Comparison with Other AOSE Methodologies

There are a number of agent development methodologies in addition to Prometheus that consider requirements modelling as an important part of the methodology. Two of the most prominent of these are Tropos [5] and MaSE [12]. One of the differences between these methodologies is in the application of use-case scenarios. Prometheus and MaSE include scenarios as an important component of the system specification activities, whereas Tropos does not use scenarios in its system specification. Tropos instead contains an extension to the early and late requirements phases in the form of a specification language for requirements modelling - Formal Tropos, which allows for representation of the dynamic aspects of the model.

Although MaSE include use-case scenarios in its System Specification phase, the scenarios in MaSE are informally described, and they do not have any structure. Consequently, scenarios in MaSE cannot readily be traced to other phases of the system development life cycle, nor linked to goals. In Prometheus scenarios are structured, providing a good basis for automated support within a use-case driven approach similar to that used by RUP, where use-case models drive all phases of a software development life cycle [2,3].

7 Conclusions

By introducing actors, and scenario-goal coupling into the Prometheus methodology we have been able to develop a systematic process for the elicitation of the initial system goals, use-case scenarios, and percepts/actions. Each revised activity of the system Specification phase is shown to be more understandable to users. Also, the users of the revised methodology have been able to produce a more complete set of use-case scenarios, actions, and percepts, than the control groups.

By making the revised approach use-case driven we made it compatible with RUP, consequently narrowing a gap between agent development methodologies and established software development processes. The modified system specification phase of Prometheus is use-case and actor driven because: i) identification of actors and associated use-cases is the first step in the modified approach; ii) Prometheus' use-cases can be traced to the architectural and detailed design artifacts; iii) use-cases provide a foundation for scoping and iterative incremental development using Prometheus [8].

This work also indicated that development of the goal hierarchy contains a lot of variance. This is possibly an area where greater systematisation could be introduced.

References

1. Padgham, L., Winikoff, M.: Developing Intelligent Agent Systems: A Practical Guide. John Wiley And Sons Ltd, West Sussex, England (2004)
2. Kroll, P., Kruchten, P.: The Rational Unified Process Made Easy. Addison-Wesley, Reading, USA (2003)
3. Kruchten, P.: The Rational Unified Process: An Introduction, Third Edition. Addison-Wesley, Boston, USA (2004)
4. van Lamsweerde, A., Letier, E.: Handling obstacles in goal-oriented requirements engineering. Software Engineering **26** (2000) 978–1005
5. Bresciani, P., Giorgini, P., Giunchiglia, F., Mylopoulos, J., Perini, A.: TROPOS: An agent-oriented software development methodology. Autonomous Agents and Multi-Agent Systems **8** (2004) 203–236
6. Rolland, C., Souveyet, C., Achour, B.: Guiding goal modelling using scenarios. IEEE Transactions on Software Engineering, Special Issue on Scenario Management **24** (1998) 1055–1071
7. van Lamsweerde, A.: Goal-oriented requirements engineering: A guided tour. In: Proceedings of the 5th IEEE International Symposium on Requirements Engineering, Toronto, Canada (2001) 249–263
8. Perepletchikov, M., Padgham, L.: Systematic incremental development of agent systems, using Prometheus. In: Proceedings of the 1st International Workshop on Integration of Software Engineering and Agent Technology (ISEAT05) *Submitted*, Melbourne, Australia (2005)
9. Levine, D., Ramsey, P., Smidt, R.: Applied Statistics for Engineers and Scientists. Prentice-Hall, Inc., New Jersey, USA (2001)
10. Cockburn, A.: Structuring use cases with goals. Journal of Object-Oriented Programming **9** (1997) 35–40,56–62
11. Anton, A., Carter, R., Dagnino, A., Dempster, J., Siege, D.: Deriving goals from a use-case based requirements specification. Requirements Engineering Journal **6** (2001) 63–73
12. DeLoach, S.: Analysis and design using MaSE and agentTool. In: Proceedings of the 12th Midwest Artificial Intelligence and Cognitive Science Conference (MAICS 2001), Ohio, USA (2001)

Agent-Based Management of Non Urban Road Meteorological Incidents*

Vicente R. Tomás and Luís A. García

AiA- Applying Intelligent Agents Research Group. University Jaume I,
12071 Castellon, Spain
{vtomas, garcial}@icc.uji.es

Abstract. Current protocols for defining and developing traffic strategies for dealing with non urban road meteorological incidents are human-centric based. These protocols are not easy to implement and, often, they do not work as well as proposed. This is mainly due to the following reasons: 1) traffic flow information is usually distributed in several equipments belonging to different traffic management centres, so the traffic operators only have a reduced view of the overall incident information; and 2) there are several traffic administrations and offices with competences in traffic management, so operators from different administrations and offices have to manually coordinated competences, resources and information. A Multiagent System (MAS) able to help traffic operators to determine the best traffic strategies and to help them in coordinating tasks is proposed in this paper. The A-3 Spanish freeway, a real traffic domain, is being used as the non urban domain where the proposed MAS is being evaluated.

1 Introduction

The evolution of the technology has made possible the application of more sophisticated systems and knowledge models to traffic control and management, the Intelligent Transportation Systems (ITS). The main purpose of an ITS is to improve the traffic flow behavior and road safety [3]. Inside ITS, one of the main research topics are the so-called Advanced Traffic Management Systems (ATMS). The basic task of an ATMS is to support road managers in road management tasks [14].

This task turns out to be especially difficult in non urban networks due to several reasons: 1) non urban roads are characterized by huge coverage extensions of road sections; 2) ATMS and, more important, traffic information are usually distributed between several traffic management centers and traffic offices and administrations; 3) data capture stations are scarce with long distances between them; and 4) data capture stations have long data integration times (so, there are long time intervals without available real traffic data). Moreover, if a traffic incident (vehicle accidents, meteorological problems, road civil works, public events, etc.) is detected, its management usually involves not only several traffic management centers, but also several

---

* This research has been partly supported by the Spanish research projects CICYT DPI2002-04357-c03-02 and Fundacio Caixa- Castello P1 1B2003-36.

M. Pĕchouček, P. Petta, and L.Z. Varga (Eds.): CEEMAS 2005, LNAI 3690, pp. 213–222, 2005.

government offices and traffic polices. The human road manager must take decisions to deal with them as soon as possible. These difficulties are clearly identifiable in meteorological incidents (for instance snowfalls). In these incidents, the problem resolution involved several organisms (road managers, civil works, red cross, etc). Thus, the traffic strategies must be defined to: 1) guarantee traffic flows and road safety and 2) facilitate the actuation of the emergency services. The application of these traffic management strategies must be able to modify the traffic behavior in the incidents zone, but these strategies should also avoid that the incident zone was moved from its original zone to another, and probably worst, zone of the road network.

The set of traffic management strategies to be developed when an incident is detected is off-line collected in the so-called Traffic Management Plans (TMPs).The implementation of these TMPs usually involves negotiations between several traffic administrations. These negotiations are currently done by human road managers.

In this paper a MAS able to works with TMPs is presented. The MAS proposed supports road managers in managing and controlling traffic in the presence of meteorological incidents. The paper is organized as follows. Next section describes the actual procedures the road manager runs to deal with traffic incidents in non urban roads, i.e. the TMPs. HTML and XML computerized approaches to TMPs are also described. In section 3 we exposed the components of the non urban traffic ontology used by the proposed MAS. Section 4 describes the Multiagent system: its software architecture and the communication protocols defined and developed. Finally, the implementation issues and the conclusions and future work are exposed.

2 Procedures to Work with Traffic Incidences

TMPs are specific procedures that define how to manage the detected traffic incidents. These procedures are structured in three levels of information: scenarios, measures and actions [16].

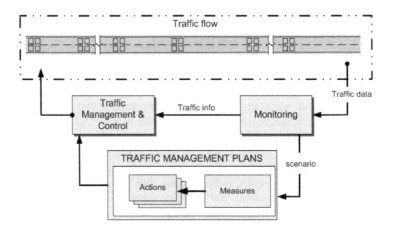

Fig. 1. Dependencies between the real traffic flow and TMPs

Figure 1 shows how TMPs are currently used to manage a traffic incident. If an incident is detected, the monitoring system warns the traffic operator. The scenario is determined from the incident information (location, severity degree, etc) and also from the values of several traffic parameters related to the incident influence area (flow rates, incident severity, weather forecast, etc). Every scenario has assigned a set of available measures that can be activated: alternative routes calculation, additional lanes, stockage of vehicles, restriction of the circulation to specific kinds of vehicles, diffusion of incident information via Internet, use of Variable Message Signal panels (VMS), etc. Every activated measure can be carrying out from the execution of one, or more, specific actions.

The information contained in TMPs is arranged in a huge document. Thus, there is a need of a computerized tool for helping road managers in browsing this document. The first developed tool was a HTML prototype following a simple client-server approach. The server stored the whole TMP document in linked HTML pages. The execution of this tool was entirely guided by the road manager, the client actor. First, the road manager chose the type of TMP from the scenario information. Then, the available measures were shown. The road manager selected the measure more appropriate. Finally, the possible actions were showed and the road manager tried to implement them by devoting resources, calling other traffic management centers, etc.

Even though the functionality of the TMP to implement had been improved and the results were the ones expected, the computerization of TMPs in HTML format still showed some problems. The most important one was related to the HTML intrinsic features: the concept of *document* does not exist; that is, there is no distinction between presentation and content. Thus, in HTML there were not possible for the road operator to modify or update a TMP.

Then, a new tool was developed: a XML prototype [16]. XML is a tag based language useful to describe tree structures with a linear syntax [5]. XML makes a distinction between the document and the representation of such document on the screen [4]. XML also allows the creation of different types of plans and it facilitates the representation of the content of the document by using different devices.

This new approach improves the performance of TMPs. However, this approach still shows several problems. The TMPs maintain a static line in the XML prototype. Thus, this prototype does not include real time support to the road operator. The road operator must determine the scenario using and validating the traffic information provided by the available traffic equipment. Therefore, he must decide what, when and how dynamic measures must be activated. So, the road traffic operator is demanding for a more advanced prototype to deal with the scenario selection and the determination of dynamic measures. The new prototype developed is a multiagent system in which several agents coordinate activities to almost automatically deal with the execution of the TMPs. The agents of the prototype use the same underlying traffic and TMP ontologies that are exposed in the following section.

3 Non Urban Traffic Road Domain

The transportation domain is composed by several objects such as roads, junctions, vehicles, signals, etc. A generic and public agreement specification of these objects is needed to be able sharing and reusing traffic knowledge between the applications executed in the transportation domain. This agreement should be based in the use of traffic ontology. However, current transportation systems do not use such ontology.

3.1 Road Traffic Ontology

A first approach of this traffic ontology has been proposed in [17]. The traffic ontology is composed by several sub domains (see fig. 2).

The road subdomain describes topological features of the roads. This subdomain is composed of the following objects: Roads, Itineraries, Segments, and Links. Link objects are also subdivided in: Origins, Destinations, Bifurcations, Unions, Weavings and Merges.

The second subdomain defines the traffic behavior model. In this subdomain, it is described the parameters related with the traffic behavior: Level of service (LOS), Traffic Volume, Flow rate (intensity), Speed and Density and weather parameters: Visibility, Road surface, Precipitations, Wind.

The third, and last, subdomain is charge of characterizing the equipment of the non urban network. The basic equipments that had been identified in this subdomain are: Data capture stations: Traffic data capture station and Meteorological station, CCTV cameras, Emergency phones and Variable Signals.

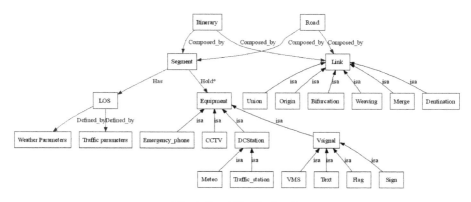

Fig. 2. Road Traffic Ontology

3.2 Traffic Management Plan Ontology

The proposed ontology models the non urban road traffic knowledge. However, we need to extend this ontology with the relevant conceptualization related to TMPs and traffic incidences.

This extension includes the following concepts:

- Severity. This object defines the seriousness of an incident.
- Incident. It identifies an incident produced in the road network. The incident produces a modification of traffic behavior. The modification depends on the severity degree. The incident is located in a segment or in a link.

- Scenario. The scenario object defines the current traffic situation. The scenario is determined by the traffic incident (location, duration, severity) and the current traffic parameters (density, flow rate, LOS).
- Measure. The measures define the set of procedures to be applied. The measures are classified in external and internal measures. The difference is related to the possibility of complete the measure internally (i.e. with the TCC own resources) or externally (other actor have to loan resources). A measure is composed by several actions.
- Action. It identifies independent and individual activities related to a measure.
- Actor. The actor defines the organization responsible of execute an action. If the action belongs to an internal measure, the actor is not necessary, but if it belongs to an external measure the related actor have to be identified. The actor object identifies not only the organism but also the way to communicate and to request the development of the action.

Figure 3 presents the TMP ontology and the relationships with the road traffic ontology.

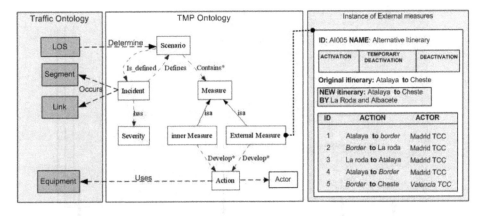

Fig. 3. TMP Ontology. The figure presents the TMP concepts and its relationship with the road traffic ontology. On the right there is an instance of an external measure: An alternative itinerary.

4   The Proposed MAS

Multiagent systems (MAS) are appropriate to manage the transportation environment [8]. MAS systems are a natural approach to work with traffic management problems [9]. This is due to the features of agents: autonomous, reactives, proactives and socials [18] and its potential to work with high complexity problems in a distributed environment. So, a MAS has been developed to improve the TMP software tool when meteorological incidents occur. The MAS developed helps the road operator to determine the scenario. It uses and it validates the traffic information provided by the available traffic equipment.

4.1 MAS Architecture

The MAS prototype developed is able to manage road traffic information and it also manages TMP. The MAS is FIPA [6] compliant. The MAS is composed by several kinds of agents: Meteo agents, Manager agent, XML Plan agent, Web agent, DF agent and Interface agent. Figure 4 shows the software architecture of this MAS prototype.

4.1.1 Meteo Agent

There exist several weather parameters that affect the traffic behavior (snow, wind, fog, etc) [13]. These weather parameters are constantly monitored through meteorological stations and its specific sensors. These Meteo stations are placed in specific road points and have a coverage area. The Meteo agent supervises the parameter provided by the sensor. It uses the parameter information to detect weather problems.

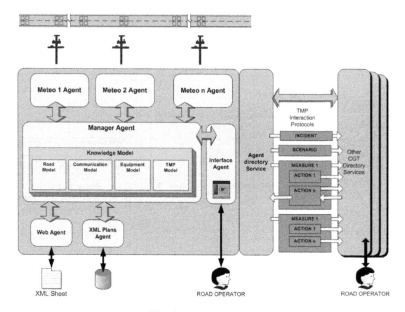

Fig. 4. MAS architecture

4.1.2 Manager Agent

This agent contains the traffic behavior model. Moreover, it contains the available resources to manage traffic incidences produced by weather problems. The manager uses the information provided by the meteo agents and it proposes the current scenario. This scenario has to be validated by the road operator. Once the operator validates the scenario, the manager agent makes a request to the XML plan agent: the TMP to activate in the current situation. The manager uses its traffic behavior model to estimate the better form to activate the measures. If the measures need external resources, it uses the DF agent to find it.

4.1.3 Interface Agent

The main purposes of the interface agent are: show graphically the entire MAS environment (road network, traffic status, equipment, active TMP) and the interaction between the road operator and the MAS system.

4.1.4 XML Plan Agent

This agent holds a database with all the TMP in XML format. This agent maintains the TMP database (TMP creation, upgrades, etc). When this agent receives information about a detected incident, it looks for the associated fired event in the database. If a TMP for this incident exits, the agent returns to the manager agent the traffic measures to be applied.

4.1.5 Web Agent

This agent translates the incident information received from the manager agent in a DATEX [10] format. DATEX is a standard format used to exchange traffic information between traffic organizations. Once the information is in DATEX format, the web agent sends it to the subscribed Traffic Control Centers.

4.1.6 DF Agent

The directory facilitator used is the DF JADE agent [12] specified by FIPA. The DF provides a yellow pages service by means of which an agent can register, deregister and search for other agents or services available in the MAS platform or in other platforms.

4.2 Communication Protocols

The communication model defines the way agents can related and exchange information. The communication model proposed follows the interaction protocols defined by FIPA [7]. It uses the JADE libraries [2] and coded in FIPA-ACL (Agent communication language) [6].

The interaction protocols govern the way of exchange of information among agents [18]. The interaction protocols are classified in three groups: Inner, Outer and External protocols. Inner protocols are used in communications inside the MAS prototype, outer protocols are used in communications between the MAS and the road traffic operator via the interface agent. The last group, external protocols, are used to communicate our MAS system with other external agents (agent belonging to other platforms) in order to implement external measures coordinately.

The outer and inner protocols are described deeply in [17]. The inner protocols are: ManagerReg, MeteoReg, AlarmReq, PlanMeasures and WebInfo and the outer protocols are: ShowPlan, ShowSignals, ForceSignal and ValidateScenario.

Next, the external protocols are described:

– WeatherInfo: Request protocol. The manager sends to external agents a message to obtain weather information.
– IncidentOccurs: Query protocol. The manager sends to the border TCCs a message containing the information of the incident produced and it forecasted evolution. (see figure 5)

- ImplementMeasure: Contract Net protocol between the Manager agent and an external agent. The external agent provides a service to implement traffic actions. First, the manager agent sends a message. It contains the incident, the measure and the actions to be developed by the external agent. The external agent evaluates the message and it respond to the manager (with: a proposal to activate his action, a rejection message or a not-understood message). If manager accepts the proposal it sends an accept-proposal message. Then, they start to implement the actions. If there are not problems implementing the actions, the measure is activated. If some problems appear, the manager can not implement the measure. Figure 5 depicts this protocol.
- SuspendTempMeasure: Query protocol to suspend temporarily the development of a measure. (E.g. if a new incident around the coverage area of the developing measure is detected).
- FinishMeasure: Query protocol to notify the finalization of a measure. This occurs when the problems are clean up. The manager sends to the related agent a message to finish the activation of the measure.

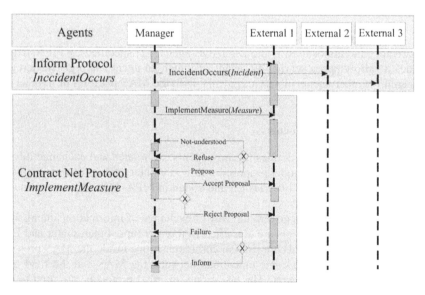

Fig. 5. Example of Interaction Protocols. IncidentOccurs: The manager sends a message to external agents subscribed in the DF. ImplementMeasure: the manager starts a Contract-Net protocol to develop coordinated actions. These actions are related to a specific TMP measure.

5 Implementation and Evaluation

The system has been implemented using the JADE platform. JADE is a software framework to develop agent applications in compliance with FIPA specifications for interoperable intelligent multiagent systems [1].

The ontologies described in section 3 have been defined by using the PROTÉGÉ-2000 ontology tool [15]. This is due to the facilities that this tool provides for editing ontologies and for developing knowledge acquisition tools from the edited ontologies. The Javabean generator PROTÉGÉ plug-in has been used [11] to convert the edited ontology to java classes. This plug-in generates automatically the java classes using the JADE specification.

A real non urban road network has been modeled to evaluate the MAS prototype, the Spanish A-3 freeway. The main characteristics of this freeway are:

- 2 traffic control centers.
- 11 different actors (traffic polices, external TCC, road work, etc).
- 3 main roads A-3, A-31, A-35 (420 km aprox.).
- 2 alternatives itineraries combining segments from roads: A-3,A-31 and A-35.
- 16 Segments.
- 20 Links.
- 13 Meteo stations.
- 22 VMS.
- A real TMP for weather problems in the A-3 freeway containing 4 scenarios and 24 measures.

The system is currently being evaluated. The evaluation is based on weather information collected from meteo stations in a XML file. Using this file, different weather situations are been simulated. The results obtained are positives, the MAS can monitor several concurrent weather problems along the road and help road manager to determine the current scenario for each road segment and the measures to apply.

6 Conclusions and Future Work

The need of defining and developing ontologies for non urban traffic is exposed in this paper. This is due to the specific characteristics of transportation environments and specillay to non urban traffic domain. This traffic domain usually involves: 1) huge road networks, 2) traffic monitoring with several distributed equipment along the road network. 3) coordinated actuations between several traffic administrations. We extend road traffic ontology with the TMP and incidents concepts. This new ontology has been used as MAS knowledge. The ontology is the component for the coordination and communication of the agents.

The proposed MAS improves the TMPs execution. The system automatically monitors weather problems that can appear in road networks. It makes easy the context and the measures to be applied. It also allows to communicate the incidents detected to other centers and traffic administrations. The proposed MAS is able to negotiate actions to develop measures with other external agents that can share resources. The MAS defines the set of actions and measures to be negotiated and implemented not only by itself but also by external agents. This negotiation has been developed using a contract-net protocol. The improvement of the negotiation protocol using more complexes negotiation strategies (multi-issue, criteria and time depending) is currently being developed.

References

1. Bellifemine F. et alt.: JADE - A FIPA-compliant agent framework, Proceedings of PAAM'99, London, April 1999, pp.97-108.
2. Caire G.: Application-Defined Content Languages and Ontologies. June 2002
3. Cascetta E.: Transportation Systems Engineering: Theory and Methods. Kluwer Academic . ress, 2001 ISBN 0792367928
4. Extensible Markup Language (XML), http://www.w3.org/XML/. September 2001.
5. Fensel D.: Ontologies: A silver Bullet for knowledge Management and Electronic commerce. Second edition. Springer-Verlag. ISBN 3-540-00302-9
6. FIPA Communicative Act Library Specification.: Foundation for Intelligent Physical Agents, December 3, 2002.
7. FIPA interaction protocol library. Technical report DC00025F. FIPA.http://www.fipa.org
8. García-Serrano et alt.: "FIPA-compliant MAS development for road traffic management with a Knowledge-Based approach: the TRACK-R agents." Challenges in Open Agent Systems '03 Workshop. Melbourne. Australia. 2003
9. Hernández, J.Z. Ossowski, S. García-Serrano, A.: Journal:Transportation Research, Part C, Pergamon Press, V 10 Issue5-6, pp:473-506, 2002
10. http://www.datex.org.
11. http://www.swi.psy.uva.nl/usr/aart/beangenerator
12. Java Agent Development framework (JADE). http://jade.cselt.it
13. Mahoney W.: An advanced weather & road condition decision support system. Proceedings of 9th World congress on Itelligent Transport systems. Chicago (EE.UU) 2002.
14. McQueen.: Intelligent transportation systems architecture   Artech House Books, 1999 ISBN 089006525
15. The Protégé Ontology Editor and Knowledge Ac. System http://protege.stanford.edu
16. Tomás, Vicente R. et al.: New technologies to work with traffic management plans. Traffic Technology International-Annual review .2003
17. Tomas V. R. Garcia Fernandez L.A.: "A cooperative multiagent system for traffic management and control". Fourth International Joint Conference on Autonomous Agents and Multi Agent Systems AAMAS 2005. Industrial Track
18. Wooldridge M.: An Introduction to Multiagent Systems.. Published in February 2002 by John Wiley & Sons (Chichester, England). ISBN 0 47149691X. 340pp

Arguing and Negotiating in the Presence of Social Influences*

Nishan C. Karunatillake[1], Nicholas R. Jennings[1],
Iyad Rahwan[2], and Timothy J. Norman[3]

[1] School of Electronics and Computer Science,
University of Southampton, Southampton, UK
{nnc02r, nrj}@ecs.soton.ac.uk

[2] Institute of Informatics, The British University in Dubai, P.O.Box 502216 Dubai, UAE
(Fellow) School of Informatics, University of Edinburgh, Edinburgh, UK
irahwan@acm.org

[3] Department of Computing Science, University of Aberdeen, Aberdeen, UK
tnorman@csd.abdn.ac.uk

Abstract. When agents operate in a society with incomplete information and with diverse and conflicting influences, they may, in certain instances, lack the knowledge, the motivation and/or the capacity to enact all their commitments. However, to function as a coherent society it is important for these agents to have a means to resolve such conflicts and to come to a mutual understanding about their actions. To this end, *argumentation-based negotiation* provides agents with an effective means to resolve conflicts within a multi-agent society. However, to engage in such argumentative encounters, agents require four fundamental capabilities; a schema to reason in a social context, a mechanism to identify a suitable set of arguments, a language and a protocol to exchange these arguments, and a decision making functionality to generate such dialogues. This paper presents formulations of all of these capabilities and proposes a coherent framework that allows agents to argue, negotiate, and, thereby, resolve conflicts within a multi-agent society.

Keywords: Argumentation-based Negotiation, Conflict Resolution.

1 Introduction

Autonomous agents usually operate as a multi-agent community performing actions within a shared social context to achieve their individual and collective objectives. In such a social context, their actions are influenced via two broad forms of motivations. First, the *internal influences* reflect the intrinsic motivations that drive the individual agent to achieve its own internal objectives. Second, as agents reside and operate within a social community, the social context itself influences their actions. Here, we categorise these latter forms as *social influences*. Now, in many cases, both these forms of influence may be present and they may give conflicting motivations to the individual

---

* The first author is a full time PhD student funded by EPSRC under the project Information Exchange (GR/S03706/01). The authors also extend their gratitude to Pietro Panzarasa, Chris Reed, and Xudong Luo for their thoughts, contributions, and discussions.

M. Pěchouček, P. Petta, and L.Z. Varga (Eds.): CEEMAS 2005, LNAI 3690, pp. 223–235, 2005.

agent. For instance, an agent may be internally motivated to perform a specific action, whereas, at the same time, it may also be subject to an external social influence not to perform it. Also an agent may face situations where different social influences motivate it in a contradictory fashion (one to perform a specific action and the other not to). Moreover, in many cases, agents have to carry out their actions in environments with incomplete information. Thus, for instance, they may not be aware of the existence of all the social influences that could or indeed should affect their actions and they may also lack the knowledge of certain specific internal influences that drive other agents' behaviours. Therefore, when agents operate in a society of incomplete information with such diverse and conflicting influences, they may, in certain instances, lack the knowledge, the motivation and/or the capacity to abide by all their social influences.

However, to function as a coherent society it is important for these agents to have a means to resolve such conflicts and to come to a mutual understanding about their actions. To this end, *Argumentation-Based Negotiation* (ABN) has been advocated as a promising means of resolving conflicts within such agent societies [1,2]. In more detail, ABN allows agents to exchange additional meta-information such as justifications, critics, and other forms of persuasive locutions within their interactions. These, in turn, allow agents to gain a wider understanding of the internal and social influences affecting their counterparts, thereby making it easier to resolve certain conflicts that arise due to incomplete knowledge. Furthermore, the negotiation element within ABN also provides a means for the agents to achieve mutually acceptable agreements to the conflicts of interests that they may have in relation to their different influences.

Now, one of the central features required by an agent to engage in such arguments within a society is the ability to generate valid arguments during the course of the dialogue. We believe this demands four fundamental capabilities: (i) a schema to reason in social settings; (ii) a mechanism to identify a suitable set of arguments; (iii) a language and a protocol to exchange these arguments; and (iv) a decision making functionality to generate such dialogues. This paper builds upon our previous conceptual grounding [3] and formulates a coherent framework that addresses all four of these issues. More specifically, apart from formulating a coherent schema that captures social influence in multi-agent systems (see Section 2.1) and systematically using it, in turn, to identify social arguments to resolve conflicts within an agent society (see Section 2.2), this paper presents three additional contributions. *First*, we construct a language that is capable of expressing such social arguments and, which allows agents to exchange them within their argumentative dialogues (see Section 3.1). *Second*, we define a dialogue game protocol identifying the different guidelines (such as locution rules, structural rules and commitment rules) which will govern these dialogues and guide its participants toward resolving their conflicts. *Finally*, we define the different decision making algorithms required by the agents to engage in such argumentative dialogues to resolve conflicts about their social influences (see Section 3.2).

2   Model for Arguing with Social Influences

Here we outline our ABN model that provides agents with a means to argue, negotiate, and, thereby, resolve their conflicts in relation to social influences. We introduce our model in two stages; first detailing how social influences within a society can be captured into a schema, and second explaining the different ways that agents can use this schema to systematically capture arguments to use within their ABN in a multi-agent community.

2.1 Capturing Social Influence

The notion of *social commitment* acts as our basic building block for capturing social influences. First introduced by Castelfranchi [4], it is one of the fundamental approaches for modelling social behaviour among agents in multi-agent systems. In essence, a social commitment ($SC_\theta^{x \to y}$) is a commitment by one agent x (termed the *debtor*) to another y (termed the *creditor*) to perform a stipulated action θ.[1] Having defined such, Castelfranchi further explains the consequences of a social commitment for both the agents involved. In detail, a social commitment results in the debtor attaining an *obligation* toward the creditor, to perform the stipulated action. The creditor, in turn, attains certain rights. These include the right to demand or require the performance of the action, the right to question the non-performance of the action, and, in certain instances, the right to make good any losses suffered due to its non-performance. We refer to these rights the creditor gains as the *rights to exert influence*. This notion of social commitment resulting in an obligation and rights to exert influence, allows us a means to capture social influences between two agents. Thus, when a certain agent is socially committed to another to perform a specific action, it subjects itself to the social influences of the other to perform that action. The ensuing obligation, on one hand, allows us to capture how an agent gets subjected to the social influence of another, whereas, the rights to exert influence, on the other hand, model how an agent gains the ability to exert such social influence upon another. Thereby, the notion of social commitment gives an elegant mechanism to capture social influence resulting between two agents.

Given this basic building block for modelling social influence between specific pairs of agents, we now proceed to explain how this notion is extended to capture social influences resulting due to factors such as roles and relationships within a wider multi-agent society (i.e., those that rely on the structure of the society, rather than the specific individuals who happen to be committed to one another). Specifically, since most relationships involve the related parties carrying out certain actions for each other, we can view a relationship as an encapsulation of social commitments between the associated roles. To illustrate this, consider the relationship between the roles supervisor and student. For instance, assume the relationship socially influences the student to produce and hand over his thesis to the supervisor in a timely manner. This influence we can perceive as a social commitment that exists between the roles supervisor and student (the student is socially committed to the supervisor to perform the stipulated action). As a consequence of this social commitment, the student attains an obligation toward the supervisor to carry out this related action. On the other hand, the supervisor gains the right to exert influence on the student by either demanding that he does so or through questioning his non-performance. In a similar manner, the supervisor may be influenced

---

[1] In the desire to maintain simplicity within our schema, we avoid incorporating the witness (see [4]) in our model (as Castelfranchi did in his subsequent expositions).

to review and comment on the thesis. This again is another social commitment associated with the relationship. In this instance, it subjects the supervisor to an obligation to review the thesis while the student gains the right to demand its performance. In this manner, social commitment again provides an effective means to capture the social influences emanating through roles and relationships of the society (independently of the specific agents who take on the roles). Given this descriptive definition of our model, we now formulate these notions to capture the social influences within multi-agent systems as a schema (refer to Figure 1 and formulae (1) through (6)):

Definition 1. For $n_A, n_R, n_P, n_\Theta \in \mathbb{N}^+$, let:
- $A = \{a_1, \ldots, a_{n_A}\}$ denote a finite set of agents,
- $R = \{r_1, \ldots, r_{n_R}\}$ denote a finite set of roles,
- $P = \{p_1, \ldots, p_{n_P}\}$ denote a finite set of relationships,
- $\Theta = \{\theta_1, \ldots, \theta_{n_\Theta}\}$ denote a finite set of actions,
- Act : $A \times R$ denote the fact that an agent is acting a role,
- RoleOf : $R \times P$ denote the fact that a role is related to a relationship, and
- In : $A \times R \times P$ denote the fact that an agent acting a role is part of a relationship.

If an agent acts a certain role and that role is related to a specific relationship, then that agent acting that role is said to be part of that relationship (as per Cavedon and Sonenberg [5]):

$$\text{Act}(a, r) \wedge \text{RoleOf}(r, p) \rightarrow \text{In}(a, r, p) \qquad \text{(Rel. Rule)}$$

Definition 2. Let SC denote a finite set of social commitments and $\text{SC}_\theta^{x \rightarrow y} \in SC$. Thus, as per Castelfranchi, $\text{SC}_\theta^{x \rightarrow y}$ *will result in the debtor attaining an obligation toward the creditor to perform a stipulated action and the creditor, in turn, attaining the right to influence the performance of that action:*

$$\text{SC}_\theta^{x \rightarrow y} \rightarrow [O_\theta^{x \rightarrow y}]_x^f \wedge [R_\theta^{y \rightarrow x}]_y, \qquad \text{(S-Com Rule)}$$

where:
- $[O_\theta^{x \rightarrow y}]_x^f$ represents the obligation that x attains that subjects it to an influence of a degree f (refer to [3] for more details) toward y to perform θ and
- $[R_\theta^{y \rightarrow x}]_y$ represents the right that y attains which gives it the ability to demand, question, and require x regarding the performance of θ.

Definition 3. Let:
- DebtorOf : $(R \cup A) \times SC$ denote that a role (or an agent) is the debtor in a social commitment,
- CreditorOf : $(R \cup A) \times SC$ denote that a role (or an agent) is the creditor in a social commitment,
- ActionOf : $\Theta \times SC$ denote that an act is associated with a social commitment, and
- AssocWith : $SC \times P$ denote that a social commitment is associated with a relationship.

If the roles associated with the relationship are both the creditor and the debtor of a particular social commitment, then we declare that social commitment is associated with the relationship (as per Section 2.1).

> An agent a_i acting the role r_i
> Leads it to be part of the relationship p
> With another agent a_j acting the role r_j
> A social commitment $SC_\theta^{r_i \to r_j}$ associated with p
> - Leads to a_i attaining an obligation O toward r_j,
>   Which subjects it to an influence of degree f
>   To perform the action θ
> - And, in turn, leads to a_j attaining the right R toward r_i
>   To demand, question, and require the performance
>   of action θ

Fig. 1. Natural Language Representation of the Schema of Social Influence

Applying the Rel. Rule to a society where: $a_i, a_j \in A \wedge r_i, r_j \in R \wedge p \in P$ s.t. $Act(a_i, r_i)$, $Act(a_j, r_j)$, $RoleOf(r_i, p)$, $RoleOf(r_j, p)$ hold true, we obtain:

$$Act(a_i, r_i) \wedge RoleOf(r_i, p) \to In(a_i, r_i, p) \tag{1}$$

$$Act(a_j, r_j) \wedge RoleOf(r_j, p) \to In(a_j, r_j, p). \tag{2}$$

Now, consider a social commitment $SC_\theta^{r_i \to r_j}$ associated with the relationship p in this society. Applying this to Definition 3 we obtain:

$$(DebtorOf(r_i, SC) \wedge RoleOf(r_i, p)) \wedge (CreditorOf(r_j, SC) \wedge RoleOf(r_j, p))$$
$$\wedge\, ActionOf(\theta, SC) \to AssocWith(SC_\theta^{r_i \to r_j}, p). \tag{3}$$

Applying the S-Comm rule to $SC_\theta^{r_i \to r_j}$ we obtain:

$$SC_\theta^{r_i \to r_j} \to \left[O_\theta^{r_i \to r_j}\right]_{r_i}^{f} \wedge \left[R_\theta^{r_j \to r_i}\right]_{r_j}. \tag{4}$$

Combining (4), (1) and (3) we obtain:

$$In(a_i, r_i, p) \wedge AssocWith(SC_\theta^{r_i \to r_j}, p) \to \left[O_\theta^{a_i \to r_j}\right]_{a_i}^{f}. \tag{5}$$

Combining (4), (2) and (3) we obtain:

$$In(a_j, r_j, p) \wedge AssocWith(SC_\theta^{r_i \to r_j}, p) \to \left[R_\theta^{a_j \to r_i}\right]_{a_j}. \tag{6}$$

2.2 Capturing Social Arguments

Having captured the notion of social influence into a schema, here we present how agents can use it to systematically identify arguments to negotiate within a society. We term these arguments *social arguments*, not only to emphasise their ability to resolve conflicts within a society, but also to highlight the fact that they use the social influence present within the system as a core means in changing decisions and outcomes within the society.[2] Specifically, we have identified two major ways in which social influence can be used to change decisions and outcomes and thereby resolve conflicts between agents (see Figure 2).

---

[2] Due to space restrictions here we present only a limited subset of social arguments. For a comprehensive list of arguments, together with their formal representation, refer to [3].

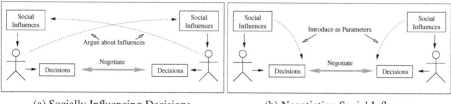

(a) Socially Influencing Decisions   (b) Negotiating Social Influence

Fig. 2. Interplay of Social Influence and Argumentation-Based Negotiation

Socially Influencing Decisions: One way to affect an agent's decisions is by arguing about the validity of that agent's practical reasoning [6,7]. Similarly, in a social context, an agent can affect another agent's decisions by arguing about the validity of the other's social reasoning. In more detail, agents' decisions to perform (or not to perform) actions are based on their internal and/or social influences. Thus, these influences formulate the justification (or the reason) behind their decisions. Therefore, agents can affect each other's decisions indirectly by affecting the social influences that determine their decisions (see Figure 2(a)). Specifically, in the case of actions motivated via social influences through the roles and relationships of a structured society, this justification to act (or not to act) flows from the social influence schema (see Section 2.1). Given this, we can further classify the ways that agents can socially influence each other's decisions into two broad categories:

1. Undercut the opponent's existing justification to perform (or not) an action by disputing certain premises within the schema that motivates its opposing decision (i.e., dispute a_i is acting role r_i, dispute SC is a social commitment associated with the relationship p, dispute θ is the action associated with the obligation O, etc.).
2. Rebut the opposing decision to act (or not) by,
   i. Pointing out information about an alternative schema that justifies the decision not to act (or act as the case may be) (i.e., point out a_i is also acting role r_i, point out SC is also a social commitment associated with the relationship p, point out θ is the action associated with the obligation O, etc.).
   ii. Pointing out information about conflicts that could or should prevent the opponent from executing its opposing decision (i.e., point out conflicts between two existing *obligations*, *rights*, and *actions*).

Negotiating Social Influence: Agents can also use social influences within their negotiations. More specifically, instead of using social argumentation as a tool to affect decisions (as above), agents can use negotiation as a tool for "trading social influences". In other words, the social influences are incorporated as additional parameters of the negotiation object itself [8] (see Figure 2(b)). For instance, an agent can promise to (or threaten not to) undertake one or many future obligations if the other performs (or does not perform) a certain action. It can also promise not to (or threaten to) exercise certain rights to influence one or many existing obligations if the other performs (or does not perform) a certain action. In this manner, the agents can use their obligations, rights, and even the relationship itself as parameters in their negotiations.

3   The Language, Protocol, and Decision Making Functionality

As mentioned in Section 1, our main objective is to formulate a society of agents that are capable of resolving their conflicts through argumentation-based negotiations. To this end, Section 2 formulated a model that allows the agents to identify such arguments to resolve conflicts in a social context. However, identifying such arguments is merely the first step. Agents also require a means to express such arguments, a mechanism to govern their interactions and guide them to resolve their conflicts, and a functionality to make decisions during the course of such dialogues. To this end, we now present the language, the protocol, and the decision making algorithms of our ABN framework.

3.1   The Language

The language plays an important role in an ABN framework. It not only allows agents to express the content and construct their arguments, but also provides a means to communicate and exchange them within an argumentative dialogue. Highlighting these two distinct functionalities, we define the language in our framework at two levels; namely the *domain language* and the *communication language*. The former allows the agents to specify certain premises about their social context and also the conflicts that they may face while executing actions within such a context. The latter, on the other hand, provides agents with a means to express these arguments and, thereby, engage in their discourse to resolve conflicts. Inspired by the works of Sierra *et al.* [9], this two tier definition not only allows us an elegant way of structuring the language, but also provides a means to easily reuse the communication component within a different context merely by replacing its domain counterpart.

In more detail, our domain language consists of ten elocutionary particles. Of these, eight allow the agents to describe their social context and these flow naturally from our social influence schema (i.e., Act, RoleOf, In, DebtorOf, CreditorOf, ActionOf, InfluenceOf, and AssocWith). Due to space restrictions we avoid repeating these definitions here (see Section 2.1). Furthermore, we define two additional predicates that provide a means to express the conflicts that the agents may face while executing their actions:

Definition 4: Let:
- do: $A \times \Theta$ denote the fact that an agent is performing an action (expressed in the abbreviated form $do(\theta)$ when the agent is unambiguous).
- Conflict: $do(A \times \Theta) \times do(A \times \Theta)$ denote the fact that performing the actions gives rise to a conflict.

On the other hand, our communication language consists of seven elocutionary particles (see Table 1). Mainly inspired form the works of Amgoud *et al.* [10], MacKenzie's system DC [11], and McBurney *et al.* [12], these form the building blocks of our dialogue game protocol explained below (see Section 3.2). Furthermore, these collectively allow the agents to use both of our identified methods of conflict resolution; namely socially influencing decisions and negotiating social influences (see Section 2.2). Due to their integrated nature with our protocol, we will detail their operational functionality and the decision making algorithms associated with each of these locutions alongside the protocol (see Section 3.2).

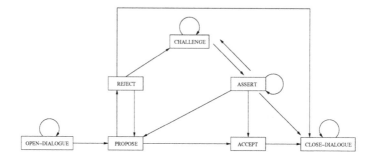

Fig. 3. Dialogue Interaction Diagram

Table 1. The Protocol

Locution	Effects on CS & IS	Next Valid Moves
OPEN-DIALOGUE	$CS(a_i) \leftarrow$ *OPEN-DIALOGUE* $CS(a_j) \leftarrow$ *OPEN-DIALOGUE*	*OPEN-DIALOGUE* *PROPOSE(l, m)*
PROPOSE(l, m)	$CS(a_i) \leftarrow$ *PROPOSE(l, m)* $CS(a_j) \leftarrow$ *PROPOSE(l, m)* $IS(a_j) \leftarrow Need(a_i, l) \wedge Capable(a_i, m)$	*ACCEPT(l, m)* *REJECT(l, m)*
ACCEPT(l, m)	$CS(a_i) \leftarrow$ *ACCEPT(l, m)* $\wedge l \wedge m$ $CS(a_j) \leftarrow$ *ACCEPT(l, m)* $\wedge l \wedge m$ $IS(a_i) \leftarrow Capable(a_j, l)$	*CLOSE-DIALOGUE*
REJECT(l, m)	$CS(a_i) \leftarrow$ *REJECT(l, m)* $CS(a_j) \leftarrow$ *REJECT(l, m)*	*CHALLENGE(l)* *PROPOSE(l, m′)* *CLOSE-DIALOGUE*
CHALLENGE(l)	$CS(a_i) \leftarrow$ *CHALLENGE(l)* $CS(a_j) \leftarrow$ *CHALLENGE(l)*	*ASSERT(l)* *CHALLENGE(l)*
ASSERT(l)	$CS(a_i) \leftarrow$ *ASSERT(l)* $CS(a_j) \leftarrow$ *ASSERT(l)*	*PROPOSE(l, m′)* *ACCEPT(l, m)* *ASSERT(¬l)* *CHALLENGE(l)* *CLOSE-DIALOGUE*
CLOSE-DIALOGUE	$CS(a_i) \leftarrow$ *CLOSE-DIALOGUE* $CS(a_j) \leftarrow$ *CLOSE-DIALOGUE*	*CLOSE-DIALOGUE*

3.2 The Protocol and the Decision Making Functionality

Given the language component of our ABN framework, we will now proceed to describe both the protocol which governs its interaction and guides the agents to resolve
their conflicts, and the various decision making algorithms that would enable the individual agents to participate in such encounters.[3] While the overall structure of our
protocol is inspired from the work on computational conflicts by Tessier *et al.* [13],
the works on pragma-dialectics proposed by van Eemeren and Grootendorst [14], and
that on dialogue games conducted by McBurney *et al.* [12], and Amgoud *et al.* [10]
contributed greatly in defining its operational guidelines.

---

[3] Even though we acknowledge the importance of distinguishing the rules of encounter governed by the protocol from the individual decision mechanisms required by the participants to
engage in such dialogues (see [12]), due to space restrictions we choose to describe both these
elements in this section.

More specifically, our protocol consists of six main stages: (i) *opening*, (ii) *conflict recognition*, (iii) *conflict diagnosis*, (iv) *conflict management*, (v) *agreement*, and (vi) *closing*. The opening and closing stages provide the important synchronisation points for the agents involved in the dialogue, the former indicating its commencement and the latter its termination [12]. The four remaining stages not only adhere to the computational conflict work by Tessier *et al.*, but also comply well with the pragma-dialectics model for critical discussion proposed by van Eemeren and Grootendorst. In more detail, in the conflict recognition stage, the initial interaction between the agents brings the conflict to the surface. Subsequently, the diagnosis stage allows the agents to establish the root cause of the conflict and also decide on how to address it (i.e., whether to avoid the conflict or attempt to manage and resolve it through argumentation and negotiation [1]). Next, the conflict management stage allows the agents to argue and negotiate, thus, addressing the cause of this conflict. Finally, the agreement stage brings the argument to an end, either with the participants agreeing on a mutually acceptable solution or agreeing to disagree due to the lack of such a solution. As mentioned above, these four stages map seamlessly to the four stages in the pragma-dialectics model; namely *confrontation*, rather infelicitously termed *opening*, *argumentation*, and *concluding* respectively.

Given the overall stages of our protocol, we now describe its internal operation. Our protocol follows the tradition of dialogue games [12] where a dialogue is perceived as a game in which each participant make moves (termed dialogue moves) to win or tilt the favour of the game toward itself. In such a context, the protocol defines the different rules for the game such as locutions rules (indicating the moves that are permitted), commitment rules (defining the commitments each participant incurs with each move), and structural rules (that define the types of moves available following the previous move).[4] To this end, Figure 3 depicts the overall structure of our protocol and Table 1 details the different commitment rules and the valid locutions that may follow each move. For ease of reference, here we address the proposing agent as a_i and its responding counterpart as a_j. The commitment rules are shown as effects on the participants' commitment (CS) and information (IS) stores (see [10]) and l and m are propositions constructed in the domain language defined above. The following describes their operation in more detail.

OPEN-DIALOGUE: This indicates the entry point of that agent to the dialogue. As shown in Table 1 this would result in an entry in either agents' commitment stores corresponding to the dialogical commitment [15] of having made the move (i.e., commitment to the fact that a_i has uttered *OPEN-DIALOGUE*). An agent receiving an *OPEN-DIALOGUE* will retort back (if it hasn't already initiated it) by uttering the same. This would put both these agents in the opening stage and their negotiation over actions can commence. For simplicity, we assume that the first agent opening the dialogue is the one attempting to make its counterpart perform (or abstain from performing) an action.

---

[4] Note, this is not intended to be an exhaustive list of rules, but rather the most important ones in our context. For instance, if the aim of the dialogue governed by the protocol is persuasion, the win-loss rules specifying what counts as a winning or losing position would become a vital component.

Algorithm 1. Decision making algorithm for *PROPOSE*.	**Algorithm 2.** Decision making algorithm for *ACCEPT* and *REJECT*.
1: **if** $(Capable(do(a_i, \theta_i))$ $\land$ $B^{a_i}_{do(a_j, \theta_j)}$ $>$ $C^{a_i}_{do(a_i, \theta_i)})$ **then** 2: $PROPOSE(do(a_j, \theta_j), do(a_i, \theta_i))$ 3: **end if**	1: **if** $(Capable(do(a_j, \theta_j))$ $\land$ $B^{a_j}_{do(a_i, \theta_i)}$ $>$ $C^{a_j}_{do(a_j, \theta_j)})$ **then** 2: $ACCEPT(do(a_j, \theta_j), do(a_i, \theta_i))$ 3: **else** 4: $REJECT(do(a_j, \theta_j), do(a_i, \theta_i))$ 5: **end if**

PROPOSE: Each such proposal is composed of two basic elements; the action θ_j that a_i requires a_j to perform and the action θ_i that a_i is willing to perform in return. Thus, in general, a proposal will have the form $PROPOSE(do(a_j, \theta_j), do(a_i, \theta_i))$. Here, θ_i could be single atomic action (e.g., I will perform (or will not perform) a certain action in return or I will make a payment of a certain amount) or a composite action (e.g., I will perform action $(\theta_1 \ and \ \theta_2)$ or $(\theta_1 \ or \ \theta_2)$). Therefore, this generic form of proposal allows the agents not only to make simple offers of payment over actions, but also to make simple or composite rewards and/or threats over actions. In this manner, it allows the agents to negotiate and also to use social influences as parameters within their negotiations to resolve conflicts (see Section 2.2). Given this, Algorithm 1 highlights the decision making required to generate such a proposal. In more detail, we assume our agents to be self-interested, thus, the proposals that they generate need to be viable on their behalf (i.e., the cost for a_i in performing the proposed action θ_i (i.e., $C^{a_i}_{do(a_i, \theta_i)}$) should not exceed the benefit it gains from a_j performing the requested action θ_j (i.e., $B^{a_i}_{do(a_j, \theta_j)}$). We also assume our agents do not intentionally attempt to deceive each other with offers that they do not believe feasible on their behalf. Therefore, they will only generate proposals that they believe to have the capability to honour.[5] Once received, as an effect of the proposal, a_j will gain the information that a_i requires θ_j and that a_i has the ability to perform θ_i (see Table 1).

ACCEPT and *REJECT*: Upon receiving a proposal, the agent a_j may choose to either accept or reject it. Now, in order to make this decision, it will need to evaluate the proposal. Similar to above, this evaluation is also based on two factors: a_j needs to have the capability to perform the requested action and the benefit of the proposal should outweigh the cost of performing the suggested action (see Algorithm 2). If both these conditions are satisfied the agent will accept the proposal, otherwise it will reject it. If accepted, both agents will incur commitments to perform their respective actions (see Table 1).

---

[5] First, under these assumptions of self-interest and non-deceit, we believe, viability and feasibility are the two most important factors to consider. Second, even though we choose to specify the algorithms at an abstract level that is independent of any domain, by defining how the agents evaluate these costs and benefits we can easily set these to reflect a given domain. Finally, even though the *PROPOSE* locution defined above has both the elements request and reward explicitly present, either can be null. This allows the agents to express proposals that are mere requests without an explicit reward (such as demands, pleads, and orders) and solitary rewards (such as offers, gifts, and suggestions) that they deem to be viable during their negotiation.

Algorithm 3. Decision algorithm for *CHALLENGE*.

- In case of *REJECT(l)*
  1: **if** $(REJECT(l) \in \Delta^{a_i} \wedge reason(REJECT(l)) \notin \Delta^{a_i})$ **then**
  2:    CHALLENGE(REJECT(l))
  3: **end if**
- In case of *ASSERT(l)*
  1: **if** $(ASSERT(l) \in \Delta^{a_i} \wedge reason(ASSERT(l)) \notin \Delta^{a_i})$ **then**
  2:    CHALLENGE(l)
  3: **end if**
- In case of *CHALLENGE(l)*
  1: **if** $(CHALLENGE(l) \in \Delta^{a_i} \wedge R_{CHALLENGE(l)} \notin \Delta^{a_i})$ **then**
  2:    CHALLENGE(CHALLENGE(l))
  3: **end if**

Algorithm 4. Decision algorithm for *ASSERT*.

- In case of *ASSERT(¬l)*
  1: **if** $(\neg l \notin \Delta^{a_i} \wedge l \in \Delta^{a_i})$ **then**
  2:    ASSERT(l)
  3: **end if**
- In case of *CHALLENGE(l)*
  1: **if** $(search\text{-}Justification(l, \Delta^{a_i}) \Rightarrow H)$ **then**
  2:    ASSERT(H)
  3: **end if**

CHALLENGE: Upon rejection of a proposal by its counterpart (a_j), a_i may choose to either forward a modified proposal (i.e., if the reason is apparent such that there can be only one possibility) or challenge a_j's decision in order to identify the underlying reasons for rejection. Apart from this, an agent may use *CHALLENGE* in two other situations (see Figure 3). First, an agent may challenge another's right to challenge (demand or question) its decision (see Section 2.1) if that right is not evident for the agent. This allows an agent to only justify its decisions to others who have the right to challenge its decision. To avoid infinite deepening of challenges, we do not allow such challenges go beyond two levels (i.e., challenge another's right to challenge its own right to challenge). Second, an agent can challenge a certain assertion by its counterpart if either that assertion or its contradiction is not within its knowledge (see Algorithm 3 where Δ^{a_i} denotes agent a_i's knowledge-base).

ASSERT: An agent can assert some fact in two possible situations. First, if the agent is challenged for some justification on its decision it can assert that justification. Second, if its counterpart has made an assertion (l), but the agent has justification to believe its contradiction $(\neg l)$, then the agent can assert this to dispute its partner's assertion.[6] This will allow agents to undercut and rebut each others' social reasoning, and, thereby, resolve conflicts (see Section 2.2). Assert can either result in the counterpart generating an alternative proposal (taking into account the reason given) or accepting the proposal (convinced by the persuasion).

CLOSE-DIALOGUE: When either the counterpart has accepted a certain proposal or the proposing agent has no other feasible and worthwhile proposals to forward, an agent will utter *CLOSE-DIALOGUE* (echoed in return by its counterpart) to bring the dialogue to an end.

Having formulated the language, the protocol, and the decision making functions of our ABN system, we now explain how these would interact to provide a means for the agents to resolve their conflicts in a social context. To this end, Figure 4 depicts an illus-

---

[6] Our current implementation uses a simple arbitration heuristic to resolve such disputes. However, this can be extended by replacing it with either a system based on the strength of justification [10] or a learning heuristic based on commitment (see Section 4).

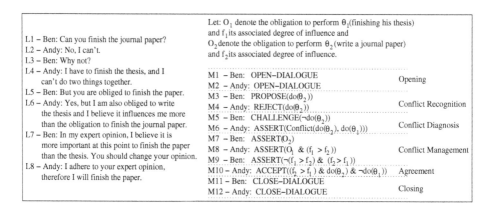

Fig. 4. Resolving Conflicts through Argumentation-based Negotiation

trative dialogue taking place between Andy, an agent acting the role of a PhD student, and Ben, acting as his supervisor. The case is set within a context where Andy has two distinct obligations, both toward Ben; to finish his thesis θ_1 and to write a journal paper θ_2. However, due to time restrictions, we assume that Andy has decided to perform θ_1 at the expense of θ_2. This choice is in conflict with Ben's own motivations. In this context, Figure 4 illustrates how he can socially influence (see Section 2.2) Andy's decision by undercutting his justification and, thereby, resolve the conflict. More specifically, Figure 4 highlights two specific aspects of our language and protocol. First, it shows how the language component allows the agents to do a straightforward encoding of the natural language locutions into its respective utterances (see locutions L1 to L8 with its corresponding utterances M3 to M10). Second, it also depicts how the dialogue progresses through the six distinct stages of conflict resolution identified above.

4   Conclusions and Future Work

The long term objective of our work is to formulate an agent society that can use argumentative dialogues to resolve their conflicts. To this end, this paper builds upon our previous conceptual grounding on social arguments [3] and formulates a coherent argumentation framework that allows agents to use ABN to resolve conflicts in a multi-agent community. In more detail, we first define a schema that captures social influences in an agent society and then illustrates the different ways that agents can use it to systematically identifying a suitable set of arguments to resolve conflicts in such a social context. Next, we formulate the language, which allows agents to construct and express such arguments, and the protocol that would guide the course of the dialogue toward resolving conflicts. Finally, we define the various decision making algorithms that would enable the individual agents to participate in such argumentative encounters. Apart from the models specified in this paper, in our current work we have implemented these in a multi-agent task allocation domain (specified in [1]) in order to empirically test the efficiency and effectiveness of these concepts. In future, we aim to expand upon our current implementation by designing different argument selection strategies, thus, allowing the agents to adopt different tactics in resolving conflicts in an agent society.

References

1. Karunatillake, N.C., Jennings, N.R.: Is it worth arguing? In: Argumentation in Multi-Agent Systems (Proc. of ArgMAS 2004). LNAI 3366, NY, USA, Springer-Verlag (2004) 234–250
2. Rahwan, I., Ramchurn, S.D., Jennings, N.R., McBurney, P., Parsons, S., Sonenberg, L.: Argumentation-based negotiation. The Knowledge Engineering Review **18** (2003) 343–375
3. Karunatillake, N.C., Jennings, N.R., Rahwan, I., Norman, T.J.: Argument-based negotiation in a social context. In: Proc. of the 2nd Int. Workshop on Argumentation in Multi-Agent Systems (ArgMAS'05), Utrecht, The Netherlands (2005) to appear
4. Castelfranchi, C.: Commitments: From individual intentions to groups and organizations. In: Proc. of the 1st Int. Conf. on Multi-agent Systems (ICMAS'95), San Francisco, CA (1995) 41–48
5. Cavedon, L., Sonenberg, L.: On social commitment, roles and preferred goals. In: Proc. of the 3rd Int. Conf. on Multi-Agent Systems (ICMAS'98). (1998) 80–86
6. Atkinson, K., Bench-Capon, T., McBurney, P.: A dialogue game protocol for multi-agent argument over proposals for action. In: Argumentation in Multi-Agent Systems (Proc. of ArgMAS 2004). LNAI 3366, NY, USA, Springer-Verlag (2004) 149–161
7. Walton, D.N.: Argumentation Schemes for Presumptive Reasoning. Erlbaum, Mahwah, NJ (1996)
8. Faratin, P., Sierra, C., Jennings, N.R.: Using similarity criteria to make trade-offs in automated negotiations. Artificial Intelligence **142** (2002) 205–237
9. Sierra, C., Jennings, N.R., Noriega, P., Parsons, S.: A framework for argumentation-based negotiation. In: Proc. of 4th Int. Workshop on Agent Theories Architectures and Languages (ATAL'97), Rhode Island, USA (1998) 167–182
10. Amgoud, L., Parson, S., Maudet, N.: Argument, dialogue and negotiation. In Horn, W., ed.: Proc. of the 14th European Conference on Artificial Intelligence (ECAI'00), Berlin (2000) 338–342
11. MacKenzie, J.: Question-begging in non-cumulative systems. Journal of philosophical logic **8** (1979) 117–133
12. McBurney, P., van Eijk, R., Parsons, S., Amgoud, L.: A dialogue-game protocol for agent purchase negotiations. Autonomous Agents and Multi-Agent Systems **7** (2003) 235–273
13. Tessier, C., Chaudron, L., Müller, H.J., eds.: Agents' Conflicts: New Issues. In: Conflicting Agents Conflict Management in Multi-Agent Systems. Kluwer Academic Publishers (2000) 1–30
14. Eemeren, F.H. van, Grootendorst, R.: Argumentation, Communication, and Fallacies. Lawrence Erlbaum Associates, Inc, Hillsdale NJ (1992)
15. Walton, D.N., Krabbe, E.C.W.: Commitment in Dialogue: Basic Concepts of Interpersonal Reasoning. State Univ. of NY (1995)

Cooperative Behavior of Agents Based on Potential Field

Takashi Katoh[1], Kensaku Hoshi[2], and Norio Shiratori[3]

[1] Iwate Prefectural Univ., Japan
[2] IBM Japan, Tokyo, Japan
[3] Tohoku Univ., Sendai, Japan

Abstract. In non-communicative environment, it is important for agents to assess the situation prevailing in the system, especially to anticipate other agents' intentions. In this paper, we argue in favor of cooperation among agents and propose a new method to utilize potential field as a tool for estimation of the environment. In our method, potential of environment gives agents some criteria to assess environmental situations from their own perspective. The potential of each object represents its influence on the environment and the environmental potential, i.e., summation of each object's potential, represents global situation of the environment. Agents' decision of their behavior will be done by refining the policy obtained from potential. We use a trash collecting problem as an example to show the effectiveness of our method. Furthermore, we show the efficiency of our method by some sets of experiments of the trash collecting problem. We also discuss the applicability of our method to hybrid systems or environments where agents' range of vision are limited.

1 Introduction

Cooperation among agents in a multi-agent system has been a major issue for the last several years. The issue becomes a more critical one in non-communicative environments. However, the area is yet to be explored thoroughly, particularly in large-scale multi-agent systems. The importance of such an investigation on cooperation in non-communicative multi-agent systems lies in ensuring future development of agents, e.g., disaster relief.

In non-communicative environment, it is important for agents to assess the situation prevailing in the system, especially to anticipate other agents' intentions. Without such assessment of agents, resources (e.g., agents' ability etc.) will be wasted. In this paper, we argue in favor of cooperation among agents in non-communicative environment and propose a new method to utilize potential field as a tool for estimation of the environment. In our method, potential of environment gives agents some criteria to assess environmental situations from their own perspective. Our purpose in this research is to realize agents' intelligent behavior by their respective decision making based on potential field and improve the efficiency of a system.

M. Pěchouček, P. Petta, and L.Z. Varga (Eds.): CEEMAS 2005, LNAI 3690, pp. 236–245, 2005.
© Springer-Verlag Berlin Heidelberg 2005

Fig. 1. Agent's behavior based on potential

2 Potential and Agent's Behavior

2.1 Agents' Assessment of a Situation

To realize efficient task processing in multi-agent systems, it is important for agents to behave appropriately depending on their situation. For this reason, agents are required to assess their situations as accurate as possible.

A trash collection example will be appropriate in this context. Suppose, agents are placed in a planar surface where trash is scattered. The goal of this system is to collect all trash on the surface as soon as possible. The simplest algorithm for agents is to go toward the nearest trash and pick it up. This method, however, has an obvious drawback that neighboring agents will go toward the same trash as their target to pick up. Thus some agents will just go after other agents and will not pick up any trash. This will thus become a cause of inefficiency. Hence each agent should find and pick up appropriate trash, i.e., the one toward which no other agent seems to be going. This means agents are required to behave cooperatively by looking ahead of other agents. To realize such cooperative behavior in non-communicative environment, agents need to assess their situation by utilizing available information (e.g., visual information via sensors) and decide their own behavior based on it.

In recent years, physics-agent-system (PAS) model [1] has been proposed. In their approach, an agent's behavior is determined by calculating potential of the environment. For example, an agent can know which trash it should go toward by using potential as its decision making function. We show such a scenario in Fig. 1. Though trash A is not the nearest one to agent A, it should go toward trash A because other trash (trash B and C) should be picked up by nearer agent B and C respectively. In this case, the gradient of potential directs to trash A, and agent A successfully picks up the most appropriate trash (trash A) accordingly. Using potential as an agent's decision making function has another merit; it needs less calculation costs because assessment of the global situation will be done by summation of potential functions of each object in the environment. However, use of potential function itself as agents' decision making function involves several serious problems. These are[1]: 1) Minimum point of potential field without any objects (Fig. 2): As we see in Fig. 2, there is a (local) minimum

---

[1] In the following examples, we use $\mp C \exp\left(-\frac{(x-a)^2}{2\sigma^2}\right)$ as potential function of an object at $x = a$ ($-$ is taken for trash and $+$ for agents. C and σ is constant). Details will be described in Sect. 3.

Fig. 2. Minimum point of potential field without any objects. Solid curve is superposition of each object's potential (dashed curve).

(a)   (b)

Fig. 3. Oscillation problem. Curves in these figures are potential due to agent A and trash. Dashed arrow drawn for agent A is derived from symmetry.

point where there are no objects. If an agent decides its behavior based only on the potential, the agent will be trapped in this well and fail to pick up trash. 2) Oscillation problem (Fig. 3): In Fig. 3 (a), both agent A and B go toward the same trash because the gradient of potential due to the trash and the other agent points to the trash. However, as a result of agents' movements, the direction of gradient will invert in the next moment because the other agent's potential cancels the trash's potential, and then agents will start going toward opposite way to the trash (Fig. 3 (b)). This process will repeat indefinitely, and thus agents will never reach the trash. 3) Detour problem (Fig. 4): The gradient will not necessarily direct to some object because potential of environment is the superposition of each object's potential and reflects the influence of multiple objects. As a result, agents may go a long way round to pick up trash if they decide their behavior based only on potential. Even though agents are able to reach the trash, it is not efficient. For example, agent A in Fig. 4 should go straight to trash A (direction denoted by dashed arrow). But at this particular moment the gradient of potential does not direct to it. As we see from these three examples, relying only on potential of environment is not appropriate to make their decision for agents.

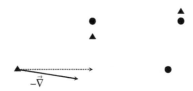

Fig. 4. Detour problem. $-\nabla V$ is calculated with V due to Agent B, Trash A and B.

To avoid these drawbacks, we interpret potential of environment as a rough indicator of an agent's behavior, not the exact strategy of the agent. Thus, agents' behavior will be decided in the following two phases: 1) calculate potential of environment and derive a general policy from it, 2) refine the policy obtained from potential and decide its behavior.

2.2 Applying Potential Field to Multi-agent Systems

Applying potential to multi-agent systems will be done in the following way: 1) Define potential functions of each object in the system, 2) Define agents' way to decide their behavior based on environmental potential. Here, we define potential of each object as representation of the object's influence to the environment, and the environmental potential as representation of a global situation of the environment. Furthermore, maintaining analogy with physics, we define the meaning of lower value of potential is desirable influence for agents, and higher value is undesirable influence. The environmental potential for some agent j is calculated by adding potentials due to other objects (superposition of potentials). This summation of potentials represents the influence due to other objects for agent j. The potential function due to some object is not necessarily the same for every agent. For example, assume there are two or more kinds of trash. If agent A collects only trash of type X, the influence of type-X trash for the agent is larger, and that of trash of other types is less (or zero).

2.3 Decision Making of Agents

Each agent decides its behavior in the following way. 1) gets the information of objects. 2) information of objects within sight of it. 3) calculates potential functions due to each object. 4) calculates an environmental potential by adding potential functions calculated in 2). 5) calculates the gradient of the environmental potential calculated in 3). 6) decides the next action based on the gradient calculated in 4).For example, if each agent can obtain the position of other objects (via its sensors), 1) gets the position of object α: (x_α, y_α), 2) calculates potential due to object α: $V_\alpha(x - x_\alpha, y - y_\alpha)$, 3) calculates environmental potential for the agent: $V^E = \sum_\alpha V_\alpha(x - x_\alpha, y - y_\alpha)$, 4) calculates gradient: $-\nabla V^E$, 5) decides the next action (direction to move) based on $-\nabla V^E$.

3   Example: Agent's Decision Making Based on Potential

Here we show how to apply our method to a multi-agent system using an example of trash collection. The settings of this example are: 1) Agents are placed on a planar surface where trash is scattered. 2) The number of agents is n and that of trash is m. 3) A piece of trash can be picked up by an agent. 4) Agents cannot communicate with each other. 5) Agents can obtain positions of other objects (agents and trash). The purpose of this system is to collect all trash on the surface as soon as possible.

3.1 Definitions and Notations

First, we define some symbols here. $A = \{A_i \mid i = 1, 2, \ldots, n\}$ is a set of the agents $A_i(i = 1, 2, \ldots, n)$ on the surface and $T = \{T_i \mid i = 1, 2, \ldots, m\}$ is a set of trash $T_i(i = 1, 2, \ldots, m)$ on the surface: $O = A \cup T$ is a set of objects on the surface[2] and $O_{\overline{\alpha}}$ is a set of objects on the surface except object α:

$$O_{\overline{\alpha}} = O - \{\alpha\} \ .$$

V_α is potential function due to object α, and V_j^E denotes environmental potential function from agent j's point of view.

3.2 Example of Potential Functions for Trash and Agents

For efficient collection of trash, agents should go toward short-handed area of agents where much trash exist and there are not enough agents. To realize agents' behavior like this, we define potential functions of the objects as follows.

Potential Function of Trash. Since the lower value of potential is defined as desirable influence for agents, agents go down potential hills. Therefore potential of trash should have lower value. We consider places where there is no influence on agents to possess a zero potential. Then in keeping with our intentions, potential of any trash will assume a negative value. The potential does not depend on an angle, but it depends only on a distance from the trash because trash can be picked up irrespective of agent's direction of approach. To satisfy these conditions, we use a function (1) as trash's potential function when the trash is located at $(0, 0)$. Here parameters of potential $A(> 0)$ and $\sigma(> 0)$ are amplitude and breadth of the trash's influence respectively.

$$V_{T_i}(x, y) = -A \exp\left(-\frac{x^2 + y^2}{2\sigma^2}\right) \ . \tag{1}$$

Potential Function of Agents. We should avoid occurrences where many agents go toward the same trash since it is a wastage of agents' efforts. If agents cannot obtain the information of other agents' velocities, potential due to the other agent spreads concentrically. Here, since a piece of trash can be picked up by an agent, we set the amplitude and breadth of potential to the same value with trash's potential (1) so that influence of an agent cancels that of a piece of trash. As a result, we obtain the following potential function due to an agent at $(0, 0)$:

$$V_{A_i}(x, y) = +A \exp\left(-\frac{x^2 + y^2}{2\sigma^2}\right) \ . \tag{2}$$

---

[2] If agent's range of vision is limited to some extent, O denotes all objects in its range of vision.

3.3   Agent's Decision Making Based on Potential in Trash Collecting Problem

Using potential functions defined above, the potential of the environment from agent j's perspective becomes

$$V_j^E(x,y) = \sum_{i \neq j} V_{A_i}(x - x_{A_i}, y - y_{A_i}) + \sum_i V_{T_i}(x - x_{T_i}, y - y_{T_i})$$

$$= \sum_{\alpha \in O_{\overline{A_j}}} V_\alpha(x - x_\alpha, y - y_\alpha)$$

where (x_α, y_α) is position of object α.

Next, we show agents' behavior based on potential. By definition, the lower value of potential means that the area is rather short-handed, and the higher value means there are enough agents in that area. Thus the direction of potential

$$-\nabla V_j^E = -\left(\frac{\partial V_j^E}{\partial x} \; \frac{\partial V_j^E}{\partial y} \right)$$

shows the direction to a short-handed area.

However, as mentioned in Sect. 2, there are several problems if agents behave according to the direction of $-\nabla V_j^E$ itself, and the task of collecting all trash ends up in failure. Therefore, agents need to refine the policy obtained from environmental potential and decide their behavior.

We propose this refinement as follows. An agent j should choose trash which is the 'nearest' to $-\nabla V_j^E$ in terms of both distance and angle as its target; otherwise the agent might need to turn back the way it has come. Here we define a function f to evaluate proximity of trash to $-\nabla V_j^E$. This function should satisfy the following conditions:

$$f(\boldsymbol{a}, -\nabla V_j^E) > f(\boldsymbol{b}, -\nabla V_j^E) \text{ if } |\boldsymbol{a}| < |\boldsymbol{b}| \; ,$$
$$f(\boldsymbol{a}, -\nabla V_j^E) > f(\boldsymbol{b}, -\nabla V_j^E) \text{ if } \theta_a < \theta_b$$

where θ_α $(0 \leq \theta_\alpha \leq \pi)$ is an angle between $-\nabla V_j^E$ and a vector to an object α from the agent j (Fig. 5). A higher value of f means the object is 'nearer' to the agent. Thus an agent should select trash which maximizes f as its target and go toward the trash. An example of a function which satisfies these conditions is

$$f(\boldsymbol{\alpha}, -\nabla V_j^E) = \cos \theta_\alpha / |\boldsymbol{\alpha}| \; . \tag{3}$$

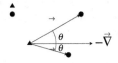

Fig. 5. Definition of θ_a and θ_b

4 Experiment

4.1 Settings

For evaluation of our proposed new method, we have performed several sets of simulations[3]. We consider the trash collecting problem described in previous sections. The settings of our experiments are as follows: 1) We consider two dimensional continuous space for a planar surface. 2) The size of the planar surface is 500×500 square units. 3) There are 100 agents on the surface. 4) Each agent can move a distance of 1 unit in any direction in unit time (1 clock). 5) Each agent can pick up trash within a distance of 1 unit from it. 6) Each agent has infinite range of vision, i.e., can acquire information of all objects on the surface. 7) Initial positions of agents and trash are determined by uniform random numbers.

In these experiments, Q takes $1, 2$ respectively, where Q is 'quorum' to pick up one trash, i.e., a trash can be picked up only when there are Q (or more) agent(s) within a distance of 1 unit from it.

m (the number of trash) takes 10, 20, 30, 50, 100, 200, 500 and 1000 respectively for setting $Q = 1$, and 10, 100 and 1000 respectively for setting $Q = 2$.

These experiments are performed with the following two types of agents. 1) Our method: Agents decide their behavior (the direction to move) in the same manner described in Sect. 3. 2) Agents without potential (we refer as 'nearest algorithm'): Agents select the nearest trash to go toward.

4.2 Results and Evaluation

Figures 6 and 7 are the results of setting $Q = 1$, and Figs. 8 and 9 are the results of setting $Q = 2$. Figures 6 and 8 show transitions of the number of collected trash (for $m = 10$ (top), $m = 100$ (middle) and $m = 1000$ (bottom)). Figures 7 and 9 show the relation between the number of trash (x-axis) and time to complete task, i.e., time to collect all trash (y-axis). These results show the average figures of 100 trials.

We now evaluate the results obtained through experiments as follows. As before, let us consider m and n be the numbers of trash and agent respectively. Figures 6 and 8 (transitions of the number of collected trash) show that there is only a little difference between the efficiency of our method and the nearest algorithm if $m \ll n$. This is because agents and trash are distributed uniformly and there are excessive agents against trash, thus agents can pick trash effectively even if agents go towards the nearest trash. On the other hand, our method works better than the nearest algorithm if $m \sim n$ or $m \gg n$. This is because agents of our method behave cooperatively by considering other agents' influence using potential. Figures 7 and 9 show the dependence of efficiency of the system against m. These graphs show that our method works more effectively for larger

---

[3] The agents on multi-agent systems of our experiments have been implemented using C++ and executed on AT compatible computers running FreeBSD 4.11-RELEASE.

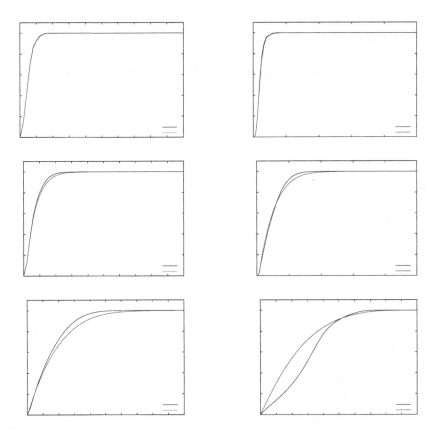

Fig. 6. Transitions of number of collected trash for $m = 10$ (top), $m = 100$ (middle) and $m = 1000$ (bottom) for $Q = 1$ (only one agent is needed to pick up one trash)

Fig. 8. Transitions of number of collected trash for $m = 10$ (top), $m = 100$ (middle) and $m = 1000$ (bottom) for $Q = 2$ (at least two agents are needed to pick up one trash)

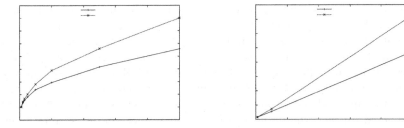

Fig. 7. Relation between the number of trash (x-axis) and time to complete task for $Q = 1$ (only one agent is needed to pick up one trash)

Fig. 9. Relation between the number of trash (x-axis) and time to complete task for $Q = 2$ (at least two agents are needed to pick up one trash)

m. Figure 8 (bottom) shows the agents without potential collect the trash faster than our method at the early stage of the experiment if $m \gg n$ when $Q = 2$. Nevertheless, the agents with potential (our method) collect all trash much faster than the agents of nearest algorithm (Fig. 9). This result suggests that switching the agents' strategies (go toward to the nearest trash (*selfish*) or the direction decided using potential (*cooperative*)) might improve the efficiency of the system. Detailed analysis of this characteristic is kept as one of our future works.

5   Discussion

There are several works regarding cooperation among agents, e.g., contract net protocol [2] and multistage negotiation protocol [3], or several works to realize cooperation among agents by forming coalitions like [4]. Furthermore, methods of the agents' dynamic organization formation based on the concept of social awareness [5] are being suggested in recent years. All of these methods need communication among agents and therefore not applicable or difficult to apply to non-communicative environments. Several works attempt to improve the performance of the system by reinforcement learning [6] (mainly Q-learning [7], profit sharing [8], or HQ-learning (hierarchical Q-learning) [9]). However, learning approaches require prior learning process and need much calculating costs, especially in continuous space. As stated in Sect. 2, physics-agent-system (PAS) model [1] by Shehory *et al.* has drawbacks like oscillation problem. This causes difference between the meaning of potential in physics and in multi-agent systems. In physics, a potential valley means stable point for an object. Meanwhile, in a multi-agent system, a potential valley does not necessarily mean the point where agents should go. In addition, there are essential differences between physics and multi-agent systems: the subjects in physics (particles etc.) are passive; the subjects in multi-agent systems (agents) are active. As such, agents should not decide their behavior depending only on the potential, and it should be refined as we proposed.

Next, we discuss the applicability of our method. Hybrid systems of our model and some other methods can improve the efficiency of systems to some extent. Imagine, for example, the hybrid system with our model and the nearest algorithm. In this case, agents of our method will collect the trash procrastinated by agents of the nearest algorithm. Figure 1 shows such situation: we can obtain the desired result if agent A uses our method even if agent B and C use the nearest algorithm. Of course, this does not work out if agent A uses the nearest algorithm even if agents B and C use our method, and we need further investigation. Our method is expected to work well even when agents' range of vision is restricted. In fact, the influence due to some object in our system described in previous sections was limited to short distance because we used the potential function which vanishes after a short distance (e^{-r^2} diminishes much faster than $1/r^n$ (n is any natural number)).

6   Conclusion

In this paper, we proposed the method to evaluate the situation of environment with potential functions to realize an effective cooperation among agents in non-communicative environments. The potential of each object represents its influence on the environment and the environmental potential, i.e., summation of each object's potential, represents global situation of the environment. Agents' decision of their behavior will be done by refining the policy obtained from potential. We used a trash collecting problem as an example to show the effectiveness of our method. Furthermore, we performed some sets of experiments of the trash collecting problem and show the efficiency of our method. We also discussed the applicability of our method to hybrid systems, environments where available information has a margin of error, or environments where agents' range of vision are limited.

The future works includes further investigation of the trash collecting problem, i.e., the behavior of the hybrid system with our model and other methods (e.g. nearest algorithm). The application of our method to real world problems is also a lucrative domain for our future work.

References

1. Onn Shehory, Sarit Kraus, and Osher Yadgar.   Emergent cooperative goal-satisfaction in large-scale automated-agent systems. *Artificial Intelligence*, 110:1–55, 1999.
2. Reid G. Smith. The contract net protocol: High-level communication and control in a distributed problem solver. *IEEE Transactions on Computers*, C-29(12):1104–1113, December 1980.
3. Susan E. Conry, Kazuhiro Kuwabara, Victor R. Lesser, and Robert A. Meyer. Multistage negotiation for distributed constraint satisfaction. *IEEE Transactions on Systems, Man, and Cybernetics*, 21(6):1462–1477, November/December 1991.
4. Onn Shehory and Sarit Kraus. Methods for task allocation via agent coalition formation. *Artificial Intelligence*, 101:165–200, 1998.
5. Lisa M. J. Hogg and Nicholas R. Jennings. Socially intelligent reasoning for autonomous agenst. *IEEE Transactions on Systems, Man, and Cybernetics—Part A: Systems and Humans*, 31(5):381–393, September 2001.
6. Richard S. Sutton and Andrew G. Barto. *Reinforcement Learning: An Introduction.* MIT Press, Cambridge, MA, 1998.
7. Ron Sun and Chad Sessions. Multi-agent reinforcement learning with bidding for segmenting action sequences. In *From Animals to Animats: Proceedings of the International Conference of Simulation of Adaptive Behavior (SAB'2000)*. MIT Press, Cambridge, MA, 2000.
8. Sachiyo Arai, Katia Sycara, and Terry R. Payne. Experience-based reinforcement learning to acquire effective behavior in a multiagent domain. In Riichiro Mizoguchi and John Slaney, editors, *The Sixth Pacific Rim International Conference on Artificial Intelligence (PRICAI 2000)*, pages 125–135. Springer-Verlag, 2000.
9. Marco Wiering and Juergen Schmidhuber. HQ-learning. *Adaptive Behavior*, 6(2):219–246, 1997.

The "Dance or Work" Problem: Why Do not all Honeybees Dance with Maximum Intensity

Ronald Thenius, Thomas Schmickl, and Karl Crailsheim

Department for Zoology, Karl-Franzens University,
Graz, Universitätsplatz 2, A-8010 Graz, Austria
theniusr@stud.uni-graz.at
schmickl@nextra.at, karl.crailsheim@uni-graz.at

Abstract. A honeybee colony has to choose among several nectar sources in the environment, each fluctuating in quality over time. Successful forager bees return to the hive and perform dances to describe the food sources they have found. Each dancer tries to recruit other forager bees to fly to the source it has found. Some individual dancers clearly dance longer for higher quality sources, other dancers distinguish little between poor and good sources; presumably the differences are genetically based [6].

Our multi-agent simulation showed that this individual heterogeneity results in optimal collective exploitation of the environment. Under all tested environmental conditions near-natural heterogeneous colonies worked more efficiently than artificially homogeneous ones. In heterogeneous colonies, dances last sufficiently long to recruit an appropriate number of waiting dance-following bees. In homogeneous colonies with good discriminating bees, the dances last longer than is efficient; the extra dancing decreases net food gains per time.

1 Introduction

1.1 Biological Background

The honeybee (*Apis mellifera* L.), an eusocial insect, lives in colonies of up to tens of thousands of individuals. The colony structure is self-organized, with no central regulatory unit. The individuals show age-polyethism, division of labour and task partitioning ([4]). A cohort of bees specialized on the same task is called a "temporal caste". The two temporal castes we modelled are the forager bees and the receiver bees.

Forager bees fly out of the hive to collect nectar, pollen, water or resins in the surrounding environment. The forager caste is subdivided into scouts, who explore for new food or other resources, and into foragers in the strict sense, who visit "known" resources. Nectar receiver bees wait near the hive's entrance to accept nectar from the returning forager bees. This nectar is then processed and stored in the colony as honey.

The colony as a whole continually chooses among different nectar sources in the environment, each with fluctuating food quality. The quality q of source i at a given moment can be expressed by the equation [6]:

$$qi = \frac{g - c}{c} \quad . \tag{1}$$

M. Pĕchouček, P. Petta, and L.Z. Varga (Eds.): CEEMAS 2005, LNAI 3690, pp. 246–255, 2005.

Here g expresses the energetic gain of the collected nectar, measured in Joules. This gain depends on the sugar concentration of the source [Mol/L] and on the collected nectar volume [µl]. c represents the costs of the foraging trip, again measured in Joules. These costs depend on the weight of the bee, the distance it must fly and the duration of the foraging trip.

In the morning, scouting bees fly out to search for new, yet unknown, nectar sources. If successful in finding food, they return to the hive and recruit other forager to the sources they discover.

Foragers or scouts returning from a successful foraging trip perform waggle-dances near the hive's entrance. These dances communicate the direction and the distance of the source to dance-following bees (here called "follower bees"). After following a dance, the follower flies to the described nectar source on its own [2].

The duration of a waggle-dance, that is, the number of waggle rounds, is correlated with the quality (q, see equation 1) of the source. This correlation can be shown in a "dance-response curve" (Figure 1, redrawn from [6]).

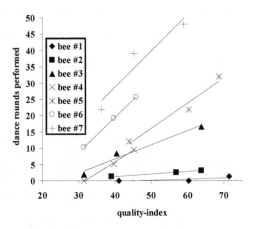

Fig. 1. Dance-response curves of real honeybees, redrawn from [6], illustrating the heterogeneity that exists within individual honeybee foragers

The curves vary remarkably among individual dancers (see figure 1). Foragers with a steep slope of the dance-response curve dance considerably longer for a high quality source than for a low quality one. In contrast, foragers with a flat slope of the curve have dances of much shorter duration, and the duration is not much longer for a good quality source than for a poorer one.

The probability that a dance is followed by a naive bee is correlated with the duration of the dance. Thus dances for a source of high quality usually attract more followers than dances for a source of low quality. The result is that more bees are recruited to fly to the sources with higher quality [6].

Some returning forager bees perform a "tremble-dance". If the search for a receiver bee takes too long after a successful foraging flight, the forager bee performs a tremble-dance, which recruits additional receiver bees. In this way an auto-balanced, self-organizing system for optimal source exploitation is accomplished:

1. The nectar influx is restricted to the current receiving workforce.
2. The receiving workforce is regulated according to the current influx.
3. The nectar sources of highest profitability are exploited to the greatest extent.

1.2   Motivation and Hypothesis

Our goal was to investigate the advantages and disadvantages of the heterogeneity of dance-response curves found in real honeybees [6]. Our hypothesis was that this "fuzziness" contributes to the robustness of the honeybee foraging decision-making system; thus we formulated the following two assumptions:

1. On the one hand, a homogeneous colony consisting only of bees with steep dance-response curves is expected to perform well in discriminating sources of different qualities in a stable environment.
2. On the other hand, in a fluctuating environment, quickly concentrating on only one source can be disadvantageous, as the quality of the chosen source can decrease rapidly. Thus, colonies with a heterogeneous set of dance-response curves are expected to perform well in fluctuating environments.

With an existing multi-agent simulation [5] we investigated the economics of colonies with these two sets of dance-response curves. In a variety of simulation runs, we compared the resulting foraging strategies and the efficiency of these two sets of dance-response curves.

1.3   Technical Relevance

Biological evolution offers numerous examples of dynamic optimization strategies. Other examples of biologically based algorithms are "ant-colony-optimization" (ACO, [1]), "genetic algorithms", "evolutionary programming" and "particle-swarm optimization" (described in detail in [3]).
Honeybee foraging algorithms offer a wide range of inspiring features, such as:

- High robustness against changes in the searched environment.

- High adaptivity to various sets of problems (e.g. optimisation of exploitation processes, search-algorithms, self organized workload balancing, etc.).

We think that honeybee foraging is a good source of inspiration in the quest for new, robust optimization algorithms. Exploration of the key features of honeybee foraging is a interesting field of studies.

2   Material and Methods

2.1   The Simulation Platform

We used a discrete-time multi-agent simulation platform of a honeybee colony (HoFoSim) [5]. In [5] HoFoSim was used to evaluate the influence of environmental fluctuations (amplitude & frequency of those fluctuations) on the efficiency of a honeybee colony. The advantages of the HoFoSim simulation platform are:

- The high adaptivity to a variety of questions.
- The nature-like individuality of honeybees regarding e.g. crop size, weight of bees, and dance-response curves.
- The detailed simulation of the forager-bee metabolism.

Contrary to the version described in [5], we implemented receiver bees instead of receiving events, to simulate the nectar-receiving act more precisely. The receiver bees have their own finite state automaton, but we did not implement the metabolism of these bees or a detailed storing process yet. Receiver bees accept nectar from returning forager bees. When a receiver bee's crop is full, the bee starts to store the nectar in a honey-store, what is simulated by the state "occupied" of the receiver bee while storing. Depending on the colony-nectar-need (cnn) the time a receiver bee spends with storing nectar varies from 10 minutes to 28 minutes.

In contrast to [5], where the amplitude and the frequency of environmental fluctuations were varied, this article focuses on a different topic: the influence of different individualities of foraging bees on the net honey gain of a honeybee colony under various environmental conditions (changing frequencies of environmental fluctuations).

2.2   The Experimental Set-Up

2.2.1   Colony Settings and the Outside Environment

We simulated a colony with 400 forager bees and 500 receiver bees[1] in an environment with three nectar sources, referred to here as sources A, B and C. Each nectar source was located within a distance of 146 patches (= 394 meters) of the hive. The sources were separated by distances of 40 patches (= 108 meters).

One experiment lasted for 8 hours, conducted in discrete time steps each corresponding to 0.5 seconds. The colony's net honey gain was recorded, as well as the distribution of foragers among the three nectar sources. Each experimental setup was repeated 14 times. Figures show mean values for each parameter setting, and each error bars expresses the standard deviation.

2.2.2   Fluctuating Environment

To simulate environmental fluctuation we repeatedly switched the sugar (sucrose) concentrations of the nectar sources from 2.5Mol/L to 0.75Mol/L[2] or vice versa. At each point in time only one nectar source was set to 2.5Mol/L (called the "good" source), while the two others were set to 0.75Mol/L ("poor sources"). The good location was switched from A to B, from B to C, from C back to A, and so on. The interval between each switch was varied to create different scenarios: "no switch", "one switch after 4 hours", "a switch every 2 hours", "every 1 hour", "every 0.5 hours" and "every 0.25 hours". In the scenario "no switch" source A was good

---

[1] A typical colony consists of 4000 to 40.000 individuals, for keeping the computational efforts in an acceptable range we chose the values of 500 foragers / 400 receivers. The ratio of foragers to receivers is comparable to the ratio found in real honeybee colonies.

throughout the whole experiment, in the scenario "one switch after 4 hours" source C was poor throughout the whole experiment, the sources A and B are switched. In figure 3, the symbol h⁺ indicates those moments when a switch of the good source took place.

2.2.3   Dance-Response Curves

The fluctuation scenarios described above were tested with two different sets of dance-response-curves (figure 2):

1. A "*heterogeneous set*" of dance-response curves, which were similar to the empirical observed ones (data calculated from [6]).
2. An artificially constructed "*homogeneous set*" of very steep dance-response curves, similar to the steepest curve observed empirically (= best discriminators only).

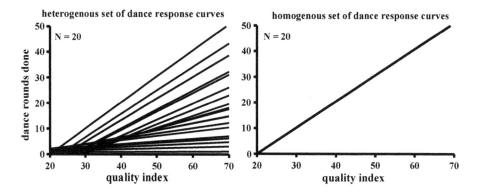

Fig. 2. Randomly picked dance-response curves from a "heterogeneous set" and the single curve (which is applied to all agents) in the "homogeneous set" used in our simulation

3   Results

3.1   Emerging Foraging Patterns

At the start of the simulation, the "homogeneous set" colonies did not recruit forager agents to the good source (source A) any faster than the "heterogeneous set" colonies. After source A changed from good to poor quality (at t = 4 hours), "homogeneous" colonies abandoned it significantly faster (between t = 5 hours and t = 6.5 hours ; Mann-Whitney U-test; $N_1=N_2=14$; $P \leq 0.05$) than "heterogeneous" colonies (for details see figure 3).

After the environmental fluctuation at t = 4 hours, colonies with the "homogeneous set" of dance-response-curves recruited agents significantly faster to the newly better source (source B) than colonies with a "heterogeneous set" (between t = 4.5 hours and

---

[2] In nature a source with a sugar concentration of 2.5Mol/L is a very good source, a source with 0.75Mol/L is a rather poor one.

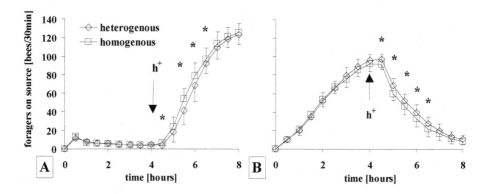

Fig. 3. Left: Number of foragers on source A from colonies with homogeneous and heterogeneous dance-response-curves. Stars indicate significant differences between the two data sets. Right: Number of foragers on source B from colonies with homogeneous and heterogeneous dance-response-curves. Stars indicate significant differences between the two data sets (P≤0.05); $N_1 = N_2 = 14$ per setting.

$t = 6$ hours; Mann-Whitney U-test; $N_1 = N_2 = 14$ per setting; P≤0.05; for details see figure 3). The graphs for source C are not shown in figure 3, for in the shown experiment source C was of poor quality throughout the whole experiment. Data of foraging patterns where evaluated for all frequencies of fluctuations (data not shown).

3.2   Energetic Efficiency of Heterogeneous Dance-Response Curves and of Homogeneous Dance-Response Curves

The cumulative net honey gain after 8 hours of both kinds of colonies are shown in table 1.

Table 1. Net honey gain of colonies with heterogeneous dance-response curves and of colonies with homogeneous dance-response curves after 8 hours under different environmental situations

fluctuations in food quality	heterogeneous dance-response curves	homogeneous dance-response curves
no fluctuations	101.6 ± 3.8 ml	93.9 ± 3.2 ml
every 4 hours	75.0 ± 3.8 ml	70.2 ± 5.4 ml
every 2 hours	56.1 ± 2.7 ml	49.3 ± 2.6 ml
every 1 hours	41.3 ± 2.1 ml	37.1 ± 3.4 ml
every 0.5 hours	40.0 ± 1.9 ml	33.8 ± 2.3 ml
every 0.25 hours	36.8 ± 3.5 ml	32.4 ± 2.4 ml

The dynamics of the cumulative net honey gain under different environmental situations is shown in Figure 4.

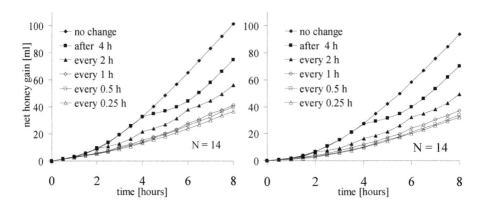

Fig. 4. Right: Cumulative net honey gains over 8 h of colonies with the "heterogeneous set" of dance-response curves under different levels of environmental fluctuation (frequency of changes in food quality), Left: Cumulative net honey gains over 8 h of colonies with the "homogeneous set" of dance-response curves under different levels of environmental fluctuation (frequency of changes in food quality)

3.3 Differences Between the Two Sets of Dance-Response Curves

The colonies having a "heterogeneous set" of dance-response-curves had a significantly higher net honey gain than those with the "homogeneous set" in every tested scenario (two-tailed Mann-Whitney U-test, N1=N2=14, P≤0.05). For details see figure 5.

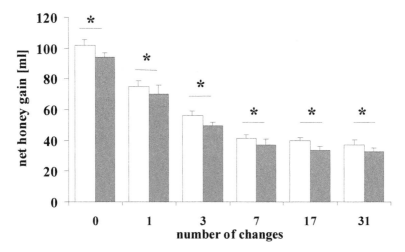

Fig. 5. Differences in net honey gain between colonies with a "heterogeneous set" of danceresponse curves (white columns) and those with the "homogeneous set" (grey columns) after 8 hours. Stars indicate significant differences between the two data sets (P≤0.05); $N_1 = N_2 = 14$ per setting.

3.4   Influence of the "In-Hive Delay" on Net Honey Gain

In this experiment, we extended the mean "in-hive" period for agents with the "heterogeneous set" of dance-response curves by adding an additional delay. We used this additional delay because the mean dance period for the "good source" lasts for 46 seconds in "heterogeneous" colonies, compared to 96 seconds in "homogeneous" colonies (calculated from [6]). To compensate for the resulting difference (50 seconds) of the foraging cycle duration, we delayed the "heterogeneous" agents by forcing them to stay in the hive for an additional 50 seconds after each bout of dancing. We used again the "no-fluctuation" scenario, which had already produced the greatest differences in net honey gain between "heterogeneous" and "homogeneous" colonies (see figure 5). The additional in-hive delay significantly decreased the net honey gains of the heterogeneous colonies (two-tailed Mann-Whitney U-test, $N_1=N_2=14$, $P<0.05$; see figure 6). These colonies no longer exceeded the homogeneous colonies in honey gains (two-tailed Mann-Whitney U-test, $N_1=N_2=14$, $P<0.05$; see figure 6).

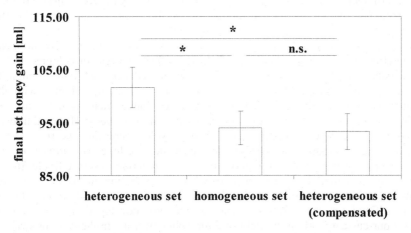

Fig. 6. Differences in net honey gain of colonies with a "heterogeneous set" of dance-response curves and colonies with the "homogeneous set" of dance-response curves after 8 hours. In "compensated" colonies, we added a delay factor that increased the time dancers stayed in the hive after dancing. Stars indicate significant differences between two data sets ($P \le 0.05$); $N_1 = N_2 = 14$ per setting

4   Discussion

Our multi-agent-simulation illuminates some global effects of distinct sets of individual behavioral settings. Fluctuations in the environment are costly for a honeybee colony (as can be seen in figure 5). The colony reacts to such fluctuations by drawing off foragers from the nectar source that has become poorer and recruiting foragers to the improved source. We found that heterogeneity of the used extent in the individual dancing dispositions of agents has no significant influence on the global dynamics of the colony's net honey gain (figure 4).

We expected a higher net honey gain in better discriminating colonies (colonies with the "homogeneous set" of dance-response curves), in scenarios with no fluctuations or a low fluctuation frequency in the environment. Furthermore, we expected that colonies with the "heterogeneous set" of dance-response-curves would be more efficient in scenarios with a high frequency of fluctuations in the environment. Because colonies with flat dance-response curves do not discriminate well between poor and good sources, they should "remember" poor sources for a longer period of time. In fluctuating environments, a poor source can suddenly turn into a good one. So we assumed that colonies with the heterogeneous set of dance-response-curves have a larger pool of available information, which should be an advantage in heavily fluctuating environments.

To our surprise, the results of our simulations confirmed only a part of our assumptions (see figures 4, 5): Except during the first hours of the simulated day, when there are not many dance-following bees, the good discriminators ("homogeneous set") recruited faster to emerging good nectar sources and were quicker to abandon worsening nectar sources (see figures 3). But in contrast to our assumption, our model found these extreme-discriminator colonies to have lower energetic efficiency. In fact, under all environmental circumstances, these colonies accumulated *less* honey within the simulation period than the colonies with the heterogeneous set of dance-response curves distributed as in nature.

The higher efficiency of "heterogeneous" colonies can be explained by the mean dance duration of the waggle-dances performed by forager bees. In colonies with a heterogeneous set of dance-response curves, foragers dance just long enough to recruit the pool of waiting follower bees, whereas foragers in colonies with the "homogeneous set" of dance-response-curves dance longer than is necessary for recruiting an appropriate number of waiting dance-following bees. These additional dance rounds increase the length of the foraging cycle, decreasing the time of the individual forager available for collecting nectar outside the hive. The impact of this delay on the nectar economics was demonstrated by simulation runs (see figure 6).

The study presented here demonstrates clearly a situation in which a nature-orientated algorithm, based on individual heterogeneity, is significantly more efficient than an artificial (engineered) homogeneous one. We developed this multi-agent model for our current work in the field of multi-robot swarms: In these robot swarms, a huge number of simple robots without sophisticated communication abilities has to suffice to reach a common swarm goal. We use algorithms from the honeybee foraging system described here to improve the performance of these robot swarms. In conclusion, this article demonstrates the advantage of heterogeneity between individuals for increasing efficiency in a distributed and decentralized system.

Acknowledgements

The writing of this article was supported by the "Fonds zur Förderung der Wissenschaftlichen Forschung (FWF)", project no. P15961-B06 and by the EU IST-FET-open project (IP) 'I-Swarm', no. 507006. Simulation experiments presented here were supported by the "University Graz / BMBWK Infrastructure Investment Program, Projekt-Nummer TUGP1" (Hard- and Software)". We also thank R. Nowogrodzki for his critical reading of the manuscript and for linguistic corrections.

References

1. Dorigo, M. and Stützle, T. Ant colony optimization. MIT Press, Cambridge, MS, London, UK, (2004)
2. Frisch, K. v. Tanzsprache und Orientierung der Bienen. Springer Verlag, Berlin, Heidelberg, New York, (1965)
3. Kennedy, J. and Eberhart, R. C. Swarm intelligence. Academic Press, San Francisco, San Diego, New York, Boston, London, Sydney, Tokyo, 2001
4. Ratnieks, F. L. W. and Anderson, C. Task partitioning in insect societies. II. Use of queueing delay information in recruitment. Am. Nat., 154, (1999), 536-548
5. Schmickl, T. Crailsheim, K. Cost of environmental fluctuations an benefits of dynamic foraging decisions in honey bees. Adapitve Behavior. 12, (2004), 263-277
6. Seeley, T. D. Honey bee foragers as sensory units of their colonies. Behav. Ecol. Sociobiol., 34, (1994), 51-62

Towards an Institutional Environment Using Norms for Contract Performance

Henrique Lopes Cardoso and Eugénio Oliveira

LIACC – NIAD&R, Faculty of Engineering, University of Porto,
R. Dr. Roberto Frias, 4200-465 Porto, Portugal
hlc@ipb.pt, eco@fe.up.pt

Abstract. A strong research emphasis is being given towards regulating inter-operable multi-agent environments through norms and institutions. We are concerned with environments in which agents form together virtual organizations leading to cooperation agreements that can be enforced. An electronic institution provides a coordination framework facilitating automatic contract establishment and providing an enforceable normative environment. We introduce the notion of contextualized norms within our institutional framework, and develop on a model of institutional reality, taking into account institutional roles and agents' statements, with the aim of providing a contract monitoring service. Our proposal describes how to use norms to formalize cooperation agreements and operational contracts, and how to monitor and detect contract violations.

1 Introduction

An increasingly important dichotomy in multi-agent systems (MAS) research is autonomy and openness versus regulation. While agent theory puts an emphasis on agents as autonomous self-interested entities interacting in open environments, the application of MAS in real-world scenarios raises an important question: how to ensure an intended cooperative behavior in environments populated with self-interested agents? A possible response to this problem is to regulate the environment, providing incentives for cooperative behavior through normative constraints [2].

In our case, we are concerned with environments in which agents may agree on cooperation efforts, involving specific interactions during a certain time frame. By this way agents may compose a virtual organization (VO), which is regulated by specific and appropriate norms. Here agents usually represent different business entities or enterprises, which come together to address new market opportunities by combining skills, resources, risks and finances no partner alone can fulfill [5].

In open environments, previous performance of potential partners (that is, their reputations) may not be assessed. A VO may comprise agents that have never worked together in the past. This makes it necessary to state, through a formal contract, what an agreement is about, and to provide an environment for enforcing those contracts.

In our view, the *Electronic Institution* (EI) concept addresses these concerns [10], as it consists of a coordination framework facilitating the establishment of contracts and providing a level of trust by offering an enforceable normative environment. This is accomplished through agent-based institutional services, including contract

M. Pěchouček, P. Petta, and L.Z. Varga (Eds.): CEEMAS 2005, LNAI 3690, pp. 256–265, 2005.
© Springer-Verlag Berlin Heidelberg 2005

monitoring and enforcement. The EI encompasses a set of norms regulating the environment. However, due to the fact that agents negotiate towards the achievement of agreements formalized in contractual norms, this normative environment is an evolving one. Through appropriate services, the EI monitors and enforces (using sanctions and reputation mechanisms) both institutional norms and those formalizing contracts.

Inside the EI, agents' illocutions are the source towards the formation of institutional reality (inspired in [17]). This reality is composed of both new organizational structures (VOs) and actions performed concerning the compliance to norms. Also, some agents perform specific institutional roles, being certified by the EI as legitimate to produce certain institutional facts. External agents may also announce themselves as performing certain roles. Instead of providing institutional services, these are general roles (such as seller or customer) which may, when performed inside the EI, have a set of attached norms. By assuming those roles, agents become committed to these norms.

In this paper we elaborate on the use of norms within our EI framework (section 2) and on the creation of institutional reality (section 3). Furthermore, we address the specification of contracts (including those devoted to VO settings) using norms regulating behavior (section 4), allowing for contract monitoring and enforcement. Finally we get to some conclusions and identify some related work (section 5).

2 Contextualized Norms

Norms play an important role in open artificial agent systems, where they improve coordination and cooperation. As in real-world societies, norms allow us to achieve social order [2] by controlling the environment, making it more stable and predictable.

Norms can be classified according to different criteria. Considering our EI framework, we find it important to classify norms according to their scope [11]. *Institutional norms* regulate the behavior of every agent inside the EI. By assuming general roles, agents become committed (before the institution) to their associated norms. Institutional norms also include general means of dealing with contract-independent occurrences, such as policies for handling norm violations. They set up the normative ground on which cooperation commitments may be established. *Constitutional norms* are used to describe the constitution of agent-based virtual organizations, which thereby commit to a certain cooperation agreement. The terms of such an agreement are specified by means of norms regulating the created consortium, which usually exists for a period of time. Finally, *operational norms* specify contracts by indicating actions to be performed by contractual agents; they may be proposed and signed within the context of a specific VO, or else may comprise a stand-alone deal.

This classification suggests that different types of norms are created at different moments. Thus, institutional norms may be pre-existent, while constitutional norms are created when agents reach cooperation agreements, and operational norms come into existence when executable contracts are signed. However, this needs not be the case. Norms with limited scopes may be predefined for a number of reasons.

An important concept in contract law theory is the use of "default rules", which facilitate contract formation, allowing contracts to be underspecified by defining default clauses. Therefore, constitutional or even operational norms may be institutionally defined: together with institutional norms, they provide a normative background in which agents can rely to build their contractual commitments.

Furthermore, just as real-world legislations are organized through hierarchies of laws, it is natural to have predefined regulations devoted to particular contexts, such as the VO setting. Agents can rely on these regulations as a ground basis to raise specific virtual organizations.

Finally, norms may be predefined when they regulate predicted coordination situations, as in the case of negotiation protocols. Agents agreeing to coordinate their negotiation efforts according to a certain protocol adhere to the norms implementing it. Differently from "default rules", however, these norms apply as they are to every adhesion to the protocol; they do not make up mere fill-in prescriptions in the absence of explicitly created norms.

According to this setting, it is possible, therefore, to predefine scoped norms that are to be imposed when the activity they regulate is adhered to by agents. This methodology may be applied to negotiation protocols, to standard cooperation commitments between a group of agents, or to norms attached to roles. Although having a limited scope, these norms can be seen as institutional in the sense that they are institutionally predefined.

Independently of the circumstances of their creation, norms define, in some context, what ought to be done in certain circumstances:

$$[Context] \; Situation \rightarrow Prescription$$

The *Context* indicates the scope of the norm. The *Situation* describes when the norm is in place. The *Prescription* specifies what should be accomplished.

In all formulae throughout this paper, we use the Prolog notation conventions for variables and relations.

3   Institutional Reality

Considering an EI as an environment where social relationships are created and enforced, it is necessary to establish how and when such relationships are in place, and how and when they are fulfilled. If we design a closed EI environment with a well-defined performative structure (as in [14]), agents' actions and their effects are restricted. If, however, we design an open environment where autonomous agents interact, we must relate those interactions with the (emergence of) social structures defining commitments among agents. This represents a much more flexible approach towards the development of a normative framework.

Following Searle's theory on "the construction of social reality" [17], inside the EI we consider *brute facts* and *institutional facts*. The latter are obtained from de former, through rules defining "counts-as" relations (constitutive rules).

3.1   Brute and Institutional Facts

Agents' illocutions are stored as brute facts in the form:

$$illocution(Agent, Content)$$

Relevant illocutions are assumed to use a well-defined institutional ontology.

Institutional facts are inferred using constitutive rules. These are fed with agents' illocutions (brute facts), and produce institutional reality. Just as norms have a context in which they apply, we associate institutional facts with the *context* within which they occur. This is important if we consider facts denoting agent behavior regarding its obligations: these facts may occur within a context (e.g. a contract).

An important issue to consider in contracting scenarios is time: every fact must occur at a given instant. We use the following representation for institutional facts:

$$[Context]\ ifact(IFact,\ Timestamp)$$

Just as brute facts, institutional facts are defined in the institutional ontology.

3.2   The Institutional Reality Engine

Institutional reality depends on the recording of brute facts, which are then processed by "systems of constitutive rules" [17]. Relevant facts include those related to commitment creation (implying the establishment of contracts) and fulfillment. Therefore, rules regulating how these facts come about are needed.

Institutional Roles. Illocutions' effects may depend on the agents uttering them. We identify a set of *institutional roles* enacted by agents providing specific services. Some institutional facts may be created only if agents performing certain institutional roles utter appropriate illocutions. Authoritative relations are established in this way between roles and institutional reality: an agent performing a given role is said to be empowered to achieve the effects expressed in its role-related constitutive rules.

Since we are concerned with the application of our model to business scenarios involving transactions, we identify three main institutional roles providing a connection to the real-world. A *messenger* role provides certified information exchange facilities; a *banking* role enables acknowledging monetary value transfers; a *delivery tracker* role certifies product delivery.

Constitutive Rules. Constitutive rules make a connection between what is said and what is taken for granted. Many of these rules will be based on institutional roles and their powers. According to our EI rationale, we identify two main focuses for constitutive rules: (1) the certification of action execution (including contract fulfillment), and (2) the establishment of commitments through contracts.

Certified action execution is important because of trustworthiness issues. Consider a situation in which an agent ought to make a certain payment to another. Although the agent may claim to have paid its debt, that does not make it the case. Still, if an independent financial agent, providing a certified institutional service, states that a currency transfer referring to a certain context (e.g. a purchase contract) has taken place, it would be safe to consider that the payment occurred, which is described as below:

$$illocution(B,\ currency\_transfered(Ctx,\ Ag1,\ Amount,\ Ag2,\ Time)) \land ibank(B)$$
$$\rightarrow [Ctx]\ ifact(payment(Ag1,\ Amount,\ Ag2),\ Time)$$

We can also say that if both agents (the payer and the receiver) acknowledge the payment, it would be safe to conclude the associated institutional fact:

---

illocution(Ag1, paid(Ctx, Amount, Ag2, _)) ∧ illocution(Ag2, collected(Ctx, Amount, Ag1, Time))
→ [Ctx] ifact(payment(Ag1, Amount, Ag2), Time)

Another exemplifying case where physical actions must be checked concerns the delivery of products. We may trust on a delivery tracking service:

---

illocution(DT, delivered(Ctx, Ag1, Item, Quantity, Ag2, Time)) ∧ idelivery_tracker(DT)
→ [Ctx] ifact(delivery(Ag1, Item, Quantity, Ag2), Time)

The same methodology can be applied concerning the exchange of messages. If message delivery recognition is a must, an institutional messenger service may be provided. This way, interactions between agents through the exchange of messages can be recorded, as long as such a service intermediates the process.

The messenger agent informs the EI that a given message was delivered. The following constitutive rule applies:

---

illocution(M, msg_delivered(Ctx, Ag1, Msg, Ag2, Time)) ∧ imessenger(M)
→ [Ctx] ifact(msg(Ag1, Msg, Ag2), Time)

In principle, any information exchange could be treated in a similar way. This opens up the possibility to verify business-related activities such as order placement, invoice issuing, or shipment notices. It also enables the verification of negotiation protocols requiring the exchange of proposals.

As for contract establishment, we must define relations between institutional facts (created from agents' illocutions) and commitment formation. These constitutive rules define how new institutionally enforceable norms can be created, describing contractual relationships between agents.

Contractual relationships may rise from an appropriate exchange of messages. For instance, a contract may be recognized if an agent accepts the terms and conditions of a standing proposal (that is, when agents reach an agreement):

---

ifact(acceptation(Ag1, Ag2), TA) ∧ ifact(proposal(Ag2, Ag1, Proposal, Timeout), TP) ∧
TP<TA<TP+Timeout
→ register_new_contract(Ag1, Ag2, Proposal, TA)

---

where *register_new_contract* would be an institutional procedure registering the contract between the involved agents. Several researchers address the issue of commitment creation from interaction protocols. A survey may be found in [12].

If, however, negotiation protocols must be enforced, or if negotiation must be mediated (besides mere message forwarding), negotiation mediation services may be provided by an institutional agent. This applies to negotiation protocols specifically devoted to formalizing VO cooperation agreements, as we have proposed before [13].

4 Specifying and Monitoring Contracts

Behavior norms prescribe the expected behavior of agents. We attribute the responsibility of monitoring and enforcing norms to the EI, which by this means establishes a trust-enabled normative environment.

A norm-aware environment can operate either preventively (making unwanted behavior impossible) or responsively (detecting violations and reacting accordingly) [18]. Taking into account the autonomous nature of agents, we rely essential on the latter practice. Norms specify states of affairs that *must* be brought about by an agent before a certain deadline. Therefore, we consider *obligations* as the means to express the prescription of behavior norms. Obligations have the following structure:

[Context] obligation(Bearer, InstitutionalFact, Deadline)

Instead of dictating the exact action an agent must perform, we prescribe the institutional fact that it must bring about. This fits with our model of institutional reality, where we specify through constitutive rules how an institutional fact may be accrued. It also enables an agent to delegate tasks conducting to the accomplishment of such state of affairs, while still being responsible for the (un)fulfillment of the obligation.

Situations in which norms apply include the achievement of institutional facts, and the fulfillment or violation of obligations. Norms prescribing behavior in case of violations are sanctioning norms: they are meant to discourage non-compliance. These norms may be defined either as institutional or as contract-specific.

4.1 Fulfillment and Violation of Obligations

Contextualized institutional facts are used to verify the fulfillment of obligations. For this, we define an obligation *fulfillment rule*:

[Context] ifact(IFact, T) ∧ obligation(Bearer, IFact, Deadline) ∧ T<Deadline
→ fulfilled(Bearer, IFact, T)

This rule indicates that if an institutional fact prescribed by an obligation is achieved before its deadline, then that obligation is fulfilled. Literals within the rule are dependent on its context. However, this rule is institutional, as it applies to all contractual relations; it thus has un-instantiated *Context*.

This rule is fundamental for enabling the chaining of obligations within a contractual relationship. It establishes a connection between the institutional facts that are added and the pending obligations.

Sanctioning norms are activated using a *violation detection rule*, which fires when deadlines have elapsed. Time events are generated as institutional facts referring to the time when obligations are due.

[Context] ifact(time, Deadline) ∧
obligation(Bearer, IFact, Deadline) ∧ not(fulfilled(Bearer, IFact, _))
→ violated(Bearer, IFact, Deadline)

This violation detection rule states that in any context, if a deadline referring to an obligation was reached, and such obligation was not fulfilled, then a violation occurred. The resulting fact may be used to activate sanctioning norms and to update the agent's reputation.

This approach allows us to distinguish violation detection from sanction imposition mechanisms. While the detection of violations is a general and institutionally defined concept, the prescription of sanctions may be contract-specific.

4.2 Virtual Organization Cooperation Agreements

A cooperation agreement aggregates the VO's constitutional information, including the cooperation effort agents are committed to, and their general business process flow. Considering situations where the intended cooperation consists of the exchange of resources, the following templates are used to specify this information:

[ ] ifact(cooperation_agreement(IdCA, Participants, Resources), CATime)

[cooperation_agreement:IdCA]
coop_effort(Participant, Resource, MinQuantity, MaxQuantity, Frequency, UnitPrice)

[cooperation_agreement:IdCA] business_process(From, Resource, To)

Cooperation efforts indicate, for each participating agent, quantity ranges for the supply of resources, within a given frequency, together with agreed prices. Business process entries indicate the resources that are supposed to flow between participants. Their effective transfer, however, is dependent on appropriate requests.

The central norm in respect to contractual promises indicates that each agent is committed to its cooperation effort. This translates to an obligation prescription:

[cooperation_agreement:IdCA]
ifact(request(Requester, Resource, Quantity, Answerer), TR) $\wedge$
business_process(Answerer, Resource, Requester) $\wedge$
coop_effort(Answerer, Resource, MinQt, MaxQt, Freq, _) $\wedge$
calculate_performed_effort(Answerer, Resource, Freq, TR, PE) $\wedge$ PE+Quantity<=MaxQt
$\rightarrow$ obligation(Answerer, acknowledge(Answerer, Resource, Quantity, Requester), TR+10)

This norm is institutionally defined: it applies to all cooperation agreements created inside the institution. Its context remains unbound until it is in use. Briefly, it states that if a predicted request (considering the stated business process and cooperation effort) is made in the context of a cooperation agreement, then the envisaged agent is obliged to accept it. An institutional procedure (*calculate_performed_effort*) is invoked for calculating the effort already performed by the agent. If it does not exceed its promised efforts, the obligation comes into effect.

4.3 Operational Contracts

Operational contracts are established in the context of a cooperation agreement. Institutional facts register their creation:

[cooperation_agreement:IdCA]
ifact(operational_contract(IdOC, Requester, Answerer, Resource, Quantity), OCTime)

Considering parties' cooperation commitments, operational contracts come into existence through a constitutive rule of the form:

[cooperation_agreement:IdCA]
fulfilled(Answerer, acknowledge(Answerer, Resource, Quantity, Requester), TA)
→ register_new_operational_contract(IdCA, Requester, Answerer, Resource, Quantity, TA)

This rule applies to every cooperation agreement, and states that when an agent fulfils its obligation to acknowledge a given request, a new operational contract comes into existence.

The cooperation agreement may also specify how operational contracts are managed, that is, what obligation chains implement such activity. This facilitates their creation, since their norms may be pre-specified. One possibility is to define norms applicable to all operational contracts within a cooperation agreement. For instance, if delivery and payment should occur:

[cooperation_agreement:IdCA, operational_contract:IdOC]
obligation(Answerer, delivery(_, Resource, Quantity, Requester), OCTime+10)

[cooperation_agreement:IdCA, operational_contract:IdOC]
fulfilled(Answerer, delivery(_,Resource, Quantity, Requester), TD) ∧
coop_effort(Answerer, Resource, _, _, _, UnitPrice)
→ obligation(Requester, payment(_, UnitPrice*Quantity, Answerer), TD+30)

where *IdOC* remains unbound, as these norms apply to all operational contracts which will be created in the future within agreement *IdCA*.

It would also be possible to define an institutional default policy, applicable to all operational contracts of all cooperation agreements.

5 Conclusions and Related Work

The regulation of multi-agent systems in environments with no central design (and thus with no cooperative assumption) is gaining much attention in the research community. Normative multi-agent systems address this issue by introducing incentives to cooperation (or discouraging deviation). After initial research on norms as constraints on behavior, it is now accepted that autonomous agents are able to deliberate whether to comply with norms [3].

Searle's work on speech acts [16] and institutional reality [17] has inspired several researchers within the MAS field (e.g. [1], [4], and [7]). In our case, we used this inspiration as a means to certify the occurrence of real-world actions, essential to contract monitoring purposes. Brute facts consist of agents' illocutions, which according to empowering relations are used to produce institutional reality.

Within the framework of our proposed electronic institution [10] providing services for the achievement of contractually specified agreements (including VO scenarios), we described the use of contextualized norms and the specification and monitoring of contracts. Norms are typically related with the deontic notions of obligation, permission and prohibition, and have been used to formalize contracts (e.g. [9] and [15]). In our case, we essentially rely on directed obligations. In the case of VO contracts, permissions are seen as rights for requesting a partner's contribution. Prohibitions may be applied as a consequence of violation detection. A formal underpinning of a logic for contract representation is given in [6], including the notion of conditional obligation with deadline (equivalent to our norm specification).

The concept of electronic institutions is gaining importance inside MAS research. Previous approaches towards regulating agent behavior through EIs include [14]. However, this model formally defines an institution using a rigid structure that implements a predefined protocol. By restricting the actions agents are allowed to perform, it does not cope well with a central property of agency: autonomy. In our approach, we avoid imposing hard constraints on behavior. By enforcing norms, we do conduct and supervise the behavior of rational agents.

Top-down normative frameworks are appropriate in situations where norms can be centrally designed, although regulating a distributed environment with autonomous self-interested agents. However, it is not amenable to contract handling: agents make agreements that are to be monitored by a trusted third-party (the EI), thus the normative structure is modified by the corresponding contracts. We aim at providing such an evolving normative framework, taking into account the creation of institutional reality.

Norms lend themselves to a rule-based implementation. We are implementing our agent-based EI framework in JADE and using the JESS shell [8] for norm representation, monitoring and enforcement. JESS incorporates features enabling also the use of default reasoning, and consists of a forward-chaining production system that fits the firing of norms and rules based on events (institutional facts in our case). It also includes the possibility to define modules for organizing sets of rules, matching our norm contexts.

References

1. Boella, G., & van der Torre, L. (2004). Regulative and Constitutive Norms in Normative Multiagent Systems. In *Proc. 9th Int. Conf. on the Principles of Knowledge Representation and Reasoning (KR'04)*, Whistler, Canada.
2. Castelfranchi C. (2000). Engineering Social Order. In A. Omicini, R. Tolksdorf, & F. Zambonelli (eds.), *Engineering Societies in the Agents World*, Springer, pp.1-18.
3. Castelfranchi, C., Dignum, F., Jonker, C., & Treur, J. (2000). Deliberative Normative Agents: Principles and Architectures. In N. Jennings & Y. Lesperance (eds.), *Intelligent Agents VI: Agent Theories, Architectures, and Languages*, Springer, pp.364-378.
4. Colombetti, M., & Verdicchio, M. (2002). An analysis of agent speech acts as institutional actions. In Castelfranchi & Johnson (eds.), *Proc. 1st Int. Joint Conf. on Autonomous Agents and Multiagent Systems*, ACM Press, pp.1157-1164.
5. Dignum, V., & Dignum, F. (2002). Towards an Agent-based Infrastructure to Support Virtual Organizations. In L.M. Camarinha-Matos (ed.), *Collaborative Business Ecosystems and Virtual Enterprises*, Kluwer, pp.363-370.

6. Dignum, V., Meyer, J.-J., Dignum, F., & Weigand, H. (2003). Formal Specification of Interaction in Agent Societies. In M. Hinchey, J. Rash, W. Truszkowski, C. Rouff & D. Gordon-Spears (eds.) *Formal Approaches to Agent-Based Systems*, Springer, pp.37-52.
7. Fornara, N., Viganò, F., & Colombetti, M. (2005). Agent Communication and Institutional Reality. In R. M. van Eijk, M.-P. Huget & F. Dignum (eds.), *Agent Communication*, Springer, pp.1-17.
8. JESS, the Rule Engine for the Java Platform (http://herzberg.ca.sandia.gov/jess/).
9. Kollingbaum, M.J., & Norman, T.J. (2002). Supervised Interaction – Creating a Web of Trust for Contracting Agents in Electronic Environments. In Castelfranchi & Johnson (eds.), *Proc. 1st Int. Joint Conf. on Autonomous Agents and Multiagent Systems*, ACM Press, pp.272-279.
10. Lopes Cardoso, H., Malucelli, A., Rocha, A.P., & Oliveira, E. (2005). Institutional Services for Dynamic Virtual Organizations. In *Proc. 6th IFIP Working Conference on Virtual Enterprises (PRO-VE'05)*, Valencia, Spain, 26-28 September 2005.
11. Lopes Cardoso, H., & Oliveira, E. (2005). Virtual Enterprise Normative Framework within Electronic Institutions. In M.-P. Gleizes, A. Omicini & F. Zambonelli (eds.), *Engineering Societies in the Agents World V*, Springer, pp.14-32.
12. Maudet, N., & Chaib-draa, B. (2002). Commitment-based and dialogue-game based protocols – new trends in agent communication languages, *Knowledge Engineering* 17(2), pp.157-179.
13. Oliveira, E., & Rocha, A.P. (2000). Agents Advanced Features for Negotiation in Electronic Commerce and Virtual Organisations Formation Process. In F. Dignum & C. Sierra (eds.), *Agent Mediated Electronic Commerce: The European AgentLink Perspective*, Springer, pp. 78-97.
14. Rodríguez-Aguilar, J.A. (2001). *On the design and construction of Agent-mediated Electronic Institutions*, Ph.D. Thesis, Universitat Autònoma de Barcelona.
15. Sallé, M. (2002). Electronic Contract Framework for Contractual Agents. In R. Cohen & B. Spencer (eds.), *Advances in Artificial Intelligence: 15th Conference of the Canadian Society for Computational Studies of Intelligence*, Springer, pp.349-353.
16. Searle, J.R. (1969). *Speech Acts: an Essay in the Philosophy of Language*. Cambridge, England: Cambridge University Press.
17. Searle, J.R. (1995). *The Construction of Social Reality*, Free Press: New York.
18. Vázquez-Salceda, J., Aldewereld, H., & Dignum, F. (2004). Implementing norms in multi-agent systems. In G. Lindemann, J. Denzinger, I. J. Timm & R. Unland (eds.), *Multiagent System Technologies*, Springer, pp.313-327.

Virtual Games: A New Approach to Implementation of Social Choice Rules

Dániel L. Kovács

Budapest University of Technology and Economics,
Faculty of Electrical Engineering and Informatics,
Department of Measurement and Information Systems, P.O.box 91,
H-1521 Budapest, Hungary
dkovacs@mit.bme.hu
http://www.mit.bme.hu/~dkovacs/index.html

Abstract. Intelligent systems play a crucial role in our everyday life. Yet there is still no general concept for designing such systems (at an individual, social, and inter-social level). Intelligent systems are designed on a case-by-case basis, mostly in an ad-hoc fashion lacking any kind of general design strategy. Nonetheless there are theories, which capture some profound aspects of the problem. One of them is the theory of implementation of social choice rules, which is concerned with the collective behavior in multi-agent systems. However the roots of the theory lie in social sciences, so its approach is not suitable enough for multi-agent system design. This article introduces a new game theoretic approach to implementation of social choice rules, which enables design of provably optimal multi-agent system without any restriction in general.

1 Introduction

Multi-agent systems (MAS) are usually considered from the perspective of intelligent agents [1]. This approach is intuitive, and holds many advantages, but has also its drawbacks. A wide variety of agent-models, communication protocols, and diverse formal methods exist, which may be effective in special design cases, but on the whole they lack the coherency to form a general theoretical basis for intelligent multi-agent system design. Even at the highest level of abstraction, the very definition of an agent is discussed. Some point out, that it is necessary for an agent to be autonomous, while others emphasize its ability to learn, etc.

From the many existing definitions this article will use one of the most widely recognized and general: an *agent* "can be anything that can be viewed as perceiving its environment through sensors and acting upon that environment through effectors." [2]. This means, that if an agent's actions depend on its senses, then it must have some representation of the environment, i.e. some kind of a *percept*. A percept is usually not equivalent to the environment, because the environment is usually not fully accessible to the agent. Using percepts an agent is able to compute its next action. Moreover, all the preceding percepts (the complete percept history) can have an effect on that choice. Consequently we may speak of *two levels* of environmental representation: an *outer representation* exterior to the agent, and an *inner representation*, inside the agent. It is the latter, upon which the agent's decision mechanism – choosing among possible

M. Pěchouček, P. Petta, and L.Z. Varga (Eds.): CEEMAS 2005, LNAI 3690, pp. 266–275, 2005.
© Springer-Verlag Berlin Heidelberg 2005

actions – may be placed. It is the task of the Designer to design this mechanism appropriately given the outer representation of the environment, and the agent's architecture (sensors, effectors, etc). This decision mechanism may depend on some special features of the environment to allow the agent to act effectively, e.g. there may be other agents, which make the environment dynamic. Such *multi-agent* situations require individual agents to consider other agents' activity for effective operation. Not only the past, or the present activity should be considered, but also events, which may occur in the future. Thus it is advantageous for an agent to *plan* its actions in advance, and to consider other agents' *planning* activity too.

Obviously the *goodness* (utility, payoff, etc.) of such agents depends not only on the plan they execute, but also on the plans executed by the others. This kind of strategic interaction is commonly modeled by *game theory* [3], where agents are called *players*, and their plans are called *strategies* [4]. Although game theory provides an elaborate description framework, it does not specify how the decision mechanism works. This makes game theory inappropriate for MAS design, where the agent society should act according to a specified (possibly optimal) rule of behavior.

Theory of implementation of social choice rules [5] (a new branch in game theory) proposes a solution to this problem. However, the roots of the theory lie in social sciences, so its approach is not universally suitable for MAS design. It considers agents to be given. Therefore it specifies the decision mechanism not inside, but outside of them. This causes some fundamental difficulties, which may be overcome, if the mechanism is specified within the agents.

This article introduces a new game theoretic approach to implementation of social choice rules: *virtual games*. Virtual games specify the mechanism within the agents enabling provably optimal MAS design. The next sections will introduce fundamentals of game theory, and implementation theory. Then they'll proceed to the definition of virtual games. After the most important definitions, some essential results are proven, followed by a conclusion and an outline of future research.

2 A Common Approach: Implementation of Social Choice Rules

Theory of implementation of social choice rules is used to handle problems of designing optimal social behavior. The population of agents is considered a *society*, which – as a collective entity – acts according to a *social choice rule* (SCR), a mapping from relevant underlying parameters to final outcomes. Thus, a SCR produces social alternatives (outcomes) depending on the private information of the agents in the society (e.g. type, individual preferences). A single-valued SCR is called a *social choice function* (SCF). The implementation problem is then formulated as: "under what circumstances can one design a mechanism so that the private information of agents is truthfully elicited and the social optimum ends up being implemented?" [5]

Fig. 1 shows the implementation problem in more detail: *a Designer must construct a mechanism that implements a given SCR* by producing the same outcomes a_1, a_2, a_3, ..., a_N, supposing that the agents *1, 2, 3, ..., N* choose their messages (e.g. actions, strategies) m_1, m_2, m_3, ..., m_N according to a given game theoretical solution concept S (e.g. dominant strategies, Nash equilibrium). If it is possible to design such a mechanism for a given SCR, then the SCR is called *S-implementable*.

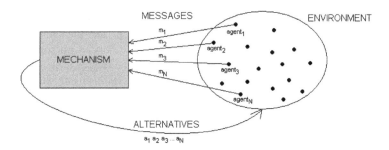

Fig. 1. The implementation problem

The above approach holds many advantages, since mechanisms can model social institutions, outer enforcement or even mutual agreement between agents. For instance it is shown [5], that if *S* is dominant (i.e. if each agent chooses its dominant strategy regardless of what the others choose), then only dictatorial SCFs are implementable (an SCR is dictatorial if it follows the preferences of one particular agent).

Despite its constructive results, the approach has also its weaknesses. In non-economical situations, e.g. in informatics, the Designer of an intelligent system (software agent, robot, etc.) has *explicit control* over the system's decision mechanism (e.g. program [6]), unlike to a game theoretical solution concept, where the assumption about agents' decision mechanism is *implicit*. Why should every agent in a MAS act according to a given solution concept *S*? It is also a weakness, that agents are forced to act "through" a *central mechanism*, which has *global access* to the environment. This assumption is generally unrealistic when designing MAS, because agents mostly act in a decentralized way, and the Designer, or any mechanism – apart from trivial cases – has only *local access* to the environment (e.g. Internet, deep sea, surface of Mars). Moreover, it is also a drawback, that the approach guarantees implementation only when certain special conditions hold for the SCR (e.g. monotonicity, ordinality, incentive compatibility). Generally only *approximate implementation* is possible, i.e. *generally* an SCR is implementable only with some error. This type of implementation is called *virtual implementation* [7].

3   A New Approach: Virtual Games

To solve the above mentioned problems a new concept of agent decision mechanism, called *virtual games*, is proposed. To give a detailed description of the concept, let us first introduce the fundamental notions of game theory: agents; pure and mixed strategies; agent-types; payoff functions; static Bayesian games; social choice functions; and finally, the notion of Bayesian Nash-equilibrium.

3.1   Game Theoretic Fundamentals

Let $N = \{1, 2, ..., n\}$ denote a finite, non-empty *set of agents*, S_i is the finite, non-empty *set of strategies* available to agent i ($i = 1, 2, ..., n$). Now $s_i \in S_i$ denotes an arbitrary member of this set. A strategy associates an elementary action with every possible contingency of an agent. Let $s = (s_1, s_2, \ldots, s_n) \in \times_{i=1}^{n} S_i = S$ denote an arbitrary *strategy combination*. A strategy combination $s \in S$ prescribes a strategy $s_i \in S_i$ to every agent i. Agents choose their strategies simultaneously, without knowing each other's choice.

For the description of the uncertainty agents may face in MAS environments (deficient sensors; dynamic, non-deterministic behavior of other agents, etc), let us introduce types [8]. Types of an agent can be used to represent the type of private information, resources, processing abilities, etc, it may possess. Thus the uncertainty of an agent about other agents (e.g. because of the imperfection of its sensors) can be modeled as the uncertainty about the types of other agents. Let T_i denote the finite, non-empty *set of types* of agent i, and $t_i \in T_i$ an arbitrary type of agent i.

Now we can define the payoff of agents. The payoff of an agent describes its success (optimality, efficiency, etc) in the environment. Let $u_i : S \times T_i \to \Re$ denote the *payoff function* of agent i, where $u_i(s_1, s_2, \ldots, s_n; t_i) = u_i(s; t_i)$ is the payoff to agent i if the agents choose strategies $s = (s_1, s_2, \ldots, s_n) \in S$, and the active type of agent i is $t_i \in T_i$. This means, that the payoff of an agent i depends only on the strategy $s_i \in S_i$ it selected, its active type $t_i \in T_i$, and the strategies $s_{-i} = (s_1, s_2, \ldots, s_{i-1}, s_{i+1}, \hbar, s_n) \in S_{-i}$ chosen by other agents.

The active type $t_i \in T_i$ of the agent i is supposed to be chosen by *Nature* with a probability $p_i(t_i)$, where $p_i \in \Delta(T_i)$ denotes a *probability distribution* over T_i. Every agent i knows only its own active type $t_i \in T_i$, but is uncertain about the active types $t_{-i} = (t_1, t_2, \ldots, t_{i-1}, t_{i+1}, \hbar, t_n) \in T_{-i}$ of others. To model this uncertainty, let us introduce a $p \in \Delta(T)$ joint probability distribution over $T = \times_{i=1}^{n} T_i$. Now the probability that the types of the agents are really $t = (t_1, t_2, \ldots, t_n)$ can be calculated as $p(t) = p_1(t_1) \cdot p_2(t_2) \cdot \hbar \cdot p_n(t_n)$, assuming that $p_1, p_2, \ldots, p_n$ are independent. The probability $p_i(t_{-i} | t_i)$ is called agent *i's belief* about other agents' types, t_{-i}, given its knowledge of its own type, t_i. Assuming, that $S_1, S_2, \ldots, S_n$, $T_1, T_2, \ldots, T_n$, $u_1, u_2, \ldots, u_n$, and $p_1, p_2, \ldots, p_n$ are *common knowledge* among the agents (i.e. everybody knows, that everybody knows, that...), the belief $p_i(t_{-i} | t_i)$ can be calculated by any of the agents using Bayes' rule:

$$p_i(t_{-i} | t_i) = \frac{p(t_{-i}, t_i)}{p(t_i)} = \frac{p(t_{-i}, t_i)}{\sum\limits_{t_{-i} \in T_{-i}} p(t_{-i}, t_i)}, \text{ where } p(t_{-i}, t_i) = p(t), \text{ and } t = (t_{-i}, t_i) . \tag{1}$$

Types enabled us to transform any incomplete information game to a game with imperfect information [8]. Incomplete information games are games, where some players are uncertain about the structure of the game (e.g. strategy sets, or utility functions of others), while imperfect information games are essentially the classic games introduced by von Neumann [3]. Collecting all of this information together, we have:

Definition 1. The ***normal-form representation of an n-player (static Bayesian) game*** specifies agents 1, 2, ..., n, their strategy spaces $S_1, S_2, ..., S_n$, their type spaces $T_1, T_2, ..., T_n$, their payoff functions $u_1, u_2, ..., u_n$, and the probability distributions $p_1, p_2, ..., p_n$. At the beginning of a play of the game Nature chooses agent types according to the independent probability distributions, and reveals type $t_i \in T_i$ only to agent i. After that agents choose their strategies simultaneously and execute them in parallel. Agent i gains a payoff depending on the chosen strategy-combination, and its active type $t_i \in T_i$. Such a game is denoted by a 5-tuple: $\Gamma = \left(N, \{S_i\}_{i \in N}, \{T_i\}_{i \in N}, \{u_i\}_{i \in N}, \{p_i\}_{i \in N}\right)$.

If agents are allowed to choose their strategies according to a probability distribution $q_i \in Q_i = \Delta(S_i)$, where $\sum_{s_i \in S_i} q_i(s_i) = 1$, and $q_i(s_i) \geq 0$ for every $s_i \in S_i$, then the strategies $s_i \in S_i$ are called *pure strategies*, while the probability distributions q_i are called *mixed strategies*. Now $q_i(s_i)$ denotes the probability, that agent i plays a given pure strategy s_i by playing the mixed strategy q_i. Thus mixed strategies generalize pure strategies. The *set of mixed strategy combinations* is constructed as $Q = \times_{i=1}^{n} Q_i$.

Utility functions also need to be generalized to support mixed strategies. Let $u_i : Q \times T_i \to \Re$ denote agent *i's payoff function*, where $u_i(q; t_i)$ is the payoff to agent i if agents choose mixed strategies $q = (q_1, q_2, ..., q_n) \in Q$, and agent i's type is $t_i \in T_i$. With a slight abuse of notation, this utility can be written as the expectation above the payoffs of all pure strategy combinations:

$$u_i(q; t_i) = \sum_{s = (s_1, s_2, \hbar, s_n) \in S} q_1(s_1) \cdot q_2(s_2) \hbar \cdot q_n(s_n) \cdot u_i(s; t_i), \text{ where } q = (q_1, q_2, ..., q_n) \in Q . \tag{2}$$

Before proceeding to the definition of the Nash equilibrium [9], let us first define strategy profiles $\{f_i(t_i)\}_{t_i \in T_i}$ of agent i $(i = 1, 2, ..., n)$, and social choice functions. A *strategy profile* is a mapping $f_i : T_i \to Q_i$, which associates a mixed strategy q_i to every type $t_i \in T_i$ of an agent i. Let $f = (f_1, f_2, \hbar, f_n) \in F = \times_{i=1}^{n} F_i$ denote a strategy profile combination, i.e. a *social choice function (SCF)*, and let $f(t) = (f_1(t_1), f_2(t_2), \hbar, f_n(t_n)) \in Q$ denote the mixed strategy combination provided by SCF f, given the agents' types are $t = (t_1, t_2, ..., t_n) \in T$. Now the expected payoff of agent i in case of an SCF f is:

$$u_i(f; t_i) = \sum_{t_{-i} \in T_{-i}} p_i(t_{-i} | t_i) \cdot u_i(f(t_{-i}, t_i); t_i), \text{ where } t = (t_{-i}, t_i) . \tag{3}$$

In (3) the payoff function $u_i : F \times T_i \to \Re$ of agent i was redefined again (with a slight abuse of notation) to support SCFs. Because of the uncertainty about other agents' types, this is the payoff, that agent i with type $t_i \in T_i$ tries to maximize, not $u_i(f(t); t_i)$. The belief $p_i(t_{-i} | t_i)$ in (3) should be calculated according to (1), and the expected payoff $u_i(f(t); t_i)$ in case of a mixed strategy combination $f(t) \in Q$ should be calculated according to (2). Now we can define Bayesian Nash equilibrium:

Definition 2. In a static Bayesian game $\Gamma = \left(N, \{S_i\}_{i \in N}, \{T_i\}_{i \in N}, \{u_i\}_{i \in N}, \{p_i\}_{i \in N}\right)$ a SCF $f^* = \left(f_1^*, f_2^*, \ldots, f_n^*\right) \in F$ is a ***Bayesian Nash equilibrium*** if for each agent i and for each $t_i \in T_i$, $f_i^*(t_i) \in Q_i$ solves $\max_{q_i \in Q_i} \sum_{t_{-i} \in T_{-i}} p_i(t_{-i}|t_i) \cdot u_i\left(f_1^*(t_1), f_2^*(t_2), \ldots, f_{i-1}^*(t_{i-1}), q_i, f_{i+1}^*(t_{i+1}), \ldots, f_n^*(t_n); t_i\right)$.

3.2 Virtual Games

Section 3.1 introduced the fundamentals of game theory. Now we can proceed to discuss the solution of the problem outlined in Section 2. A new approach for implementation of social choice rules is proposed, called *virtual games*. This concept enables the construction of mechanisms, which provably implement any SCF exactly. Roughly speaking a virtual game is a part of this mechanism. Fig. 2 illustrates this concept:

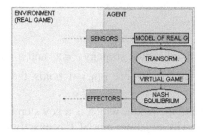

Fig. 2. A new approach to the implementation problem

The mechanism is distributed among the agents. Every agent has a *decision mechanism*, which has three parts: a *transformation*, a *virtual game*, and a *function for selecting Nash-equilibrium*. First the agent senses the outer representation of the environment: the *real game*. From that percept it creates an inner representation of the real game: the *model of the real game*. This is the input for the decision mechanism choosing among strategy profiles. Finally, the agent acts according to that profile.

Thus, virtual games are artificial constructs built from the model of the real game. They are not models of the real game, they are components of the decision mechanism of agents, and as such, they may be arbitrarily "far" from the model of the real game. Technically they differ from the model of the real game only in that they have different pure strategy spaces, called *pure virtual strategies*, and payoff functions, called *virtual payoff functions*. Formally this means, that every agent i has a finite, non-empty *set of pure virtual strategies* $V_i \subset Q_i$, a subset of the set of mixed strategies. These are the feasible strategies for agent i. Now the *virtual payoff function* of agent i is denoted by $v_i : V \times T_i \to \Re$, where $V = \times_{i=1}^n V_i$. Virtual payoff represents an agent's private valuation of the feasible strategic outcomes. A *virtual game* is then a normal-form static Bayesian game $\Gamma^* = \left(N, \{V_i\}_{i \in N}, \{T_i\}_{i \in N}, \{v_i\}_{i \in N}, \{p_i\}_{i \in N}\right)$. In this game the concepts of mixed strategies, mixed strategy combinations, their payoff, strategy profiles, social choice functions, their payoff, and Bayesian Nash equilibrium are defined similarly to the concepts introduced in Section 3.1.

A *mixed virtual strategy* of agent i is denoted by $r_i \in R_i = \Delta(V_i)$, where $r_i(q_i)$ denotes the probability, that agent i plays the pure virtual strategy $q_i \in V_i \subset Q_i$ by playing the mixed virtual strategy $r_i \in R_i$. The *set of mixed virtual strategy combinations* is denoted by $R = \times_{i=1}^{n} R_i$. The *virtual payoff function* for them is denoted by $v_i : R \times T_i \to \Re$, and the *virtual payoff* is calculated similarly to (2). Let $g_i : T_i \to R_i$ denote a *virtual strategy profile* of an agent i in a virtual game. An SCF g of the virtual game is called a *virtual social choice function (VSCF)*. The *virtual payoff* for a VSCF is calculated similarly to (3). A mixed virtual strategy $r_i \in R_i$ in the virtual game is *equivalent* to a mixed strategy $q_i \in Q_i$ in the model of the real game, and denoted $r_i \equiv q_i$, if

$$q_i(s_i) = \sum_{q_i^{(j)} \in V_i} r_i\left(q_i^{(j)}\right) \cdot q_i^{(j)}(s_i)$$ holds for every $s_i \in S_i$. A mixed virtual strategy combination

$r \in R$ is *equivalent* to a mixed strategy combination $q \in Q$, and denoted $r \equiv q$, if $r_i \equiv q_i$ holds for every $i = 1, 2, ..., n$. A VSCF g is *equivalent* to a SCF f, and denoted $g \equiv f$, if $g(t) \equiv f(t)$ holds for every $t \in T$.

Corollary 1. If given a mixed virtual strategy $r_i \in R_i$ and a mixed strategy $q_i \in V_i \subset Q_i$ which is also pure virtual strategy, where $r_i(q_i) = 1$ holds, then $r_i \equiv q_i$.

Now it is possible to state the result, which is a key step in showing that with decision mechanisms based on virtual games any SCF is exactly implementable.

Theorem 1. If in a virtual game $\Gamma^* = \left(N, \{V_i\}_{i \in N}, \{T_i\}_{i \in N}, \{v_i\}_{i \in N}, \{p_i\}_{i \in N}\right)$ constructed for a static Bayesian game $\Gamma = \left(N, \{S_i\}_{i \in N}, \{T_i\}_{i \in N}, \{u_i\}_{i \in N}, \{p_i\}_{i \in N}\right)$ for every $i = 1, 2, ..., n$ and $t_i \in T_i$ exists a $q^{(t_i)} = \left(q_1^{(t_i)}, q_2^{(t_i)}, ..., q_n^{(t_i)}\right) \in V \subset Q$ pure virtual strategy combination such that

$$v_i(q, t_i) = \begin{cases} 1, & q = q^{(t_i)} \\ 0, & q \in V \setminus \left\{q^{(t_i)}\right\} \end{cases}$$ holds, then the unique Bayesian Nash equilibrium of the virtual

game Γ^* is the VSCF $g^* = \left(g_1^*, g_2^*, ..., g_n^*\right)$, where for every $t = (t_1, t_2, \hbar, t_n) \in T$ $g^*(t) = \left(g_1^*(t_1), g_2^*(t_2), ..., g_n^*(t_n)\right) \in R$ is a mixed virtual strategy combination, and $g_i^*(t_i)\left(q_i^{(t_i)}\right) = 1$ holds for every $i = 1, 2, ..., n$ and $t_i \in T_i$, i.e. $g^*(t) \equiv q^{(t)} = \left(q_1^{(t_1)}, q_2^{(t_2)}, \hbar, q_n^{(t_n)}\right) \in Q$ for every $t \in T$.

Theorem 1 constructively guarantees a unique Bayesian Nash equilibrium of a virtual game Γ^* with special binary virtual payoff functions (see Appendix). To use this result, game theoretical solution concepts and implementation need to be defined. Let $\mathbb{S}$ be a *game theoretical solution concept*. Given a game Γ we denote by $\mathbb{S}(\Gamma) \in 2^F$ the set of strategy profiles (SCF's) that are recommended by $\mathbb{S}$ in game Γ. An SCF f in Γ is $\mathbb{S}$-*implementable* if there exists a virtual game Γ^* constructed from Γ, such that $f \equiv \mathbb{S}\left(\Gamma^*\right)$. Now the main result can be stated as:

Theorem 2. Any SCF of any static Bayesian game is Bayesian Nash-implementable.

In a game theoretical sense these results are independent of the accuracy of agents modelling abilities. Theorem 2 states only that any SCF of any static Bayesian game can be implemented (even by virtual games with binary payoffs) in case when agents act according to the Bayesian Nash equilibrium of the virtual game constructed for the given static Bayesian game (see Appendix). Nonetheless, when players are considered agents, there is no guarantee, that they will use the same virtual game, because – by definition – they construct virtual games upon their model of the real game (see Fig. 2), and this model may be different among the agents. Thus, the results in Theorem 2 apply only to situations, when agents have the same virtual game. I assume that it is the task of the Designer to construct agents that way. Any relaxation of the assumptions is the task of future research.

4 Conclusions

The results in this article enable the design of decision mechanisms that implement arbitrary SCFs. Consequently optimal (e.g. Pareto-optimal, bounded optimal [6]) SCFs are implementable exactly in a uniform way. These results overcome the weaknesses of the theory of implementation of social choice rules. Moreover, they make it possible to design optimal MAS, e.g. to optimize agents' communication protocols (strategic interaction); resource usage (in connection with the utility of agents); or the quality of various services of MAS (in connection with the optimality of the SCF). A uniform framework is provided to design optimal social behaviour. Nonetheless it can be used also to analyze MAS. Elaborate distinctions can be made in the incentives, private valuation and preferences of agents if modelling their decision mechanism via virtual games. However, only virtual games with binary payoffs were discussed. The examination of virtual games with non-binary payoff functions is the task of future research. This research will mainly concentrate on connecting the concept of virtual games to existing low-level agent architectures (e.g. [10], [11]) and integrating it into a unified theory of designing and analysing intelligent multi-agent systems.

References

1. Weiss, G.: Multiagent Systems. MIT Press (1999)
2. Russell, S., Norvig, P.: Artificial Intelligence: A Modern Approach. Prentice Hall (1995)
3. Neumann, J., Morgenstern, O.: Theory of games and economic behavior. Princeton University Press (1947)
4. Bowling, M., Jensen, R., Veloso, M.: A Formalization of Equilibria for Multiagent planning. In: Proceedings of IJCAI'03 Workshop (2003) 1460-1462
5. Serrano, R.: The Theory of Implementation of Social Choice Rules. In: SIAM Review, Vol. 46. (2004) 377-414
6. Russell, S., Subramanian, D.: Provably bounded-optimal agents. In: Journal of AI Research, Vol. 2. (1995) 1-36
7. Abreu, D., Sen, A.: Virtual Implementation in Nash Equilibrium. In: Econometrica, Vol. 59. (1991) 997-1021

8. Harsányi, J. C.: Games with incomplete information played by Bayesian players I-II-III. In. Management Science, Vol. 14. (1967-1968) 159–182, 320–334, 486–502
9. Nash, J. F.: Non-cooperative games. In. Annals of Mathematics, Vol. 54. (1951) 286–295
10. Ferguson, I. A.: TouringMachines: An Architecture for Dynamic, Rational, Mobile Agents. Ph.D. Thesis, Clare Hall, University of Cambridge, UK (1992)
11. Kovács, D. L.: Evolution of Intelligens Agents: a new approach to automatic plan design. In. Proceedings of IFAC Workshop on Control Applications of Optimization, Elsevier (2003)

Appendix

Proof of Theorem 1. Suppose that g^* is not a Bayesian Nash equilibrium of Γ^*. Therefore there must be an agent j, a type $t_j \in T_j$ and a mixed virtual strategy $r_j \in R_j$ such that agent j has the incentive to change to it from the mixed virtual strategy $g_j^*(t_j)$ prescribed by g^*. From definition 2 it follows, that:

$$\sum_{t_{-j} \in T_{-j}} p_j(t_{-j}|t_j) \cdot v_j\Big(g_1^*(t_1) \cdot g_2^*(t_2) \hbar \ldots g_{j-1}^*(t_{j-1}) \cdot r_j \cdot g_{j+1}^*(t_{j+1}) \hbar \ldots g_n^*(t_n); t_j\Big) > \hbar$$

$$\hbar > \sum_{t_{-j} \in T_{-j}} p_j(t_{-j}|t_j) \cdot v_j\Big(g_1^*(t_1) \cdot g_2^*(t_2) \hbar \ldots g_{j-1}^*(t_{j-1}) \cdot g_j^*(t_j) \cdot g_{j+1}^*(t_{j+1}) \hbar \ldots g_n^*(t_n); t_j\Big)$$

Using formula (2) we have:

$$\sum_{t_{-j} \in T_{-j}} \left[p_j(t_{-j}|t_j) \cdot \sum_{q=(q_1,q_2 \wedge \ldots q_n) \in V} g_1^*(t_1)(q_1) \cdot g_2^*(t_2)(q_2) \hbar \ldots g_{j-1}^*(t_{j-1})(q_{j-1}) \cdot r_j(q_j) \cdot g_{j+1}^*(t_{j+1})(q_{j+1}) \hbar \ldots g_n^*(t_n)(q_n) \cdot v_j(q_1,q_2 \wedge \ldots q_n; t_j) \right] > \hbar$$

$$\hbar > \sum_{t_{-j} \in T_{-j}} \left[p_j(t_{-j}|t_j) \cdot \sum_{q=(q_1,q_2 \wedge \ldots q_n) \in V} g_1^*(t_1)(q_1) \cdot g_2^*(t_2)(q_2) \hbar \ldots g_{j-1}^*(t_{j-1})(q_{j-1}) \cdot g_j^*(t_j)(q_j) \cdot g_{j+1}^*(t_{j+1})(q_{j+1}) \hbar \ldots g_n^*(t_n)(q_n) \cdot v_j(q_1,q_2 \wedge \ldots q_n; t_j) \right]$$

Using the definition of v_j we have:

$$\sum_{t_{-j} \in T_{-j}} p_j(t_{-j}|t_j) \cdot g_1^*(t_1)\Big(q_1^{(t_j)}\Big) g_2^*(t_2)\Big(q_2^{(t_j)}\Big) \hbar \ldots g_{j-1}^*(t_{j-1})\Big(q_{j-1}^{(t_j)}\Big) r_j\Big(q_j^{(t_j)}\Big) g_{j+1}^*(t_{j+1})\Big(q_{j+1}^{(t_j)}\Big) \hbar \ldots g_n^*(t_n)\Big(q_n^{(t_j)}\Big) > \hbar$$

$$\hbar > \sum_{t_{-j} \in T_{-j}} p_j(t_{-j}|t_j) \cdot g_1^*(t_1)\Big(q_1^{(t_j)}\Big) g_2^*(t_2)\Big(q_2^{(t_j)}\Big) \hbar \ldots g_{j-1}^*(t_{j-1})\Big(q_{j-1}^{(t_j)}\Big) g_j^*(t_j)\Big(q_j^{(t_j)}\Big) g_{j+1}^*(t_{j+1})\Big(q_{j+1}^{(t_j)}\Big) \hbar \ldots g_n^*(t_n)\Big(q_n^{(t_j)}\Big)$$

This can also be written in the following form:

$$r_j\Big(q_j^{(t_j)}\Big) \cdot \sum_{t_{-j} \in T_{-j}} p_j(t_{-j}|t_j) \cdot g_1^*(t_1)\Big(q_1^{(t_j)}\Big) g_2^*(t_2)\Big(q_2^{(t_j)}\Big) \hbar \ldots g_{j-1}^*(t_{j-1})\Big(q_{j-1}^{(t_j)}\Big) g_{j+1}^*(t_{j+1})\Big(q_{j+1}^{(t_j)}\Big) \hbar \ldots g_n^*(t_n)\Big(q_n^{(t_j)}\Big) > \hbar$$

$$\hbar > g_j^*(t_j)\Big(q_j^{(t_j)}\Big) \cdot \sum_{t_{-j} \in T_{-j}} p_j(t_{-j}|t_j) \cdot g_1^*(t_1)\Big(q_1^{(t_j)}\Big) g_2^*(t_2)\Big(q_2^{(t_j)}\Big) \hbar \ldots g_{j-1}^*(t_{j-1})\Big(q_{j-1}^{(t_j)}\Big) g_{j+1}^*(t_{j+1})\Big(q_{j+1}^{(t_j)}\Big) \hbar \ldots g_n^*(t_n)\Big(q_n^{(t_j)}\Big)$$

This implies $r_j\Big(q_j^{(t_j)}\Big) > g_j^*(t_j)\Big(q_j^{(t_j)}\Big) = 1$, which is a contradiction.

Now lets suppose that there exists also another Bayesian Nash equilibrium $g^{*'} = \Big(g_1^{*'}, g_2^{*'}, \ldots, g_n^{*'}\Big)$, where $g^{*'} \neq g^*$. Therefore for every agent j, type $t_j \in T_j$, and mixed virtual strategy $r_j \in R_j$ the following must hold (see Definition 2):

$$\sum_{t_{-j} \in T_{-j}} p_j(t_{-j}|t_j) \cdot v_j\left(g_1^{**}(t_1) \cdot g_2^{**}(t_2) \hbar \cdot g_{j-1}^{**}(t_{j-1}) \cdot g_j^*(t_j) \cdot g_{j+1}^{**}(t_{j+1}) \hbar \cdot g_n^{**}(t_n); t_j\right) \geq \hbar$$

$$\hbar \geq \sum_{t_{-j} \in T_{-j}} p_j(t_{-j}|t_j) \cdot v_j\left(g_1^{**}(t_1) \cdot g_2^{**}(t_2) \hbar \cdot g_{j-1}^{**}(t_{j-1}) \cdot r_j \cdot g_{j+1}^{**}(t_{j+1}) \hbar \cdot g_n^{**}(t_n); t_j\right)$$

Similarly to the previous half of the proof, using (2) and the definition of v_j we have:

$$g_j^{*}(t_j)\left(q_j^{(t_j)}\right) \cdot \sum_{t_{-j} \in T_{-j}} p_j(t_{-j}|t_j) \cdot g_1^{**}(t_1)\left(q_1^{(t_j)}\right) g_2^{**}(t_2)\left(q_2^{(t_j)}\right) \hbar \cdot g_{j-1}^{**}(t_{j-1})\left(q_{j-1}^{(t_j)}\right) g_{j+1}^{**}(t_{j+1})\left(q_{j+1}^{(t_j)}\right) \hbar \cdot g_n^{**}(t_n)\left(q_n^{(t_j)}\right) \geq \hbar$$

$$\hbar \geq r_j\left(q_j^{(t_j)}\right) \cdot \sum_{t_{-j} \in T_{-j}} p_j(t_{-j}|t_j) \cdot g_1^{**}(t_1)\left(q_1^{(t_j)}\right) g_2^{**}(t_2)\left(q_2^{(t_j)}\right) \hbar \cdot g_{j-1}^{**}(t_{j-1})\left(q_{j-1}^{(t_j)}\right) g_{j+1}^{**}(t_{j+1})\left(q_{j+1}^{(t_j)}\right) \hbar \cdot g_n^{**}(t_n)\left(q_n^{(t_j)}\right)$$

This implies $g_j^*(t_j)\left(q_j^{(t_j)}\right) \geq r_j\left(q_j^{(t_j)}\right)$ for every agent j, type $t_j \in T_j$, and $r_j \in R_j$, even for $r_j = g_j^*(t_j)$. In this case we have $g_j^*(t_j)\left(q_j^{(t_j)}\right) \geq r_j\left(q_j^{(t_j)}\right) = g_j^*(t_j)\left(q_j^{(t_j)}\right) = 1$ implying $g^* = g^*$, which is a contradiction. ∎

Proof of Theorem 2. Let $\Gamma = \left(N, \{S_i\}_{i \in N}, \{T_i\}_{i \in N}, \{u_i\}_{i \in N}, \{p_i\}_{i \in N}\right)$ denote an arbitrary static Bayesian game, f an arbitrary SCF, and B the solution concept of Bayesian Nash equilibrium. SCF f is B -implementable, if there exists a virtual game $\Gamma^* = \left(N, \{V_i\}_{i \in N}, \{T_i\}_{i \in N}, \{v_i\}_{i \in N}, \{p_i\}_{i \in N}\right)$ such that $f \equiv B\left(\Gamma^*\right)$. Constructing the virtual game Γ^* so that $V_i = \{f_i(t_i) | t_i \in T_i\}$, and $v_i(q, t_i) = \begin{cases} 1, & q = q^{(t_i)} \\ 0, & q \in V \setminus \{q^{(t_i)}\} \end{cases}$, where $q^{(t_i)} = \left(q_1, q_2, \ldots, q_{i-1}, f_i(t_i), q_{i+1}, \ldots, q_n\right) \in V \subset Q$ (and $q_{-i} \in V_{-i} \subset Q_{-i}$ is arbitrary) we have (from Theorem 1), that the only Bayesian Nash equilibrium of the virtual game Γ^* is the VSCF $g^* = \left(g_1^*, g_2^*, \ldots, g_n^*\right)$, where for every $t = (t_1, t_2, \hbar, t_n) \in T$ $g^*(t) = \left(g_1^*(t_1), g_2^*(t_2), \ldots, g_n^*(t_n)\right) \in R$ is a mixed virtual strategy combination, where $g_i^*(t_i)(f_i(t_i)) = 1$ holds for every $i = 1, 2, \ldots, n$ and $t_i \in T_i$, and thus $g^*(t) \equiv f(t) = \left(f_1(t_1), f_2(t_2), \hbar, f_n(t_n)\right)$ for every $t \in T$, i.e. $g^* \equiv f$. ∎

How Our Beliefs Contribute to Interpret Actions[*]

Guillaume Aucher[**]

University of Otago (NZ) - University Paul Sabatier (F)
aucher@cs.otago.ac.nz

Abstract. In update logic the interpretation of an action is often assumed to be independent from the agents' beliefs about the situation (see [BMS04] or [Auc05]). In this paper we deal with this type of phenomenon. We also deal with actions that change facts of the situation. We use probability to model the notion of belief and our probabilistic update mechanism satisfies the AGM postulates of belief revision.

Often in everyday life we interpret an action on the basis of our beliefs about the situation. For example, assume that you see somebody drawing a ball from an urn containing black balls and white balls. If you *believe* there is no particular distribution in the urn then you will consider it equally probable that he draws a white ball or a black ball; but if you *believe* there are more black than white balls in the urn then you will consider it more probable than he draws a black ball than a white ball: the interpretation of the same action is different in both cases. The literature about update logic does not deal with this kind of phenomenon (see [BMS04] or [Auc05]). Likewise, actions that change the truth of propositions are also neglected in the literature about update logic although they are quite common in everyday life and hence interesting to formalize.

This paper is a continuation of [Auc05] and solves the problems raised there. However, instead of using plausibilities we use probabilities because in this context it is technically easier to deal with probability, and because I believe the modeling of the notion of belief is better rendered with a subjective probability. A novelty is also our use of infinitesimals in order to express what would surprise the agents and by how much.

In Sect.1 we motivate and define a structure slightly different from the hyperreals where the probabilities of worlds take value. In Sect.2 we present the core of the system in three parts : static (where we model static situations), dynamic (where we model actions) and the update mechanism. Finally, in Sect.3 we compare it with the AGM postulates and other relevant literature.

---

[*] An extended version of this paper with proofs is available on my homepage.
[**] I thank my PhD supervisors Hans van Ditmarsch and Andreas Herzig for useful comments and discussions.

M. Pěchouček, P. Petta, and L.Z. Varga (Eds.): CEEMAS 2005, LNAI 3690, pp. 276–285, 2005.

1   Mathematical Preliminaries

In the proposed system, the probabilities of worlds and formulas will take value in a particular mathematical structure $(\mathbb{V}, \lesssim)$ (abusively denoted $(\mathbb{V}, \leq)$) different from the real numbers, based on hyperreal numbers $(^{*}\mathbb{R}, \leq)$ (see [Adams75] which uses them as well to give a probabilistic semantics to conditional logic).

Roughly speaking, hyperreal numbers are an extension of the real numbers to include certain classes of infinite and infinitesimal numbers. A hyperreal number, typically denoted ε, is said to be infinitesimal iff $|\varepsilon| < 1/n$ for all integers n; and finite if $|x| < n$ for some integer n (in that case $St(x)$ is the unique real number closest to x). For an account on the hyperreal numbers, see chapter 1 of [Keis86].

What we would like to do is to approximate our expressions. That is to say, in case an hyperreal number a is infinitely smaller than b (that is to say, there is an infinitesimal ε such that $a = \varepsilon.b$), then we would want $b + a = b$; for example '$1 + \varepsilon = 1$','$\varepsilon + \varepsilon^2 = \varepsilon$',... Unfortunately, the hyperreal numbers do not allow us to do that, so we are obliged to introduce a new structure $(\mathbb{V}, \lesssim)^1$ defined in the footnote 1.

2   Dynamic Proba-Doxastic Logic

2.1   The Static Part

Definition 1. *A proba-doxastic model (pd-model) $M = (W, \{\sim_j; j \in G\}, \{P_j; j \in G\}, V, w_0)$ is a tuple where:*

1. *W is a finite set of possible worlds.*
2. *w_0 is the possible world corresponding to the actual world.*
3. *$\sim_j$ is an equivalence relation defined on W for each agent j.*
4. *P_j is an operator for each agent j which assigns to each world w a number in $]0;1]$ such that $\sum\{P_j(v); v \sim_j w\} = 1$ (*).*
5. *V is a valuation.*
6. *G is a set of agents.*

Intuitive Interpretation. Items 1,2,5,6 are clear. It remains to give interpretations for items 3 and 4. The probabilistic operator P_j together with $\sim_j$ intuitively model the epistemic state of mind of any agent $j \in G$. We set $w \sim_j v$ iff agent j can not distinguish world w from world v. This relation does not model the notion of knowledge and we do not deal with this notion in this paper (see general conclusion).

Among the worlds that agent j can not distinguish, there are some that j conceives as potential candidates for the world in which j dwells, and some

---

[1] $\mathbb{V}$ is the quotient structure of the set of positive hyperreal numbers $^{*}\mathbb{R}^{+}$ by the equivalence relation $\approx$ defined by $x \approx y$ iff $((St(\frac{x}{y}) = 1$ and $y \neq 0)$ or $x = y = 0)$. We define a total order $\lesssim$ on $\mathbb{V}$ by $\overline{x} \lesssim \overline{y}$ iff there are $x \in \overline{x}, y \in \overline{y}$ such that $x \leq y$. Elements of $\mathbb{V}$ containing an infinitesimal (resp. real) are abusively called infinitesimals (resp. reals) and we abusively denote $\lesssim$ by $\leq$.

that j would be surprised to hear somebody claiming that they correspond to the world in which j dwells (whatever it is). The first ones are called *conceived worlds* and the second *surprising worlds*. The conceived worlds are assigned by P_j a real value and the surprising worlds are assigned an infinitesimal value (both different from 0). For example, some people would be surprised to hear somebody claiming that some swans are black, although it is true. So for them the actual world is a surprising world, indistinguishable from the only conceived world where all swans are white.

Of course j might conceive some (conceived) worlds as better candidates than others and this is expressed by the value of the probability of the world: the larger the real probability value of the (conceived) world is, the more likely it is for j. But that is the same for the surprising worlds: j might be more surprised to hear some worlds than others. For example, if you play poker with your brother (or a friend), you will never suspect that he cheats. However he does so, and so carefully that you do not suspect anything. Then at the end of the game if he announces to you that he has cheated, you will be surprised (although it is something true in the actual world, which is then a surprising world). But you will be even more surprised if he tells you that he has cheated five times than if he has cheated only once. So the world where he has cheated five times will be more surprising than the world where he has cheated once, and these are both surprising worlds for you. Infinitesimals enable us to express this: the larger the infinitesimal probability value of the (surprising) world is, the less j would be surprised by this world. Anyway, that is why we need to introduce these hyperreal numbers: to express these degrees of surprise that can not be expressed by a single number like 0 (which then becomes useless for us).

Finally, the natural condition (*) ensures us that $([w]_j, \mathcal{P}([w]_j), P_j)$ (with $[w]_j := \{v; v \sim_j w\}$) is a (nonstandard) probability space.

So, dwelling in one of the world of $[w]_j$, j does not think consciously that her respective surprising worlds in $[w]_j$ are possible (unlike conceived worlds), she is just not aware of them. So they are useless to represent her beliefs which I assume are essentially conscious. But still, these worlds are relevant for the (objective) modelisation. Indeed they provide some information about the epistemic state of mind of j : namely what would surprise her. Intuitively, something that you do not consider consciously as possible and that contradicts your beliefs is often surprising for you when it is claimed by somebody else. These worlds will moreover turn out to be very useful technically in case j has to revise her beliefs.

Definition 2. *The syntax of the language $\mathcal{L}_{St}$ is defined by,*
$\phi := \bot \mid p \mid \neg\phi \mid \phi \wedge \psi \mid P_j(\phi) \geq x \mid C_j\phi$ *where* $x \in [0;1[$.
Its semantics is defined by,
$M, w \models P_j(\phi) \geq x$ *iff* $\sum\{P_j(v); w \sim_j v$ *and* $M, v \models \phi\} \geq x$
$M, w \models C_j\phi$ *iff* $\sum\{P_j(v); w \sim_j v$ *and* $M, v \models \phi\} = 1$.

$M, w \models P_j(\phi) \geq x$ should be read "in world w and for j, ϕ has a probability greater than x ". $M, w \models C_j\phi$ should be read "in world w, j is convinced (sure) of ϕ ".

Note that above, if x is real then only the conceived worlds have to be considered in the sum (see Sect.1). Similarly the semantics of C_j amounts to say that ϕ is true only in all the *conceived* worlds of $[w]_j$ (see Sect.1). This is not surprising since only the conceived worlds describe the beliefs of the agent as we just said above. So it is quite possible to have a surprising actual world where $\neg\phi$ is true and still j being convinced of ϕ (i.e. $C_j\phi$): see the swan example above with $\phi :=$ "All swans are white".

Moreover, we can also express in this language what would surprise the agent, and by how much. Indeed, in case x is infinitesimal, $M, w \models (P_j(\phi) = x)$ should be read "in world w, j would be surprised with intensity x to hear somebody claiming that ϕ ". (Note that the smaller x is, the higher the intensity of surprise is.)

Remark 1. If we define the operator $B_j\phi$ by $P_j(\phi) > \frac{1}{2}$, then the meaning of the operators B_j and C_j are respectively exactly the same as the Lenzen's notion of (weak) belief and conviction (see [Len03]).Often these notions are confused and we use in everyday life the same word "belief" to denote both of them.

Example 1. Consider two friends A and B in a fair, and an urn containing $n = 2.k > 0$ balls which are either white or black. A knows how many black balls there are in the urn but B does not know it. Now say there are actually 0 black ball in the urn. This situation is depicted in Fig.1, where p_i stands for: "there are i black balls in the urn " and the double bordered world is the actual world. In Fig.1 the probabilities of worlds are $P_A(x) = 1$ and $P_B(x) = \frac{1}{n+1}$ for all worlds x, so B believes there is no particular distribution in the urn.

Example 2. Consider the same example as before but now B is *convinced* (sure) that there are more black balls than white balls (i.e. $C_B(p_{k+1} \vee ... \vee p_n)$). For example her friend A might have lied to her by telling her so, and she fully believed him. This situation is still depicted in Fig.1 but the probabilities of worlds here are $P_A(x) = 1$ for all worlds x, and $P_B(w_i) = \epsilon$ for all $i \in \{0, .., k\}$, $P_B(w_i) = \frac{1}{k}$ for all $i \in \{k + 1, .., n\}$. The worlds where there are less black balls than white balls are all (equally) surprising.

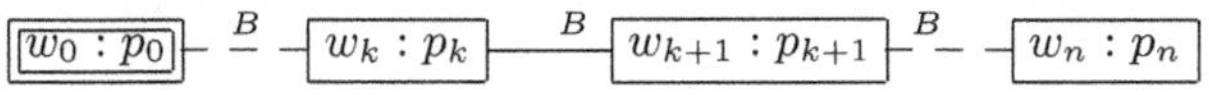

Fig. 1. 'urn' Examples 1 and 2 (without specifications of the probabilities of worlds for each example: see text)

Throughout this paper we apply our system to the example of the introduction. So note that Examples 1 and 2 only differ in what the agent B believes.

2.2   The Dynamic Part

Definition 3. *A generic action model is a structure* $\Sigma = (\Sigma, S, \{\sim_j ; j \in G\}, \{P_j^\Gamma ; \Gamma$ *is a maximal consistent subset of S and $j \in G\}, \{Post_\sigma ; \sigma \in \Sigma\}, \sigma_0)$ *where*

1. Σ is a finite set of possible actions.
2. σ_0 is the actual action.
3. $\sim_j$ is an equivalence relation defined on Σ for each agent j.
4. S is a set of formulas of $\mathcal{L}_{St}$ and their negations.
5. P_j^Γ is an operator indexed by each agent j and each maximal consistent subset Γ of S which assigns to each possible action a number in $[0;1]$, such that for each possible action σ and agent j_0
   if $P_{j_0}^\Gamma(\sigma) = 0$ then $P_j^\Gamma(\sigma) = 0$ for all $j \in G$ (*).
6. $Post_\sigma$ is a function which takes as argument a propositional letter p and gives two formulas of $\mathcal{L}_{St}$ $Post_\sigma(p) := (Post_\sigma^+(p), Post_\sigma^-(p))$ such that $\models \neg(Post_\sigma^+(p) \wedge Post_\sigma^-(p))$ (**).
7. G is a set of agents.

Intuitive Interpretation. Items 1,2,3,7 are totally similar to definition 1. It remains to give interpretation to items 4,5,6 of the definition.

Item 4. S corresponds to the set of formulas (and their negation) that are relevant for the agents in a particular world in order to assign a probability to an action occurring in this world. Consequently, the larger the size of S will be, the more the interpretation by the agents of the actions will be dependant on their beliefs (see Sect.2.3).

Item 5. P_j^Γ is the probability for j, if *she assumes* she is in a particular world where the set of formulas Γ is true, that the action σ is occurring.

Just as in the static case, relatively to a world w satisfying Γ and among indistinguishable actions for the agent j, we have *conceived* actions (which are assigned a real number) and *surprising* actions (which are assigned an infinitesimal). The former are possible actions that the agent conceives as possible candidates while one of the indistinguishable actions actually takes place. The latter are possible actions that j would be surprised to hear somebody claiming that they took place while one of the indistinguishable actions actually took place. For example, if you play poker with your brother (or a friend) and at a certain point he cheats while you do not suspect anything, then the actual action of cheating will be a surprising action for you (of value ε) and will be indistinguishable for you from the conceived action where nothing particular happens (of value 1).

Just as in the static case, the relative strength for j of the indistinguishable actions (conceived and surprising), relatively to a world where Γ is true, is expressed by the value of the operator P_j^Γ.

Finally, note that we can have $P_j^\Gamma(\sigma) = 0$. This means that the action σ can not *physically* be performed in a world where Γ is true. This impossibility is public and inherent to the possible action, that is why we have the condition (*). That replaces the notion of precondition in [BMS04] and [Auc05].

From now on, we note $P_j^w(\sigma) := P_j^\Gamma(\sigma)$ **for the unique** Γ **such that** $M, w \models \Gamma$.

Item 6. The function $Post_\sigma$ deals with the problem of determining what facts will be true in a world after the action σ takes place. Intuitively, $Post_\sigma^+(p)$ (resp.

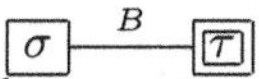

$$S = \{p_i, \neg p_i; i = 0..n\}.$$
$$P_B^{\{p_i\}}(\sigma) = \tfrac{i}{n}, \ P_B^{\{p_i\}}(\tau) = 1 - \tfrac{i}{n} \text{ for all } i.$$
$$P_A^{\{p_i\}}(\sigma) = 1 \text{ for all } i \neq 0, \ P_A^{\{p_0\}}(\sigma) = 0.$$
$$P_A^{\{p_i\}}(\tau) = 1 \text{ for all } i \neq n, \ P_A^{\{p_n\}}(\tau) = 0.$$
$$P_A^\Gamma(\sigma) = P_A^\Gamma(\tau) = P_B^\Gamma(\sigma) = P_B^\Gamma(\tau) = 0 \text{ for all } \Gamma \neq \{p_i\}.$$
$$Post_\sigma^+(p_n) = \bot, \ Post_\sigma^-(p_n) = \top.$$
$$Post_\sigma^+(p_i) = p_{i+1}, \ Post_\sigma^-(p_i) = \neg p_{i+1} \text{ for all } i < n.$$
$$Post_\tau^+(p_n) = \bot, \ Post_\tau^-(p_n) = \top.$$
$$Post_\tau^+(p_i) = p_i, \ Post_\tau^-(p_i) = \neg p_i \text{ for all } i < n.$$

Fig. 2. A draws a (white) ball, observes it and puts it in his pocket

$Post_\sigma^-(p))$ represents the precondition in any world w for p to become true (resp. false) in (w, σ) after the performance of σ. The role of condition (**) is to avoid the case where the performance of an action σ in a world w could provoke at the same time both p and $\neg p$ to be true in the resulting world (w, σ).

Example 3. Now, let us resume the 'urn' example. Consider the action whereby A draws a ball from the urn (which is actually white), looks at it and puts it in his pocket, B sees A doing that but can not see the ball. This action is depicted in Fig.2. The maximal consistent sets are represented by their 'positive' components, so $\{p_i\}$ refers to the set $\{p_i, \neg p_k; k \neq i\}$.

It looks quite complicated but the ideas behind are quite simple. Action σ (resp. τ) stands for "A draws a black (resp. white) ball, observes it and puts it in his pocket". Clearly B can not distinguish σ from τ. However if B assumes she is in a world where there are i black balls then for her the probability that A draws a black (resp. white) ball is $\tfrac{i}{n}$ (resp. $1 - \tfrac{i}{n}$): $P_B^{\{p_i\}}(\sigma) = \tfrac{i}{n}$ and $P_B^{\{p_i\}}(\tau) = 1 - \tfrac{i}{n}$. Moreover there can not be n black balls in the urn since A put one ball in his pocket ($Post_\sigma^+(p_n) = \bot$, $Post_\sigma^-(p_n) = \top$ and $Post_\tau^+(p_n) = \bot$, $Post_\tau^-(p_n) = \top$), but if he draws one black ball then there is one black ball less ($Post_\sigma^+(p_i) = p_{i+1}$, $Post_\sigma^-(p_i) = \neg p_{i+1}$ for all $i < n$), otherwise the number of black balls remains the same ($Post_\tau^+(p_i) = p_i$, $Post_\tau^-(p_i) = \neg p_i$ for all $i < n$).

2.3   The Update Mechanism

Definition 4. *Given a pd-model $M = (W, \{\sim_j; j \in G\}, \{P_j; j \in G\}, V, w_0)$ and a generic action model $\Sigma = (\Sigma, S, \{\sim_j; j \in G\}, \{P_j^\Gamma; \Gamma \text{ is a m. c. subset of } S \text{ and } j \in G\}, \{Post_\sigma; \sigma \in \Sigma\}, \sigma_0)$, we define their update product to be the pd-model $M \otimes \Sigma = (W \otimes \Sigma, \{\sim_j'; j \in G\}, \{P_j'; j \in G\}, V', w_0')$, where:*

1. $W \otimes \Sigma = \{(w, \sigma) \in W \times \Sigma; P_j^w(\sigma) > 0\}$.
2. $(w, \sigma) \sim_j' (v, \tau)$ *iff* $w \sim_j v$ *and* $\sigma \sim_j \tau$.
3. *We set*

$$P_j^{[w]_j}(\sigma) = \frac{\sum \{P_j(v) . P_j^v(\sigma); w \sim_j v\}}{\sum \{P_j(v) . P_j^v(\tau); w \sim_j v, \sigma \sim_j \tau\}}.$$

Then

$$P'_j(w, \sigma) = \frac{P_j(w).P_j^{[w]_j}(\sigma)}{\sum\{P_j(v); w \sim_j v \ and \ P_j^v(\sigma) > 0\}}.$$

4. $V'(p) = \{(w, \sigma) \in W \otimes \Sigma; M, w \models Post_\sigma^+(p) \vee (p \wedge \neg Post_\sigma^-(p))\}$.
5. $w'_0 = (w_0, \sigma_0)$.

Intuitive Interpretation and Motivations.

Items 1,2,5 are completely similar to the 'BMS' system ([BMS04] or [Auc05]) except for item 1 where the precondition is replaced by $P_j^w(\sigma) > 0$ (see section above). So, we only motivate items 3 and 4.

Item 3. We want to determine $P'_j(w, \sigma) = P_j(W \cap A)$ where W stands for 'we were in world w before σ occurred' and A for 'action σ occurred'. More formally, in the probability space $[(w, \sigma)]_j := \{(v, \tau); (v, \tau) \sim_j (w, \sigma)\}$, W stands for $\{(w, \tau); \tau \sim_j \sigma\}$ and A for $\{(v, \sigma); v \sim_j w\}$ and we can check that $W \cap A = \{(w, \sigma)\}$.

Probability theory tells us that

$$P_j(W \cap A) = P_j(W|A).P_j(A).$$

We first determine $P_j(W|A)$, that is to say the probability that j was in world w *given* the extra assumption that action σ occurred in this world. We reasonably claim

$$P_j(W|A) = \frac{P_j(w)}{\sum\{P_j(v); w \sim_j v \ and \ P_j^v(\sigma) > 0\}}.$$

That is to say, we *conditionalize* the probability of w for j (i.e. $P_j(w)$) to the worlds where the action σ took place and that may correspond for j to the actual world w (i.e. $\{v; w \sim_j v \ and \ P_j^v(\sigma) > 0\}$). That is how it would be done in classical probability theory. The intuition behind it is that we now possess the extra piece of information that σ occurred in w. So the worlds indistinguishable from w where the action σ did *not* occur do not play a role anymore for the determination of the probability of w. We can then get rid of them and conditionalize on the remaining relevant worlds.

It remains to determinate $P_j(A)$ which we also denote $P_j^{[w]_j}$; that is to say the probability for j that σ occurred. Agent j does not know in which world of $[w]_j := \{v; v \sim_j w\}$ she dwells. So this action could occur for j in any world v of $[w]_j$, each time with probability $P_j^v(\sigma)$. So we would first be tempted to take the average of them: $P_j(A) = P_j^{[w]_j}(\sigma) = \frac{\sum\{P_j^v(\sigma); v \sim_j w\}}{n}$, where n is the number of world in $[w]_j$.

But we have more information than that. j does not know in which world of $[w]_j$ she is, but she has a preference among them, which is expressed by P_j. So we can refine our expression above and take the *center of mass* (or barycenter) of the $P_j^v(\sigma)$s balanced respectively by the weights $P_j(v)$s (whose sum equals 1), instead of taking roughly the average (which is actually also a center of mass but with weights $\frac{1}{n}$). We get $P_j(A) = P_j^{[w]_j}(\sigma) = \sum\{P_j(v).P_j^v(\sigma); v \sim_j w\}$.

Finally, we would naturally want $\sum\{P_j^{[w]_j}(\tau); \tau \sim_j \sigma\} = 1$ so that $([\sigma]_j, \mathcal{P}([\sigma]_j), P_j^{[w]_j})$ (where $[\sigma]_j := \{\tau; \tau \sim_j \sigma\}$) forms a (nonstandard) probabilistic space. So we set

$$P_j(A) = P_j^{[w]_j}(\sigma) = \frac{\sum\{P_j(v).P_j^v(\sigma); w \sim_j v\}}{\sum\{P_j(v).P_j^v(\tau); w \sim_j v, \sigma \sim_j \tau\}}.$$

We then get the expected result by multiplication. We can easily check that its sum on $[(w, \sigma)]_j$ is equal to 1.

Item 4. Intuitively, this formula says that a fact p is true after the performance of σ in w iff the condition for p to become true after σ was satisfied in w, or else if p was already true in w but the condition to switch it to false was not satisfied in w.

Remark 2. Note the difference between $P_j^w(\sigma)$ and $P_j^{[w]_j}(\sigma)$: the former is determined by what is *true* in w and the latter by what j *believes* in w (see Examples 4 and 5 below). Moreover, since what j believes is the same in every world of $[w]_j$, we indeed have $P_j^{[w]_j}(\sigma) = P_j^{[w']_j}(\sigma)$ for all $w' \in [w]_j$.

From this product mechanism, we can easily define a dynamic language in the line of [BMS04] or [Auc05] that we do not spell out here.

Example 4. Let us come back to our 'urn' Example 1. Assume now that A draws a (white) ball from the urn, looks at it and puts it in his pocket, action depicted in Fig.3. Then because B does not have any particular preference about the distribution of the urn, she should believe equally that A draws a black ball and a white ball (see introduction). That is indeed the case : $P_B^{[w_i]_B}(\sigma) = P_B^{[w_i]_B}(\tau) = \frac{1}{2}$. Note the difference between $P_B^{w_i}(\sigma)(= \frac{i}{n})$ and $P_B^{[w_i]_j}(\sigma)(= \frac{1}{2})$ (see remark 2).

If we perform the full update mechanism, then we get the pd-model of Fig.3 with probabilities $P_A(x) = 1$ and $P_B(x) = \frac{1}{2n}$ for all worlds x. In this model all the worlds are equally probable for B and there can not be n black balls in the urn (p_n) since one has been withdrawn.

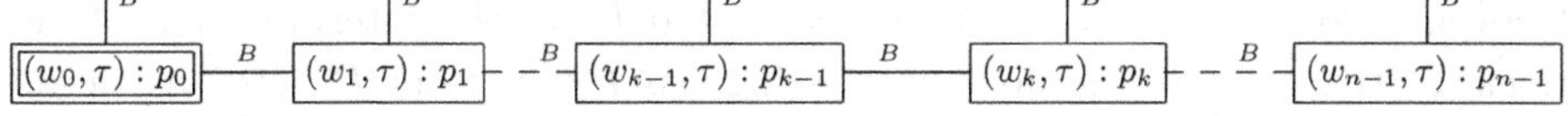

Fig. 3. situation of Examples 1 and 2 after A draws a white ball, looks at it and puts it in his pocket (without specification of the probabilities of worlds for each example: see text).

Example 5. Let us now come back to our 'urn' Example 2. Assume the same action as above occurs (depicted in Fig.2). However, now B is convinced that there are more black balls than white. Consequently, she should consider it more likely that A draws a black ball than a white ball (see introduction). That is the case indeed: $P_B^{[w_i]_B}(\sigma) = \frac{3}{4} + \frac{1}{4k} > P_B^{[w_i]_B}(\tau) = \frac{1}{4} - \frac{1}{4k}$.

If we perform the full update, then we still get the pd-model of Fig.3 but with different probability values: $P_A(x) = 1$ for all worlds x; $P_B(w_i, \sigma) = \varepsilon.(\frac{3}{4} + \frac{1}{4k})$ for $i = 1..k$; $P_B(w_i, \sigma) = \frac{1}{k}.(\frac{3}{4} + \frac{1}{4k})$ for $i = k+1..n$; $P_B(w_i, \tau) = \frac{\varepsilon}{4}$ for $i = 0..k$; $P_B(w_i, \tau) = \frac{1}{4k}$ for $i = k+1..n-1$. Note the grading of the surprising worlds. It states that B would be a bit more surprised to hear somebody claiming that "there were as many or less black balls than white balls *and* A drew a white ball" (worlds $(w_i, \tau), i = 0..k$), than to hear somebody claiming that "there were as many or less black balls than white balls *and* A drew a black ball" (worlds $(w_i, \sigma), i = 1..k$). This is coherent since she believed more that A drew a black ball than she believed that he drew a white ball (i.e. $P_B^{[w_i]_B}(\sigma) > P_B^{[w_i]_B}(\tau)$).

3   Comparisons

Comparison with the AGM postulates. We can prove that, under the assumption that the AGM notion of 'belief' (see [GardRott95]) corresponds to the Lenzen's notion of conviction (see remark 1), the 8 AGM postulates are fulfilled.

Comparison with Reiter's situation calculus. It turns out (surprisingly) that the way we deal with change of facts is completely similar to the way Reiter solves the frame problem in the situation calculus (see [Reit01]), and the assumptions he makes about actions are fulfilled in our framework.

Comparison with Kooi's system. Kooi's dynamic probabilistic system (see [Kooi03]), based on the static approach by Fagin and Halpern in [FH94], does not make any particular assumption about the relation between probability and epistemic relation (explored in [FH94]); contrary to our approach. Moreover, he deals only with public announcement, and in this particular case our update mechanism is basically the same as his.

Comparison with van Benthem's system. van Benthem's system (see [vBen03]) seems similar to ours, but he does not deal with actions changing facts and does not show the influence of *beliefs* on the interpretation of actions. In that respect, he does not distinguish $P_j^w(\sigma)$ from $P_j^{[w]_j}(\sigma)$ as we do (see Remark 2), and his ambiguous $P_j^w(\sigma)$ seems to be different from ours if we refer to his example. His probabilistic update rule (without motivations) is also different. Besides, his update product can not be iterated because he deals with worlds rather than maximal consistent sets in the probabilities of actions. Anyway, his comparison with the Bayesian setting and other insights are still valid here.

4   Conclusion

We have proposed a system which models belief with probability and whose update performs genuine belief revision (unlike the existing approaches in the literature). So it indirectly offers a new probabilistic approach to belief revision.

Moreover, in our modeling we have introduced surprising worlds necessary to model incorrect beliefs. Their relative degrees of surprise for the agent is expressed by infinitesimals. This use of infinitesimal has also enabled us to express what would surprise the agent and by how much. This is of importance since we want to describe with most accuracy any epistemic state of mind of any agent, including what would surprise her. In that respect the notion of knowledge can also be added to this dynamic epistemic system, which then validates all the Lenzen's axioms for belief and knowledge (that I consider as most accurate and expressive to describe epistemic states).

Finally, we have also incorporated actions that change facts of the situation and showed from a formal point of view how our beliefs can affect our interpretation of actions. In a sense this last point complements and reverses the classical view whereby only our interpretation of actions affects our beliefs and not the other way around, as in belief revision theory.

References

[Auc05] G. Aucher. A combined System for Update Logic and Belief Revision. In M. W. Barley and N. Kasabov (Eds.): *PRIMA 2004*, LNAI 3371 Pages 1-17, 2005.

[Adams75] E. W. Adams. The Logic of Conditionals. In *Synthese Library* Volume 86, D. Reidel, Dordrecht, Netherlands, 1975.

[BMS04] A. Baltag, L.S. Moss,and S. Solecki. Logic for epistemic program. In *Synthese* Volume 139(2) Pages: 165 - 224.

[FH94] R. Fagin and J. Y. Halpern. Reasoning about knowledge and probability. In *Journal of the ACM* (JACM) Volume 41(2) Pages: 340 - 367.

[GardRott95] P. Gardenfors and H. Rott, 1995, 'Belief Revision', in D. M. Gabbay, C. J. Hogger and J. A. Robinson, eds., *Handbook of Logic in Artificial Intelligence and Logic Programming* 4, Oxford University Press, Oxford 1995.

[Keis86] H. J. Keisler. *Elementary Calculus: An Approach Using Infinitesimal.* Prindle, Weber and Schmidt (eds), 1986. Online edition on the website http://www.math.wisc.edu/ keisler/calc.html .

[Kooi03] B.P. Kooi (2003). Probabilistic Dynamic Epistemic Logic. In *Journal of Logic, Language and Information* Volume 12(4) Pages: 381-408.

[Len03] W. Lenzen. Knowledge, Belief, and Subjective Probability: Outlines of a Unified System of Epistemic/Doxastic Logic. In: V. F. Hendricks and Al. (eds.), *Knowledge Contributors*, Dordrecht (Kluwer) 2003, Pages: 17-31.

[Reit01] R. Reiter. *Knowledge in Action: Logical Foundations for Specifying and Implementing Dynamical Systems*, MIT Press, 2001.

[vBen03] J. van Benthem. Conditional probability meets update logic. In *Journal of Logic, Language and Information* Volume 12(4) Pages: 409 - 421.

The Effect of Flag Introduction on the Explosion of Nogood Values in the Case of ABT Family Techniques

Ionel Muscalagiu

The Politehnica University of Timisoara,
The Engineering Faculty of Hunedoara, Revolutiei, nr.5, Hunedoara, Romania
mionel@fih.utt.ro

Abstract. Starting from the algorithm of asynchronous backtracking, a unifying framework for some of the asynchronous techniques has recently been suggested. Within this unifying framework, several techniques have been derived, known as the ABT family. The asynchronous backtracking technique is characterized by an explosion of nogood values for the large dimensions problem. The storing of these values, needed within the asynchronous backtracking technique needs a very large quantity of space. Recently, a derivate technique called asynchronous backtracking with flags allowed the reduction of nogood values explosion. In this article, a solution of flag technique application is suggested for the ABT family. It implies the indexing of local values in the domain of each flagged agent. This eliminates the nogood value storing and, therefore, for great dimension problems, allows avoiding the nogood value explosions. The allocated memory space is considerably reduced in the case of flag technique. Solutions are being suggested for the derivation of the common kernel in order to reach two known techniques: Asynchronous Backtracking and Distributed Dynamic Backtracking.

1 Introduction

The constraint programming is a model of software technology used to describe and solve large classes of problems as, for instance, combinatorial problems. The idea of sharing various parts of the problem among agents that act independently and that collaborate among themselves using messages, in the prospective of gaining the solution, proved useful, as it lead to obtaining a new modeling type called Distributed Constraint Satisfaction Problem (DCSP)[5].

According to the IT literature the backtracking algorithm distributed in an asynchronous way, existing for the DCSP model, is considered the first complete algorithm for the asynchronous search [5]. Starting from the algorithm of asynchronous backtracking (ABT), it has recently been suggested in [1], [2] a unifying framework, a starting kernel for some of the asynchronous techniques. From this kernel, several techniques have been derived, known as the ABT family. These techniques start from a common core which can lead to some of the known techniques, including the algorithm of asynchronous backtracking, by eliminating the obsolete information among agents.

M. Pěchouček, P. Petta, and L.Z. Varga (Eds.): CEEMAS 2005, LNAI 3690, pp. 286–295, 2005.

The appearance of the nogood values has as an effect the introduction of some new constraints. Although the nogood list indicates the cause of the failure and its incorporation as a new constraint, it will teach the agents not to repeat the same mistake and it is expected that during the course of the algorithm the nogood values be as few as possible, because they have as an effect the increasing of the execution time. The number of recordings of nogood messages determines the exponential complexity of the algorithm in the unfavorable case in the first place. The stocking complexity refers to the memory quantity used by an algorithm; contoured with a different measure unit. This measure unit is very important to be used in the analyzing of some techniques, like the ABT, like the learning techniques or the caching techniques. It is possible that those costs linked to the quantity of memory used, make a certain technique unusable, even if from the calculations' point of view it is very efficient.

Recently, a derivate technique [3] called asynchronous backtracking algorithm with flags, allows eliminating the explosion effect for the nogood values. In [3] more types of nogood values received by an agent are identified in the case of ABT technique. They show that only certain classes of nogoods should be stored. Moreover, in [3], it is suggested to replace these classes of nogood values, by labeling the values in the domain of variables.

This article suggests a solution of applying the flag technique in the case of ABT family. Instead of storing the nogood values, they are labeled by two types of flags. This solution is applied for the ABT kernel and the resulting variant will be called ABTkernel with flags. Starting from this nucleus, two known techniques are reached: ABT and DisDB (with flags).

The article also investigates the efficiency of this derivative technique reported to the messages stream, the calculating necessary effort and the cycles consumed for finding the solution, as compared to the basic techniques derived from the ABT kernel.

2   The Framework

In order to do the analysis of the impact of the nogood values, this paragraph presents some notions known from the IT literature related to the DCSP modeling, ABT algorithm [5], ABT family [1],[2] and ABT with flags [3].

2.1   The Distribution Constraint Satisfaction Problem

Definition 1. *The model based on constraints CSP-Constraint Satisfaction Problem, existing for centralized architectures, consists in:*

- n variables X1,...,Xn, whose values are taken from finite domains D1, D2,..., Dn.
- a set of constraints on their values.

The solution of a CSP implies to find an association of values to all the variables so that all the constraints should be fulfilled.

Definition 2. *A problem of satisfying the distributed constraints (DCSP) is a CSP, in which the variables and constraints are distributed among autonomous agents that communicate by transmitting, messages.*

The Asynchronous Backtracking algorithm uses 3 types of messages:

- the OK message, which contains an assignment variable-value, is sent by an agent to the constraint-evaluating-agent in order to see if the value is good.
- the nogood message which contains a list (called nogood) with the assignments for which the looseness was found is being sent in case the constraint-evaluating-agent found an unfulfilled constraint.
- the add-link message, sent to announce the necessity to create a new direct link, caused by a nogood appearance.

Each agent keeps its own agent-view and nogood store. Considering a generic agent self, the agent-view of self is the set of values that it believes to be assigned to agents connected to self by incoming links. A nogood is a subset of agent view. If a nogood exists, it means the agent can not find a value from the domain consistent with the nogood. When agent X_i finds its agent-view including a nogood, the values of the other agents must be changed. The nogood store keeps nogoods as justifications of inconsistent values. When self makes an assignment, it informs those agents connected to it by outgoing links. Self always accepts new assignments, updating its agent-view accordingly. When self receives a nogood, it is accepted if it is consistent with self's agent view, otherwise it is discarded as obsolete. An accepted nogood is added to self's nogood store to justify the deletion of the value it targets. When self cannot take any value consistent with its agent-view, new nogoods are generated as inconsistent subsets of the agent-view, and are sent to the closest agent involved, causing backtracking. The process terminates when achieving quiescence, meaning that a solution has been found, or when the empty nogood is generated, meaning that the problem is unsolvable.

2.2   The ABT Family

Starting from the algorithm of asynchronous backtracking, in [1],[2] several derived techniques were suggested, based on this one and known as the ABT family. They differ in the way that they store nogoods, but they all use additional communication links between unconnected agents to detect obsolete information. These techniques are based on a common core (called ABT kernel) hence some of the known techniques can be obtained, including the algorithm of asynchronous backtracking, by eliminating the old information among the agents. In [1],[2] the starting point is a simple procedure that includes the main characteristics of the asynchronous search algorithms.

The ABTkernel algorithm requires, like ABT, that constraints are directed-from the value-sending agent to the constraint-evaluating agent-forming a directed acyclic graph. Agents are ordered statically in agreement with constraint orientation. Agent i has higher priority than agent j if i appears before j in the total ordering. Considering a generic agent self, $\Gamma^-(self)$ is the set of agents constrained with self appearing above it in the ordering. Conversely, $\Gamma^+(self)$ is the set of agents constrained with self appearing below it in the ordering.

The ABT kernel algorithm, is a new ABT-based algorithm that does not require to add communication links between initially unconnected agents. The ABT kernel algorithm is sound but may not terminate (the ABT kernel may store obsolete information). In [1],[2] were suggested several solutions for the elimination of the old information among agents. A first way to remove obsolete information is to add new communication links to allow a nogood owner to determine whether this nogood is obsolete or not. A second way to remove obsolete information is to detect when a nogood could become obsolete. These two alternative ways lead to the following four algorithms:

1. Adding links as preprocessing: This algorithm adds all the potentially useful new links during a preprocessing phase. New links are permanent.
2. Adding links during search:ABT. This algorithm adds new links between agents during search. A link is requested by self when it receives a Back message containing unrelated agents above self in the ordering.
3. Adding temporary links.This algorithm adds new links between agents during search. The diference is that new links are temporary. A new link remains until a fixed number of messages have been exchanged through it.
4. No links:DisDB. No new links are added among the agents. To achieve completeness, this algorithm has to remove obsolete information in finite time. To do so, when an agent backtracks forgets all nogoods that hypothetically could become obsolete.

2.3   The Asynchronous Backtracking Algorithm with Flags (ABTWF)

In [3] more types of nogood values received by an agent are identified in the case of ABT technique. Moreover, in [3] four classes of nogood values that come up with a nogood type message have been identified, namely:

(1) (x_i, d_i): the value of d_i is the same as the current value.
(2) (x_i, d_i): the value of d_i is different from the current value.
(3) $(x_j, d_j),...,(x_i, d_i)$: is consistent with the agent-view of X_i and (x_i, d_{x_i})
(4) $(x_j, d_j),...,(x_i, d_i)$: is not consistent with the agent-view of X_i and (x_i, d_{x_i}).

In the ABT algorithm [5], agent X_i will change the current value under two conditions: (1) when it receives an OK? message or (2) when it receives a nogood message consistent with agent view of X_i. So, class 2 and class 4 nogoods are out-of-date information to agent X_i. When X_i receives a class 1 nogood, it means that the current value of X_i does not satisfy at least one constraint between the agent which sends the nogood message to X_i. However, when X_i receive a class 3 nogood, it means that the nogood in the nogood message is consistent with the agent-view of X_i and $(X_i,$ current value). The nogood in the message is useful information to X_i in the current agent-view, so we must record it. The recording of nogoods will avoid the same wrong combination from being produced again when agent X_i selects a new current value. But the agent-view of X_i will change when the values of related agents are changed. Thus, when the agent-view of X_i changes, the nogood becomes out-of-date information. For the above mentioned reason, the class 3 nogood should be recorded temporarily.

Starting from these observations, in [3] a derivate technique has been suggested, called asynchronous backtracking with flags (ABTWF). This algorithm is obtained starting from the basic ABT algorithm by replacing the storing of nogood values by indexing the local values with flags. Two types of flags are being used, corresponding to classes 1 and 3 of nogoods:

(1) The Permanent Flag (PF): when the received nogood is class 1, agent Xi will set the flag of the current value of local variable to PF. This PF flag will not be cleared in the running processes all the time.

(2) The Temporary Flag (TF): when the receiving nogood is class 3, agent X_i will set the flag of the current value of the local variable to TF. When agent X_i receives an OK? message or sends a nogood message, it means that the agent with a higher priority than agent Xi will change its value or has changed value already. In this situation, the TF will be cleared, so the value labeled by the TF flag before it can be selected again.

3   The ABT Family with Flags

Analyzing the nogood message flux, we identified the same types of nogood values, similar to those identified in [3]. Therefore, only the class 1 and 2 nogood values have to be stored, the class 2 and 4 values being old. Moreover, the class 3 nogood values need to be stored only temporarily.

Starting from these observations we will replace the storage of the nogood values by the flag indexation of the local values. We will use two types of flags, corresponding to the two nogood classes:

1 The Permanent Flag (PF): when the receiving nogood is class 1
2 The Temporary Flag (TF): when the receiving nogood is class 3

Each agent will keep a list of flags associated to the values in its field, flags of the type given previously. This list of flags will be used by each agent in selecting a value from its field. The list of flags will be permanently consistent with the context of each agent. The consistency conditions shall consist in checking the *myAgentView* list with the current value meant to meet all the constraints, respectively the flag associated to the correct value shall not be labeled with any of the values PF or TF. It is to be noticed that an extra condition has been added for the consistency of the values, namely that the flag corresponding to the current value should not be labeled PF or TF.

In figure 1 is shown the algorithm ABT kernel with flags. The modifications are labeled by character * and the annulled code portions start with // and are labeled **. In figure 1 one can notice a few essential modifications in the initial code of the ABT kernel. They are going to be analyzed hereinafter.

First, on receiving an "info"-type message that informs the "self" agent of the change in another agent's value, the local context of the "self" agent is being updated. This involves updating the *myAgentView* list and also updating the flag list by deleting the temporary flags. One can notice that there is no more need to update the nogood list, as it does not exist any more.

Secondly, on receiving a nogood message, this is accepted only if it is consistent with $\Gamma^-(self) \cup self$. Then, the *myAgentView* list is being updated with the values of the agents included in the nogood message but not in $\Gamma^-(self)$. It is to be noticed that we no longer need to update the list of stored nogood values, as their role has been taken over by the flags. Practically, the class of nogood values is being identified in this moment (either class 1 or 3) the associated flags being labeled accordingly.

Another modification that appears in the body of the BackTrack procedure, a routine that is being called when no value consistent with the context of the "self" agent is found. First, the new nogood is not of the "Nogood resolution" type, but it is constituted as an inconsistent subset of the agent's context. On this occasion the flags associated to the values in the domain of the current variable are being updated and the temporary flags are being reset. Secondly, the flag attached to the value of agent x_j is being reset, so that this value can be chosen again. The last modification needed relates to the ChooseValue function, in which only the flag list has to be updated and not the list of nogood values stored.

Some observations have to be made with respect to the updating of the flag list. In [3] it is suggested to delete the temporary flags and to keep the permanent ones. In [4] a slight improvement is suggested, consisting in restarting the search process by also resetting the permanent flags, not only the temporary ones. This idea is applied here, both temporary and permanent flags being reset.

In [1],[2] it is shown that the ABT kernel can lead to the appearance of old information among the agents. This situation leads to an infinite cycle of the algorithm for certain classes and instances of problems. Starting from the ABT kernel, in [2], the old information among agents are being eliminated by various methods. Starting at this procedure, we could reach the known algorithms or versions close to this (such as ABT or DisDB).

Applying the same methods of information elimination, we can reach various variants of techniques, variants that use flags instead of nogood storing. We shall hereinafter analyze two notorious techniques that can be reached. The variants obtained shall be called Asynchronous Backtracking with flags(ABTWFL), Distributed Dynamic Backtracking with flags (DisDBWFL).

A first way of removing obsolete information is to add new communication links to allow a nogood owner to determine whether this nogood is obsolete or not. Applying this method to the ABT kernel (the flag variant), we reach the technique of asynchronous backtracking with flags(ABTWFL). This algorithm adds new links between agents during search. A link is requested by self when it receives a Back message containing unrelated agents above self in the ordering. The necessary modifications in the ABT kernel with flags, meant to eliminate

---

procedure ABTkernel()
1   myValue ←empty; end←false; CheckAgentView();
3   while (not end) do
4   msg←getMsg();
5   switch(msg.type)
6   Info : ProcessInfo(msg);
7   Back : ResolveConflict(msg);
8   Stop : end ← true;
end

procedure CheckAgentView(msg)
1   if not consistent(myValue;myAgentView) then
2   myValue← ChooseValue();
3   if (myValue) then for each child∈ $\Gamma^+(self)$ do sendMsg:Info(child;myValue);
4   else Backtrack();
end

procedure ProcessInfo(msg)
1   add(newAssig; myAgentView); //remove Update(myAgentView; msg.Assig); **
2   Clear TF Flags on domain values;* CheckAgentView();
end

procedure ResolveConflict(msg)
1   if Coherent(msg.Nogood;$\Gamma^-(self) \cup \{self\}$) then
2   for each assig ∈ lhs(msg.Nogood)$\setminus \Gamma^-$(self) do
            add(newAssig;myAgentView); * //remove Update(myAgentView; assig); **
3   //remove add(msg:Nogood;myNogoodStore); **
4   when nogood only contains $(x_i, d_i$) and is consistent with $(x_i$, current-value) do *
            label current-value Flag PF ; end do;
5   when nogood is consistent with agent-view and $(x_i$, current-value) do *
            label current-value Flag TF ; end do;
6   myValue ← empty; CheckAgentView();
7   else if msg.sender ∈ $\Gamma^+(self)\wedge$ Coherent(msg.Nogood; self) then
            SendMsg:Info(msg.sender; myValue);
end

procedure Backtrack()
1   newNogood← {V|V=inconsistent subset of myAgentView}*
2   if (newNogood = empty) then
3   end ← true; sendMsg:Stop(system);
4   else sendMsg:Back(newNogood, x_j); /*where x_j has the lowest priority in V */
5   Update(myAgentView; x_j ← unknown);
6   Clear TF Flags on domain values; *
7   Label value-of x_j Flag unknown; *
8   CheckAgentView();
end

function ChooseValue()
1   for each v∈D(self)not eliminated by myFlagList do *
2   if consistent(v; myAgentView) then return (v);
3   else label current-value Flag TF * /*v is inconsistent with x_j 's value */
4   // remove add($x_j = val_j$) self ≠ v;myNogoodStore); **
5   return (empty);
end

procedure Update(myAgentView; newAssig)
1   add(newAssig;myAgentView);
2   for each v∈ D(self) do
3   if not consistent (v; myAgentView) then label v Flag TF; *
5   else label v Flag unknown
end

Fig. 1. The ABTkernel with flags algorithm for asynchronous backtracking search

the old information are the same as those given in [2], in order to reach the asynchronous backtracking technique.

A second way to remove obsolete information is to detect when a nogood could become obsolete. In that case, the hypothetically obsolete nogood and the values of unrelated agents are forgotten. By applying this technique to the ABT kernel (the flag variant), one can reach the technique of Distributed Dynamic Backtracking with flags (DisDBWFL). Let's remember that there is certain difference from the variant derived from [1],[2]: the new nogood is not of the "nogood resolution" type, but it is built as an inconsistent subset of the agent's context (the list of *myAgentView*).

4   Experimental Results

This paragraph will present our experimental results, obtained by implementing and evaluating the asynchronous techniques that were introduced. In order to make such estimation, these techniques have been implemented in NetLogo 2.0.2, a distributed environment, using a special language named NetLogo [6], [7].

The asynchronous techniques were applied for a classical problem: the problem of colouring a graph in the distributed versions. For the problem of graph colouring we took into consideration two types of problems (we kept in mind the parameters n-number of knots, k=3 colours and m-the number of connections between the agents). We evaluated two types of graphs: graphs with few connections (called sparse problems, having m=n x 2 connections) and graphs with a special number of connections (called difficult problems and having m=n x 2.7 connections). For each version a number of 100 trials were carried out, retaining the average of the measured values (for each class 10 graphs are generated randomly, for each graph being generated 10 initial values).

The message stream was counted down, the number of constraint checks (the local effort), the number of concurrent constraint checks and the number of cycles necessary for obtaining each solution. We have also kept in mind the number of stored nogood values (respectively the flag lists for the flag versions). The four evaluated versions were called ABT, ABTWFL, DisDB and DisDBWFL. The values obtained for the three graph classes (with 20, 25 and 30 knots) are stored in the table 1 (the ABT versions) and table 2 (the DisDB versions).

The first measuring unit for the analyzed asynchronous techniques performances was the cycle. Out of the value analysis it can be noticed that the two versions have close values regarding the necessary cycle numbers, nevertheless pointing out to the good results for the flag versions that needed a small number of cycles. This shows a good behavior also in the case of difficult problems with great dimensions.

As known, the verified constraints quantity evaluates the local effort given by each agent, but the number of concurrent constraint checks allows the evaluation of this effort without considering that the agents work concurrently (informally,

Table 1. The results for ABT versions (Distributed n-Graph-Coloring Problem)

		n=20		n=25		n=30	
		m=nx2	m=nx2.7	m=nx2	m=nx2.7	m=nx2	m=nx2.7
ABT	Nogood	279.70	928.05	1213.23	1393.19	4152.59	5498.03
	Ok	1012.81	3242.26	4205.35	5389.66	14648.67	23741.29
	Nogood store	137.55	289.61	592.42	477.98	1719.31	1546.79
	Cycles	211.52	490.74	634.17	736.62	2294.85	2427.14
	Constraints	59372.05	186777.62	368304.06	376304.06	1328756.54	1892342.32
	c-ccks	12393.31	34358.36	48201.90	56843.21	270280.68	240830.17
ABTWFL	Nogood	242.51	621.54	694.04	972.76	2859.54	3004.56
	Ok	908.85	2218.59	2684.29	3677.43	10091.74	13021.04
	Nogood store	119.20	194.80	338.98	343.35	1207.56	882.73
	Cycles	183.09	329.63	56.06	472.31	1585.63	1313.81
	Constraints	24535.72	67371.98	91516.39	115722.67	426475.21	406482.49
	c-ccks	7349.29	18365.84	32865.54	27624.41	119371.28	79695.95

Table 2. The results for DisDB versions (Distributed n-Graph-Coloring Problem)

		n=20		n=25		n=30	
		m=nx2	m=nx2.7	m=nx2	m=nx2.7	m=nx2	m=nx2.7
DisDB	Nogood	288.12	824.89	697.92	1066.35	3397.69	5956.57
	Ok	629.39	1927.99	1393.93	2728.78	6980.30	13620.43
	Nogood store	168.88	330.75	402.67	474.35	1951.72	2442.77
	Cycles	158.05	403.42	400.58	534.55	1814.48	1770.23
	Constraints	38258.77	112446.82	122533.57	178043.25	719449.09	1196721.64
	c-ccks	9364.67	25255.19	31541.98	33845.25	184218.86	1866897.88
DisDBWFL	Nogood	215.38	648.08	446.74	775.30	1976.57	6434.89
	Ok	480.37	1502.50	839.75	1974.85	4601.43	14589.85
	Nogood store	127.61	269.74	238.72	346.38	1046.07	2862.95
	Cycles	115.50	284.23	233.32	327.37	1053.68	1912.38
	Constraints	24723.56	73457.67	52843.36	103938.15	401034.94	1081615.49
	c-ccks	6357.37	16447.37	13569.45	19069.65	107099.27	169949.27

the number of concurrent constraint checks approximates the longest sequence of constraint checks not performed concurrently). Analyzing these values, there is an obvious difference between the basic technique and the two flag versions, those needing a local effort much reduced (at half).

In the case of the message stream the two versions need a close number of messages for problems with small dimension and low density. But in the case of problems with great dimension and density, the flag versions needed a smaller message stream. It is obvious that the number of stored nogood values, respectively the number of flags for the flag versions are close, but the quantity of necessary memory is much smaller for the last versions.

By analyzing the table values it is to be remarked that the two flag versions, need much smaller calculating costs.

5   Conclusions

The ABT family techniques are characterized by an explosion of the nogood values, particularly for the bulky problems. Another characteristic, specific for the asynchronous techniques in the ABT family is that the storage of the nogood values is necessary, so that the agents don't repeat the same mistake. This requires a large amount of memory, particularly for the bulky problems. One solution meant to eliminate the explosion of nogood values is to label the values in the the field of each flag variable.

This article suggests a solution to replace the nogood value storage by labeling the values in the field by two types of flags. This solution is applied for the ABT kernel, thus obtaining a new variant that only requires the storage of the nogood values. Starting from this kernel, one can reach two notorious techniques: the ABT and the DisDB.

The ABT and DisDB flag technique is a derived one from the basic ABT kernel technique with flags. It implies the indexing of local values in the domain of each flagged agent. This eliminates the nogood value storing and, therefore, for great dimension problems, allows avoiding the nogood values explosions. The allocated memory space is considerably reduced in the case of flag technique.

The evaluations realized in the conditions of various problems, with initial random values, for the problems with various densities, show that the flag techniques need a memory space for flags much smaller comparative to the basic technique. This flag technique could be enhanced by restarting the searching process when arriving an ok type message. The experiments show a greater efficiency of this version, but without bringing spectacular results.

References

1. Bessiere, C., Maestre, A., Meseguer P.:The ABT family. In Proceedings of JFNP (2002).
2. Bessiere, C., Brito, I., Maestre, A., Meseguer P.:Asynchronous Backtracking without Adding Links: A New Member in the ABT Family. Journal of Artificial Intelligence **161** (2005) 7-24.
3. Gwen-Hua C., Wei-Li Lin, Chan-Lon Wang: Asynchronous Backtracking Algorithm with no effect of nogood explosion. In Proceedings International Conference on Computer, Communication and Control Technologies, Orlando, Florida (2003).
4. Muscalagiu I., Balan M.: The Effect Of Flag Introduction On The Explosion Of Nogood Values When Using The Asynchronous Backtracking Technique, CSCS14, Bucuresti, Romania (2005).
5. Yokoo, M., Durfee E.H., Ishida T., Kuwabara K.: The distributed constraint satisfaction problem: formalization and algorithms. IEEE Transactions on Knowledge and Data Engineering **10(5)** (1998) 673-685.
6. Wilensky U.: NetLogo itself: NetLogo. http://ccl.northwestern.edu/netlogo/. Center for Connected Learning and Computer-Based Modeling, Northwestern University. Evanston, (1999).
7. MAS Netlogo Models. Available:
   http://ccl.northwestern.edu/netlogo/models/community, (2005).

Toward a Formal Theory of Belief, Capability and Promise Incorporating Temporal Aspect[*]

Xinyu Zhao, Shaofeng Fan, Runjie Zhang, Anbu Yue, and Zuoquan Lin

LMAM, Department of Information Science,
School of Mathematical Sciences,
Peking University, Beijing 100871, China
{xinyua, fsf, zrj, yueanbu, lz}@is.pku.edu.cn

Abstract. In this paper, a logical model for reasoning about rational agent's three attitudes *Belief*, *Capability* and *Promise*, incorporating the temporal aspect, is proposed. Diverse axioms that can reflect different properties of the agents are presented in a precise way by appropriate conditions according to the accessibility relations of the models. The inter-relations among the operators are also explored to characterize the interactions and cooperations between the agents. An illustrative reasoning example in the trading agent competition for supply chain management(TAC SCM) is presented to show the potential applications of the model.

1 Introduction

From last two decade, there has been much interest in the use of logic for developing formal theories of rational agents, such as *BDI* logics[1], *KARO* framework[2] and *LORA* logic[3]. When formalizing the properties of rational agents, the first fundamental problem is to determine which combination of attitudes is appropriate for modeling their cognitive states and functional components.

For a type of complex systems, we discuss the necessity of the three attitudes, i.e. belief, promise and capability. It's necessary for agents to be provided with an informative component, called *belief*, to keep the states of the systems and the environments. In order to achieve their goal, there must be a functional component, called *capability*, to carry out the plans and bring them to success. Before cooperation, the participants must make an agreement in some way and a model about *promise* must be built to establish cooperation relationship between them. In multi-agent systems, the decision-making processes, based on the individual belief, are commonly impacted by whether the other agents would like to make promises to accept the tasks and whether they can fulfill the tasks. Thus, an agent is required to be able to reason about other agents' promises and capabilities to decide whether they can accept and accomplish tasks most effectively.

---

[*] This paper was partially supported by NKBRPC (2004CB318000) and NSFC (60373002, 60496322).

M. Pěchouček, P. Petta, and L.Z. Varga (Eds.): CEEMAS 2005, LNAI 3690, pp. 296–305, 2005.

As pointed out in [4], there may not be a unique agent model suitable for all applications, since different domains have different characteristics and different requirements regarding rational behavior. Although such three notions, i.e. belief, capability and promise, have been separably explored in the literature, there has been very little work on combining them as a whole framework and studying the relationship between them. This is the central issue of what we will do in the following sections.

In this paper, a logical model for reasoning about the agent's *Belief, Capability* and *Promise*(abbreviated as BCP) incorporating temporal aspect is proposed. We use *modal logic*, which provides an intuitively acceptable, uniform formalization of intensional notions, to model rational agents. Inspired by [5], we use time lines instead of normal worlds, because they provide a simple way of introducing time into the model. The standard *Kripke*-style semantics for B and P is combined with *minimal* semantics[6] for C to interpret the well-formed formulas. The intended meaning of $P_{ij}(t, \phi)$ is that at time t, the agent j makes a promise to the agent i that j would like to achieve ϕ, while $C_{ij}(t, \phi)$ means at time t, i considers that j has the capability to perform action ϕ[1]. A sound and complete model is given as the basis for introducing more properties to the three attitudes. Afterwards, diverse axioms that can reflect different properties of agents, are presented in a precise way by appropriate conditions according to the accessibility relations of the models. The inter-relations among operators are explored to characterize multi-agent interactions in different domains. In addition, an illustrative case of (TAC SCM)[8] is presented to show the potential applications of the model.

This paper is organized as follows. In section 2, we provide the syntax, semantics and axioms of the basic temporal BCP model plus the properties of the three attitudes and the inter-relation among the mixed operators are explored with intuitive meanings. A reasoning example in TAC SCM is illustrated in section 3. In section 4, related works are compared and distinguished in detail. Section 5 concludes with a discussion and indicates the future work.

2   The Logical Model

2.1   The Logic BCP

We will combine Kripke-style semantics for agents' belief and promise with *minimal structures*[6] style semantics for capability. Inspired by [5], we use time lines instead of normal worlds, because they provide a simple way of introducing time into the system. At every time point in the each time line, some propositions are true as well as the rest are false. We denote by *Agents* the set of agents. We have a set TC of time point constants, a set TV of time point variables (t, t_1, t_2, ...), a set AC of agent constants, a set AV of agent variables (i, j, ...), and a set *Pred* of predicate symbols. We denote by *Variables* the set of all variables

---

[1] Be similar to [7], we will not distinguish between actions and facts, and the occurrence of an action will be represented by the corresponding fact holding.

(including TV and AV), by $Constants$ the set of all constants (including TC and AC), and by $Terms$ the set of variables and constants. We also use the term nil. Then the set of the well-formed formulas(wff) of the temporal BCP model is defined as follows:

(1) if $t_1, t_2 \in TC \cup TV$, then $t_1 < t_2$ is a wff.
(2) if $x_1, x_2 \in Terms$, then $x_1 = x_2$ is a wff.
(3) if $P \in Pred$ is a k-ary predicate, $x_1, ..., x_n$ are terms, and $t \in TC \cup TV$, then $P(t, x_1, ..., x_n)$ is a wff ($P(t, x_1, ..., x_n)$ is true at time t).
(4) if φ and ψ are wffs, then so are $\varphi \wedge \psi$ and $\neg\varphi$. If φ is a wff and $x \in Variables$, then $\forall x\varphi$ is a wff. $\exists, \vee, \supset$ are defined as usual.
(5) if φ and ψ are wffs, $t \in TC \cup TV$, $i, j \in AC \cup AV$, then the following expressions are wffs:
   (a) $B_i(t, \varphi)$ (i believes φ at time t),
   (b) $P_{ij}(t, \varphi)$ (at time t, j promises i that φ could be done),
   (c) $C_{ij}(t, \varphi)$ (at time t, i considers that j is capable of performing φ).
   (d) $Agent(t, \phi, i)$ (i is the agent of ϕ).

Formally, time is a pair $\langle T, \prec \rangle$, where T is a set of time points and $\prec$ is a total order on T (unbounded in both directions). A BCP model is a tuple $M = \langle \Xi, L, Agents, A, R^B, R^C, R^P, \Phi, v \rangle$, where

- Ξ is a set of elements in the agent's environment.
- L is a set of time lines.
- $Agents$ is a set of agents.
- $R^B : L \times T \times Agents \rightarrow 2^L$ is the belief-accessibility relation.
- $R^C : L \times T \times Agents \times Agents \rightarrow 2^{2^L}$ is the capability-accessibility relation.
- $R^P : L \times T \times Agents \times Agents \rightarrow 2^L$ is the promise-accessibility relation.
- Φ interprets predicates and v interprets constants.
- $A : L \times T \times 2^{2^L} \rightarrow Agents \cup nil$ associates an agent or nil with each proposition for any given time period.

The domain of quantification is $\Theta = \Xi \cup T \cup Agents$. Given this, $\Phi : Pred^k \times L \times T \rightarrow \Theta^k$. $\overline{v}$ is the extension of v to all $Variables$. If for any extension v' of v $M, l, v' \models \psi$, we say that M, l satisfy ψ ($M, l \models \psi$). Given a structure M, and a wff ψ, we denote by $\|\psi\|$ the set $\{l | l \in L, M, l, \overline{v} \models \psi\}$. The satisfaction relation is defined inductively as follows:

(1) If $t_1, t_2 \in TC \cup TV$, then $M, l, \overline{v} \models t_1 < t_2$ iff $\overline{v}(t_1) \prec \overline{v}(t_2)$.
(2) If $x_1, x_2 \in Terms$, then $M, l, \overline{v} \models x_1 = x_2$ iff $\overline{v}(x_1) = \overline{v}(x_2)$.
(3) If $P \in Pred$ is a k-ary predicate, $x_1, ..., x_k$ are terms, and $t \in TC \cup TV$, then $M, l, \overline{v} \models P(t, x_1, ..., x_k)$ iff $\langle \overline{v}(x_1), ..., \overline{v}(x_k) \rangle \in \Phi(P, l, \overline{v}(t))$.
(4) If φ is a wff, ψ is a wff and $x \in Variables$, then:
   (a) $M, l, \overline{v} \models \neg\varphi$ iff $M, l, \overline{v} \not\models \varphi$;
   (b) $M, l, \overline{v} \models \varphi \wedge \psi$ iff $M, l, \overline{v} \models \varphi$ and $M, l, \overline{v} \models \psi$;
   (c) $M, l, \overline{v} \models \forall x\varphi$ iff for every $\overline{v}'$ which agrees with $\overline{v}$ everywhere, except possibly on x $M, l, \overline{v}' \models \varphi$.

(5) If φ and ψ are wffs, $t \in TC \cup TC$, $i, j \in AC \cup AV$, then:
(a) $M, l, \overline{v} \models B_i(t, \varphi)$ iff $l' \in L$, if $l' \in R^B(l, \overline{v}(t), \overline{v}(i))$, $M, l', \overline{v} \models \varphi$;
(b) $M, l, \overline{v} \models C_{ij}(t, \varphi)$ iff $\|\varphi\| \in R^C(l, \overline{v}(t), \overline{v}(i), \overline{v}(j))$;
(c) $M, l, \overline{v} \models P_{ij}(t, \varphi)$ iff $l' \in L$, if $l' \in R^P(l, \overline{v}(t), \overline{v}(i), \overline{v}(j))$, $M, l', \overline{v} \models \varphi$;
(d) $M, l, \overline{v} \models Agent(t, \varphi, i)$ iff $A(l, \overline{v}(t), \|\varphi\|) = \overline{v}(i)$.

A temporal BCP model $M = \langle \Xi, L, Agents, A, R^B, R^C, R^P, \Phi, v \rangle$ is said to *validate* a formula φ if for every $l \in L, M, l \models \varphi$. A formula φ is valid if it is validated by any BCP model.

Until now, the agents in our model are provided with rather limited reasoning power because of lacking appropriate properties for their attitudes. As the following theorem states, all tautologies and inferences of first-order logic are valid in temporal BCP model. The axiom **(B1)** formalizes that operator B satisfies the K-axiom. The operator P is similar to B. It means that if the agent j makes a promise of goal φ to the agent i, it also gives all logical consequence of φ. **(R3)** is an instance of rule of necessitation which states that the valid wff is believed and promised in advance. **(R4)** indicates that if an agent is considered to be capable of performing a wff, then the consequence of the wff is all the same.

Theorem 1. *The following axiomatic system is sound and complete for validity in BCP models:*

(A0) *All tautologies of first-order logic.*
(B1) $B_i(t, \varphi) \wedge B_i(t, \varphi \supset \psi) \supset B_i(t, \psi)$.
(P1) $P_{ij}(t, \varphi) \wedge P_{ij}(t, \varphi \supset \psi) \supset P_{ij}(t, \psi)$.
(R1) *From φ and $\varphi \supset \psi$ infer ψ.*
(R2) *From φ infer $\forall x \varphi$.*
(R3) *From φ infer $B_i(t, \varphi)$ and $P_{ij}(t, \varphi)$.*
(R4) *From $\varphi \supset \psi$ infer $C_{ij}(t, \varphi) \supset C_{ij}(t, \psi)$.*

Due to space limitations here we omit the proof of the theorem, which can be gained by the standard technique of canonical model construction in [6].

Even though the agents in BCP model are still simple now, this model can be the basis for introducing diverse properties to the attitudes, characterizing multi-agent interactions and cooperations in different domains, meanwhile preserving the soundness and completeness results. Furthermore, different properties of the attitudes can satisfy different axioms, which can be presented in a precise way by appropriate conditions according to the accessibility relations of the models.

2.2   Properties of the Attitudes

In all the following axiom schemas, we will assume that the unbounded variables are universally quantified as follows: $\forall l, l', l'' \in L, a, b \in Agents, \tau, \tau' \in T$. In addition, we assume that $i, j \in AC \cup AV, t \in TC \cup TV$ and that φ and ψ represent any wff in the language.

Let's start with the properties of belief. We would like to introduce three constraints on the belief-accessibility relation R^B, which formalize that the operator B satisfies the consistency, positive introspection and negative introspection axioms relating to the serial, transitive and Euclidean properties of the R^B:

(CB2) *For every $l \in L$, there is a $\hat{l} \in L$, such that $l \in R^B(\hat{l}, \tau, a)$.*
(CB3) *If $l \in R^B(l', \tau, a)$ and $l' \in R^B(l'', \tau, a)$, then $l \in R^B(l'', \tau, a)$.*
(CB4) *If $l \in R^B(l', \tau, a)$ and $l \in R^B(l'', \tau, a)$, then $l' \in R^B(l'', \tau, a)$.*

The following axioms are sound with respect to the above conditions.

Proposition 2. *A BCP model that satisfies conditions (CB2)-(CB4) validate the following axioms:*

(B2) $\neg B_i(t, false)$.
(B3) $B_i(t, \varphi) \supset B_i(t, B_i(t, \varphi))$.
(B4) $\neg B_i(t, \varphi) \supset B_i(t, \neg B_i(t, \varphi))$.

We will make similar restriction on the operator P. It is required that the restriction on P should eliminate the possibility for an agent to make contradictory promises. We introduce the following proposition about the promise, which exhibits the D dimension(D axiom in modal logic) of the BCP model.

Proposition 3. *A BCP model that satisfies the condition*

(CP2) *For every $l \in L$, there is a $\hat{l} \in L$, such that $l \in R^P(\hat{l}, \tau, a)$*

validate the axiom:

(P2) $\neg P_{ij}(t, false)$.

For capability, an agent is required to be capable of doing something at least, as well as performing actions that are not contradictory. This can be achieved by introducing two constraints on the capability-accessibility relation R^C:

Proposition 4. *A BCP model that satisfies conditions*

(CC1) $\varnothing \notin R^C(l, \tau, a)$.
(CC2) $\varnothing \neq R^C(l, \tau, a)$.

validate the following axioms:

(C1) $\neg C_{ij}(t, false)$.
(C2) $C_{ij}(t, true)$.

There are several other properties of capability that are controversial, for example when the agent i considers that the agent j is capable of performing φ and is capable of performing ψ, whether it believes that j has the capability of achieving the conjunction, vice versa, i.e., if i considers that j is capable of achieving $\varphi \wedge \psi$, whether it believes that j has the capability of achieving them separately. The later is more acceptable(see [14]). Here is an counterexample for the former. Let's consider an agent j that is designed for helping a handicapped person i. It is possible for i to consider that j can at time t go either upstairs to serve a cup of milk, or at time t downstairs to fetch an express parcel, depending on the order of the person. But this does not mean that i believes that at time t, j has the capability to accomplish the two tasks at the same time.
The latter property is captured by the following condition and proposition:

Proposition 5. *A BCP model that satisfies condition*

(CC3) *If $U \in R^C(l, \tau, a, b)$, and $U \subseteq V$, then $V \in R^C(l, \tau, a, b)$*

validate the axiom:

(C3) $C_{ij}(t, \varphi \wedge \psi) \supset C_{ij}(t, \varphi) \wedge C_{ij}(t, \psi)$.

From the above example, we can see that some formulas are valid whereas their converses are not. This will be further discussed in the illustrative case section. Axiom **(C3)** is also a special case of the inference rule **(R4)** which is also valid in models that satisfy condition **(CC3)**.

2.3   Inter-relations Among Attitudes

Until now, the relations R^B, R^C and R^P are still independent. In such model, an agent's belief can not be updated with what other agents promise to it and changes of other agents' capabilities. This scenario can not reflect our original motivations, therefore it is not what we want. In this section, we will focus on the inter-relations among the mixed attitudes.

First, an agent is self-aware of its attitude towards other agents' capabilities:

(M1) $C_{ij}(t, \varphi) \equiv B_i(t, C_{ij}(t, \varphi))$.

The restriction on the model as stated in the following proposition:

Proposition 6. *A BCP model that satisfies the condition*

(CM1) $U \in R^C(l, \tau, a, b)$ *iff* $\{l' | U \in R^C(l', \tau, a, b)\} = R^B(l, \tau, a)$

validates axiom (M1).

We assume that an agent's attitude towards other agents' capabilities does not contradict its beliefs:

(M2) $C_{ij}(t, \varphi) \supset \neg B_i(t, \neg \varphi)$.

The corresponding restriction on the R^C and R^B is as follows:

Proposition 7. *A BCP model that satisfies the condition*

(CM2) $U \in R^C(l, \tau, a, b)$, *then* $L \backslash U \cap R^B(l, \tau, a) = \emptyset$

validates axiom (M2).

According to **(M2)**, if an agent starts believing that one of its attitude towards other agents' capabilities is not feasible, it will abandon the attitude:

Proposition 8. *BCP models that validate (M2) also validate following axiom*

(M2') $C_{ij}(t, \varphi) \wedge B_i(t + 1, \neg \varphi) \supset \neg C_{ij}(t + 1, \varphi)$.

In large scale multi-agent systems, the decision-making processes, based on the individual belief, are impacted by whether the cooperating agents would like to make promises to accept the tasks and whether they can fulfill the tasks. During the processes of interactions and cooperations, an agent would update its belief, and establish the relationships with those capable agents, whose promises can build on. In such system, the individual agent might be required to be able to reason about other agents' promises and capabilities to decide whether they can accept and accomplish new tasks most effectively. Thus we are more interested in the model satisfying the following proposition:

Proposition 9. *A BCP model that satisfies condition*

(CM3) *If $U \in R^C(l, \tau, a, b)$, $U' = U \cap \{l''|l'' \in R^B(l', \tau, a), l' \in R^P(l, \tau, a, b)\}$, then $R^B(l, \tau, a) \subseteq U$*

validates the axiom:

(M3) $B_i(t, P_{ij}(t, \varphi)) \wedge C_{ij}(t, \varphi) \supset B_i(t, \varphi)$

We should emphasize here that the axiom **(M3)** ties the three attitudes of agents up. An agent's belief is affected by what other agents promise to it and changes of other agents' capabilities. More specially, if the agent j promises the agent i to perform an action, meanwhile i considers that j has the capability to carry out the action, then i will also believe the action could be done.

Sometimes an agent may have deficient information about its opponent, therefore it is hard to judge whether its opponent actually has the capability to carry out the specific action. However the agent can take advantage of the information from other correlative agents assisting in its decision-making. Consider the following proposition:

Proposition 10. *A BCP model that satisfies condition*

(CM4) *If $U \in R^C(l, \tau, a, c)$, $U' = U \cap \{l''|l'' \in R^B(l', \tau, a), l' \in R^P(l, \tau, b, c)\}$, then for every $V \in R^C(l, \tau, a, b)$, such that $V \subseteq U'$*

validates the axiom:

(M4) $B_i(t, P_{jk}(t, \varphi)) \wedge C_{ik}(t, \varphi) \supset C_{ij}(t, \varphi)$

It indicates that if the agent i believes that the agent k has the capability to carry out the task φ, and k promises the agent j to achieve φ, then i will consider j has the capability to accomplish the task φ.

The system, composed of the BCP model and the axiom **(B2-B4)**, **(P2)**, **(C1-C3)** and **(M1-M4)** can also be proved to be sound and complete with the standard technique of canonical model construction in [6].

3   Illustrative Cases of TAC SCM

TAC SCM[8] provides a competition stage for researchers interested in both artificial intelligence agents and supply chain management. Agents in the chain should hold the belief about the information flowing across the supply chain. When making sourcing strategy, the agent has better to affirm that the supplier agent will be provided with sufficient supply capability and will keep its promise to offer materials on time. Trades with the suppliers, as well as with the customers, are negotiated through a request-for-quotes (RFQ) mechanism. If the supplier can satisfy the order specified in the RFQ in its entirety, the supplier will make promises to the agent meanwhile an offer is sent as a response. It may be necessary for an agent to maintain a model of promise and capability for the suppliers and their suppliers in order to keep the track of their production.

For the agent i, its supplier j and j's supplier k, let φ and ψ denote respectively the facts "obtaining sufficient materials" and "producing sufficient components". We may have the fact $\varphi \supset \psi$. Then from (**R4**), the agent i may have the fact $C_{ij}(t, \varphi) \supset C_{ij}(t, \psi)$. It is one of the possible instances that the agent i will consider that k has the sufficient materials and k would supply j with its materials. Therefore the agent i has the facts $C_{ik}(t, \varphi)$ and $B_i(t, P_{jk}(t, \varphi))$. From (**M4**), $C_{ij}(t, \psi)$ is deduced. Building on the facts of $B_i(t, P_{ij}(t, \psi))$ and $C_{ij}(t, \psi)$, the agent i will believe ψ from (**M3**). Although the agent i has deficient information about its supplier j, for example $B_j(t, P_{jk}(t, \psi))$ and $C_{jk}(t, \psi)$ which can be regarded as the business secrets of j, the agent i can also come to the conclusion of $B_i(t, \psi)$ when it plans production and delivery, as follows:

(1) $C_{ij}(t, \varphi) \supset C_{ij}(t, \psi)$ $\qquad\qquad\qquad$ $\varphi \supset \psi$ and (**R4**)

(2) $B_i(t, P_{jk}(t, \varphi)) \wedge C_{ik}(t, \varphi) \supset C_{ij}(t, \varphi)$ $\qquad\qquad$ (**M4**)

(3) $[C_{ij}(t, \varphi) \supset C_{ij}(t, \psi)] \wedge C_{ij}(t, \varphi) \supset C_{ij}(t, \psi)$ $\qquad$ (1)(2) and (**R1**)

(4) $B_i(t, P_{ij}(t, \psi)) \wedge C_{ij}(t, \psi) \supset B_i(t, \psi)$ $\qquad\qquad$ (3) and (**M3**)

In the previous discussion, we have mentioned that some formulas are valid whereas their converses are not. Let us dwell on this further with the following example in TAC SCM. Let φ and ψ denote the facts "delivering the requested quantity specified in RFQ" and "delivering on due date", respectively. But the delivered quantity depends upon the different strategies of the supplier(i.e. *Likelihood* of the agent). Thus it is possible for the agent i to consider that supplier j has the capability to achieve either φ or ψ depending upon j's strategy, but this does not mean that i believes j can satisfy the order entirely on due date, i.e. $C_{ij}(t, \varphi) \wedge C_{ij}(t, \psi) \supset C_{ij}(t, \varphi \wedge \psi)$ is not valid. On the contrary, if i is convinced of both φ and ψ, it will believe that j has the capability to satisfy the order either in quantity or on due date, i.e. $C_{ij}(t, \varphi \wedge \psi) \supset C_{ij}(t, \varphi) \wedge C_{ij}(t, \psi)$ is valid.

4 Related Works

Capability, on which we place strong emphasis, is one of the necessary conditions for agents to interact and cooperate successfully. The very beginning of the research on capability can be cast back to Ryle's book[9], in which the author argued the key difference between stupidity, that is, not knowing how, and ignorance, not knowing that. *Singh*[10] introduced an abstract concept *Know How* to characterize the agent's capability from the view of external system designers.

He suggested that it is not sufficient for an agent to be capable of performing something, moreover the agent must have the knowledge required to form the complete plans before acting. The KARO[2] framework is one of the best known theories of rational agency which combined dynamic and epistemic logic into one modal system perfectly. The authors of KARO consider composite abilities to be built up from a set of atomic abilities using a variety of constructors. *Padgham*[11] extended the well-known BDI architecture by adding Cap operator in order to eliminate mismatch between theory and practice for actual systems. A style of commitment was defined to enrich the existing formal models in [11], which allowed a self-aware agent to modify its goals and intentions when its capabilities changed. *Fisher*[12] incorporated more flexible motivational attributes, such as ability and confidence, then introduced ABC model. The main advantage of the ABC modeling is that it provided a simple but flexible foundation for a formal development method.

In [14], a logic was proposed to reason about perceptions and belief. The logic contains three modalities: B stands for belief, P for actual perception, whereas C for the sets of perceptions agent can perceive. Similar to ours, the modalities of [14] use the standard semantics in modal logic and the neighborhood semantics. [14] only deals with a single agent and not considering the temporal aspect. Capability delivered in the BCP model is an abstract, high-level ability of agents, and not limited to any kind of special abilities.

It is worthy to mention that the notion of capability is analogous to the *individual power-of* an agent[15]. The individual power-of describes the powers that an agent has without considering other agents, whereas the capability in BCP model indicates the attitude of an agent towards other agents' abilities. In some sense, the term of *social power*[16] is more similar to the notion of capability proposed here.

5   Conclusions

This paper aims to present a logical model for reasoning about belief, capability and promise of rational agents incorporating temporal aspects. The basic temporal BCP model plus properties of the three attitudes and the inter-relation among the operators are explored with intuitive meanings. A reasoning example is presented to show how the model is applied in an actual agent competition.

There are several possible directions for future investigations. For example, the formalization presented here suffers from the logical omniscience problem. Accordingly an agent believes and promises all logical consequences of its beliefs and promises. In addition, a potential application of the model is to incorporate with the contract net protocol (CNP). The self-interested agents may embellish their bids and delude their manager to get more bids in order to maximize profits, even if they cannot accomplish the tasks on time. In this case, it is necessary for the manager to reason about the bidders' capabilities to avoid an unexpected delay of its task. In the future, we will keep improving the temporal BCP model as well as apply it in more realistic domains.

References

1. Rao, A.S., and Georgeff, M.P.: Modeling Rational Agents within a BDI Architecture. In: Proc. of the Second Conference on Knowledge Representation and Reasoning (KR91), Morgan Kaufman, (1991) 473–484
2. Van Linder, B., van der Hoek, W., Meyer, J.-J. C.: Formalising Abilities and Opportunities of Agents. Fundamenta Informaticae, **34** (1998) 53–101
3. Wooldridge, M.: Reasoning About Rational Agents. The MIT Press: Cambridge, MA, 2000
4. Rao, A.S., and Georgeff, M.P.: Decision procedures for BDI logics. Journal of Logic and Computation, **8**(3) (1998) 293–342
5. Kraus, S., Sycara and K., Evenchik, A.: Reaching agreements through argumentation a logical model and implementation Artificial Intelligence, **104** (1998) 1–69
6. Chellas, B.F.: Modal Logic: An Introduction. Cambridge University Press, Cambridge, 1980
7. Shoham, Y.: Agent-oriented programming. Artificial Intelligence, **60**(1) (1993) 51–92
8. The Supply Chain Management Game for the Trading Agent Competition (TAC SCM) 2005. Available at http://www.sics.se.
9. Ryle, G.: The Concept of Mind. Barnes and Noble, New York, 1949.
10. Singh, M.P.: A Logic of Situated Know-how. In Proceedings of the Ninth National Conference on Artificial Intelligence, (AAAI91), California, (1991) 343–348
11. Padgham, L., Lambrix, P.: Agent Capabilities: Extending BDI Theory. In Proceedings of Seventeenth National Conference on Artificial Intelligence, (AAAI00), Austin, Texas, (2000) 68–73
12. Fisher, M. and Ghidini, C.: The ABC of Rational Agent Modelling. In Proceedings of the First International Joint Conference on Autonomous Agents and MultiAgent Systems, (AAMAS02), Bologna, Italy, (2002) 849-856
13. Churn-Jung L.: Belief, Information Acquisition, and Trust in Multi-Agent Systems-a Modal Logic Formulation. Artificial Intelligence, **149**(1) (2003) 31–60
14. Del Val, A., Maynard-Reid, P., Shoham, Y.: Qualitative Reasoning about Perception and Belief. In Proceedings of the Fifteenth International Joint Conference on Artificial Intelligence, (IJCAI97), Nagoya, Japan, (1997) 508–513
15. Castelfranchi, C.: A micro and macro definition of power. ProtoSociology C An International Journal of Interdisciplinary Research, **18-19** (2002) 208-268
16. Carabelea, C., Boissier, O., Castelfranchi, C.: Using Social Power to Enable Agents to Reason about Being Part of a Group. In Fifth International Workshop Engineering Societies in the Agents World, (ESAW04), Toulouse, France, (2004)

A Multi-agent Fuzzy-Reinforcement Learning Method for Continuous Domains

Erkan Duman, Mehmet Kaya, and Erhan Akin

Firat University, Department of Computer Engineering, 23119, Elazig, Turkey
{erkanduman, kaya, eakin}@firat.edu.tr

Abstract. This paper proposes a fuzzy reinforcement learning based method for improving the learning ability of multi-agents acting in continuous domains. The previous studies in this area generally solved multi-agent learning problem by using discrete domains. However, the most of real-world problems use the continuous state spaces. Also, it is really a difficult task to handle the continuous domains for multi-agent learning systems. In this paper, proposing a novel approach, we will have two significant advantages according to the conventional multi-agent learning algorithm. One of them is that the number of state spaces of learning agents in multi-agent environment only depends on the number of fuzzy sets which were used to represent the state of an agent. Whereas, in the previous approaches, the visual area of agent or the size of domain were taken into consideration for the state space. The other advantage is that the employed environment has a continuous domain as in the real-world problems. Experimental results obtained on a well-known pursuit domain show the effectiveness of the proposed approach.

Keywords: Multi-agent Systems, Fuzzy Logic, Reinforcement Learning, Continuous Domain.

1 Introduction

Multi-agent systems form a particular type of distributed artificial intelligence systems. They are different from single agent systems in the sense that there is no global control and globally consistent knowledge. So, limitations on the processing power of a single agent are eliminated in a multi-agent environment. In other words, since data and control are distributed, multi-agent systems include the inherent advantage of distributed systems, such as scalability, fault-tolerance and parallelism, among others [1].

The realization of cooperative behavior in multi-agent systems is an interesting topic from the viewpoint of engineering and cognitive science. In particular, reinforcement learning of cooperative behaviors has attracted recent attention because of its adaptability to dynamic environments. For this purpose, reinforcement learning has been applied to multi-agent systems such as pursuit games, soccer, the prisoners' dilemma game, and coordination games.

One approach to model multiagent learning is to augment the state of each agent with the information about other existing agents [2-4]. However, as the number of

M. Pĕchouček, P. Petta, and L.Z. Varga (Eds.): CEEMAS 2005, LNAI 3690, pp. 306–315, 2005.

agents in a multiagent environment increases, the state space of each agent grows exponentially. Another solution is to generalize visited states to unvisited ones as in supervised learning. In order to handle this problem, functional approximation and generalization methods seem to be more feasible solutions. Unfortunately, optimal convergence of functional approximation implementation of reinforcement learning algorithms has not been proven yet [5, 6, 10]. As the alternative approaches, we proposed some fuzzy-reinforcement learning based methods for multi-agent discrete domains [7, 8].

However, how agents acquire and maintain knowledge is an important issue in reinforcement learning. When the state space of the task is small and discrete as it is the case with the above studies, the Q-values are usually stored in a lookup table. But, this method is either impractical in case of large state-action spaces, or impossible with continuous state spaces. The main drawback of look-up tables is their scaling problem. In case of a task with a huge state space, it is difficult and unlikely to store all states in a limited memory and to visit each state in reasonable time. In order to handle the problems of large and continuous state spaces, in this paper, we present a novel multi-agent fuzzy-reinforcement learning method. It uses a fuzzy inference mechanism in continuous domain. The each learning agent in the environment acts observing its nearest partner and prey. Also, with the proposed reward mechanism, a cooperation behavior is exhibited.

The rest of the paper is organized as follows. Section 2 gives an introduction of reinforcement learning and Q-learning algorithm. Section 3 describes the proposed algorithm. Section 4 presents the experimental results of the algorithm. Section 5 includes the conclusions.

2 Reinforcement Learning

Reinforcement Learning (RL) is used to answer the questions of how an autonomous agent perceives the environment and make the optimum decision to reach its own goal. It is very interesting that such an agent does not need any previous information about the search space [9].

In the RL algorithm, an agent interacts with the environment by using its sensors and actuators as shown in Figure 1. The agent receives the information of the current state s by its sensors then it applies the making decision algorithm and determines an output action a. It gets a feedback information r from environment after acting a. If the new state of the agent is a goal state, r will be positive, otherwise, it will have a negative value.

The RL might be modeled as a Markov Decision Process and this model is the most widely mathematical model of RL. This is formalized as follows:

- S is the finite set of the states.
- A is the finite set of the actions.
- R is the function determining the expected reward r $(R : SxA \rightarrow r)$
- T is the translation function between the current and the next states $(T, SxA \rightarrow \pi(S))$

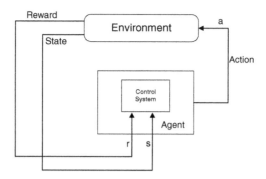

Fig. 1. The model of the Reinforcement Learning

The notation of $T(s, a, s^I)$ indicates the probability of the transition from state s to s^I by acting a. As a result of Markov Decision Process, the function of $T(\ )$ does not consider the previous states. It is only concerned with the current state and the available actions.

The Q-Learning is the most popular technique in RL applications, where the pairs of (state,action) are saved in a look-up table. The following learning equation is used to update the cells of the Q-table in the run time.

$$Q(s,a) = (1-\alpha).Q(s,a) + \alpha.\left[r + \gamma.\max_{a^I \in A} Q(s^I, a^I) \right] \qquad (1)$$

The notations of the α and γ indicates the learning rate and the discount factor at the interval of the [0,1] respectively. $Q(s^I, a^I)$ indicates the action with the maximum reward in the next state.

3 The Proposed Method

In this study, a new approach based on fuzzy inference system is proposed to improve the ability of the multi-agent reinforcement learning in continuous domain. Q-learning is used as learning algorithm in this method. It could be understood from the title of this study that all the hunter agents move together in order to reach a common goal. The number of the hunter agents determined arbitrary is four and their common goal is to surround the single prey agent in continuous pursuit problem. The cooperation of the hunter agents is provided by using same structure of Q-tables and the learning algorithm. However, they are not able to observe the search space entirely. Each agent can see objects at a certain distance, the radius of which is r and does not have any information about the remaining of the search space as seen in Figure 2.

So far, many researchers have proposed various methods to improve the learning ability in multi-agent systems in discrete domain. However most of them are not appropriate for continuous domain because the state space of each learning agent grows exponentially in terms of the number of partners in environment and visual

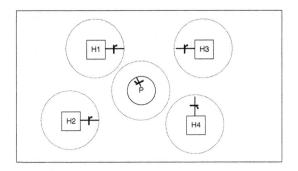

Fig. 2. A Multi-agent system in the continuous pursuit problem

depth of each agent. In our method, the size of Q-tables is independent from these terms; it is only related to the number of linguistic labels of input variables in fuzzy inference system used to decide the optimal action in current state. This underlying idea causes reducing the requirements of time and memory in Q-learning algorithm. Also, the search space of the agents that has been transformed from a simple grid to a continuous environment is very important advantage for the proposed method to be able to be used in real world problems.

As you can see in Figure 3, each agent has a fuzzy inference mechanism in order to choose the optimal action in its current state. There are four fuzzy input variables representing the distances and the angles of the nearest and the prey hunters and, one output variable for an action produced by inference mechanism in this structure.

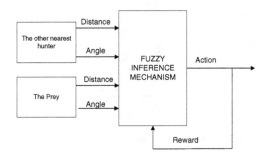

Fig. 3. The fuzzy inference mechanism of each agent

First, each agent must perceive the nearest hunter and the prey available in its visual area in order to start choosing an action. If they are inside, it must measure the distance and the angle of them by crisp values as shown in above figure, which are the input variables of the fuzzy inference mechanism. Here, the first step is fuzziness of the input values as linguistic variables. So, each agent is able to determine its own state by these fuzzy sets. In such a case, the action to be done is determined by using relative rows.

Table 1. The structure of Q-table in the proposed method

state/action	action-1	action-2	.....	....	.....	action-m
state-1	Q_{11}	Q_{12}	....	....	....	Q_{1m}
state-2	Q_{21}	Q_{22}	.....	.....	....	Q_{2m}
$\vdots$	$\vdots$	$\vdots$	$\vdots$	$\vdots$	$\vdots$	$\vdots$
$\vdots$	$\vdots$	$\vdots$	$\vdots$	$\vdots$	$\vdots$	$\vdots$
state-n	Q_{n1}	Q_{n2}	.....	.....	.....	Q_{nm}

As the rows in the Q-table indicates the states which agent can perceive, the columns shows the possible actions. The Q_{ij} values in cells represent the amount of the reward in the case agent chooses action j in state i. If the agent observes state i, it must calculate the probabilities of the actions which is able to be done in that state according to Q_{ij} values in relative cells by using Equation 1. This equation is known as Boltzmann distribution in literature, where τ represents the temperature which will be decreased in the following iterations so as to reduce the probabilities of small Q_{ij} values. After the probabilities are calculated, the agent uses the Roulette Wheel being a popular selection method in Genetic Algorithms to choose the action a_i as seen in figure $4 \left(1 \leq i \leq m\right)$.

$$\pi[a_i \mid s] = \frac{e^{Q(s,a_i)/\tau}}{\sum_{a_k \in A} e^{Q(s,a_k)/\tau}} \qquad (2)$$

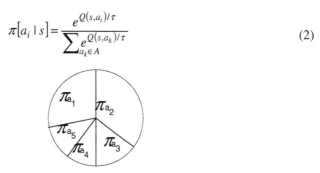

Fig. 4. Roulette Wheel method for choosing an action according to their probabilities

However, the following equation as the learning rule is different from the conventional structure by adding two gains: μ and μ^I. They represent the degrees of the memberships of the agent in state s and s^I respectively.

$$Q(s,a) = (1 - \alpha\mu).Q(s,a) + \alpha\mu^I \left[r + \gamma.\max_{a^I \in A} Q(s^I, a^I) \right] \qquad (3)$$

Each of the agents has a visual area whose radius is $r_i (1 \leq i \leq 5)$. Through this study, all the visual areas are defined as same and the agents cannot observe the remaining of the search space because this is generally a disadvantage if we decide to apply the proposed method to the real-world problems.

The information received from the environment by agent is about the distances and angles of the other nearest hunter agent and the prey present in its own visual area. If there is no other hunter and the prey in that area, the agent moves at random exactly.

This paper proposes a generalization method based on fuzzy sets to decrease the state spaces of the agents in the continuous domain. For this case, the membership functions representing states of each agent are given in Figure 5.

The both of the distance axes shown in Figure 5 have three uniform membership functions and the definitive intervals of them are bounded with $[0,100]$, because the radius of the agent's visual area is assumed to be 100. The angle linguistic variables for the other nearest hunter agent and the prey have four triangular membership functions at interval of $[0^o, 360^o]$.

After the fuzzification of $\theta_{nearest\ hunter}$ variable which represents the angle of the other nearest hunter, the agent will has two linguistic labels from the set of (East[E], North[N], West[W] and South[S]) with m_1 and m_2 that indicate the membership degrees of fuzzy sets it belongs to. With $d_{nearest\ hunter}$ representing the distance of the other nearest hunter agent, it will receive two linguistic labels more from the set of (Small[S}, Medium[M] and Large[L]) with m_3 and m_4.

Similarly, θ_{prey} and d_{prey} representing the angle and the distance of the prey are fuzzified as explained.

The steps of observing a current state can be explained better by using a numerical example as follows: Consider that the agent j is the nearest hunter inside the visual area of the agent i and the agent i will measure $\theta_{ij} = 30^o$ and $d_{ij} = 60$. In this case, $[m_1, m_2]$ and $[m_3, m_4]$ are computed by above fuzzy sets as shown in Figure 6.

In this example case, the agent j, as the other nearest hunter, is assumed to be located at North [N] with weight of $m_1 = 0.33$ and at East [E] with weight of $m_2 = 0.67$ according to the agent i. Besides, it belongs to Large [L] and Medium [M] membership functions with weight of $m_3 = 0.2$ and $m_4 = 0.8$ respectively.

So, the agent i will observe the following four states with $\mu_1, \mu_2, \mu_3, \mu_4$.

s_1 = EM (The agent j's angle is East and its distance is Medium).
s_2 = EL (The agent j's angle is East and its distance is Large).
s_3 = NM (The agent j's angle is North and its distance is Medium).
s_4 = NL (The agent j's angle is North and its distance is Large).

The agent i observes state s_1 with weight of $\mu_1 = m_2.m_4$. Similarly, the other three membership degrees are computed:

s_1 = EM (The agent j's angle is East and its distance is Medium) $\Rightarrow \mu_1 = m_2.m_4$
s_2 = EL (The agent j's angle is East and its distance is Large) $\Rightarrow \mu_2 = m_2.m_3$
s_3 = NM (The agent j's angle is North and its distance is Medium) $\Rightarrow \mu_3 = m_1.m_4$
s_4 = NL (The agent j's angle is North and its distance is Large) $\Rightarrow \mu_4 = m_1.m_4$

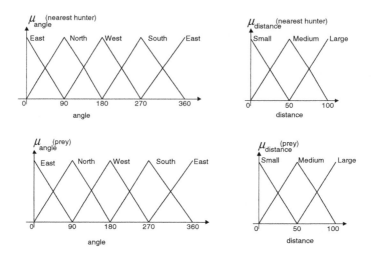

Fig. 5. Membership functions representing the state of an agent

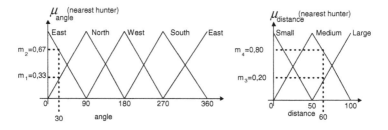

Fig. 6. The fuzzification of the $\theta_{ij} = 30^{o}$ and the $d_{ij} = 60$

We can assume that the prey agent p is inside the visual area of the agent i at the same time. Then, the number of the states observed by the agent i will be 4x4=16. Each of them is represented as a row in the agent's own Q-table. However, these rows can have different membership degrees. The membership degrees of all the states are computed by minimum function using relative pairs of weights as two arguments.

In Q-table, the number of states depends on the number of the membership functions, rather than the visual area of the agent. The agent's decision space resolution decreases if the radius of the agent's visual area increases while the number of the membership functions is constant. However, the agent perceives a larger area. On the other hand, the agent exhibits a finer resolution if the number of membership functions increases while the radius of the agent's visual area is constant.

In this study, the number of the states is computed as shown in equation 5. It could be thought as the number of the rows in each of the agent's Q-tables.

$$\text{The number of states} = L_1 x L_2 x L_3 x L_4 + L_1.L_2 + L_3 x L_4 + 1 \qquad (4)$$

In the above equation, the L_i variable indicates the number of the linguistic labels for fuzzy input variables $(1 \le i \le 4)$. The size of the Q-table depends on the number of the other agents or the radius of the agent's visual area. L_1 indicates the number of the agent j's angle variable according to the agent i. Similarly, L_2 for the agent j's distance, L_3 for the prey's angle and L_4 for the prey's distance are used to determine the size of the state space. Each of L_i is added with 1 because the relative input variable is able to exceed the bounds of defined interval.

As an example, if we assume $L_1 = L_3 = 4$ and $L_2 = L_4 = 3$ as in Figure 5 and Figure 6, then the number of states evaluates to 12x12+12+12+1, where 12×12 is the number of states in case both the prey and the other hunter are observed in the visual environment of the hunter under consideration, 12+12 is the number of states in case only one agent, either the prey or a hunter, is observed and 1 is the number of states in case no agent is perceived.. The agent i will chose an action a_i from the set of actions $A = (a_1, a_2, a_3, a_4, a_5)$ after it observed the current state according to the Q-values in corresponding cells. The action a_i can be one of the (right, up, left, down and none).

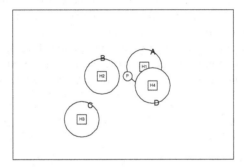

Fig. 7. The performed pursuit problem with 4 hunters and single prey

The proposed method was applied to a continuous pursuit problem with four hunter and single prey as shown in Figure 7. If hunter 1 observes the its own current state, it will see the area of A meaning the other nearest hunter is 4 and the prey is inside the visual area. Similarly, the area of B for hunter 2, C for hunter 3 and D for hunter 4 will be drawn imaginary. The hunter 2 and 3 will chose an action at random exactly because any other agent is not inside their visual area but hunter 4 will move according to hunter 1's location.

Hunter 1 will get a reward r computed as shown in Equation 5 from the environment on moving a new state s^I. r_s represents the special reward that is proportional with only the distance between hunter 1 and prey. It is limited to 50 because the goal is to surround the prey by all hunters, not only by one. r_g indicates the general reward according to the distances of all hunters to the prey and it is limited to 50 too. Thus, when all hunters surrounded the prey, the r will be 100.

$$r = r_s + r_g \tag{5}$$

4   Experimental Results

We used a pursuit game containing a single prey and four hunter agents in the continuous domain to evaluate the performance of the proposed method. In the experiment environment, we tested it in 10000 trials. Each trial begins with a single prey and four hunter agents placed at random positions inside the search space, and ends when either the prey is captured or at 2000 time steps.

When the all hunter agents surround the prey, they get the reward of 100 from environment. Otherwise, each hunter agent gets a special reward according to its distance to the prey and others. The size of domain is fixed as 5000x5000. Besides, we determined the parameters of the Q-learning as the following.

- The learning rate, $\alpha = 0.8 \rightarrow 0.2$
- The discount factor, $\gamma = 0.9$
- The initial value of the Q-cells are 0.1

We determined that the learning rate α was 0.8 at the beginning of the experiment but when the learning process had been well advanced it begun to decrease until 0.2. Specially, having chosen the initial values of the cells in the Q-tables as 0.1 accelerated the learning processes of the agents.

We applied the practice in an environment that it was developed by using a visual object-oriented programming language. The search space and the agents were represented by a continuous toroidal grid object and geometrical shapes objects respectively.

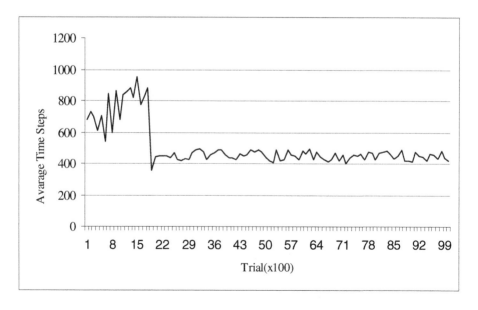

Fig. 8. The experimental result of the proposed method

The average time steps per trial were calculated for 10000 trials after a small number of tests as seen in figure 8. There was a rapid learning process between 1500 and 2000 trials then the learning curve started to converge, because the learning rate reached the minimum value after 2000 trials.

5 Conclusion

We have proposed a novel multi-agent fuzzy-reinforcement learning method for multi-agent system in continuous domain as the real world problems to improve the performance of it. There were a few disadvantages for traditional RL algorithms to be able to be used in real applications. For instance, the size of Q-tables and the time requirement would grow up exponentially for the most conventional methods so we adapted it by using fuzzy sets. Besides, in the our proposed method, we considered that an agent was not be able to see the entire of the search space and the requirements were not depend upon the visual depth and the number of the agents. There were two significant criteria for the sensitiveness of the system that the number of the linguistic labels used in fuzzy logic and the parameters of these labels in the our proposed method.

References

1. P. Stone and M. Veloso, "Multiagent systems: A Survey from a Machine Learning Perspective," *Autonomous Robots*, Vol.8 No.3, 2000.
2. M.L. Littman, "Markov Games as a Framework for Multiagent Reinforcement Learning," *Proceedings of the International Conference on Machine Learning*, pp.157-163. San Francisco, CA, 1994.
3. T.W. Sandholm and R. H. Crites, "Multiagent Reinforcement Learning in the Iterated Prisoner's Dilemma," *Biosystems*, Vol.37, pp.147-166, 1995.
4. M. Tan, "Multi-agent Reinforcement Learning: Independent vs. Cooperative Agents," *Proceedings of the International Conference on Machine Learning*, pp.330-337, 1993.
5. R.S. Sutton, "Generalization in reinforcement learning: Successful Examples Using Sparse Coarse Coding," *Advances in Neural Information Processing Systems*, 1996.
6. R.S. Sutton and A.G. Barto, Reinforcement Learning: An Introduction, Cambridge, MA: MIT Press, 1998.
7. M. Kaya and R. Alhajj, "Modular Fuzzy-Reinforcement Learning Approach with Internal Model Capabilities for Multiagent Systems", *IEEE Transactions on Systems, Man and Cybernetics-Part B, vol. 34 (2), pp. 1210-1223*, April 2004.
8. M. Kaya and R. Alhajj, "Reinforcement Learning in Multiagent Systems: A Modular Fuzzy Approach with Internal Model Capabilities", *14th IEEE International Conference on Tools with Artificial Intelligence*, November 2002, Washington DC.
9. L.P. Kaelbling, M.L. Littman and A.W. Moore, "Reinforcement learning: A survey," *Artificial Intelligence Research*, Vol.4, pp.237-285, 1996.
10. H. Berenji and D. Vengerov, "Advantage of Cooperation between Reinforcement Learning Agents in Difficult Stochastic Problems," *Proceedings of IEEE International Conference on Fuzzy Systems*, 2000.

An Adaptive Approach for the Exploration-Exploitation Dilemma for Learning Agents

Lilia Rejeb[1], Zahia Guessoum[1,2], and Rym M'Hallah[3]

[1] CReSTIC, MODECO Team, Rue des Crayères, Reims Cedex2, France
[2] Université de Paris-VI, LIP6, OASIS Team, 4 place Jussieu, 75252 cedex 5, France
[3] Kuwait University, Dep. of Statistics and Operations Research, P.O. Box 5969, Safat 13060

Abstract. Learning agents have to deal with the exploration-exploitation dilemma. The choice between exploration and exploitation is very difficult in dynamic systems; in particular in large scale ones such as economic systems. Recent research shows that there is neither an optimal nor a unique solution for this problem. In this paper, we propose an adaptive approach based on meta-rules to adapt the choice between exploration and exploitation. This new adaptive approach relies on the variations of the performance of the agents. To validate the approach, we apply it to economic systems and compare it to two adaptive methods: one local and one global. Herein, we adapt these two methods, which were originally proposed by Wilson, to economic systems. Moreover, we compare different exploration strategies and focus on their influence on the performance of the agents.

1 Introduction

The exploration-exploitation dilemma, which is an important problem frequently encountered in reinforcement learning [17], is defined as follows. When an agent is faced with a state of the environment, it either chooses to explore its environment and try new actions in search for better ones to be adopted in the future [12], or exploit already tested actions and adopt them. When opting to explore, the agent is considering its long term performance whereas when opting to exploit tested actions, the agent is considering its short term performance [15].

Formally, the agent has to resolve two subproblems. The first subproblem consists of choosing an exploration method. The exploration can be either directed or undirected. The second subproblem consists of identifying a method that switches the agent's mode between exploration and exploitation according to the state of the agent and the state of its environment. The two subproblems are important since they influence the learning speed, the performances and the actions of an agent. This influence is more critical when the agent environment is dynamic, which is the case of economic systems.

In this paper, we study the aforementioned two subproblems in the context of an economic system characterized by a set of firms in competition in a shared market. We propose an adaptive approach to the exploration-exploitation problem in a dynamic economic context where firms are modeled using the XCS-learning classifier system for their decision process [9]. We show that a firm performance can be improved when

M. Pěchouček, P. Petta, and L.Z. Varga (Eds.): CEEMAS 2005, LNAI 3690, pp. 316–325, 2005.

it opts for directed exploration and uses a meta-rules based approach to choose between exploration and exploitation.

This paper is organized as follows. Section 2 presents the firm model and an overview of the learning classifier system XCS. Section 3 investigates exploration techniques. Section 4 presents the proposed meta-rules approach and the adaptation of Wilson's techniques to our context. Section 5 presents and analyzes the experimental results. Finally, Section 6 summarizes the contributions of this paper and provides future extensions.

2   Adaptive Firms

We study the exploration-exploitation dilemma in the context of a dynamic economic system where a set of firms are in indirect interaction in a shared market. We model the firms as adaptive agents with the XCS-learning classifier system for their learning. In Section 2.1, we present the model of a firm while in Section 2.2, we detail the characteristics of the XCS classifier system, and explain how agents learn when using it.

2.1   The Firm Model

We model firms using a resource-based approach [10]. We regard a firm as a collection of physical and human resources. We stipulate that the survival of a firm depends on the way it allocates its resources. A firm is characterized by a set X of resources, a set $Y_t = (Y_t[1], Y_t[2])$ of performance indicators, where $Y_t[1]$ is profitability and $Y_t[2]$ is market share at time t, a capital K, a budget B (which when allocated updates the status of the firm resources), and a set S of strategies available for the firm. The performance of a firm is measured using the statistical Lisrel Model. The allocation of the budget B to the different resources X according to the firm priority defines the firm strategy.

A firm behavior is dynamic over time. Each time period, a firm

- observes its environment and updates its competition model;
- updates its internal parameters (eg., its capital K and budget B);
- opts for a strategy; and
- updates its performance.

A firm chooses the strategy that best suits its current context. The context of a firm is determined by the firm's internal parameters ($K, B, X,$ and Y_t), and its perception of the environment, which is strongly competitive and non-stationary. At the end of a time period, firms can either join or leave the market. A firm leaves the market either when its performance decreases over a number of successive periods or when its capital decreases and reaches an exit threshold. Its exit or extinction is the result of a bad strategy used by the firm not disposing of all the information about its rivals.

Each firm, represented by an agent, bases its perception of its current context on its environment. This perception is an aggregation of the performances and the capital of the firms present in the environment. Based on this perception, the firm chooses the most suited strategy. The dynamic nature of the environment makes it difficult for a firm to anticipate all the possible outcomes of its strategy and/or to take into account the inadequate outcomes of its prior strategies. A firm gradually builds its rule base as it acquires knowledge from its environment. Herein, the XCS classifier systems defined by Wilson [16] constructs the model of the firm environment, updates the model as a firm acquires experience and foresees the possible consequences of the decision before it is undertaken.

2.2   XCS and Adaptive Firms

We use XCS [16] to model the decision process of adaptive firms. XCS constructs a complete and accurate model of a firm environment. It develops a readable set of "condition-action" rules or classifiers which explain the evolution of the environment [8].

A classifier is also characterized by three parameters: its prediction p, its prediction error e and its fitness F which evaluates the quality of the prediction p. The condition part of a classifier is a representation of the perception of the environment; that is of the context of the firm. The set of possible actions or strategies is defined by the economist. In our case, the set has twenty strategies oriented towards customers, suppliers and production.

At each decision period, XCS undertakes a perception, prediction, action cycle. It determines the set [M] of classifiers whose conditions match the context of the firm. If [M] is empty, covering takes place; else the average prediction PS_i of each action a_i proposed by the classifiers in [M] is calculated:

$$PS_i = \frac{\sum F_{cl_j} p_{cl_j}}{\sum F_{cl_j}}, \tag{1}$$

where F_{cl_j} and p_{cl_j} are respectively the fitness and the prediction of classifier j when undertaking action a_i. The PS_i serves as the decisional basis for the firm action selection which is either done by exploration (random choice) or exploitation (choice of the action having the largest PS_i). Exploration encourages a firm to take risks whereas exploitation incites a firm to avoid risks.

The firm adopts the chosen action or strategy and gets a reward r_t at time t. This reward is an aggregation of the firm performances variations:

$$r_t = aggreg \left(\frac{Y_t[1] - Y_{t-1}[1]}{Y_{t-1}[1]}, \frac{Y_t[2] - Y_{t-1}[2]}{Y_{t-1}[2]} \right) \tag{2}$$

where $aggreg$ is the average aggregation operator. r_t is used by the reinforcement learning component represented by the Q-Learning algotithm [14] to update the p, e and F of the classifiers proposing the chosen action. These classifiers are blocked in a set [A] which is updated by a Michigan genetic algorithm when possible.

3   Exploration Techniques

Exploration techniques are classified as undirected and directed [13]. Undirected techniques are random. They are difficult to use in real-valued domains and in large state-action spaces. They increase the learning time exponentially. Directed exploration techniques seek to improve the knowledge of the environment by adopting more informative actions. They include techniques such as recency-based exploration and frequency-based exploration.

To compare the performance of firms under directed and undirected techniques, we need to integrate directed exploration techniques in XCS. Indeed, the current version of XCS randomly chooses between exploration and exploitation, and allows undirected exploration only. In the following, we explain how we integrate, within XCS, the best known directed exploration techniques: recency based approach and frequency based approach.

The *recency-based technique* selects the least recently selected action independently of its number of occurrences. It finds, for each action a, the matching classifiers $j, j = 1, \ldots, n$ and determine the recent activation-time

$$Rec(a) = \min_{j=1,n} \{t - ActivationTime(cl_j)\} \tag{3}$$

where $ActivationTime(cl_j)$ is the last activation date of classifier cl_j, and t is the current time. It chooses then the action with the maximal Recency value.

The *Frequency-based exploration* selects the least frequently used action a. It tallies for each action the frequency $Freq(a)$ of the corresponding matching classifiers that were previously used at least once and rewarded.

$$Freq(a) = \min\{ \sum_{j=1,n} (cl_j) : experience(cl_j) \geq 1 \} \tag{4}$$

where $experience$ is the activation frequency of cl_j in a similar context of the firm.

Wiering [15] states that when the firm is interested in immediate reward, it has to switch to exploitation and has to gradually increase its rate of switching to exploitation. An exploitation-exploration tradeoff is therefore needed.

4   Exploration-Exploitation Tradeoff

Finding a balance between exploration and exploitation is not an easy task [5,6]. Most existing methods, such as the "interval estimation" [6,7] and the "Gittings index" [5,1] techniques, deal with small non-complex problems [13]. Methods that are applicable to more complex contexts such as a multi-agent context are limited in number [11,4]. Peres [11] underlined the necessity to link the changing rate of exploration and the changing indicators of performance to the changing prediction, but proposed no solution. Carmel [4] integrated an exploration technique to a learning-based model and applied to game theory with a small number of agents.

Wilson [17] proposed ten techniques that were tested on small simple test problems only. Their performance is sensitive to the constant gain factor fixed by the designer. The behavior of these techniques in complex systems remains however an open issue. In the following, we propose to test the behavior of two of these techniques in more complex settings.

4.1   Wilson Techniques

Wilson techniques focus on an "on-line "choice between exploration and exploitation in a dynamic environment. They are based on the rate of variation of the performance (prediction) or the prediction errors. In this section, we adapt two adaptive Wilson techniques : a local and a global one.

The adaptive **local technique** is applied at each activation of XCS. When all the classifiers matching the current context are identified, the values of the moving average $\widehat{E}_i$ of the difference between the current and estimated error of action a_i are computed for all actions. The exploration probability p_1 is then determined:

$$p_1 = min \left\{ 1, f\left(\widehat{E}_i\right) \times Gf \right\}, \tag{5}$$

where Gf is a given gain factor, and

$$f\left(\widehat{E}_i\right) = \frac{\sum_{i=1,na}\left(\widehat{E}_i\right)}{na} \tag{6}$$

where na is the number of the identified actions in the set of matching classifiers [M].

The adaptive **global technique** estimates $\widehat{E}$ the average prediction error during exploration periods and determines the rate of change $g\left(\widehat{E}\right)$ which is the difference between the moving averages of $\widehat{E}$ before and after **n** periods of exploration (where **n** is usually set to 100). The rate of change is then used to determine the probability p_1:

$$p_1 = min \left\{ 1, g\left(\widehat{E}\right) \times Gf \right\}. \tag{7}$$

Thus, if the average prediction error changes, **n** other steps of exploration are executed prior to switching to exploitation.

The performance of both of Wilson strategies -the local and the global- are sensitive to Gf, n, and $p_{exploration}$. We avoid this shortcoming by using an approach based on meta-rules.

4.2   A Meta-Rules Based Approach

We use meta-rules to control the activation of exploration and exploitation. These meta-rules adapt the choice between exploration and exploitation to the evolution of the firm performance. They account for the new variations of the environment, once the firm has learned. They are simple and make the behavior of the classifier system close to that of a decision maker. Contrary to some techniques of Wilson, they allow the return of a firm to exploration and do not use the gain factor.

After **n** periods of exploration and **m** periods of exploitation, the following meta-rules are applied:

- If $MY_{t+n} > MY_{t+n+m}$, the system must continue learning. Subsequently, **m** must be decreased: $m = m * (1 - Exploitation\_Rate)$.
- If $MY_{t+n} \le MY_{t+n+m}$, the system has achieved enough learning. Subsequently, **m** must be increased: $m = m * (1 + Exploitation\_Rate)$.

MY_{t+n} and MY_{t+n+m} correspond to the moving average of the aggregation of Y[1] and Y[2] during the exploration and exploitation periods, respectively. $Exploitation\_Rate$ represents the variation rate of m. Once the system has acquired enough learning, the value of m becomes very large. The value of n is maintained positive to allow the system to adapt to small changes of the environment.

5   Experimental Results

The objective of this experimentation is twofold. First, we investigate the impact of exploration techniques on the performance of a firm. Second, we study the impact of the meta-rules approach and compare it to other choice techniques of exploration and exploitation.

The XCS parameters are fixed as follows: the population size is 6000 (allowing the system to represent all the possible classifiers when the generalization is not used), the generalization probability is 0.5; the learning rate is 0.001; the crossover rate is 0.8; the mutation rate equals 0.02; the minimum error is 0.01; the genetic algorithm frequency is 10 (allowing an update of the classifiers population), and the exploration probability equals 0.5. Each simulation is replicated 20 times. The reported results correspond to the average values of these 20 replications.

5.1   Exploration Techniques

The first series of experiments compares exploration techniques. The comparison is based on the results of the simulation of three populations involving 300 firms each. These populations use respectively recency, frequency, and random based exploration techniques. The three populations use identical initial parameters and the same exploration-exploitation method.

Figures 1 and 2 show the difference between the directed and undirected exploration techniques. They show that directed exploration is interesting at the beginning of the

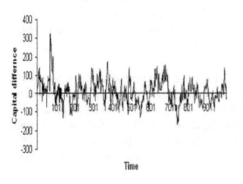

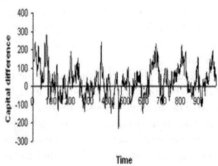

Fig. 1. Random vs. Recency-based exploration techniques

Fig. 2. Random vs. Frequency-based exploration techniques

Table 1. Summary statistics for the capital of firms

Technique	Run	1	2	3	4	5
Random	Standard deviation	99.78	104.22	111.21	128.57	50.11
	Average	869.63	854.64	880.57	875.57	862.43
Frequency	Standard deviation	58.72	123.48	123.53	113.77	125.35
	Average	882.66	874.73	861.91	870.71	883.02
Recency	Standard deviation	123.87	118.44	131.30	122.32	55.35
	Average	872.38	869.61	880.31	886.91	877.57

simulation period. It directs the exploration towards the use of new actions; which is not always the case for random exploration. It enriches the classifier population at the beginning better than random exploration, and results in a larger accumulation of the environment knowledge. On average, directed exploration does not greatly improve the performance of a firm. The average percent improvement is 3.4 %, reaching a maximum of 9.1% and a minimum of -7%. Table 1 displays the mean and standard deviation of the capital of firms from different simulation runs. The mean of the two techniques of directed exploration is greater than that of the random exploration but this difference is not statistically significant at the 99.95 % level. Therefore, directed-exploration alone is not sufficient to improve the performance of a firm. A balance between exploration and exploitation remains needed.

5.2   Exploration-Exploitation Techniques

The second series of experiments compares the techniques of choice between exploration and exploitation. First, we compare the proposed meta-rules based approach to a random switch approach. Second, we compare the proposed meta-rules based approach to the adapted Wilson techniques.

Meta-rules vs. Random Switch Techniques. To compare the proposed meta-rules approach to a random switch approach, we run a simulation involving two types of populations of firms. The first population uses a random choice between exploration and exploitation whereas the second uses the meta-rules with an $exploitation\_Rate = 20$ %. To focus on the exploration-exploitation switch technique, we endow these populations with identical parameters and with the same exploration technique. We set **n** = 20 and **m** = 10.

Figure 3 shows that the use of meta-rules improves the performance of surviving firms. The comparison of the average life span for firms adopting meta-rules (112 periods) to the average life span for random-XCS firms (107 periods) shows that meta-rules improve the resistance of firms. The important degradation of the performance of firms when meta-rules are applied coincides with the beginning of the exploitation period. This degradation shows that firms should have pursued learning and that it was too early for them to consider exploitation.

Despite their positive impact on the performance of firms, the meta-rules are sensitive to the values of **n** and **m**. Large periods of exploration are advantageous at the beginning when a firm has not learned enough. However, large **n** values could become

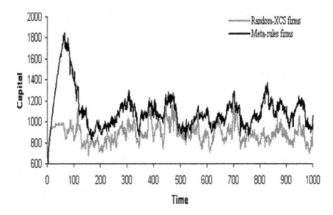

Fig. 3. Comparison of the capital of random XCS firms and meta-rules firms

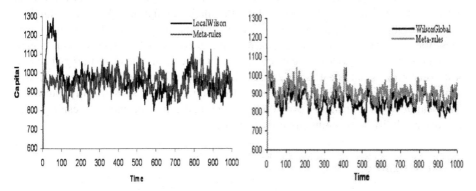

Fig. 4. Comparison of the meta-rules based approach to Wilson local technique

Fig. 5. Comparison of the meta-rules based approach to Wilson global technique

hazardous when the firm has acquired enough learning. At the end of the simulation, shorter periods of exploration are preferred.

Meta-rules vs. Wilson Techniques The following results are obtained by two simulations. The first includes a population of 300 firms adopting the meta-rules based approach and a population of 300 firms using Wilson adaptive local technique. The second includes the first population and a population of 300 firms using Wilson global adaptive technique. The gain factor for Wilson techniques is set to 0.5. The three populations share the same parameters and strategies except for the exploration-exploitation switch strategy. We compare Wilson local strategy to the meta-rules strategy on Figure 4 while we compare Wilson global strategy to the meta-rules strategy on Figure 5.

These graphics show that the use of meta-rules improves the performance of firms. This improvement is more pronounced with respect to Wilson global adaptive technique. In fact, this strategy does not allow firms to return to exploration once they have acquired enough knowledge and the environment has changed. The improvement is less

Table 2. Summary statistics for the average capital of firms under different exploitation-exploration strategies

	Meta-rules	GlobalWilson	LocalWilson
Standard Deviation	44.65	47.97	85.07
Average	912.50	862.19	962.75

pronounced when comparing the meta rules to Wilson local technique as the latter re-considers the choice for each period. The local Wilson strategy is clearly better at the beginning of the simulation period as the meta-rules based approach engages only in exploration for long periods, at the beginning of the simulation. However, in the long run, meta-rules outperform Wilson local strategy. Basing decisions only on current information is not wise on the long run. The meta-rules based approach is promising and could be improved by adapting the $exploitation\_Rate$ to the age of the firm.

These conclusions are further confirmed when we compare the standard deviation and mean capital, displayed in Table 2, of the three populations. A smaller standard deviation of the capitals reflects a more stable behavior of an approach; thus, the meta-rules strategy is more stable than either Wilson local or global strategies. Even though its mean is the largest, Wilson local strategy is not necessarily the best strategy because of its very high variation: it could cause a large drop of the capital due to successive erroneous choices between exploration and exploitation and subsequently cause the disappearance of the firm. However, on the long run, the average capital doesn't greatly improve as all firms are simultaneously learning.

6   Conclusion

In this paper, we studied the exploration-exploitation dilemma and learning in the context of large scale economic systems. The experiments demonstrated that directed exploration is useful at the beginning for the construction of the classifiers population as it decreases the learning time of firms. However, these techniques are insufficient to improve the performance of a firm. We proposed an adaptive approach that determines the choice between exploration and exploitation. This approach is based on meta-rules that adapt the choice to the evolution of the performance and knowledge of the firm. We compared the proposed approach to two adaptive techniques, originally proposed by Wilson, and adapted herein to a dynamic environment. The obtained results show that the approach is promising. However, the adaptation of the rate of change of the meta-rules to the age of the firm is needed.

References

1. Azoulay-Schwartz, R., Kraus, S., Wilkenfeld, J.: Exploration vs. exploitation: choosing a supplier in an environment of incomplete information. Elsevier Science (2003).
2. Baum, J.A.C., Rao, H.: Handbook of Organizational Change and Development: Evolutionary Dynamics of Organizational Populations and Communities. Oxford University Press (1999).

3. Butz, M. V., Wilson, S. W.: An algorithmic description of XCS. Journal of Soft Computing, **6** (2002) 144–153.
4. Carmel, D., Markovitch, S.: Exploration Strategies for Model-Based Learning in Multi-agent Systems. Autonomous Agents and Multi-agent systems. Nicholas Jennings and Katia Sycara and Michael Georgeff (eds.). **2(2)** (1999) 141–172.
5. Gittings, J. C.: Multi-armed bandit allocation indices. NY: John Wiley and sons (1989).
6. Kaelbling, L. P., Moore, A. W.: Reinforcement learning: A survey. Journal of Artificial Intelligence Research, **4**, (1996) 237–285.
7. Meuleau, N., Bourgine, P.: Exploration of multi-state environments: Local measure and back-propagation of uncertainty. Machine Learning. **35(2)** (1999) 117–154.
8. Miramontes Hercog, L., Fogarty, T. C.: Social Simulation Using a Multi-agent Model Based on Classifier Systems: The emergence of Vacillating Behavior in the " El Farol" Bar Problem. In P.L. Lanzi, W. Soltzman and S. Wilson eds.: IWLCS 2001, Volume **2321** of Lecture Notes in Artificial Intelligence. (2002) 88-111.
9. Rejeb, L., Guessoum, Z.: Adaptive Firms. In Proc. AISTA'04 International Conference on Advances in Intelligent Systems - Theory and Applications. In cooperation with the IEEE Computer Society. Luxembourg November (2004).
10. Penrose, E. T.: The theory of the growth of the firm. Basil Blackwell, (1959).
11. Peres-Uribe, A., Hirsbrunner, B.: The risk of Exploration in multi-agent learning systems: a case study. Proc. Agents-00 Joint workshop on learning agents, Barcelona, June 3–7, (2000) 33–37.
12. Sutton, R. S., Barto, A.G.: Reinforcement learning, an introduction. The MIT Press, (1998).
13. Thrun S. B.: The role of exploration in learning control. In D A. Sofge (eds.). Handbook of Intelligent Control: Neural, Fuzzy and Adaptive Approaches. Florence, Kentucky: Van Nostrand Reinhold (1992).
14. Watkins, C., Dayan, P.: Q-Learning. Machine Learning, 8 (1999) 279-292.
15. Wiering, M.: Explorations in Efficient Reinforcement Learning. Ph.D. thesis. February (1999).
16. Wilson, S.W.: Classifiers Fitness Based on Accuracy. Evolutionary computation, **3(2)** (1995) 149-175.
17. Wilson, S.W.: Explore/Exploit Strategies in Autonomy. In P. Maes, M. Mataric, J. Pollac, J.-A. Meyer and S. Wilson eds. From Animals to Animats 4, Proc. of the 4th International Conference of Adaptive Behavior, Cambridge (1996).

A Multi Agent Approach to Interest Profiling of Users

P.H.H. Rongen[1], J. Schröder[1], F.P.M. Dignum[2], and J. Moorman[2]

[1] IBM Nederland - Center for Advanced Studies
{erik, jasper}@nl.ibm.com
[2] Institute of Information and Computing Sciences
Utrecht University
{dignum, jmoorman}@cs.uu.nl

Abstract. Intelligent applications deliver personalized experiences and services to the user. This is done by creating and using a profile of the user: user profiling. Several approaches and algorithms are developed for user profiling. This paper describes a multi agent approach that allows multiple algorithms to be combined dynamically to generate a knowledge and interest profile of a user. IBM's ABLE environment was used for the implementation of the multi agent system. To test the system, the user interest profile is build on browse behavior and this profile is applied in a TV program recommender system. The results of implemented system show that multi agent systems provide an excellent platform for an extendible user profiling system that can use multiple classifiers.

1 Introduction

The amount of channels that provide us with information increases rapidly. These channels get more and more available to us at any time and any place. In the last ten years the clear distinction between places and activities has faded away. As a result daily life is becoming more and more complex, despite the increasing capabilities of intelligence in applications and services [SC04]. Intelligent applications provide personalized services and experiences, based on user profiles. A user profile is a collection of attributes that belong to an individual. This includes address books in mobile phones, browser history information, and messages, emails and documents authored by the user. This data can be processed to obtain additional user profile information. Examples are the extraction of a user's social network from address books, the deduction of user interests from the browser history and the extraction of expertise from messages and documents written by the user.

User profiles can be created explicit or implicit by the subject or can be created by others. When signing up to a web site like hotmail, a user has to fill out a form containing amongst others name and address. This is defined as the explicit creation of a user profile. Implicit creation of a user profile happens automatically during other activities. Examples of implicit user profiling are Amazon that keeps an interest user profile based on bought books and your computer keeping track of visited web pages. Doctors create medical records for their patients which is a sample of explicit profile creation by others.

M. Pĕchouček, P. Petta, and L.Z. Varga (Eds.): CEEMAS 2005, LNAI 3690, pp. 326–335, 2005.

Explicit creation of a user profile by a user has a number of disadvantages amongst which that users get annoyed at them and thus do not fill in correct and/or complete information. In the other hand, implicitly build profiles can be very incomplete.

Besides the distinction of explicitly and implicitly build profiles we can also distinguish profiles on the basis of whether they are structured or unstructured. Many implicitly build profiles are unstructured. I.e. they are not predefined in any way and will either be defined ad hoc during the profiling process, or remain undefined while the profile data is just stored in raw form. Unstructured profilers are often used by systems that use the profile directly in local applications. A good example of such a system is WebMate[CH97]. WebMate is a personal assistant that produces a personalized news paper by observing multiple news sources and selecting the news articles that match with the current user profile.

A good example of a structured profiler is the Quickstep system [MI04] that acts as a recommender system for a group of researchers within a computer science laboratory. The Quickstep system monitors the browsing behavior of a specific researcher by recording the visited web pages, classifying them onto an existing ontology of topics.

A major drawback of unstructured user profiles is that it is difficult to reuse them in different systems or to compare them. In addition structured profiles can more easily be visualized, reviewed and modified by a user.

The different user profiling systems use different approaches and techniques for the internal representation of the user profile. Samples of these techniques are the vector space model, n-grams, semantic networks, associative networks, and classifiers including neural networks, decision trees, inducted rules and Bayesian networks [MO02]

In situations where multiple techniques and profilers compete with each other to be the best and perform differently in different environments, the best solution is to combine multiple techniques and profilers into one system. This is possible through the use of a multi agent system, which also provides the possibility to distribute the application over multiple systems.

In the remainder of this paper, a flexible multi agent system approach is presented that is able to create and manage the profile of a user dynamically. The profiling system is split up into several autonomous entities that all take care of a specific part of the profile and combine their results in an overall user profile. The agents collaborate in producing an appropriate profile and compete with each other in delivering the best results.

This multi-agent system is tested with the personal television guide created by the Telematica Institute [TE04]. The multi-agent system builds the user profile on browse behavior and the profile is used by the television recommender to create viewing advises.

2 Multi Agent System Architecture

The profiling system presented here is able to generate a profile from the data that is obtained by observing user behavior. This data can for instance be the number of web pages the user has visited the past hour, the e-mail the user received today or the transcripts from a number of chats. Both unstructured and structured approaches to the classification of profiling data are considered. The general design of the presented profiling system is based on a structured approach. It consists of a structured hierarchy of profiling agents, each of which is responsible for a sub topic of the total profile. At the top level of this hierarchy, a single agent called the root, can be found. The root agent observes the behavior of a certain user and sends this information through to agents that are connected to it. When no agents are connected yet or the current set of agents is unable to profile the current data, the root will try to connect to other agents by requesting them from an agent pool. Whenever the root obtains data, it will request new agents from the agent pool to profile this new data.

The newly connected agents themselves may request other agents to create more specific profiling data. Figure 1 shows the profiling hierarchy after a number of new agents has been connected to the previously connected ones.

Fig. 1. An iteratively extended profiling hierarchy

An important reason to use a hierarchical agent structure is that generally, a classifier performs better within a limited domain. Classifying algorithms often locate and use the most distinguishing set of elements from the data to be able to determine the right class. In limited domains it is much easier to locate these distinguishing elements. A soccer agent for instance, can assume the incoming information is classified as sports, since it is placed beneath the sports agents within the hierarchy. Such a soccer agent therefore only has to find the distinguishing factors of soccer compared to other sports and doesn't have to worry about distinguishing the data from other topics that don't concern sports.

Another reason for using a hierarchical agent structure is performance. If all agents are connected directly to the root, the system will become increasingly slow, when the number of agents grows, since the root will have to pass the new information to all other agents, and they all have to process it.

The current approach doesn't enforce the agents to use a specific structure for building the hierarchy. The hierarchy is initiated with a root and whatever will be added to this hierarchy is up to the agents. In the current design approach, the agent pool is responsible for defining the structure of the hierarchy. Whenever an agent of the profiling hierarchy requests a new node agent from the agent pool, a specialized agent called the pool keeper will determine which agents will be advised to the requester and therewith the structure of the hierarchy

2.1   The Profiling Agents

The profiling agents can decide autonomously whether the incoming information can be profiled as belonging to their designated topic, or not. To increase the flexibility of the classification, different algorithms can be applied to different domains and different algorithms can be combined to produce a weighted average. This is achieved by connecting a profiling agent to multiple classifiers. These classifiers are specialized in classifying documents on a certain topic with a certain algorithm. A number of classifiers are connected to the profiling agent. The profiling agent forwards the information it retrieves from super-nodes to the classifiers and combines their results to determine the outcome of the profiling process.

Whenever the profiling process is successful, indicating that the incoming information could be classified according to the designated topic of the profiling agent, the agent will forward the data to its connected profiling agents or, if the current agents are unable to process it, will contact the pool keeper to obtain new profiling agents for the new data.

Figure 2 shows the resulting model for the multi agent profiling system. The model indicates the different types of agents and their relationships. The profile root can be connected to multiple pool keepers and a pool keeper can be connected to multiple profiling roots, for instance a web profiling root and a mail profiling root. The profile root is connected to at least one pool keeper, since the profile root needs to obtain new agents from at least one agent pool. Besides the pool keeper each profile root is also connected to the profile portal of the centralized profile. This connection is needed for obtaining the appropriate profile keepers that assemble the profile data from the several profile hierarchies.

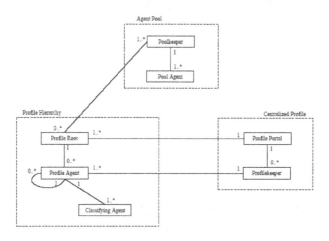

Fig. 2. The multi agent profiling system model

Furthermore the profiling agents are connected to a set of classifiers, or at least one, that perform the classification tasks on the specified topic in the specified domain, each using their own algorithm. The agent pool consists of the pool keeper and a number of agents of any type.

The centralized profile is the portal to the outside world. It contains a profile portal, an agent that is connected to all profile roots in a one-to-many relationship. A web profile root may for instance track the internet behavior of a user while a mail profile root observes the activity within a mail application.

This agent can be contacted by any outside agents or applications for obtaining an up-to-date profile of a user.

2.2 Collaboration Model

The agent collaboration model in Figure 3 specifies how agents collaborate and communicate. Basically the data streams within the collaboration model can be separated into three parts: a profiling part, a hierarchy management part and a profile extracting part. In the profiling part the user is observed by the several profiling roots.

When a root is presented with new data for profiling, this data is forwarded to the connected profiling agents. A profiling agent in turn collaborates with several classifiers to produce a profiling result for the incoming data. It forwards the data to the connected classifiers and combines the returned classifying results. When the profiling agent concludes that the current data can't be classified according to its assigned topic, the data flow will stop at this point. However, if the agent decides the current information can be classified according to the topic, the profiling agent will forward the information to its connected children and the profiling process will iteratively be repeated until the end of the hierarchy is reached or the profiling agents were not able to classify the incoming information anymore. The profiling agents send feedback to their parent nodes, indicating whether they were able to classify the incoming data. The sender of the data can use this feedback information to keep track of the information flow and is able to decide when agents should be added to or removed from the hierarchy.

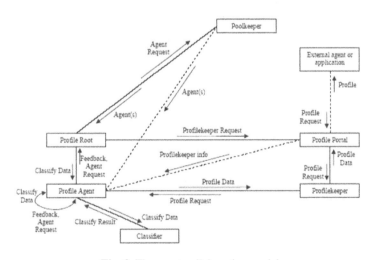

Fig. 3. The agent collaboration model

The data streams that concern hierarchy management are used for extending the hierarchy with new agents. Agents within the hierarchy can extend their set of connected agents by requesting a new agent from the agent pool. The pool keeper takes the request into consideration, checks the pool for the availability of the appropriate agents and returns a set of selected agents.

The pool keeper receives agent requests only from the profile roots. This approach makes the system more flexible since the roots of the profiling hierarchies are the only agents that are responsible for maintaining a connection to the agent pools. Whenever a pool is added or removed, only the profile roots have to be informed.

3 Classifiers

In the current system, a classifier receives a text document as input and will either conclude that the document can be classified as belonging to the specified topic or not. Neural networks have been used in a number of text classifying projects. In [CA01] a neural network approach is used to classify financial news articles, [RU02] describes a hierarchical text classification approach using neural networks and in [SE03] the application of neural networks for classifying web pages is investigated. We follow this approach in this project as well.

The network does not get fed the actual text, but rather the distinguishing features of the text such as length, language, number of words and number of sentences that could be useful for classifying.

The text classifier in our system uses trigrams, sets of three letters like AAA and IBM, as input to the network. In [HO99], a project for determining the author of a poem with neural networks, it was shown that trigrams in comparison with other n-gram (n-letter words) distributions produced the optimal results in classifying text. For the 26 characters in the alphabet, $26^3 = 17576$ trigrams are possible, but in practice only about 9000 actually occur. Therefore, there is no direct need for pre-selection of trigrams. Maybe a smaller amount of trigrams would do for the current problem domain but, during the trainings process, the network itself should be able to figure out which trigrams are the most important and will increase the weights of these trigrams. In the neural text classifier, the input of the network is composed by collecting all the occurring trigrams within the documents of the training set. This set of trigrams is then trimmed down by the least and most occurring trigrams to exclude trigrams from stop-words and trigrams that only occur in very few documents of the training set. Every input of the network is then linked to one of the trigrams of the remaining set. The output layer of the network consists of a single neuron that should be activated when a document about the classifiers topic is fed to the network. Reinforced training is then applied and the network is tested with a test set to avoid overfitting of the training set.

3.1 The Neural Web Classifier

The web classifier is part of the hierarchy of agents that is able to monitor the web behavior of a user by observing the pages the user has visited. A single classifier within this agent network determines whether a certain html page can be classified to the topic it has been trained to classify. The web classifier receives a web document from a profiling agent that in its turn received the data directly from the root agent or from a peer profiling agent. The web classifier should be able to classify an incoming web document and adjust his current profile if needed. For this purpose the neural web classifier is trained with positive and negative sample data about the assigned topic of the agent. The positive sample data contains representative web documents on the specific topic while the negative sample data contains any other web documents as long as they fall within the domain the classifier is placed. For example, if an agent that is specialized in managing a profile about soccer within the field of robotics, it should contain negative sample data about other robotics topics. An agent that is not trained within the right domain might still be a good classifier but will have a high misclassification than agents that are trained with the appropriate domain specific data. The ratio between the positive and negative samples is a reflection of reality. Thus, if the current domain is very large and a topic covers only a small part of this domain, this then a relatively small positive and a large negative data sample set of web documents is provided to the agent.

3.2 Other Classifying Algorithms

As shown in fig 2, one profiling agent can use multiple classifiers, using different algorithms. In the current implementation a simple title classifier is created that extracts the title from a web page and classifies the page according to that title by mapping it to a predefined set of key phrases. This approach is very simple but is a good example of the classifiers that can be used for special sources of information.

3.3 Accuracy of the Classifiers

Currently two types of classifiers have been implemented to assist the profiling agents in obtaining a profile on a specific topic. The results of these classifiers basically determine the performance of the profiling process, since the other agents of the system depend on the outcome of the classifiers.

The results of the simple title classifiers show the expected results. When topics contain a number of specific and unique key phrases the classifier can produce reasonable results. The title classifier however only has been added to the system to show the ease of adding new classifiers and to show the collaboration with other classifiers. In a professional environment, the title classifier should therefore either be replaced by a more sophisticated one or be extended with some machine learning features to be really useful to the system. The current profiling system leans heavily on the results of the neural classifying agents. The neural classifiers show good results across multiple domains. During the training process, the neural classifiers show up 80 to 100% accuracy on the test sets, indicating that the training process is able to create good (and sometimes perfect) classifiers. It is hard to obtain exact precision and recall rates however, since there is no such thing as a test database for web classifying systems similar to the Reuters-21578 database that is often used to test text classifying algorithms. In general the results of the neural classifiers show a tendency to a higher accuracy within limited domains.

Experiments were performed to discover the ideal network topology of the neural classifiers. Multi layer networks structurally outperform the single layer network.

Although the neural classifiers perform well on the test sets, the classifiers may perform differently in practice if the training and test sets are a bad reflection of reality. The actual performance of the classifiers thus depends heavily on collecting representative data on the specified topics. In the current implementation this data selection process is done manually and can be very time consuming since the performance of the neural classifier improves when more training data is made available. Experiments show that at least 40 to 60 positive samples of web pages per topic are needed to train a good classifier.

Besides the positive samples, a classifier needs a set of negative sample data that represents the other topics within the domain a specific agent is classifying.

In the current implementation the neural network are trained automatically by providing sets of negative and positive sample data. In practice the negative sample database is built by using the positive sample data of other topics and adding some sample web pages of the remaining topics within the domain. In this approach still a lot of data has to be assembled manually though.

4   The TV Program Recommender

To show the easy use of the currently implemented profiling system, the profiler is connected to an actual recommender system, a TV program recommender that is currently being developed by the Dutch Telematica Institute [TE04] in association with public broadcasting (omroep.nl). The TV program recommender takes a constructed profile in the form of an XML document, as in figure 4 as input and is able to recommend TV programs to the user based on this profile. The genre field is determined by the profiling system, and is used to determine the user's interest for TV programmes.

```
<profile>
  <pages> <page>
   <id>thePageId</id>
      <url>http://someurl.com
      </url>
      <title>Voetbal
          International
      </title>
    <genre>Sport</genre>
    <date>2004-2-23</date>
    <time>06:59:00</time>
  </page> </pages>
</profile>
```

Fig. 4. Example XML input document of the TV Program recommender

If for instance the profile indicates that a user is interested in sport and news, TV programs that cover these topics will be recommended to the user.

More complex profiles make it possible to advise the user in a more specific and sophisticated way. The TV recommender shows the straightforward use of a constructed profile by other applications. A special profile tracking agent is generated that requests and receives the profile from the profile portal once in a while and informs the recommendation application when modifications to the profile have occurred. Furthermore, a specific taxonomy for the profiling system defines what categories can be handled by the recommender. The 17 categories the TV recommender can handle are specified in the taxonomy as classes directly placed under the root and classifiers have been trained especially for this purpose. Due to the flexible agent structure the changes in the taxonomy and the new classifiers in the agent pool automatically lead to the forming of a new kind of profile hierarchies.

5 Conclusions

The implemented profiling system is able to create a profile of a user that is based on its internet browse behavior. The platform agents work well together in building the hierarchy and consulting each other about incoming web documents.

A number of advantages result from the agent approach to the profiling system. One of the most important advantages of the agent approach is the ease of adding new profilers and classifiers to the system dynamically without having to change any code within the other parts of the system. Currently two classifying algorithms are used. New algorithms and agents can be attached easily by adding them to the agent pool. This approach to the combination of multiple algorithms has shown to be easy and flexible. By delegating the responsibilities to the appropriate agent the architecture and implementations are simplified significantly.

Furthermore, the general agent approach makes it easy to retract the profile from the profiling system. Currently an XML version of the created profile is extracted for the use in a TV recommender system but the profiling system can be connected to any other application that is able to benefit from a structured profile of a user. As discussed above, we have connected our profiling system to a TV program recommender system, without these systems having been designed to collaborate

Another emerging advantage of the multi agent approach to profiling is the ability to distribute parts of the profiling systems when needed. This ensures scalability when a large number of agents are added to the profiling hierarchies.

Besides the mentioned advantages, the agent approach inevitably also results in some shortcomings, especially for development and maintenance. Since the agent system is basically a system of independent running threads, debugging the agent community has shown to be a difficult and time consuming task.

Another effect of agent oriented programming is the inability to access and interpret the state of the overall agent system in an easy way.

Agent oriented programming thus has shown to take some extra time in the development phase but the approach also offers major advantages in extending the system and connecting the agent system to new applications. Especially in the field of profiling where many different classifiers can be implemented to assist in the profiling process, the advantages of the agent approach have shown to be a suitable solution.

While the system provides promising results for user profiling, its major drawback for using it as a cross-domain profiling approach is the lack of openness of the architecture. In a world where profiles provided by different owners are to be combined, the use of open standards such as Web Services and Semantic Web Services is crucial. Other classifying algorithms are also being considered. Natural Text analysis seems a promising technology to provide additional information about texts above what trigrams may provide. Finally, the combination of other sources of information such as email with web pages is also being considered to provide additional profiling information. In the case of using email as a source, the issues related to privacy become very important, especially in the case where a company enforces a classifying solution upon its employees.

Acknowledgements

We wish to thank Peter Fennema for integration with the TV Recommender. This work is part of the MultimediaN project (http://www.multimedian.nl). MultimediaN is sponsored by the Dutch government under contract BSIK 03031.

References

[CA01]   Calvo R.A. (2001) Classifying financial news with neural networks, 6th Australasian Document Symposium
[CH97]   Chen, L. and Sycara K. (1997) WebMate: A Personal Agent for Browsing and Searching
[HO99]   Hoorn, J.F. et al (1999) Neural Network Identification of Poets Using Letter Sequences, Literary and Linguistic Computing, 14(3), 311-338.
[IE04]   IE Canvas, http://www.nothome.com/IECanvas/
[MI04]   Middleton, S. E., Shadbolt, N. R. and De Roure, D. C. (2004) Ontological User Profiling in Recommender Systems, ACM Transactions on Information Systems (TOIS), 22(1), 54-88
[MO02 Montaner M, Lopez B, and de la Rosa J. (2003) A taxonomy of recommender agents on the internet. Artificial Intelligence Review, 19:285 - 330
[PA02]   Padgham, L and Winiko, M. (2002) Prometheus: A methodology for developing intelligent agents, Third International Workshop on Agent-Oriented Software Engineering
[PR04]   Protégé,   Ontology   Editor   and   Knowledge   Acquisition   System, http://protege.stanford.edu/
[RU02]   Ruiz, M.E. and Srinivasan, P (2002) Hierarchical Text Categorization Using Neural Networks Information Retrieval, 5, 87–118
[SC04]   Schuurmans J, Zijlstra E (2004). Towards a continuous personalization experience. ACM International Conference on Dutch directions in HCI
[SE03]   Selamat, A. et al (2003) Web page classification method using neural networks, Transactions of The Institute of Electrical Engineers of Japan, 123(5), 1020-1026
[TE04]   Telematica Instituut, http://www.telin.nl/

vBroker: Artificial Agents Helping to Stock Up on Knowledge

Gábor Tatai, László Gulyás, László Laufer, and Márton Iványi

AITIA Inc, Infopark sétány 1. V. em,
H-1117, Budapest, Hungary,
{tatus, gulya, laufer, mivanyi}@aitia.ai

Abstract. Hungary, a former socialist country, has a thriving financial market (Budapest Stock Exchange, BSE) 15 years after the systems change. Yet, the general public's knowledge about the BSE, or about stock markets in general, is very limited and most small investors are only aware of a single investment option: the savings account. The vBroker project (funded by the Hungarian Financial Supervisory Authority) aimed at familiarizing the Hungarian public with the workings of the stock market. It consisted of a combination of three elements: an e-learning portal with material on financial markets, an intelligent training assistant agent (an intelligent chatter robot connected to a specialized knowledge base) and a multi-agent based simulated stock market, packaged as an online investment game. This paper describes the vBroker portal, gives an overview of its main modules, and discusses its embodied communicational agent and its artificial stock market in more detail.

1 Introduction

Hungary, a former socialist country, has a thriving financial market (Budapest Stock Exchange, BSE) 15 years after the systems change. Yet, the general public's knowledge about the BSE, or about stock markets in general, is very limited and most small investors are only aware of a single investment option: the savings account. To change this, the Hungarian Financial Supervisory Authority (*PSZÁF* – the Hungarian equivalent of the Securities and Exchange Commission) solicited proposals for educational materials. Our funded proposal, *vBroker* (virtual broker), consisted of a combination of three elements: an e-learning *portal* with material on financial markets, an intelligent training assistant agent (an intelligent chatter robot connected to a specialized knowledge base) and a multi-agent based simulated stock market, packaged as an online investment game. Our ambition was to make this online application as interactive as possible in order to motivate the visitors to gain enough information and experience to try out themselves on the Budapest Stock Exchange in the future.

In this paper we introduce the vBroker project, give an overview of its architecture and provide a summary of the lessons and experiences that we have gained from running the system for one year. We believe that we had a special opportunity, since we were able to follow the students' way from the very beginning of acquiring knowledge in a certain area, till they mastered the subject. We were able to observe the trial of the newly acquired knowledge in an almost realistic environment, without having the heavy consequences of possible bad decisions.

M. Pěchouček, P. Petta, and L.Z. Varga (Eds.): CEEMAS 2005, LNAI 3690, pp. 336–345, 2005.

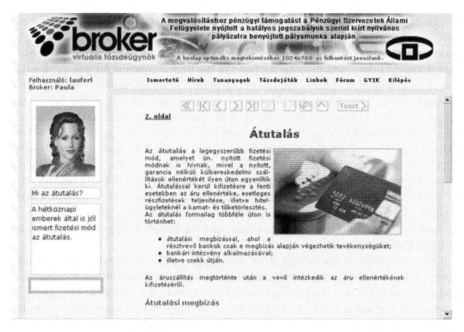

Fig. 1. The interface of vBroker. The user asked the tutoring agent what does transfer mean. The agent replied and showed the bit in the curricula where this concept is being explained.

Registering on the site, the user meets the chatterbot first, his tutoring agent, and virtual broker in one person. After choosing the convenient character, the chatbot becomes the person, who accompanies the students throughout the whole time spent on the site. He/she has a mediatory function between the online curriculum and the student, and also between the complex interface of the artificial stock market and the client. The chatbot provides the consistency in the site, someone, who is always there to ask, if the user does not understand something. His/her continuous presence and proactive behavior gives a constant motivation to go through the chapters of the course and to try out the different functions of the stock exchange, to learn how BSE, the real life counterpart functions.

There is no learning without evaluation and feedback; therefore we put an emphasis on implementing these functions of the chatbot in our system. The tutoring agent is assisting the evaluation in the learning process, and also provides proper feedback on the gains and losses of the user on the stock market.

The Internet has hosted a number of online stock market games in the past, superficially similar to vBroker's simulation game. [6-10] These simulations generally belonged to one of the following two classes. They were either *trailing games* or *participatory* markets. In the former ones the traded papers correspond to stocks in a real stock-market and the price of a given good equals the real price (usually with a certain delay). The advantage of this setup is that the stock market is rooted in a real economic system, and thus, neither extensive modeling of the fundamentals, nor that of the information flow is necessary. However, the real economic base also prevents the online community of the artificial market to have any influence on the running prices. In fact, this setup consists of two separate markets connected through a narrow, one-directional flow of information: the price-taking. The latter case of *participatory* markets is basically an online trading game. Participants can freely determine their bids and offers, and the running price of the traded goods is fully determined by the simulated market. Therefore, this setup places a strong emphasis on the implemented market micro-structure. However, it also poses several, rather hard challenges. In order to maintain the realism of the market and its prices, the institutions must provide enough control and 'momentum' to prevent the participants to have extreme influence. Unrealistic bubbles or crashes must be avoided (especially when caused by only a few human users). Similarly, price setting by the coordinated action of participants must also be made impossible. A related matter is that a realistic level of market liquidity must also be guaranteed, even in periods when the participants happen to be passive. Finally, the simulated market's prices must somehow be grounded in an 'artificial economic system' and the information generated by it must be channeled to the users.

Given *vBroker*'s focus on education, our design emphasized realistic market institutions (i.e., real trading rules and market micro-structure), realistic market behavior, and the availability of (fundamental) information about the traded stocks. These requirements yielded a model that is closer to participatory markets than to trailing games, but where control over the underlying fundamentals and information flow is maintained. Our answers to the participatory setup's challenges are mostly based on the use of artificial agents. Therefore the *vBroker* simulated stock market is a heterogeneous multi-agent system, where human and artificial agents trade together.

In the second chapter we describe the usability of our tutoring agent in it's relation with the e-learning module and the virtual stock exchange. In the third chapter we explain the architecture and the functioning of the artificial stock market; and in the last chapters we provide some conclusions of our experiences with the system.

2   BotCom as a Tutoring Agent: From Theory to Practice

Before vBroker we developed an embodied communicational agent (ECA) capable of carrying out dialogues in Hungarian language with the users on general conversational issues and on specific topics as well. We put an emphasis on detecting the users' emotions and reacting on them verbally and by presenting an adequate animation. We applied several psychological and communicational theoretical models in order to provide the possibilities for expressing complex behaviors, as well as for leaving possibilities for further improvement. The details of the agent's characteristics are discussed elsewhere. [11, 14]

The ECA system consists of 3 main parts. The backbone is a multi-layered dialogue management sub-system working on a knowledge base of dialogue fragments enhanced with knowledge representation. There is an emotional modeling sub-system in conjunction with an expression-emotion mapping database. We also use a set of facial and upper-body animations integrated with the other two previously mentioned modules.

The most plausible application for an ECA, besides the normal website navigation task that web-integrated ECAs generally provide, is that of a tutoring agent. The vBroker project was a trial of our communicational agent both in roles.

2.1 Pedagogical Agents

According to recent approaches [12] tutoring agents should have at least four capabilities in order to paralelly fulfill both their embodied communicational agent role and their tutoring function [13].

The first skill is the ability to adapt. The agent has to be able to evaluate student's understanding of the subject during knowledge acquisition, and it has to move on if the user acquired the certain segment of knowledge on an acceptable level. Similarly to real classroom situations, the teacher has to determine timing, taking the initiative to move on.

The second important function for a tutoring agent is giving motivation. It has to ask questions, encourage the students during learning and give appropriate feedback. When the student is asking the agent about the subject, it has to present relevant information and provide excellent examples. In order to carry out these tasks it has to interpret the student's responses.

Another important aspect of tutoring is engaging the student in the studying process. This greatly depends on the personality of the teacher. It is not any different in the case of pedagogical agents. A successful tutoring system must present an interesting personality as a teacher, who in the meantime, has specific areas of expertise. The proper use of humor is also a powerful tool from this perspective. We are dealing with this topic in a separate section.

The forth aspect of a tutoring agent is its ability to evolve or learn. The paradigm of Life Long Learning applies to virtual educators, too. There should be a possibility to revise and update their knowledge as often as required

Of course there aren't any real teachers fulfilling all these requirements perfectly. If there were, there wouldn't be a need for tutoring agents at all!

2.2 E-Learning with Tutoring Agents

We developed our vBroker curriculum in cooperation with the MBA program of the Budapest University of Economics. We used all the materials of the Financial Markets course, created a detailed structure suitable for e-learning, assigned keywords and topics for each section and subsection. We have also assembled a phrase book with definitions, tests for each section, and summaries of the longer segments. Moreover we have created cross linked sections for better navigation. The most important part, however, was the integration of the knowledge base with the communicational agent.

If we want our agent to adapt to the learning process, it has to follow the user's learning procedure. By this we don't simply mean the history of the browser session, but also the other aspects of navigation, such as how much time was spent on each section, or if the user looked up all the definitions on a page in the phrase book. Whether the student skip some pages or stopped somewhere in the course, is also relevant. All of these aspects give us important information about the user, and they are also possibilities for a virtual agent to enhance the learning procedure with its interaction.

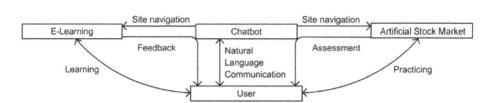

Fig. 2. The schema of learning with the chatterbot in vBroker

When skipping to the next section, ahead of the estimated time required for properly reading it, the agent can ask if the topic was familiar for the student. When some expressions weren't looked up, we can draw the user's attention to their importance by asking their meaning, and when not getting the proper answer navigating the site back to the skipped section.

For an ECA to fulfill its role of motivation, besides reflecting on the students' action, it must be able to get engaged in conversations on the subject. We created a wide variety of dialogue segments about each subtopic, and about financial markets in general, and fed it in the ECA's knowledge base. This may sound simple, but in reality, it takes combining domain expertise and everyday communication skills to define these conversational sequences and the proper clues for their activation.

Giving proper feedback is another area where natural language is a significantly better tool than any other means of communication: e.g., than test score or statistical data, etc. Students need to be compared to others, but this comparison happening in a conversation is less harmful. In addition, using relevant sentences encourages students for further improvement more than simple numeric feedback.

In vBroker this ability of the agent is used not only in the e-learning module, but also when providing feedback on the user's accomplishments in the virtual stock exchange. In addition to its tutoring tasks, the agent also helps navigating the virtual exchange's site. When doing so, the agent not only answers questions (e.g. about the current value of a particular share), but also shows the table with the relevant values.

In order to carry out these tasks, the agent has to track the topic of discussion very precisely. It has to know when to skip from the virtual stock exchange part to the curriculum, e.g. when the user was asking about a definition of a certain term in the course: "What is the BUX index?", and when it has to stay in the same section, only jumping to another part: "How much is the BUX index?".

The chatterbot also gives feedback about the results of the tests, turning the test results into an interactive discussion about the incorrectly answered questions. In this way, the VBroker system turns the traditional self-paced web-based training method into a live, synchronous and interactive teaching technique without using expensive, rarely used technologies such as satellite video conferencing etc. Of course, a real life trainer can never be replaced by a virtual agent, but a web-based virtual tutoring system offers a cost-efficient solution for e-learning training developers.

3 The vBroker Artificial Stock Market Participatory Simulation

The *vBroker* artificial stock market simulation is an online virtual market where registered users trade virtual papers for virtual money over the Internet 24 hours a day, 7 days a week. The orders are matched according to rules similar to those of the Budapest Stock Exchange (BSE), a NYSE-like modification of the continuous double auction (CDA). The clearing of the orders is automatic, executed by the artificial stock market system. The *vBroker* system charges a flat rate for submitting or canceling orders, plus a percentage for the trades made.

The liquidity of the market is ensured by *specialists* or *market makers* (one per share). These are autonomous software agents that follow the internal processes of the simulated market, and the news about those processes, and change their orders according to them. The *vBroker* system hosts two other types of artificial agents. *Contestant agents* apply various artificial intelligence (AI) techniques to do their trade. They face the exact same set of information and costs than human participants and their goal is to collect as much wealth as possible. *Simulator (noise) agents*, on the other hand, are responsible for maintaining a moderate level of trade when no human user is active. Note that as the *vBroker* system operates *24x7*, human participants cannot be assumed to be uniformly present. Yet, they may potentially enter the virtual floor *anytime*. Therefore, the dynamic system of temporarily active simulator (noise) agents was introduced. *Contestant agents* cannot be used for this purpose, since this would require a much higher trading frequency on their part than on that of the human participants. This would contradict the requirement of fairness and thus the performance of the human participants and the contestant agents would not be comparable. Another important difference between the contestant and the simulator (noise) agents is that the goal of the latter is to provide a level of trade and not to accumulate wealth. Since a trade always requires both a buyer and a seller, the population of simulator agents collects an average of 0% profit. When determining the simulated trades' prices, special care is taken to ensure that these virtual price movements do not affect any valid orders made by specialists, contestant agents, or human participants.

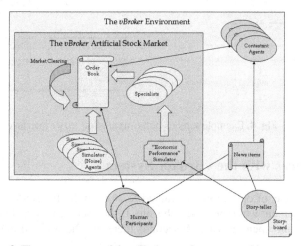

Fig. 3. The components of the vBroker environment and its connections

The behavior of the artificial market is grounded in a raw simulation of the stocks' economic performance. This simulation provides the fundamental value of the given instrument by determining its general trend and volatility. The trend is fed to the specialist of the given paper, who tunes its orders accordingly. The *vBroker* system is configured in such a way that with its default settings each stock is in balance without any pronounced trends. Trends are introduced by a human operator, the *story-teller*, by tuning the stocks' 'economic performance' simulator. The story-teller follows a *storyboard*, written before the start of the *vBroker* game. It is important to note, however, that trends and market prices can only be controlled to a certain limit using the 'economic performance' simulator. This is because the traders (the human participants and the contestant agents) have the capacity to influence trends. The degree to which the storyteller may counter-balance the traders' behavior is also a parameter of the system (to be set for each paper). Naturally, the challenge here is to determine this sensitivity in such a way that no single user has too much influence, but yet, the simultaneous actions of the traders could build enough pressure to turn a trend.

In addition to implementing the storyboard by tuning the stocks' 'economic performance' simulators, the story-teller also informs the traders about the imaginary economic events underlying the trade changes. This is done via the imaginary news agency *vBroker-Press* whose reports (in natural language) are published on the *vBroker* site. The pre-written storyboard contains the news items, as well as the simulator parameters to be tuned. The publication of news items does not necessary imply changing the related paper's parameters.

Figure 3. summarizes the main components of the *vBroker* system with their connections, while Figure 4. shows example screens of the simulation's user interface.

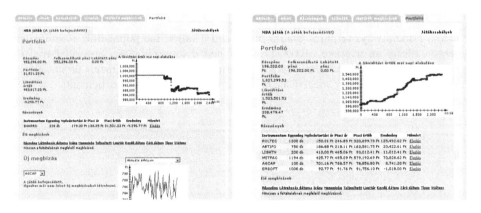

Fig. 4. Example screens of the simulation's user interface

4   Experiences with the vBroker System

During its one year of operation we wanted to capture the tutoring agent's influence on user's engagement while browsing the site. If the user was interested in the content of the website, and spent at least 30 seconds there, he/she was willing to browse the average of 3 times more on vBroker (back row) then on the scientific portal (middle row) and 7 times more then on the company website (front row).

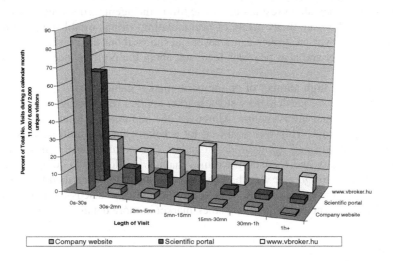

Fig. 5. Distribution of visit lengths among 3 different types of websites during a calendar month. In this particular month our company's website, an AI portal and the vBroker site had approx. 2000, 6000, 11000 unique visitors respectively.

During this 12 month period it hosted 8 games for a total of 177 trading days. The 8 games were run according to different storyboards, changing the economic scenario in a relatively wide range. The number of stocks also varied across games ranging from 4 stocks only (in the first game) to a selection of 18 papers. On rare occasions, the storyboard also contained the mid-game entrance of a new paper.

In the simulation game the motivation of the (human) traders was ensured by prizes offered by our sponsors. (The prizes included computer equipment, money, etc.) Two games were organized in cooperation with the Master of Business Administration program of the Budapest University of Technology and Economics. In these games the students of the program had the chance to practice their trading skills. The best performing class received an additional exam week from the program administration.

5   Conclusions

This paper introduced the vBroker project, an effort aimed at familiarizing the Hungarian public with the workings of the stock market. vBroker was a year-long service that consisted of an e-learning portal with material on financial markets, enhanced by the presence of an intelligent training assistant agent (an intelligent chatter robot connected to a specialized knowledge base and with responses based on emotional modeling of the user). In addition, the portal also hosted a virtual stock market based on multi-agent based simulation.

In vBroker the chatter robot is used in two functions. It helps website navigation and also serves as a tutoring agent. In its latter function, it can draw the user's attention to understudied topics, it is able to get engaged in conversations on the subject, and provides feedback about test results. In addition, the agent also serves as a virtual broker assisting the user in its effort of accumulating virtual wealth on the virtual stock market. This virtual broker can answer questions about the current trends and prices on the market and also provides feedback about the performance of the user's portfolio.

In contrast to the high number of online stock market games hosted by the Internet in the past, the *vBroker* participatory stock market applied real trading rules, realistic market institutions and infrastructure. Moreover, the simulated market was rooted in an 'artificial economy'. This was achieved by a heterogeneous multi-agent system, where human and artificial agents traded together. For example, artificial agents ensured market liquidity and realistic price movements, in addition to competing with human participants for greater wealth. The current publication described the vBroker portal as a whole, gave an overview of its main modules and discussed its embodied communicational agent and its artificial stock market in more detail.

References

1. GULYÁS, L., ADAMCSEK, B.: Charting the Market: Fundamental and Chartist Strategies in a Participatory Stock Market Experiment, In: International Conference Experiments in Economic Sciences: New Approaches to Solving Real-world Problems, Okayama and Kyoto, Japan,14-17 December 2004.
2. GULYÁS, L., ADAMCSEK, B., KISS, Á.: An Early Agent-Based Stock Market: Replication and Participation, Rendiconti Per Gli Studi Economici Quantitativi, Volume unico (2004) 47-71.
3. GULYÁS, L., ADAMCSEK, B., KISS, Á.: Experimental Economics Meets Agent-Based Finance: A Participatory Artificial Stock Market, Proceedins of the 34th Annual Conference of International Simulation and Gaming Association (ISAGA 2003), August 25-29 (2003)
4. LAUFER, L., TATAI, G.: Learn, Chat and Play – An ECA supported stock markets e-learning curricula, In Proceedings of the IASTED International Conference on Web-Based Education (WBE 2004), ACTA Press, Innsbruck, Austria 16-18 February 2004.
5. LAUFER, L., TATAI, G., CSORDÁS, A.: Use of Communicational Agents in Distance Learning Environments, In Proceedings of the First Central European International Multimedia and Virtual Reality Conference (CEIMVRC04), Veszprém University Press. Veszprém, Hungary, 6-8 May 2004.
6. RABERTO, M., CINCOTTI, S., FOCARDI, S., MARCHESI, M.: Agent-based simulation of a financial market, Physica A, 299 (1 October 2001) 320-328
7. TERNA, P.: Cognitive Agents Behaving in a Simple Stock Market Structure, Agent-Based Methods in Economics and Finance: Simulations in Swarm, LUNA, F., PERRONE, A. (eds.), Kluwer Academic Publishers (2001)
8. WEB: Foundation for Investor Education: The Stock Market Game, electronic resource, http://www.smg2000.org/
9. WEB: Stock-Trak, Inc: The Florida Stock Market Simulation, electronic resource, http://www.floridasms.com/

10. WEB: TERNA, P., CAPPELLINI, A.: SumWeb: A Live Stock Market Simulation, electronic source: http://eco83.econ.unito.it/sumweb/

11. TATAI, G., CSORDÁS A., KISS Á., LAUFER L., SZALÓ A.: The chatbot who loved me. Pelachaud, C., Marriott, A. and Ruttkai, Z. eds.: Proceedings of the AAMAS 2003 workshop on Embodied Conversational Characters as Individuals. pp. Melbourne, Australia, 2003.

12. JOHNSON, W.L., RICKEL, J.W.: Animated pedagogical agents: Face-to-face interaction in interactive learning environments, International Journal of Artificial Intelligence in Education 11 2000 47-78.

13. RICKEL, J.W., JOHNSON, W.L.: Integrating pedagogical capabilities in a virtual environment agent, In Proceedings of the First International Conference on Autonomous Agents (Agents'97), New York, USA 1997 30-38

14. TATAI, G., CSORDÁS A., SZALÓ A., LAUFER L.:.The chatbot feeling - Towards a usable emotional model for Internet ECAs: Proceedings of EPIA'03 - 11th Portuguese Conference on AI. pp. 336-341, Springer Verlag, 2003

Cooperative Planning in the Supply Network – A Multiagent Organization Model

Péter Egri and József Váncza

Computer and Automation Institute, Hungarian Academy of Sciences,
H-1518 Budapest P.O.B. 63, Hungary
{egri, vancza}@sztaki.hu

Abstract. The paper presents an approach for modelling the planning processes in supply networks at various partners, on different horizons and aggregation levels. After introducing an overall planning framework, we apply the Gaia agent-oriented analysis and design methodology to construct an organizational model for supply networks that operate in markets of customized mass products. The paper presents the main elements of this model, the necessary extensions of Gaia, and discusses the next steps towards developing and validating a portfolio of cooperation mechanism.

1   Introduction

The question all manufacturers have to answer time and again can be put simply as how to produce what is needed, neither more, nor less, neither earlier, nor later, just in the required quality. Giving appropriate answer is hard because market demand is uncertain and distributed, while production processes are complex, involving geographically dispersed producers of raw materials, components and end-products operating in a *supply network*. Furthermore, acceptable order lead times are much shorter than production lead times. This is the case when retailers require shipment within one day, or customers configuring their cars will expect delivery within a couple of weeks, or even days.

Taking high *service level* as their main priority, manufacturers can hedge against demand uncertainty only by maintaining capacity and/or material *buffers*. This however, incurs extra equipment, labor and inventory *costs*, as well as the risk of producing *obsolete* components and/or products. Partners within the supply network must find their own *trade-offs* between service level and cost that are acceptable both for their markets and other partners. Such a solution can emerge only from the interaction of local and asynchronous decisions.

The problem is essentially a *planning problem*: manufacturers would like to exercise control over some future events based on information what they know at the moment for certain (about products, technologies, resource capabilities, sales histories) and only anticipate (demand, resource and material availability).

The aim of our research is to develop planning methods that improve the *overall logistic and production* performance of a supply network. We assume

M. Pěchouček, P. Petta, and L.Z. Varga (Eds.): CEEMAS 2005, LNAI 3690, pp. 346–356, 2005.
© Springer-Verlag Berlin Heidelberg 2005

that members of the network are independent entities, with their own resources, performance objectives and internal decision mechanisms. Hence, there is an inevitable need to coordinate logistics and production related decisions and to facilitate and sustain cooperation among network members [13].

Since in a supply net there are various, in some cases very complex and often interacting planning tasks, we have chosen the *agent-based* approach for modelling them, analyzing their interactions, as well as for developing and validating novel cooperation mechanisms. However, when building directly a multiagent system we would get lost in the details. First one has to set up the *organizational model* of the network. We applied *Gaia methodology* that supports modelling of a complex organization in terms of abstract role and interaction models [15]. Later on, in the design phase, the roles will be realized by agents.

Below we present our application domain, give an overview of the main planning functions, and specify the requirements towards our modelling approach. Next we show how the various planning functions and interactions can be mapped to the abstract layer of Gaia, and describe the necessary extensions of the framework. Finally, we conclude by outlining future research directions.

2 Problem Statement

2.1 Customized Mass Production

The scope of our study is *customized mass production* in a large-scale, real-life production network, where the ultimate goal is to satisfy demand on a market of mass products (like cosmetics, food, mobile phones, light bulbs, low-tech electronics, etc.), where the demand appears for a complex and ever changing variety of products, both for small and large quantities, in hardly predictable temporal patterns. Such a market is typically served by a consumer goods manufacturer that works in a *focal point* of a supply network whose other nodes provide necessary raw materials, components and packaging materials (see Fig. 1). Market demand is transmitted to the manufacturer by distribution centers (DC). Some of the suppliers (e.g., packaging material providers) serve several manufactures acting on different markets. Guaranteeing extremely high service level and, at the same time, keeping operation costs low requires the integration of the traditionally extreme principles of mass production and customization.

Customer orders specify the quantity, due date and shipment location of final products. Production is carried out on production lines that are able to process several products, but the changeover cost between them are considerable. At any moment, a large number of product variants are produced by the manufacturer (in our case, the size of the mix is in the order of thousand.). Due to the volatile market conditions, production is based mostly on *forecasts*, thus inventories are inevitable to provide service at the required level and to enable local resource optimization. After all, the partners in the network cannot store too much products because the inventory holding costs are high, some components are perishable, and some products have short life-cycles. In a focal supply network, a strong buyer may not maintain inventory: it gives only forecasts and suppliers have

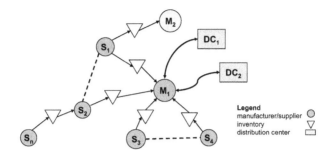

Fig. 1. Typical elements and connections of the supply network

to decide the production quantities and store the goods until the buyer needs and calls-off them. This is the so-called *consignment vendor managed inventory* (VMI) [5]. Lateral cooperation of suppliers—when they mutually help each other in critical shortage situations—is also possible, though atypical.

Forecasts and plans must be shared with the suppliers in order to improve performance, hence long-term relations and trust are prerequisites for managing the network. Fortunately, the networks can be considered *stable*: there are tight relations between the nodes (e.g., key supplier and customer partnering, dedicated warehouses, etc.), and there are few and rare newcomers.

2.2   The Planning Matrix

In a supply network, the traditional boundaries of firms are getting dissolved: decisions on the use of resources should concern both internal and external capacities, the internal flow of materials should be synchronized with the incoming and outgoing flows. There are long-standing recipes to handle such structural complexity. *Aggregation* merges details in the representation of products and orders, forecasts, production processes, resource capacities, and time [11]. Problems formulated with more details are limited by shorter planning horizons. Solutions are generated in a hierarchical process where higher level solutions provide constraints to lower level problems. At the same level, *decomposition* separates planning problems into easier-to-solve subproblems.

The evolution of planning functions in production management, and recently, in supply network management resulted in a planning hierarchy [2,8] that we adopt to our modelling purpose. This so-called *planning matrix* shows long-term, medium-term and short-term planning functions organized along the main flow of materials (Fig. 2). The functions are common at each node of a supply network, though, of course, manifest themselves in different forms and complexity.

We assume an existing running network, hence network planning is out of the scope of this study. We have a special interest in *master* and *demand planning*—that specify the required output of a factory on the medium-term; in *production* and *distribution planning*—that determine what to do so as to produce the required output on medium-term; in *scheduling* that determines on the short-

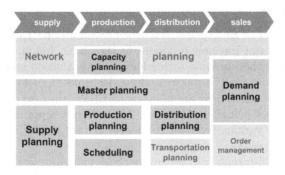

Fig. 2. Planning functions in supply networks. Functions in our scope are dark.

term how to execute production plans; and, finally, in *supply planning*—that is responsible for providing the necessary materials. Later on, we present how the selected planning function and their interrelationships can be represented in terms of roles (Sect. 3.1) and interactions (Sect. 3.2).

2.3   Requirements Towards the Organization Model

The main requirements towards modelling the organization of a supply network together with the main planning functions that must be realized at the nodes, along the entire hierarchy of the planning matrix, are as follows:

– **Generic approach** The model should be adaptable for each enterprise.
– **Common information model** Models at various levels of the planning hierarchy must be built up from common product, resource, technology, order etc. related data, stored in existing—so-called legacy—information systems.
– **Aggregation** High-level planning models should be built on lower level ones by aggregation. It must be guaranteed, that high level plans can be executed in reality; e.g., a production plan can be refined into an executable schedule.
– **Local planning and optimization** Optimization of resource usage and material management should be the responsibility of the individual nodes. In any case, a solution must be found for a problem that is posed by temporal and capacity constraints, even in case of multiple, conflicting objectives.
– **Reuse of existing planners** In a running network, at the various nodes there may be functions supported by some planner systems. The organizational model should cover such tools by providing wrappers around them.
– **Planning at various, rolling horizons** The model should capture that planning, at all levels, is performed on *rolling horizon*. As approaching actual production, the length and time units of these horizons become shorter.
– **Portfolio of mechanism** The model should enable the design, implementation and verification of a portfolio of various coordination mechanisms, ranging from cooperation to competition.

2.4 Related Work

There exists a number of *Enterprise Resource Planning* (ERP) systems for integrating data of all major business functions at the nodes, but these systems are rather transactional: they provide technology for information storing, retrieval and sharing, but do not really support making decisions [2,4]. The so-called *Advanced Planning Systems* (APS) are add-ons to ERPs: they extract some data, generate and feed back solutions. However, APSs do not support each planning function, systems at various levels of the hierarchy are hardly integrated, and behave like black boxes [8].

An object oriented framework for supply chain modelling is presented in [1]. It consists of a modelling library with design patterns and a collection of solution methods, but it does not facilitate organizational design. In contrast, a generic framework for designing multiagent systems by using principles of organizational design is presented in [9]. There are also a number of simulation studies: e.g., [3] developed a multiagent simulation based on the SCOR reference model for analyzing collaborative inventory management. More enterprise modelling tools are reviewed in [12]. We also developed a multiagent system that combined demand planning, production planning and scheduling decisions, where the distributed decisions where coordinated and the overall performance of the system was controlled by a market-based incentive mechanism [10].

3 Representation Approach: The Gaia Model

As a high-level methodology, we use Gaia [15], a specification framework for analyzing and designing the organizational model of multiagent systems. Gaia has two aspects of the modelled system: the *abstract* viewpoint helps one to conceptualize and analyze the organization, while the *concrete* viewpoint is used during the design phase to model entities which will have realization in the runtime system. Now we are dealing only with the analytic part, since the design must be preceded by an extensive research.

Analysis consists of two models: *roles* and *interactions*. Since an organization is considered a collection of roles, the main challenge is to distinguish different roles, describe them and define their interactions. A role can have a set of *permissions*—typically access rights to certain *shared information resources*—and *responsibilities*: *liveness* properties which declare what the role must do and *safety* properties which are invariants stating situations to be avoided. Liveness properties, that resemble regular expressions, consist of *activities*, which are autonomous computations, and *protocols*, which denote interactions between roles.

The main assumption of Gaia—that the structure of the system must be static—is not a real drawback in our case, since both the inter- and inner-organizational relations are sufficiently stable. However, the original framework has to be extended in several ways. Firstly, with the capability to express periodic activities. Besides the reactive functions (e.g., receiving a customer order), there are periodic activities, such as daily scheduling. This also raises the question of modelling the granularity of time. In our case, the discrete model is proper, but

the time units and horizons can differ according to different roles. We extended
the roles model also with *optimization objectives* to measure their performance.

3.1   Roles

We have distinguished the roles presented below. Most of them fit in the planning
matrix but we have introduced a few other non-planning roles, too.

ORDERMANAGER (OM) receives orders and uncertain forecasts from the
buyers. DEMANDPLANNER (DP) determines the forecasted output of the factory on the long-term, and also the safety stock levels which are held to cope
with unforeseen demand. CAPACITYPLANNER (CP) sets the capacity calendars
(e.g., number of shifts in the factory) in such a way that they should support balanced production on long-term. Notice, that under capacity planning we do not
understand the strategic decisions about the number and type of new machines,
but the usage of extant production lines and workforce. MASTERPLANNER (MP)
determines the output of the factory by specifying what actual orders have to be
satisfied on medium-term, and tunes the capacity levels so as to match resources
with expected future load. PRODUCTIONPLANNER (PP) determines what to produce on short-term: it makes the master plan actual and executable by inserting
additional orders, doing stock manipulations, and performing resource allocation
and optimization. SUPPLYPLANNER (SP) ensures the necessary raw materials for
the manufacturer by creating medium-term material requirement plans, ordering
from suppliers and maintaining the raw material inventory. SCHEDULER (SCH)
makes the assignment of smaller production units—tasks—to production lines,
the sequencing of the tasks, and determines the setup of lines between different products. DISTRIBUTION PLANNER (DiP) assigns finished goods in stock to
the buyers. TRANSPORTATIONPLANNER (TP) organizes the delivery of products,
which is usually performed by a *third party logistics* (3PL) company. MANUFAC-
TURER (M) is not a planner role—its responsibility is to execute the schedule.

While previously described roles occur in almost every node of a supply
network, we introduce a special CUSTOMER (C) role, which is attached to retailers or DCs. Customers can generate demand in at least three ways: with (1)
medium-term, certain, often periodical orders, (2) medium-term forecasts and
instant call-off and (3) short-term, unique, urgent orders.

All of these roles have different responsibilities, permissions and measurements. We have modelled them using the Gaia formalism. For instance, the
schema in Table 1 defines the SUPPLYPLANNER role with a brief description,
enumerates its protocols and activities (which are underlined), and contains the
rights of the role to access the information resources. In this schema we have
omitted the comments of the shared resources, because we will detail them in
Sect. 3.3. The liveness property states that the role does two things in parallel:
it periodically generates the medium-term material requirement plan—an internal activity—which may be followed by ordering, giving material requirement
forecast to suppliers and calling-off raw products from supplier's inventory. We
have extended Gaia's liveness operators by x^p, which can be interpreted as "x
occurs periodically" to distinguish such actions from stochastic events. Secondly,

Table 1. Schema for the SUPPLYPLANNER role

Role Schema: SUPPLYPLANNER
Description:
Ensures raw materials by creating medium-term material requirement plan, ordering and maintaining the raw product inventory.
Protocols and Activities:
Order, CustomerForecast, Call-off, Transport, Exception, CreateMaterialRequirementPlan
Permissions:
reads   *forecasts, plannedOrders, schedule, technologicalData* changes *rawProductInventoryLevels*
Responsibilities
Liveness:
SUPPLYPLANNER = (CreateMaterialRequirementPlan . [Order] . [Call-off] . [CustomerForecast])^p ∥ (Transport | Exception)$^\omega$
Safety:
• execution of the schedule must not stop because of material shortage
Objectives:
• minimal raw product inventory level
• minimal obsolete raw product inventory

it accepts incoming transports, receives and sends exceptions, which may come infinitely often—as x^ω means. Safety property in our case is a text instead of a formula, which states that raw product inventory levels cannot be too small, even if the objective of SUPPLYPLANNER is to minimize inventories.

3.2   Interactions

Most of the communication in the system is periodical and is done through shared resources. For example PRODUCTIONPLANNER creates *plannedOrders* and stores them as a shared resource, then SUPPLYPLANNER reads and processes it. For this cooperation no further interaction is needed.

There are also some cases, when no such shared resource is available— especially in interactions between nodes—and thus well-defined protocols are required. Since most of the roles occur in every node, we have to distinguish the roles at different nodes. During an interaction between two nodes, one node is in requester (R), the other is in supplier (S) position, so we differentiate them by denoting their node's position (e.g., S.ORDERMANAGER means the ORDER-MANAGER role of the supplier node). Simultaneously, a node can be in supplier position in one interaction and in requester position in another. The most important types of interactions are the following:

– Order: The ORDERMANAGER receives an external order from one of his buyers (CUSTOMER or SUPPLYPLANNER). This interaction may include due date and/or price negotiation, auctions, etc.

- **CustomerForecast**: Buyers can give forecasts instead of orders, then the supplier's DEMANDPLANNER has the responsibility to determine the quantity to produce and transport.
- **Call-off**: In case of consignment VMI, buyer (CUSTOMER or SUPPLYPLANNER) calls-off raw products from the supplier, exactly before their utilization.
- **Exception**: Due to the uncertainties, there is a need to handle deviations from plans. Exceptions can occur between any roles of the same or connected nodes, but there are some typical ones: (1) urgent order, when the factory must skip the hierarchical planning process and insert the order into the short-term plan, and (2) delayed delivery, when raw products will not be available when expected, planners should be informed to revise affected plans.
- **Transport**: This is mainly a physical interaction—transferring goods—but also some communication is needed to coordinate the process.

In Table 2 the definition of the **Order** protocol is shown. It contains the initiator and the responder roles, a brief description, as well as the input and output data.

Table 2. The **Order** Protocol Definition

Protocol name: **Order**		
Initiator: R.SUPPLYPLANNER or R.CUSTOMER	Partner: S.ORDERMANAGER	Input: order information
Description: Supplier receives an order from one of his buyers. This may include due date and/or price negotiation, auctions, etc.		Output: acceptance or rejection

Table 3. Shared information resources of SUPPLYPLANNER

Name	Description	Roles using
forecasts	Order forecasts: information about uncertain demand (product, buyer, quantity, priority, etc.). It can contain various groupings (product lines, regions, etc.).	DP, CP, MP, SP
technologicalData	Detailed BOMs, routings, resource models, etc.	CP, SCH, SP
rawProduct-InventoryLevels	Actual levels of the component inventory.	SCH, M, SP
plannedOrders	Medium-term master production plan contains the planned output of the factory.	MP, PP, SP
schedule	Short-time detailed production schedule, which will be executed on the shop floor.	SCH, M, SP

3.3 Shared Information Resources

Although it is not part of Gaia, we have found it necessary to describe shared resources—which are the main instruments of information changing—separately from the role model. In our case, most of these resources are data held in ERP systems. The following resource types can be distinguished according to the type of information they store: *demand, production resource, inventory* and *plan related* information.

Table 3 presents the resources related to SUPPLYPLANNER. There are also several non-shared resources—i.e., the SUPPLYPLANNER stores historical information about its past orders and their fulfillment for calculating service levels—but we disregard them in this high-level model. They are hidden inside the realization of roles and are not involved directly in interactions.

4 Towards Cooperative Planning

Since supply networks are unique and complex, furthermore local planning at the nodes is done in many different ways, there is no "one-size-fits-all" solution. Instead, there is a need for a portfolio of coordination mechanisms, where relations between the partners can be represented on a range of colors: from cold (competitive auctions, single business relations), through warm (cooperative planning), to hot (full integration). For reasons discussed above our interest is in cooperative planning. Hence, we assume that partners have definite incentive and commitment to cooperate, to share both their *risks* and *benefits*.[1]

The main driver for cooperation is uncertainty, which has its roots in market demand, manufacturing and supply. Uncertainty can be managed only, if:

- Powerful planner systems fill in the various planner roles locally [7]. Plans which are really executable and cost efficient make the future—even market demand—more predictable, and the actual production more profitable.
- Novel information channels are established between the partners to share the results of local planning, from detailed production schedules up to demand plans, on all the horizons and levels.

As for handling supply uncertainty, all partners need inventory buffers which are not only costly, but incur also the risk of obsolete production. Cooperation can be seen as a method of managing these buffers. A focal manufacturer can pass the responsibility of handling inventories to its suppliers, or alternatively, it can keep the raw product inventory, but the supplier sets its level (VMI) [5]. In the traditional way the manufacturer manages the inventory and decides its level. Finally, in some cases, just-in-time production with no inventories is adequate.

In the next steps the organizational model will be refined and transformed into a multiagent model. The granularity of the design will depend on the position of the nodes: planning functions of the focal manufacturer will be realized

---

[1] Tendencies in other industries, like the U.S. automotive industry point also towards strong, lasting relationships of autonomous companies. [6].

by several agents, while some of the roles at supplier nodes can be realized by single agents. Some agents will hide legacy planner systems that we have to accept as granted. We intend to use parts of the multiagent system in simulation experiments to explore weak links in the supply network, and also to provide benchmarks for validating the novel cooperation and planning mechanisms.

5 Conclusions

The paper exposed the problem of cooperative planning in supply networks, with special regard to the field of customized mass production. It was suggested, that such a complex system should be modelled with a multiagent framework. For this purpose, Gaia methodology was used in an extended form. An abstract organizational model of the network was designed by separating and describing roles, interactions and information resources. Gaia had sufficient representation power and flexibility to model planning functions and interactions in a supply network.

Acknowledgments

This work has been supported by the NKFP grant No. 2/010/2004 and the OTKA grant No. T046509.

References

1. Biswas, S., Narahari, Y.: Object Oriented Modeling and Decision Support for Supply Chains. *Eur. J. Operational Research*, **153**, 704–726, (2004).
2. Fleischmann, B., Meyr, H.: Planning Hierarchy, Modeling and Advanced Planning Systems. In: de Kok, Graves (eds): *Handbooks in OR & MS, 11, Supply Chain Management: Design, Coordination and Operation*, Elsevier, 457–523, (2003).
3. Fu, Y., Piplani, R., de Souza, R., Wu, J.: Multi-agent Enabled Modeling and Simulation Towards Collaborative Inventory Management in Supply Chains. *Proceedings of the 32nd Conference on Winter Simulation*, 1763–1771, (2000).
4. Holsapple, C.W., Sena, M.P.: ERP Plans and Decision-Support Benefits. *Decision Support Systems*, **38**, 575–590, (2005).
5. Lee, C.C., Chu, W.H.J.: Who Should Control Inventory in a Supply Chain? *Eur. J. Operational Research*, **164**, 158–172, (2005).
6. Liker, J.K., Choi, T.Y.: Building Deep Supplier Relationships. *Harvard Business Review*, **82**(12), 104–113, (2004).
7. Márkus A., Váncza J., Kis T., Kovács A.: Project Scheduling Approach to Production Planning. *CIRP Annals Manuf. Tech.*, **52**(1), 359–362, (2003).
8. Stadtler, H.: Supply Chain Management and Advanced Planning – Basics, Overview and Challeges. *Eur. J. Operational Research*, **163**, 575–588, (2005).
9. van Art, Ch.J., Wielinga, B., Schreiber, G.: Organizational Building Blocks for Design of Distributed Intelligent System. *Int. J. Human-Computer Studies*, **61**, 567–599, (2004).

10. Váncza, J., Márkus, A.: An Agent Model for Incentive-based Production Scheduling. *Computers in Industry*, **43**(2), 173–187, (2000).
11. Váncza, J., Kis, T., Kovács, A.: Aggregation - The Key to Integrating Production Planning and Scheduling. *CIRP Annals Manuf. Tech.*, **53**(1), 377–380, (2004).
12. Vernadat, F. B.: Enterprise Modelling and Integration: Principles and Applications, *Chapman & Hall*, (1996).
13. Wiendahl, H.-P., Lutz, S.: Production in Networks. *CIRP Annals Manuf. Tech.*, **51**(2), 1–14, (2002).
14. Wooldridge, M.: An Introduction to Multiagent Systems. *Wiley*, (2002).
15. Zambonelli, F., Jennings, N.R., Wooldridge, M.: Developing Multiagent Systems: The GAIA Methodology. *ACM Trans. on Software Engineering and Methodology*, **12**(3), 317–370, (2003).

Diagnosis of Plans and Agents

Nico Roos[1] and Cees Witteveen[2]

[1] Department of Computer Science, Universiteit Maastricht,
P.O.Box 616, NL-6200 MD Maastricht
roos@cs.unimaas.nl
[2] Faculty EEMCS, Delft University of Technology,
P.O.Box 5031, NL-2600 GA Delft
witt@ewi.tudelft.nl

Abstract. We discuss the application of Model-Based Diagnosis in (agent-based) planning. Here, a plan together with its executing agent is considered as a system to be diagnosed. It is assumed that the execution of a plan can be monitored by making partial observations of the results of actions. These observations are used to explain the observed deviations from the plan by qualifying some action instances that occur in the plan as behaving abnormally. Unlike in standard model-based diagnosis, however, in plan diagnosis we cannot assume that actions fail independently. We focus on two sources of dependencies between failures: such failings may occur as the result of malfunctioning of the executing agent or may be caused by dependencies between action instances occurring in a plan. Therefore, we introduce causal rules that relate health states of the agent and health states of actions to abnormalities of other action instances. These rules enable us to determine the underlying causes of plan failing and to predict future anomalies in the execution of actions.

1 Introduction

The well-known quote: *"No plan survives its first contact with the enemy"* should remind us that *diagnosis* constitutes an unavoidable part of the plan execution process.[1] Here, plan diagnosis might refer to quite different aspects of a failing plan in execution. Since there is a huge number of potential factors that might influence, or even prevent, correct plan execution, it is not surprising that current approaches to plan diagnosis are rather diverse.

The aim of this paper is to adapt and extend a classical Model-Based Diagnosis (MBD) approach to the diagnosis of plans. First, we will first show how a plan consisting of a partially ordered set of actions can be viewed as a system to be diagnosed by proposing an object oriented description of an action's behavior. Given this view, a diagnosis can be established using *partial observations* of a plan in progress.

Second, we introduce the concept of a *causal diagnosis*. Traditional MBD focuses on minimal diagnosis based on the intuitively acceptable assumption that components qualified as abnormal are failing *independently* from each other. However, as soon as *dependencies* exist between such components, the choice for minimal diagnoses cannot

---

[1] The quote is attributed to the Prussian Field Marshall Von Moltke.

M. Pěchouček, P. Petta, and L.Z. Varga (Eds.): CEEMAS 2005, LNAI 3690, pp. 357–366, 2005.
© Springer-Verlag Berlin Heidelberg 2005

be justified. As we will argue, the existence of dependencies between failing actions in a plan is often the rule instead of an exception.

Finally, we will introduce causal rules and causal diagnoses to predict future failings of actions.

Related Work. We briefly discuss some other approaches to plan diagnosis. Similar to our use of MBD as a starting point to plan diagnosis, Birnbaum et al. [1] apply MBD to *planning agents* relating health states of agents to *outcomes* of their planning activities, but they do not take into account faults that can be attributed to actions occurring in a plan as a separate source of errors.

de Jonge et al. [5] propose another approach that directly applies model-based diagnosis to plan execution. Their paper focuses on agents each having an individual plan, and where conflicts between these plans may arise (e.g. if they require the same resource). Diagnosis is applied to determine those factors that are accountable for *future* conflicts. The authors, however, do not take into account dependencies between health modes of actions and do not consider agents that collaborate to execute a common plan.

Kalech and Kaminka [9,10] apply *social diagnosis* in order to find the cause of an anomalous plan execution. They consider hierarchical plans consisting of so-called *behaviors*. Such plans do not prescribe a (partial) execution order on a set of actions. Instead, based on its observations and beliefs, each agent chooses the appropriate behavior to be executed. Each behavior in turn may consist of primitive actions to be executed, or of a set of other behaviors to choose from. Social diagnosis then addresses the issue of determining what went wrong in the joint execution of such a plan by identifying the disagreeing agents and the causes for their selection of incompatible behaviors (e.g., belief disagreement, communication errors).

Lesser et al. [2,8] also apply diagnosis to (multi-agent) plans. Their research concentrates on the use of a *causal model* that can help an agent to refine its initial diagnosis of a failing component (called a *task*) of a plan. While their approach in its ultimate intentions comes close to our approach, their approach to diagnosis concentrates on specifying the exact causes of the failing of one single *component* (tasks) of a plan. Diagnosis is based on observations of a single component without taking into account the consequences of failures of such a component w.r.t. the remaining plan.

Paper Outline. This paper is organized as follows. Section 2 introduces the preliminaries of plan-based diagnosis, while Section 3 formalizes plan-based diagnosis. Section 4 extends the formalization to determining the agent's health state. Section 5 concludes the paper.

2   Preliminaries

Model Based Diagnosis. Classical Model-Based Diagnosis (MBD) [3,4,12] uses a model of a system to identify causes of discrepancies between the observed behavior of the system and the behavior predicted by the model. The model that is applied consists of a set $Comp$ of components, a set M_c of health modes for each component $c \in Comp$, and a specification of a component's behavior given a health mode. The result of MBD is a suitable assignment of health modes to the components, called a *diagnosis*, such that the actually observed output is *consistent* with this health mode qualification or can be *explained* by this qualification. Usually, in a diagnosis one requires the number of components qualified as abnormal to be minimized.

States. We consider plan-based diagnosis as a simple extension of the model-based diagnosis where the model is not a description of an underlying system but a *plan* of an agent. Before we discuss plans, we discuss our *object-* or *resource-based* view on the world, assuming that for the planning problem at hand, the world can be simply described by a set $Obj = \{o_1, o_2, \ldots, o_n\}$ of objects, their respective *value domains* S_i and and their (current) values $s_i \in S_i$.[2] A *state of the world* σ then is an element of $S_1 \times S_2 \times \ldots \times S_n$. It will not always be possible to give a complete state description. Therefore, we introduce a *partial state* as an element $\pi \in S_{i_1} \times S_{i_2} \times \ldots \times S_{i_k}$, where $1 \leq k \leq n$ and $1 \leq i_1 < \ldots < i_k \leq n$. We use $O(\pi)$ to denote the set of objects $\{o_{i_1}, o_{i_2}, \ldots, o_{i_k}\} \subseteq Obj$ specified in such a state π. The value s_j of object $o_j \in O(\pi)$ in π will be denoted by $\pi(j)$. The value of an object $o_j \in Obj$ not occurring in a partial state π is said to be unknown (or unpredictable) in π, denoted by $\perp$. Partial states can be ordered with respect to their information content: π is said to be contained in π', denoted by $\pi \sqsubseteq \pi'$, iff $O(\pi) \subseteq O(\pi')$ and $\pi'(j) = \pi(j)$ for every $o_j \in O(\pi)$. We say that two partial states π, π' are *equivalent* modulo a set of objects O, denoted by $\pi =_O \pi'$, if for every $o_j \in O$, $\pi(j) = \pi'(j)$. Finally, we define the partial state π restricted to a given set O, denoted by $\pi \upharpoonright O$, as the state $\pi' \sqsubseteq \pi$ such that $O(\pi') = O \cap O(\pi)$.

Goals. An (elementary) goal g of an agent specifies a set of states an agent wants to bring about using a plan. Here, we specify each such a goal g as a constraint, that is a relation over some product $S_{i_1} \times \ldots \times S_{i_k}$ of domains.

We say that a goal g is satisfied by a partial state π, denoted by $\pi \models g$, if the relation g contains at least one tuple $(v_{i_1}, v_{i_2}, \ldots, v_{i_k})$ such that $(v_{i_1}, v_{i_2}, \ldots v_{i_k}) \sqsubseteq \pi$. We assume each agent to have a set G of such elementary goals $g \in G$. We use $\pi \models G$ to denote that all goals in G hold in π, i.e. for all $g \in G$, $\pi \models g$.

Actions and Action Schemes. An *action scheme* or plan operator α is represented as a function that replaces the values of a subset $O_\alpha \subseteq Obj$ by other values, dependent upon the values of another set $O'_\alpha \supseteq O_\alpha$ of objects. Hence, every action scheme α can be modeled as a (partial) function $f_\alpha : S_{i_1} \times \ldots \times S_{i_k} \to S_{j_1} \times \ldots \times S_{j_l}$, where $1 \leq i_1 < \ldots < i_k \leq n$ and $\{j_1, \ldots, j_l\} \subseteq \{i_1, \ldots, i_k\}$. The objects whose value domains occur in $dom(f_\alpha)$, the *input resources* of α, will be denoted by $dom_O(\alpha) = \{o_{i_1}, \ldots, o_{i_k}\}$ and, likewise $ran_O(\alpha) = \{o_{j_1}, \ldots, o_{j_l}\}$ denotes the *output resources* of α. Note that $ran_O(\alpha) \subseteq dom_O(\alpha)$. This functional specification f_α constitutes the *normal* behavior of the action scheme, denoted by f_α^{nor}.

The correct execution of an action may fail either because of an inherent malfunctioning or because of a malfunctioning of an agent responsible for executing the action, or because of unknown external circumstances. In all these cases we would like to model the effects of executing such failed actions. To keep the discussion simple, in the sequel we only consider two health modes, the normal behavior mode: *nor*, and the

---

[2] In contrast to the conventional approach to state-based planning, cf. [7].

most general abnormal behavior mode: ab. The most general abnormal behavior of action α is specified by the function f_α^{ab}, where $f_\alpha^{ab}(s_{i_1}, s_{i_2}, \ldots, s_{i_k}) = (\perp, \perp, \ldots, \perp)$.[3]

Given a set $\mathcal{A}$ of action schemes, we will need to consider a set $A \subseteq inst(\mathcal{A})$ of *instances* of actions in $\mathcal{A}$. Such instances will be denoted by small roman letters a_i. If $type(a_i) = \alpha \in \mathcal{A}$, a_i is said to be of type α. If the context permits we will use "actions" and "instances of actions" interchangeably.

Plans.   A plan is a tuple $P = \langle \mathcal{A}, A, < \rangle$ where $A \subseteq Inst(\mathcal{A})$ is a set of instances of actions occurring in $\mathcal{A}$ and $(A, <)$ is a partial order. The partial order relation $<$ specifies a precedence relation between these instances: $a < a'$ implies that the instance a must finish before the instance a' may start. We will denote the *transitive reduction* of $<$ by $\ll$, i.e., $\ll$ is the smallest subrelation of $<$ such that the transitive closure $\ll^+$ of $\ll$ equals $<$.

We assume that if in a plan P two action instances a and a' are independent, in principle they may be executed concurrently. This means that the precedence relation $<$ at least should capture all resource dependencies that would prohibit concurrent execution of actions. Therefore, we assume $<$ to satisfy the following *concurrency requirement*:

If $ran_O(a) \cap dom_O(a') \neq \varnothing$ then $a < a'$ or $a' < a$.[4]

That is, for concurrent instances, domains and ranges do not overlap.

Example 1. Figure 1 gives an illustration of a plan. Arrows relate the objects an action uses as inputs and produces as its outputs to the action itself. In this plan, the dependency relation is specified as $a_1 \ll a_3$, $a_1 \ll a_4$, $a_2 \ll a_4$, $a_2 \ll a_5$, $a_4 \ll a_7$, $a_5 \ll a_8$ and $a_4 \ll a_6$. Note that the last dependency has to be included because a_6 changes the value of o_2 needed by a_4. The actions a_4, a_5 and a_6 show that not every object occurring in the domain of an action needs to be affected by the action.   ∎

3   Standard Plan Diagnosis

Let us assume, for the moment, that each action instance can be viewed as an independent component of a plan. To each action instance a a health mode $m_a \in \{nor, ab\}$ can be assigned and the result is called a *qualified* plan. In establishing which part of the plan fails, we are only interested in those actions qualified as abnormal. Therefore, we define a qualified version P_Q of a plan $P = \langle \mathcal{A}, A, < \rangle$ as a tuple $P_Q = \langle \mathcal{A}, A, <, Q \rangle$, where $Q \subseteq A$ is the subset of instances of actions qualified as abnormal (and therefore, $A - Q$ the subset of actions qualified as normal).

Since a qualification Q corresponds to assigning the health mode ab to every action in Q and since $f_a^{ab}(s_{i_1}, s_{i_2}, \ldots, s_{i_k}) = (\perp, \perp, \ldots, \perp)$ for every action $a \in Q$ with $type(a) = \alpha$, the results of anomalously executed actions are unpredictable.

Qualified Plan Execution.   For simplicity, when a plan P is executed, we will assume that every action takes a unit of time to execute. We are allowed to observe the execution

---

[3] This definition implies that the behavior of abnormal actions is essentially unpredictable.

[4] Note that since $ran_O(a) \subseteq dom_O(a)$, this requirement excludes overlapping ranges of concurrent actions, but domains of concurrent actions are allowed to overlap as long as the values of the object in the overlapping domains are not affected by the actions.

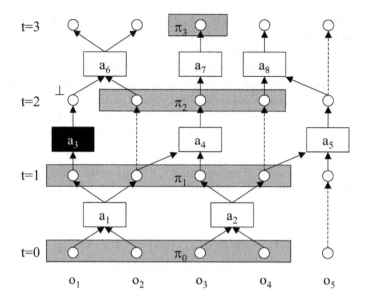

Fig. 1. Plan execution with abnormal actions

of a plan P at discrete times $t = 0, 1, 2, \ldots, k$ where k is the depth of the plan, i.e., the longest $<$-chain of actions occurring in P. Let $depth_P(a)$ be the depth of action a in plan $P = \langle \mathcal{A}, A, < \rangle$.[5] We assume that the plan starts to be executed at time $t = 0$ and that concurrency is fully exploited, i.e., if $depth_P(a) = k$, then execution of a has been completed at time $t = k + 1$. Thus, all actions a with $depth_P(a) = 0$ are completed at time $t = 1$ and every action a with $depth_P(a) = k$ will be started at time k and will be completed at time $k + 1$. Note that thanks to the above specified concurrency requirement, concurrent execution of actions having the same depth leads to a well-defined result.

Let P_t denote the set of actions a with $depth_P(a) = t$, let $P_{>t} = \bigcup_{t'>t} P_{t'}$, $P_{<t} = \bigcup_{t'<t} P_{t'}$ and $P_{[t,t']} = \bigcup_{k=t}^{t'} P_k$. Execution of P on a given initial state σ_0 will induce a sequence of states $\sigma_0, \sigma_1, \ldots, \sigma_k$, where σ_{t+1} is generated from σ_t by applying the set of actions P_t to σ_t. Generalizing to partial states and transitions from partial states, we define the (predicted) effect of the execution of plan P on a given (partial) state π at time $t \geq 0$, denoted by (π, t).

We say that $(\pi', t + 1)$ is (directly) generated by execution of P_Q from (π, t), abbreviated by $(\pi, t) \to_{Q;P} (\pi', t + 1)$, iff the following conditions hold:

1. $\pi' \restriction ran_O(a) = f_a^{nor}(\pi \restriction dom_O(a))$ for each $a \in P_t - Q$ such that $dom_O(a) \subseteq O(\pi)$, that is, the consequences of all actions a enabled in π can be predicted and occur in π'.[6]

---

[5] Here, $depth_P(a) = 0$ if $\{a' \mid a' \ll a\} = \varnothing$ and $depth_P(a) = 1 + max\{depth_P(a') \mid a' \ll a\}$, else. If the context is clear, we often will omit the subscript P.

[6] An action a is enabled in a state π if $dom_O(a) \subseteq O(\pi)$.

2. $O(\pi') \cap ran_O(a) = \varnothing$ for each $a \in Q \cap P_t$, since the result of executing an abnormal action cannot be predicted (even if such an action is enabled in π);
3. $O(\pi') \cap ran_O(a) = \varnothing$ for each $a \in P_t$ with $dom_O(a) \not\subseteq O(\pi)$, that is, even if an action a is enabled in (the complete state) σ_t, if a is not enabled in $\pi \sqsubseteq \sigma_t$, the result is not predictable and therefore does not occur in π', since it is not possible to predict the consequences of actions that depend on values not defined in π.
4. $\pi'(i) = \pi(i)$ for each $o_i \notin ran_O(P_t)$, that is, the value of any object not occurring in the range of an action in P_t should remain unchanged. Here, $ran_O(P_t)$ is a shorthand for the union of the sets $ran_O(a)$ with $a \in P_t$.

For arbitrary values of $t \leq t'$ we say that (π', t') is (directly or indirectly) generated by execution of P_Q from (π, t), denoted by $(\pi, t) \rightarrow^*_{Q;P} (\pi', t')$, iff the following conditions hold:

1. if $t = t'$ then $\pi' = \pi$;
2. if $t' \geq t + 1$ then $(\pi, t) \rightarrow_{Q;P} (\pi'', t+1)$ and $(\pi'', t+1) \rightarrow^*_{Q;P} (\pi', t')$.

Note that $(\pi, t) \rightarrow^*_{\varnothing;P} (\pi', t')$ denotes the normal execution of a normal plan $P_\varnothing$.

Example 2. Figure 1 gives an illustration of an execution of a plan with abnormal actions. Suppose action a_3 is abnormal and generates a result that is unpredictable ($\bot$). Given the qualification $Q = \{a_3\}$ and the partially observed state π_0 at time point $t = 0$, we predict the partial states π_i as indicated in Figure 1, where $(\pi_0, t_0) \rightarrow^*_{Q;P} (\pi_i, t_i)$ for $i = 1, 2, 3$. Note that since the value of o_1 and of o_5 cannot be predicted at time $t = 2$, the result of action a_6 and of action a_8 cannot be predicted and π_3 contains only the value of o_3.   ∎

Diagnosis. Suppose now that we have a (partial) observation $obs(t) = (\pi, t)$ of the state of the world at time t and an observation $obs(t') = (\pi', t')$ at time $t' > t \geq 0$ during the execution of the plan P. We would like to use these observations to infer the health states of the actions occurring in P. Assuming a normal execution of P, we can (partially) predict the state of the world at a time point t' given the observation $obs(t)$: if all actions behave normally, we predict a partial state $\pi'_\varnothing$ at time t' such that $obs(t) \rightarrow^*_P (\pi'_\varnothing, t')$. Since we do not require observations to be made systematically, $O(\pi')$ and $O(\pi'_\varnothing)$ might only partially overlap. Therefore, if all actions are executed normally, the values of the objects that occur in both the predicted state and the observed state at time t' should match, i.e, we should have

$$\pi' =_{O(\pi') \cap O(\pi'_\varnothing)} \pi'_\varnothing.$$

If this is not the case, the execution of some action instances must have gone wrong and we have to determine a qualification Q such that the predicted state derived using Q agrees with π'. This is nothing else then a straight-forward extension of the diagnosis concept in MBD to plan diagnosis (cf. [4]):

Definition 1. *Let $P = \langle \mathcal{A}, A, < \rangle$ be a plan with observations $obs(t) = (\pi, t)$ and $obs(t') = (\pi', t')$, where $t < t' \leq depth(P)$ and let $obs(t) \rightarrow^*_{Q;P} (\pi'_Q, t')$ be a derivation assuming a qualification Q.*
Then Q is said to be a plan diagnosis *of $\langle P, obs(t), obs(t') \rangle$ iff $\pi' =_{O(\pi') \cap O(\pi'_Q)} \pi'_Q$.*

So in a plan diagnosis Q the observed partial state (π') at time t' and the predicted state (π'_Q) assuming the qualification Q at time t' agree upon the values of all objects occurring in both states.

Example 3. Consider again Figure 1 and suppose that we did not know that action a_3 was abnormal and that we observed $obs(0) = ((s_1, s_2, s_3, s_4), 0)$ and $obs(3) = (s'_1, s'_3, s'_5), 3)$. Using the normal plan derivation relation starting with $obs(0)$ we will predict a state $\pi'_\varnothing$ at time $t = 3$ where $\pi'_\varnothing = (s''_1, s''_2, s''_3)$. If everything is ok, the values of the objects predicted as well as observed at time $t = 3$ should correspond, i.e. we should have $s'_j = s''_j$ for $j = 1, 3$. If, for example, only s'_1 would differ from s''_1, then we could qualify a_6 as abnormal, since then the predicted state at time $t = 3$ using $Q = \{a_6\}$ would be $\pi'_Q = (s''_3)$ and this partial state agrees with the predicted state on the value of o_3. ∎

Note that for all objects in $O(\pi') \cap O(\pi'_Q)$, the qualification Q provides an *explanation* for the observation π' made at time point t'. Hence, for these objects the qualification provides an *abductive diagnosis* [3] for the normal observations. For all observed objects in $O(\pi') - O(\pi'_Q)$, no value can be predicted given the qualification Q. Hence, by declaring them to be unpredictable, possible conflicts with respect to these objects if a normal execution of all actions is assumed, are resolved. This corresponds with the idea of a *consistency-based diagnosis* [12].

If Q is a plan diagnosis of $\langle P, obs(t), obs(t') \rangle$, then every superset $Q' \supseteq Q$ is also a plan diagnosis, since in that case we have $\pi'_{Q'} \sqsubseteq \pi'_Q$ and therefore $\pi' =_{O(\pi') \cap O(\pi'_Q)} \pi'_Q$ implies $\pi' =_{O(\pi') \cap O(\pi'_{Q'})} \pi'_{Q'}$. Clearly then, the smaller a diagnosis is, the more values it will predict that are also actually observed in the resulting plan state. This, like in MBD, is a reason for us to prefer *minimum* diagnoses among the set of minimal diagnoses.

But there is a caveat: a minimum diagnosis only minimizes abnormalities to explain deviations; as important however for a diagnosis might be its *information content*, i.e. the exactness it provides in predicting the values of the variables occurring in the observed state π'. This means that besides *minimizing* the cardinality of abnormalities another criterion could be *maximizing* $|O(\pi') \cap O(\pi'_Q)|$.

Definition 2. *Given plan observations* $\langle P, (\pi, t), (\pi', t') \rangle$, *a qualification Q is said to be a* minimum plan diagnosis *if for every plan diagnosis Q' it holds that* $|Q| \leq |Q'|$.

Q *is said to be a* maximum informative plan-diagnosis *iff for all plan diagnoses Q^*, it holds that* $|O(\pi') \cap O(\pi'_Q)| \geq |O(\pi') \cap O(\pi'_{Q^*})|$.

Note that every maximum informative diagnosis is a minimal diagnosis. So both minimum plan diagnoses and maximum informative plan diagnoses are the result of different criteria for selecting minimal diagnoses, as the following example shows:

Example 4. To illustrate the difference between minimum plan diagnosis and maximum informative diagnosis, consider again the plan execution depicted in Figure 1. Given $obs(0)$ and $obs(3)$ and a deviation in the value of o_2 at time $t = 3$, there are three possible minimum diagnoses: $D_1 = \{a_1\}$, $D_2 = \{a_3\}$ and $D_3 = \{a_6\}$. D_2 and D_3 are also maximum-informative diagnoses. ∎

4   Causes of Plan-Execution Failures

Unlike in classical MBD, minimum diagnosis and maximum-informative diagnosis need not provide the best explanation for the differences between observed effects of a plan execution and the predicted effects. The reason is that often in a plan, instances of actions do not fail independently. For example, suppose that we have a plan for carrying luggage from a depot to a number of waiting planes. Such a plan might contain several instances of a drive action pertaining to the same carrier controlled by an agent. Suppose that an instance a_i of some drive action (type) α behaves abnormally because of malfunctioning of the carrier. Then it is reasonable to assume that other instances a_j of the same drive action that occur in the plan *after* a_i can be predicted to behave abnormally, too. Another possibility is that a number of instances of actions is related to the malfunctioning of an *agent* executing several actions in the plan. For example, in the luggage example, the carrier is controlled by a driving agent. If this agent itself is not functioning well, all driving actions as well as loading and unloading actions might be affected.

Such dependencies between action instances and between agent health states and action instances imply that sometimes qualifying an instance of an action as being abnormal implies that other instances of actions must be qualified a being abnormal, too. Minimum and information-maximum diagnosis do not take these dependencies between action failures into account. Therefore, we must take into consideration the underlying *causes* of a plan-execution failure.

Causal Rules.   We consider a plan together with its executing agent as the system to be diagnosed. An agent will be represented by a set H of specific health states. To identify causes of action failures, we use a set R of *causal rules* in combination with plan diagnosis. The intuitive idea behind causal rules is that the rules enables us to predict failures of future actions given the agent's health state and a set of failed actions. A causal rule is a rule that can appear in the following forms:

> $(h; \alpha_1, \alpha_2, \ldots, \alpha_k) \to \alpha_{k+1}$, where $k \geq 0$, $h \in H$ is a health state of the plan executing agent and, for $i = 1, 2 \ldots, k+1$, $\alpha_i \in \mathcal{A}$ are action types. This type of rule relates the occurrence of an agent health state h and a set of action abnormalities occurring at time t to the inference of a failed action at time $t+1$. If $k = 0$ and $h \neq nor$, this rule establishes a health state as a single cause for action failure.

To define the effect of applying R to a set of (unique) instances of actions occurring in a plan, we first construct the set $inst(R)$ of instance of actions with respect to given plan $P = \langle \mathcal{A}, A, < \rangle$ as follows:

> For every rule r of the form $(h; \alpha_1, \alpha_2, \ldots, \alpha_k) \to \alpha_{k+1} \in R$, $inst(R)$ contains the instances $(h; a_{i_1}, a_{i_2}, \ldots, a_{i_k}) \to a_{i_{k+1}}$, whenever there exists a $t \geq 0$ such that $\{a_{i_1}, a_{i_2}, \ldots, a_{i_k}\} \subseteq P_{\leq t}$ and $a_{i_{k+1}} \in P_{>t}$.

Note that the failure of an action $a_{i_{k+1}}$ only depends on $a_{i_1}, a_{i_2}, \ldots, a_{i_k}$ if the agent is healthy: $h = nor$.

The intuitive idea behind a causal diagnosis is to be able to explain a given plan diagnosis Q by a (usually smaller) set of qualifications (causes) Q' together with some health state h of the agent established at time t using the set of causal rules R. Using such a pair consisting of a health state and a qualification should enable us to generate, using the rules in R, a set containing Q.

Definition 3. *The set of a causal consequence $C_{R,h}(Q)$ of a qualification $Q \subset A$ given the health state $h \in H$ and the causal rules R is defined as:*

$$C_{R,h}(Q) = Cn_A(inst(R) \cup Q \cup \{h\}).$$

Here, the instances of causal rules are interpreted as Horn clauses, Q and $\{h\}$ as sets of atoms, and Cn denotes the logical consequence operator.

To simplify the notation, we will omit the subscripts R and h from the operator C.

Now we define a causal diagnosis as a qualification Q such that its set of consequences $C(Q)$ constitutes a diagnosis:

Definition 4. *Let $P = \langle A, A, < \rangle$ be a plan, R a set of causal rules and let $obs(t)$ and $obs(t')$ be two observations with $t < t'$. Then a qualification $Q \subseteq A$ is a causal diagnosis of $(P, obs(t), obs(t'))$ if $C(Q) \cap P_{[t;t']}$ is a diagnosis of $(P, obs(t), obs(t'))$.*

Among the causal diagnoses, we distinguish *minimum* and *maximum informative* causal diagnoses. Moreover, we distinguish *closed set* causal diagnoses; i.e. causal diagnoses Q such that $C(Q) = Q$.

Causal Diagnoses and Prediction.   Except for playing a role in establishing causal *explanations* of observations, (causal) diagnoses also can play a significant role in the *prediction* of future results (states) of the plan or even the attainability of the goals of the plan. First of all, we should realize that a diagnosis can be used to enhance observed state information as follows: Suppose that Q is a causal diagnosis of a plan P based on the observations $obs(t)$ and $obs(t')$ for some $t < t'$, let $obs(t) \rightarrow^*_{C(Q);P} (\pi'_Q, t')$ and let $obs(t') = (\pi', t')$. Since $C(Q)$ is a diagnosis, π' and π'_Q agree upon the values of all objects occurring in both states. Therefore we can combine the information contained in both partial states by merging them into a new partial state $\pi'_{\sqcup} = \pi'_Q \sqcup \pi'$. Here, the merge $\pi^1 \sqcup \pi^2$ of two partial states π^1 and π^2 is simply defined as the partial state π where $\pi(j) = \pi^i(j)$ iff $\pi^i(j)$ is defined for $i = 1, 2$ and undefined else. $\pi'_{\sqcup}$ can be seen as the partial state that can be obtained by direct observation at time t and indirectly by making use of previous observations and plan information.

In the same way, we can use this information and the causal consequences $C(Q)$ to derive a prediction of the partial states derivable at times $t'' > t'$:

Definition 5. *Let Q is a causal diagnosis of a plan P based on the observations (π, t) and (π', t') where $t < t'$. Furthermore, let $obs(t) \rightarrow^*_{C(Q);P}(\pi'_Q, t')$ and let $obs(t') = (\pi', t')$. Then, for some time $t'' > t'$, (π'', t'') is the partial state predicted using Q and the observations if $(\pi'_Q \sqcup \pi', t') \rightarrow^*_{C(Q);P}(\pi'', t'')$.*

In particular, if $t'' = depth(P)$, i.e., the plan has been executed completely, we can predict the values of some objects that will result from executing P and we can check which goals $g \in G$ will still be achieved by the execution of the plan, based on our current knowledge. That is, we can check for which goals $g \in G$ it holds that $\tau \models g$. So causal diagnosis might also help in evaluating which goals will be affected by failing actions.

5 Conclusion

We have presented a new object-oriented model to specify plans and to apply techniques developed for model-based agent diagnosis. We distinguished two types of diagnosis: minimum plan diagnosis and maximum informative diagnosis to identify (*i*) minimum sets of anomalously executed actions and (*ii*) maximum informative (w.r.t. to predicting the observations) sets of anomalously executed actions. Assuming that a plan is carried out by a single agent, anomalously executed action can be correlated if the anomaly is caused by some malfunctions in the agent. Therefore, (*iii*) causal diagnoses have been introduced and we have extended the diagnostic theory enabling the prediction of future failure of actions. We intend to extend our model along three lines. First, we wish to extend the model such that the agent might evolve through several abnormal states. The resulting model will be related to diagnosis in Discrete Event Systems [6,11]. Second, we intend to investigate plan repair in the context of the agent's current (abnormal) state. Third, we would like to extend the diagnostic model with sequential observations and iterative diagnoses.

References

1. L. Birnbaum, G. Collins, M. Freed, and B. Krulwich. Model-based diagnosis of planning failures. In *AAAI 90*, pages 318–323, 1990.
2. N. Carver and V.R. Lesser. Domain monotonicity and the performance of local solutions strategies for cdps-based distributed sensor interpretation and distributed diagnosis. *Autonomous Agents and Multi-Agent Systems*, 6(1):35–76, 2003.
3. L. Console and P. Torasso. Hypothetical reasoning in causal models. *International Journal of Intelligence Systems*, 5:83–124, 1990.
4. L. Console and P. Torasso. A spectrum of logical definitions of model-based diagnosis. *Computational Intelligence*, 7:133–141, 1991.
5. F. de Jonge and N. Roos. Plan-execution health repair in a multi-agent system. In *PlanSIG 2004*, 2004.
6. R. Debouk, S. Lafortune, and D. Teneketzis. Coordinated decentralized protocols for failure diagnosis of discrete-event systems. *Journal of Discrete Event Dynamical Systems: Theory and Application*, 10:33–86, 2000.
7. R. E. Fikes and N. Nilsson. Strips: A new approach to the application of theorem proving to problem solving. *Artificial Intelligence*, 5:189–208, 1971.
8. Bryan Horling, Brett Benyo, and Victor Lesser. Using Self-Diagnosis to Adapt Organizational Structures. In *Proceedings of the 5th International Conference on Autonomous Agents*, pages 529–536. ACM Press, 2001.
9. M. Kalech and G. A. Kaminka. On the design of social diagnosis algorithms for multi-agent teams. In *IJCAI-03*, pages 370–375, 2003.
10. M. Kalech and G. A. Kaminka. Diagnosing a team of agents: Scaling-up. In *AAMAS 2004*, 2004.
11. Y. Pencolé, M. Cordier, and L. Rozé. Incremental decentralized diagnosis approach for the supervision of a telecommunication network. In *DX01*, 2001.
12. R. Reiter. A theory of diagnosis from first principles. *Artificial Intelligence*, 32:57–95, 1987.

Dialectical Theory for Multi-agent Assumption-Based Planning

Damien Pellier and Humbert Fiorino

Laboratoire Leibniz, 46 avenue Félix Viallet F-38000 Grenboble, France
{Damien.Pellier, Humbert.Fiorino}.imag.fr

Abstract. The purpose of this paper is to introduce a dialectical theory for plan synthesis based on a multi-agent approach. This approach is a promising way to devise systems based on agent planners in which the production of a global shared plan is obtained by conjecture/refutation cycles. Contrary to classical approaches, our contribution relies on agents' dialectical reasoning: in order to take into account the partial knowledge and the heterogeneous skills of the agents, we propose to consider the planning problem as a defeasible reasoning where agents exchange proposals and counter-proposals and are able to conjecture *i.e.,* formulate plan steps based on hypothetical states of the world. The dialogue between agents is a joint investigation process allowing agents to progressively prune objections, solve conjectures and elaborate solutions step by step.

1 Introduction

The problem of plan synthesis achieved by autonomous agents in order to solve complex and collaborative tasks is still an open challenge. Increasingly new application areas can benefit from this research domain: for instance, cooperative robotics [1] or composition of semantic web services [2] when considering actions as services and plans as composition schemes. From our point of view, multi-agent planning can be likened to the process used in automatic theorem proving. In a sense, a plan can be considered to be a particular proof based on specific rules, called actions. In this paper, we draw our inspiration from the proof theory described by Lakatos. According to [3], a correct proof does not exist in the absolute. At any time, an experimentation or a test can refute a proof. If one single test leads to a refutation, the proof is reviewed and it is considered as mere conjecture which must be repaired in order to reject this refutation and consequently to become less questionable. The new proof can be subsequently tested and refuted anew. Therefore, the proof elaboration is an iterative non monotonous process of conjectures - refutations - repairs.

The same is true of our approach. The plan synthesis problem is viewed as a dialectical and collaborative goal directed reasoning about actions. Each agent can refine, refute or repair the ongoing team plan. If the repair of a previously refuted plan succeeds, it becomes more robust but it can still be refuted later. If the repair of the refuted plan fails, agents leave this part of the reasoning and explore another possibility: finally "bad" sub-plans are ruled out because there is no agent able to push the investigation process further. As in an argumentation with opponents and proponents, the current plan

M. Pěchouček, P. Petta, and L.Z. Varga (Eds.): CEEMAS 2005, LNAI 3690, pp. 367–376, 2005.
© Springer-Verlag Berlin Heidelberg 2005

is considered as an acceptable solution when the proposal/counter-proposal cycles end and there is no more objection.

The originality of this approach relies on the agent's capabilities to elaborate plans under partial knowledge and/or to produce plans that partially contradict its knowledge. In other words, in order to reach a goal, such an agent is able to provide a plan *which could be executed if certain conditions were met*. Unlike "classical" planners, the planning process does not fail if some conditions are not asserted in the knowledge base, but rather proposes an Assumption-Based Plan or *conjecture*. Obviously, this conjecture must be *reasonable*: the goal cannot be considered "achieved" and the assumptions must be as few as possible because they become new goals for the other agents. For instance, suppose that a door is locked: if the agent seeks to get into the room behind the door and the key is not in the lock, the planning procedure fails even though the agent is able to fulfill 100% of its objectives behind the door. Another possibility is to suppose for the moment that the key is available and then plan how to open the door etc. whereas finding the key might become a new goal to be delegated. To that end, we designed a planner that relaxes some restrictions regarding the applicability of planning operators.

Our approach differs from former ones in two points. First of all, unlike approaches that emphasize the problem of controlling and coordinating a posteriori local plans of independent agents by using negotiation [4], argumentation [5], or synchronization [6] *etc.*, the dialectical theory for plan synthesis presented here focuses on generic mechanisms allowing agents to jointly elaborate a global shared plan and carry out collective actions. Secondly, by elaboration, we mean plan production and not instantiation of predefined global plan skeletons [7,8]. This is achieved by composing agents' skills *i.e.,* the actions they can execute for the benefit of the group. Thus, the issues are: how can agents produce plans as parts of the global proof with their partial and incomplete beliefs? what kind of refutations and repairs agents can propose to produce robust plans? and how to define the conjecture - refutation protocol so as to converge to an acceptable solution plan?

In this paper, we introduce a multi-agent assumption-based planning approach. In section 2, we present the primary notions used in this approach. Then, in section 3, we define the concept of *proof board* used by agents to collaboratively build a solution plan and finally, in section 4, the dialectical mechanisms for the conjecture-refutation process is presented.

2   Primary Notions

We start by defining the language used to describe agents' beliefs. This language is based on a first-order language $\mathcal{L}$ in which there is a finite number of predicates symbols and constants symbols but no function symbols. A *state* is a set of ground atoms of $\mathcal{L}$. Since $\mathcal{L}$ has no functions symbols, the set S of all possibles states s is guaranteed to be finite. An atom p holds in s iff $p \in s$. If g is a set of literals (*i.e.,* atoms and negated atoms), we will say that s *satisfied* g (denoted $s \models g$).

Now, let us introduce, the definition of a planning operator used by agents. An planning operator defines a transition operation from a state to another one.

Definition 1 (Planning Operator). *A* planning operator *is a triple* $o = \langle name(o),$
$precond(o), effects(o) \rangle$ *whose elements are as follows:*

- *name*(o), *the name of the operator,* $n(x_1, \ldots, x_k)$ *where* n *is a symbol and* $x_1, \ldots,$
  x_k *define operator's parameters.*
- *precond*(o) *and effects*(o), *the* preconditions *and* effects *of* o, *respectively defining*
  the literals that must be held in the state where the operator is applied and the
  literals that must be added (denoted effect$(o)^+$*) or removed (denoted effect*$(o)^-$*),*
  to compute the transition operation.

Although we use the same operator representation as in classical planning, the operator semantic in our approach is different. In classical planning, an operator is applicable to a state s if o is ground and s is a state such precond$(o) \subseteq s$. Our approach relaxes
this constraint: all operators are applicable to a state s. Hence, we must distinguish
facts that hold in s and facts that do not hold. The second are called *assumptions*. An
assumption defines a literal $p \in$ precond(o) such p do not hold in s. We use assump(o)
to denote the set of assumptions needed to apply an operator o in a particular state s.
The state resulting of the application of o to s_i is the state:

$$s_{i+1} = ((s_i \cup \text{assump}(a)) - \text{effects}^-(a)) \cup \text{effects}^+(a)$$

For instance, consider the initial belief state of an agent $s_0 = \{at(cont,loc1)\}$ and a
simple operator that can be performed by this agent to move a container from a location
to another one: name$(o) = $ move$(c,l1,l2)$; precond$(o) = \{$connected$(l1,l2)$, at$(c,l1)\}$ and
effect$(o) = \{\neg at(c,l1), at(c,l2)\}$. In this example, the agent has no information about the
connection between the locations loc1 and loc2. In order to apply the move operator, the
agent must assume the assumption connected(loc1,loc2). The state resulting of the application of the move operator is the state: $s_1 = \{$connected(loc1, loc2), at(cont,loc2)$\}$.

Before going further and introducing our multi-agent planning model, we must clarify one point. We say that an assumption is a precondition of an operator o that do not
hold in the state s where the operator is applied. Thus, there are two cases: i) if a precondition p is not contained in s, the fact must be added to the agent's belief and simply
considered as a *hypothetical fact*; ii) if a precondition does not hold because its negation
is contained in s, the agent must first remove the negation before adding the precondition. We call this kind of assumption a *fact negation*.

Assumptions are important opportunities for improving collaborative synergy between agents. They can be refined by the other agents in order to produce the supposed
facts (*e.g.*, by connecting the two locations loc1 and loc2). They are viewed as subgoals
that must be fulfilled by other agents.

Definition 2 (Agent). *An agent is a triple* $ag = \langle name(ag), operators(ag), beliefs(ag) \rangle$,
where:
- *name*(ag), *the name of the agent;*
- *operators*(ag), *a set of operators, i.e., the skills of the agent;*
- *beliefs*(ag), *a set of literals, i.e., the initial beliefs of the agent.*

In classical planning, a planning domain is defined by a set of operators. In our
approach, operators are included in agents' description. Thus, we define a multi-agent
planning domain as a set of agents.

Definition 3 (Multi-Agent Planning Domain). *A* multi-agent planning domain $\mathcal{D}$ *is defined as a set of agents.*

Finally, we need to define the notion of multi-agent planning problem. A multi-agent planning problem must define the goals that must be reached and the set of agents that must solve it.

Definition 4 (Multi-Agent Planning Problem). *A* multi-agent planning problem *is a couple* $\mathcal{P} = \langle \mathcal{AG}, g \rangle$, *where:*

- *$\mathcal{AG}$ defines a set of agents' names;*
- *g is a set of literals that must be reached by the agents defined in $\mathcal{AG}$.*

Consider a simple domain containing four agents: a farmer, a miller, a baker and a conveyor. The farmer sows wheat, which must be harvested. The miller grinds the farmer's wheat to produce flour. The baker makes bread with miller's flour and finally the conveyor is in charge of moving the goods needed by the other agents. An instance of a multi-agent planning problem can define with $\mathcal{AG} = \{\text{famer}, \text{miller}, \text{baker}, \text{convoyor}\}$ and $g = \{\text{has-goods}(\text{baker}, \text{bread}, 2)\}$.

3 Conjectures Space Search

The plan synthesis relies on dialectical exchanges between agents as expected in a debate. Agents interact collaboratively in the dialogue so as to construct a plan without assumption, fulfilling the assigned goals. In order to build such a plan and organize the dialog between agents, we need a structure, called *proof board*. This structure has two main functions: it must be able to represent the space search as in classical planning and it must be able to specify the dialectical rules used by agents to interact.

3.1 Conjectures and Plans

First, let us refine the notion of conjecture used in our approach. We have informally introduced a conjecture as a plan that can be executed if certain conditions were met. In classical planning, a plan is a set of ground operators organized into some structure, *e.g.*, a sequence. However, a sequence of operators is a particular plan that reflects the intrinsic constraints of the operators. It seems to be to much restrictive for a multi-agent approach of collaborative planning, *e.g.*, it is no possible to define concurrent actions. Therefore, to find out what is needed in a conjecture, consider an informal planning step (shown figure 1) on the simple example previously introduced with the farmer, the miller, the baker and the conveyor.

baker$_1$:   "I can make 2 breads to solve the goal, but I need 2 flour containers available in loc1."

conveyor$_1$: "I can transport the flours containers at loc1, but I don't know where I must load the goods."

miller$_1$:   "I propose to sell you the flours containers. I needed to be payed 4 euros for that and find someone to transport flour containers from loc2 to loc1. Moreover, I need a wheat container available in loc2 to grind the flour."

baker$_2$:   "Thank you for your help, miller, but I have not enough money."
miller$_2$:   "Ok, give me only 2 euros."
baker$_2$:   "Good deal, I pay you."
conveyor$_2$: "Thus, I understand that I must load the flour in loc2."
farmer$_1$:   "I propose to sell you a wheat container. I need to be payed 1 euros for
               that and find someone to transport the container from loc3 to loc2."
miller$_3$:   ...

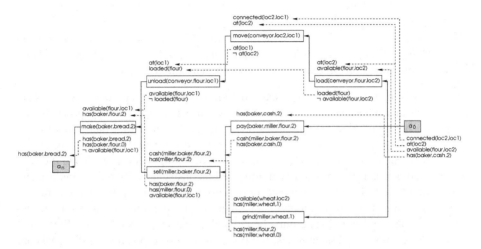

Fig. 1. Example of conjecture: each boxes is an operator with preconditions above and effects below. Solid arrows are ordering constraints, dashed arrows are causal links and binding constraints are implicit or shown directly in the operator parameters. This representation is based on [9].

Operators. Initially, baker$_1$ proposes to add the operator make-bread to reach the goal $g = \{$ has(baker,bread,2)$\}$. This operator make two assumptions: available(flour, loc1) and has(baker,flour,2). These assumptions must be refined. Thus, conveyor$_1$ and miller$_1$ propose recursively to add others operators or sub-conjecture to reach these two new goals.

Ordering Constraints. Consider the sub-conjecture added by conveyor$_1$; it achieves its purpose only if it is constrained to come *before* the make-bread operator. But should this conjecture come before or after the miller conjecture? Both options are possible. We use the least commitment principle of not adding constraints unless it is strictly needed. If no constraint are specified the conjecture between conveyor$_1$ and miller$_1$, these two conjectures will be able to run concurrently.

Causal links. Because there is no explicit notion of current state (distributed on the agents), an ordering constraint does not say, for instance, that the flour stays available at loc1 until make-bread operator is performed. Hence, we need to encode explicitly in the conjecture the reason why the conveyor$_1$ sub-conjecture was added: to satisfy the assumption available(flour, loc1). The relation between the baker's conjecture and the conveyor's one with respect to available(flour, loc1), is called a *causal link*.

Binding Constraints. Operators are added in a conjecture with systematic variable renaming. For instance, we must ensure that the conveyor conjecture concerns the same container flour and the same location loc1 as those in operator make-bread.

Definition 5 (Conjecture). *A conjecture is a tuple* $\chi = \langle \mathcal{A}, \prec, \mathcal{B}, \mathcal{C} \rangle$, *where:*

- $\mathcal{A} = \{a_1, \ldots, a_k\}$ *is a set of partially instantiated operators.*
- $\prec$ *is a set of ordering constraints on $\mathcal{A}$ of the form $(a_i \prec a_j)$.*
- $\mathcal{B}$ *is a set of binding constraints on $\mathcal{A}$ of the form $x = y$, $x \neq y$ or $x \in D_x$, where D_x is the domain of x.*
- $\mathcal{C}$ *is a set of causal links of the form $(a_i \xrightarrow{p} a_j)$, such that a_i and a_j are operators in $\mathcal{A}$, the constraint $a_i \prec a_j$ is in $\prec$, assumption p is an effect of a_i and a precondition of a_j and finally the binding constraints between a_i and a_j about p are in $\mathcal{B}$.*

The proof board is a conjecture space defining a directed graph whose vertices are conjectures and whose edges correspond to the *transition operation* proposed by the agent. An outgoing edge from a vertex χ is a transition operation that transforms χ into a successor χ'. A transition operation can be: a refinement (*i.e.*, adding operators to prove an assumption), a refutation (*i.e.*, highlighting inconsistencies in the conjecture) and a repair of a previously highlighted inconsistency. Therefore, multi-agent assumption-based planning is a search in the proof board from a initial conjecture to a node recognized as a solution plan. Note that due to no explicit current state representation, goals and initial state must be defined as particular conjectures. Since preconditions are possibly assumptions, the propositions corresponding to the goals are represented as preconditions of a dummy operator a_n. Similarly, the initial state is represented as the effects of a dummy action a_0. The effects of a_0 define the union of the agents' beliefs. We make the assumption that the agents' beliefs are consistent.

3.2 Solution Plan

Let us now specify what is a solution plan to a planning problem $\mathcal{P} = \langle \mathcal{AG}, g \rangle$. A solution plan is a conjecture that has particular properties. First, a conjecture is a solution plan if the conjecture makes no assumption. But according to the conjecture definition, it is not enough. A solution conjecture must define a consistent set of ordering constraints, binding constraints and causal links. These properties allow us to define three kinds of refutations.

Proposition 1 (Solution Plan[1]). *A conjecture $\chi = \langle \mathcal{A}, \prec, \mathcal{B}, \mathcal{C} \rangle$ is a solution plan to a planning problem $\mathcal{P} = \langle \mathcal{AG}, g \rangle$, if χ has no assumption and χ can not be refuted.*

Definition 6 (Ordering Refutation). *An action a_k of a conjecture χ refutes an ordering constraint $a_i \prec a_j$ iff $a_k \prec a_i$ and $a_j \prec a_k$.*

Definition 7 (Binding Refutation). *An action a_k of a conjecture χ refutes an binding constraint iff one of the following condition holds:*

---
[1] Can be proved inductively on the number of operators in $\mathcal{A}$.

1. *if there is an operator a_k that contains a variable x such that $x \in D_x$ and x is not consistent with $\mathcal{B}$.*
2. *if there is an operator a_k that contains two variables x and y such that $x = y$ is not consistent with $\mathcal{B}$.*
3. *if there is an operator a_k that contains two variables x and y such that such that $x \neq y$ is not consistent with $\mathcal{B}$.*

Definition 8 (Causal Refutation). *An action a_k of a conjecture χ refutes a causal link $a_i \xrightarrow{p} a_j$, iff:*

- *a_k has an effect $\neg q$ and $\neg q$ is not consistent with p, i.e., p and q are unifiable.*
- *ordering constraints $(a_i \prec a_k)$ and $(a_k \prec a_j)$ are consistent with $\prec$.*
- *binding constraints resulting of the unification of p and q are consistent with $\mathcal{B}$.*

4 Dialectical Mechanisms

In order to tackle the dialectical mechanisms to collaboratively build a solution plan, let us remember the definition of the proof board. The proof board defines a conjectures space where edges represent transition operations: refine, refute or repair. A conjecture is a solution plan if it does not contain assumption and if no agent is able to refute it. This definition gives us two tips to specify the dialectical mechanism. Indeed, the first condition can be reached by refining or repairing. On the contrary, the second condition needs a deliberation process to guarantee that no agent can refute the conjecture. Therefore, we distinguish two layers: i) an *informational layer* that defines the rules to exchange refinements, refutations and repairs about the current conjecture. Each new conjecture suggested by an agent produces new goals to be achieved by the other agents; ii) a *contextualization layer* in which agents can decide to stop interacting when they believe a solution was found or not reachable. Moreover agents can decide to change the dialogue context by forwarding or backtracking into the proof board if the current conjecture has been refuted or none of the agents can refine its assumptions.

4.1 Informational Layer

The characterization of the solution plan brings elements needed for the specification of the speech acts used in the informational layer. The main principle of the multi-agent assumption based planning is to let the agents choose a transition operation to apply to the proof board until χ contains no more assumptions and until χ cannot be refuted. The basic steps of agent's dialectical mechanisms are the following:

- Select a conjecture χ on which to apply a transition operation.
- Select a transition operation to apply to χ.
- Find ways to resolve the transition operation.
- Select a resolver for the transition operation.
- Assert the resolver, *i.e.,* refine, refute or repair.

For each transition operation that can be applied, we introduce a speech act: i) a speech act *refine* is performed by an agent to express the refinement of a conjecture. A refinement can be specified by adding a set of operators, a set of ordering constraints, a set of binding constraints and finally a set of causal links (*e.g.,* miller$_1$ in example 1); ii) a speech act *refute* is performed by an agent to express the refutation of a conjecture. A refutation highlights that an action produces a set of ordering inconsistencies or a set of binding inconsistencies or finally a set of causal inconsistencies. The computation of the inconsistencies are based on the formal definition of the three kinds of refutation previously presented (*e.g.,* baker$_2$ in example 1); iii)a speech act *repair* is performed by an agent to express that a conjecture can be repaired by adding and removing respectively a set of operators, a set of ordering constraints, a set of binding constraints and finally a set of causal links (*e.g.,* miller$_2$ in example 1). Note that all informational speech acts can be performed only if they were not already proposed by other agents. This condition guarantees that the proof board defines a loop free directed graph. In order to find ways to resolve a transition operation agents use the following mechanisms:

Refinement. If a conjecture χ contains an operator a_j that makes an assumption p (see figure 2): i) If a causal link $(a_i \xrightarrow{p} a_j)$ can be established such that a_i is already in the conjecture, the refinement will contain the causal link $(a_i \xrightarrow{p} a_j)$, the ordering constraint $(a_i \prec a_j)$ and the binding constraints to unify p with the effects of a_i; ii) Otherwise, agents must compute a sub conjecture χ' to prove p. The refinement will contain all the elements of χ', a causal link $(a_i \xrightarrow{p} a_j)$ to specify which operator a_i of χ' reaches the assumption p done by a_j and a ordering constraint $(a_i \prec a_j)$. Note that we have already shown in [10] how an agent can produce such conjecture.

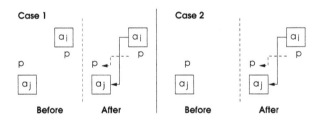

Fig. 2. The left figure shows a refinement when an operator already reached an assumption and right figure shows a refinement by adding a new conjecture

Repair [2]. If there is a causal refutation on $(a_i \xrightarrow{p} a_j)$ by an action a_k that has an effect $\neg q$, and q is unifiable with p, then the resolvers are any of the following: i) add an ordering constraint such that a_k occurs before the causal link; ii) add an ordering constraint such that a_k occurs after the causal link; iii) add a binding constraint that makes q and p non-unifiable.

Refutation. The causal refutation can be computed by testing all triples of actions of a conjecture χ. The ordering refutation can be computed by testing that the ordering

---

[2] Repairs of binding refutation and ordering refutation are not discussed here.

constraint represent a loop free graph. Finally, the binding refutation of type 1 and 2 (see definition 7) can be computed in linear time, whereas the type 3 raises a general NP-complete Constraint Satisfaction Problem (CSP).

4.2 Contextualization Layer

The informational layer defines the basic mechanisms to build a solution plan. Is that enough? Not quite. The dialectical mechanism must guarantee the soundness and the completeness of the collaborative plan synthesis process. Now let us consider the proof board as a search in an AND/OR tree. The assumptions and the refutations correspond to AND branches because all of them must be resolved in order to find a solution. For each assumption and refutation the possible resolvers (*i.e.,* refinement and repair) correspond to OR branches because only one of them is needed in order to find a solution. In order to guarantee the completeness, agents must coordinate their exploration. Therefore, we consider that agents can apply a transition operation only on a specific conjecture in the proof board, called *current conjecture*. This conjecture defines the dialog context. The speech acts define in the contextualization layer allow agents to change the dialog context. We introduce four contextualization speech acts: i) a speech act *prop.solve* is performed by an agent when it believes that a solution plan χ is reached. When the speech act *prop.solve* is proposed each agent checks if it can refute χ. If χ cannot be refuted each agent acknowledges the solve proposition. Otherwise, they refute χ and the dialectical process is extended; ii) a speech act *prop.failure* is performed by an agent when it believes that no solution plan exists. Like the previous speech act, when speech act *prop.failure* is performed, each agent checks if there is a conjecture in the proof board on which they can apply a transition operation. In this case, each agent acknowledges the failure proposition. Otherwise, the dialectical process continues; iii) a speech act *prop.backward* is performed by an agent when it believes that no resolver can be proposed to go further in the current conjecture exploration; iv) a speech act *prop.foreward* is performed by an agent when it believes that agent have no more resolvers to apply at the current conjecture.

Note that all contextualization speech acts define a joint commitment between agents. For instance, all agents must agree on the plan solution before stopping the dialectical plan synthesis process. The computation of the next current conjecture when the speech acts *prop.backward* and *prop.foreward* are proposed by agents is based on A* heuristics. Recall that A* uses a heuristic estimate $f(\chi)$ of the overall solution cost consisting of, in the one hand $g(\chi) = $ cost of the current conjecture χ and in the other hand $h(\chi) = $ estimate of the additional cost of the best complete solution that extends χ. We propose to think $f(\chi)$ as a measure of conjecture *complexity, i.e.,* "good" conjecture are simple conjectures. What is significant to compute $f(\chi)$? [11] indicates that the most promising heuristic measure for conjecture selection is the number of actions contained in the conjecture and the number of assumptions done. Therefore, we define $g(\chi)$ as the number of action of χ, *i.e.,* the complexity of the conjecture and $h(\chi)$, the number of assumptions done, since each remaining assumption must be established by some sub-conjecture. Note that this heuristic can be used locally by the agent to choose the best resolver to submit to the other agents.

5   Conclusion

The dialectical plan synthesis theory model presented in this paper relies on plan production and revision by conjecture/refutation cycles: for a given goal, agents try collaboratively to produce a valid proof, *i.e.,* a plan. In order to demonstrate the goal assigned to the system, agents interact by using a conventional dialogue approach that can be split in two layers: *informational layer*, which defines the conventions to refine, refute or repair conjectures and *contextualization layer*, which defines the conventions to allow agents to change the dialogue state. The dialogue rules are described according to the *proof board*. The proof board represents the public part of the communication storing the different exchanges between agents. The advantage of the dialectical plan synthesis is to merge in the collaborative plan generation, the composition and the coordination steps. It also includes the notion of uncertainty in the agents' reasoning and allows the agents to make conjectures and to compose their heterogeneous competences. Moreover, we apply conjecture/refutation to structure the multi-agent reasoning as a collaborative investigation process. However, former works on synchronization, coordination and conflict resolution are integrated through the notions of refutation/repairs. From our point of view, this approach is suitable for applications in which agents share a common goal and in which the splitting of the planning and the coordination steps (when agents have independent goals, they locally generate plans and then solve their conflicts) becomes difficult due to the agents strong interdependence.

References

1. Alami, R., Fleury, S., Herrb, M., Ingrand, F., Robert, F.: Multi robot cooperation in the martha project. IEEE Robotics and Automation Magazine **5** (1997) 36–47
2. Wu, D., Parsia, B., Sirin E, Hendler, J., Nau, D.: Automating daml-s web services composition using shop2. In: Proceedings of International Semantic Web Conference. (2003)
3. Lakatos, I.: Proofs and Refutations: The Logic of Mathematical Discovery. Cambridge University Press, Cambridge, England (1976)
4. Zlotkin, G., Rosenschein, J.: Negotiation and conflict resolution in non-cooperative domains. In: Proceedings of the American National Conference on Artificial Intelligence, Boston, Massachusetts (1990) 100–105
5. Tambe, M., Jung, H.: The benefits of arguing in a team. Artificial Intelligence Magazine **20** (1999) 85–92
6. Clement, B., Barrett, A.: Continual coordination through shared activities. In: Proceedings of the International Conference on Autonomous Agent and Muti-Agent Systems. (2003) 57–67
7. Grosz, B., Kraus, S.: Collaborative plans for complex group action. Artificial Intelligence **86** (1996) 269–357
8. D'Inverno, M., Luck, M., Georgeff, M., Kinny, D., Wooldridge, M.: The dmars architecture: A specification of the distributed multi-agent reasoning system. Autonomous Agents and Multi-Agent Systems **9** (2004) 5–53
9. Ghallab, M., Nau, D., Traverso, P.: Automated Planning Theory and Practice. Morgan Kaufmann Publishers (2004)
10. Pellier, D., Fiorino, H.: Assumption-based planning. In: In Proceedings of the International Conference on Advances in Intelligence Systems Theory and Applications, Luxemburg (2004)
11. Gerevini, A., Schubert, L.: Accelerating partial-order planners: Some techniques for effective search control and pruning. Journal of Artificial Intelligence Research **5** (1996) 95–137

Keeping Plan Execution Healthy[*,**]

Femke de Jonge, Nico Roos, and Jaap van den Herik

Universiteit Maastricht, IKAT,
P.O. Box 616, NL-6200, Maastricht
{f.dejonge, roos, herik}@cs.unimaas.nl

Abstract. Unexpected events during the execution of a plan may lead to conflicts: we then say that the plan execution is unhealthy. This paper presents a new model that enables agents (1) to control plan-execution health and (2) to regain health when necessary. The agents can utilize the model to predict consequences of occurring disruptions and thus detect unhealthy situations. With the help of the model's predictions, agents can correct the execution of tasks within the plan to regain health. The applicability of the presented model is demonstrated by introducing two multi-agent protocols to keep the plan execution healthy. Finally, we investigate the solving capabilities and the efficiency of our method in experiments using randomly generated plans. Our conclusion is that a reasonable proportion of unhealthy situations can be solved adequately by corrections in the plan execution instead of performing a replanning procedure.

1   Introduction

Plan development and plan execution in complex, dynamic environments are difficult tasks. This explains the tendency to apply intelligent computer programs to support these tasks. Currently, the (initial) plan development in fields such as Air Traffic Control (ATC) is to a large extent performed by planning software. For plan execution, however, such software is not widely available, even though the execution of plans in complex and dynamic environments requires continuous control and adaptation. Our research focusses on employing a multi-agent system for plan-execution control and adaptation. Multi-agent systems seem an obvious means to this end since the plans in environments such as ATC are mainly distributed.

An adequate plan normally satisfies all constraints imposed by its environment and by other plans. Hence, such a plan is conflict free. This is a property that should be kept persistently during the execution of the plan. We denote a plan execution as healthy, when during the execution of the plan no constraints are violated. A conflict-free plan can have an unhealthy plan execution when unexpected changes in the environment occur. The process of keeping a plan execution healthy can be viewed as a continuous cycle of detecting unhealthy situations and regaining health. Plan-execution health can be regained by either correcting the execution or changing the plan (i.e., replanning).

---

[*] A more elaborated version appeared in [1].

[**] This research is supported by the Technology Foundation STW, applied science division of NWO and the technology programme of the Ministry of Economic Affairs (the Netherlands).

M. Pěchouček, P. Petta, and L.Z. Varga (Eds.): CEEMAS 2005, LNAI 3690, pp. 377–387, 2005.

In our opinion, corrections within the execution of a plan have three advantages when compared to replanning, viz. (1) they are often easier to accomplish, (2) they are less influential for the environment and the rest of the plan, and (3) especially within domains such as ATC, plan changes are more costly than changes in execution. For instance, gate changes require a large amount of organization as the passengers need to be informed, the engaged ground handling needs to be relocated, and so on. Not surprisingly, within the ATC practice, the first attempt to regain health is always to try and find solutions within the execution of the current plan. Therefore, we emphasize that before applying replanning, agents should try to regain health by correcting the execution of the plan without changing the plan itself.

In summary, the contribution of this paper is that it enables agents to keep the plan execution healthy by applying small corrections within the plan execution. For this purpose, we developed a model that agents can apply (1) to control the health of the plan execution and (2) to find corrections to regain health when necessary.

The outline of the paper is as follows. Section 2 discusses the background of our approach. In section 3, we present our model for plan-execution health control and repair in a multi-agent system. Section 4 provides formal definitions of when a plan execution is healthy, and how plan-execution health can by regained by applying small corrections to the execution. In section 5, we present two protocols that implement our model and in section 6, we applied these protocols in experiments to evaluate the applicability of our model. Section 7 concludes the paper.

2   Background

Planning notions. As stated in the introduction, we address the execution of a plan after it is created. Therefore, we assume that a plan is already developed. We view a plan as a partially ordered set of steps. These steps are actions carried out at specific points in the plan, while the actions are instantiations of general operations [2]. The execution of the steps usually has a certain duration and may require resources that have to be shared with other steps of the same plan or of other plans. We assume that a set of constraints describes requirements with respect to shared resources. Within ATC, for instance, we can think of safety constraints and of environmental constraints on noise pollution. Since we consider a multi-agent context, we assume that the plan is distributed over the agents. For example, in the ATC case, we can think of a multi-agent system containing one agent for each aircraft (controlling its plan).

Plan descriptions generally see the steps as atomic parts that make up the plan. Here, we view them as tasks that require several, often reactive, activities of the executing agents. These activities cannot be planned because they depend on the status of the environment (cf. when driving a car from A to B, not every overtaking manoeuvre can be planned in advance). Therefore, the way the plan should be executed is not specified exactly and we may state that the tasks have some boundaries or margins within which the execution may vary. In particular in air traffic, it is common to specify margins for the duration of tasks. For instance, it is the primary responsibility of a pilot or aircraft agent, flying from one waypoint to the next one, to keep the aircraft in the assigned flight path within an assigned time interval. The activities of adjusting speed, height, and directions are not specified in the plan, but are assumed to be applied within the boundaries. However, the activities contribute to the attempt to follow the plan, i.e., to keep plan execution within the specified margins such as the flight path and the time interval. So, the unplannable activities within plan execution influence whether the constraints are satisfied or violated. Even when a plan is executed within its margins, it still may happen that constraint violations occur (e.g., due to overtaking manoeuvres when driving a car from A to B).

Related research. The main contribution of this paper is the model for plan-execution health control and repair. A fundamental property of such a model is, in our opinion, the ability to represent the current and future states of the plan and its environment. Models that are at the basis of such a property are Discrete Event Systems (DESs) and Markov Decision Models (see, for an overview [3]). A DES models (1) the states that a task (or object) can reach by nodes, and (2) the changes of states by events. Markov Decision Models are a specific type of DES, in which changes of states are probabilistically determined. Our model is partially inspired by these two models.

The TÆMS modelling framework used by [4] is also related to our model, since their plan representation is rather similar. In TÆMS, a plan is represented by task descriptions that express the uncertainty in plan execution. Raja et al. use TÆMS for plan development. Instead of determining how agents can execute a plan cooperatively, our research focusses on predicting the states that the tasks will reach, and how to influence this to regain plan execution health.

Our goal to keep plan execution healthy somewhat overlaps the goal of so-called continual planning (for an overview of distributed continual planning, see [5]). In continual planning, the processes of planning and execution are interleaved so as to deal with uncertainties in a dynamic environment. desJardins et al. [5] state that the most preferred planning technique for continual planning is hierarchical plan refinement. It is our opinion that plan refinement cannot resolve all possible unhealthy situations, since there is a level within each plan for which its (sub)activities are unplannable.

Running example. The following example will be used as a running example throughout the text. Consider a small airport with only one runway used for both arrival and departure. Assume that two aircraft agents, agent A and agent B, each have their own (sub)plan, connected through a constraint. A's plan is (1) to taxi from the gate to the runway, and (2) to take off from the runway. B's plan is (1) to arrive at the airport (at the runway), and then (2) to taxi from the runway to its gate. The obvious constraint that connects the two plans is that the runway cannot be used by more than one aircraft at the same time. Therefore, the agents have agreed on a mutual plan in which B lands before A takes off. Although the plan satisfies the constraint, still, small changes in the execution can cause a violation of constraints imposed on the plan execution. For instance, assume that A is a bit early as the aircraft speeded up while taxiing, and B is a bit delayed because of heavy head wind during its flight. Then, they still may not use the (same part of the) runway at the same time, but the two aircraft might pass one another at a close distance. However, a close distance could cause a violation of the safety constraints on the distance that should be kept between the two aircraft.

3   Model Description

The model assigns a health state to each task in a plan. This health state may change during the execution of a task caused by unforeseen environmental influences or by activities of the agent executing the task. The external influences of the environment will be modelled as disruption events and the activities of agents, assuming that agents do not deliberately disrupt the execution of tasks, as repair events.

The assignment of health states to tasks will enable us to evaluate the effects of disruption events that have occurred during the execution of tasks. Our first (implicit) assumption of the model is that disruption events are observable. This assumption will not hold in general, especially in environments where not all possible disruption events can be known. However, the model is also useable, with minor adaptations, if agents are able to determine the actual health states of tasks, for instance through plan diagnosis (see, e.g., [6]). A second assumption is that the plans of the individual agents are linear. This assumption is mainly made for the clarity of the presentation of the model. Moreover, it is a common practice in ATC. The model is, however, also applicable if agents have partially ordered plans.

Formally, we model a multi-agent plan as a quadruple consisting of four sets: $MAP = (A, PD, R, Cst)$. The sets are: (1) a set of agents A, (2) a set of plan descriptions PD, containing one plan description for each agent: $PD = \bigcup_{i=1}^{|A|} PD_i$, (3) a set of common rules R specifying the execution of the plan in general, and (4) a set of constraints Cst between the agents' plans. In the remainder of this section, these four sets will successively be explained in more detail.

We assume that each *agent* in set A has its individual plan. All plans are gathered within MAP. There are no other plans outside MAP that the agents should consider.

A *plan description* $PD_i = (P_i, \mathcal{S}_i, \mathcal{E}_i, \tau_i, \sigma_i)$ describes how the plan of agent i will be executed. The base of the plan description is the sequence of tasks $P_i = \langle t_{i,0}, t_{i,1}, ..., t_{i,n} \rangle$ which the agent wants to execute in this specific order. We use $\overline{P_i}$ to denote the corresponding set of all tasks in sequence P_i. To describe the health of a task, we have the sets $\mathcal{S}_i$ and $\mathcal{E}_i$ containing for each task a set of states and a set of events respectively. The functions τ_i and σ_i formalize, in combination with the common rules R, the execution of tasks within a plan (we will specify this further on).

During the execution of an agent's plan, a task $t_{i,j}$ is in a certain *state*. Each task has its own set of possible states: $S_{i,j} \in \mathcal{S}_i$. We distinguish three types of state: pending, active, and finish. For each task $t_{i,j}$ holds: $S_{i,j} = S_{i,j}^{pending} \cup S_{i,j}^{active} \cup S_{i,j}^{finish}$. There is only one pending state for each task, this is the state in which the task is awaiting before it is being executed. Thus, $S_{i,j}^{pending} = \{s_{i,j}^{pending}\}$. When the current task (task1) finishes, the next task (task2) will become active by changing from the pending state to an active state (which state that is, depends on the execution of the previous task). Finally, when task2 is completed, task2 changes from an active state to a finish state and consequently, the then subsequent task (task3) is triggered.

Each plan has one start task: $t_{i,0}$, with $S_{i,0} = \{s_{i,0}^{pending}, s_{i,0}^{finish}\}$. The start task has only one pending and one finish state. When the start conditions are fulfilled, this start task will change from the pending to the finish state, which will cause the next task to begin execution (viz. go from the pending state to an active state).

State changes are caused by *events*. Each task $t_{i,j}$ has its own set of events: $E_{i,j} \in \mathcal{E}_i$, with $E_{i,j} = E_{i,j}^{finish} \cup E_{i,j}^{disrupt} \cup E_{i,j}^{repair}$. Finish events are triggered when pre-defined conditions are fulfilled and they change tasks from an active to a finish state. Disruption events are externally caused and represent unexpected changes in the execution of a task that might effect the plan-execution health. Finally, the repair events are executed by the agent to regain the plan-execution health when necessary. They represent the corrections in the plan execution. A task's state is the result of the sequence of events during the plan execution, and will be represented by predicate $ts(t_{i,j}, s, E)$, where $t_{i,j} \in \overline{P_i}$ is the task for which event sequence $E = \langle e_1, ..., e_k \rangle$ leads to state $s \in S_{i,j}$. We use the predicate $ats(t, s)$ to denote that task t will achieve state s during the actual plan execution, i.e., the past, current, and expected events lead to s.

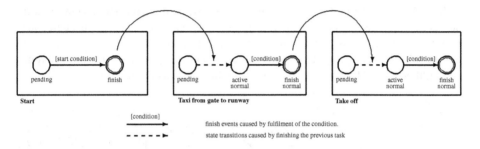

Fig. 1. Normal plan execution of agent A

Figure 1 illustrates the normal execution of a plan of the departing agent A in our running example. The plan consists of three tasks: $P_1 = \langle t_{1,\text{Start}}, t_{1,\text{Taxi}}, t_{1,\text{Take\_off}} \rangle$, and sequence $\langle e_{\text{finish\_Start}}, e_{\text{finish\_Taxi}}, e_{\text{finish\_Take\_off}} \rangle$. Note that, for reasons of clarity, the figure does not present the whole model, but shows only the occurring states.

As stated above, we formalize the execution of tasks within an agent's plan by the partial functions τ_i and σ_i, and by the set of common rules R from MAP. The partial function τ_i maps a task, its state, and an event to a new state: $\tau_i : \overline{P_i} \times \bigcup_j S_{i,j} \times \bigcup_j E_{i,j} \nrightarrow \bigcup_j S_{i,j}$. (with $\nrightarrow$ denoting a partial mapping). τ_i is defined such that only events in $E_{i,j}$ can change the state of a task $t_{i,j}$ into a new state in $S_{i,j}$. We assume that there is exactly one finish event for each task. A task can, by the definition of τ_i, reach different finish states depending on the previous state the task is in. The partial function σ_i returns the new state in the next task based on the previous task and its finish state: $\sigma_i : \overline{P_i} \times \bigcup_j S_{i,j}^{finish} \nrightarrow \bigcup_j S_{i,j}$.

The *set of common rules* R in MAP consists of three rules. The first rule in R describes how a state transition of a task is caused by an event e_k:

$$(ts(t_{i,j}, s, \langle e_1, ..., e_{k-1} \rangle) \wedge \tau_i(t_{i,j}, s, e_k) = s') \rightarrow ts(t_{i,j}, s', \langle e_1, ..., e_k \rangle) \quad (1)$$

The second rule in R describes the immediate activation of the next task when the previous task is finished:

$$(ts(t_{i,j}, \text{pending}, \langle e_1, ..., e_{k-1} \rangle) \wedge ts(t_{i,j-1}, s, \langle e_1, ..., e_k \rangle) \wedge \sigma_i(t_{i,j-1}, s) = s')$$
$$\rightarrow ts(t_{i,j}, s', \langle e_1, ..., e_k \rangle) \quad (2)$$

The third rule in R defines which states will or will not be reached during the plan execution. We use the predicate $Events(\{E_1, ..., E_m\})$ to denote that these sequences of events will occur (a sequence E_i for each P_i).

$$\exists e_1, ..., e_k (Events(\{\langle e_1, ..., e_k, ..., e_n \rangle_i, ...\}) \wedge ts(t_{i,j}, s, \langle e_1, ..., e_k \rangle)) \leftrightarrow ats(t_{i,j}, s) \tag{3}$$

We denote RPD as the set of all instantiations of the rules in R for all plan descriptions PD_i.

The set Cst in MAP is the set of *constraints*, with each constraint composed of predicates $ats(,)$ and logic symbols $\{\vee, \wedge, \neg\}$. Moreover, constraints are only defined on finish states, as they can be viewed as a summary of the execution of a task. An example of a constraint is $cst = \neg(ats(t, s) \wedge ats(t', s')) \vee ats(t'', s'')$, in which s, s', s'' are finish states. The constraints are 'demands' on the plan execution that should be fulfilled. A constraint violation or conflict occurs when the expected execution is inconsistent with a certain constraint. We will assume that when plans are executed normally (only finish events occur), all constraints will hold and the plan execution is in good health. Consequently, the constraint violations are caused by disruption events, and might be solved by repair events to regain the plan-execution health.

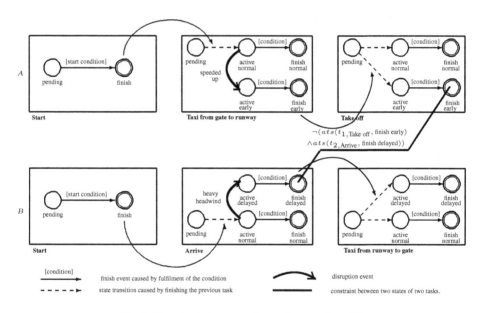

Fig. 2. Disturbed plan executions of agents A and B

Figure 2 illustrates a disrupted execution of the plans of the departing agent A and arriving agent B in our running example. Both plans consist of three tasks: $P_1 = \langle t_{1,\text{Start}}, t_{1,\text{Taxi}}, t_{1,\text{Take\_off}} \rangle$, and $P_2 = \langle t_{2,\text{Start}}, t_{2,\text{Arrive}}, t_{2,\text{Taxi}} \rangle$. The event sequences of the plan execution are $\langle e_{\text{finish\_Start}}, e_{\text{Speeded\_up}}, e_{\text{finish\_Taxi}}, e_{\text{finish\_Take\_off}} \rangle_1$ and $\langle e_{\text{finish\_Start}}, e_{\text{Heavy\_head\_wind}}, e_{\text{finish\_Arrive}}, e_{\text{finish\_Taxi}} \rangle_2$. In this setting, the constraint $\neg(ats(t_{1,\text{Take\_off}}, \text{finish\_early}) \wedge ats(t_{2,\text{Arrive}}, \text{finish\_delayed}))$ between the two plans is violated.

In general, we assume that each agent has knowledge (i) of its individual plan description PD_i, (ii) of the common rules R, (iii) of the constraints $Cst_i \subseteq Cst$ that are relevant for its plan. Moreover, we assume that each agent i is able to communicate to the other agents to which subplans the constraints Cst_i apply.

4   Health and Health Repair

We assume that an agent notices when disruption events occur during the execution of a plan (for instance through its sensors). Based on the detected disruption events, an agent can construct the sequence of past events (up to and including the current or latest events) in the so-called current event history CEH_i (with $CEH = \bigcup_i CEH_i$). We assume that in the future, from current task $t_{i,j}$ on, no disruption or repair events will occur. Hence, for each task in the remaining plan, one finish event will occur. The resulting sequence of events $FE_i = \langle e_j, e_{j+1}, ..., e_n \rangle$, with $e_h \in E_{finish}$, will be called the future event sequence. The current event history can be combined with the future events sequence into the future event history: $FEH_i = CEH_i \circ FE_i$ (with $\circ$ denoting a concatenation of the two sequences, and $FEH = \bigcup_i FEH_i$). Based on the set of future event histories, FEH, we can define plan-execution health as follows.

Definition 1. *A plan execution is healthy iff $Events(FEH) \cup RPD \vdash Cst$.*

When an unhealthy plan execution has been detected, the agents should correct the execution of the plans such that no constraint violations will occur in the future and the plan-execution health is restored. To achieve this, each agent can insert repair events in the future event history in order to create new state paths in its plan execution.

A plan-execution health repair FER is a set of event sequences containing all future event sequences with some repair events inserted, in such a way that by applying FER, all constraints hold again.

Definition 2. *A plan-execution health repair FER is a set of sequences $FER = FE \uplus RE$ where RE is a minimal subset of E_{repair} s.t. $Events(CEH \circ FER) \cup RPD \vdash Cst$.*

We use $FER = FE \uplus RE$ to denote that the events in RE are placed at specified places within the sequences collected in FE. Note that for the same FE and RE different sets $FER = FE \uplus RE$ are possible, depending on the placement of the repair events in the sequences in FE. With a minimal RE we limit the subsets of RE to those which have no subset that will construct a plan-execution health repair as well.

Note that computing a plan-execution health repair corresponds to applying abduction. Without proof, we state that definition 2 is equivalent to a FER such that $Events(CEH \circ FER) \cup RPD \cup Cst \nvdash \perp$ holds. This corresponds to applying consistency checks. Since both abduction and consistency-check problems are known to be NP-equivalent, in general, plan-execution health repair is NP-equivalent as well.

In our example, A can apply an event e_{Wait} during the taxi task, which changes the state of task $t_{1,\text{Taxi}}$ from 'active_early' to 'active_normal', and subsequently the state of task $t_{1,\text{Taxi}}$ to 'active_normal'. This correction of plan execution resolves the constraint violation. Therefore, an example of a plan execution health repair is $FER = \{ \langle e_{\text{fin\_Start}}, e_{\text{Speeded\_up}}, e_{\text{fin\_Taxi}}, e_{\text{Wait}}, e_{\text{fin\_Take\_off}} \rangle_1, \langle e_{\text{fin\_Start}}, e_{\text{Head\_wind}}, e_{\text{fin\_Arrive}}, e_{\text{fin\_Taxi}} \rangle_2 \}$.

5   Two Protocols

Health control During the execution of a plan, agents control its development to detect unhealthy states (conflicts) as follows. Based on the detected disruption events and the expected future events, the agents construct a future event history. Using the future event history, agents are able to predict which states will be reached in the future. If these expected states are part of a possible constraint violation, the agents communicate the new values to other agents that participate in this constraint. This way, the agents individually have sufficient information to determine whether a constraint will be violated and an unhealthy plan execution is reached. The corresponding protocol for health control is presented below. When one or more conflicts are detected, i.e., when the plan-execution health is disturbed, the protocol for finding repair events to restore plan-execution health is activated.

Health control protocol of agent i
    while executing plan
        if disruption event occurs **then**
            determine expected future states;
            send message STATE_CHANGE to related agents;
        if message STATE_CHANGE received **then** update view on other agent's states;
        check for conflicts;
        if conflict detected **then** agent 0 start *health repair* protocol;

Health repair The protocol for health repair is based on a mapping from the problem of finding a plan-execution health repair to a constraint satisfaction problem. Simplified, through assignment of an events path, agents choose a state for each task such that all constraints hold. In this article, we sketch the protocol in broad outlines. For a more detailed description of the underlying algorithm, we refer to [1].

Health repair protocol of agent 0
    all agents start *consistency* subprotocol;
    if consistency succeeded **then** agent 0 start *path assignment* subprotocol;
    else health repair failed, no solution possible;
Consistency subprotocol of agent i
    repeat until no domain changes occur anymore
        apply domain reduction, check consistency;
        if domains changed **then** send message DOMAIN_CHANGE to related agents;
        receive all DOMAIN_CHANGE messages,
        update internal representation;

Path assignment subprotocol of agent i
    while not path assigned **and not** failed :
        assign a new event path (including repair events);
        if succeeded **then**
            all agents: start *consistency* subprotocol;
            if consistency succeeded **then**
                path assigned;
                if agent i+1 exists **then** agent i+1 start *path assignment* subprotocol;
                else all agents apply repairs
            else if i $\neq$ 0 **then** failed, agent i-1 start *path assignment* subprotocol;
            else failed, no solution possible;

The principal part of the protocol is the *path assignment subprotocol*, in which agents one by one assign an event path they want to follow during their plan execution (to this end, the existing event path is extended by inserting repair events in the future part of the path). An event path is chosen only if it does not violate constraints given the already chosen paths. When an agent is not able to assign a conflict-free event path, the process backtracks to the previous agent, that should assign a new event path.

The *consistency subprotocol* is applied in between path assignments to increase efficiency. In this subprotocol, two steps are repeated. (1) Agents (with no path assignment yet) propagate all possible event paths to verify which states are still reachable given the current assignments. By removing the unreachable states, the agents achieve domain reduction (and thus search space reduction). (2) Changed domains are communicated to agents related through constraints, which, based on this new knowledge, apply domain reduction (step 1). The consistency subprotocol finishes when no domains change anymore and subsequently a state of consistency with maximal domain reduction is achieved. When during the consistency subprotocol a domain becomes empty, no solution is possible given the current path assignments. Consequently, the assignment subprotocol should backtrack, or when backtracking is not possible, the protocol fails.

6 Experiments

As stated in the introduction, the goal of the experiments is to gain insight into which unhealthy situations are suitable for our approach of correcting plan execution. Moreover, we would like to test the efficiency of the proposed protocols with respect to the communication overhead. For these two purposes, the protocols presented in the previous section have been implemented and tested with randomly generated plans. During the experiments, the complexity of the problem of finding repair events has been varied by altering two constraint parameters: (i) the percentage of constraints on the variables (or tasks), $p1$, and (ii) the percentage of value combinations that are allowed within a constraint between the variables, $p2$. The performance of the protocols is measured by the number of messages on state or domain changes.

In each experiment, a random plan is generated. Subsequently, an initial value assignment is made based on the expectations of a normal plan development. Then, a number of randomly generated disruption events are executed, which causes state changes. Consequently, the agents detect constraint violations. When an unhealthy plan execution is detected, the agents start the repair protocol to regain plan-execution health.

Figure 3 illustrates typical results of our experiments. The figure shows for a series of settings of constraint parameters ($10 < p1 < 100$ and $10 < p2 < 100$), the average percentage of problems solved and the average number of messages on domain changes that were sent during the plan-execution health repair protocol. The other parameter settings for these specific experiments are: # agents = 5; # tasks per agent = 5; # states per task = 5; # tasks per constraint = 2; # possible repair events per state = 2; # executed disruption events = 10; # runs per constraint-parameter setting = 1000.

The results show that problems with high constraint density are unsolvable with health repair, as was to be expected since increasing the constraint density causes a

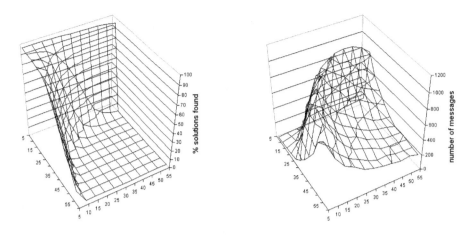

Fig. 3. Results of experiment

decrease in the solution space. Given the settings of the experiments described, the phase transition from solvable to unsolvable problems lies roughly around the boundary $p1 + p2 = 100$. The ridge in the bottom figure shows that problems situated at the phase transition need the largest amount of messages.

7   Conclusion and Future Research

In this paper, we presented a model that enables agents to maintain plan-execution health. With help of the predicting capabilities of the model, agents can control and regain health by correcting the plan execution. The protocols for health control and health repair together with their implementations demonstrate the applicability of the model in a multi-agent system. From the experiments we may conclude that a substantial proportion of unhealthy situations are solvable by small corrections in plan execution with a reasonable amount of communicative costs. In view of the observations presented in section 6, we may conclude that health repair is best applicable in problems with constraint density considerably lower than the transition area. Our overall conclusion is that a reasonable range of unhealthy situations can be solved adequately by a well-thought correction in plan execution instead of performing a replanning procedure.

We wish to examine three topics in the near future. First, the efficiency of the protocols can be increased to reduce communication overhead. Second, the balance between health repair and replanning can be examined to gain a better insight into which unhealthy situations should be solved by execution corrections, and which by replanning. Third, we can extend the model to take into account the probabilities that a disruption event will occur in the future. This will improve the controlling power of the agents, as they can anticipate on bad health in a much earlier stage.

References

1. de Jonge, F., Roos, N., van den Herik, H.: How to keep plan execution healthy. In: Proceedings IJCAI05 workshop on Agents in Real-Time and Dynamic Environments. (2005)
2. Ghallab, M., Nau, D., Traverso, P.: Automated planning. Theory and practice. Morgan Kaufmann Publishers (2004)
3. Cassandras, C.G.: Discrete event systems: modeling and performance analysis. Aksen associates series in electrical and computer engineering. Homewood: Irwin (1993)
4. Raja, A., Lesser, V., Wagner, T.: Towards robust agent control in open environments. In: Proceedings of 5th International Conference of Autonomous Agents. (2000)
5. desJardins, M., Durfee, E., C.L. Ortiz, J., Wolverton, M.: A survey of research in distributed, continual planning. AI Magazine **4** (2000) 13–22
6. Witteveen, C., Roos, N., de Weerdt, M., van der Krogt, R.: Diagnosis of single and multi-agent plans. In: Proceedings of AAMAS 2005. (2005)

Stochastic Reactive Production Scheduling by Multi-agent Based Asynchronous Approximate Dynamic Programming

Balázs Csanád Csáji[1] and László Monostori[1,2]

[1] Computer and Automation Research Institute,
Hungarian Academy of Sciences
[2] Faculty of Mechanical Engineering,
Budapest University of Technology and Economics
{csaji, monostor}@sztaki.hu

Abstract. The paper investigates a stochastic production scheduling problem with unrelated parallel machines. A closed-loop scheduling technique is presented that on-line controls the production process. To achieve this, the scheduling problem is reformulated as a special Markov Decision Process. A near-optimal control policy of the resulted MDP is calculated in a homogeneous multi-agent system. Each agent applies a trial-based approximate dynamic programming method. Different cooperation techniques to distribute the value function computation among the agents are described. Finally, some benchmark experimental results are shown.

1 Introduction

Scheduling is the allocation of resources over time to perform a collection of tasks. Near-optimal scheduling is a prerequisite for the efficient utilization of resources and, hence, for the profitability of the enterprise. Therefore, scheduling is one of the key problems in a manufacturing production control system. Moreover, much that can be learned about scheduling can be applied to other kinds of planning and decision making, therefore, it has general practical value.

The paper suggests an agent-based closed-loop solution to a stochastic scheduling problem that can use information, such as actual processing times, as they become available, and can control the production process on-line. For this reason, the stochastic scheduling problem is reformulated as a Markov Decision Process. Machine learning techniques, such as asynchronous approximate dynamic programming (namely approximate Q-learning with prioritized sweeping), are suggested to compute a good policy in a homogeneous multi-agent system.

Using approximate dynamic programming (also called as reinforcement learning) for job-shop scheduling was first proposed in [12]. They used the $TD(\lambda)$ method with iterative repair to solve a static scheduling problem, namely the NASA space shuttle payload processing problem. Since then, a number of papers have been published that suggested using reinforcement learning for scheduling problems. However, most of them investigated static and deterministic problems, only, and the suggested solutions were mostly centralized. A reinforcement

M. Pěchouček, P. Petta, and L.Z. Varga (Eds.): CEEMAS 2005, LNAI 3690, pp. 388–397, 2005.
© Springer-Verlag Berlin Heidelberg 2005

learning based centralized closed-loop production scheduling approach was first briefly described in [10]. Recently, several machine learning improvements of multi-agent based scheduling systems were proposed, for example [2] and [3].

2   Production Scheduling Problems

First, a static deterministic scheduling problem with unrelated parallel machines is considered: an instance of the problem consists of a finite set of *tasks* T together with a partial ordering $C \subseteq T \times T$ that represents the *precedence constraints* between the tasks. A finite set of *machines* M is also given with a partial function that defines the *durations* (or processing times) of the tasks on the machines, $d : T \times M \to \mathbb{N}$. The tasks are supposed to be non-preemptive (they may not be interrupted) thus a *schedule* can be defined as an ordered pair $\langle \varrho, \mu \rangle$ where $\varrho : T \to \mathbb{N}_0$ gives the starting (release) times of the tasks ($\mathbb{N}_0 = \mathbb{N} \cup \{0\}$), and $\mu : T \to M$ defines which machine will process which task. A schedule is called *feasible* if and only if the following three properties are satisfied:

(s1) Each machine processes at most one operation at a time:
$\neg \exists (m \in M \wedge u, v \in T) : \mu(u) = \mu(v) = m \wedge \varrho(u) \le \varrho(v) < \varrho(u) + d(u, m)$

(s2) Every machine can process the tasks which were assigned to it:
$\forall v \in T : \langle v, \mu(v) \rangle \in dom(d)$

(s3) The precedence constraints of the tasks are kept:
$\forall \langle u, v \rangle \in C : \varrho(u) + d(u, \mu(u)) \le \varrho(v)$

Note that $dom(d) \subseteq T \times M$ denotes the domain set of the function d. The set of all feasible schedules is denoted by S, which is supposed to be non-empty (thus, e.g., $\forall v \in T : \exists m \in M : \langle v, m \rangle \in dom(d)$). The objective of scheduling is to produce a schedule that minimizes a *performance measure* $\kappa : S \to \mathbb{R}$, which usually depends on the task completion times, only. For example, if the completion time of the task $v \in T$ is denoted by $C(v) = \varrho(v) + d(v, \mu(v))$ then a commonly used performance measure, which is often called total production time or make-span, can be defined by $C_{max} = \max\{C(v) \mid v \in T\}$.

However, not *any* function is allowed as a performance measure. These measures are restricted to functions which have the property that a schedule can be uniquely generated from the order in which the jobs are processed through the machines, e.g., by semi-active *timetabling*. *Regular* measures, which are monotonic in completion times, have this property. Note that all of the commonly used performance measures (e.g., maximum completion time, mean flow time, mean tardiness, etc.) are regular. As a consequence, S can be safely restricted to these schedules and, therefore, S will be finite, thus the problem becomes a *combinatorial optimization* problem characterized by the 5-tuple $\langle T, M, C, d, \kappa \rangle$.

It is easy to see that the presented parallel machine scheduling problem is a generalization of the standard *job-shop* scheduling problem which is known to be *strongly NP-hard* [7], consequently, this problem is also strongly NP-hard. Moreover, if the used performance measure is C_{max}, there is no good polynomial time approximation of the optimal scheduling algorithm [9]. Therefore, in practice, we have to satisfy with sub-optimal (approximate) solutions.

The stochastic variant of the presented problem arises, when the durations are given by independent finite random variables. Thus, $d(v, m)$ denotes a random variable with possible values $d_{vm1}, \ldots, d_{vmk}$ and with probability distribution $p_{vm1}, \ldots, p_{vmk}$. Note that $k = k(v, m)$, it can depend on v and m. If the functions ϱ and μ are given, we write d_{vi} and p_{vi} for abbreviation of $d_{v\mu(v)i}$ and $p_{v\mu(v)i}$. In this case, the performance of a schedule is also a random variable.

In stochastic scheduling there are some data (e.g. the actual durations) that will only be available during the execution of the plan. According to the usage of these information, we consider two basic types of scheduling techniques.

A *static* (*open-loop, proactive* or *off-line*) scheduler has to make all decisions before the schedule actually being executed and it cannot take the actual evolution of the process into account. It has to build a schedule that can be executed with high probability. For a *dynamic* (*closed-loop, reactive* or *on-line*) scheduler it is allowed to make the decisions as the scheduling process actually evolves and more information becomes available. In this paper we will focus on dynamic techniques and will formulate the stochastic scheduling problem as a Markov Decision Process. Note that a dynamic solution is not a simple $\langle \varrho, \mu \rangle$ pair, but instead a scheduling *policy* (defined later) which controls the production.

3   Markov Decision Processes

Sequential decision making under uncertainty is often modeled using MDPs. This section contains the basic definitions and some preliminaries. By a (finite state, discrete time, stationary, fully observable) *Markov Decision Process* (MDP) we mean a 8-tuple $\langle \mathbb{S}, \mathbb{T}, \mathbb{A}, \mathcal{A}, p, g, \alpha, \beta \rangle$, where the components are:

(m1) $\mathbb{S}$ is a finite set of discrete *states*.

(m2) $\mathbb{T} \subseteq \mathbb{S}$ is a set of *terminal states*.

(m3) $\mathbb{A}$ is a finite set of control *actions*.

(m4) $\mathcal{A} : \mathbb{S} \rightarrow \mathcal{P}(\mathbb{A})$ is an *availability function* that renders each state a set of control actions available in that state. Note that $\mathcal{P}$ denotes the power set.

(m5) $p : \mathbb{S} \times \mathbb{A} \rightarrow \Delta(\mathbb{S})$ is a *transition function*, where $\Delta(\mathbb{S})$ is the space of probability distributions over $\mathbb{S}$. We denote by $p_{ss'}(a)$ the probability of arriving to state s' after executing control action $a \in \mathcal{A}(s)$ in a state s.

(m6) $g : \mathbb{S} \times \mathbb{A} \times \mathbb{S} \rightarrow \mathbb{R}$ is an *immediate cost* (or reward) function, $g(s, a, s')$ is the cost of moving from state s to state s' with control action $a \in \mathcal{A}(s)$.

(m7) $\alpha \in [0, 1]$ is a *discount rate* or also called *discount factor*. If $\alpha = 1$ then the MDP is called *undiscounted* otherwise it is *discounted*.

(m8) $\beta \in \Delta(\mathbb{S})$ is an *initial probability distribution*.

An interpretation of a MDP can be given if we consider an agent that acts in a stochastic environment. The agent receives information about the state of the environment $s \in \mathbb{S}$. At each state s the agent can choose an action $a \in \mathcal{A}(s)$. After the action is selected the environment moves to the next state according to the probability distribution $p(s, a)$ and the decision-maker collects its one-step penalty (cost). The aim of the agent is to find an optimal control policy that minimizes the expected cumulative costs over an infinite horizon or until it reaches an absorbing terminal state. The set of terminal states can be empty. Theoretically, the terminal states can be treated as states with only one available control action that loops back to them with probability 1 and cost 0.

A (stationary, randomized, Markov) control *policy* $\pi : \mathbb{S} \to \Delta(\mathbb{A})$ is a function from states to probability distributions over actions. We denote by $\pi(s, a)$ the probability of executing control action $a \in \mathcal{A}(s)$ in the state $s \in \mathbb{S}$.

The initial probability distribution β, the transition probabilities p together with a control policy π completely determine the progress of the system in a stochastic sense, namely, it defines a homogeneous Markov chain on $\mathbb{S}$.

The *cost-to-go* or *value* function of a policy is $J^\pi : \mathbb{S} \to \mathbb{R}$, where $J^\pi(s)$ gives the expected costs when the system is in state s and it follows π thereafter:

$$J^\pi(s) = \mathbb{E}_\pi \left[\sum_{t=0}^{\infty} \alpha^t g(s_t, a_t, s_{t+1}) \,\middle|\, s_0 = s \right], \tag{1}$$

whenever this expectation is well-defined. Naturally, it is always well-defined if $\alpha < 1$. Here, we consider problems with expected total [un]discounted cost, only.

A policy $\pi_1 \leq \pi_2$ if and only if $\forall s \in \mathbb{S} : J^{\pi_1}(s) \leq J^{\pi_2}(s)$. A policy is called (uniformly) *optimal* if it is better than or equal to all other control policies.

There always exits at least one optimal stationary deterministic control policy. Although, there may be many optimal policies, they all share the same unique optimal cost-to-go function, denoted by J^*. This function must satisfy the (Hamilton-Jacoby-) *Bellman optimality equation* [1] for all $s \in \mathbb{S}$:

$$J^*(s) = \min_{a \in \mathcal{A}(s)} \sum_{s' \in \mathbb{S}} p_{ss'}(a) \left[g(s, a, s') + \alpha J^*(s') \right] \tag{2}$$

Note that from a given cost-to-go function it is straightforward to get a control policy, for example, by selecting in each state in a deterministic and greedy way an action that produces minimal costs with one-stage lookahead. The problem of finding a good policy will be further investigated in Section 5.

4 Stochastic Reactive Scheduling as a MDP

In this section a dynamic stochastic scheduling problem is formulated as a Markov Decision Process. The actual task durations will be only incrementally available during production and the decisions will be made on-line.

A state $s \in \mathbb{S}$ is defined as a 6-tuple: $s = \langle t, \mathcal{T}_S, \mathcal{T}_F, \varrho, \mu, \varphi \rangle$, where $t \in \mathbb{N}_0$ is the actual time, $\mathcal{T}_S \subseteq \mathcal{T}$ is the set of tasks which have been started before time t and $\mathcal{T}_F \subseteq \mathcal{T}_S$ is the set of tasks that have been finished, already. The functions $\varrho : \mathcal{T}_S \to \mathbb{N}_0$ and $\mu : \mathcal{T}_S \to \mathcal{M}$, as previously, give the starting times of the tasks and the task-machine assignments. The function $\varphi : \mathcal{T}_F \to \mathbb{N}$ stores the task completion times. We also define a starting state $s_0 = \langle 0, \emptyset, \emptyset, \emptyset, \emptyset, \emptyset \rangle$, that corresponds to the situation at time 0 when none of the tasks have been started. The initial probability distribution β renders 1 to the starting state s_0.

We introduce a set of terminal states, as well. A state $s = \langle t, \mathcal{T}_S, \mathcal{T}_F, \varrho, \mu, \varphi \rangle$ is considered as a terminal state if and only if $\mathcal{T}_F = \mathcal{T}$ and it can be reached from a state $\hat{s} = \langle \hat{t}, \mathcal{T}'_S, \mathcal{T}'_F, \hat{\varrho}, \hat{\mu}, \hat{\varphi} \rangle$ where $\mathcal{T}'_F \neq \mathcal{T}$. If the system reaches a terminal state (all tasks are finished), then we treat the control process completed.

At every time t the system is informed which tasks have been finished, and it can decide which unscheduled tasks it starts (and on which machines).

The control action space contains task-machine assignments $a_{vm} \in \mathbb{A}$, where $v \in \mathcal{T}$ and $m \in \mathcal{M}$, and a special a_{wait} control that corresponds to the action when the system does not start a new task at the present time.

In a non-terminal state $s = \langle t, \mathcal{T}_S, \mathcal{T}_F, \varrho, \mu, \varphi \rangle$ the available actions are:

(a1) $a_{wait} \in \mathcal{A}(s) \Leftrightarrow \mathcal{T}_S \setminus \mathcal{T}_F \neq \emptyset$
(a2) $\forall v \in \mathcal{T} : \forall m \in \mathcal{M} : a_{vm} \in \mathcal{A}(s) \Leftrightarrow (v \in \mathcal{T} \setminus \mathcal{T}_S \wedge \forall u \in \mathcal{T}_S \setminus \mathcal{T}_F :$
$\quad m \neq \mu(u) \wedge \langle v, m \rangle \in dom(d) \wedge \forall u \in \mathcal{T} : (\langle u, v \rangle \in \mathcal{C}) \Rightarrow (u \in \mathcal{T}_F))$

If an $a_{vm} \in \mathcal{A}(s)$ is executed in a state $s = \langle t, \mathcal{T}_S, \mathcal{T}_F, \varrho, \mu, \varphi \rangle$, the system moves with probability 1 to a new state $\hat{s} = \langle t, \mathcal{T}'_S, \mathcal{T}'_F, \hat{\varrho}, \hat{\mu}, \hat{\varphi} \rangle$, where $\mathcal{T}'_F = \mathcal{T}_F$, $\mathcal{T}'_S = \mathcal{T}_S \cup \{v\}$, $\hat{\varrho}\big|_{\mathcal{T}_S} = \varrho$, $\hat{\mu}\big|_{\mathcal{T}_S} = \mu$, $\hat{\varrho}(v) = t$, $\hat{\mu}(v) = m$ and $\varphi = \hat{\varphi}$.

The effect of the a_{wait} action is that it takes from $s = \langle t, \mathcal{T}_S, \mathcal{T}_F, \varrho, \mu, \varphi \rangle$ to a state $\hat{s} = \langle t+1, \mathcal{T}_S, \mathcal{T}'_F, \varrho, \mu, \hat{\varphi} \rangle$ where $\mathcal{T}_F \subseteq \mathcal{T}'_F \subseteq \mathcal{T}_S$ and for all $v \in \mathcal{T}_S \setminus \mathcal{T}_F$: the task v will be in $\mathcal{T}'_F$ (v terminates) with probability as follows:

$$\mathbb{P}(v \in \mathcal{T}'_F \mid s) = \mathbb{P}(F(v) = t \mid F(v) \geq t) = \frac{\sum_{i=1}^{k} p_{vi} \, \mathbb{I}(f_i(v) = t)}{\sum_{i=1}^{k} p_{vi} \, \mathbb{I}(f_i(v) \geq t)}, \quad (3)$$

where $F(v)$ is a random variable that gives the finish time of task v (according to $\langle \varrho, \mu \rangle$), $f_i(v) = \varrho(v) + d_{vi}$ and $\mathbb{I}$ is an indicator function, viz. $\mathbb{I}(A) = 1$ if A is true, otherwise it is 0. Recall that $p_{vi} = p_{vmi}$ and $d_{vi} = d_{vmi}$, where $m = \mu(v)$; k can also depend on v and m; $\hat{\varphi}\big|_{\mathcal{T}_F} = \varphi$, $\forall v \in \mathcal{T}_F \setminus \mathcal{T}'_F : \varphi(v) = t$.

The cost function, for a given κ performance measure (which depends only on the task completion times), is defined as follows. Let $s = \langle t, \mathcal{T}_S, \mathcal{T}_F, \varrho, \mu, \varphi \rangle$ and $\hat{s} = \langle \hat{t}, \mathcal{T}'_S, \mathcal{T}'_F, \hat{\varrho}, \hat{\mu}, \hat{\varphi} \rangle$. Then $\forall a \in \mathcal{A}(s) : g(s, a, \hat{s}) = \kappa(\varphi) - \kappa(\hat{\varphi})$.

It is easy to see that the MDPs defined by this way have finite state spaces and their transition graphs are acyclic. Therefore, these MDPs have a *finite horizon* and, thus, the discount rate α can be safely set to 1, without risking that the expectation in the cost-to-go function becomes not well-defined. Note that these type of problems are often called *Stochastic Shortest Path* (SSP) problems. For the effective computation of a control policy it is important to try reducing the number of states. Domain specific knowledge can help to achieve this: if κ is non-decreasing in the completion times (which is mostly the case in practice), then an optimal policy can be found among those policies which only start new tasks at times when another task has been finished or at the initial state s_0.

5   Approximate Dynamic Programming

In the previous section we have formulated a dynamic production scheduling task as an acyclic stochastic shortest path problem (a special MDP). Now, we face the challenge of finding a good control policy. We suggest a homogeneous multi-agent system in which the optimal policy is calculated in a distributed way. First, we describe the operation of a single adaptive agent that tries to learn the optimal value function with Watkins' Q-learning. Next, we examine different cooperation techniques to distribute the value function computation.

In theory, the optimal value function of a finite MDP can be computed exactly by dynamic programming methods, such as value iteration or the Gauss-Seidel method. Alternatively, an exact optimal policy can be directly calculated by policy iteration. However, due to the "curse of dimensionality" (viz. in practical situations both the needed memory and the required amount of computation is extremely large) calculating an exact optimal solution by these methods is practically infeasible. We should use Approximate Dynamic Programming (ADP) techniques to achieve a good approximation of an optimal control policy.

The paper suggests using the Q-learning algorithm to calculate a near optimal policy. Like most ADP methods, the aim of Q-learning is also to learn the optimal value function rather than directly learning an optimal control policy. The Q-learning method learns state-action value functions, which are defined by:

$$Q^\pi(s,a) = \mathbb{E}_\pi\left[\sum_{t=0}^{\infty} \alpha^t g(s_t, a_t, s_{t+1}) \;\middle|\; s_0 = s, a_0 = a\right] \tag{4}$$

An agent can search in the space of feasible schedules by simulating the possible occurrences of the production process with the model. The trials of the agent can be described as state-action pair trajectories. After each episode the agent makes updates *asynchronously* on the approximated values of the visited pairs. Only a subset of all pairs are updated in each trial. Note that the agent does not need a uniformly good approximation on all possible pairs, but instead on the *relevant* ones which can appear with positive probability during the executing of an optimal policy. Therefore, it can always start the simulation from s_0.

The general version of the one-step Q-learning rule can be formulated as:

$$Q_{t+1}(s,a) = Q_t(s,a) + \gamma_t(s,a)\left[g(s,a,s') - Q_t(s,a) + \alpha \min_{b \in \mathcal{A}(s')} Q_t(s',b)\right], \tag{5}$$

where s' and $g(s,a,s')$ are generated from the pair (s,a) by simulation, that is, according to the transition probabilities $p_{ss'}(a)$; $\gamma_t(s,a)$ are sequences that define the *learning rates* of the system. Q-learning can also be seen as a Robbins-Monro type stochastic approximation method. Note that it is advised to apply *prioritized sweeping* during backups. Q-learning is called an *off-policy* method, which means that the value function converges almost surely to the optimal state-action value function *independently* of the policy being followed or the starting Q values. It is known [1], that if the learning rates satisfy: $\sum_{t=1}^{\infty} \gamma_t(s,a) = \infty$ and $\sum_{t=1}^{\infty} \gamma_t^2(s,a) < \infty$ for all s and a, the Q-learning algorithm will converge with probability one to the optimal value function in the case of lookup table representation (namely, the value of each pair is stored independently).

However, in systems with large state spaces, it is not possible to store an estimation for each state-action pair. The value function should be approximated by a parametric function. We suggest a *Support Vector Machine* (SVM) based regression for maintaining the Q function, as in [4], which then takes the form:

$$Q(s,a) \approx \tilde{Q}(x,w,b) = \sum_{i=1}^{n} w_i K(x,x_i) + b, \qquad (6)$$

where $x = \phi(s,a)$ represents some peculiar features of s and a, x_i denotes the features of the training data, b is a bias, K is the *kernel* function and $w \in \mathbb{R}^n$ is the parameter vector of the approximation. As a kernel we choose a Gaussian type function $K(x_1,x_2) = \exp(-\|x_1 - x_2\|^2/\sigma^2)$. Basically, an SVM is an approximate implementation of the *method of structural risk minimization*. Recently, several on-line, incremental methods have been suggested that made SVMs applicable for reinforcement learning. For more details, see [8].

Now, we give some ideas about the possible features that can be used in the stochastic scheduling case. Concerning the environment: expected relative ready time of each machine with their standard deviations and the estimated relative future load of the machines. Regarding the chosen action (task-machine assignment): its expected relative finish time with its deviation and the cumulative estimated relative finish time of the tasks, which succeeds the selected task.

In order to ensure the convergence of the Q-learning algorithm, one must guarantee that each state-action pair is continue to update. An often used technique to balance between *exploration* and *exploitation* is the *Boltzmann formula*:

$$\pi(s,a) = \frac{\exp(\tau/Q(s,a))}{\sum_{b \in \mathcal{A}(s)} \exp(\tau/Q(s,b))}, \qquad (7)$$

where $\tau \geq 0$ is the Boltzmann (or Gibbs) temperature. Low temperatures cause the actions to be (nearly) equiprobable, high ones cause a greater difference in selection probability for actions that differ in their value estimations. Note that here we applied the Boltzmann formula for minimization, viz. small values mean high probability. Also note that it is advised to extend this approach by a variant of *simulated annealing*, which means that τ should be increased over time.

6   Distributed Value Function Computation

In the previous section we have described the learning mechanism of a single agent. In this section we examine cooperation techniques in homogeneous multi-agent systems to distribute the computation of the optimal value function. Our suggested architectures are *heterarchical*, in which the agents communicate as peers and no master/slave relationships exist. The advantages of these systems include: self-configuration, scalability, fault tolerance, massive parallelism, reduced complexity, increased flexibility, reduced cost and emergent behavior [11].

An agent-based (holonic) reference architecture for manufacturing systems is PROSA [5]. The general idea underlying this approach is to consider both the machines and the jobs (sets of tasks) as active entities. There are three types of standard agents in PROSA: order agents (internal logistics), product agents (process plans), and resource agents (resource handling). In a further improvement of this architecture the system is extended with mobile agents, called ants. As we have shown in [2], it is advised to extend the ant-colony based approach with ADP techniques. Another way for scheduling with PROSA is to use some kind of market or negotiation mechanism. We have presented a market-based scheduling approach with competitive adaptive agents in [3].

Now, we return to our original approach and present ways to distribute the value function calculation. The suggested multi-agent architectures are homogeneous, therefore, all of the agents are identical. The agents work independently by making their trials in the simulated environment, but they share information.

If a common (global) storage is available to the agents, then it is straightforward to parallelize the value function computation: each agent searches independently by making trials, however, they all share (read and write) the same value function. They update the value function estimations asynchronously.

A more complex situation arises when the memory is completely local to the agents, which is realistic if they are physically separated (e.g. they run on different computers). For that case, we suggest two cooperation techniques. A way of dividing the computation of a good policy among several agents is when there is only one "global" value function, however, it is stored in a distributed way. Each agent stores a part of the value function and it asks for estimations which it requires but does not have from the other agents. The applicability of this approach lies in the fact that the underlying MDP is acyclic and, thus, it can be effectively partitioned among the agents, for example, by starting each agent from a different starting state. Partitioning the search space can be very useful for the other distributed ADP approaches, as well. The policy can be then computed by using the aggregated value function estimations of the agents.

Another approach is, when the agents have their own completely local value functions and, consequently, they could have widely different estimations on the optimal state-action values. In that case, the agents should count that how many times did they update the estimations of the different pairs. Finally, the values of the global Q-function can be combined from the estimations of the agents:

$$Q(s,a) = \sum_{i=1}^{n} w_i(s,a)\, Q_i(s,a), \qquad w_i(s,a) = \frac{\exp(h_i(s,a)/\eta)}{\sum_{j=1}^{n} \exp(h_j(s,a)/\eta)}, \qquad (8)$$

where n is the number of agents, Q_i is the state-action value function of agent i, $h_i(s,a)$ contains the number of how many times did agent i update its estimation for the (s,a) pair and $\eta > 0$ is an adjustable parameter. Naturally, for large state spaces, the counter functions can be parametrically approximated, as well.

The agents can also help each other by communicating estimation information, episodes, policies, etc. A promising way of cooperation is, when the agents periodically exchange a fixed number of their best episodes after an adjustable amount of trials and, by this way, they help improving each others value functions. After an agent receives an episode (a sequence of states), it updates its value function estimation as if this state trajectory was produced by itself.

7   Experimental Results

We have tested our ADP based approach on Hurink's benchmark dataset [6].
It contains flexible job-shop scheduling problems with 6-30 jobs (30-225 tasks)
and 5-15 machines. These problems are "hard", which means, for example, that
standard dispatching rules or heuristics perform poorly on them. This dataset
consists of four subsets, each subset contains about 60 problems. The subsets
(sdata, edata, rdata, vdata) differ on the ratio of machine interchangeability,
which are shown in the "parallel" column in the table (left part of Figure 1).
The columns with label "x es" show the global error after carrying out altogether
"x" episodes. The execution of 10000 simulated trials (after on the average the
system has achieved a solution with less than 5% global error) takes only a few
seconds on a computer of our day. In the tests we have used a decision-tree based
state-aggregation. The left part of Figure 1 shows the results of a single agent.

dataset	parallel	1000 es	5000 es	10000 es
sdata	1	8.54 %	5.69 %	3.57 %
edata	1.2	12.37 %	8.03 %	5.26 %
rdata	2	16.14 %	11.41 %	7.14 %
vdata	5	10.18 %	7.73 %	3.49 %
average	2.3	11.81 %	8.21 %	4.86 %

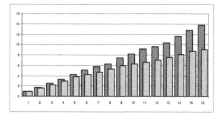

Fig. 1. Benchmarks; left: average global error on a dataset of "hard" flexible job-shop
problems; right: average speedup (y axis) relative to the number of agents (x axis);
dark grey bars: global value function; light grey bars: local value functions

We have also investigated the speedup of the system relative to the number
of agents. The average number of iterations was studied, until the system could
reach a solution with less than 5% global error on Hurink's dataset. We have
treated the average speed of a single agent as a unit. In the right part of Figure 1
two cases are shown: in the first case, all of the agents could access a global value
function. In that case, the speedup was almost linear. In the second case, each
agent had its own (local) value function and, after the search was finished, the
individual functions were combined. The experiments show, that the computation of the ADP based scheduling technique can be effectively distributed among
several agents, even if they do not have a commonly accessible value function.

8   Concluding Remarks

Efficient allocation of manufacturing resources over time is one of the key problems in a production control system. The paper has presented an approximate
dynamic programming based stochastic reactive scheduler that can control the
production process on-line, instead of generating an off-line rigid static plan. To

achieve closed-loop control, the stochastic scheduling problem was formulated as a special Markov Decision Process. To compute a (near) optimal control policy, homogeneous multi-agent systems were suggested, in which cooperative agents learn the optimal value function in a distributed way by using trial-based ADP methods. After each trial, the agents asynchronously update the actual value function estimation according to the Q-learning rule with prioritized sweeping. For large state spaces a Support Vector Machine regression based value function approximation was suggested. Finally, the paper has shown some benchmark results on Hurink's flexible job-shop dataset, which illustrate the effectiveness of the ADP based approach, even in the case of deterministic problems.

Acknowledgements

This research was partially supported by the National Research and Development Programme (NKFP), Hungary, Grant No. 2/010/2004 and by the Hungarian Scientic Research Fund (OTKA), Grant Nos. T049481 and T043547.

References

1. Bertsekas, D. P., Tsitsiklis J. N.: Neuro-Dynamic Programming (1996)
2. Csáji, B. Cs., Kádár, B., Monostori, L.: Improving Multi-Agent Based Scheduling by Neurodynamic Programming. Holonic and Mult-Agent Systems for Manufacturing, Lecture Notes in Computer Science **2744**, HoloMAS: Industrial Applications of Holonic and Multi-Agent Systems (2003) 110–123
3. Csáji, B. Cs., Monostori, L., Kádár, B.: Learning and Cooperation in a Distributed Market-Based Production Control System. Proceedings of the 5th International Workshop on Emergent Synthesis (2004) 109–116
4. Dietterich, T. G., Xin Wang: Batch Value Function Approximation via Support Vectors. Advances in Neural Information Processing Systems **14** (2001) 1491–1498
5. Hadeli, Valckenaers, P., Kollingbaum, M., Van Brussel, H.: Multi-Agent Coordination and Control Using Stigmergy. Computers in Industry **53** (2004) 75–96.
6. Hurink, E., Jurisch, B., Thole, M.: Tabu Search for the Job Shop Scheduling Problem with Multi-Purpose Machine. Operations Research Spektrum **15** (1994) 205–215
7. Lawler, E. L., Lenstra, J. K., Rinnooy Kan, A. H. G., Shmoys, D. B.: Sequencing and Scheduling: Algorithms and Complexity. Handbooks in Operations Research and Management Science (1993)
8. Martin., M.: On-line Support Vector Machine Regression. Proceedings of the 13th European Conference on Machine Learning (2002) 282–294
9. Williamson, D. P., Hall L. A., Hoogeveen, J. A., Hurkens, C. A. J., Lenstra, J. K., Sevastjanov, S. V., Shmoys, D. B.: Short Shop Schedules. Operations Research **45** (1997) 288–294
10. Schneider, J., Boyan, J., Moore, A.: Value Function Based Production Scheduling. Proceedings of the 15th International Conference on Machine Learning (1998)
11. Ueda, K., Márkus, A., Monostori, L., Kals, H. J. J., Arai, T.: Emergent Synthesis Methodologies for Manufacturing. Annals of the CIRP **50** (2001) 535–551
12. Zhang, W., Dietterich, T.: A Reinforcement Learning Approach to Job-Shop Scheduling. IJCAI: Proceedings of the 14th International Joint Conference on Artificial Intelligence (1995) 1114–1120

Do Agents Make Model Checking Explode (Computationally)?

Wojciech Jamroga and Jürgen Dix

Institute of Computer Science, Clausthal University of Technology, Germany
{wjamroga, dix}@in.tu-clausthal.de

Abstract. ATL is a logic for multi-agent systems that enjoys model checking *linear in the size of the models*. Here, we point out that the size of an ATL model is usually *exponential in the number of agents*. We establish the precise ATL model checking complexity when the number of agents is considered a *parameter*: it turns out that the problem is $\Sigma_2\mathbf{P}$-complete for concurrent game structures, and **NP**-complete for alternating transition systems. We also show that ATL model checking over the broader class of nondeterministic alternating transition systems is still **NP**-complete, which suggests that using the more general class of models may be convenient in practice.

Keywords: multi-agent systems, model checking, temporal logic.

1   Introduction

Alternating-time Temporal Logic [1, 2] is one of the most interesting frameworks that emerged recently for multi-agent systems. One of the most appreciated features of ATL is its model checking complexity—*linear in the size of the model* (more precisely: the number of transitions in the model) *and the formula*. While the result is certainly attractive, we point out that the amount of transitions in an ATL model is usually exponential in the number of agents. Following this observation, we show that ATL *model checking is intractable when the number of agents is considered a parameter of the problem*. It turns out that the problem is $\Sigma_2\mathbf{P}$-complete for the ATL semantics based on concurrent game structures, and "only" **NP**-complete when the previous semantics, based on alternating transition systems, is used. We also show that ATL model checking over the broader class of nondeterministic alternating transition systems is still **NP**-complete, which suggests that using the more general class of models may be a good choice in practice.

2   ATL: A Logic of Strategic Ability

ATL [1, 2] is a generalization of the branching-time logic CTL, and can be seen as a logic for systems involving multiple agents, that allows one to reason about what agents can achieve in game-like scenarios. ATL introduces *cooperation modalities* $\langle\!\langle A \rangle\!\rangle$, where A is a coalition of agents; formula $\langle\!\langle A \rangle\!\rangle \varphi$ expresses that A have

M. Pĕchouček, P. Petta, and L.Z. Varga (Eds.): CEEMAS 2005, LNAI 3690, pp. 398–407, 2004.
© Springer-Verlag Berlin Heidelberg 2004

a collective strategy to enforce φ. ATL formulae include temporal operators: "$\bigcirc$" ("in the next state"), $\square$ ("always from now on") and $\mathcal{U}$ ("until"). An additional operator $\diamondsuit$ ("sometime") can be defined as $\diamondsuit\varphi \equiv \top\mathcal{U}\varphi$. Like in CTL, every occurrence of a temporal operator is preceded by exactly one cooperation modality. A number of different semantics and model classes have been defined for ATL, most of them equivalent (cf. [6, 7]). In what follows, we begin with a brief presentation of the two most prominent semantics, based on concurrent game structures and alternating transition systems.

2.1 Strategic Abilities with Concurrent Game Structures

Models for ATL, *concurrent game structures* (CGS) [2], can be defined as tuples $M = \langle \text{Agt}, Q, \Pi, \pi, Act, d, o \rangle$, where $\text{Agt} = \{a_1, ..., a_k\}$ is the set of all agents, Q is the set of states, Π the set of atomic propositions, $\pi : Q \to \mathcal{P}(\Pi)$ a valuation of propositions, and Act the set of (atomic) actions; function $d : \text{Agt} \times Q \to \mathcal{P}(Act)$ defines actions available to an agent in a state, and o is the (deterministic) transition function that assigns outcome states $q' = o(q, \alpha_1, ..., \alpha_k)$ to states and tuples of actions.

A *strategy* of agent a is a conditional plan that specifies what a is going to do in every possible situation (state).[1] Thus, a strategy can be represented with a function $s_a : Q \to Act$, such that $s_a(q) \in d_a(q)$. A *collective strategy* for a group of agents $A = \{a_1, ..., a_r\}$ is simply a tuple of strategies $S_A = \langle s_{a_1}, ..., s_{a_r} \rangle$, one per agent from A. A *path* in M is an infinite sequence of states that can be effected by subsequent transitions, and refers to a possible course of action (or a possible computation). Function $out(q, S_A)$ returns the set of all paths that may result from agents A executing strategy S_A from state q onward. Now, the semantics of ATL formulae can be given via the following clauses:

$M, q \models p$ iff $p \in \pi(q)$ (where $p \in \Pi$);

$M, q \models \neg\varphi$ iff $M, q \not\models \varphi$;

$M, q \models \varphi \vee \psi$ iff $M, q \models \varphi$ or $M, q \models \psi$;

$M, q \models \langle\!\langle A \rangle\!\rangle \bigcirc \varphi$ iff there is a collective strategy S_A such that, for every path $\lambda \in out(S_A, q)$, we have $M, \lambda[1] \models \varphi$;

$M, q \models \langle\!\langle A \rangle\!\rangle \square \varphi$ iff there exists S_A such that, for every $\lambda \in out(S_A, q)$, we have $M, \lambda[i]$ for every $i \geq 0$;

$M, q \models \langle\!\langle A \rangle\!\rangle \varphi \mathcal{U} \psi$ iff there exist S_A and $i \geq 0$ such that, for every $\lambda \in out(S_A, q)$, we have that $M, \lambda[i] \models \psi$, and $M, \lambda[j] \models \varphi$ for every $0 \leq j < i$.

2.2 Semantics of ATL Based on ATS

The previous version of ATL was defined over alternating transition systems [1]. An *alternating transition system* (ATS) is a tuple $M = \langle \text{Agt}, Q, \Pi, \pi, \delta \rangle$ where

---

[1] This is a deviation from the original semantics of ATL [1, 2], where strategies assign agents' choices to *sequences* of states, which suggests that agents can recall the whole history of each game. It should be pointed out, however, that both types of strategies yield equivalent semantics for ATL [9].

$\delta : Q \times \text{Agt} \to \mathcal{P}(\mathcal{P}(Q))$ is a function that maps a pair $\langle state, agent \rangle$ to a non-empty family of choices of possible next states. The idea is that, at state q, agent a chooses a set $Q_a \in \delta(q, a)$ thus forcing the outcome state to be from Q_a. The resulting transition leads to a state which is in the intersection of all Q_a for $a \in \text{Agt}$. Since the system is required to be deterministic (given the state and the agents' decisions), $Q_{a_1} \cap ... \cap Q_{a_k}$ must always be a singleton.

In an ATS, the type of a strategy function is slightly different since choices are sets of states now, and a strategy is represented as a mapping $s_a : Q \to \mathcal{P}(Q)$, such that $s_a(q) \in \delta(q, a)$. The rest of the semantics looks exactly the same as for concurrent game structures. It is worth pointing out that ATS's are usually less natural and more difficult to come up with than CGS's; they are also larger in most cases (more precisely: for every ATS there exists an isomorphic CGS, but the reverse does not hold). This issue was discussed in more detail in [7].

3   Complexity of ATL Model Checking Revisited

One of the main results concerning ATL states that its formulae can be model-checked in deterministic polynomial time. More precisely, the complexity of ATL model checking is PTIME-complete, and can be done in time $O(ml)$, where m is the number of transitions in the model and l is the length of the formula [1, 2]. While the result is certainly attractive, it should be kept in mind that it is only relative to the size of models and formulae, and these can be very large for most application domains. Indeed, it is well known that the number of states in a model is usually exponential in the size of a higher-lever description of the problem domain (Boolean variables, for example) for both CTL and ATL models. Moreover, for higher-lever system descriptions, the computation of $\langle\langle A \rangle\rangle \bigcirc$ may require PSPACE or even NEXPTIME [3, 4]. We point out that the complexity of $O(ml)$ includes potential intractability even *on the model level* when a finer-grained analysis is performed.

Remark 1. Let n be the number of states in an ATL model M. It was already observed in [2] that the number of transitions in M is *not* bounded by n^2, because transitions are labelled with tuples of agents' choices. Now, let k denote the number of agents, and d the maximal number of available decisions per agent per state. Obviously, $m = O(nd^k)$. In consequence, the ATL model checking algorithms from [1, 2] run in time $O(nd^k l)$, and hence their complexity is exponential if the number of agents is a parameter of the problem.

In this section, we establish the complexity of model checking ATL formulae over concurrent game structures, with n, k, d, l as input parameters. We show that the problem is $\mathbf{\Sigma_2 P}$-complete, where $\mathbf{\Sigma_2 P} = \mathbf{NP^{NP}}$ is the class of problems that can be solved by a nondeterministic Turing machine in polynomial time with calls to an $\mathbf{NP}$ oracle. Note that the transition function o must be kept externally to the Turing machine, or represented in a somehow "compressed" way. Otherwise the function requires exponential amount of memory, and in consequence the problem is not even in PSPACE.

3.1   ATL **Model Checking over** CGS **Is** Σ_2P**-Hard**

We show this through a polynomial reduction of $QSAT_2$ to the model checking problem. In $QSAT_i$ (satisfiability for quantified Boolean formulae with i alternations of quantifiers), we are given k propositional variables $p_1, ..., p_k$ (partitioned into i sets $P_1, ..., P_i$) and a Boolean formula θ that includes no other variables. $QSAT_i$ asks if $\exists P_1 \forall P_2 \exists P_3 ... \Delta P_i\ \theta$ (where $\Delta = \forall$ if i is even, and $\exists$ if i is odd). $QSAT_i$ is known to be Σ_iP-complete [8].

   To obtain the reduction, we construct a concurrent game structure M with 3 states: $Q = \{q_0, q_\top, q_\bot\}$, and k agents: $Agt = \{a_1, ..., a_k\}$ that "decide" at q_0 upon valuations of propositions $p_1, ..., p_k \in P_1 \cup P_2$, respectively. Thus, agent a_i can "declare" proposition p_i true (action $\top$) or false (action $\bot$); Every tuple of actions from Agt corresponds to a valuation $v_1, ..., v_k$ of the propositions, and vice versa. Now, the transitions from q_0 are defined in the following way: $o(q_0, v_1, ..., v_k) = q_\top$ if $v_1, ..., v_k \models \theta$ and $q_\bot$ otherwise. Transitions from $q_\top$ and $q_\bot$ do not matter. Note that $v_1, ..., v_k \models \theta$ can be verified in time and space linear in $|\theta|$, so o has a polynomial representation with respect to the size of the original problem. Finally, we define proposition sat to hold only in state $q_\top$. Note that the agents "controlling" propositions from P_1 can enforce the next state to be $q_\top$ if, and only if, they can declare such a valuation of "their" propositions that θ is satisfied regardless of the opponents' choices:

Lemma 1. *Let A be the group of agents "responsible" for propositions P_1, i.e. $a_i \in A$ iff $p_i \in P_1$. Then, $\exists P_1 \forall P_2\ \theta$ iff $M, q_0 \models \langle\!\langle A \rangle\!\rangle \bigcirc$ sat.*

3.2   ATL **Model Checking over** CGS **Is** Σ_2P**-Easy**

In order to demonstrate Σ_2P-easiness of the model checking problem, we show an algorithm that computes the set of states in which formula φ holds, and lies in $\mathbf{NP^{NP}}$. A careful analysis of the algorithms proposed in [1, 2] reveals that the intractability is due to the pre-image operator Pre, which is called at most n times for every subformula of φ. Indeed, as we saw in the previous section, checking what a coalition can enforce in a single step (e.g., $M, q \models \langle\!\langle A \rangle\!\rangle \bigcirc$ sat) lies very close to the standard Σ_2P-complete problem of $QSAT_2$. We show that checking a more sophisticated ATL formula is no more complex than this. The main idea of the algorithm is as follows. First, we guess nondeterministically *all* the choices that will be needed for any call to function Pre (that is, for each coalition A that occurs in φ, and for each state $q \in Q$). Then we employ the standard model checking algorithm from [2] with one important modification: every time function $Pre(A, Q_1)$ is called, it assumes the subsequent A's choices from the tuple and checks whether $q \in Pre(A, Q_1)$ by calling an $\mathbf{NP}$ oracle (*is there a response from the opposition in q that leads to a state outside Q_1?*) and reversing its answer. The detailed algorithm is shown in Figure 1.

Lemma 2. *Function mcheck defines a nondeterministic Turing machine that runs in time $O(nkl)$, making calls to an $\mathbf{NP}$ oracle. The size of the witness is $O(nkl)$. The oracle is a nondet. Turing machine that runs in time $O(n + k)$.*

Proposition 1. *Model checking* ATL *formulae over* CGS *is Σ_2P-complete.*

---

function $mcheck(M, \varphi)$;
  Returns the set of states in M, in which formula φ holds.

- assign cooperation modalities in φ with subsequent numbers $1, ..., c$;
  - // note that $c \le l$; by $c(\varphi)$, we denote the number of cooperation modalities in φ
  - // we will denote the coalition from the ith cooperation modality in φ as $\varphi[i]$
- for every $i = 1, ..., c$, assign the agents in $\varphi[i]$ with numbers $1, ..., k_c$;
  - // note that $k_c \le k$ and $k_c \le l$
  - // we will denote the jth agent in A with $A[j]$
- guess an array $choice$ such that, for every $i = 1, ..., c$, $q \in Q$, and $j = 1, ..., k_c$, we have that $choice[i][q][j] \in d_{\varphi[i][j]}(q)$;
  - // at this point, the optimal choices for all coalitions in φ are guessed
  - // note that the size of $choice$ is $O(nkl)$
  - // by $choice|_i$, we will denote the array $choice$ with rows $1, ..., i-1$ removed
- return $eval(M, \varphi, choice)$;

---

function $eval(M, \varphi, choice)$;
  Returns the states in which φ holds, given choices for all the coalitions from φ.

case $\varphi \in \Pi$: return $\{q \mid \varphi \in \pi(q)\}$;
case $\varphi = \neg\psi$: return $Q \setminus eval(M, \psi, choice)$;
case $\varphi = \psi_1 \vee \psi_2$: return $eval(M, \psi_1, choice) \cup eval(M, \psi_2, choice|_{c(\psi_1)+1})$;
case $\varphi = \langle\langle A \rangle\rangle \bigcirc \psi$: return $pre(A, eval(M, \psi, choice|_2), M, choice[1])$;
case $\varphi = \langle\langle A \rangle\rangle \square \psi$: $Q_1 := Q$; $Q_2 := Q_3 := eval(M, \psi, choice|_2)$;
  while $Q_1 \not\subseteq Q_2$ **do** $Q_1 := Q_1 \cap Q_2$; $Q_2 := pre(A, Q_1, M, choice[1]) \cap Q_3$ **od**;
  return Q_1;
case $\varphi = \langle\langle A \rangle\rangle \psi_1 \mathcal{U} \psi_2$: $Q_1 := \varnothing$; $Q_2 := eval(M, \psi_1, choice|_2)$;
  $Q_3 := eval(M, \psi_2, choice|_{c(\psi_1)+2})$;
  while $Q_3 \not\subseteq Q_1$ **do** $Q_1 := Q_1 \cup Q_3$; $Q_3 := pre(A, Q_1, M, choice[1]) \cap Q_2$ **od**;
  return Q_1;
end case

---

function $pre(A, Q_1, M, thischoice)$;
  Returns the set of states, for which the A's choices from $thischoice$ enforce that the next state is in Q_1, regardless of what agents from $\mathbb{A}gt \setminus A$ do.

- $Q_2 := \varnothing$;
- for each $q \in Q$: **if** $oracle(A, Q_1, M, thischoice, q) = yes$ **then** $Q_2 := Q_2 \cup \{q\}$ **fi**;
- return Q_2;

---

function $oracle(A, Q_1, M, thischoice, q)$;
  Returns yes if, and only if, the A's choices from $thischoice$ in q enforce that the next state is in Q_1, regardless of what agents from $\mathbb{A}gt \setminus A$ do.

- guess an array $resp$ such that, for every $a \in \mathbb{A}gt \setminus A$, we have $resp[a] \in d_a(q)$;
  - // at this point, the most dangerous response from the opposition is guessed
  - // note that the size of $resp$ is $O(k)$
- **if** $o(q, thischoice[q], resp) \in Q_1$ **then** return yes **else** return no **fi**;

Fig. 1. Nondeterministic algorithm for model checking formulae of ATL

4   Model Checking with Alternating Transition Systems

The transition function in a CGS refers to choices that are abstract, while in alternating transition systems the function already encodes some information about possible outcomes of actions. In this section, we show that this implies some advantage in terms of model checking complexity: it still sits in the nondeterministic polynomial hierarchy, but it is "only" **NP**-complete. First, we demonstrate that the model checking is in **NP** in Section 4.1. Then, in Sections 4.2 and 4.3, we define a variant of the Boolean satisfiability problem that we call "single false clause SAT" (*sfc-SAT*), prove that it is **NP**-complete, and present a reduction of *sfc-SAT* to the model checking problem.

Modelling systems via ATS is usually troublesome in practice, mostly due to the "singleton" requirement. In Section 4.4, we point out that, if we relax the requirement and allow for nondeterministic ATS's, the model checking problem remains **NP**-complete – that is, we obtain the same model checking complexity for a strictly larger class of models.

4.1   Model Checking ATL over ATS Is NP-Easy

Unlike in concurrent game structures, choices in alternating transition systems already contain some information about which states can possibly be achieved through them. More precisely, α includes *all* the states that can be achieved through α. Had it contained *only* such states, checking if it enforces φ would have been easy (it would have been sufficient to check whether φ holds in all $q' \in \alpha$). However, the latter condition is not true in general. [6] introduces the notion of a *tight* ATS: all states q' to which no transition exists from q are removed from agents' choices at q (i.e. from the elements of $\delta(q, a)$ for all $a \in \text{Agt}$). Still, this is not enough for our purposes, because $\alpha \in \delta(q, a)$ may include states that are reachable from q in general, but not by executing α. In the following, we assume without loss of generality that $A = \{a_1, ..., a_r\}$ for some $r \leq k$.

Definition 1. *Let $\alpha_A = \langle \alpha_1, ..., \alpha_r \rangle$ be a collective choice of A at q, i.e. $\alpha_i \in \delta(q, a_i)$. State q' is α_A-reachable from q if there is a combination of responses from the rest of agents: $\alpha_{r+1}, ..., \alpha_k$, $\alpha_i \in \delta(q, a_i)$ such that $q' \in \alpha_1 \cap ... \cap \alpha_k$.*

Definition 2. ATS *M is strongly tight if, for each $q \in Q, a \in \text{Agt}$, we have that for every $q' \in \alpha_a \in \delta(q, a)$, q' is α_a-reachable from q.*

Lemma 3. *Let M be strongly tight, $\alpha_1, ..., \alpha_r$ be choices of $a_1, ..., a_r$ at q, and $q' \in \alpha_1 \cap ... \cap \alpha_r$. Then q' is $\langle \alpha_1, ..., \alpha_r \rangle$-reachable from q.*

Every ATS can be made strongly tight via the procedure in Figure 2A. Moreover, ATL formulae can be model-checked over strongly tight ATS's via the original ATL model checking algorithm from [1], with function $Pre(A, Q1)$ implemented as in Figure 2B. We observe that – if we assign numbers $1, ..., |\delta(q, a)|$ to choices from $\delta(q, a)$ for all q, a at the beginning, so that the choices are further identified by abstract labels rather than their content – all the "guessing" operations are

function $tighten(M)$; (A)	function $Pre(M, A, Q1)$; (B)

For every $a_i \in$ Agt, $q \in Q$, $\alpha_i \in \delta(q, a_i)$, and $q' \in \alpha_i$:
 	
 ■ guess the "opposition" responses $\alpha_1, ..., \alpha_{i-1}, \alpha_{i+1}, ..., \alpha_k$;
 ■ if $q' \notin \alpha_1 \cap ... \cap \alpha_k$ then remove q' from α_i;
	■ $pre := \varnothing$;
	 ■ for every $q \in Q$:
	   – guess $\alpha_a \in \delta(q, a)$ for each $a \in A$;
	   – if $\bigcap_{a \in A} \alpha_a \subseteq Q1$ then $pre := pre \cup \{q\}$;
	 ■ return pre;

Fig. 2. Algorithms for model checking ATL over alternating transition systems

independent from each other. Thus, we can apply the same trick as in Section 3.2, and guess *all* the necessary information beforehand. The size of the witness is $O(n^2 k^2 d + nkl)$, hence we obtain an **NP** algorithm for the model checking. We do not present the algorithm in more detail here due to lack of space.

4.2   Single False Clause SAT

Definition 3. [Single false clause SAT (**sfc-SAT**)].   *We define the following variant of the SAT problem.*
Input: *(1) n clauses: $C_1, ..., C_n$, in k propositions: $p_1, ..., p_k$ such that for each valuation of $p_1, ..., p_k$, exactly one clause is false; (2) numbers $m \leq n$, $r \leq k$.*
Problem: *Is there a valuation of $p_1, ..., p_r$ such that all clauses $C_1|_r, ..., C_m|_r$ are satisfied? Clause $C|_r$ is obtained from clause C by deleting all literals that refer to propositions $p_{r+1}, ..., p_k$ (i.e., we keep only the literals up to r).*

Obviously, *sfc-SAT* is in **NP** (it is sufficient to guess a valuation and check whether it is a good one). In order to show that *sfc-SAT* is **NP**-hard, we show that 3-SAT can be reduced to it. In 3-SAT, we are given m clauses $C_1, ..., C_m$ over r propositions $p_1, ..., p_r$ such that each clause C_i contains at most three literals: $C_i = l_{i,1} \vee l_{i,2} \vee l_{i,3}$ ($l_{i,j}$ are p_l or $\neg p_l$, $1 \leq i \leq m$). This special instance of the satisfiability problem is also **NP**-complete [8]. Note that the m and the r are the respective numbers occurring as inputs in Definition 3. To show that 3-SAT can be reduced to *sfc-SAT*, we demonstrate that there are propositions $p_{r+1}, ..., p_k$, and clauses $C'_1, ..., C'_n$, with $m \leq n$, $C_i \subseteq C'_i$ and $C'_i|_r = C_i$ for $i \leq m$, such that for each valuation of $p_1, ..., p_k$, exactly one of C'_i is false.

What does the last condition mean for a set of clauses $C'_1, ..., C'_n$? Basically, it means that these clauses represent all 2^k possibilities of choosing truth values for $p_1, ..., p_k$. So, the problem in the reduction is to *extend the given clauses by new variables* and to *add new clauses*. This has to be done so that the length of the new problem is still polynomial in the length of the given 3-SAT instance.

We assume without loss of generality that none of $C'_1, ..., C'_m$ contains a complementary pair of literals (otherwise the clause would be satisfiable under all valuations and could be safely discarded as it does not matter for the overall satisfiability problem). In order to extend clauses $C_1, ..., C_m$ in an appropriate way, we use auxiliary formulae α_i and β, defined in the following way:

α_i: We construct formulae α_i stating that *a selected clause number is $i \leq m$*. To be more precise, we introduce $t := \lceil \log m \rceil$ new variables $y_1, \ldots, y_t$ and define conjunctions α_i ($i = 1, \ldots, m$) over these variables as follows (this idea is due to Thomas Eiter [5]). We write each number $1, \ldots, m$ in binary and represent each (of the t) digits by the new variables (a 1 is represented by the variable itself, a 0 by the negation of the variable). The i'th digit is then represented by y_i if it is 1 and by $\neg y_i$ if it is 0. Thus, for each valuation of the new variables, only one conjunction α_i can be true, namely the one representing the number coded in the binary representation.

Note that we can also represent numbers greater than m (up to the next power of 2, namely 2^t). These conjunctions do not correspond to the m original clauses from the 3-SAT problem. In our reduction, we have to distinguish between them. Therefore we introduce a formula β in the next step.

β: We construct a formula β stating that the selected clause number is less than or equal to m. Thus, β satisfies the following equivalences: $\beta \Leftrightarrow \bigvee_{i=1}^{m} \alpha_i \Leftrightarrow \bigwedge_{i=m+1}^{2^{\lceil \log m \rceil}} \neg \alpha_i$. Note that the last formula is a set clauses (because all $\neg \alpha_i$ are clauses), and hence we need at most $2^{\lceil \log m \rceil} - m$ many clauses to represent β (which is never more than m). We denote these clauses by $C_1^\beta, \ldots, C_m^\beta$. Each clause C_j^β states, that *the selected clause has not the number $m + j$*.

Extending the clauses: For each $C_i = l_{i,1} \vee l_{i,2} \vee l_{i,3}$ we construct the *remaining* 7 clauses (all parities of the 3 variables) and add $\neg \alpha_i$. So, for each C_i we get 8 clauses $C'_{i,0}, \ldots C'_{i,7}$, where $C'_{i,0} = C_i \vee \neg \alpha_i$ and $(C'_{i,0} \wedge \ldots \wedge C'_{i,7}) \Leftrightarrow \neg \alpha_i$. Note, again, that $\neg \alpha_i$ is always a clause. We observe also that the m clauses $C_1, \ldots, C_m$, which we originally started with (as an instance of 3-SAT), are, by construction, exactly $C'_{1,0}|r, C'_{2,0}|r, \ldots, C'_{m,0}|r$.

Reduction: The (at most) $s := m + m \times 8$ clauses:

$$C_1^\beta, \ldots, C_m^\beta, \quad \text{and} \quad C'_{i,j} \ (1 \leq i \leq m, 0 \leq j \leq 7),$$

over $k = r + \lceil \log m \rceil$ variables, represent an instance of *sfc-SAT*, such that if we choose $m \leq n$ and $r \leq k$, then we get the 3-SAT problem we started with.

Why are the clauses above an instance of *sfc-SAT*? The fact that we get back the 3-SAT problem has already been shown. It is also obvious that the constructed instance is polynomial in the size of the instance we started with. So it remains to show that for each valuation of all the variables, *exactly one clause is false*. Let a valuation be given. We must consider two cases:

1. Exactly one of the $\alpha_1, \ldots, \alpha_m$ is true, say α_{i_0}. Then all clauses $C'_{i,j}$ with $i \neq i_0$ are true (because $\neg \alpha_i$ is true and it occurs as a disjunct in all these clauses). Of the 8 clauses $C'_{i_0,j}$ ($0 \leq j \leq 7$), exactly one is false, namely the one contradicting the valuation of the three old variables occurring in the original C_i. Clearly, β (i.e all clauses C_j^β) is true as well.
2. None of the $\alpha_1, \ldots, \alpha_m$ is true. But then all clauses $C'_{i,j}$ are true and only β is false, i.e. exactly one of the clauses C_j^β.

These are all the cases, because α_i (resp. C_j^β) are pairwise inconsistent by construction: any two different conjunctions α_i, α_j (resp. C_i^β, C_j^β) with $i \neq j$ contain at least one pair of complementary literals. This gives us the following result:

Proposition 2. *Sfc-SAT is* **NP***-complete.*

4.3   Reduction of *sfc-SAT* to ATL Model Checking over ATS

To obtain the reduction, we construct an ATS M with states $Q = \{q_0, C_1, ..., C_n\}$, i.e. one state per clause plus an initial state. Next, we "simulate" propositions $p_1, ..., p_k$ with agents $a_1, ..., a_k$. Each agent "declares" his proposition true or false in the initial state q_0. Thus, agent a_i has two available choices at q_0: to declare p_i true or to declare p_i false; a choice of a_i is represented with the set of clauses that are *not* made true by setting the value of p_i in this particular way. There is only one atomic proposition, therest, with $\pi(\text{therest}) = \{C_{m+1}, ..., C_n\}$.

Note that each combination of choices from $a_1, ..., a_k$ at q_0 corresponds to a single valuation of $p_1, ..., p_k$, and vice versa. Moreover, a clause is not satisfied by a valuation iff no proposition "makes" it true. Thus, the set of clauses, unsatisfied by a valuation, is equal to the intersection of sets of clauses that are not "made" true by each single proposition. By definition of *sfc-SAT*, such an intersection is always a singleton, which proves that M is indeed an ATS.

Lemma 4. *There is a valuation of $p_1, ..., p_r$ such that all clauses $C_1|r, ..., C_m|r$ are satisfied   iff $M, q_0 \models \langle\langle a_1, ..., a_r \rangle\rangle \bigcirc \text{therest}$.*

Note that the reduction can be done in time polynomial in n, k. Computing the agents' choice sets is the hardest point here, and it can be done in time $O(k^2 n)$. The resulting model includes $n + 1$ states, k agents, and $d = 2$ choices per agent per state – and the length of the resulting formula is $l = r + 2 \leq k + 2$, which concludes the reduction.

Proposition 3. *Model checking* ATL *formulae over* ATS *is* **NP***-complete.*

4.4   Model Checking with Nondeterministic Transition Systems

Alternating transition systems were proposed as models for open computational systems, and the way in which the transition function is constructed reflects this intention. The problem with ATS's is that they are *not* modular, partly due to the "singleton intersection" requirement: legality of a choice cannot be defined in isolation from the rest of the choices model. Adding another process to the system usually requires thorough re-construction of the model: in particular, new states must be added, and agents' choices extended so that *every* intersection is again a singleton. We suggest that the requirement can be relaxed, yielding a more general (and more flexible) class of models with the same ATL model checking complexity. To show this, we define *non-deterministic alternating transition systems* (NATS) in the same way as ATS, except that no requirement on function δ is imposed. Obviously, model checking ATL formulae over NATS is **NP**-hard, because ATS are special cases of NATS. Moreover, the model checking algorithm, depicted in Section 4.1, can be applied to NATS as well.

Proposition 4. *Model checking* ATL *formulae over* NATS *is* **NP***-complete.*

This suggests that using the more general class of NATS may be beneficial for most purposes. Note, however, that defining ATL semantics over NATS may have some disadvantages too. For example, CTL cannot be syntactically embedded in ATL over NATS, because $\mathsf{E}\varphi$ is not equivalent to $\langle\!\langle \mathrm{Agt} \rangle\!\rangle\varphi$ anymore. A more detailed analysis of ATL expressivity over NATS is beyond the scope of this paper.

5 Conclusions

In this paper, we establish the precise ATL model checking complexity when the number of agents is considered a parameter of the problem. Most importantly, we prove that the model checking is intractable for both major ATL semantics. The problem sits very close to QSAT_2 in the case of concurrent game structures, and indeed, it turns out to be $\mathbf{\Sigma_2 P}$-complete. For the previous semantics, based on alternating transition systems, the problem is "only" **NP**-complete, which suggests that using ATS may have some advantage over CGS. Finally, we show that ATL model checking over the broader class of nondeterministic ATS is still **NP**-complete, which suggests that using NATS may be also convenient.

We would like to thank Thomas Eiter for his help in the **NP**-hardness proof of the *sfc-SAT* problem.

References

1. R. Alur, T. A. Henzinger, and O. Kupferman. Alternating-time Temporal Logic. *Lecture Notes in Computer Science*, 1536:23–60, 1998.
2. R. Alur, T. A. Henzinger, and O. Kupferman. Alternating-time Temporal Logic. *Journal of the ACM*, 49:672–713, 2002.
3. L. de Alfaro, T.A. Henzinger, and F.Y.C. Mang. The control of synchronous systems. In *Proceedings of CONCUR 2000*, pages 458–473, 2000.
4. L. de Alfaro, T.A. Henzinger, and F.Y.C. Mang. The control of synchronous systems, part II. In *Proceedings of CONCUR 2001*, pages 566–580, 2001.
5. T. Eiter. Oral communication. March 2005.
6. V. Goranko. Coalition games and alternating temporal logics. In *Proceedings of TARK VIII*, pages 259–272. Morgan Kaufmann, 2001.
7. V. Goranko and W. Jamroga. Comparing semantics of logics for multi-agent systems. *Synthese*, 139(2):241–280, 2004.
8. C.H. Papadimitriou. *Computational Complexity*. Addison Wesley : Reading, 1994.
9. P. Y. Schobbens. Alternating-time logic with imperfect recall. *Electronic Notes in Theoretical Computer Science*, 85(2), 2004.

Multiagent Resource Allocation in the Presence of Externalities

Paul E. Dunne

Dept. of Computer Science,
University of Liverpool, Liverpool L69 7ZF, UK
ped@csc.liv.ac.uk

Abstract. In studies of settings concerning the allocation of a finite resource collection among a set of agents it is, usually, assumed that each agent associates a value with each subset of resources via a utility function that is free from so-called *externalities*, i.e. that these values are independent of the distribution of the remaining resources among the other agents. While this assumption is valid in many application domains, it is, however, by no means universally so. Thus, one can identify a number of circumstances wherein an agent's assessment of a given subset is dependent not only on the elements of this set but also on the *context* in which it is held, i.e. on the resources owned by other agents. In this paper a general model for considering resource allocation settings with externalities is presented and its properties reviewed with reference to a select number of issues that have been widely-studied in externality–free settings.

Keywords: Multiagent Resource allocation; Computational Complexity.

1 Introduction

In studies of multiagent negotiation traditional models of activities such as resource allocation implicitly assume that the settings are free from so-called *externalities*, i.e. that the "value" placed by an agent on a given subset of the resources is unaffected by the distribution of the remaining resources among the other agents. For example, although not always explicitly stated, this is the view adopted in, among others, [4,5,9,11,13,14]. While suitable for many situations that arise in practice, it is, however, not appropriate for *every* domain. Thus, one may identify a number of cases where the effective utility of some collection of resources to an agent is dependent on how the remainder are allocated. As examples consider the following.

Example 1. Card games such as Contract Bridge: a standard (52 card) deck is dealt among four players (conventionally named N, S, E and W) grouped as two separate partnerships of two players (N with S; E with W). The "utility" of the cards dealt to a given player cannot be assigned a definitive value since its worth may depend on the distribution of the remaining cards among the other players.

Example 2. The "value" of shares in a company: as viewed by different groups of shareholders this may vary considerably, so that those seeking to obtain a majority controlling interest find the cost of shares escalating the closer they come to realising their objective. If the attempts are unsuccessful the "share price" may collapse, e.g. if a group

M. Pěchouček, P. Petta, and L.Z. Varga (Eds.): CEEMAS 2005, LNAI 3690, pp. 408–417, 2005.

seeking control disposes of its shares having decided the cost of obtaining a majority holding is excessive.

Despite the differing applications domains identified in these examples some common features can be noted. In each case a given subset of the resources (cards, shares) has some notional "intrinsic" value, e.g. in the Bridge example this might be assessed in terms of how many "high cards" are held: this intrinsic valuation may, however, fail to be a true reflection of a resource set's actual worth *relative to the holdings of other agents*. A further similarity concerns how an agent's view of a given resource set evolves with its knowledge of what other agents are allocated: the decisions taken concerning resource usage when an agent has complete information about an allocation may be different from those made when only its own holding is known.

That the utility of a collection of resources may be affected by factors other than the resource set itself has, of course, long been recognised outside the particular arena of multiagent systems issues. Thus the terminology "externality" originates from game-theoretic models of exchange economies. There has, however, been little work carried out regarding, for example, algorithmic and other implications arising from such behaviour in terms of multiagent systems settings.

For example, one issue of interest is the following: in the standard setting various concepts have been mooted in order to capture the idea of how an allocation P of $\mathcal{R}$ among $\mathcal{A}$ "compares with" a different allocation Q, e.g. social welfare, Pareto optimality, etc. in [3,4,11]. To what extent do these measures continue to be "sensibly defined" in settings with externalities? Are there alternative or additional comparative standards for distinct allocations in this case? Thus, there are highly non-trivial aspects from, for example, the perspective of properties of negotiation mechanisms both in semantic – e.g. protocol formalisms as considered in [2,8,10], – and algorithmic terms, e.g. as reviewed in [7,12].

The aim of this paper is to present a model of resource allocation with externalities and to discuss its properties. The basic model is described in the next section. In Section 3 it is argued that if allocations are to be negotiated using distributed autonomous mechanisms, then some provision for all agents to discover complete information about the current allocation is needed. In Section 4, we examine decision questions relating to settings with externalities together with strategic considerations that might motivate a coalition of agents to form. Conclusions and discussion occupy the final section.

2   Belief Contexts: Partial and Complete Information

Throughout the sequel $\mathcal{A}$ is a system of n agents $\langle a_1, \ldots, a_n \rangle$ and $\mathcal{R}$ a collection of m indivisible and non-shareable *resources*, $\{r_1, \ldots, r_m\}$. The set $\mathcal{P}_{n,m}$ of *partial allocations* of $\mathcal{R}$ among $\mathcal{A}$, is

$$\mathcal{P}_{n,m} = \{ \langle P_1 ; P_2 ; \cdots ; P_n \rangle : P_i \subseteq \mathcal{R} \text{ and } P_i \cap P_j \neq \emptyset \Rightarrow i = j \}$$

The set $\mathcal{F}_{n,m}$ of *full allocations* of $\mathcal{R}$ among $\mathcal{A}$ is

$$\mathcal{F}_{n,m} = \left\{ \langle F_1 ; F_2 ; \cdots ; F_n \rangle \in \mathcal{P}_{n,m} : \bigcup_{i=1}^{n} F_i = \mathcal{R} \right\}$$

In order to deal with the notion of utility functions with externalities, it is necessary to distinguish full allocations F as they are *in "reality"* from what agents *believe to be true* of them. To this end each agent, a_i, maintains a structure $B^{(i)} \in \mathcal{P}_{n,m}$ called its *belief context*: if $F \in \mathcal{F}_{n,m}$ describes the full allocation currently in force, then the only condition imposed on the belief context, $B^{(i)} = \langle B_1^{(i)} ; B_2^{(i)} \cdots B_n^{(i)} \rangle$ for a_i is that $B_i^{(i)} = F_i$, i.e. it is assumed that every agent knows its own allocation within F.

Informally, these model the following idea: a_i knows its own resource holding ($B_i^{(i)} = F_i$) and, in the course of resources being moved around, a_i may collect information concerning the holdings of other agents, e.g. if a_1 transferred resource r_1 to a_2, then a_1 could subsequently update $B^{(i)}$ to record $\{r_1\} \subseteq B_2^{(i)}$. The critical aspect is that, other than the requirement $B_i^{(i)} = F_i$, the set $B_j^{(i)}$ (when $j \neq i$) could be unrelated to the subset F_j actually held by a_j under F: a_i "believes" that $B_j^{(i)} \subseteq F_j$, this may, however, not be the case.

Combining these elements leads to the following basic model of resource allocation settings with externalities.

Definition 1. *A resource allocation setting with externalities is defined by $\langle \mathcal{A}, \mathcal{R}, \mathcal{V}, \mathcal{U} \rangle$: $\mathcal{V}$ describes the valuation functions $v_i : \mathcal{P}_{n,m} \to \mathbb{Q}$ whereby agents associate values with their belief contexts; $\mathcal{U}$ defines the utility functions $u_i : 2^{\mathcal{R}} \to \mathbb{Q}$ through which a_i associates a value with its assigned resource set.*

For a full allocation $F \in \mathcal{F}_{n,m}$ an n-tuple $B = \langle B^{(1)}, B^{(2)}, \ldots, B^{(n)} \rangle$ of belief contexts is F-consistent if for each $1 \leq i \leq n$, $B_i^{(i)} = F_i$; B is consistent if it is F-consistent for at least one $F \in \mathcal{F}_{n,m}$.

Although the component $\mathcal{U}$ does not feature significantly in our subsequent discussion, we include this to model the concept of an agent's "intrinsic valuation" of subsets of $\mathcal{R}$.

We note one important aspect of Defn. 1: the mechanism defined for evaluating full allocations relies *only* on an agent's knowledge of its own resource holding and its beliefs concerning what is held by other agents, i.e. agents may form a (subjective) view of "how good" a full allocation is without possessing complete and/or correct information about it. We thus distinguish valuation functions whose domain is $\mathcal{F}_{n,m}$ (which implicitly assume agents have complete knowledge) and those with domain $\mathcal{P}_{n,m}$. While it is certainly the case that the effect of externality could be modelled using the former, one significant drawback to doing so concerns how such valuations are implemented at the level of *individual* agents: in order accurately to evaluate the full allocation, F, an agent would need to know each subset F_j, i.e. a_i cannot determine $v_i(F)$ unless its "belief" is that $B^{(i)} = F$. In many situations, for example in settings involving a large number of agents and within which there are frequent local reallocations of resources occurring, the overhead needed to ensure that all agents have complete knowledge of the present allocation will become prohibitive: in these cases the assumption of complete knowledge seems unrealistic. In contrast, by allowing agents to determine the influence of external factors by maintaining a (partial) record of what other agents are thought to own, an agent may be able to assess its allocation in the light of information which is locally gathered, e.g. by forming inferences based on observed transactions.

A reliance on partial information does, however, create one problem: an agent can determine a valuation through its belief context but may find itself making decisions on the basis of *incorrect* and/or *insufficient* information, since its belief context does not describe the full allocation in use. Such inaccuracy may arise even in the absence of "malicious" action by other agents, e.g. an agent deliberately giving the wrong response to a query about its ownership of some resource: if a_i reassigns some subset, X, of its original holding to a_j, then although a_i may be able to update its belief context to reflect $X \subseteq F_j$, a_i (unless explicitly informed) cannot know if a_j subsequently disposes of some subset Y of X to a different agent.

In total the contrasting approaches give rise to a dichotomy confronting how an agent *ought* to view its allocation with how an agent *believes* it should be viewed. This conflict can be interpreted as clash between global and local perspectives: the former that of an "external" observer who is aware of the full allocation, F, of $\mathcal{R}$ that is in place; the latter that of individual agents, who, although able to form hypotheses about F may not be in a position easily to verify such. Some of the difficulties that these dual viewpoints create in the areas of defining and negotiating "optimal" allocations, are examined in the next section.

3   Concepts of Optimality

In presenting formulations of "optimal allocation", a widely studied idea has been that of "*social welfare*". The assessment made of a full allocation, F, within the standard externality-free model, defines the social welfare of F – denoted $\sigma(F)$ – to be the value $\sum_{i=1}^{n} u_i(F_i)$, (where $u_i : 2^\mathcal{R} \to \mathbb{Q}$ is the (externality-free) valuation function for a_i) so that an optimal allocation is one that *maximises* this value. This measure has been examined in the multiagent systems arena with respect to computational complexity issues, e.g. [4],[7, p. 43], and frameworks for identifying allocations with maximum social welfare, e.g. [3,11].

In the setting of Defn. 1, one natural reformulation of $\sigma(F)$ for $F \in \mathcal{F}_{n,m}$, is as

$$\sigma^{(\tau)}(F) =_{\text{def}} \sum_{i=1}^{n} v_i(F)$$

Thus, v_i is evaluated from the (global) perspective in which $B^{(i)} = F$ for each agent's belief context. It is certainly the case that $\sigma^{(\tau)}$ defines the *attained* social welfare from the viewpoint of an external, independent observer, thus one may describe $\sigma^{(\tau)}$ as the *true* social welfare. Equally, however, such an observer may be unaware of the exact allocation and, in order to calculate the sum of the agents' valuations must rely on each agent reporting their *local* assessment. In such cases, the *perceived* social welfare of F will be

$$\sigma^{(\pi)}(F, B) =_{\text{def}} \sum_{i=1}^{n} v_i(B^{(i)})$$

That is, the assessment is via the F-consistent system B formed by the belief contexts of the agents.

Now given that $\mathcal{P}_{n,m}$ is finite, it is certainly the case that there are full allocations, $\{F^{\mathrm{opt}}, F^{\mathrm{bad}}\}$ for which

$$F^{\mathrm{opt}} =_{\mathrm{def}} \text{A full allocation that } maximises\ \sigma^{(\tau)}$$
$$F^{\mathrm{bad}} =_{\mathrm{def}} \text{A full allocation that } minimises\ \sigma^{(\tau)}$$

It was earlier noted that requiring agents to have complete knowledge about the current allocation may impose unrealistic overheads. The following result indicates one significant problem if all negotiations about redistributing resources between agents take place in an environment where decisions are made *solely* on the basis of what agents believe about the current allocation.

Phrased less formally, Theorem 1 below asserts the existence of resource allocation settings with externalities in which a *genuine* "best" allocation (F^{opt}) is perceived as a worst possible one (F^{bad}); and (for the *same* setting) a genuine "worst possible" allocation (F^{bad}) is perceived to be optimal (F^{opt}).

Theorem 1. *There are resource allocation settings with externalities,* $\langle A, \mathcal{R}, \mathcal{V}, \mathcal{U} \rangle$ *in which* $\langle F^{\mathrm{opt}}, F^{\mathrm{bad}}, B^{\mathrm{bad}}, B^{\mathrm{opt}} \rangle$ *can be defined so that* B^{bad} *is* F^{opt}*–consistent,* B^{opt} *is* F^{bad}*–consistent and with*

a. $\sigma^{(\pi)}(F^{\mathrm{opt}},, B^{\mathrm{bad}}) = \sigma^{(\tau)}(F^{\mathrm{bad}})$
b. $\sigma^{(\pi)}(F^{\mathrm{bad}}, B^{\mathrm{opt}}) = \sigma^{(\tau)}(F^{\mathrm{opt}})$

Proof: (Outline) Assume that, for some $k > 1$, $n = 2k$ and $m = n$. Let F be the full allocation in which $F_i = \{r_i\}$ and G that in which $G_i = \{r_{n-i+1}\}$.[1] Define the belief contexts, $B^{(i)}$, via

$$B_j^{(i)} = \begin{cases} \emptyset & \text{if } i \text{ is odd and } j \notin \{i, i+1\} \\ \emptyset & \text{if } i \text{ is even and } j \notin \{i-1, i\} \\ \{r_i\} & \text{if } j = i \\ \mathcal{R} \setminus \{r_i\} & \text{if } i \text{ is odd and } j = i+1 \\ \mathcal{R} \setminus \{r_i\} & \text{if } i \text{ is even and } j = i-1 \end{cases}$$

and, similarly, the belief contexts $D^{(i)}$ as

$$D_j^{(i)} = \begin{cases} \emptyset & \text{if } i \text{ is odd and } j \notin \{i, i+1\} \\ \emptyset & \text{if } i \text{ is even and } j \notin \{i-1, i\} \\ \{r_{n-i+1}\} & \text{if } j = i \\ \mathcal{R} \setminus \{r_{n-i+1}\} & \text{if } i \text{ is odd and } j = i+1 \\ \mathcal{R} \setminus \{r_{n-i+1}\} & \text{if } i \text{ is even and } j = i-1 \end{cases}$$

For $P \in \mathcal{P}_{n,m}$, the valuation functions, v_i, are given by

$$v_i(P) = \begin{cases} 1 & \text{if } P = B^{(i)} \\ n & \text{if } P = D^{(i)} \\ n & \text{if } P = F \\ 1 & \text{if } P = G \\ 2 & \text{if } P \notin \{F, G, B^{(i)}, D^{(i)}\} \end{cases}$$

---

[1] Combined with the assumption that n is even, choosing G as the "reverse" ordering of F ensures that for every a_i, $G_i \neq F_i$.

To complete the proof it suffices to observe that $\langle B^{(1)}, \ldots, B^{(n)} \rangle$ is F–consistent and $\langle D^{(1)}, \ldots, D^{(n)} \rangle$ is G-consistent. In the former case – the full allocation being F and a_i holding the belief context $B^{(i)}$ –

$$\sigma^{(\tau)}(F) = n^2$$
$$\sigma^{(\pi)}(F, \langle B^{(1)}, \ldots, B^{(n)} \rangle) = n$$

while in the latter case – the full allocation being G and a_i holding the belief context $D^{(i)}$ –

$$\sigma^{(\tau)}(G) = n$$
$$\sigma^{(\pi)}(G, \langle D^{(1)}, \ldots, D^{(n)} \rangle) = n^2$$

It is straightforward to show that $n \leq \sigma^{(\tau)} \leq n^2$ so that (a) follows using the full allocation F with the F-consistent system B and (b) from G with the G-consistent system D.   □

The construction outlined above, employs systems of belief contexts, $\{B, D\}$, which although F^X–consistent (for $X \in \{\text{opt, bad}\}$) involve each agent taking an incorrect view of the full allocation, e.g. for the pairing $\langle F, B \rangle$, when i is odd, a_i wrongly believes $\mathcal{R} \setminus \{r_i\} \subseteq F_{i+1}$. It is not difficult, however, to devise a belief context system B, say, which is F^{opt}-consistent, has the property that every agent's beliefs are correct, i.e. $B_j^{(i)} \subseteq F_j^{\text{opt}}$, yet nevertheless is such that $\sigma^{(\pi)}(F^{\text{opt}}, B) = \sigma^{(\tau)}(F^{\text{bad}})$. One such choice for B is,

$$B_j^{(i)} = \begin{cases} \emptyset & \text{if } j = i - 1 \text{ and } i \geq 2 \\ \emptyset & \text{if } j = n \text{ and } i = 1 \\ \{r_j\} & \text{otherwise} \end{cases}$$

The system B is F^{opt}–consistent, but, as in the proof of Theorem 1, combined with valuation functions v_i that assign 1 to the context P if $P = B^{(i)}$, n if $P = F^{\text{opt}}$, and 2 in all other cases, has $\sigma^{(\pi)}(F^{\text{opt}}, B) = \sigma^{(\tau)}(F^{\text{bad}})$. In this construction the problem is not that the beliefs of agents are incorrect, since $B_j^{(i)} \subseteq F_j^{\text{opt}}$, but that their knowledge of the allocation if *incomplete*: the agent a_1 is not aware of who owns the resource r_n; similarly, for $i \geq 2$, a_i does not know the owner of r_{i-1}.

One further straightforward consequence is that the difference between $\sigma^{(\pi)}(F, B)$, and $\sigma^{(\tau)}(F)$ when B is F–consistent, can be arbitrarily large, even when F is a full allocation that maximises $\sigma^{(\tau)}$.

Corollary 1. *Given* $\langle \mathcal{A}, \mathcal{R} \rangle$, *a full allocation* $F \in \mathcal{F}_{n,m}$, *and* $K \in \mathbb{N}$, *there is a choice of* V *and* F–*consistent systems of belief contexts* B *and* D, *for which*

$$\left. \begin{array}{l} \sigma^{(\tau)}(F) - \sigma^{(\pi)}(F, B) \\ \sigma^{(\pi)}(F, D) - \sigma^{(\tau)}(F) \end{array} \right\} \geq K$$

Furthermore, these hold even when V *must be chosen so that* F *maximises* $\sigma^{(\tau)}$ *in the setting* $\langle \mathcal{A}, \mathcal{R}, V, \mathcal{U} \rangle$.

Proof: The proof is, in essence, simply a variation of the device used in proving Theorem 1. Details are omitted.   □

Although the extremes indicated by Theorem 1 are established through the use of, what are arguably, "artificial" valuation functions, the possibilities represented – optimal allocations being perceived as sub-optimal; or sub-optimal distributions seen as optimal ones – clearly pose problems for mechanisms that attempt practically to address systems of utility functions with externalities. In summary, faced with such environments:

a. To enforce "complete knowledge" of allocations at the level of individual agents imposes unrealistic maintenance overheads especially in large volatile settings.
b. Relaxing the "complete knowledge" condition to the extreme in which each agent is responsible for locally maintaining its own view of the allocation may result in situations where no "useful" allocation is obtained: agents lack any incentive to deviate from (wrongly perceived to be) optimal forms; and/or may attempt to change already optimal allocations in the mistaken belief that the current distribution is sub-optimal.

4   Profiles and Coalitions

In this section our concern is with the complexity of various decision properties arising in settings with externalities. We first define the *profile* of a full allocation.

Definition 2. *For a full allocation $F \in \mathcal{F}_{n,m}$ the* profile *of F within $\langle \mathcal{A}, \mathcal{R}, \mathcal{V}, \mathcal{U} \rangle$ is the n-tuple, $\pi(F) \in \mathbb{Q}^n$ given by $\langle v_1(F), v_2(F), \ldots, v_n(F) \rangle$. For a given n-tuple $\mathbf{q} \in \mathbb{Q}^n$, we say that $\mathbf{q} = \langle q_1, \ldots, q_n \rangle$ is an* attainable profile *within $\langle \mathcal{A}, \mathcal{R}, \mathcal{V}, \mathcal{U} \rangle$, if there exists $F \in \mathcal{F}_{n,m}$ with which $\pi(F) \geq \mathbf{q}$ where n-tuples $\mathbf{p}, \mathbf{q}$ are ordered $\mathbf{q}$ via $\mathbf{p} \geq \mathbf{q}$ if and only if $p_i \geq q_i$ for each $1 \leq i \leq n$.*

A natural decision question within this setting is the following.
Attainable Profile (AP)
Instance: $\langle \mathcal{A}, \mathcal{R}, \mathcal{V}, \mathcal{U} \rangle; \mathbf{q} \in \mathbb{Q}^n$.
Question: Is there a full allocation $F \in \mathcal{F}_{n,m}$ for which $\pi(F) \geq \mathbf{q}$?

In presenting instances of this problem there is, of course, the issue of how the structures $\mathcal{V}$ and $\mathcal{U}$ are encoded, bearing in mind that the domains $\mathcal{P}_{n,m}$ and $\mathcal{F}_{n,m}$ have size exponential in m: we adopt the so-called "straight-line program" model (SLP) proposed in [4, Defns. 9–10].

Theorem 2. AP *is* NP–*complete.*

Proof: (Outline) Membership in NP is immediate from the non-deterministic algorithm that guesses a full allocation $F \in \mathcal{F}_{n,m}$ and checks $\pi(F) \geq \mathbf{q}$. For NP–hardness we prove a rather stronger result: AP is NP–hard even when instances are restricted to 2 agents, with the profile $\langle q_1, q_2 \rangle = \langle 1, 1 \rangle$ and for a fixed pair of valuation functions $\langle v_1, v_2 \rangle$ whose definition, given a full allocation $F = \langle F_1, F_2 \rangle$, is

$$v_1(F) = \begin{cases} 0 & \text{if } u_1(F_2) > u_1(F_1) \\ 1 & \text{if } u_1(F_2) \leq u_1(F_1) \end{cases} \quad v_2(F) = \begin{cases} 0 & \text{if } u_2(F_1) > u_2(F_2) \\ 1 & \text{if } u_2(F_1) \leq u_2(F_2) \end{cases}$$

We employ a reduction from 3-SAT, with instances $\Phi(Z_t)$ limited to those for which the number of propositional variables, t, is *odd*. We need only specify $\mathcal{R}$ and the functions $\langle u_1, u_2 \rangle$. Fix $\mathcal{R} = \{z_1, z_2, \ldots, z_t\}$, i.e. the resource set consists of the propositional variables defining $\Phi(Z_t)$. For $W \subseteq \mathcal{R}$, the instantiation $pos(W)$ is given by $z_i = \top$ if

$z_i \in W$, $z_i = \bot$ if $z_i \notin W$; similarly, the instantiation $neg(W)$ is given by $pos(\mathcal{R}/W)$. The utility functions, $\langle u_1, u_2 \rangle$ are:

$$u_1(S) = \begin{cases} 2t & \text{if } \Phi(pos(S)) = \top \\ |S| & \text{if } \Phi(pos(S)) \neq \top \end{cases} \qquad u_2(S) = \begin{cases} 2t & \text{if } \Phi(neg(S)) = \top \\ |S| & \text{if } \Phi(neg(S)) \neq \top \end{cases}$$

For space reasons we omit the straightforward argument that $\langle 1, 1 \rangle$ is attainable in the constructed setting if and only if $\Phi(Z_t)$ is satisfiable. $\qquad\qquad\qquad\qquad\square$

From Theorem 2 the decision problems considering whether there are full allocations under which a_i *strictly* improves v_i (*Subjective Improvement* – SI); or under which *every* agent strictly improves its valuation, (*Objective Improvment* – OI) are also seen to be NP–complete. In addition we have the following consequence: for (externality–free) resource allocation settings $\langle \mathcal{A}, \mathcal{R}, \mathcal{U} \rangle$, a full allocation, F, is said to be *envy–free* ([6]) if for every pair $\langle i, j \rangle$ it holds that $u_i(F_i) \geq u_i(F_j)$; thus no agent views the holding of another agent as having greater worth than its own resources. The decision problem *Envy-Freeness* (EF) asks of a given $\langle \mathcal{A}, \mathcal{R}, \mathcal{U} \rangle$ if there exists any envy–free full allocation within it.

Corollary 2. EF *is* NP–*complete.*[2]

Proof: Given $\langle \mathcal{A}, \mathcal{R}, \mathcal{U} \rangle$, define the valuation function, $v_i : \mathcal{F}_{n,m} \to \mathbb{Q}$ as

$$v_i(F) = 1 - |\{ j : u_i(F_j) > u_i(F_i) \}|$$

With this, $\langle \mathcal{A}, \mathcal{R}, \mathcal{U} \rangle$ admits an envy–free allocation if and only if the profile $\langle 1, 1, \ldots, 1 \rangle$ is attainable, so that with $\langle u_1, u_2 \rangle$ constructed as in in Theorem 2 it follows that the resulting setting admits an envy–free allocation if and only if its source formula $\Phi(Z_n)$ is satisfiable. $\qquad\qquad\qquad\qquad\square$

There are properties of given settings $\langle \mathcal{A}, \mathcal{R}, \mathcal{V}, \mathcal{U} \rangle$ that a set of agents may seek to exploit, e.g. assuming a competitive environment of self-interested agents, one reason why a *coalition*, $\mathcal{X} \subset \mathcal{A}$ of agents may form within resource allocation settings with externalities, is that by acquiring and distributing some subset S of $\mathcal{R}$, the members of $\mathcal{X}$ achieve an allocation they regard as optimal, irrespective of how $\mathcal{R} \setminus S$ is distributed among $\mathcal{A} \setminus \mathcal{X}$. Such resource subsets, S, may assume greater importance to the coalition if not only can it achieve a locally optimal allocation with S but also ensure that $\mathcal{A} \setminus \mathcal{X}$ are unable to to realise a locally optimal distribution with only $\mathcal{R} \setminus S$ available. This leads to the idea of a coalition being able to *block* another. Noting that, even if a coalition is unable to realise an optimal outcome, its members might be content with one which guarantees a certain return while ensuring that of other agents is smaller, motivates the decision problem below.

Blocking Coalition (BC)
Instance: $\langle \mathcal{A}, \mathcal{R}, \mathcal{V}, \mathcal{U} \rangle$; $\mathcal{X}, \mathcal{Y} \subseteq \mathcal{A}$ (with $\mathcal{X} \cap \mathcal{Y} = \emptyset$); $\langle q_{\mathcal{X}}, q_{\mathcal{Y}} \rangle \in \mathbb{Q}^2$ ($q_{\mathcal{X}} \geq q_{\mathcal{Y}}$)
Question: Is there a subset $S_{\mathcal{X}}$ of $\mathcal{R}$ and a full allocation, P, of $S_{\mathcal{X}}$ among $\mathcal{X}$ for which: if Q is *any* allocation in $\mathcal{F}_{n,m}$ with $Q_i = P_i$ for each $a_i \in \mathcal{X}$, then $v_i(Q) \geq q_{\mathcal{X}}$ and for every $a_j \in \mathcal{Y}$, $v_j(Q) < q_{\mathcal{Y}}$?

---

[2] A similar result, within a different formalism for representing utility functions, has been independently obtained in recent work of Bouveret and Lang [1].

Theorem 3. BC *is* Σ_2^p*-complete.*

Proof: (Outline) For membership in Σ_2^p it suffices to observe that

$$\langle\langle \mathcal{A}, \mathcal{R}, \mathcal{V}, \mathcal{U}\rangle, \mathcal{X}, \mathcal{Y}, \langle q_{\mathcal{X}}, q_{\mathcal{Y}}\rangle\rangle$$

is accepted as an instance of BC if and only if: $\exists\, \langle P_{i_1}, \ldots, P_{i_k}\rangle \,\forall\, Q \in \mathcal{F}_{n,m}$, should it be the case that $\wedge_{i_j \in \mathcal{X}} P_{i_j} = Q_{i_j}$ then

$$\left(\bigwedge_{i_j \in \mathcal{X}} v_{i_j}(Q) \geq q_{\mathcal{X}} \wedge \bigwedge_{i_k \in \mathcal{Y}} v_{i_k}(Q) < q_{\mathcal{Y}} \right)$$

The proof that BC is Σ_2^p–hard, uses a reduction from QSAT$_2^\Sigma$ instances of which comprise a CNF formula $\Phi(X_t, Y_t)$ defined over 2 disjoint sets of propositional variables. An instance of QSAT$_2^\Sigma$ is accepted if there is an instantion, α_X of X_t under which for all instantiations, β_Y of Y_t we have $\Phi(\alpha_X, \beta_Y) = \bot$.

The basic idea of the construction is to form a four agent system – $\{a_1, a_2, b_1, b_2\}$ – in which the resource set is formed by the propositional variables $X_t \cup Y_t$. The valuation functions, $\langle v_1, v_2, v_3, v_4\rangle$ are designed so that the coalition formed by $\{a_1, a_2\}$ is able to block the coalition $\{b_1, b_2\}$ if it can partition the X_t resources in such a way that when a_1 sets its alloted subset of X_t to $\top$ while a_2 sets its variables to $\bot$ then the instantiation of $\Phi(X_t, Y_t)$ evaluates to $\bot$ no matter what setting of Y_t is used.   □

5   Conclusions and Further Work

The principal focus of this paper has been directed towards defining a framework for resource allocation settings involving utility functions with externalities, it being maintained that there are many application domains to which such treatments are most appropriate. The technical matter that has been the basis of the results discussed above, has largely been concerned with highlighting reasons why issues such as negotiation and coalitional strategy pose non-trivial questions. In particular, as a consequence of Theorem 1 it is apparent that highly autonomous negotiation protocols schemes require additional apparatus, over and above that suitable to externality–free settings, in order to effect practical algorithmic solutions.

The nature of appropriate algorithmic methods, e.g. within the centralised approach of combinatorial auctions, is one area with considerable potential for development. Although we have not discussed such schemes in detail, it is observed that unless the bidding protocols allow agents to express conditions under which offers are made, e.g. that a price p is offered for S subject to a particular allocation being in force, the full allocation generated may be found unsatisfactory by both agents and auctioneer alike. A second area, of interest to autonomous environments, concerns the investigation of reasoning mechanisms by which agents can "reliably" make use of their belief contexts in reaching decisions about offers, e.g. so that the extremes highlighted at the conclusion of Section 3 are avoided. Both of these are the subject of work currently in progress.

References

1. S. Bouveret and J. Lang. Efficiency and envy–freeness in fair division of indivisible goods: logical representation and complexity. (to appear, *Proc. 19th International Joint Conf. on A.I. (IJCAI'05)*, Edinburgh, 2005)
2. F. Dignum (Editor). Advances in Agent Communication. Lecture Notes in A.I., 2922, Springer, 2004
3. P. E. Dunne. Extremal behaviour in multiagent contract negotiation. *Jnl. of Artificial Intelligence Research*, 23:41–78, 2005
4. P. E. Dunne, M. J. Wooldridge, and M. Laurence. The complexity of contract negotiation. *Artificial Intelligence*, 164:23–46, 2005
5. U. Endriss and N. Maudet. On the Communication Complexity of Multilateral Trading. *Proc. 3rd International Joint Conf. on Autonomous Agents and Multiagent Systems* (AAMAS'04), July 2004, ACM Press, pages 622–629
6. U. Endriss and N. Maudet. Welfare Engineering in Multiagent Systems. *Proc. 4th International Workshop on Engineering Societies in the Agents World (ESAW-2003)* LNAI 3071, Springer-Verlag, pages 93–106
7. S. Kraus. *Strategic negotiation in multiagent environments*. MIT Press, 2001.
8. P. McBurney and S. Parsons. Games that agents play: A formal framework for dialogues between autonomous agents. *J. Logic, Language and Information*, 11:315–334, 2002
9. D. C. Parkes and L. H. Ungar. Iterative combinatorial auctions: theory and practice. In *Proc. 17th National Conf. on Artificial Intelligence (AAAI-00)*, pages 74–81, 2000
10. C. Reed. Dialogue frames in agent communications. In: Y. Demazeau (ed.): *Proc. 3rd International Conference on Multi-agent systems (ICMAS-98)*. pp. 246–253. 1998
11. T. W. Sandholm. Contract types for satisficing task allocation: I theoretical results. In *AAAI Spring Symposium: Satisficing Models*, 1998.
12. T. W. Sandholm. Distributed rational decision making. In *Multiagent Systems* (Editor: G. Weiß) pages 201–258, MIT Press, 1999.
13. M. Tennenholz. Some tractable combinatorial auctions. In *Proc. 17th National Conf. on Artificial Intelligence (AAAI-00)*, 2000.
14. M. Yokoo, Y. Sakurai and S. Matsubara. The effect of false-name bids in combinatorial auctions: new fraud in internet auctions. *Games and Economic Behavior*, 46(1):174–188, 2004

On Communication in Solving Distributed Constraint Satisfaction Problems

Hyuckchul Jung[1] and Milind Tambe[2]

[1] Florida Institute for Human and Machine Cognition, USA
[2] Department of Computer Science, University of Southern California, USA

Abstract. Distributed Constraint Satisfaction Problems (DCSP) is a general framework for multi-agent coordination and conflict resolution. In most DCSP algorithms, inter-agent communication is restricted to only exchanging values of variables, since any additional information-exchange is assumed to lead to significant communication overheads and to a breach of privacy. This paper provides a detailed experimental investigation of the impact of inter-agent exchange of additional legal values among agents, within a collaborative setting. We provide a new run-time model that takes into account the overhead of the additional communication in various computing and networking environments. Our investigation of more than 300 problem settings with the new run-time model (i) shows that DCSP strategies with additional information-exchange can lead to big speedups in a significant range of settings; and (ii) provides categorization of problem settings with big speedups by the DCSP strategies based on extra communication, enabling us to selectively apply the strategies to a given domain. This paper not only provides a useful method for performance measurement to the DCSP community, but also shows the utility of additional communication in DCSP.

1 Introduction

Distributed, collaborative agents play an important role in large-scale multiagent applications such as sensor networks [1]. Collaborative agents in such applications must coordinate their plans, resolving conflicts, if any, among their action or resource choices. Distributed Constraint Satisfaction Problems (DCSP) is a major technique in multiagent coordination and conflict resolution in collaborative settings [2]. DCSP provides rich foundation for the representation of multiagent coordination and conflict resolution, and there exist highly efficient baseline algorithms [3,4,5,2].

In most DCSP algorithms, inter-agent communication is restricted to only exchanging values of variables, since any additional information-exchange is assumed to lead to significant communication overheads, a breach of privacy, and knowledge transformation cost [2]. We refer to this restriction of only communicating values of variables as *value-only communication*. However, as large-scale systems based on such value-only communication get developed, it is critical to re-examine this commitment to value-only communication that has now become the foundation of DCSP. Indeed, it is feasible that, by unnecessarily subscribing to such value-only communication, researchers may be forced to compromise on correctness or quality of solutions; and/or forced to develop unnecessarily complex algorithms. Could eliminating or diluting this restriction

M. Pěchouček, P. Petta, and L.Z. Varga (Eds.): CEEMAS 2005, LNAI 3690, pp. 418–429, 2005.

of value-only communication lead to significant speedups, or would that lead to additional overheads? Such a re-examination of the communication commitment in DCSP may imply potentially significant enhancements to the current DCSP algorithms.

We examine the impact of value-only communication in collaborative agent applications, where agents are homogeneous or at least do not face significant difficulties in communicating their potential choices of values to each other. In such collaborative agent applications, some of the key reasons for restricting to value-only communication do not hold. In particular, there are three key reasons provided in the literature [2] for value-only communication: (i)Maintaining privacy, (ii) Difficulty of knowledge transformation in heterogeneous agent settings; (iii) Overheads of extra communication.

However, collaborative agents have no reason to maintain privacy from other agents, and many domains with homogeneous agents do not have a problem in knowledge transformation. The central remaining question is thus of communication overheads, and loosening the restriction of value-only communication can indeed add to the communication cost in DCSP. This tradeoff in the potential speedup due to extra communication vs the cost of communication is the central tradeoff that is at the heart of this paper. Various aspects of different types of domains need to be considered in the analysis (e.g., communication or local computation cost).

In earlier work, we introduced DCSP techniques with additional information exchange [6]. However, since the investigation was limited to limited settings, the performance of such DCSP techniques was not fully evaluated in a large set of realistic domains. Furthermore, the overhead from extra communication was never analyzed. In this paper, we present a comprehensive, detailed analysis over a large range of realistic domain settings. For the analysis, we develop a new run-time model that takes into account extra communication overhead in various computing and networking environments since the performance metric widely used in the DCSP literature, *cycles* explained in Section 3, does not take into account the overhead of additional information exchange (i.e., increased message size and number).

To evaluate the performance of DCSP techniques based on extra communication in different domains, we systematically investigate more than 300 problem settings in a large problem space with more than 200,000 experimental runs, using the new run-time model. Our investigation (i) shows that DCSP strategies with additional information-exchange can lead to big speedups in a significant range of settings; and (ii) provides categorization of problem settings where big speedups are achieved by the DCSP strategies to guide which DCSP strategy to apply given a domain.

2   Background

DCSP provides an abstract formal framework to model coordination and conflict resolution in many multiagent applications such as distributed sensor networks [1]. DCSP is a distributed version of CSP (Constraint Satisfaction Problems) [2]. CSP is commonly defined by a set of n variables, $X = \{x_1, ..., x_n\}$, each element associated with value domains $D_1, ..., D_n$ respectively, and a set of k constraints, $\Gamma = \{C_1, ..., C_k\}$. A solution in CSP is the value assignment for the variables which satisfies all the constraints in Γ. In DCSP, variables and constraints are distributed among multiple agents. A constraint defined only on variables belonging to a single agent is called a *local constraint*. In contrast, an *external constraint* involves variables of different agents. Solving a DCSP requires that agents not only solve their local constraints, but also communicate with other agents to satisfy external constraints.

A major characteristic of most DCSP algorithms is that they have focused on *value-only communication*: agents communicate only their intended values for the objects on which they need to agree [3,4,2]. That is, while the value selection is based on each agent's local knowledge and local situation, agents do not communicate such information. However, a few different approaches (based on the communication of local information between agents) were recently presented [6,7,5].

In this section, we describe two algorithms as representative examples. One is Asynchronous Weak Commitment search algorithm [2], one of the most advanced DCSP algorithms, in which agents communicate only selected values, and the other is Locally Cooperative DCSP algorithm [6] in which agents communicate selected values plus local information and the communicated information is used for value ordering.

2.1 Asynchronous Weak Commitment (AWC) Search Algorithm

In the AWC algorithm, agents asynchronously assign values to their variables and communicate the values to neighboring agents with shared binary constraints. Each variable has a priority that changes dynamically during search. A variable is consistent if its value does not violate any constraints with higher priority variables. A solution is a value assignment in which every variable is consistent.

To simplify the description of the algorithm, suppose that each agent has exactly one variable. When the value of an agent's variable is not consistent with the values of its neighboring agents' variables with higher priorities, there can be two cases: (i) a *good* case where there exists a consistent value in the variable's domain; (ii) a *nogood* case that lacks a consistent value. In the good case with one or more value choices available, an agent selects a value that minimizes the number of conflicts with lower priority agents. On the other hand, in the nogood case, an agent selects a new value that minimizes the number of conflicts with all of its neighboring agents, and increases its priority to *max+1*, where *max* is the highest priority of its neighboring agents.

2.2 Locally Cooperative DCSP (LCDCSP) Algorithm

In the LCDCSP algorithm [6], agents take into account the flexibility (choice of values) given to other agents by their value choices in selecting new values. The LCDCSP algorithm is based on the AWC but has a different mechanism in value ordering (which is enabled by extra communication of local constraints). To elaborate this notion of cooperative value selection, the followings was defined in [6]:

- **Definition 1:** For a value $v \in D_i$ and a set of agents $N_i^{sub} \subseteq N_i$, *flexibility function* is defined as $f^{\oplus}(v, N_i^{sub}) = \oplus(c(v, A_j))$ where (i) $A_j \in N_i^{sub}$; (ii) $c(v, A_j)$ is the number of values of A_j that are consistent with v; and (iii) $\oplus$, referred to as a *flexibility base*, can be *sum*, *min*, *max*, *product*, etc.

Based on the flexibility, four different techniques are defined for value selection:

- $S_{min-conflict}$: Each agent A_i selects a value based on min-conflict heuristics (the original value ordering method in the AWC algorithm);
- S_{high} (S_{low}): Each agent A_i attempts to give maximum flexibility towards its higher (lower) neighboring agents by selecting a value v that maximizes $f^\oplus(v, N_i^{high})$ ($f^\oplus(v, N_i^{low})$);
- S_{all}: Each agent A_i selects a value v that maximizes $f^\oplus(v, N_i)$, i.e. max flexibility to all neighbors.

These four different techniques can be applied to both the *good* and the *nogood* case described in Section 2.1. (Refer to [6] for detailed information.) Therefore, there are sixteen combinations for each flexibility base. While the LCDCSP apporach has relation to a popular centralized CSP technique, the *least constraining value* heuristic [8], it is not a simple mapping of the *least constraining value* heuristic onto the DCSP framework. Agents can explicitly reason about which agents to consider most with respect to the constrainedness given towards neighboring agents.

3   Performance Measurement

To evaluate approaches with different types of information exchange (as shown above), we need a new run-time model (Section 3.2) that takes into account the overhead of extra communication (required for the LCDCSP algorithm) since existing performance metrics (described in Section 3.1) do not properly assess such communication overhead.

3.1   Existing Method

Since it has been practically difficult to access a real large-scale distributed system (with hundreds of nodes), the standard methodology in the field [3,5,2] is to implement a synchronized distributed system which is a model of distributed system where every agent synchronously performs the following three steps (called a *cycle*): (i) Agents receives all the messages sent to them in the previous cycle; (ii) Agents resolve conflicts, if any, and determine which message to send; (iii) Agents send messages to neighboring agents. Given such a synchronized distributed system, it is difficult to directly measure the run-time for real distributed conflict resolution. However, in the literature, as a compromise, researchers have used hardware independent metrics such as *cycles* and *constraint checks* defined below.

- *Cycles*: The number of cycles until a solution is found. Total time for conflict resolution is expected to be proportional to *cycles* [2].
- *Constraint checks*: The total number of the maximum number of constraint checks at each cycle until a solution is found. More specifically, at each cycle, a bottleneck agent (which performs the most constraint checks) is identified, and the numbers of constraint checks from bottleneck agents (which may vary at each cycle) are summed up over all cycles. This is a main indicator for local computation time.

In the DCSP research community, *cycles* is used as a major metric for performance evaluation since the amount of local computation and communication that each agent solves mostly remains same in most of previous DCSP approaches [3,5,2]: the difference is in the protocol for passing values and controlling backtracking. However, *cycles* has the following shortcomings:

- Local computation overhead: For the hardware with limited computing power, the time for local computation may not be ignored, and there can be a variation in local computation depending on constraint checks.
- Message communication overhead: While *cycles* assumes that uniform time is taken at each communication phase, the time for message communication often depends on the size/number of messages.

3.2   Analytical Model for Run-Time

While the *cycles* (a major DCSP metric) described above can be used as approximate measurements, it does not properly assess the performance of algorithms like LCDCSP which do not properly assess the additional computation and communication overhead from the local information exchange. Therefore, we need a new model to take into account such overheads as part of the run-time. In this section, we present an analytical model for run-time measurements which takes into account various message processing/communication overhead in different computing/networking environments.

The local computation processed by an agent at each cycle consists of processing received messages, performing constraint checks, and determining which message to send for its neighbors. The run-time taken by an agent for a cycle is the sum of the local computation time and the communication time for the agent's outgoing messages. Our new run-time model is based on the data collected from the experimentation on a synchronized distributed system. The following terms are defined for the model:

- n_i^k: incoming message number for agent i at cycle k
- $s_i^k(j)$: size of jth incoming message for agent i at cycle k
- $\mathcal{I}(l)$: computation time to process one incoming message (whose size is l)
- c_i^k: number of constraint checks by agent i at cycle k
- t: computation time to perform one constraint check
- o_i^k: number of outgoing message for agent i at cycle k
- u_i^k: size of an outgoing message for agent i at cycle k
- $\mathcal{O}(m)$: computation time to process an outgoing message (whose size is m)
- $\mathcal{T}(d)$: communication time to transmit an outgoing message (whose size is d)

In a synchronous distributed system, at each cycle, agents synchronously start their local computation and communication. Thus, the run-time for a cycle is dominated by an agent which requires maximum time for its local computation and communication.

- *Run-time for a cycle* k $(\mathcal{R}(k)) = max_{i \in Ag}(\mathcal{L}_i^k + \mathcal{C}_i^k)$ where Ag is a set of agents in a given system, $\mathcal{L}_i^k$ is the *local computation time of agent i at cycle k*, and $\mathcal{C}_i^k$ is the *communication time of agent i at cycle k*.

Here, $\mathcal{L}_i^k$ and $\mathcal{C}_i^k$ are computed by the following equations:

- *Local computation time of agent i at cycle k* $(\mathcal{L}_i^k) = \sum_{j=1}^{n_i^k}(\mathcal{I}(s_i^k(j)))$ (time to process received messages) $+ c_i^k \times t$ (time to perform constraint checks) $+ o_i^k \times \mathcal{O}(u_i^k)$ (time to process outgoing messages)
- *Communication time of agent i at cycle k* $(\mathcal{C}_i^k) = o_i^k \times \mathcal{T}(u_i^k)$ (time for transmitting a message whose size is u_i^k for o_i^k times)

Finally, the total run-time is the sum of run-time $(\mathcal{R}(k))$ for each cycle:

- *Total run-time* $= \sum_{k=1}^{K}(\mathcal{R}(k))$ where K is the number of total cycles.

While the above model aims to provide a metric which takes into account message processing/communication overhead (based on message size/number), it is flexible enough to subsume the existing method of performance measurement (Section 3.1):

- *Constraint checks* corresponds to the total run-time (defined above) where $t = 1$, $\mathcal{I}(\cdot) = \mathcal{O}(\cdot) = 0$ and $\mathcal{C}_i^k = 0$ (i.e., no communication/message-processing cost).
- *Cycles* corresponds to the total run-time under the assumption that $t = 0$ (the cost for constraint checks is zero), $\mathcal{I}(\cdot) = \mathcal{O}(\cdot) = 0$ (message processing cost is zero), and $\mathcal{C}_i^k = 1$ (a constant communication time independent of message size/number).

As the first analytical model for the performance measurement in DCSP which takes into account the overhead based on message size and number, the above model could provide a useful method for performance measurement to the DCSP community. Furthermore, as shown below, the model shows interesting results as the parameters for message processing/communication overhead vary.

4   Performance Analysis

While we focus on the domain where agents' interaction topology is regular[1], there can be variations (e.g., problem hardness) in different problem settings that arise within the domain. In this section, we provide various problem settings controlled by several parameters. Systematic changes in the parameters generate a wide variety of problem settings, and enable us to evaluate the performance of the strategies and find their communication vs. computation trade-offs in different situations. Here, parameter selection is motivated by the experimental investigation in the CSP/DCSP literature [2].

First, we vary the density of regular graphs by changing the number of neighboring agents: (i) *Hexagonal topology*: Each agent is surrounded by three agents (separated by 120 degrees); (ii) *Grid topology*: Each agent is surrounded by four neighboring agents (separated by 90 degrees); (iii) *Triangular topology*: Each agent is surrounded by eight neighboring agents (separated by 45 degrees). The purpose of trying three different regular graphs is to investigate the impact on performance by the degree of connectivity (number of interactions for each agent).

---

[1] In real applications such as sensor networks [1], agents are often arranged in regular networks.

Second, given a topology (among the three topologies above), we make variations in constraint compatibility which has shown a great impact on the hardness of problems [2]. We distinguish external constraints from local constraints in defining the constraint tightness to analyze the effect from each constraint:

1. External constraint compatibility: Given an external constraint, for a value in an agent's domain, the percentage of compatibility with neighboring agents' values is defined. The percentage varies from 30% to 90% with intervals of 30%. Note that 0% case and 100% case are not tried since there is no solution for 9% case and every value assignment is a solution for 100% case.
2. Local constraint compatibility: Given a local constraint, a portion of agents' original domains is not allowed. We make the following two variations in local constraint: (i) The percentage of locally constrained agents changes from 0% to 100% (0%, 30%, 60%, 90%, 100%); and (ii) Given a local constraint, the portion of allowed values varies from 25% to 75% (25%, 50%, 75%). Here, 0% and 100% are not tried since 0% case gives agents empty domain and 100% case has no effect of having a local constraint.

Third, we vary the number of domain values from 10 to 80 (10, 40, 80) to check how different domain sizes have an impact on the performance and trade-offs of the strategies. Given the above variations, the total number of settings is 351, and we evaluate the performance of the two DCSP strategies (presented in Section 2) on each setting. Note that the LCDCSP strategy can have different value selection techniques introduced in Section 2.2. For a given problem setting, the performance of strategies is measured on 35 problem instances which are randomly generated by the problem setting (defined with the above parameters).

For each setting, seventeen strategies (sixteen strategies defined in this paper plus the original AWC strategy) are tried for each problem instances. Thus, the total number of experimental runs is 208,845 ($= 351 \times 35 \times 17$).[2] Note that, for the sixteen LCDCSP strategies, *sum* is used as a flexibility base (the original AWC strategy is *min-conflict* strategy without extra communication of local information). We set the number of agents as 512 since, in real applications such as sensor networks [1], the number of agents in hundreds is considered to be large-scale.

4.1 Categorization of Problem Settings with Big Speedups by LCDCSP

In Figure 1, the horizontal axis plots problem hardness for each individual problem instance (based on the *cycles* by the AWC strategy), and the vertical axis plots how many speedup (i.e., how many fold reduction in cycles) is achieved by the best LCDCSP strategies for each problem instance. [3] The results in Figure 1 indicates that LCDCSP strategies show performance improvement for majority of problem instances across different problem hardness: while there is a variation in performance improvement, the speedups do not come from only a few exceptional cases.

---

[2] To conduct the experiments within a reasonable amount of time, the number of cycles was limited to 1000 for each run (a run was terminated if this limit exceeded).

[3] Selecting the best LCDCSP strategies were based on empirical results.

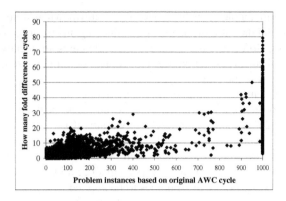

Fig. 1. Speedup by LCDCSP strategies for individual problem instances

Table 1. Speedups based on problem class

Local constraint compatibility	External constraint compatibility	Domain size	Ratio of locally constrained agents	Speedup at Each Topology Hexagonal	Grid	Triangular
25%	30%	10	30%		High	
			60%		Moderate	
			others		Low	
		40 & 80	60%	Low	Moderate	Low
			others		Low	
	60%	40	90%	Low	High	Low
		10 & 80	others		Low	
	90%	*	*		Low	
50% & 75%	*	*	*		Low	

Table 2. Maximum speedup in the problem settings where topology is grid, and external constraint compatibility is 60%

Local constraint compatibility	Domain size	Ratio of locally constrained agents	Speedup
25%	10	0 ∼ 100%	Low
25%	40	90%	High
		others	Moderate
25%	80	0 ∼ 100%	Moderate
50%	10, 40, 80	0 ∼ 100%	Moderate
75%	10, 40, 80	0 ∼ 100%	Moderate

Table 1 and 2 show how much speedu can be achieved by the best LCDCSP strategies for a group of problem settings classified by the parameters introduced above. Note that this categorization is not exhaustive, and focuses on problem settings (not on individual problem instances). In Table 1 and 2, high/moderate/low speedup respectively indicates "more than five"/"between three and four"/"less than two"-fold speedup by LCDCSP strategies over the AWC strategy. The following is the summarized result shown in Table 1 and 2:

- When external constraint compatibility is low (30%),
  - For each topology, high performance improvement is achieved when local constraint compatibility is low (25%) and domain size is small (10).
    * A big speedup by LCDCSP strategies is shown unless agents are either totally unconstrained in local constraints(0%) or totally constrained (100%).

  * For grid topology, a big speedup is shown when domain size is large (80), and the ratio of locally constrained agents is moderate (60%) or high (90%). However, little speedup when all agents are locally constrained.
- When local constraint compatibility increases or domain size gets larger, LCD-CSP shows low speedup.
- When external constraint compatibility is moderate (60%) in grid topology,
  - High performance improvement is achieved when local constraint compatibility is low (25%) and domain size is moderate (40).
    * A big speedup by the best LCDCSP strategy is shown when the ratio of locally constrained agents is high (90%). However, note that, when the ratio is 100%, there is no big speedup since all the problems in the setting are easy regardless of strategies to be applied.
- When external constraint compatibility is 90%, the speedup is relatively small since the problem settings with 90% external constraint compatibility is easier than other settings (taking less than 30 *cycles* in general) so that there is no big difference in *cycles* between the AWC strategy and LCDCSP strategies.

4.2   Performance in Run-Time Analytical Model

In this section, we present how the performance results (e.g., speedup) changes with the analytical run-time model in Section 3.2 compared with the results based on *cycles*. The parameters specified in this section assume a realistic domain where message communication overhead dominates local computation cost and message processing overhead is relatively smaller than communication overhead (but cannot be ignored). In defining the parameters for such a domain, two different properties for message processing and communication overhead are considered:

- Property 1: Message processing/communication overhead mainly depends on the size of messages to process/communicate.
- Property 2: Message processing/communication overhead mainly depends on the number of messages to process/communicate: Message is processed as a bundle or message communication delay is dominated by message contention.

Message Size as a Main Factor for Message Processing & Communication Overhead. For a domain where message size is a main factor for message processing and communication overhead, parameters for the run-time model are set as follows:

- $\mathcal{I}(l) = l \times t \times \alpha$ and $\mathcal{O}(m) = m \times t \times \alpha$: Message processing is assumed to be slower than a constraint check by two order of magnitude. To simulate such a difference, α is set as 100 or 1000.
- $\mathcal{T}(d) = d \times t \times \beta$: To simulate the situation where communication overhead dominates local computation cost, β is set as 1000 or 10000.

Table 3 shows the speedup by the best LCDCSP strategy for prototypical settings given different α and β. In Table 3, the speedup based on the run-time model for different α and β is less than the speedup based on *cycles*: i.e., the performance of LCDCSP strategies with the run-time model appear to be worse than the *cycle*-based performance.

Table 3. Speedup change in run-time model

Case	Based on cycles	Speedup by LCDCSP strategies Based on run-time model			
		$\alpha = 100\ \beta = 1000$	$\alpha = 100\ \beta = 10000$	$\alpha = 1000\ \beta = 1000$	$\alpha = 1000\ \beta = 10000$
1	11	7	7	7	7
2	10	9	9	8	9
3	37	21	21	20	21
4	14	4	7	5	7
5	11	7	8	7	8
6	44	33	33	31	33

The decrease in speedup with the *run-time* model is due to the fact that LCDCSP strategies have larger message size to process/communicate and more constraint checks (to compute flexibility towards neighbors) than the AWC strategy. The analysis with other α and β values show similar results.

While we present limited data because of space limit, the analysis shows that, as domain size or graph density (i.e., the number of neighbors) increases, the difference in message size and constraint checks between the AWC strategy and LCDCSP strategies also increases, leading to significant decrease in speedup for LCDCSP strategies.

Message Number as a Main Factor for Message Processing & Communication Overhead. For a domain where message number is a main factor for message processing and communication overhead (message processing & communication time is independent of message size), parameters for the run-time model are set as follows:
- $\mathcal{I}(l) = t \times \alpha$ and $\mathcal{O}(m) = t \times \alpha;\ \mathcal{T}(d) = t \times \beta$

Table 4. Speedup change in run-time model

Case	Based on cycles	Speedup by LCDCSP strategies Based on run-time model			
		$\alpha = 100\ \beta = 1000$	$\alpha = 100\ \beta = 10000$	$\alpha = 1000\ \beta = 1000$	$\alpha = 1000\ \beta = 10000$
1	11	9	10	9	10
2	10	10	10	9	10
3	37	37	37	38	37
4	14	6	12	9	13
5	11	10	10	9	10
6	44	46	44	54	47

Here, the values of α and β are same as above. Table 4 shows the speedup by the best LCDCSP strategy for the same prototypical settings (presented in Table 3). In Table 4, the speedup based on the run-time model for different α and β is very similar with the speedup based on *cycles* in general. The main reason is that the number of messages to communicate is decided by the number of neighbors (i.e., graph density) which is static. While there can be a large difference in constraint checks depending on the graph density and the domain size, when the message processing or communication overhead dominates (the difference in *constraint checks* becomes insignificant), the performance of the AWC strategy and LCDCSP strategies depends on *cycles* because of little difference in message size.

This analysis shows that, when the overhead of message processing and communication is mainly decided by message number (not size) and dominates local computation overhead (the difference in *constraint checks* is not significant), *cycles* can be a reasonable measurement to compare strategy performance. Note that, using this analytical model, we can simulate various computing and networking environments by changing (i) the values of α and β (different weights to message processing/communication overheads) or (ii) the cost functions.

5   Related Work and Conclusion

While significant works have focused on variable or agent ordering in DCSP [9,3,2], value ordering techniques which exploit additional information-exchange have not received enough attention, and little investigation has been done for performance measurement which takes into account extra communication overhead. While communicating local information [7,5] and partial centralization [10] have been investigated in DCSP, the communication overhead in different computing/networking environments was not properly evaluated. Fernandez et al. investigated the effect of communication delays on the performance of DCSP algorithms [11]. However, their investigation was limited to the effects from random delays, not from extra value communication. A run-time model by Davin and Modi [12] used a fixed communication latency rather than the latency based on message size/number used in our run-time model (Section 3) which can have a significant impact on performance in a certain network architecture.

In this paper, we investigated the impact of inter-agent exchange of additional information. We provided a new run-time model for DCSP performance measurement that takes into account the overhead of extra communication. Extensive systematic experiments show that exploiting additional information-exchange can improve performance in a significant range of problem settings. We also provided categorization of problem settings with big speedups by the DCSP strategies to guide strategy selection.

References

1. Lesser, V., Ortiz, C., Tambe, M., eds.: Distributed Sensor Networks: a Multiagent Perspective. Kluwer Academic Publishers (2003)
2. Yokoo, M.: Distributed Constraint Satisfaction: Foundations of Cooperation in Multi-Agent Systems. Springer (2000)
3. Hamadi, Y., Bessière, C., Quinqueton, J.: Backtracking in distributed constraint networks. In: Proceedings of European Conference on Artificial Intelligence. (1998)
4. Modi, P., Jung, H., Tambe, M., Shen, W., Kulkarni, S.: A dynamic distributed constraint satisfaction approach to resource allocation. In: Proceedings of International Conference on Principles and Practice of Constraint Programming. (2001)
5. Silaghi, M., Sam-Haroud, D., Faltings, B.: Consistency maintenance for abt. In: Proceedings of International Conference on Principles and Practice of Constraint Programming. (2001)
6. Jung, H., Tambe, M.: Performance models for large scale multiagent systems: Using pomdp building blocks. In: Proceedings of International Joint Conference on Autonomous Agents and Multi-Agent Systems. (2003)
7. Monfroy, E., Rety, J.H.: Chaotic iteration for distributed constraint propagation. In: ACM Symposium on Applied Computing. (1999)
8. Haralick, R.M., Elliot, G.L.: Increasing tree search efficiency for constraint satisfaction problems. Artificial Intelligence **14** (1980) 263–313

9. Armstrong, A., Durfee, E.: Dynamic prioritization of complex agents in distributed constraint satisfaction problems. In: Proceedings of International Joint Conference on Artificial Intelligence. (1997)
10. Mailler, R., Lesser, V.: Solving distributed constraint optimization problems using cooperative mediation. In: Proceedings of International Joint Conference on Autonomous Agents and Multi-Agent Systems. (2004)
11. Fernandez, C., Bejar, R., Krishnamachari, B., Gomes, C., Selman, B.: Communication and computation in distributed csp algorithms. In Lesser, V., Ortiz, C., Tambe, M., eds.: Distributed Sensor Networks. Kluwer Academic Publishers (2003)
12. Davin, J., Modi, P.: Impact of problem centralization in distributed constraint optimization algorithms. In: Proceedings of International Joint Conference on Autonomous Agents and Multi-Agent Systems. (2005)

Towards Reliable Large-Scale Multi-agent Systems

Zahia Guessoum[1,2] and Nora Faci[2]

[1] LIP6, Université Paris 6, 8 rue du Capitaine Scott, F-75015 Paris
Zahia.Guessoum@lip6.fr
[2] MODECO-CReSTIC - IUT de Reims, 51687 Reims Cedex 2, France
faci@leri.univ-reims.fr

Abstract. In this paper, we propose an approach for fault-tolerance of multi-agent systems (MASs). The starting idea is the application of replication strategies to agents, the most critical agents being replicated to prevent failures. As criticality of agents may evolve during the course of computation and problem solving, and as resources are bounded, we need to dynamically and automatically adapt the number of replicas of agents, in order to maximize their reliability and availability. We will describe our approach and related mechanisms for evaluating the criticality of a given agent and for deciding how to parameterize the strategy (e.g., number of replicas). We also will report on experiments conducted with our prototype architecture (named DimaX).

1 Introduction

The possibility of partial failures is a fundamental characteristic of distributed applications. The fault-tolerance research community has developed solutions [4] [10] [3], mostly based on the concept of replication, applied for instance to data bases. Replication of data and/or computation is thus an effective way to achieve fault tolerance in distributed systems. A replicated software component is defined as a software component that possesses a representation on two or more hosts [4]. But, these techniques are almost always applied explicitly and statically, at design time. In such approaches, this is the responsibility of the designer of the application to identify explicitly which critical servers should be made robust and also to decide which strategies (active or passive replication...) and their configurations (how many replicas, their placement...).

New cooperative applications, e.g., air traffic control, cooperative work, and e-commerce, are much more dynamic and large scale . It is thus very difficult, or even impossible, to identify in advance the most critical software components of the application. Furthermore, criticality can vary over run time, information that should be used to best allocate the scarce replication resources. Such cooperative applications are now increasingly designed as a set of autonomous and interactive entities, named agents, which interact and coordinate (MAS). In such applications, the roles and relative importance of the agents can greatly vary during the course of computation, of interaction and of cooperation, the

M. Pěchouček, P. Petta, and L.Z. Varga (Eds.): CEEMAS 2005, LNAI 3690, pp. 430–439, 2005.

agents being able to change roles, strategies. Also, new agents may also join or leave the application (open system). In addition, such applications may be large scale. And the fact that the underlying distributed system is large scale makes it unstable by nature, at least in currently deployed technologies. That increases the needs for mechanism for adaptive fiabilisation of the application.

Our approach is in consequence to give the capacity to the MAS itself to dynamically identify the most critical agents and to decide which fiabilisation strategies to apply to them. This is analog to "load balancing" but for fiabilisation. We want to **automatically** and **dynamically** apply fiabilisation (mostly through replication mechanisms) **where** (to which agents) and **when** they are most needed. To guide the adaptive fiabilisation, we intend to use various levels of information, system level, like communication load, and application/agent level, like roles or plans.

This paper is organized as follows: Section 2 introduces our monitoring-agent architecture. Sections 3 et 4 introduce a dynamic and adaptive control mechanism of replication. Section 5 presents the DimaX platform that we developed to implement this solution and the realized experiments.

2   Monitoring Multi-agent Architecture

Monitoring consists in acquiring necessary information to dynamically and automatically apply replication to agent when it is almost needed. This information may be based on standard measurements (communication load, processing time...) or multi-agent characteristics such as the roles of agents or their interdependences.

In most existing multi-agent architectures, the observation mechanism is centralized. The acquired information is typically used off-line to explain and to improve the system's behavior. Moreover, the considered application domains typically only involve a small number of agents and *a priori* well-known organizational structures. These centralized observation architectures are not suited for large-scale and complex systems where the observed information needs to be analyzed in real-time to adapt the MAS to the evolution of its environment.

We thus proposed to distribute the observation mechanism to improve its efficiency and robustness (see [6] for details). This distributed mechanisms relies on a reactive-agent organization. These agents have two roles: they observe the domain agents and control their replication, and they build global information and minimize communication. These two roles are assigned to two kinds of agents: domain agent monitors (named agent-monitors) and host monitors (named host-monitors). An agent-monitor is associated to each domain agent and a host-monitor is associated to each host (see Figure 1).

The monitoring agents (agent-monitors and host-monitors) are hierarchically organized. Each agent-monitor communicates only with one host-monitor. Host-monitors exchange their local information to build global information (global number of messages, global exchanged quantity of information...).

After each interval of time Δt, the host-monitor sends the collected events and data to the corresponding agent-monitors. Each agent-monitor activates then

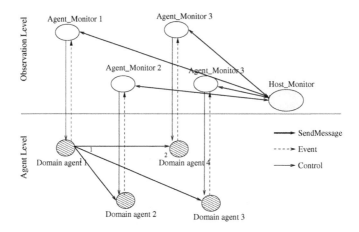

Fig. 1. Multi-agent architecture

the adaptation algorithm. When the arcs of a node are significantly modified, the concerned agent-monitor notifies its host-monitor. The latter informs the other host-monitors to update global information. In turn, agent-monitors are informed by their host-monitors when global information changes significantly.

3   Agent Criticality

We will now detail our approach for dynamically evaluating criticality of each agent in order to perform dynamic replication where and when best needed. In the proposed dynamic approach, the agent criticality relies on two kinds of information:

- System-level information. It is based on standard measurements (communi- cation load, processing time...). We are currently evaluating their significance to measure the activity of an agent.
- Semantic-level information. Several aspects may be considered (importance of agents, interdependence of agents, importance of messages...). We decided to use the concept of interdependence graph, because it captures the impor- tance of an agent in its organization.

In a MAS, each agent is defined as an autonomous entity. However, the agents do not always have all the required competences or resources and thus depend on other agents to provide them. Interdependence graphs [1] were introduced to describe the interdependences of these agents. These graphs are defined by the designer before the execution of the MAS. However, complex MASs are characterized by emergent structures [9] which thus cannot be statically defined by the designer.

In our architecture, a MAS is therefore represented by a graph which reflects an emergent organizational structure. This structure can be interpreted to define each agent criticality.

3.1   Interdependence Graph

For each domain agent, we associate a node. The set of nodes (see Figure 2), named interdependence graph, is represented by a labelled oriented graph (N, L, W). N is the set of nodes of the graph, L is the net of arcs and W the set of labels.

$$N = \{N_i\}_{i=1,n}, \ L = \{L_{i,j}\}_{i=1,n,j=1,n}, \ W = \{W_{i,j}\}_{i=1,n,j=1,n} \tag{1}$$

$L_{i,j}$ is the link between the nodes N_i and N_j and $W_{i,j}$ is a real number which labels $L_{i,j}$. $W_{i,j}$ reflects the importance of the interdependence between the associated agents ($Agent_i$ and $Agent_j$). These weights can be used, for example, to detect which links become too heavy or if the system relies too much on few agents.

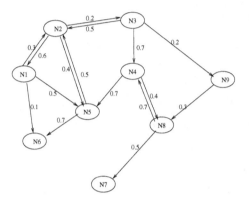

Fig. 2. Example of interdependence graph

A node is thus related to a set of other nodes that may includes all the nodes of a system. This set is not static: it can be modified when a new domain agent is added or an existing one disappears.

The proposed adaptation algorithms of the interdependence graph are described in the next section.

3.2   Adaptation Algorithms

Several parameters may be used to define the interdependences between agents such as communication load, executed tasks, roles of agents. An adaptation algorithm gives an outline of the adaptation mechanism of the interdependence graph. This adaptation relies on local information (communication load ...) and on global information (aggregation of the local information). The adaptation algorithm is thus used by each agent-monitor to manage the associated node.

Let us consider an interval of time Δt. The agent-monitors are activated each Δt. At each step, an agent-monitor executes an adaptation algorithm. However, the domain agents act continuously according to their goals and the evolution of their environment.

In this section, we propose two algorithms to compute the interdependence between two agents. The first one considers only the number of messages exchanged by agents and the second one deals with speech acts (performatives).

Algorithm 1. relies on the global number of sent messages $NbM(\Delta t)$ which is calculated as follows by the host-monitors:

$$NbM(\Delta t) = op1(NbM_{i,i}(\Delta t)) \text{ with } i = 1, n \ j = 1, n \text{ and } i \neq j \qquad (2)$$

where

- n is the number of the domain agents,
- $NbM_{i,j}(\Delta t)$ is the number of messages sent by $agent_i$ to $agent_j$ during the interval of time Δt,
- $op1$ is an aggregation operator.

Algorithm 1 Basic adaptation of the interdependences

1: **for** each j different of i **do**
2:    Calculate:
$$\Delta W_{i,j}(t) = (NbM_{i,j}(\Delta t) - NbM(\Delta t))/NbM(\Delta t) \qquad (3)$$
3:    Update the weights by using the following rule:
$$W_{i,j}(t + \Delta t) = W_{i,j}(t) + \Delta W_{i,j}(t) \qquad (4)$$

4: **end for**

Algorithm 2. relies on the semantics proposed by FIPA and the influence of the reception of a message on the receiver. Based on the work of Colombetti and Verdicchio [2], we propose the following six classes of performatives:

- class 1 ={request, request-whenever, query-if, query-ref, subscribe}
- class 2 = {inform, inform-done, inform-ref}
- class 3 = {cfp, propose}
- class 4 = {reject-proposal, refuse, cancel}
- class 5 = {accept-proposal, agree}
- class 6 = {not-understood, failure}.

To represent the influence of a message on its receiver, we use a granulation of the interval of possible variations [0, 1]: 0 corresponds to no influence and 1 corresponds to the maximum influence. Various methods and techniques can be used to represent this granulation. These methods fall mainly into two categories: crisp and fuzzy. Fuzzy granulation mimics the human reasoning and manipulation of information resulting from perception [11]. It provides a better representation of the various classes of influences and a very good decision-making process. So, we choose the fuzzy granulation. An influence is thus described by symbolic

Table 1. Symbolic values of the six classes and their weights

Classes	Symbolic Values	Weights
classes 4, 6	Low	0.17
classes 2, 3, 5	medium	0.47
class 1	high	0.85

values such as *low, medium, high* which correspond respectively to the intervals: $[0, 0.35]$, $]0.30, 0.65]$ and $]0.60, 1]$. The average value of each symbolic value is the median of its interval. It is used to define the weight of a message. Table 1 gives the symbolic values of the six classes. The weight of a message is defined by the median of the interval corresponding to the fuzzy value of its performative.

Algorithm 2 Performative-based adaptation of the interdependences

1: $S_{i,j}$: the set of messages sent by $Agent_i$ to $Agent_j$.
2: $\Delta W(t)$: the average value of $\Delta W_{i,j}(t)$ for $i = 1, n$, $j = 1, n$ and $i \neq j$.
3: **for** each j different from i **do**
4:     Calculate the variation of $W_{i,j}$:

$$\Delta W_{i,j}(t) = \sum_{m \in S_{i,j}} weight(m) \tag{5}$$

5:     $weight(m)$ relies on the performative of m It is provided by Table 1.
6:     Update $W_{i,j}$ by using the following rule:

$$W_{i,j}(t + \Delta t) = W_{i,j}(t) + (\Delta W_{i,j}(t) - \Delta W(t))/\Delta W(t) \tag{6}$$

7: **end for**

The analysis of an agent criticality allows to define its importance and the influence of its failure on the behavior and reliability of the MAS. We propose to use the interdependences of each agent to define its criticality. The criticality of $Agent_i$ is thus defined as an aggregation of $W_{j,i}$ with $j = 1, n$. Each $W_{j,i}$ may increase or decrease depending on the considered parameters (number of messages and their weight). The agent criticality and the number of its replicas may thus increase or decrease.

4   Resource Management

The resource set is dynamic as new hosts could be added or removed (fail) dynamically. To deal with the problem of management of resources and the problem of agent replication, we propose to use ideas from economics [7]. We first define some useful parameters: resource cost, budget, and negotiation behaviors of the agent-monitors and the host-monitors to allocate resources. These agents interact by using the contract net and request protocols.

Each host provides a number of resources (number of replicas that can be used). This number is defined and can be changed by the designer or the host owner. Each resource has an initial cost which is defined by the designer. This cost is then updated by the host-monitor. At time t, the resource cost of $host_i$ is defined as follows:

$$CM_i(t) = CM_i(t0) * (1 - pp_i(t)) \tag{7}$$

where:

- $pp_i(t)$ is the failure probability of $host_i$, at $time t$. This probability is given by the observation module of DarX.
- $CM_i(t0)$ is the initial cost of $host_i$,
- $pp_i(t0)=0$.

Moreover, the criticality of each agent represents a quantitative value for evaluating its relevance in a MAS. At time t, $agent - monitor_j$ computes its budget $B_j(t)$ which depends on the criticality $W_j(t)$ of the associated domain level $Agent_j$:

$$B_j(t) = W_j(t) * CM(t)/W(t) \tag{8}$$

$$W(t) = \sum_{i=1,n} W_i(t) \text{ and} CM(t) = \sum_{i=1,m} CM_i(t) * Nb_i \tag{9}$$

where n is the number of agents, m is the number of hosts and Nb_i the number of resources of $host_i$.

The resources allocation mechanism is based on the contract net protocol. After each Δt and when the variation of the budget is positive, an agent-monitor sends a call for proposal to host-monitors. A host-monitor responds if it has an available resource. In that case, it sends a proposal which includes the cost of its resources to the initiator. The agent-monitor (initiator) uses then a strategy to select the most suited resources. Agent-monitors use two criteria to evaluate the proposals: communication time between the two hosts (the initiator host and the participant one) and resource cost. The communication time is very important because it can affect the performances of the whole system. For instance, an important communication time between the leader agent and its replicas could overload the network.

When the variation of the budget is negative, agent-monitor decreases the number of replicats. It thus uses this budget variation and the already allocated replicas costs to select the replicats and sends a request to the corresponding host-monitors to cancel the allocation and kill the replicas.

5   Implementation and Experiments

This section gives an overview of the realized platform (named DimaX) which implements our adaptive replication mechanism. It then describes the example that we use for the experiments and give some results.

5.1   Overview of DimaX

The DIMA multi-agent framework [5] and the fault-tolerant DarX framework [8] have been integrated to build a fault-tolerant multi-agent platform (named DimaX). DimaX provides MASs with several services such as distribution, replication, and naming service [8]. In order to benefit from fault tolerance mechanisms, the agent behavior is wrapped in a task of the DarX framework (see Figure 3). Moreover, for a dynamic control of replication, the monitoring architecture has been introduced. Figure 3 gives an overview of DimaX.

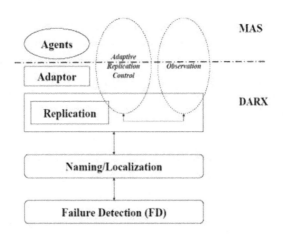

Fig. 3. Overview of DimaX

5.2   Experiments

Note: The experiments presented in this section were carried out on twenty machines with Intel(R) Pentium(R) 4 CPU at 2 GHz and 526 Mb of RAM. They are based on the example of a distributed multiagent system that helps at scheduling meetings. Each user has a personal assistant agent which manages its calendar.

This series of experiments evaluates the robustness of our fault-tolerant MASs. For these experiments, we use a failure simulator. This simulator chooses randomly an agent and stops its thread. If the killed agent is critical then the MAS fails. We considered a MAS with 200 agents distributed on 10 machines. Each experiment aims to schedule a set of fixed set if meeting. We run each experiment 10 minutes and we introduce 100 faults. We repeated several times the experiment with a variable number of extra resources Rm. Rm defines the number of extra replicas that can be used by the whole MAS. These experiments measure the rate of succeeded simulations SR which is defined as follows:

$$SR = \frac{NSS}{TNS} \qquad (10)$$

where NSS is the number of simulations which did not fail and TNS is the total number of simulations. A simulation fail when the fault simulator stops a critical agent which is not replicated. The set of meetings cannot be thus completely scheduled.

We considered three cases: 1) the replication is random, 2) the replication is based on algorithm 1 and 3) the replication is based on algorithm 2.

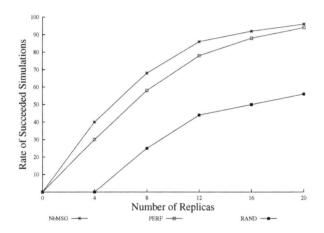

Fig. 4. Rate of succeeded simulations for each number of replicas

Figure 4 shows the success rate SR as a function of the number of extra replicas. It shows that algorithm 2 gives the best results for the considered application. Meanwhile the two algorithms require a number of extra resources which is at least equal to the number of critical agents.

6   Conclusion

Large-scale MASs are often distributed and must run without any interruption. To make these systems reliable, we proposed a new approach to evaluate dynamically the criticality of agents. This approach is based on the concepts of interdependence, an agent criticality relies thus on it interdependences with other agents. The agent criticality is then used to replicate agents in order to maximize their reliability and availability based on available resources and their costs.

We thus proposed a generic architecture to augment an already-built MAS with a basic adaptation mechanism to dynamically and automatically update the replication strategy. To make concrete this architecture, we have implemented a fault-tolerant multi-agent platform (named DimaX). DimaX is the result of an integration of the DIMA multi-agent platform [5] and the DarX replication framework [8]. Any MAS can be thus made fault-tolerant with a small effort.

References

1. C. Castelfranchi. *Decentralized AI*, chapter Dependence relations in multi-agent systems. Elsevier, 1992.
2. Marco Colombetti and Mario Verdicchio. An analysis of agent speech acts as institutional actions. In *AAMAS*, pages 1157–1164, 2002.
3. A. Fedoruk and R. Deters. Improving fault-tolerance by replicating agents. In *AAMAS2002*, pages 373–744, Bologna, Italy, 2002.
4. R. Guerraoui, B. Garbinato, and K. Mazouni. Lessons from designing and implementing GARF. In *Object-Based Parallel and Distributed Computation*, number 791 in LNCS, pages 238–256, 1995.
5. Z. Guessoum and J.-P. Briot. From active objects to autonomous agents. *IEEE Concurrency*, 7(3):68–76, 1999.
6. Zahia Guessoum, Mikal Ziane, and Nora Faci. Monitoring and organizational-level adaptation of multi-agent systems. In *AAMAS*, pages 514–521, 2004.
7. N. Jamali, P. Thati, and G. Agha. An actor-based architecture for customizing and controlling agent ensembles. *IEEE Intelligent Systems, Special Issue on Agents*, 1999.
8. O. Marin, M. Bertier, and P. Sens. DARX - a framework for the fault-tolerant support of agent software. In *14th International Symposium on Software Reliability Engineering (ISSRE'2003)*, pages 406–417, Denver, Colorado, USA, 2003. IEEE.
9. J. S. Sichman and R. Conte. Multi-agent dependence by dependence graphs. In *AAMAS2002*, pages 483–490, Bologna, Italy, 2002. ACM.
10. R. van Renesse, K. Birman, and S. Maffeis. Horus: A flexible group communication system. *Communications of the ACM*, 39(4):76–83, 1996.
11. L. A. Zadeh. A new direction in ai: Toward a computational theory of perceptions. *AI Magazine*, 22(1):73–84, 2001.

Emergent Timetabling Organization

Gauthier Picard, Carole Bernon, and Marie-Pierre Gleizes

IRIT, Université Paul Sabatier,
F-31062 Toulouse Cedex, France
{picard, bernon, gleizes}@irit.fr

Abstract. This paper presents the usage of cooperative self-organization to design adaptive artificial systems. Cooperation can be viewed as a local criterion for agents to self-organize and then to perform a more adequate collective function. This paper shows an application of cooperative behaviors to a dynamic distributed timetabling problem, ETTO, in which the constraint satisfaction is distributed among cooperative agents. This application has been prototyped and shows positive results on adaptation, robustness and efficiency of this kind of approach.

1 Introduction

Kohonen networks or ant algorithms are two examples of artificial transcription of self-organizing mechanisms [1,2]. To be applied to less specific tasks, the mechanisms need to equip some parts –agents– of systems with cognitive capabilities in order to decide when to reorganize to adapt to the environmental pressure and to reach the global goal. As a response to this need of decision-making, the AMAS (*Adaptive Multi-Agent Systems*) approach proposes *cooperative attitude* as the local criterion which agents use to reorganize. Here, coooperation is not limited to ressource or task sharing, but is a behavioral guideline. Cooperation is viewed in a proscriptive way: agents have to locally change their way to interact when they are in *non cooperative situations* (or NCS). In AMAS, an agent is cooperative if it verifies the following meta-rules [3]: (c_{per}) perceived signals are understood without ambiguity *and* (c_{dec}) received information is useful for the agent's reasoning *and* (c_{act}) reasoning leads to useful actions toward other agents. If an agent detects it is in a NCS ($\neg c_{per} \vee \neg c_{dec} \vee \neg c_{act}$), it has to act to come back to a cooperative state. The functional adequacy theorem [4] ensures that the function of the system is adequate – the system produces a function which is cooperative for its environment – if every agent has such a cooperative behavior.

This paper aims at showing that with only local rules based on cooperative attitude and without global knowledge, a solution is provided by the system and local changes lead to global reorganization and then to a more adapted global function. In the next sections, this approach is illustrated by defining a cooperative behavior for agents having to dynamically solve an academic timetabling problem. Teachers and student groups have to find partners, time slots and rooms to give or to assist at some courses. Each actor has some constraints concerning

M. Pěchouček, P. Petta, and L.Z. Varga (Eds.): CEEMAS 2005, LNAI 3690, pp. 440–449, 2005.
© Springer-Verlag Berlin Heidelberg 2005

his availabilities or required equipment. Moreover, a teacher can add or remove constraints at any time during the solving process via an adapted interface. Such an application clearly needs adaptation and robustness. The system must be able to adapt to environmental disturbances (constraints modifications) and not to compute new solutions at each constraint changing. The correct organization has to emerge from actors interactions. This problem has been called ETTO, for *Emergent TimeTabling Organization*. To solve this problem, two kinds of agents were identified and are presented in section 2. These agents respect several cooperation rules that are expounded in section 3. Experiments exhibit results on adaptation and robustness of the AMAS approach in section 4.

2   ETTO Cooperative Agents

Two different classes of agents have been identified to tackle the ETTO problem: *Representative Agents* (RA) and *Booking Agents* (BA). The exploration of the solution space, a n-dimensional grid of cells, is delegated to Booking Agents. Each cell c_i of the grid is constrained (time slots, number of places,...). All the constraints of a cell are regrouped in a set $C(c_i)$. Cooperation between agents must lead to a correct organization by efficiently exploring the grid.

Representative Agents. RAs are the interface between human actors (teachers or student groups) and the timetabling system. They own constraints (called *intrinsic constraints*) about availability, equipment requirements (projectors), or any other kind of personal constraint. To efficiently explore the possibilities of partnership and room reservation, those agents delegate exploration to Booking Agents. A RA (called *proxy*) creates as many BAs (called *delegates*) as it has courses to give (for teachers) or to take (for student groups), and randomly positions them on the planning grid at the beginning of the solving. BAs from a same RA are called *brothers*. The task of a RA is simple: to warn its delegate BAs when its user adds or removes constraints and to inform all its delegate BAs when one of its delegate BAs produces new constraints (called *induced constraints*), to ensure coherence.

Booking Agents. BAs are the real self-organizing agents in ETTO. They have to reserve time slots and rooms and to find partners (student groups for teachers and vice versa) in accordance with constraints owned by their proxy. In a cooperative situation, a BA, which is in a grid cell (i.e. a time slot in a room for a given day) books it and partners with another BA. But this nominal situation is not ensured at the beginning since BAs are randomly positioned. BAs then need to reorganize, i.e. to change their partnership and reservations, to find an adequate timetable. Such situations are NCS (see section1). Therefore, BAs must be able to respond to NCS by respecting cooperation rules (see section 3).

Actions a BA can perform are simple: to partner (or unpartner) with another BA, to book (or unbook) a cell (by marking it with a virtual *post-it* with its address), to move to another cell and to send messages to other agents *it knows*. BAs do not know the whole grid, so moving to another cell implies defining the visible cells from a given cell. A BA only knows its proxy and the BAs it encounters at runtime. The life-cycle of a BA is a classical "perceive-decide-act" process as proposed in [3]:

1. During the *perception* phase, the BA checks its messages (coming from other BAs or its proxy) and updates data about the cell (BAs in the cell, post-its, properties of the cell) in which it is positioned,
2. During the *decision* phase, the BA must choose the next action to perform to be as cooperative as possible, in accordance with the cooperation rules,
3. During the *action* phase, the BA performs the chosen action.

To perform its tasks, a BA ba_i has the following *local* properties, capabilities and knowledge:

- its current position in the grid $(cell(ba_i))$, which is the only cell the BA ba_i can view since it does not have a global knowledge of the whole grid,
- its current partner $(partnership(ba_i, ba_j)$ with $i \neq j)$,
- its current reservation of the cell c_j $(reservation(ba_i, c_j)$ and $rCell(ba_i))$,
- its proxy $(proxy(ba_i))$,
- its search time $(time(ba_i))$ for a reservation,
- the time slot of a cell $(slot(c_j))$,
- a limited memory of known BAs to send messages to $(knows(ba_i, ba_j)$ or $knows(ba_i))$, which is empty at the beginning of the solving and will be updated during the grid exploration,
- a set of intrinsic constraints (CI_{ba_i}) which are attached to the BA when created by its proxy RA,
- a set of constraints induced by its brothers (CB_{ba_i}) which are attached to and updated by its proxy RA when one of its brother reserves a cell to avoid ubiquity situations (two BAs of the same RA book the same time slot, for example),
- a set of constraints induced by its partner (CP_{ba_i}) which are attached to each partnership and updated when the partner changes its constraints to take into account its preferences,
- a set of constraints induced by its reservation (CR_{ba_i}) to avoid partnering with a BA which is not available at certain time slots,
- the set of constraints from a first set which are non compatible with constraints of a second set $(nonCompatible(C_i, C_j) \subseteq C_i)$ to process potential partners or cells to reserve,
- a function to weight constraints $(w(c_i) > 0)$. The higher the weight is the more difficult the constraint can be relaxed. A constraint c_i cannot be relaxed if $w(c_i) = +\infty$.

A macro, NC, is defined to simplify notations:

Definition 1. *The set of non compatible constraints between two BAs is*
$$NC_{ba_i, ba_j} = nonCompatible(CI_{ba_i} \cup CB_{ba_i} \cup CR_{ba_i}, CI_{ba_j} \cup CB_{ba_j} \cup CR_{ba_j}).$$

To determine the non compatible constraints between two BAs, the constraints coming from partners (CP) are not taken into account. In the same manner, for determining if a cell is compatible with a BA's constraints, constraints from the current reservation (CR) are not included:

Definition 2. *The set of non compatible constraints between a BA and a cell is*
$NC_{ba_i,c_j} = nonCompatible(CI_{ba_i} \cup CB_{ba_i} \cup CP_{ba_i}, C_{c_j}).$

Definition 3. $compatible(x, y) \equiv (NC_{x,y} = \emptyset).$

Before starting the solving, there is no absolute way to decide what are the most difficult sub-problems to solve. Moreover, the difficulty degree may evolve because of the dynamic evolution of the problem description. Therefore, during the solving, each agent must be able to evaluate the difficulty it has to find a partner or a reservation. A BA ba_i can calculate the cost of a reservation of a cell c_j $(rCost(ba_i, c_j))$ and the cost of a partnership with another BA ba_j $(pCost(ba_i, ba_j))$ as following:

- $rCost(ba_i, c_j) = (\sum_{c \in NC_{ba_i,c_j}} w(c))/time(ba_i),$
- $pCost(ba_i, ba_j) = \sum_{c \in NC_{ba_i,ba_j}} w(c).$

Dividing by the $time(ba_i)$ of search prioritizes the BA which is searching a cell for a long time. In fact, informally, helping agents having difficulties to find a position within the organization is cooperative.

Basic Behavior. BAs have two orthogonal goals: *find a partner* and *find a reservation*. The main resolution algorithm is distributed among BAs and is based on the cooperation between agents. Solving is the result of dynamic interactions between distributed entities (BAs). As BAs have to reach two main individual goals, the nominal behavior they follow can be expressed in terms of the achievement of these goals, as shown in the algorithm 1. During the perception phase, the BA checks its mailbox, in which other BAs can put messages about partnership requests or reservations. If these messages let it know that its goals are reached (partnership and reservation), the BA moves to its reserved cell only if this reservation is not too constrained. If the agent has relaxed some constraints or if it lacks partner or reservation, it will explore the grid to find a (better) solution and analyze encountered BAs and known cells, i.e. it verifies whether encountered BAs or cells better fit its constraints. Exploring the grid implies the capability for the agent to choose a next cell to explore. In the experiments of section 4, this is randomly done.

Constraint Management and Related Works. Actions may lead to add new induced constraints. For example, a BA which books a cell corresponding to a given hour at a given day warns its brothers, via its proxy, that this time slot is forbidden to avoid ubiquity situations. Conversely, if a BA unbooks a cell, it must inform its brothers. Therefore, a BA must process two kinds of constraints: intrinsic ones, which come from the actor its proxy RA represents, and induced ones, that come from its brother BAs. Of course, some problems may not have any solution without constraint relaxation. As a consequence, BAs

Algorithm 1 – Basic behavior for a Booking Agent.

```
while alive do
  processMessages()
  if partner AND reservation then                //reservation is optimal
    if rCost(ba_i,rCell(ba_i)) == 0 then
      moveTo(reservedCell)
    else
      processCurrentCell()        //analyze cell to find either partner or reservation
    endif
  else
    moveTo(nextCell);                         //choose another cell to explore
    addBAsToMemory();                             //memorize BAs on the cell
    processEncounteredBAs();              //verify if they fit with constraints
    if NOT (reservation OR partner) then                    //goals not reached
      processCurrentCell()                       //analyze the current cell
    endif
  endif
done
```

must be able to affect priorities and weights to constraints as in fuzzy CSP or weighted CSP [5]. But, contrary to classical dynamic CSP [6], memory of previous states is sprayed within all the BAs which could be distributed within several servers. Finally, contrary to all these approaches, BAs only reason on a limited number of known BAs to find a good solution as in distributed CSP [7]. Since BAs are agents, they do not have any global knowledge. Therefore, constraint satisfaction is shared by BAs, and the solution emerges from their local peer-to-peer interactions. Nevertheless, our approach remains different from above-mentioned ones, because the main objective is not to provide an algorithm that is sound, complete, and terminates, but to define local and robust mechanisms, able to implement a global solving. Similarly to applications of ant algorithms on scheduling problems [8], BAs alter their environment (the grid) with markers to indicate the cells they book and to constrain the other agents. The main difference with the usage of pheromone is the way the markers disappear. In the ant approach, markers evaporate with time. In our algorithm, markers are removed consequently to negotiation between BAs in booking conflict (see section 3.4). Finally, this work is close to local search based CSP approaches such as [9], but by using the agent paradigm to encapsulate constraints.

3   Cooperative Self-organization Rules

The solving algorithm is distributed among BAs and lies in cooperative self-organization. Five different situations for reorganization are identified. The two firsts do not respect the c_{dec} meta-rule of AMAS. The three next ones do not respect c_{act}. In this example, there is no c_{per} violation because all BA agents are identical and can understand each other. The idea is to design these rules as *exceptions* in classical object programming, at the agent level and not at the instruction level. This concept really fits with the proscriptive approach proposed by [3]. As for exceptions, designers have to specify the condition of the exception throwing and the action to perform in the exception case. The following cooperation rules are then presented as condition-action pairs. Conditions are not exclusive. Nevertheless, a policy must be defined if several NCS have to be processed: from c_{dec} to c_{act}, for example.

3.1   Partnership Incompetence ($\neg c_{dec}$)

One of the goals a BA has to reach is to find a partner. If a BA ba_i encounters, in a cell, another BA ba_j it cannot partner with; ba_i is, using the AMAS terminology, incompetent [3]. For example, a BA representing a teacher's course meets another BA representing another teacher's course. As the only entity able to detect this partnership incompetence is the agent itself, this latter is the only one which changes the state of the organization by changing its position to encounter other more relevant BAs. Moreover, to enable a more efficient exploration of partnership possibilities, ba_i will memorize the location and the BAs known by ba_j for exchanging them during further encounters. The $pCost$ comparison allows ba_i to decide if the potential new partner ba_j is less constraining than the current one.

Name: **Partnership Incompetence** (for agent ba_i)
Condition: $\exists j(j \neq i \wedge knows(ba_i, ba_j) \wedge (\neg compatible(ba_i, ba_j) \vee (pCost(ba_i, ba_j) \geq pCost(ba_i, partnership(ba_i)))))$
Action: `memorize(ba`$_i$`,knows(ba`$_j$`));move`

3.2   Reservation Incompetence ($\neg c_{dec}$)

In the same manner than partnership incompetence, BAs must be able to change organization when their reservations are not relevant. This reservation incompetence NCS occurs when a BA ba_i occupies a cell which constraints do not fit its own constraints. For example, a BA representing a teacher's course is in a cell representing a room with not enough seats for this course. Then ba_i must move to explore the reservation possibility space. To improve the exploration of the grid, a BA memorizes the cells in which this NCS occurs to share it during negotiation or to avoid it when moving, like in tabu search.

Name: **Reservation Incompetence** (for agent ba_i)
Condition: $\neg compatible(ba_i, cell(ba_i)) \vee (rCost(ba_i, cell(ba_i)) \geq rCost(ba_i, reservation(ba_i)))$
Action: `memorize(ba`$_i$`,cell(ba`$_i$`));move`

3.3   Partnership Conflict ($\neg c_{act}$)

Situations during which a BA wants to partner with another partnered BA may append. The agent must react to this partnership conflict by partnering or by moving. In this case, the cooperation is directly embedded within the resolution action: the partnership will be performed with the agent that has more difficulties to find partners (by comparing the $pCost$). When it partners, a BA also unpartners with its previous partner and informs its previous partner and its proxy.

Name: **Partnership Conflict** (for agent ba_i)

Condition:
$\exists j \exists k (j \neq i \wedge i \neq k \wedge knows(ba_i, ba_j) \wedge compatible(ba_i, ba_j) \wedge partnership(ba_j) = ba_k)$

Action:

```
if (pCost(ba_i,ba_j) < pCost(ba_i,partnership(ba_i)))
   then partner(ba_i,ba_j)
   else move
```

3.4   Reservation Conflict ($\neg c_{act}$)

As for partnership, reservation may lead to conflict: a BA wants to reserve an already booked cell. When it books a cell, a BA also warns its previous partner and its proxy to inform not to book in the same time slot and unbooks the previous cell.

Name: **Reservation Conflict** (for Agent ba_i)

Condition:
$\exists j (j \neq i \wedge (reservation(ba_j, cell(ba_i)) \vee \exists k (reservation(ba_j, c_k) \wedge slot(cell(ba_i)) = slot(c_k) \wedge proxy(ba_i) = proxy(ba_j))) \wedge compatible(ba_i, cell(ba_i))$

Action:

```
if (rCost(ba_i,cell(ba_i)) < rCost(ba_i,reservation(ba_i)))
   then book(ba_i,cell(ba_i))
   else move
```

3.5   Reservation Uselessness ($\neg c_{act}$)

In the case a BA is in the same cell than one of its *brothers*, reservation is useless. Therefore it can leave the cell without analyzing it, and its occupants, to find another more relevant one. Processing encountered BAs corresponds to verifying, in a limited memory list of BAs the agent has already encountered or another agent has shared during a negotiation, whether the agents can find a relevant partner with minimum partnership cost.

Name: **Reservation Uselessness** (for agent ba_i)

Condition: $cell(ba_i) = cell(partnership(ba_i))$

Action: processEncounteredBAs();move

---

4   Prototyping and Experiments

Experiments are based on a French benchmark for the timetabling problem[1]. This requirements set is decomposed into four variants from simple problem

---

[1] http://www-poleia.lip6.fr/~guessoum/asa/BenchEmploi.pdf

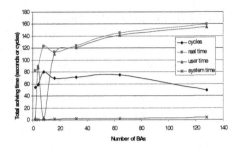

Fig. 1. Variation of solving time in terms of the number of BAs

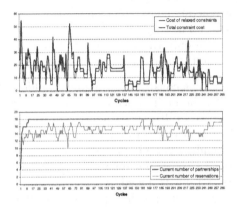
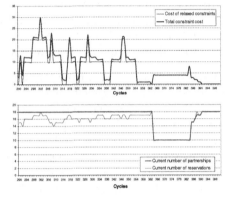

Fig. 2. Global constraint (*at top*) and partnership (*at bottom*) variations at run time for a solution requiring constraint relaxing

Fig. 3. Global constraint (*at top*) and partnership (*at bottom*) variations with a removing of 8 agents after the system stabilization

solving without constraint relaxing to system openness by adding or removing agents and constraints at run time. For each one of them, we proposed a solution – not unique in many cases.

Influence of Cardinality. Figure 1 shows the evolution of solving time as a consequence of the growing number of BAs in the system. For these experiments, we keep the same exploration space size by increasing the number of cells in the grid proportionally to the number of agents. Only availability constraints are owned by teachers: one time slot per day is forbidden. Once the maximum reached (average 8 BAs), the number of cycles (during which every agent acts one time) decreases as the number of BAs increases. The time that varies the less is the real time. Therefore, it is the most relevant indicator of the solving time evolution. Beyond 32 BAs, it has a logarithmic curve. More BAs the system has more efficient the solving is – if a solution exists.

Constraint Relaxing and Dynamic Solving. Figure 2 shows the efficiency of ETTO solving, for a variant with 36 BAs requiring constraint relaxing. Reservations are set later than partnerships. ETTO found a solution with a constraint cost of 10 in 265 cycles. This cost represents the sum of all the constraints BAs had to relax, i.e. the sum of the weights of relaxed constraints. Nevertheless, the current prototype does not manage the cooperative slot sharing during negotiation and therefore, when a BA moves, it randomly chooses the next cell. A third series of experiments tests the benefit in terms of robustness and dynamics. In these experiments, constraints become dynamic. Rooms or actors' availabilities may change at run time. Moreover, some agents can appear or disappear. By taking into account the chosen modeling, adding constraints is not different from adding agents that carry constraints. The figure 3 shows results on an experiment with initially 36 BAs. At cycle 364 – at the stabilization of the system – 8 BAs were removed, increasing the cost of relaxing constraints since each agent cannot find a relevant partner. 20 cycles later, 8 new agents with adequate constraints are plunged into the grid. The system only runs 7 cycles (from 384 to 391) to find an adequate organization with null constraint cost.

Discussion. Restarting from scratch each time a constraint is modified (added, removed) would not be efficient and usually, the main objective is to have the smallest impact possible on the current solution. In [10], this is done by introducing a new search algorithm that limits the number of additional perturbations. In [11], explanations are used as well to handle dynamic problems, especially, new operators are given to re-propagate once a constraint removed and its past effects undone. In ETTO, as soon as a constraint is added or removed for an agent, this latter questions its reservations and its possible partnership; if it judges that they are inconsistent with its new state, it tries to find new ones by roaming the grid and applying its usual behavior. If a new agent is added, it immediately begins searching for a partnership and if it is removed, then all its reservations and constraints are deleted from the system and its possible partner warned. The main feature of ETTO is that modifications are then done *without stopping the search* for a solution while this latter is in progress.

But, in ETTO, processing over-constrained problems is not fully efficient because even if agents have found a solution, they *continue to explore the grid* to find more relevant solutions. As agents usually have a *limited view* of the environment, they cannot take into account the global constraint cost to stop the exploration. To use ETTO, we consider an oracle exists who will halt the solving process when the organization fits his requirements. The search for a cell in the grid is not efficient either because it is *randomly* made by an agent. For the time being, we just wanted to show that our approach by self-organization is *feasible* and can produce positive results as it has been shown. Nevertheless, a future step would be to enhance this search by *adding a memory* to agents concerning, for instance, the cells they visited in the past.

5   Conclusion

We presented a cooperative self-organization approach to model a university timetabling solver which function emerges from inter-agent interactions. This work consists in defining local reorganization rules and cooperative behaviors to equip agents with, and then building an adaptive multi-agent system: ETTO. Experiments show relevant results on adaptivity and robustness to environmental dynamics and openness –by addind/removing agents or constraints to the running system. One perspective is to apply ETTO to a more realistic timetabling problem or to a benchmark such as the one given by the *Metaheuritics Network* (http://www.metaheuristics.org/), to compare our results with other ones.

References

1. Kohonen, T.: Self-Organising Maps. Springer-Verlag (2001)
2. Bonabeau, E., Theraulaz, G., Deneubourg, J.L., Aron, S., Camazine, S.: Self-Organization in Social Insects. Trends in Ecology and Evolution **12** (1997) 188–193
3. Capera, D., Georgé, J., Gleizes, M.P., Glize, P.: The AMAS Theory for Complex Problem Solving Based on Self-organizing Cooperative Agents. In: 1st International TAPOCS Workshop at IEEE 12th WETICE, IEEE (2003) 383–388
4. Georgé, J.P., Edmonds, B., Glize, P.: Making Self-Organising Adaptive Multiagent Systems Work. In: Methodologies and Software Engineering for Agent Systems, Kluwer (2004) 321–340
5. Bistarelli, S., Fargier, H., Mantanari, U., Rossi, F., Schiex, T., Verfaillie, G.: Semiring-based constraints CSPs and valued CSPs: frameworks, properties, and comparison. Constraints: an International Journal **4** (1999) 199–240
6. Dechter, Meiri, Pearl: Temporal constraint networks. Artificial Intelligence **49** (1991) 61–95
7. Yokoo, M., Durfee, E., Ishida, Y., Kubawara, K.: The Distributed Constraint Satisfaction Problem : Formalization and Algorithms. IEEE Transactions on Knowledge and Data Engineering **10** (1998) 673–685
8. Socha, K., Knowles, J., Sampels, M.: A MAX-MIN Ant System for the University Timetabling Problem. In: Proceedings of 3rd International Workshop on Ant Algorithms, ANTS'02. Volume 2463 of LNCS. (2002) 1 –13
9. Minton, S., Johnston, M., A., P., Laird, P.: Minimizing Conflicts: a Heuristic Repair Method for Constraint Satisfaction and Scheduling Problems. **58** (1992) 160–205
10. Müller, T., Rudova, H.: Minimal Perturbation Problem in Course Timetabling. In: Proc. of the 5th International Conference of the Practice and Theory of Automated Timetabling (PATAT), Pittsburg, USA. (2004)
11. Cambazard, H., Demazeau, F., Jussien, N., David, P.: Interactively Solving School Timetabling Problems using Extensions of Constraint Programming. In: Proc. of the 5th International Conference of the Practice and Theory of Automated Timetabling (PATAT), Pittsburg, USA. (2004)

Experiments in Emergent Programming Using Self-organizing Multi-agent Systems

Jean-Pierre George and Marie-Pierre Gleizes

IRIT, Université Paul Sabatier, 118 route de Narbonne, 31062 Toulouse cedex, France
{george, gleizes}@irit.fr

Abstract. We propose to investigate the concept of an Emergent Programming Environment enabling the development of complex adaptive systems. For this we use as a foundation the concept of *emergence* and a multi-agent system technology based on cooperative self-organizing mechanisms. The general objective is then to develop a complete programming language in which each instruction is an autonomous agent trying to be in a cooperative state with the other agents of the system, as well as with the environment of the system. The work presented here aims at showing the feasibility of such a concept by specifying, and experimenting with, a core of *instruction-agents* needed for a sub-set of mathematical calculus.

1 Introduction

In the last few years, the use of computers has spectacularly grown and classical software development methods run into numerous difficulties. The classical approach, by decomposition into modules and total control, cannot guaranty the functionality of the software given the complexity of interaction between the increasing and variable number of modules, and the shear size of possibilities. Adding to this, the now massive and inevitable use of network resources and distribution only increases the difficulties of design, stability and maintenance.

This state is of interest to an increasing number of industrials, including IBM who wrote in a much relayed manifesto : "*Even if we could somehow come up with enough skilled people, the complexity is growing beyond human ability to manage it. [...]increasing system efficiency generates problems with more variables than any human can hope to solve. Without new approaches, things will only get worse*" [9]. Their answer to that is a scientific challenge they call *autonomic computing*, whose objective is to design systems able to execute themselves, adjust their behaviour in face of various circumstances, manage at best their resources and self-repair when needed.

These kind of applications are what we call *neo-computation problems*, namely: autonomic computing, pervasive computing, ubiquitous computing [12], emergent computation, ambient intelligence, amorphous computing... This set of problems have in common the inability to define the global function to achieve, and by consequence to specify at the design phase, a derived evaluation function for the learning process. Thus, *neo-computation* systems are characterized by :

- a great number of interacting components (intelligent objects, agents, software);
- a variable number of these components during runtime (open system);

M. Pěchouček, P. Petta, and L.Z. Varga (Eds.): CEEMAS 2005, LNAI 3690, pp. 450–459, 2005.

- the impossibility to impose a global control;
- a dynamic and unpredictable environment;
- a functional adequacy[1] to reach in respect to the environment.

1.1   Problem Solving by Emergence

Given the previous characteristics, the challenge is to find new approaches to conceive these new systems by taking into account the increasing complexity and the fact that we want reliable and robust systems. Looking at natural systems [3] -biological, physical, sociological-,there is a common factor among theses systems : the emergent dimension of the observed behaviour. Thus it is quite legitimate to study emergence so as to understand its functioning or at least to be able to adequately reproduce it for the design of artificial systems. This would enable the development of more complex, robust and adaptive systems, needed to tackle the difficulties inherent to *neo-computation* problems. In this way, interesting and useful emergent phenomena will be used in artificial systems when needed. Contrariwise, they will still appear sooner or later the more complex the systems are getting but will be unexpected and unwanted. To prevent this, one orientation would be, in our opinion, that the scientific community studies and develops new theories based upon emergence.

It is noteworthy that some research is already being done for quite some years now to bring emergence into artificial systems, but it is still very localized. For example, the *Santa Fe Institute* [2] has acquired an international renown for its works on complexity, adaptive complex systems and thus emergence. These are also the preoccupations of *Exystence* [1], the European excellence network on complex systems. More recent (Mars 2000), this network wants to promote collaboration between researchers from any field interested in it, from fundamental concepts to applications.

1.2   Going to the Lowest Level: The Instructions

If we suppose that we can manage to use the emergent phenomena to build artificial systems, this will be by specifying the behaviour of the parts of the systems so that it will enable their interactions to produce the expected global emergent behaviour of the system. A relevant question would be to ask about what parts we are focusing on and on which level. As with classical software engineering, any decomposition could be interesting, depending on the nature of the system being build.

We propose here to focus on the lowest possible level for any artificial system : the instruction level. We will explain our theoretical and experimental exploration of the concept of *Emergent Programming*. This concept is explained in the next section (section 2). Its use relies on emergence and self-organization (section 3) on one hand, and on a multi-agent approach called *AMAS* (Adaptive Multi-Agent System) [7] on the

---

[1] "Functional" refers to the "function" the system is producing, in a broad meaning, i.e. what the system is doing, what an observer would qualify as the behaviour of a system. And "adequate" simply means that the system is doing the "right" thing, judged by an observer or the environment. So "functional adequacy" can be seen as "having the appropriate behaviour for the task".

other hand. A sub-problem (a *mathematical example*) has been thoroughly explored and is presented in section 4 where we then show how the learned lessons can lead us forward in our exploration of *Emergent Programming* and more generally of problem solving using emergence.

2   Emergent Programming

In its most abstract view, *Emergent Programming* is the automatic assembling of instructions of a programming language using mechanisms which are not explicitly informed of the program to be created. We may consider that for a programmer to produce a program comes down to finding which instructions to assemble and in which precise order. This is in fact the exploration of the search space representing the whole set of possible programs until the right program is found. However, if this exploration is easy when the programmer has a precise knowledge about the program he wants and how to obtain it, it grows more and more difficult with the increase of complexity of the program, or when the knowledge about the task to be executed by the program becomes imprecise or incomplete. Then are we not able to conceive an artificial system exploring efficiently the search space of the possible programs instead of having the programmer do it ? Only very few works exists on this topic. One noteworthy try has been done by Koza using Genetic Algorithms and a LISP language [10], but the main hindrance of GA is the need for a specific evaluation function for each problem, which can be very difficult to find. At the opposite, we aim at an as generic as possible approach.

To solve the problem of *Emergent Programming* concretely, we chose to rely on an adaptive multi-agent system using self-organizing mechanisms based on cooperation as it is described in the *AMAS* theory [7]. This theory can be considered as a guide to endow the agents with the capacity to continuously self-organize so as to always tend toward cooperative interactions between them and with the environment. It then claims that a cooperative state for the whole system implies the functional adequacy of the system, i.e. that it exhibits a behaviour which satisfies the constraints of the parts of the system as well as from the environment (e.g. a user).

2.1   The Instruction-Agents and the Reorganization Process

In this context, we define an agent as an instruction of a programming language. Depending on the type of the instruction he is representing, the agent possesses specific competences which he will use to interact with other *instruction-agents*. A complete program is then represented by a given organization of the *instruction-agents* in which each agent is linked with partners from which he receives data and partners to which he sends data. The counterpart of the execution of a classical program is here simply the activity of the multi-agent system during the exchange of data between the agents.

We can now appreciate all the power of the concept : a given organization codes for a given program, and thus, changing the organization changes the final program. It comes down to having the agents self-organize depending on the requirements from the environment so as to continuously tend toward the adequate program (the adequate global function). In principle, we obtain a system able to explore the search space of the possible programs in place of the programmer. Everything depends on the efficiency of the exploration to reach an organization producing the right function. An important part of our work on *Emergent Programming* has been the exploration of the self-organization mechanisms which enable the agents to progress toward the adequate function, depending on the constraints of the environment but without knowing the organization to reach or how to do it (since this is unknown for the problems we are interested in).

2.2 A Neo-Programming Environment

The system will not be able to grow *ex nihilo* all by itself, all the more if we want to obtain higher level programs. As the programmer with his classical programming environment, the *neo-programmer* will affect the development of the system through a *neo-programming environment*, at least at the beginning. It is a matter of supplying the tools to shape the environment of the system so as to have this environment constrain the system toward the adequate function. In a pure systems theory's view, the *neo-programmer* is simply part of the environment of the system.

But the *neo-programming environment* will certainly have to be more than a simple envelope for the developing system. We will probably need to integrate some tools for the observation of the evolution of the system, means to influence this evolution, the type and proportions of *instruction-agents*, to affect some aspects of the structure. Moreover, a complex program is generally viewed as a modular construct and the *neo-programmer* may want to influence this modular structure, either by manipulating some sorts of "bricks", each being an *emergent programming* system, or by letting these "bricks" self-organize in the same manner as their own components.

At the end, we will obtain a system able not only to "find" *how* to realize the adequate function, but also to continuously adapt to the environment in which it is plunged, to react to the strongly dynamic and unpredictable nature of real world environments, and all this by presenting a high grade of robustness. Indeed, because of its nature, the system would be able to change its internal structure any time and by consequence its performed function, or even grow by adding instructions to respond to some partial destruction or to gain some new competences.

The research we did on *Emergent Programming* was to explore the feasibility of the concept. For this, we restrained the programming language to the instructions needed for a subset of mathematical calculus, of which the *mathematical example* (section 4) is a representative. We specified such a core of agents and put it through experimentation. For this an environment has been implemented : *EPE* (*Emergent Programming Environment*) [6]. These experimentations enabled us to explore different self-organization mechanisms for the *instruction-agents* so as to find those who lead to the emergence of the adequate function. Part of these mechanisms are described here.

3   Emergence and Self-organization

If we study specialized literature on emergence or self-organization, we can see that these are tightly linked. Yet, at the same time, we can see a lot of works focusing exclusively on the second without any mention, or only a brief, about the first. One explanation could be that the notion of emergence is quite abstract, even philosophical, making it difficult to fully grasp and therefore delicate to manipulate. At the opposite, self-organization is more concrete by its description in terms of mechanisms and thus, more easily used. But by concentrating solely on the mechanisms, are we not taking the risk to leave the frame of emergence? We give here a description of self-organization integrating emergence.

Whereas emergence has been studied for a long time only as a philosophical concept manipulable only as it, the self-organization field has from the very beginning tried to explore its internal mechanisms. They tried to find the general functioning rules explaining the growth and evolution of the observed systemic structures, to find the shapes the systems could take, and finally to produce methods to predict the future organizations appearing out of changes happening at the component level of the systems. And these prospective results had to be applicable on any other system exhibiting the same characteristics (search for generic mechanisms).

3.1 Using Emergence in Artificial Systems

There are abundant definitions and descriptions of characteristics of emergence and self-organization in literature. To resume, we can sum it up as this :

Definition. *Self-organization is the set of processes within a system, stemming from mechanisms based on local rules which lead the system to produce structures or specific behaviours which are not dictated by the outside of the system* [5][8][11].

Our work in this domain during the last decade lead us to give a "technical" definition of emergence in the context of multi-agent systems, and therefore with a strong computer science colouration. It is based on three points: what we want to be emergent, at what condition it is emergent and how we can use it [4].

1. **Subject**. The goal of a computational system is to realize an adequate function, judged by a relevant user. It is this function (which may evolve during time) that has to emerge.
2. **Condition**. This function is emergent if the coding of the system does not depend on the knowledge of this function. This coding has to contain the mechanisms facilitating the adaptation of the system during its coupling with the environment, so as to tend toward an adequate function.
3. **Method**. To change the function the system only has to change the organization of its components. The mechanisms which allow the changes are specified by self-organization rules providing autonomous guidance to the components' behaviour without any explicit knowledge of the collective function nor how to reach it.

3.2 The Engine for Self-organization

According to the *AMAS* theory[7],the designer provides the agents with local criterion to discern between cooperative and non-cooperative situations (NCS). The detection and then elimination of NCS between agents constitute the engine of self-organization. Depending on the real-time interactions the multi-agent system has with its environment, the organization between its agents emerges and constitutes an answer to the aforementioned difficulties of *neo-computation problems* (indeed, there is no global control of the system). In itself, the emergent organization is an observable organization that has not been given first by the designer of the system. Each agent computes a partial function, but the combination of all the partial functions produces the global emergent function. Depending on the interactions between themselves and with the environment, the agents change their interactions i.e. their links. This is what we call self-organization.

By principle, the emerging purpose of a system is not recognizable by the system itself, its only criterion must be of strictly local nature (relative to the activity of the parts which make it up). By respecting this, the *AMAS* theory aims at being a theory of emergence.

4   Emergence of a Mathematical Function

We tried to find an *emergent programming* system as simple as possible (i.e. with the smallest number of agents with the simplest functioning), but still needing reorganizations so as to produce the desired function. The advantages of such a case study are that it is more practical for observation, that it leads to less development complexity and that it presents a smaller search space.

4.1   Description

The specification of each agent depends on the task he has to accomplish, of his *"inputs"* and *"outputs"*. The agents communicate by messages but to accomplish the actual calculation, we can consider that the agents are expecting values as inputs to be able to provide computed values as outputs. Schematically, we can consider exchanges between agents as an electronic cabling between outputs and inputs of agents.

The mathematical example we choose is constituted of 6 agents : 3 *"constant"* agents, an *"addition"* agent, a *"multiplication"* agent and an *"output"* agent. A *"constant"* agent is able to provide the value which has been fixed at his creation. The 3 the system contains have been given sufficiently different values so as to prevent calculation ambiguity : *AgentConstantA* (value = 2), *AgentContantB*(value = 10) and *AgentConstantC* (value = 100). Combined with *AgentAddition* and *AgentMultiplication*, the values produced by the system are results from organizations like $(A + B) * C$ or any other possible combination. *AgentOut* simply transmits the value he receives to the environment. But he is also in charge of retrieving the feedback from the environment and forward it into the system.

The size of the complete search space is 6^5, that is 7776 theoretically possible organizations, counting all the incomplete ones (i.e. where not every agent has all his partners). There are 120 complete organizations and among those, 24 are functional (they can actually calculate a value) if we count all the possible permutations on the inputs which do not change the calculated value. In the end, we have 6 types of different organization (cf. Figure 1) producing these 6 values : 120, 210, 220, 1002, 1020 and 1200. The aim is to start without any partnerships between agents and to request that the system produces the highest value for example.

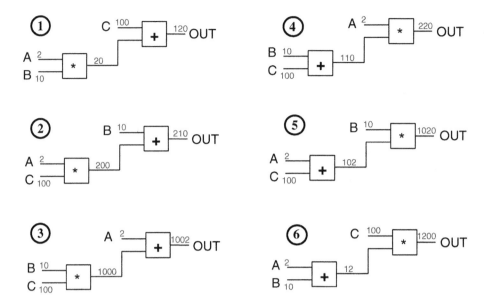

Fig. 1. The 6 different possible types of functional organizations for the mathematical example

4.2   Reorganization Mechanisms

In accordance with the *AMAS* theory, the agent's self-organizing capacity is induced by their capacity to detect NCS (Non-Cooperative Situations), react so as to resorb them and continuously act as cooperatively as possible. This last point implies in fact that the agent also has to try to resorb NCS of other agents if he is aware of them: to ignore a call for help from another agent is definitely not cooperative. We will illustrate this with the description of two NCS and how they are resorbed.

Detection

NCSNeedIn : the agent is missing a partner on one of his inputs. Since to be cooperative in the system he has to be useful, and to be useful he has to be able to compute his function, he has to find partners able to send values toward his input.

Most NCS lead the agent to communicate so as to find a suitable (new) partner. These calls, because the agents have to take them into account, also take the shape of NCS.

NCSNeedInMessage : the agent receives a message informing him that another agent is in a *NCSNeedIn* situation.

Resorption

NCSNeedIn : this is one of the easiest NCS to resorb because the agent only has to find any agent for his missing input. And the agents are potentially always able to provide as many values on their outputs for as many partners as needed. The agent has simply to be able to contact some agent providing values of the right type (there could be agents handling values of different types in a system), i.e. corresponding to his own type. So he generates a *NCSNeedInMessage* describing his situation (his needs) and send it to his acquaintances (because they are the only agents he knows).

NCSNeedInMessage : the agent is informed of the needs of the sender of the NCS and his cooperative attitude dictates him to act. First, he has to judge if he is relevant for the needs of the sender, and if it is the case, he has to propose himself as a potential partner. Second, even if he is not himself relevant, one of its acquaintances may be. He will do what the *AMAS* theory calls a resorption by restricted propagation : he tries to counter this NCS by propagating the initial message to some acquaintances he thinks may be the most relevant.

For each NCS the agent is able to detect (there are 10 NCS in total for these agents), a specific resorption mechanism has been defined. It is a precise description of the decision making of the agent depending on his state and on what it perceives. For other NCS, the mechanisms become quite complicated, and require a long description. For an exhaustive presentation, please refer to [6].

These NCS and their symmetric for a missing partner on an output enable the system to produce an organization where each agent has all his needed partners. To obtain the functional adequacy for the system means that the final organization is able to produce the expected result. The main question is how to introduce mechanisms in the resorption of the NCS to enable the agents as a whole to reach this organization. For this, they need some kind of *"direction"* (but on local criterion) to get progressively closer to the solution, a local information to judge this proximity. The information used here is simply a "smaller/bigger" feedback type that the environment sends to the system and that will be dispatched between the agents by propagation and by taking other the goal (smaller or bigger). The agent then tries to satisfy its new goal and staying at the same time the most cooperative possible with the other agents. This will bring the system as a whole to produce a smaller or bigger value.

Of course, the agents will get into conflict with other agents when trying to reach these goals and the self-organizing mechanisms take that into account. Each agent also manipulates a knowledge about the prejudice he inflicts or may inflict following changes he induces in the organization. By minimizing these prejudices (which is a form of cooperation), the whole organization progresses.

It is important to note that the information which is given as a feedback is not in any way an explicit description about the goal and *how* to reach it. Indeed, this information does not exist : given a handful of values and mathematical operators, there is no explicit method to reach a specific value even for a human. They can only try and guess, and this is also what the agents do. That is why we believe the solving we implemented to be in the frame of emergence.

4.3   Results and Discussion

Results. First of all, the internal constraints of the system are solved very quickly : in only a few reorganization moves (among the 7776 possible organizations), all the agents find their partners and a functional organization is reached. Then, because the system is asked to produce the highest value for example (configuration 6, Figure 1), other NCS are produced and the system starts reorganizing toward its goal.

On a few hundred simulations, the functional adequacy is reached in a very satisfactory number of organization changes. Since the search space if of 7776 possible organizations, a blind exploration would need an average of 3.888 checked organizations to reach a specific one. Since a functional organization possesses 4 identical instances for a given value (by input permutations), we would need 972 tries to get the right value. Experimentation shows that, whatever the initial organization (without any links or one of the 6 functionals), the system needs to explore less than a hundred organizations among the 7776 to reach one of the 4 producing the highest value. We consider that this self-organization strategy allows a relevant exploration of the search space. A noteworthy result is also that whatever organization receives the feedback for a better value, the next organization will indeed produce a better value (if it exists).

Emergent Programming : A Universal Tool. If we define all the agents needed to represent a complete programming language (with agents representing variables, allocation, control structures, ...) and if this language is extensive enough, we obtain maximal expressiveness : every program we can produce with current programming languages can be coded as an organization of *instruction-agents*. In its absolute concept, *Emergent programming* could then solve any problem, given that the problem can be solved by a computer system. Of course, this seems quite unrealistic, at least for the moment.

Problem Solving Using Emergence. But if we possess some higher-level knowledges about a problem, or if the problem can be structured at a higher level than the instruction level, then it is more efficient and easier to conceive the system at a higher level. This is the case for example when we can identify entities of bigger granularity which therefore have richer competences and behaviours, maybe adapted specifically for the problem.

Consequently, we will certainly be able to apply the self-organizing mechanisms developed for Emergent Programming to other ways to tackle a problem. Indeed, *instruction-agents* are very particular by the fact that they represent the most generic type of entities and that there is a huge gap between their functions and the function of a whole program. The exploration of the search space, for entities possessing more information or more competences for a given problem can only be easier. In the worst case, we can always try to use Emergent Programming as a way to specify the behaviour of higher-level entities (recursive use of emergence).

Let us consider for instance the problem of ambient intelligence : in a room, a huge number of electronic equipments controlled each by an autonomous microchip have as a goal the satisfaction of the users moving around it from day to day. The goal itself, user satisfaction, is really imprecise and incomplete, and the way to reach it even more. We claim that this problem is an ideal candidate for a problem solving by emergence approach: let us endow the entities with means to find by themselves the global behaviour of the system so as to satisfy the users. The challenge is to define the "right" self-organizing behaviours for the different equipments for them to be able to modify the way they interact to take into account the constraints of every one of them plus the external stimuli from the users (order, judgement, behaviour, ...). And we are convinced that this can only be done if the self-organization mechanisms tightly fit the frame of emergence.

5   Conclusion

We aimed at studying the feasibility of the concept of *Emergent Programming* by using self-organizing *instruction-agents*. We presented in this paper the concept and how we studied it. For this, we first described the frame of self-organization and emergence as we think can be applied in artificial systems. Then we described a generic approach for adaptive systems based upon a multi-agent system where the agents are endowed with self-organizing mechanisms based upon cooperation and emergence.

A mathematical example has been used as a case study. Its implementation, and experimentation with, lead to the definition of the self-organizing mechanisms of the *instruction-agents* so as to enable them to make the system reach a given goal.

This study has been an interesting work to explore self-organization in MAS when confronted to difficult problems that we are persuaded need an Emergent solution. We claim that this approach would be really relevant for *neo-computation* problems such as ambient intelligence, if not directly with *instruction-agents*, by using the same kind of cooperative self-organization mechanisms.

References

1. Web site of exystence : the complex systems network of excellence. http://www.complexityscience.org.
2. Web site of the santa fe institute. http://www.santafe.edu.
3. S. Camazine, J.-L. Deneubourg, N. Franks, J. Sneyd, and E. Theraulaz, G.and Bonabeau. *Self-organization in biological systems*. Princeton University Press, 2002.
4. D. Capera, J. Georgé, M.-P. Gleizes, and P. Glize. Emergence of organisations, emergence of functions. In *AISB'03 symposium on Adaptive Agents and Multi-Agent Systems*, April 2003.
5. J. Georgé, B. Edmonds, and P. Glize. *Self-organizing adaptive multi-agent systems work*, chapter 16, pages 321–340. Kluwer Publishing, 2004.
6. J.-P. Georgé. *Résolution de problèmes par émergence - Étude d'un Environnement de Programmation Émergente*. PhD thesis, Université Paul Sabatier, Toulouse, France, 2004. http://www.irit.fr/SMAC/EPE.html.
7. M.-P. Gleizes, V. Camps, and P. Glize. A theory of emergent computation based on cooperative self-oganization for adaptive artificial systems. In *Fourth European Congress of Systems Science*, Valencia, Spain, 1999.
8. F. Heylighen. *Encyclopedia of Life Support Systems*, chapter The Science of Self-organization and Adaptivity. EOLSS Publishers Co. Ltd, 2001.
9. P. Horn. Autonomic computing - ibm's perspective on the state of information technology. http://www.ibm.com/research/autonomic, 2001.
10. J. R. Koza. Evolution and co-evolution of computer programs to control independently-acting agents. In *From animals to animats : proceedings of the first international conference on Simulation of Adaptative Behavior (SAB)*. MIT Press, 1991.
11. I. Prigogine and G. Nicolis. *Self Organization in Non-Equilibrium Systems*. J. Wiley and Sons, New York, 1977.
12. M. Weiser and J. S. Brown. Designing calm technology. *PowerGrid Journal*, 1(1), 1996.

A Direct Reputation Model for VO Formation

Arturo Avila-Rosas[1] and Michael Luck[2]

[1] Instituto Mexicano del Petróleo,
Eje Central 152, México DF, CP 07730, México
aavilar@imp.mx

[2] School of Electronics and Computer Science,
University of Southampton,
Southampton, SO17 1BJ, United Kingdom
mml@ecs.soton.ac.uk

Abstract. We show that reputation is a basic ingredient in the Virtual Organisation (VO) formation process. Agents can use their experiences gained in direct past interactions to model other's reputation and deciding on either join a VO or determining who is the most suitable set of partners. Reputation values are computed using a reinforcement learning algorithm, so agents can learn and adapt their reputation models of their partners according to their recent behaviour. Our approach is especially powerful if the agent participates in a VO in which the members can change their behaviour to exploit their partners. The reputation model presented in this paper deals with the questions of deception and fraud that have been ignored in current models of VO formation.

1   Introduction

Recently, a large number of new collaborative, networked organisations have emerged, having as motivation the explosive progress in computer networks and communication systems, but also as a reaction to market pressures that demand customised, high quality products and services at lower costs and, at the same time, shorter production and marketing times. Promising greater flexibility, resource optimisation and responsiveness in *competitive open environments*, VOs are an example of this trend that has pervaded not only business domains but other areas such as e-science. The concept of a VO has been used to describe the aggregation of autonomous and independent organisations connected through a network and brought together to deliver a product or service in response to a customer need [6]. In this paper we take a VO to be *a temporary alliance composed of a number of autonomous entities (representing different individuals, departments and organisations) each of which has bounded problem solving capabilities and limited resources at their disposal, that come together to share skills or core competences and resources in order to better respond to customer needs or business opportunities, and whose cooperation is supported by computer networks* (adapted from [5]).

What distinguishes VOs from other forms of organisation is the full mutual dependence of their members to achieve their goal and therefore the need for

M. Pĕchouček, P. Petta, and L.Z. Varga (Eds.): CEEMAS 2005, LNAI 3690, pp. 460–469, 2005.

cooperation. However, open environments in which VOs are embedded involve organisations and individuals that do not necessarily share the same objectives and interests that they might not know in advance, and where they might not trust each other, but should work together and help each other to achieve a common goal. One of the key omissions in the computational representation of VOs relates to the need to take into account more subjective facets like the *reputation* of the individuals, which helps to cope with heterogeneity, autonomy and diversity of interests among members. We observe that current solutions underestimate the possibility of swindle in VOs. A common flaw is assuming that the partners selected are fully competent and honest. Since partners represent organisations or individuals who want to maximise their utilities by joining a VO, they have a strong incentive to misrepresent the value of their contributions and enjoy more benefits of cooperative associations [1]. Further, partners are selected in relation to the abilities they claim to have, but it is possible that they do not have such abilities. However, due to lack of information about past interactions, it is difficult to detect and control these situations. This paper considers the introduction of reputation into VOs, by providing a reputation model based on the adaptive evaluation of direct experiences to identify trustworthy individuals to join VO.

The remainder of this paper is organised as follows. The requirement for reputation systems for VOs are discussed in Section 2. In Section 3 we present our reputation model for VOs which is based on reinforcement learning techniques. In Section 4, we describe the experiments undertaken to support the validity of our model, the results of which (and their comparison with two other models) are presented in Section 5. Section 6 reviews related work, and Section 7 present our conclusions.

2   Requirements

The objective of this section is to delineate the requirements for building a reputation system in order to serve as a decision-making variable in the selection of partners, promote cooperation, produce trust and induce *good* behaviour in the members of a VO.

1. *Distributed reputation management.* As they are distributed and dynamic, VOs do not depend on the presence of any centrally trusted authority. Moreover, individuals must maintain personalised models of the trustworthiness of others at a capability level so that they will be able to know which capability caused cooperation to fail and why [3]. By contrast, centralised management of reputation offers a biased perspective of reputation because it aggregates feedback, making no distinction between the preferences of partners submitting feedback that may not coincide with the interests of the VO.

2. *Dynamism.* VOs integrate multiple autonomous, diversely skilled partners under intense time pressures to create complex products or services [4]. Due to limitations in time and intense task pressures, VOs require that their

members develop mutual trust fast. Partners should be able to quickly use a reduced number of interactions to estimate the reputation of a partner and; at the same time, take partner selection decisions without having a significant impact, in terms of time consumption, on the formation of a VO.

3. *Adaptability.* VOs operate under high levels of demand uncertainty generated by unknown and rapid shifts in consumer preferences [4]. Demand uncertainty creates changes in the structure of the VO, which is forced to adapt itself by reallocating tasks or redefining them. In these circumstances, organisations feeds into periodic evaluations of the VO which, in turn, leads partners to make adjustments to their relationships and identify when changes in the efficiency of partners is due to the adaptation process or due to abusive behaviour [4]. This suggests that the updating process of reputation values should be a *learning* process about another's true abilities, that captures the observed performance through the reputation of the partner.

4. *Predictability.* The behaviour of each partner in a VO usually offers clues to the others about its capabilities and *intentions*, so it is possible to make predictions about its future behaviour. The main objective of *predictions* is to detect any misconduct of the partner early enough, so that the VO can take necessary steps to protect itself from adverse effects of partner misbehaviour. Reputation must provide information to predict the future performance of a partner and eventually the risk involved of interacting with it.

3   Direct Reputation Model

In this section we introduce our model of reputation, which meets some of the requirements discussed in the previous section. We start by defining mathematically the concepts of reputation and impressions. Next we describe the methods used in our model for updating reputation.

3.1   Reputation

We define the reputation of an agent as *a perception regarding its intention and competences, which is held by other agents through the formation and dissemination of subjective evaluations based on experiences and observations of past actions.* Here, these evaluations are called *impressions*. From the definition, the observed behaviour of others is collected through: (i) direct experiences, with interaction histories serving as a strong evidence for estimating someone reputation or (ii) via the testimony of others, known as recommenders. On the basis of the source of reputation, two concepts of reputation may be derived, namely *direct reputation* and *social reputation*. Although important, the concept of social reputation lies beyond the scope of our research and is not defined; we only make reference to it as another source of reputation different from direct reputation.

3.2   Direct Reputation

Direct reputation (DR) is defined as the weighted average evaluation that an agent makes of another's competence, and gives the extent to which the target is *good* or *bad* with respect to a given behaviour or action. Direct reputation is context-dependent so that an agent is reputed according to the service provided. For example, an agent may be well reputed as a printing service provider but poorly reputed as a file storing service provider. VOs provide an environment in which agents may offer the same service with different qualities for different reasons such as demand uncertainty or as a result of dishonest behaviour. In this sense, we adopt the ideas of Shapiro [8] expressed in his analysis of the economic effects of reputation in such environments. Shapiro proved that the most efficient way to estimate a seller's reputation (i.e., the way that induces the seller to produce at the highest quality level) is a time-discounted average of the recent ratings evaluating its reputation. Hence, direct reputation is computed as the average of *impressions* received within the most recent time window,

$$W = [t - \epsilon, t],\tag{1}$$

where ϵ defines a time interval that limits the set of interactions and in which impressions are used to compute a direct reputation value. Impressions are weighted from 0 to 1 to indicate the notion of importance of an impression in relation to others for calculating reputation. Taking only the most recent impressions is equivalent to using an average calculation where weights are non-zero for impressions received within the time window and 0 otherwise. The direct reputation values vary in the range of [0,1] and are used only to represent comparative values in this continuous space from bad reputation (values near 0) to good reputation (values near 1). The direct reputation of i in the perspective of j in context k is represented as:

$$DR_{ij}^k \in [0,1].$$

3.3   Impression

We define an impression as an evaluative opinion that is formed by any entity (individual, organisation, etc.) based on a discrete experience with another partner, coupled with the partner's performance. Computationally, an impression is the value assigned to a service that indicates the proximity of the service provided by an agent i to the expectations of agent j requesting the service. An impression is related with a dimension that describes just one of the qualities of the service as required by agent j. For example, a partner can get different impressions for its efficiency or the quality of its services. The group of dimensions needed for evaluating the whole performance of a service provider is denoted by the set of enabling qualities Q and it is context-dependent. For example, to evaluate an agent in the context of a printing service, two dimensions may be taken into account: printing quality and rapidity. Mathematically, the impression appear as follows,

$$imp_{ij}^d \in [0,1],$$

$$Q_{ij} = \{d \in k | k \text{ is a context}\},\tag{2}$$

where i is the service provider whose interaction with the service consumer j left in it the strong impression imp in relation to dimension d, and Q_{ij} is the set of dimensions for evaluating a service provider in context k. The numbers used for impressions are merely reference values for making comparisons, each consumer establishes a personal threshold of *acceptable* values for the dimension d evaluated. This personal threshold may be based on:

– the agreed values of a contract, when interactions are fixed by contractual terms; or
– the values that constitute a standard for delivering a service, when standards are available to indicate the permissible values of a particular dimension; or
– the values obtained empirically, when the consumer has previous experience of consuming a particular service and can estimate optimal values for the dimensions involved.

Once a personal threshold of acceptable values is established, it is compared with the actual values of each dimension after providing a service.

3.4   Updating Direct Reputation

Each agent updates its reputation value of a service provider every time it receives impressions from either direct (immediate or observed interactions) or indirect experiences. Our first proposal to update the reputation values (after receiving t rated experiences or impressions) consists in the use of the following reinforcement learning based action update rules:

$$DR_t = DR_{t-1} + \alpha \cdot [imp_t - DR_{t-1}]. \tag{3}$$

Reputation, in Eq.(3), can be interpreted as the aggregation of the previous value of reputation plus a factor that strengthens or weakens that value. This factor indicates the proximity of the recent impression to the past reputation, and shows of how well the previous reputation predicts the latest given impression. Note that although we omit the indices k, i and j to make the expression more readable, DR_t makes reference to the reputation of an agent i in the opinion of agent j for the context k. The update rule in Eq.(3) is a linear function which is required in an open environment where the number of prior interactions may be reduced, and reputation cannot be updated in the long term through a non-linear function because an agent could cheat on many occasions before the reputation is updated. Instead, reputation must be updated immediately after any interaction. If α is near 1 then all the previous history will be forgotten, otherwise, if α is near 0 then the previous history will be preserved.

The factor α is also known as a learning rate, and is an indicator of how long past experiences will last in the memory of the system. For example, while low values of α mean that early experiences will have more influence in the system than recent ratings, high values of α indicate that early experiences will soon be forgotten. For our purposes, we consider α as a function $\alpha(DR_{t-1}, imp_t)$ with the following properties that are based on the ideas of Carbo et al. [2]:

– The function $\alpha(DR_{t-1}, imp_t)$ determines how fast the reputation value changes after an experience and how this affects the memory of the system.

This depends on the accuracy of the predictions suggested by the *impressions* received; that is, how much similarity exists between the expectation formed by the previous reputation values and the last rating. We consider the initial value for the function $\alpha(DR_{t0}, imp_{t0}))$ to be 0.5. That is, as the agent starts to learn, it will be careful with the first impressions until it learns how to better estimate its predictions.

- Similarity will be estimated through a similarity function $\beta(DR_{t-1}, imp_t) \in (0, 1)$:

$$\beta(DR_{t-1}, imp_t) = 1 - e^{-10 \cdot ABS(E-imp)}, \tag{4}$$

where E is the estimated rating based on the past reputation and rating:

$$E = \frac{DR_{t-1} + imp_{t-1}}{2}. \tag{5}$$

- Finally, the function $\alpha(DR_{t-1}, imp)$ is updated as follows:

$$\alpha(DR_t, imp) = \frac{\alpha(DR_{t-1}, imp) + \beta(DR_{t-1}, imp)}{2}. \tag{6}$$

4 Experiments

We performed two sets of experiments to evaluate DIRECT (our algorithm for computing reputation based on direct interactions) and show its feasibility and effectiveness. For comparison purpose, we use two existing models of reputation, SPORAS [9] and REGRET [7]. These models were chosen because reputation systems for VOs should consider the time when the interactions take place in order to update their reputation values, and both SPORAS and REGRET meet this requirement. In order to compare similar values of reputation, SPORAS and REGRET were modified to produce reputation values normalised in the range [0,1]. Additionally, in the case of REGRET, just the *individual dimension* of reputation is considered because it is the only one associated with direct interactions.

4.1 Accuracy

The objective of this experiment is to evaluate the accuracy of the reputation model. The value of reputation must provide a measure of the true capabilities of a service provider (SP) for providing a service. We generate 10 series of data representing the quality perceived of a service (QP) during 60 interactions. This data varies randomly in the interval $[-z, +z]$ from a mean value q of the actual quality (QoS). We want to model the fact that although SP delivers its services with the same quality, that is $q = 0.5$, the consumer (CA) may perceive such a quality in distinct ways. In our experiment, CA's perceptions vary around the actual quality q with a standard deviation $\sigma = 0.03$, and according to a normal distribution.

4.2   Abuse

The experiment here described is similar to that described in [9] where a SP who joins a VO behaves reliably until it reaches a high reputation value and then starts committing fraud. Thus, in this experiment we aim to show quantitatively which model of reputation offers a mechanism for dealing with deceit. Deceit in a VO is found when a partner deteriorates the quality of its services once it has reached a certain level of reputation, in order to exploit others. We measure the rapidity with which agents *learn* the *new* behaviour of their partners in terms of the minimum number of interactions to adjust the reputation of a partner towards true quality of a service. We generated two sets of 10 data series representing the quality of a service during 120 interactions, both data varying using a normal distribution in the interval $[-z, +z]$ from a mean value $q1$ and $q2$ of quality. In the first set of data the agent provides the highest quality during the first 25% of the interactions and, after that it decreases the quality in 6.25%, 12.5%, 18.75%, 25%, 31.25%, 37.5%, 43.75% and 50% for the rest of the interactions. We want to model the fact that after delivering its services with the same quality, $q1 = 0.8$, during the first 30 interactions, this may be perceived by CA in distinct way. SP then reduces the quality of its services to milk the reputation already built. As in the previous experiment, CA's perceptions vary around the actual qualities $q1$ and $q2$ with a standard deviation $\sigma = 0.03$, and according to a normal distribution.

5   Results

5.1   Results of Reputation Evaluation Accuracy

In Figure 1 the reputation values computed with the three algorithms are shown. As can be seen, our proposal obtains similar results as REGRET in a similar number of interactions. DIRECT and REGRET establish the reputation value faster than SPORAS. Although REGRET and our proposal DIRECT use different aggregation algorithms for computing reputation, both obtain accurate results when a SP maintains the provision of its service without change. In our simulations, we compute the number of interactions before the reputation curves generated by each of the algorithms converge towards the actual QoS. The convergence is considered when the calculated values of reputation are in the interval $[q - \sigma, q + \sigma]$.

5.2   Results of Abuse of Prior Performance

In Figure 2 we can see that REGRET requires in general more interactions to adapt its reputation values to the change of behaviour of service providers. In contrast, DIRECT and SPORAS show a more adaptive behaviour and require fewer interactions. On the other hand, REGRET updates reputation values very slowly, and opportunistic providers might take advantage of this by getting high values of reputation to be considered as well reputed and then start to cheat.

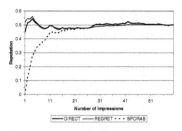
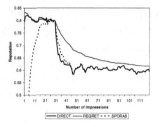

Fig. 1. Building Reputation   **Fig. 2.** Reputation is decreased in 25.0%

In Figure 3 the minimum number of interactions is shown to adjust the decrement in the reputation value of 6.25%, 12.5%, 18.75%, 25%, 31.25%, 37.5%, 43.75% and 50%. As can be seen SPORAS and DIRECT require less than 20 interactions to adjust their reputation values to the change in quality of the service, regardless of the percentage in which the quality is reduced. In RE-GRET, due to the accumulation of experiences, the effect of past experiences on the computation of reputation provokes accelerated increment in number of interactions required to adjust its reputation value.

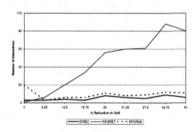

Fig. 3. Minimum number of interaction to adjust reputation values

The key difference between SPORAS and DIRECT is the ability to distinguish changes in behaviour based on the accuracy of the predictions. That is, DIRECT adjusts its values of reputation faster than SPORAS when the expectations created by the reputation values are closer to latest impressions. This can be seen in the slope of both curves. While the rapidity to detect the change in the quality of a service is alike for both curves, DIRECT presents values of reputation closer to the true quality of service.

6   Related Work

Zacharia and Maes in [9] present SPORAS, which is a *centralised* reputation system that establishes reputation for users in an on-line community, based on the aggregation of *rates* given by users after each transaction. Reputation in SPORAS aims to predict future performance of the users. In order to make accurate predictions using a small computational space, a recursive and adaptive algorithm for updating reputation is used. Reputation is calculated continuously using the previous value of reputation; and the previous value of reputation is reinforced or weakened depending on the rates obtained. This aggregation method then allows newer rates to count more than older ones. Because SPORAS is a centralised reputation system, it is not viable for VOs where partners need personalised reputation values calculated from assembled rates of those they trust already rather than those they do not know. Although the assumption made in SPORAS to make reputation values dependent on the reputation of the entity who is providing a feedback is correct, it mixes two different dimensions of reputation. While a user can be reputed as completely unable to cheat on deals, nonetheless that same user may be a bad evaluator of other users. That is, being an excellent service provider does not mean being an honest evaluator.

REGRET is a reputation system developed by Sabater and Sierra [7] that adopts a sociological approach for computing reputation in societies of agents trading well defined products inside an e-commerce environment. Although RE-GRET provides a very simple method for aggregating rates (or *impressions* that are the result of evaluating direct interactions) based on the weighted sum of the impressions (more relevance is given to the recent ones), its major contribution is the vision of reputation through of three dimensions. These dimensions are called the *individual dimension, social dimension* and *ontological dimension*. RE-GRET emphasises both individual and social components of social evaluations. That is, whereas the individual dimension is the effect of past experience with a given agent, the social dimension refers to reputation inherited by individuals from the *groups* they belong to. However, as discussed earlier, VOs require to a certain extent that the reputation of a partner is assessed in a *reactive* form to detect possible opportunistic behaviour. However, REGRET's main idea consists of emphasising the freshness of information. Computations in REGRET give a *fixed* high relevance to recent rates over older ones according to a time dependent function, and, moreover the rates are aggregated in a way that can be sensitive to noise since they are simply summed. Furthermore, VOs require that reputation be assessed swiftly in order to detect misbehaviour. REGRET, on its part, requires a minimum number of interactions to make correct evaluations of reputation but it is likely that partners will not interact the minimum number of times to provide a reliable reputation value. Finally, REGRET does not handle the problem of lying (strategically) among agents. Rates are obtained in a cooperative manner rather than in a competitive environment.

7   Conclusions and Future Work

We have provided a critical overview of the state of the art in the field of VOs and reputation. We argue that subjective aspects of partners such as their *competences* and *trustworthiness* should be taken into account in partner selection decisions, since these aspects ultimately influence cooperation between partners.

Moreover, we assert that reputation plays an important role in VOs when members decide who to interact with and when to interact, by providing information about the past behaviour of potential partners, their abilities and reliability. Additionally, we discussed the requirements for building reputation systems that pursue three basic objectives in the formation and operation of VOs: (1) they provide useful information about potential partners for selecting the most *appropriate*, and eventually enable the formation of VOs; (2) they foster trust among the partners of the VO by revealing each partner's capabilities and predicting its future behaviour; and (3) they offer a means for enhancing cooperation by detecting and deterring deceptive behaviour through imposing *collective sanctions* on defectors. Finally, we have provided experimental evidence to demonstrate the validity of the model developed and the fulfilment of the requirements mentioned above, including a comparative analysis of the model proposed in this thesis and two other models. In particular, two aspects were analysed regarding the accuracy of the values calculated and the ability to detect abuses.

Although this paper has answered how reputation is relevant to recognise cooperative partners through direct interactions, it opens up more research opportunities and questions that are unanswered. Moreover, there are other issues that were not faced in this paper, due to the bounds imposed on the research, and still need to be addressed.

References

1. S. Braynov and T. Sandholm. Trust revelation in multiagent interaction. In *Proceedings of CHI'02 Workshop on Philosophy and design of Socially Adept Technologies*, pages 57–60, Minneapolis, USA, 2002.
2. J. Carbo, J. Molina, and J. Davila. Trust management through fuzzy reputation. *International Journal of Cooperative Information Systems*, 12(1):135–155, 2003.
3. N. Griffiths and M. Luck. Coalition formation through motivation and trust. In *Proceedings of the Second International Joint Conference on AAMAS*, pages 17–24, Melbourne, Australia, 2003.
4. C. Jones, W.S. Hesterly, and S.P. Borgatti. A General Theory of Network Governance: Exchange Conditions and Social Mechanisms. *Academy of Management Review*, 22:911–945, 1997.
5. T. Norman, A. Preece, S. Chalmers, N. R. Jennings, M. Luck, V. Dang, T. Nguyen, V. Deora, J. Shao, W. Gray, and N. Fiddian. Agent-based formation of virtual organisations. *International Journal of Knowledge Based Systems*, 17(2–4):103–111, 2003.
6. E. Oliveira and A. Rocha. Agents advanced features for negotiation in electronic commerce and virtual organisations formation processes. In *Agent Mediated Electronic Commerce, the European AgentLink Perspective*, volume 1991 of *Lectures Notes in Artificial Intelligence*, pages 77–96, 2000.
7. J. Sabater and C. Sierra. Reputation and social network analysis in multi-agent systems. In *Proceedings of the First International Joint Conference on AAMAS*, pages 475–482, Bologna, Italy, 2002.
8. Carl Shapiro. Consumer information, product quality, and seller reputation. *The Bell Journal of Economics*, 13:20–35, 1982.
9. G. Zacharia and P. Maes. Trust management through reputation mechanisms. *Applied Artificial Intelligence*, 14(8):881–907, 2000.

Adversarial Behavior in Multi-agent Systems

Martin Rehák, Michal Pěchouček, and Jan Tožička

Department of Cybernetics, Czech Technical University in Prague,
Technická 2, Prague 6, 166 27 Czech Republic
{rehakm1, pechouc, tozicka}@labe.felk.cvut.cz

Abstract. Adversariality of the agents with respect to the multi-agent
system can be a serious issue in the design of open multi-agent systems.
Until now, many incoherent definitions of such behavior were used, preventing the consolidation of the knowledge about the domain. By basing
ourselves on the valid and accepted results from economics, law and conflict theory, we propose a consistent definition of adversariality in the
multi-agent systems and discuss the characteristics of the behavior that
falls into this definition.

1 Introduction

The current trend in the multi-agent systems field is to emphasize the openness
of systems, their ad-hoc integration capability and to capitalize on their syntactic
and semantic interoperability. In open environments, we can no longer assume
that the agents are cooperative. The agents in these system can have their own,
sometimes partially or completely antagonistic goals and they often compete for
the shared resources or opportunities.

In such environments, we must ensure that the system as a whole will autonomously maintain its sustainability and efficiency, that self-interested agents
will be able to agree at least on some goals and that their cooperation will
leverage their capabilities. To do so, agent researchers frequently introduce the
concepts from microeconomics and game theory, most notably mechanism design [1]. Mechanism design is used to design interaction patterns in the system to
promote globally desirable behavior and reduce incentive for undesirable behavior. However, despite the fact that it will provide the basis of the algorithms and
protocols of such systems, it still suffers from some serious limitations. Mechanism design techniques have achieved some spectacular results, but their applicability is in general restricted to static environments, where the fine-tuned
mechanisms perform well. However, the problems like bounded rationality of
the agents, their possible polyvalence, strategic behavior and willingness to keep
some of their knowledge private can not be completely addressed by the current
mechanisms [2].

Alternatively, similar results can be achieved achieved using norms [3], enforcing flexible social commitments [4], adjustable policies [5] or trust and reputation
[16,6]. But in general, these approaches rely on the fact that the agents are able
to distinguish the undesirable behavior in all possible contexts. Therefore, as

M. Pěchouček, P. Petta, and L.Z. Varga (Eds.): CEEMAS 2005, LNAI 3690, pp. 470–479, 2005.

the system adapts to its environment, the norms, policies and trust mechanisms must be adapted as well to avoid becoming an obstacle of system efficiency, rather than to support it.

In this contribution, we will look at the problem from somewhat different perspective – after the brief analysis of existing approaches in the multi-agent field, we will use the conflict theory and some fundamental principles from the economy and law (Section 2) to consistently define the adversarial behavior in the multi agent system (Section 3) and provide a specific example that instantiates the definition in Section 4.

Currently, adversariality in the multi-agent systems is a concept that has been defined in many different contexts. Most of the current definitions are mutually exclusive, but they provide a valuable guidance in our attempt to formalize the definition using their overlaps.

In the field of multi-agent systems, **adversarial planning** was introduced [7]to analyze the behavior of two opponents. However, even if the approach remains interesting due to the analysis of planning in conflicting environment, it is of limited importance for the definition of adversarial behavior. The definition proposed by the authors, where they define adversariality by "opposite goals" doesn't fit our needs, as the agents in the general system we consider (i) are not always adversarial and at least some of their goals are common, (ii) communicate by other means than pure actions, (iii) have asymmetric and partial knowledge and (iv) are deliberative, therefore possibly adversarial within the limited scope of time or issues.

In the mechanism-design field, [2] defines adversarial entities as the entities who's goals can not be described by a utility function and assumes these actors to be irrational. This definition well captures the fact of bounded rationality of agent perceptions - some agents can have goals that are impossible to capture and understand during normal system operations and that are justified by large scale (time or space) behavior of their owners.

2   Conflict Theory and Economics of Conflict

We shall use the conclusions from the field of the conflict theory to (i) determine the defining properties of adversariality as they are currently understood.

In his contribution [8], James Fearon analyzes the war between two or more perfectly rational states. For Fearon, the most important distinguishing property of the war from the rationalist point of view is the war's **ex-post inefficiency** – he argues that the states can reach the same result by negotiation, eliminating the cost of the adversarial actions: "...ex-post inefficiency of war opens up an ex-ante bargaining range..."([8], page 390). This is clearly visible from the simple conflict specification proposed by author.

In the work of **Posner** and **Sykes** [9], approaching the problem of optimal war from the legal perspective, the aggression (unilateral beginning of the war) is defined as an action that is *socially undesirable and imposing net social cost*, while the authors assume that the aggression is motivated by the expected profit of the aggressor, either as a result of war or the threat. They argue that this definition of aggression is consistent with the studies on the economics of crime [10], where the *gains of criminal are smaller than the social cost of act*.

In his breakthrough article, **Gary Becker** [10] analyzes the economics of crime, incentives of criminals, their economic motivation and dissuasive effect of punishments and functional justice system. Besides the definition of criminal activity stated above, the notion of indirect costs is also important. Costs of crime are not only direct, but we must consider the cost of law enforcement as inseparable from the direct crime costs. In a multi-agent system, the well designed mechanisms and trust maintenance models come with a cost that may harm the system efficiency through their computational requirements and other associated requirements. This doesn't mean a refusal of the principle of trust maintenance and mechanism design, but it means that the mechanism must be efficient and well adapted to the current environment.

3   Adversarial Behavior Definition

This section is devoted to the formal definition and characterization of adversarial behavior in the multi-agent systems. We will depart from the conflict theory premise stated above that conflict is an *ex-post inefficient* method of resolving competitive issues that imposes a net cost on the society, and we will base our formal definition on these notion. Similar classification was done in [11], but focused on interaction between different types of agents rather than on definition of types of behavior and didn't use the conflict theory. However, some preliminary technical definitions are necessary.

In the following, we will use capitals to denote agents.

Utility is defined as *"a value which is associated with a state of the world, and which represents the value that the agent places on that state of the world"* by [12].

To simply state our problems, we will define a simple abstract game model featuring agent set $Ag = \{A, B, C, ...\}$ with the agents playing a non-extensive (single round) game with that is not strictly competitive – sum of all agents' utilities is not constant. Each agent X has a set of available actions denoted a_X^*, with actions $a_X^i \in a_X^*$ (whenever possible, we only write a_X). From this set, agent selects its action using its strategy. The final state, *outcome* of the game[1] $o(a_A, a_B, ...)$ is determined by strategies of the agents and determines both the individual agents' utilities $u_A(o), u_B(o), u_C(o), ...$ and the social choice function $u(o) = u_A(o) + u_B(o) + u_C(o) + ...$, considered to represent the *social welfare*[1].

In this simplistic game, we can define cooperative, competitive and adversarial behavior in accordance with the principles from section 2. Simplified graphical form of the definitions is presented in Fig. 1.

In the cooperative environment, all agents do share a single utility function.

---

[1] The exact form of the outcome is irrelevant, if we are able to obtain the utility values. To simplify the notation, we will also write $u(a_A, a_B, ...)$ instead of technically more correct $u(o(a_A, a_B, ...))$.

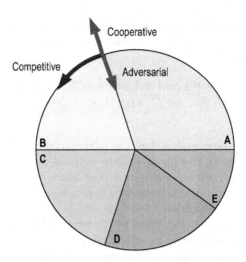

Fig. 1. Cooperative, Competitive and Adversarial actions. Pie represents the total utility u and individual utilities $u_A, u_B, ...$ We can see that purely cooperative action increases social welfare, purely competitive action doesn't modify the social welfare, but only changes its distribution among agents, while the purely adversarial action reduces the social welfare without any benefit for the agent. In practice, real actions are rarely pure and are a combination of the above types.

Definition 1. *We say that agent's A action* a_A^{coop} *is a **cooperative action** provided that* $a_A^{coop} = \arg\max_{a_X^*} u(a_A^{coop}, a_B, ...)$.

In the competitive environment, agents select actions to maximize their own private utility, but they restrict their choice to the actions that at least conserve the social welfare.

Definition 2. *We say that agent's A action* a_A^{comp} *is a **competitive action** provided that* $a_A^{comp} = \arg\max_{a_X^{**}} u_A(a_A^{comp}, a_B, ...)$, *where the set* a_X^{**} *contains the actions* $a_A^i \in a_X^*$ *that conserve or increase the social welfare* $u(a_A^i, a_B, ...)$.

In many contexts, the above terms self-interestedness and competitiveness are considered to be synonymous. However, we consider the competitiveness to be more strict - in [11], self interestedness is defined as not taking the utility of the others into the consideration while maximizing their own utility, while [13] requires the trust between competitors, allowing them to avoid globally undesirable outcomes. In the systems with carefully programmed mechanisms, the results are equivalent in both cases. However, in many real-world cases the total utility may decrease, even if each agent optimizes locally (see [14] for a nice analogy).

Definition 3. *We say that agent's A action* a_A^{si} *is a **self-interested action** provided that* $a_A^{si} = \arg\max_{a_X^*} u_A(a_A^{si}, a_B, ...)$.

And finally, the adversarial action is defined as an action that significantly decreases the social welfare while it causes loss or provides only small profit to the actor of the action.

Definition 4. *We say that agent's A action a_A^{adv} is an **adversarial action** if $\exists a_A^i \in a_A^* : i \neq adv$ such that $u(a_A^{adv}, a_B, ...) \ll u(a_A^i, a_B, ...)$ and $u_A(a_A^{adv}, a_B, ...) \lesssim u_A(a_A^i, a_B, ...).$*

The definition 4 above states that the adversarial action a_A^{adv} selected by A from the set a_A^* of hurts the social welfare without strong incentive. To make the formalism simpler, we have assumed that there is only single action a_A^{adv} of agent A that hurts the social welfare. There are several interesting points to consider in the general definition.

The first point is the non-emptiness of the set $a_A^* \setminus \{a_A^a dv\}$ - we don't consider the behavior with no alternative as adversarial.

Motivation and justification of the adversarial action is closely related to two relational operators used in the definition: $\ll$ and $\lesssim$. The first inequality $\ll$ signifies that the agent shall not cause significant harm to the common welfare, while the inequality $\lesssim^2$ means that the agent remains self-interested and it will not lose a significant part of its welfare to save the utility of other agents. The concept is illustrated by Fig. 2. In this context, it is important not to take our simplification of the game formalism literally and to consider only immediate payoff as the utility – in most systems, agents expect to encounter their partners again in the future and we suppose that the attitudes of their partners towards them and expected future profits are included in the utility $u_X{}^3$. Formally, we may pose:

Definition 5. *We say that **action** a_A^j of agent A is **rationally adversarial** if it is both self-interested and adversarial. In the action is not self-interested and is adversarial, it is **irrationally adversarial**.*

In this context, we may mention the relationship between adversariality and Pareto-Optimality: [4]

An outcome of an Adversarial action is not Pareto optimal. Rationally adversarial action is not Pareto optimal in the situations where the agents may negotiate and transfer the utility - in such situations, the agents may always transfer enough utility to motivate the adversarial agent to behave cooperatively, therefore achieving socially acceptable outcome. When the utility is not

---

[2] We actually mean that the agent has no, or very little motivation to make an adversarial move. In Def. 5, we treat the special case when we fall into the $\sim$ case.

[3] In this point, we are consistent with the utility definition given above. We have omitted the explicit future gains member in the definitions to simplify the notation by using this broader definition of utility.

[4] Following [15], we denote as o^* a set of all achievable outcomes and we define: Outcome o is considered to be **Pareto optimal** if : (i) it is achievable (i.e. $o \in o^*$) and (ii) not majored by any other outcome $o' \in o^* \setminus \{o\}$, where we define majoring as: $\forall_{X \in Ag} u_X(o') \geq u_X(o)$ and $\exists_{X \in Ag} u_X(o') > u_X(o)$.

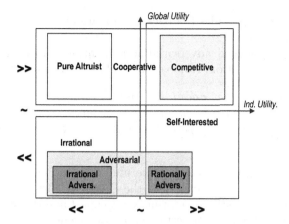

Fig. 2. Classification of action with respect to global utility (social welfare) and individual utility of acting agent

transferable (e.g. indivisibility as defined in [8]), the set o^* is severely restricted and even an action that causes the overall social loss may be considered non-adversarial due to the lack of alternative. In the irrationally adversarial case, Pareto optimality does not hold neither, as the utility is lost both by adversarial agent and the society as a whole.

On the other hand, Pareto optimality as such doesn't preserve social welfare (due to the indivisibility), it only ensures that all agents behave rationally given the knowledge about the action of the others.

Another point to address is the predictability of the outcome. The uncertainty of o arises from the simultaneity of all players' moves, while the uncertainty of values $u_X(o)$ and $u(o)$ exists due to the privacy of functions u_X. This seems to make the definition useless – but social knowledge and norms can provide solutions. In most situations, the individuals are able to estimate the actions of others (denoted a_X^{exp}) and the effects of different outcomes on their utility.

Therefore, without considering norms, we pose:

Definition 6. *We say that **action** a_A^{ia} of agent A is **intentionally adversarial** if the action is adversarial and the agent A **knows that** $\exists a_A^i \in a_A^* : i \neq ia$ such that $u(a_A^{ia}, a_B^{exp}, ...) \ll u(a_A^i, a_B^{exp}, ...)$ and $u_A(a_A^{ia}, a_B^{exp}, ...) \lesssim u_A(a_A^i, a_B^{exp}, ...)$. Otherwise, the action is **unintentionally adversarial**.*

More specifically, the lack of norms or conventions is a possible cause of unintentional adversariality – the adversarial outcome may arise due to the limited computational power or knowledge of agents, private knowledge or the environmental noise. Important question of attribution must be solved by each agent – we can not expect that all agents will agree on the cause of the common loss.

Existence of shared normative system reduces the uncertainty regarding the expected actions of other agents (a_X^{exp}). In our future work, we will use this system in the adapted definition of adversarial action. On the other hand, definition

4 remains valid, as it provides feedback for update of the normative system in changing environment.

So far, we have defined adversarial action, rational adversarial action and intentional adversarial action. However, we still have to define *adversarial agent*.

Definition 7. *We say that **agent** A **is adversarial** (or there exists **adversarial behavior** performed by the agent A) if the agent A performed at least one adversarial action in the past –* $adv(A) \Leftrightarrow \exists a_A^{adv}$ *: so that* $adv(a_A^{adv}) \wedge$ $P(\texttt{Perform } A\, a_A^{adv})$.

In the definition, we assume that the predicate adv classifying the actions is defined according to the property 4, the P operator to be a temporal logic operator representing validity of a formula in the past and the operator $\texttt{Perform}$ linking an agent and the action performed by the agent.

There are clear extensions of this definition of adversarial behavior that define adversariality in a time window, or agent's adversarial behavior with relation to a specific agent community. In the definition 7 we assume by default the whole of the community as a target of agent's adversariality and the whole past as the relevant time window.

We are interested in the impact of the adversarial action on the global social welfare of the community Ag. We say that:

- decrease of social welfare implies existence of an adversarial behavior in the community, while
- existence of an adversarial behavior in the community does not imply decrease of social welfare.

For the proof of these statements, let us consider only types of actions according to the definitions 1, 2 and 4. No combination of cooperative and competitive actions may cause an overall decrease of the social welfare, thus an existence of at least one adversarial action is inevitable. In contrary, for a combination of adversarial actions there may exist a compensating combination of cooperative or competitive actions that can be carried out by any member of the community in the finite time t so that in t the social welfare does not decrease.

The definition 7 does not classify performance of an action that has got a direct inevitability (or possibly an option) of an adversarial action as its effect as adversarial behavior.

4   Example: Adversariality in Coalition Formation

In this example, we will illustrate rather abstract definitions provided above with the real example, the coalition formation, approaching the problem from the utility side. We will start by introducing the necessary notation. In this section, we consider the coalition to be short-lived and therefore the terms adversarial action of agent A and adversarial agent A will be used interchangeably.

Using the concept of the marginal utility[5], we may now define cooperative and competitive behavior in our example.

We say that agent A is **collaborative** provided that: if an agent A makes an attempt to join the coalition C then always $mu_{A \mapsto C}(C) > 0$. We shall note that even if all agents are collaborative, the optimum result is not guaranteed. A typical case can be described as follows: $mu_{B \mapsto C}(C \cup B) > mu_{A \mapsto C}(C \cup A) \geq 0$ and $mu_{B \mapsto (C \cup A)}(B) < 0$. If A joins the coalition first, it blocks the entry of B and only local optimum is reached.

We say that agent A is **competitive** provided that: if an agent A makes an attempt to join the coalition C then always $mu_{A \mapsto C}(A) > 0$ and $mu_{A \mapsto C}(C) \geq 0$. Similarly, we say that agent A is **self-interested** provided that: if an agent A makes an attempt to join the coalition C then always $mu_{A \mapsto C}(A) > 0$.

As we have already stated before, self-interested agent considers only its own profit while it takes coalition entry decision. Competitive agent is both self interested and collaborative, as it maximizes its own profit, but it at least maintains the social welfare that is represented by the coalition utility. Therefore, in both competitive and cooperative behavior, the social welfare is maintained. This is not necessarily true in the self-interested or adversarial behavior.

In this example, we will use the marginal utility defined above to define adversarial behavior. We say that an agent is **adversarial** provided:

- $mu_{A \mapsto C}(A) \lesssim 0$
- $mu_{A \mapsto C}(C) \ll 0$
- agent A makes an attempt to join the coalition C

Informally, an agent is adversarial with respect to coalition C provided that the increase of his direct marginal utility is significantly smaller than the harm (decrease of the total payoff) caused to the coalition.

If the condition $mu_{A \mapsto C}(A) \geq 0$ holds, agent's action is rationally adversarial, otherwise it is irrationally adversarial, as defined in definition 5.

Main advantage of the above definition is that it provides a basis for the detection of adversarial agents, by defining the metrics measuring the adversariality.

Gathering and maintaining such experience is not trivial. However, we may reuse the existing work on trust, where one of the components of the trust[16] - intentional trust (willingness)- is a complement of intra-community adversariality defined above. Therefore, if we establish a reasonable value for trust (that may be actually lower, due to the capability trust), we may deduce an acceptable estimation of agent's adversariality.

---

[5] Agent's A *marginal utility* (mu) from joining the coalition C (an activity denoted as $A \mapsto C$) is a derivation of the agent's utility before and after it joins the coalition ($mu_{A \mapsto C}(A) = u_{A \in C}(A) - u_{A \notin C}(A)$, where $u_{A \in C}(A)$ is a utility the agent A (in parentheses) receives as a member of the coalition C (situation is described by subscript), while $u_{A \notin C}(A)$ denotes the utility agent A receives if it doesn't join the coalition C). The marginal utility of a coalition C in agent's A joining the coalition is defined as a derivation of the collective utility (such as social welfare) of the coalition before and after the agent joins the coalition ($mu_{A \mapsto C}(C) = u(C \cup A) - u(C)$).

5   Conclusion

The definition of the adversarial behavior that we present provides a useful complement of the current approaches to the open systems engineering. Even if the system is based on carefully designed mechanisms and/or norms, the changing system social structure and the environment or agent's strategic behavior may modify the system and make it inefficient or dysfunctional. To counter such danger, the agents in the system shall continuously monitor the behavior of the others and their own and detect potentially adversarial actions. As soon as these actions are identified, protocols or normative systems can be altered to counter the undesirable tendencies, or the adversarial agents can be completely cut-away from the system. Such detection can be done on peer-to-peer basis, but can be also entrusted to dedicated agents that would implement not the norm enforcement, but norm creation and maintenance.

The problem of adversariality in the multi-agent systems is real. While the irrationally adversarial agents may be easy to identify, it may be much more difficult to identify the rationally adversarial behavior, especially if all the agents in the system are self-interested. In this context, the question of *bounded rationality* of agent's reasoning is crucial. For example, some agents may be willing to leave the local optimum to bring the system into the globally optimal (or simply better) state. However, if the other agents in the system lack this insight, they may consider this behavior as adversarial because they fail to see the long-term benefits. To better illustrate the concept, we will cite several accepted causes for the emergence of the conflict between the rational actors. It is easy to realize that most of these causes can plausibly exist in the multi-agent system and shall be considered while designing autonomous agents.

Private information of each agent is not available to the others, providing one of the causes of **miscalculation** about **capabilities or attitudes** of the other party. Such miscalculation may cause an adversarial behavior, as the agents will not be able to correctly estimate the utility function of the partners. Agents are often willing to **misrepresent** the reality about themselves, in order to obtain better payoff or negotiation position in the future. However, if such behavior becomes widespread in the system (It can be often prevented by careful mechanism design.), agents are unable to communicate efficiently. In the more sophisticated extension of this behavior, agents can behave strategically and harm the others to gain higher relative power in the long term. In some situations, the system may even become purely competitive – agents or their groups have nothing to gain from cooperation, for example when the payoff is indivisible.

Acknowledgment

Effort sponsored by the Air Force Office of Scientific Research, Air Force Material Command, USAF, under grant number FA8655-04-1-3044. The U.S. Government is authorized to reproduce and distribute reprints for Government purpose notwithstanding any copyright notation thereon[6]. We also gratefully acknowledge the support of the presented research by ARL project N62558-03-0819.

References

1. Dash, R.K., Jennings, N.R., Parkes, D.C.: Computational-mechanism design: A call to arms. IEEE Intelligent Systems **18** (2003) 40–47
2. Feigenbaum, J., Shenker, S.: Distributed algorithmic mechanism design: Recent results and future directions. In: Proceedings of the 6th International Workshop on Discrete Algorithms and Methods for Mobile Computing and Communications, ACM Press, New York (2002) 1–13
3. Conte, R., Castelfranchi, C.: From conventions to prescriptions - towards an integrated view of norms . Artif. Intell. Law **7** (1999) 323–340
4. Pasquier, P., Flores, R., Chaib-draa, B.: Modeling flexible social commitments and their enforcement. (In Gleizes, M.P., Omicini, A., Zambonelli, F., eds.: Proceedings of Engineering Societies in the Agents World V, Toulouse, October 2004)
5. Suri, N., Carvalho, M.M., Bradshaw, J.M., Breedy, M.R., Cowin, T.B., Groth, P.T., Saavedra, R., Uszok, A.: Enforcement of communications policies in software agent systems through mobile code. In: POLICY. (2003) 247–250
6. Ramchurn, S., Huynh, D., Jennings, N.R.: Trust in multiagent systems. The Knowledge Engineering Review **19** (2004)
7. Willmott, S., Bundy, A., Levine, J., , Richardson, J.: An adversarial planning approach to go. In: Proceedings of the Firstrst International Conference on Computers and Games, Springer-Verlag, LNCS 1558 (1998) 93–112
8. Fearon, J.D.: Rationalist explanations for war. International Organization **49** (1995) 379–414
9. Posner, E.A., Sykes, A.O.: Optimal war and jus ad bellum (2004)
10. Becker, G.S.: Crime and punishment: An economic approach. The Journal of Political Economy **76** (1968) 169–217
11. Brainov, S.: The role and the impact of preferences on multiagent interaction. In: ATAL '99: 6th International Workshop on Intelligent Agents VI, Agent Theories, Architectures, and Languages (ATAL),, Springer-Verlag (2000) 349–363
12. Parsons, S., Wooldridge, M.: Game theory and decision theory in multi-agent systems. Autonomous Agents and Multi-Agent Systems **5** (2002) 243–254
13. Gambetta, D., ed.: Trust: Making and Breaking Cooperative Relations. Basil Blackwell (1990)
14. Goldratt, E.M.: The Theory of Constraints. N.Y.: North River Press, Croton-on-Hudson, N.Y. (1990)
15. Mares, M.: Fuzzy coalition structures. Fuzzy Sets Syst. **114** (2000) 23–33
16. Castelfranchi, C., Falcone, R.: Principles of trust for mas: Cognitive anatomy, social importance, and quantification. In: Proceedings of the 3rd International Conference on Multi Agent Systems, IEEE Computer Society (1998) 72

---

[6] The views and conclusions contained herein are those of the author and should not be interpreted as necessarily representing the official policies or endorsements, either expressed or implied, of the Air Force Office of Scientific Research or the U.S. Government.

Bayesian Dynamic Trust Model

Dimitri Melaye and Yves Demazeau

Laboratoire Leibniz 46, avenue Felix Viallet, 38031 Grenoble Cedex, France

Abstract. In this paper we propose a Bayesian dynamic trust model based on Castelfranchi and Falcone's works, thanks to which we can determine the agent's trust in another agent. Trust is not only a static mental state: it changes over time. Either some new observations are perceived and modify the trust level, or no observation is perceived and so trust is eroded. Our model takes into account these dynamic aspects by a Bayesian Kalman filter. We present, experiment and discuss our formalism compared with others models. The results obtained with our model are relevant and account for the particular dynamic aspects of trust.

1 Introduction

The expansion of the distributed systems highlights new problematics: need for acting in an open, dynamic, unpredictable environment, need for guaranteeing security, and need for providing the best services for other services and users. As all distributed systems where knowledge is distributed and handled locally, the concept of trust is naturally primordial in these systems. Regarded as a crucial phenomenon by social sciences ([1,2,3]), trust is a concept difficult to define because of its abstract and heterogeneous character. Trust is initially regarded as a central mechanism of coordination in situation of ignorance and a mechanism of social integration. We consider trust as a belief concerning an action to except from another, in connection with something in a precise field or context. It is a hypothesis about a future behaviour and refers to a possibility of the realization of other's action. It is neither a doubt nor a certainty: the one who knows all need not to trust, the one knows nothing cannot trust [4].

The aim of this article is to regard trust as a cognitive process and to take into account some of its dynamic aspects. Following the work of [5], we distinguish on the one hand the "one-to-one" trust model that calculates a level of trust, and on the other hand the decision-taking, i.e. the act of trust called reliance by Castelfranchi. In this paper, we concentrate on the trust model and we adopt the Castelfranchi and Falcone's model [6]. The cognitive approach of this model is adapted to the social dimension of trust.

Furthermore, trust is a dynamic phenomenon. Thus two main aspects of trust dynamics must be supported: the erosion of trust due to the absence of new observations and corresponding to an increasing uncertainty, and the particular increase/decrease of trust. As far as we know, the erosion of trust has not really been studied in the trust literature yet, and particular dynamics of trust has not been integrated in a cognitive-based model of trust yet.

M. Pěchouček, P. Petta, and L.Z. Varga (Eds.): CEEMAS 2005, LNAI 3690, pp. 480–489, 2005.

First we present Castelfranchi and Falcone's model that we choose to formalize by a Bayesian approach. Secondly, we show how this approach can take into account some dynamic aspects of the trust by using a Kalman filter. Finally we experiment and discuss this approach in regard to other approaches.

2   Castelfranchi and Falcone's Trust Model

We consider trust as a cognitive process in order to account for its complexity whether it concerns the social aspects or internal working of an agent. So the cognitive approach of Castelfranchi and Falcone's model ([5,6]) is adapted to this view.

In Castelfranchi and Falcone's view, trust is regarded as a mental state and consists of beliefs: the degree of trust is a function of the subjective certainty of the pertinent beliefs, and the subjective certainty of this beliefs is derived from the credibility of their sources. In that way, trust is decomposed in internal factors and external factors. The idea is that these factors have some different influences on the final trust level and produce completely different intervention strategies. In [6], internal factors and external factors are formalized in the same way (with Fuzzy Cognitive Map). However, considering the importance of the external factors in the interpretation of some internal components [7], we think internal factors and external factors are so different that they should not be processed in the same way. Thus, in this paper, we concentrate on the internal factors (how we can calculate them) and we do not consider the external factors. These latter should be associated with the notion of context, where a context would be the fact of a domain and a situation, i.e. the circumstances and the conditions in which the agents are immersed. Thus the environment could be taken into account in a well-different conceptual way from the internal factors.

These factors are decomposed themselves in relevant basic beliefs. These beliefs are assumed to be independent of each other. In particular, concerning the internal factors, the ability and the willingness of the trustee are considered. However, they are not exhaustive, other beliefs could be added like dependence or integrity (i.e. ethical dimension connected to the notion of honesty).

Each belief depends on belief sources. [6] distinguishes four belief sources: direct experience, categorization, reasoning, and reputation. They are assumed to be independent of each other. According to the context, we have not to use all belief sources, but only the ones we have at one's disposal. What's more, another belief source that is not taken into account is the institution. It generates and facilitates the trust between anonymous entities [8]: living under the same institution, members are imbued with these normative ideas. However, for the moment, we are not interested in this belief source whose the implications (norms, laws and guarantees) extend beyond the aim of this article.

3   Bayesian Formalization

By relying on Castelfranchi and Falcone's cognitive model [5], we could think a logical approach (i.e. a manipulation of knowledge) is the most relevant one.

However, a pure logical approach is in connection only with knowledge, pure reasoning and interests, and is not a choice any more where you "risk your trust". Therefore we adopt a Bayesian approach. As we have written it in the introduction, trust is a hypothesis about a future behaviour. Thus, we can take into account the non-fulfilment of the information, and the uncertainty of knowledge. What's more it provides a flexible well-formalized framework on which reasoning and learning process is possible.

Proposition 1. *We formalize the notion of trust of a truster agent and a trustee agent in a context ω by a Bayesian network structured in three layers as figure 1 illustrates it :*

- *The final trust is represented by the variable T*
- *The i-th basic belief is represented by the variable B_i, with $1 \leqslant i \leqslant N_c$*
- *The j-th belief source of the i-th basic belief is represented by the variable S_{ij}, with $1 \leqslant i \leqslant N_c$ and $1 \leqslant j \leqslant N_s$*
- *The belief sources S_{ij} influence the i-th basic belief, and the basic beliefs influence the final level trust. These influences are taken into account by the conditional probabilities existing between the aleatory variables.*

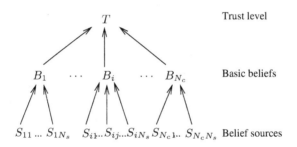

Fig. 1. Bayesian network modeling

Each trust component is associated with a probability of satisfaction. In other words, the trust value $P(X)$ of the concept carried by X can be calculated from the distribution of the aleatory variables. Thus $P(T) = 1$ represents a blind trust and $P(T) = 0$ represents a fully distrust. Our approach does not prevent from supporting a more symbolic qualitative view of trust: the range $[0, 1]$ can be divided in several ranges corresponding to different trust levels as [6] shows it.

The trust level is calculated by Bayesian inference (by starting from the belief source, and by inferring the probabilities from the belief sources until the trust level). These influences are supported by the conditional probabilities thanks to which a concept can have more influence than another concept on the superior concept (e.g. to favour the direct experiences rather than reputation). The beliefs and sources are assumed to be independent for a same level of the hierarchy. Nevertheless, this assumption can be discussed. The independence between the beliefs is not intuitive. For instance, low willingness could decrease competence, or competence could encourage to perform a task in a complex way. However, in a first approach, for simplicity we assume the beliefs are orthogonal. The marginal independence of the sources can be justified if their nature are different : for example, generalization are static, and personal experience does not influence reputation in a large system significantly. Concerning the scalability of the model, the conditional probability table is exponential in the number of parent nodes. However, from a cognitive standpoint, this number is not large (e.g. three beliefs and four sources for [6]).

So, now we may wonder how the belief sources can be determined actually and how this model can take into account some dynamic aspects of trust.

4   Dynamic Trust System

Trust is not only a static mental state: it changes over time. Moreover, as presented in the previous section, the level of the belief sources should be calculable at any moment to infer the trust level. For this purpose, in this section, we propose a formalism based on the previous Bayesian formalism of Castelfranchi and Falcone's model.

4.1   Trust Dynamics

The dynamic aspects of trust have been discussed in several papers. [9] proposes trust dynamics by learning. However, this approach is based on game theory and it is may not be adapted to a more social approach [10]. [11] assumes that trust is based on some events perceived in the environment (the direct experiences). It distinguishes several types of trust dynamics, according to whether positive evolution is more or less fast than negative evolution. However, this approach does not integrate other belief sources in a more general computation of trust. In [7], the influence of the external factors on trust dynamics is tackled. Nevertheless, in our article, we assume that these contextual and situational aspects are treated in a different way from the internal factors. Except for this aspect, no dynamic aspect is treated in Castelfranchi and Falcone's model ([5,6]).

In this article we concentrate on two aspects of the trust dynamics: the erosion of trust in the absence of new observations and the increase/decrease of trust.

As trust is viewed as a function of the subjective certainty of the pertinent beliefs [5], it is submitted to the phenomenon of erosion evoked in [12]. Thus, the trust level drifts towards a default value corresponding to an increase of the uncertainty when no information brings up to date the beliefs. This aspect of trust dynamics is crucial and pertinent in practice, as it supports the absence of regular information.

Rather than considering the increase and decrease of trust as a multi-type phenomenon [11], we group the different types by considering an only property: the inertia of trust and distrust. The inertia of trust (resp. distrust) accounts for the speed of trust (resp. distrust) to swing to distrust (resp. trust). For instance, blindly positive dynamics corresponds to a high inertia of trust and a low inertia of distrust.

In this paper, like [11], we are interested in an only belief source: the direct experience. Indeed we assume that trust dynamics is mainly the outcome of the evolution of this only belief source: the institution and categorization sources are the most static belief source (it is more confidence than trust [1]), and the reputation source evolves in a large system slowly (it can be considered as a level-headed average of other's trust). On the contrary, the direct experience source is submitted to some significant variations. This assumption is based on another assumption: the direct experience source is function of some observations perceived by the truster. Let us stress the fact that these signs are not the outcome of previous reliance (successes and failures), but more generally some relevant clues. Moreover, for simplicity we consider trust dynamics for a fixed context. Thus, the question of the influence of the external factors on the direct experiences [7] can be neglected.

4.2   Formalization

We propose a formalism that supports trust dynamics concerning its direct experience aspects. In the Bayesian framework, we propose a stochastic estimation by Kalman filter. It supports the dynamic evolution of a system, whether new information are observed or not. So it is an appropriate mathematical tool for our purpose. We distinguish two phases: the state model accounts for the inertia and the erosion of trust based on the propagation of the present trust state (prediction). Then, the system proposes a revision of the trust state from new observations (correction). If no observation is perceived, trust computation is supported only by the prediction step. In the remainder of this paper, for simplicity we omit the name of the fixed context ω.

Formally, as the figure 2 shows, $p(x_{k+1}|x_k)$ represents the state model. We assume that trust dynamics is supported by a dependence between the present state of the components and the previous one. So the Bayesian decomposition of (1) gives a product of three terms:

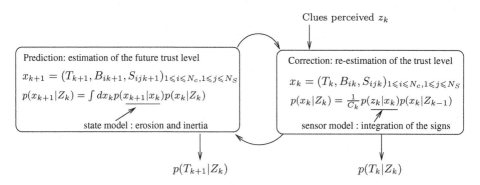

Fig. 2. Kalman filter process for trust

– the term $\prod_{ij} p(S_{ijk+1}|S_{ijk})$ with $1 \leqslant i \leqslant N_c$ and $1 \leqslant j \leqslant N_S$ takes into account dynamics of the belief sources, as a state of a belief source is statistically dependent on the previous one.

– The term $\prod_{ij} p(B_{ik+1}|B_{ik}S_{ijk+1})$ with $1 \leqslant i \leqslant N_c$ and $1 \leqslant j \leqslant N_S$ accounts for dynamics of the basic beliefs and the influence of the belief sources on the basic beliefs.

– the term $p(T_{k+1}|T_k B_{1k+1}...B_{N_ck+1})$ integrates the basic beliefs in final trust, and takes into account dynamics of final trust.

$p(z_k|x_k)$ is the sensor model: it accounts for the integration of the signs perceived. As the observations influence only the direct experience belief sources, the Bayesian decomposition gives $p(z_k|x_k) = \prod_{im} p(z_{ijk}^m|S_{ijk})$, where the j-th source corresponds to the direct experience belief sources, and z_{ijmk} is the m-th observation that influences the direct experience source of the i-th belief.

5 Experimentation and Discussion

In this section, we illustrate our dynamic model with some outputs of experimentation, and discuss its contribution in regard to other approaches.

5.1 Experimental Protocol and Results

We consider a Bayesian network that instantiates an agent's trust model in a target agent according to a fixed context. The agent observes the target agent by two fixed signs. Trust dynamics corresponds to a common sense inertia: trust is fragile, it takes efforts to build trust but only a few acts to completely destroy it (the decrease is faster than the increase). To simplify computation, we decide that each component of the model can be in two different states (satisfactory or unsatisfactory), following Bernoulli distribution. As we are interested in the direct experiences especially, we consider this only belief source and two beliefs (competence and willingness). The influence between the beliefs is the same, and the a priori distribution of the state vector is uniform.

We present four experiments (figures 3, 4, 5, and 6). In each figure, three curves are displayed. The dotted curve is the percentage of positive signs perceived by the agent at each time step. The thicker curve describes the trust level calculated from our trust system. The thin curve is the mean of the positive signs. It corresponds to a statistical approach that counts the positive observations naively.

In the first experiment, the trust system becomes the signs from the target agent with a probability 0.90 that this sign is positive. Between time 20 and time 50, no observation is perceived. The outputs are presented in figure 3. This graph illustrates the trust erosion from time 20 through time 50 (the full curve decreases gradually). Three slow increases are observable after a low trust level (from time 0, from time 50 and from time 80).

In the second experiment, the positive signs come with a low probability, except from time 30 through time 70. Thus, the curve of figure 4 illustrates the

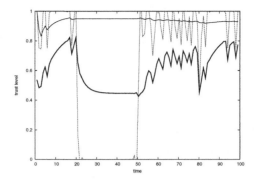

Fig. 3. Trust dynamics with a high probability of positive observations

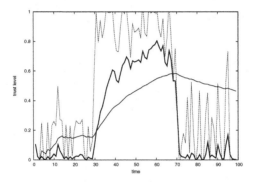

Fig. 4. Trust dynamics with a high probability of positive observations

increase of trust, and the sharp decrease from time 70. Compared to the naive statistical approach, our model is more efficient and versatile: it is more similar to the target agent's trustworthiness (in particularly from time 70, by using this naive model, the trust level is too high compared with the effective observations).

The third experiment (figure 5) illustrates the inertia of trust. All perceived observations are positive, except at time 40. This only negative observation makes the trust level decrease sharply. It corresponds to a sudden doubt due to a contradiction perceived in regard to the previous positive observations. After that, trust increases slowly before getting back its previous value. Thus, our model accounts for this negative sign, whereas it is transparent for the classic statistical approach.

Finally, figure 6 shows the inertia of distrust. On the contrary of the previous experiment, the perceived observations are negative, except an only one at time 40. As we have defined, the inertia of distrust is high, so that the "positive accident" is transparent for the trust system. Although the observations are the opposite of the previous experiment, we notice that the trust level is not complementary of the previous trust level. This non-symmetry is only due to

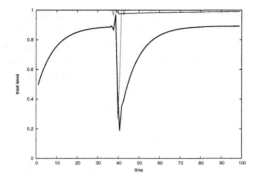

Fig. 5. Trust dynamics with a low probability of negative observations

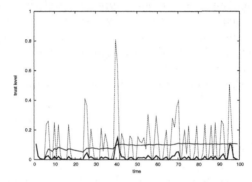

Fig. 6. Trust dynamics with a low probability of negative observations

dynamics of trust. It illustrates the relevant idea that trust and distrust have peculiar dynamic, and are not both terms of a same unidimensional concept.

As the results show it, our model is more relevant than a naive statistical approach: first, like [13], trust is viewed as a cognitive multi-component notion. Secondly, particular dynamics are taken into account: the "accidents" have a real impact on the final trust level, and target agent's versatility is taken into account. The main difficulty is to determine the parameters of the model. In this experimentation, they are defined by an "expert". However, in the future, they should be learned autonomously by the agent considering the outcome of the reliance (e.g. with an expectation-maximization process).

5.2   Discussion

Our model is based on a stochastic approach: we assume that trust is not provable, but it is only predictable. The behaviour's trustee cannot be predicted exactly, but we assume that it can be modeled by a probabilistic distribution for a fixed context. Moreover, in our system, the outcome of an execution is statically dependent of previous executions. Thus, trust dynamics can be supported, as we have shown it with the previous experiments.

We do not think as [13] implies, that a statistical approach is necessary less relevant than a pure cognitive approach. First, our approach is subtler than the one described in [13]: it does not count the failures and successes, but integrates in the trust cognitive process some perceived signs. In addition, our system supports trust dynamics and erosion (in [13], internal behaviour's agents are fixed and constant, so experiments are biased). Thus, although it is numerical, it can account for complex trust characteristics as well as more cognitive approaches.

Our approach is based on the fact that an agent behaves in a regular way for a same context. So, the drawback is that it requires one instance of the model per context. If several contexts must be considered, it can become heavy and expensive. In order to avoid this problem, we think that the influence of the contexts on the trust model should be managed with a more symbolic cognitive approach like [14].

In fact, we think that the symbolic approach and the statistical approach should not be opposed: both of these views are necessary to account for the complexity of the trust notion. Two layers should be considered: a low level (statistical approach) as presented in this paper for the integration of observations and basic dynamics, and a high level (symbolic approach) for the influence of the contexts and the manipulation of the cognitive components (trust, beliefs, sources) calculated by the low layer.

6   Conclusions and Perspectives

We have presented a Bayesian trust model based on Castelfranchi and Falcone's works, and we have added to it trust dynamics by using Kalman filter. As far as we know, the phenomenon of the erosion of trust has not really been studied in the multi-agent literature yet, and dynamics of trust has not been integrated in a cognitive-based model of trust yet. In our system, the inertia of trust and distrust is fixed a priori. In the future, it could be learned with experiences (successes and failures of reliance). What is more, in this paper, we have been interested only in the direct experience: we will study dynamics of the other belief sources in next papers. Finally, we have experimented our model. The results of our experiments confirm the relevance of our approach. Nevertheless, in a second shot, we must conduct an evaluation in a real-world context.

We think that a statistical approach and a symbolic approach are complementary. They form a low-level and high-level layer. The low-level layer integrates the signs perceived by the agent, calculates the strength of the components of the model (sources, beliefs, trust), and takes into account basic trust dynamics. The high-level layer should support the aspects in connection with a more symbolic approach:

- The influence of context: as the fact of a situation and a domain, the context has an influence on the components of the trust model [7] and trust dynamics (the more uncertain the environment is, the more abrupt the erosion is).
- The manipulation of the trust cognitive components.

– By relying, a truster becomes dependent on the trustee, and the trustee is in duty situation to respect social norms. Trust, dependence, and social norms are connected and take part in the dynamic phenomena of trust reinforcement. It will be interesting to study them in a more high-level approach.

These symbolic cognitive aspects of trust will make up our future works, as well as the connections between both layers.

References

1. Luhmann, N.: Familiarity, confidence, trust: Problems and alternatives. In Blackwell, ed.: Trust: Making and Breaking of Cooperative Relations. Diego Gambetta (1988) 94–107
2. Deutsch, M.: Cooperation and trust: Some theoretical notes. In Jones, M.R., ed.: Nebraska Symposium on Motivation, Nebrask University Press (1962)
3. Gambetta, D.: Trust. In Gambetta, D., ed.: Trust: Making and Breaking Cooperative Relations. Department of Sociology, University of Oxford (2000) i–x
4. Simmel, G.: The Sociology of Georg Simmel. Glencoe: Free Press (1950)
5. Castelfranchi, C., Falcone, R.: Principles of trust for mas : cognitive anatomy, social importance, and quantification. In: ICMAS'98, Paris (1998) 72–79
6. Castelfranchi, C., Falcone, R., Pezzulo, G.: Trust in information sources as a source for trust: a fuzzy approach. In: AAMAS'03, ACM Press (2003) 89–96
7. Castelfranchi, C., Falcone, R.: Trust dynamics: How trust is influenced by direct experiences and by trust itself. In: AAMAS'04. Volume 2., New-York, IIE (2004)
8. Offe, C. Democracy and Trust. In: How Can We Trust Our Fellow Citizens? ed. M. E. Warren, Cambridge University Press (1999) 42–87
9. Birk, A.: Learning to trust. In: Trust in Cyber-societies, Integrating the Human and Artificial Perspectives. Volume 2246., Springer-Verlag (2001) 133–144
10. Williamson, O.: Calculativeness, trust and economic organization. Journal of Law & Economics **36** (1993) 453–486
11. Jonker, C.M., Treur, J.: Formal analysis of models for the dynamics of trust based on experiences. In Garijo, F.J., Boman, M., eds.: MAAMAW'99. Volume 1647., Berlin, Springer-Verlag: Heidelberg, Germany (1999) 221–231
12. Fabiani, P.: Dynamics of beliefs and strategy of perception. In: ECAI'96. (1996) 8–12
13. Falcone, R., Pezzulo, G., Castelfranchi, C., Calvi, G.: Why a cognitive trustier performs better: Simulating trust-based contract nets. In: AAMAS'04, IEEE Computer Society (2004) 1394–1395
14. Liau, C.J.: Logical systems for reasoning about multi-agent belief, information acquisition and trust. In: ECAI'04, Berlin, IOS Press (2000)

Behavior Evaluation with Actions' Sampling in Multi-agent System*

Krzysztof Cetnarowicz[1], Renata Cięciwa[2], and Gabriel Rojek[3]

[1] Institute of Computer Science,
AGH University of Science and Technology,
Al. Mickiewicza 30, 30-059 Kraków, Poland
cetnar@agh.edu.pl
[2] Department of Computer Networks,
Nowy Sącz School of Business — National-Louis University,
ul. Zielona 27, 33-300 Nowy Sącz, Poland
rcieciwa@wsb-nlu.edu.pl
[3] Department of Computer Science in Industry,
AGH University of Science and Technology,
Al. Mickiewicza 30, 30-059 Kraków, Poland
rojek@agh.edu.pl

Abstract. Behavior evaluation is an approach to the problem of the detection of intruders that are undesirable in the computer system. Considering multi–agent architecture each agent should execute continuous and autonomous behavior evaluation of other agents existing in the environment of the secured system. This means that an agent is evaluated separately by all agents in the environment. The distributed character of behavior evaluation in multi–agent system requires an algorithm of management and collection of the results of autonomous behavior evaluations of agents. The algorithm of results' collection should enable to elect the worst agent or agents which have to be eliminated. The main topic of this article is a modified approach to the behavior evaluation process. This approach reduces the number of evaluations which have to be done by agents. The main idea is to evaluate only sampled actions (e.g. every second action) which are undertaken by agents in the secured system.

1 Introduction

Behavior based detection of unfavorable activities in multi–agent systems is inspired by ethically–social processes that function in human societies. An individual in a society seems trustworthy if its behavior can be observed by others and considered (or in other words *evaluated*) by majority as good and secure. The decision about trustworthy of an individual takes place in a society in the decentralized and distributed way — all individuals in a society make their own decisions which form one decision of this society. Inspired by ethically–social

---

* This work was partially supported by AGH founds — grant no 11.11.110.660.

M. Pěchouček, P. Petta, and L.Z. Varga (Eds.): CEEMAS 2005, LNAI 3690, pp. 490–499, 2005.

mechanisms in computer security systems induce decentralization of security mechanisms which should be based on the observation and evaluation of the behavior of an agent functioning in a secured system.

Behavior based detection of unfavorable activities in multi–agent systems could be also applied in intelligent information systems which assure security in real–world systems e.g. air ports, shop centers etc. The problems of application behavior evaluation algorithm in the real-world security systems and first results were presented in [2].

2   Related Work

One of the ideas, considering the real difficulties at building security systems,is the approach to using the mechanisms of the immunological system. The main idea of this approach is to create autonomic detectors, that can detect everything, that differs from "self elements". In the nature such a detector set is the set of T–lymphocytes. Intruders' detection in computer environment has to be done on the basis of certain characteristic structures. In case of an immunological system of a human organism, these structures are peptides and proteins.

Some works in the area of artificial immune mechanisms, in which the place of peptides is assigned to short sequences of data in a computer system are presented in [7,8,10]. It is shown, that short sequences of executed codes could be significant to distinguish normal and abnormal behaviour of the system. The mechanisms presented in [7,8,10] enable to distinguish "self" and "nonself" resources. The "self" resources are some data, codes, that are desirable in a secured computer system. "Nonself" resources are some data, codes, that (in certain simplification) were created e.g. outside computer system or with tools from outside computer system. The "nonself" resources should be treated as undesirable, harmful intruders.

Rapidly developing agent technology makes full flow of resources among open computer systems possible . Autonomous agents can yet freely migrate in the net without knowledge of an owner or an administrator. In open systems, resources recognized by immunological system as the "nonself", can actually be desirable as well as useful. Resources defined as the "self" do not necessarily have to be useful for the system and resources recognized as the "nonself" do not have to be harmful. The more adequate discrimination turns out to be the distinction between the *bad* resources — harmful, and the *good* ones — useful, although the origin of supply ("self"/"nonself") does not play essential part in the system.

In our work we would like to obtain the method for distinguishing between the *good* and the *bad* resources. One of our ideas is to apply immunological mechanisms to the sequences of actions (which means behavior) instead of the sequences of codes or data. An agent should be evaluated on the basis of his behavior (actions that he undertakes) instead of his code. The security mechanisms in open multi–agent systems should be distributed in the same way as some security mechanisms that act in human societies.

3   Distributed Behavior Evaluation

The decentralization of security mechanisms is realized in multi–agent systems by means of equipping all agents with some additional goals, tasks and mechanisms. Those goals, tasks and mechanisms are named *division profile* and should be designed in order to assure security for agents and the multi–agent system those agents are situated. So the agents will execute tasks that they have been created for and simultaneously will execute tasks connected with security. The name *division profile* is inspired by M–agent architecture which could be used to describe an agent (M–agent architecture was introduced among others in [1,3]).

Actions undertaken by agents are the base for behavior evaluation. They are perceived as objects, which create a sequence registered by all agents in the environment. Registered objects–actions could be processed in order to qualify whether it is a *good* or a *bad* acting agent in this particular system, in which evaluation takes place. A *bad* agent also could be named an *intruder*.

3.1   Division Profile

The description of the division profile was presented in [4,5,6]. Because of the limitation of the acceptable length of this paper, this section contains only some information that is crucial to understand the main ideas presented in this article. In this paper we would like to focus on the algorithms of collection and processing of the results of the division profile of agents functioning in the environment, what is presented in Sect. 4 and in Sect. 6.

Each agent in a multi–agent system has his own autonomous calculated division profile. In division profile the immunological mechanisms are applied to estimate the behavior of an agent. The division profile of an agent has three stages of functioning:

1. creation of collection of *good* (*self*) sequences of actions,
2. generation of detector set,
3. behavior evaluation.

An agent a, which division profile is at his behavior evaluation stage, has division state m_a represented as a vector:

$$m_a = (m_a^1, m_a^2, ..., m_a^{j-1}, m_a^j) \qquad (1)$$

where j is the number of neighboring agents (neighboring agents are agents which are visible for an agent a) and m_a^k is the coefficient assigned to neighboring agent number k. The coefficient m_a^k indicates whether the agent number k is evaluated by an agent a as *good* (if the coefficient has a small value) or *bad* (if the coefficient has a great value). The coefficient m_a^k is a number of counted matches between:

– detectors of an agent a which evaluates behavior and possesses division state m_a,
– the sequence of actions undertaken by an agent number k.

The presented process of setting of division state m_a is a realization of behavior evaluation in multi–agent system.

Marking the length of a detector as l and the length of the sequence of actions as h, the coefficient m_a^k is a number from a range $\langle 0, h - l + 1 \rangle$. The maximum of counted matches is equal to $h - l + 1$, because every fragment of the sequence of actions, which has a length equal to the length of a detector, can match only one detector.

4   Algorithms of Distributed Evaluation Management, Collecting and Processing

An algorithm of agent's evaluations management is used to specify which agent or agents should be evaluated by other entities in the secured multi–agent system at given time period. In order to choose an agent, which should be removed from the system, division states of all agents are collected and processed, what is specified by the algorithm of evaluation's collecting and processing. Also an agent's algorithm, which specifies how to co-operate with the environment's management and collection algorithm, is attached to the group of the algorithms of evaluation process.

4.1   Algorithm of an Agent

An agent a in case of receiving a request of evaluation of an agent number k sends back only the coefficient o_a^k in the range $0 \le o_a^k \le 1$. The coefficient o_a^k is given by function:

$$o_a^k = \left(\frac{m_a^k}{h - l + 1} \right)^4 \tag{2}$$

where $h - l + 1$ is the maximum of counted matches of agent a. An agent a does not have to calculate the whole division state m_a, but only the coefficient m_a^k.

The power function of evaluation behavior increases a weight of high coefficient m_a^k. As a result, an agent with high number of counted matches obtains coefficient o_a^k much higher than an agent with low number of counted matches. The exponent of power function has been set empirically [9].

4.2   Algorithms of an Environment

An elimination table o_* represented as a vector is used in the environment:

$$o_* = (o_*^1, o_*^2, ..., o_*^{j-1}, o_*^j) \tag{3}$$

where j is the number of neighboring agents and o_*^k is the coefficient assigned to the agent number k.

Each action undertaken by an agent may cause the change of the results of behavior evaluations that are done by other agents in the system. This approach lets us formulate *the algorithm of evaluation management* as follows:

If an agent k undertakes an action, a request of evaluation the agent k is sent to all agents (except the agent k) by the environment.

After sending the request of evaluation of an agent number k the environment uses *the algorithm of evaluation's collecting and processing*, which consists of following actions:

1. The coefficient o_*^k in the elimination table is set to 0. In this way the information about earlier evaluation's results is dismissed.
2. Agents send back coefficients as it is described in Sect. 4.1.
3. Gained coefficients are summed and then this sum is divided by $j - 1$ (j is the number of agents):

$$o_*^k = \frac{o_1^k + o_2^k + ... + o_{k-1}^k + o_{k+1}^k + ... + o_{j-1}^k + o_j^k}{j - 1} \tag{4}$$

The coefficients in the elimination table o_* are looked up permanently. If the coefficient o_*^k is greater than $\frac{1}{2}$ agent k is eliminated.

5   Behavior Evaluation Experiment

In this experiment a multi–agent system with asynchronously acting agents was implemented. In the simulated environment there are two types of resources: resources of type A and resources of type B. This situation reflects these operations in computer system which should be executed in couples e.g. opening / closing a file. Resources are used by agents, but refilling all resources is only possible when each type of resources reaches the established low level. The simulated system has three types of agents:

- *type g=0* – agents which take one unit of randomly selected (A–50%, B–50%) resource in every full life cycle;
- *type g=1* – agents which take one unit of randomly selected (A–75%, B–25%) resource in every full life cycle; type g=1 agents can be treated as intruders, because increased probability of undertaking only actions of one type can cause blocking the system (what is presented in [4,5]);
- *type g=2* – agents which take one unit of A resource in every full life cycle; type g=2 agents are also called intruders.

Actions of agents of type g=1 are similar to actions of agents of type g=0 but they are also undesirable in the secured system.

The case in which initially there are 64 agents of type g=0, 8 agents of type g=1 and 8 agents of type g=2 is presented below. All agents in the system are equipped with the division profile mechanisms with parameters $h = 18$ and $l = 5$. The simulations are run to 2000 constant time periods Δt and 10 simulations were performed. The diagram in Fig. 1 shows the average number of agents in separate time periods.

During the first 18 time periods Δt all agents were acting synchronously. In 18th time period all agents have generated their detectors and achieved the

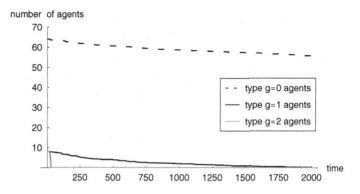

Fig. 1. Number of agents in separate time periods

third stage of their division profiles — behavior evaluation. From 19th time period agents were acting asynchronously — an agent could be activated in one time period Δt, but had to be activated at least once during ten time periods Δt.

From 19th time period all agents used their detectors to evaluate agents which undertook an action according to algorithms presented in Sect. 4. As a result of evaluation processes all bad agents (agents of type g=2) were being deleted successively from 19 constant time period Δt to 28 constant time period Δt. At the end of presented simulation the agents of type g=1 were eliminated in 96%, but agents of type g=0 were eliminated in 13% as well.

The elimination of good agents (type g=0) has been named *the phenomenon of self–destruction*. The phenomenon of self–destruction could be caused by the random choice of undertaken action. For example an agent of type g=0 deciding about action randomly, can undertake such sequence of action: AAAAAAAAAB-BAAABBBB. As a result, this agent will be evaluated as bad because his actions are very similar to actions of bad agents.

The other problem is the rate of deleting type g=1 agents whose actions are similar to actions undertaken by type g=0 agent. However, they are also unfavorable for the system (probability of taking resource A–75%, B–25%). An exemplary action sequence of type g=1 agent could be presented as follows: AABBAAAAABABAAABAA, so probably this agent could be evaluated better than the type g=0 agent from the example mentioned above.

6   Actions' Sampling

In previous simulations an agent was evaluated each time he tried to undertake an action (according to the algorithm of evaluation management presented in Sect. 4.2). The difference between coefficients obtained during two (or even more) following evaluation processes of an agent was very slight as it is presented in Fig. 2. Therefore the new idea (which has been named actions' sampling) in the algorithm of evaluation management is proposed. Actions' sampling means that agents will not be evaluated after each of their actions. An example of actions' sampling can be: only every second action of an agent, this agent will be evaluated. *The algorithm of evaluation management with actions' sampling* could be presented as follows:

> An environment sends a request of evaluation the agent k to all agents (except the agent k) when the agent k undertakes an action every s-th time.

Parameter s is a positive integer. $s = 1$ means that behavior evaluation is without actions' sampling, because after each action of an agent this agent is evaluated.

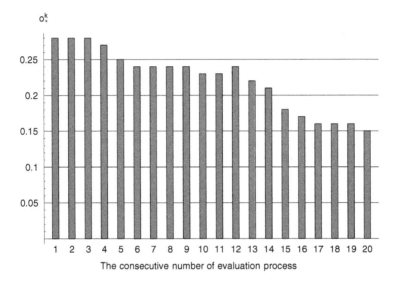

Fig. 2. Evaluation results for an exemplary agent k

7   Behavior Evaluation with Actions' Sampling Experiments

A multi–agent system with asynchronously acting agents of type g=0, type g=1 and type g=2 was implemented, as it was specified in Sect. 5. All agents in the system are equipped with the same division profile parameters — $h = 18$ and $l = 5$. The multi–agent system analogous to the experiment in Sect. 5 in which initially there were 64 type g=0 agents, 8 agents of type g=1 and 8 agents of type g=2 was researched, but additionally the actions' sampling with parameter s with value from 1 to 18 was applied. The simulations were run to 2000 constant time periods Δt. Presented results are in all cases the average of 10 runs of simulation.

The case for $s = 1$ is presented in Fig. 1, $s = 1$ means that there is behavior evaluation without actions' sampling, because after each action of an agent, this

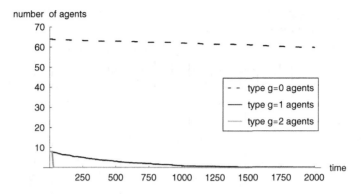

Fig. 3. Number of agents in separate time periods in the case of actions' sampling with parameter $s = 2$

agent is evaluated. The results for $s = 2$ are presented in Fig. 3, $s = 2$ means that only after every second action of an agent, this agent is evaluated.

Till the 18th time period Δt all agents were acting synchronously. As it was described in Sect. 5, in 18th time period all agents have generated their detectors and achieved the third stage of their division profiles — behavior evaluation (agent can use their detectors in order to evaluate an agent). From 19th time period an agent was evaluated after his first action and after his every s-th action according to algorithms with actions' sampling. As a result of evaluation processes all bad agents (agents of type g=2) were being deleted successively from 19 constant time period Δt to 28 constant time period Δt.

The phenomenon of self–destruction and the rate of deleting an agent of type g=1 seem to be similar for two presented cases ($s = 1, 2$). More precise deductions can be gathered from Fig. 4. Figure 4 presents number of type g=0 agents and type g=1 agents for different values of parameter $s = 1, 2, 3, ..., 18$ remained after 2000 constant time periods Δt (at the end of simulations). In all those cases agents of type g=2 were deleted as quickly as it was possible (from 19 constant time period Δt to 28 constant time period Δt).

Considering the phenomenon of self–destruction, actions' sampling can reduce the rate of destruction of good agents. Improvement of self–destruction rate can be noticed for $s = 2$ and bigger. However, the best results are obtained for $s = 5$, $s = 6$, $s = 9$ or bigger. This improvement can be induced by the fact, that agents are not evaluated very often. Less frequent evaluation can reduce the number of destructed agents whose actions can be sometimes similar to actions of bad agents.

Considering the problem of deleting agents of type g=1 whose actions are similar to type g=0 agents' actions unfavorable for the system, actions' sampling can increase the number of remained agents of type g=1 in the system. This occurrence is unfavorable in research computer system. However, actions' sampling increases number of type g=1 agents remained in environment in general, actions' sampling with parameter s with value no bigger than 6 increases this unfavorable occurrence with very small rate.

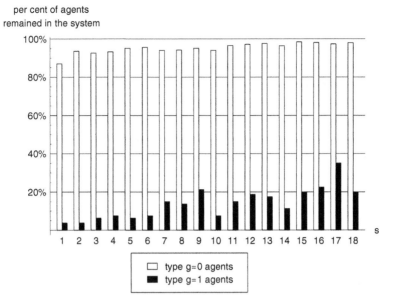

Fig. 4. Final number of agents after 2000 constant time periods Δt in the cases of actions' sampling with parameter $s = 1, 2, 3, ..., 18$

There is another advantage of usage of actions' sampling with parameter s with bigger values — it reduces the computational complexity of behavior evaluation process. In some applications low computational complexity of applied solutions (and/or small self–destruction rate) could be more important than the most exact removal of intruders that undertake an action slightly similar to desirable agents.

8   Conclusion

The main mechanisms of distributed behavior evaluation in multi–agent systems were presented in this article. Results of experiments indicate that the difference between coefficients obtained during two (or even more) following evaluation processes of an agent was very small. This observation permits us to formulate a proposition of actions' sampling. Actions' sampling with parameter s means that an agent will be evaluated only after his every s-th action. Solutions with actions' sampling will have reduced the level of computational complexity.

A multi–agent system with agents which are responsible for behavior evaluation with actions' sampling was simulated. Considering the phenomenon of self–destruction and the problem of deleting agents of type g=1, it could be stated that in general actions' sampling with parameter $s = 2, 3, 4, 5, 6$ is desirable in evaluations algorithm. Actions' sampling with parameter $s > 6$ reduces the rate of self–destruction of good agents strongly, but reduces also the rate of removing agents of type g=1 which are undesirable in the researched system. However, there could be applications of behavior evaluation algorithms in which the value of parameter s bigger than 6 will be profitable, instead of problems with recognition agents that should be evaluated as bad, but whose actions are similar to good agents.

References

1. Cetnarowicz K.,: M–agent architecture based method of development of multiagent systems, in Proc. of the 8th Joint EPS-APS International Conference on Physics Computing, ACC Cyfronet, Kraków (1996)
2. Cetnarowicz K., Nawarecki E., Rojek G.: Behavior Based Detection of Unfavorable Events Using the Multiagent System, in Monitoring, Security, and Rescue Techniques in Multiagent Systems, Advances in Soft Computing, Springer-Verlag Berlin Heidelberg (2005) 579–588
3. Cetnarowicz K., Nawarecki E., Żabińska M.: M–agent Architecture and its Application to the Agent Oriented Technology, in Proc. of the DAIMAS'97, St. Petersburg (1997)
4. Cetnarowicz K., Rojek G.: Unfavourable Beahvior Detection with the Immunological Approach, in Proc. of the XXVth International Autumn Colloquium ASIS 2003, MARQ, Ostrava (2003) 41–46.
5. Cetnarowicz K., Cieciwa R., Rojek G.: Behavior Based Detection of Unfavorable Activities in Multi–Agent Systems, in MCPL, Conference on Management and Control of Production and Logistics, Santiago - Chile (2004) 325–330.
6. Cetnarowicz K., Rojek G.: Behavior Based Detection of Unfavorable Resources, in Lecture Notes in Computer Science, Volume 3038, Springer-Verlag Berlin Heidelberg (2004) 607–614.
7. Forrest S., Hofmeyer S.A., Somayaji A.: Computer Immunology, in Communications of the ACM Vol. 40, No. 10, (1997) 88–96 .
8. Forrest S., Allen L., Perelson A.S., Cherukuri R.: Self-Nonself Discrimination in a Computer, in Proc. of the 1994 IEEE Symposium on Research in Security and Privacy, Los Alamitos, IEEE Computer Society Press, Oakland, CA (1994) 202–212
9. Rojek G., Cięciwa R., Cetnarowicz K., Algorithm of Behavior Evaluation in Multi-agent System, in Lecture Notes in Computer Science, Volume 3516, Springer-Verlag Berlin Heidelberg (2005), 711–718.
10. Wierzchoń, S.: Artificial Immune Systems [in polish], Akademicka Oficyna Wydawnicza EXIT, Warszawa (2001)

Agent-Based Control of a Municipal Water System

Lucilla Giannetti[1,2], Francisco P. Maturana[2], and Frederick M. Discenzo[2]

[1] Department of Electronic and Information Engineering,
University of Perugia, Perugia, Italy
[2] Rockwell Automation, Mayfield Heights, OH, USA
{lgiannetti, fpmaturana, fmdiscenzo}@ra.rockwell.com

Abstract. In this project, we discuss the implementation of an intelligent agent-system for controlling a municipal water system. This work presents an agent-based approach to establishing the expected water requirements, operating constraints, and evaluation criteria and the use of collaborating agents to prescribe an optimal control scheme. A distributed control strategy is implemented and evaluated in a simulation of a municipal water system.

1 Introduction

A Municipal Water System (MWS) can be defined as a combination of utility components and services that are involved in providing drinking-quality water to the local population. The system includes:

- Water: Service or product with a defined flow and quality requirement.
- Tanks: A cylindrical vessel with storage capacity.
- Pumps: Links that impart energy to a fluid thereby raising its hydraulic head.
- Pipes: Links that transport water from one point in the network to another.
- Valves: Links that limit the pressure or flow at a specific point in the network.
- Reservoirs: Large water deposit which can be natural or artificial.
- Controllers: Hardware and software components.
- Sensors: Instrumentation that extracts data from the physical system (sensors).
- Consumers: System end points or boundaries with service requirements.

Due to increased levels of urbanization and consumer demand, most water distribution systems have become increasingly complex and energy prices have continued to escalate. There is a growing need efficiently schedule pump operation to minimize energy consumption and other operating costs while insuring the reliable delivery of high quality water to meet dynamic consumer demands. The security and safety of urban water distribution system is now an extremely critical problem that must be considered in the design and operation of water systems. The control and monitoring system must allow for the implementation of different surveillance techniques to detect the presence of hazardous elements in the water to prevent their transmission to the public. These control systems must have complete and immediate knowledge and initiate an appropriate coordinated response to safely and efficiently maintain operations of the water system. We explore these dimensions by introducing agent-based control as the core monitoring and control element. The following

M. Pěchouček, P. Petta, and L.Z. Varga (Eds.): CEEMAS 2005, LNAI 3690, pp. 500–510, 2005.

sections describe the implementation of autonomous agents to meet local demand for fresh water in a reliable, efficient and safe manner.

Optimizing the operation of a pump system in a municipal water-distribution system can reduce energy costs and also realize other economic and operational benefits. Theoretical and empirical studies of pump scheduling in various water supply systems suggest that 10% of the annual energy cost and related costs may be saved if by optimizing pump operation [1]. The additional benefits include more reliable delivery of water, improved water quality, and greater protection for consumer safety. However, optimal control requires a precise prediction of the short-term water demand and complete state information such as pump capacities and efficiencies. This information permits establishing minimum cost pumping schedules in advance to meet future demand. One objective of this work is to develop an intelligent agent system for monitoring and controlling a municipal water-supply system that ensures optimal control to reduce energy costs, while maintaining water quality and demand [2].

Our focus is on the operation of the pumping stations and the collaboration between the pumps and the water storage tanks. As a first step, we present the reasoning behind the creation of the agent-based rules using a simple system. Although we use a simple system, we will follow well-defined steps to scale up the solution into a multi agent system. In one way, our intention is to frame the procedure for creating agents for the water distribution system. The study of a MWS can be divided into three concepts that define the system requirements and its associated constraints: (1) Water quality, (2) Energy costs, and (3) Demand.

Water quality is affected by the time a parcel of water is retained in a storage tank. New water entering a tank from a reservoir is assumed to have age zero. The cumulative age of the water is a factor that helps define the quality of the water.

The aging of water in a tank is primarily a function of water demand, system operating strategy, and the system design or topology. As water demand increases, the amount of time a given water element is resident in the distribution system decreases. Demand is in turn related to land use patterns, commercial/industrial activity, weather (i.e., temperature and lawn watering), and water use habits by the community (i.e., conservation and reuse practices). The use of reclaimed water on-site or through separate distribution systems will tend to lead toward reduced demand and consequently greater water age when all other factors are held constant [3].

Energy costs are an important aspect affecting the operation of a MWS. An energy-efficient system should minimize cost of supplying water. This includes establishing a control strategy that keeps the water level within physical and operational constraints, minimizing the time pumps operate when energy costs are high and reducing peak energy demands and while maintaining sufficient water in storage tanks to meet the time varying demand.

Demand is another critical aspect affecting the control of a MWS. The instantaneous consumption of water in an urban system also depends on the environment, commercial and community factors. Moreover, a particular day of the week or an observed holiday will considerably influence water consumption.

It is necessary to know the current and future demand in order to define how much water is needed in the tanks and at what time. This information then provides the basis to prescribe a time-based control strategy that meets the predicted demand while achieving cost and quality objectives.

There are many different methods to predict the demand [4]. A simple method is to predict demand using historical data for the specific time period of interest. Based on the predicted demand it is possible to determine if water currently in the tank is adequate for the next time period or if water needs to be added or possibly refreshed. Historical demand information is needed for different times of the day, different days of the week, and for different seasons. It is useful to establish estimates of predicted demand for multiple scheduling periods beyond the current planning period. This information is used to establish more global optimum solutions and control strategies that are more stable and reliable particularly when demand is near peak capacity or upsets may impact the ability of the system to meet the expected demand.

2   General Architecture of Agents

We use a distributed control architecture based on automation controllers with an extended firmware that supports intelligent agents [7]. With these extensions, component-level intelligence is possible by associating a logical processing program with a physical device such as a pump or a valve. The physical devices can then be operated as intelligent nodes with negotiation capabilities. The intelligence of the system is distributed among multiple controllers by placing standalone or multiple agents inside the controllers. The relationship among the agents is loosely coupled but their association is cohesive and adaptable [6] and [8]. The agent architecture is organized according to the following characteristics:

1.   Autonomy: Each agent makes its own decisions and is responsible for carrying out its decisions (i.e. performing control) to successful completion;
2.   Cooperation: Agents combine their capabilities and simple rules of interaction into clusters to negotiate, adapt and respond to events and goals;
3.   Communication: Agents share a common language;
4.   Fault tolerance: Agents possess the capability to detect equipment failure and to isolate failures from propagating; and
5.   Pro-action: Agents periodically or asynchronously propose strategies to enhance the system performance, improve reliability, or to prevent the system from entering harmful or otherwise undesirable states.

Intelligent agents possess characteristics that make them well suited to control a municipal water system. A suite of collaborating autonomous agents can reduce operating cost and provide increased control flexibility by concurrently looking at constraints, changing system economics and uncertain future demand and develop a response using negotiation scenarios. For example, a water storage tank can request water from a supplier pumping station. The pumping station can then consult with the utility company about the cheapest electricity period to schedule for inexpensive pumping. These types of agents can be programmed to evaluate control strategies based on water quality requirements that are affected by high system complexity and unpredictability. The most appropriate use of agents in a municipal water system will be to establish an association with the plant physical devices with agent-based autonomous software elements that comprise a multi-agent system.

Agents are autonomous, problem-solving entities capable of effective operation in dynamic and open environments. Agents can follow two types of collaboration: centralized and decentralized.

The centralized approach has only one agent with knowledge about the complete system. This agent makes decisions and sends these decisions to the interested parts of the system. This kind of control may be more efficient from the agent's point of view, since only the central agent has to have substantial computing capacity. However, it is less desirable from a reliability and security point of view. For example, if the central agent breaks, the whole system stops.

Instead, decentralized control has more agents with the same capability, and each agent controls only one small part of the system. Agents communicate with each other using agent language [5] and exchange information about the system status. Furthermore, distributed agents may self-organize into clusters to insure efficient communications and coordinated operation.   Central failures are avoided and parallelism is increased. However, there is a trade off between parallelism and optimality of the solutions.

This paper presents algorithms to control a MSW based only on the demand, with a distributed agent system. The aim of the control system is to guarantee enough water in the tank to satisfy consumers, avoiding empty or full tank.   The framework presented is readily extended to accommodate reliability and economic considerations.

3   System Analysis

To simplify the study, we established a reduced scale model of a municipal water system. The model is comprised of: a single water reservoir, a single tank, a pump station with only one electrical pump, and pipes and valves. The model was simulated using Simulink, where we placed the simulation of the plant, the control and agent programs. After we conclude the baseline architecture we will expand the system into a complex one, with more than one tank and more than one pump. In that case, the complexity will arise for the simulation model but we will just replicate the agent behavior. We believe that this is a very important and practical observation. For example, by adding the model of a junction among the pump station and the tanks, the agent has to schedule the activity of more than one pump and it has to regulate the opening and closing of the valves of each tank. In such a case, it will make more sense to create multiple agents to handle the new scenarios and components. In particular with a more complex system the agent must be divided into multiple agents to be consistent with the distributed control approach. An idea can be to have an agent at the pumping station and an agent for each tank. In this way, the agents speak with each other to schedule the transportation of water and let the control system operate the low level devices such as valves.

The pumping station takes water from the reservoir and moves it into the tank through a main trunk line (distribution pipe). In between the tank and the pump station, there is an electrically operated valve. The tank is assumed of cylindrical shape. For each of these components, there are intelligent behaviors to control and monitor in the simulation. These intelligent behaviors are defined as controller and agent behaviors, as shown in Figure 1.

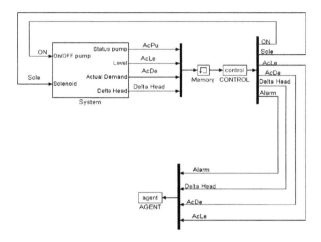

Fig. 1. Simple water system simulation with controller and agent

Both the control and agents were implemented as S-functions in Simulink. The algorithms will be converted into formal languages to build agents and control charts for implementation in a hardware automation controller. The approach used is that the simulation will act as test bed to validate the behavior of the algorithms. In addition, the same algorithms may be directly employed for operating the real equipment. In fact the simulation model of the plant may also be employed in the control of the actual MWS to analyze what-if scenarios and to assist in isolating faults or analyzing unusual disturbances. A training system is also an option.

The agents collaboratively evaluate the condition or state of the system, make decisions about the operation of the system, establish execution plans, and initiate the prescribed change in operation. In this simulation study, an agent establishes the operating schedule of the pump such as when to turn it on or off. The agent generates the schedule. The control function reads the schedule to control the pump. The schedule's structure is shown in Table 1.

Table 1. Schedule generated by agent

T_{start_1}	T_{end_1}	Pump activity	$Predicted\_level_{start\_1}$	$Predicted\_level_{end\_1}$
...	...	...	...	...
T_{start_n}	T_{end_n}	Pump activity	$Predicted\_level_{start\_n}$	$Predicted\_level_{end\_n}$

Where,
- T_{start_i} is the beginning of the *ith* interval;
- T_{end_i} is the end of the *ith* interval;

- Pump activity is the binary variable that indicates if pump is on (1) or off (0);
- Predicted_level$_{start\_i}$ is the predicted level at the beginning of the *ith* interval; and
- Predicted_level$_{endt\_i}$ is the predicted level at the end of the *ith* interval.

Time is expressed in seconds and because of the continuity of the schedule, $T_{end\_i}=T_{start\_(i+1)}$. The same applies for the predicted level, a value that denotes the expected water level in the tank in feet. The pump activity is expressed as a binary value indicating the state of the pump.

The control module reads this file and stores the data in memory. It commands the simulation to carry out the actions affecting the different simulation subsystems. Later, the same control signals will be emitted by a control program from a hardware-based controller(s) to affect the real equipment. The control signals correspond to Inputs and Outputs (I/O) of the control system which are associated with the devices.

3.1 Agent Function

The agent is being created to generate schedules using the demand. The problem is that the future demand is not known accurately because it is a dynamic, probabilistic factor (independent variable). An altered version of the historical demand is used to estimate the actual demand inside the simulation and to establish a difference between the actual and historical demands and for calculating the expected demand schedule. The historical demand trend is shown in Figure 2.

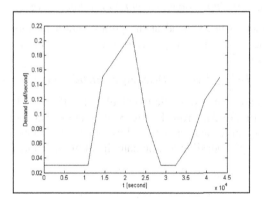

Fig. 2. Historical demand

With this information, we calculate the predicted level after fixed intervals (e.g., 30 minutes and 60 minutes, as shown in Equation 1).

$$\text{Pr}edicted\_Level_{30'} = Level_{now} - Demand_{30'}$$
$$\text{Pr}edicted\_Level_{60'} = Level_{30'} - Demand_{60'}$$
$$\vdots$$
$$\text{Pr}edicted\_Level_{n'} = Level_{(n-DeltaT)'} - Demand_{n'}$$

Equation 1. Equations to calculate the predicted level

The minimum level of water in the tank is chosen be to one foot. The trigger level was another important value that was also arbitrarily chosen. This variable indicates the level at which the pump needs to be on. However, if due to a fault or inaccurate forecast, the level reaches the minimum level, an alarm signal is generated into the agent by the control module. Knowing the predicted level, a set of rules can be generated to control the level in the tank, as shown in Equation 2.

$$\boxed{\begin{array}{l}(\Pr edicted\_Level_{n'} - Level\_Trigger) > 0 \Rightarrow PumpOn = 0\\(\Pr edicted\_Level_{n'} - Level\_Trigger) = 0 \Rightarrow PumpOn = 1\\(\Pr edicted\_Level_{n'} - Level\_Trigger) > 0 \Rightarrow PumpOn = 1\end{array}}$$

Equation 2. Rules for the pump

- Rule 1: PumpOn = 0. This rule indicates that the tank contains enough water and that there is no need for additional pumping;
- Rule 2: PumpOn = 1 (a). This rule says that the level of water is low and that pumping is needed to recover the safety buffer; and
- Rule 3: PumpOn = 1 (b). This rule tells that the demand was more than the previous prediction and that water is needed now.

The needed water was calculated to reach the level trigger value plus an error:

*HowMuchWaterToPump = level_trigger * (1 + Percentage) - prediceted_level*

Knowing the suction head (head at the pump station location) and the discharge head (head at the water in the tank location), it is possible to calculate the "Delta_Head", as follows:

$$Delta\_Head = Disch\arg e\_Head - Suction\_Head$$

With this information, it is possible to calculate the flow out to the pump, knowing the pump curves (Figure 3). From Figure 3, it is clear that more water in the tank means a higher discharge head and less flow out to the pump. Knowing the pump curves (from OEM), it is possible to calculate the pumping time, i.e. t_{ON}.

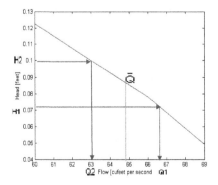

Fig. 3. Head versus flow

The actual flow leaving the pump is calculated as the average between the flow at the beginning of the pumping interval and the flow at the end of the interval based on the variable discharge head, which is affected by the level in the tank. With these assumptions, we can formulate the next set of rules:

- Rule 1: Let $Level_1$ be the level of water at the beginning of the pumping interval. The agent decides the value of *"HowMuchWaterToPump"* (the amount of water that will be needed in 30 minutes). And so after 30 minutes *Delta_Head* is changed because the level in the tank will be $Level_2 = Level1 + HowMuchWaterToPump$;
- Rule 2: Let Q_1 be flow out of the pump associated with $Level_1$ and Q_2 flow associated with $Level_2$. The average flow $\overline{Q}$ used to calculate t_{ON} is obtained as the average between the boundary flows: $\overline{Q} = \dfrac{Q_1 + Q_2}{2}$. t_{ON} is calculated as follows:

$t_{ON} = HowMuchWaterToPump * AreaTank / \overline{Q}$;

- Rule 3: In this way, we calculate the average time that the pump has to be on and so it is possible to fill out the schedule table for the next period. Hence, the predicted level in the tank can be approximated as follows:

$$\Pr edicted\_Level_i = \Pr edicted\_Level_{i-1} + HowMuchWaterToPump;\ \text{and}$$

- Rule 4: At the end of the scheduled period, a new plan for the pump is created using the predicted level. Practically, the schedule can be done more often. The control actuates the commands decided by the agent, but it always monitors the condition of the system to prevent harmful conditions from happening (e.g., excessive or lack of pumping into the tank).

3.2 Control Function

The task of the control module is to activate the pump based on the schedule done by the agent. So the first job of the control module is to check the pumping intervals. The control module sets the pump start and end times in the control table by indicating the corresponding times. Because the schedule is created using a prediction, there is a need to monitor the system to periodically correct the predicted demand, if required.

The second task of the control module is to change the pump activity before an anomalous state occurs. It generates alarms to notify the agent that something is deviating from a desired trend. Given this condition, the agent re-schedules the activity to compensate for the dynamic changes. An alarm signal is generated under the following states:

- State 1: When the predicted level value is different than the actual level and greater than an acceptance threshold;
- State 2: When the level in the tank is near less than a fixed percentage of the maximum level admissible;
- State 3: When the predicted level value is very different from the actual level and the actual level is very close to the level trigger; and
- State 4: When the actual level is very close to the minimum level.

We have observed that usually the last state doesn't occur because preceding states change the pump activity before the level can reach the minimum level.

4 Simulation Results

In this section, preliminary simulation results are reported. The duration of each simulation trail is 43200 seconds (12 hours).

The predicted level is calculated looking at the historical demand after 30 minutes from the actual simulation time. So, the agent calculates a new schedule every four hours using 30 minutes intervals. The agent also creates a new schedule if an alarm occurs. This interval of time is chosen to guarantee an accurate prediction. In fact, the time interval does not have to be too long to avoid missing sudden changes in the demand. But it does not have to be too short either to know the demand in advance. Figure 4 illustrates the demand curves, actual (green) and historical (blue).

The curves in Figure 4 represent a typical morning demand. During the first hours of the morning, the demand is not very high, but about 3 a.m. until 8 a.m. the demand increases, people are getting up. Then about 11 a.m., the demand increases again.

Figure 5 represents the simulation results for the actual demand with correction actions. The real level in the tank is the green line. The predicted level is the blue line. The trigger level is the red line and the minimum level is the cyan color line.

In particular, we can see that at time 14400 sec (4 hours), the predicted level changes instantly because the first schedule is finished and the agent has scheduled the next four hours of water consumption. The agent adjusts the predicted value with the real value, as shown in Figure 6.

Another case corresponds to the schedule at time 36645 sec (about 10 hours), as shown in Figure 7. This change is due to the difference between the two levels. The difference in the levels was more than the 30% of the maximum level (10 ft) allowed in the tank, and so the control module sent an alarm signal to the agent to re-schedule the pumping.

From Figure 5, it can be established that there is no need to pump water because the levels are higher than the trigger level. But the pump, instead, is turned on anyway. The agent decides that to have enough water in the future, when the demand is high, the pump has to be on very soon. This behavior is proactive, purely autonomous and emergent. It was triggered by the agent itself with no explicit rules, just looking at the future trying to have always the water requested.

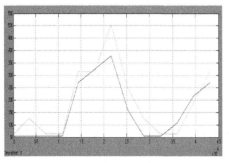
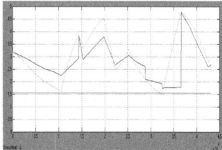
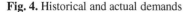

Fig. 4. Historical and actual demands   **Fig. 5.** Levels

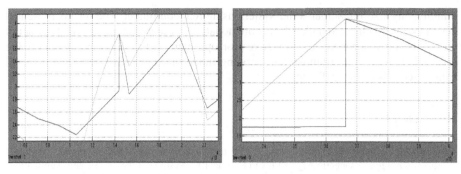

Fig. 6. Particular at time 14400 sec   **Fig. 7.** Particular at time 36645 sec

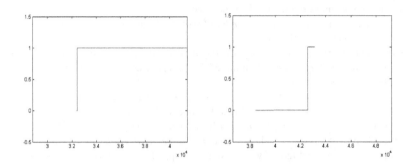

Fig. 8. a) First hypothesis b) Correction and second hypothesis

In Figure 8, there is an example of the correction of pump activity. For the last four hours of simulation, the agent made another hypothesis for the schedule and it was like shown in Figure 8(a). But as seen at time 36645 sec in Figure 7, the levels were too different from each other, and so after the correction of the predicted level, the agent generated a new hypothesis for the schedule to pump less, as shown in Figure 8(b). The agent assumed that because of a prediction error, there is enough water in the tank, and so the pump must be turned off earlier.

5 Conclusion

In this paper, a method to schedule pump activity in a municipal water system was presented. Preliminary results were obtained using simulation, a single agent, and a control program written as S-functions. The algorithms proposed looked at only the control of the water level in the tank. Water in the tank was kept at a level enough to satisfy the demand, but also it was always away from saturating the tank. The algorithms proposed were able to change the schedule when unforeseen situations happened in the actual demand.

The system proposed is the bases for a larger system. The behavior of the agent will need to be split to isolate the pump behavior from the tank behavior, so to create pump agents and tank agents. These agents will serve as the template behaviors for building any size municipal water system using real equipment. The results presented here may be readily expanded to accommodate a variable rate structure for energy costs, machinery prognostics, objectives for optimizing life cycle cost or optimizing asset utilization, or to establish an operating mode that is less brittle or more secure from externally induced disruption.

References

1. G.Mackle, D.A.Savic, G.A.Walters "*Application of genetic algorithms to pump scheduling for water supply*". Genetic Algorithms in Engineering Systems: Innovations and Applications 12-14 September 1995, Conference Publication No. 414, © IEEE, 1995.
2. "*Effects of water age on distribution system water quality*". By AWWA with assistance from Economic and Engineering Services, Inc.
3. An, C.Chan et al. "*Applying knowledge discovery to predict water-supply consumption*". Knowledge discovery IEEE, 1997.
4. G.McCormick, R.S.Powell "*Optimal pump scheduling in water supply systems with maximum demand charges*". Journal of water resources planning and management © ASCE. September/October 2003
5. FIPA: *The Foundation for Intelligent Physical Agents, Geneva, Switzerland*, 1997.
6. Mařík, V., Pěchouček, M., Štěpánková, O.: *Social Knowledge in Multi-Agent Systems. In Multi-Agent Systems and Applications*, LNAI 2086, Springer, Berlin (2001) 211-245
7. Maturana F.P., Staron R., Hall K.: "*Methodologies and Tools for Agents in Distributed Control*". In IEEE Intelligent Systems Magazine, pp. 42-49, January/February 2005.
8. Shen W., Norrie D., and Barthès J.P.: "*Multi-Agent Systems for Concurrent Intelligent Design and Manufacturing*". Taylor & Francis, London, 2001.

Agent-Based Framework for Simulation and Support of Dynamic Engineering Design Processes in PSI

Vladimir Gorodetsky[2], Vadim Ermolayev[3], Wolf-Ekkehard Matzke[1],
Eyck Jentzsch[1], Oleg Karsaev[2], Natalya Keberle[3], and Vladimir Samoylov[2]

[1] Cadence Design Systems, GmbH, Mozart str., 2, 85622, Feldkirchen, Germany
{wolf, jentzsch}@cadence.com
[2] SPIIRAS, 39, 14-th Liniya, St. Petersburg, 199178, Russia
{gor, ok, samovl}@mail.iias.spb.su
[3] Zaporozhye National Univ., 66, Zhukovskogo st., 69063, Zaporozhye, Ukraine
{eva, kenga}@zsu.zp.ua

Abstract. The paper reports on the first results of the Productivity Simulation Initiative (PSI) project of Cadence Design Systems GmbH. The project addresses the problem of fine-grained modeling and simulation of dynamic engineering design processes in order to attempt to assess and to enhance their productivity. The application domain of PSI is Semiconductor and Electronic Systems design. PSI uses multi-agent approach and models design processes as collaborative orchestrated activities of designers' teams. Rational collaboration and team formation is arranged through enhanced Contract Net negotiations. The paper outlines the modeling approach, reports on the methodology, and the rapid prototyping tool used for PSI Simulation Prototype implementation.

1 Introduction

"Design – a signature of human intelligence – was always a great challenge for artificial intelligence (AI) research" (cf. [22]). Observations of how humans act in design inspired several fundamental ideas in AI, e.g., automated problem solving and reasoning [20]. In return, AI community has attacked the problems of design domain by attempting to engineer systems and infrastructures that are capable of supporting humans in accomplishing intelligent tasks.

Engineering design processes are far from being fully automated yet in a satisfactory way, though some attempts have been undertaken. These attempts have used agents to create intelligent software systems to support design processes performed by designer teams and comprising contributions from various disciplines ([1], [3], [4], [5], [18], [19]). These attempts revealed the fact that automating a design process is the task, which due to its complexity is similar to that of AI challenges like natural language processing, human-like decision making, etc. In both cases available theories, frameworks, methodologies, and technologies are still too immature to approach a solution (the state of the art is discussed in [8]). However, some of the vital problems in design process analysis, optimization and management may be solved at least partially automatically.

One of these problems is the modeling, the assessment and the prediction of the productivity of the teams performing design in order to be capable to optimize and

M. Pěchouček, P. Petta, and L.Z. Varga (Eds.): CEEMAS 2005, LNAI 3690, pp. 511–520, 2005.

manage a time-cost trade-off "on the fly" preserving the high quality of the expected final design product.

The task of building a software system able to reliably assess, predict and optimize the productivity in a Dynamic Engineering Design Process (DEDP) is at least threefold. The first aspect is that the system needs the adequate representation model of the world – i.e., the environment comprising the processes and the collaborative teams of autonomous actors who play these processes. The second aspect is that the system needs the adequate model of a DEDP. And the third aspect is that the system needs well defined and reliable productivity metrics and their assessment and prediction mechanisms. It is also important to notice that the mentioned representation models, metrics and mechanisms should be well grained and balanced to constitute adequate, feasible, and reliable framework.

The goal of the first phase of the PSI project is to develop and to validate an agent-based simulation framework designated for future use in DEDP planning, as well as in assessment and prediction of the design process productivity. It forms the prerequisites for the design process optimization and on-line management. Particular subtasks of this phase are: to develop the formal framework for modeling the world and the processes, to implement the demonstrator of this framework in the form of multi-agent simulator prototype (further on referred to as DEDP-MAS), and to use it for experimenting with several application scenarios for assessing the feasibility and the further development of the approach.

The paper is structured accordingly. Section 2 presents our problem statement and the rationale for the focus of our activities. Section 3 sketches the approach, modeling and implementation methodology used. Section 4 describes the two of our application scenarios and the experimental settings. Section 5 reports on the simulation experiments of different types. The reminder of the paper discusses the related work, provides conclusions and our plans for future work.

2 Problems Addressed and Benefits Gained

PSI project bases itself on the understanding that engineering design processes in the vast majority of cases and industrial branches are weakly defined and heavily influenced by human and uncertainty factors. Therefore, these processes should be performed in quite a flexible manner to ensure meeting the objectives and to demonstrate at least near-optimal productivity and quality of results. Gaining such flexibility seriously depends on the capability to assess the feasibility of the initial plan, to react to the changes in the process in timely and flexible manner through re-planning, to evaluate the plan in terms of the predicted productivity and the result quality. Hence, one of the tasks of PSI was to implement a software tool capable to play DEDP simulation games for both:

– Evaluating the initial plan for an engineering design project using predictive simulation, and
– Partially automating the process of dynamic planning of collaborative activities of a designer team through the simulation of their negotiations

Another goal of the reported PSI phase was to create the initial DEDP Simulation Testbed by recording the logs of the DEDPs of the application scenarios (Section 4). This testbed contains the logs of the DEDPs application scenarios and the mental models of the agents playing the roles of design team members in experiments (Section 5).

The initial set of experiments performed on the created prototype clearly showed the approach feasibility to model engineering design processes. E.g., experimenting with the PSI application scenarios showed that DEDP-MAS simulator may be efficiently used for the planning and the adjustment of the project design plans according to the unexpected changes in designers' capabilities. DEDP-MAS framework prototype is now used in PSI project as the basis for further development of a more accurate model of design processes. We finally aim to obtain a software tool which will help in enhancing the productivity of DEDPs.

3 Approach, Methodology, and Agent Platform

DEDP participants are conceptually structured and form a kind of organization comprising individual human **Actors**[1] and groups of **Actors** at different hierarchical levels. **Activities** of an organization and its members are regulated by **Policies**. **Actors** form dynamic **Teams** on **Project** and/or **Task** basis. The organization and its members own certain knowledge. Substantial part of this knowledge is the **Capabilities** of the **Actors** to perform certain activities. Sub-sets of these **Capabilities** together with respective **Authority** specifications form human **Roles** in a design process. The environment of the above organization is formed by the structured specification of DEDPs under performance which actually imposes partial ordering and other relations on activities being composed in the design process.

DEDP-MAS prototype has been designed and implemented in Multi Agent System Development Kit (MASDK) [14]. According to the Gaia methodology [23] forming the methodological basis of the MASDK platform the system's organization is described at analysis stage in terms of *Roles*, *Protocols,* and *Agent classes*. Fig.1 illustrates the organization of the current version of DEDP-MAS prototype as it looks in the window of the *Meta-model editor* provided by MASDK. It comprises three problem-oriented (*Task_manager*, *Executor* and *Tool_Provider*) and one auxiliary (*Time_Simulator*) roles. A human actor can play *Task_manager* and *Executor* roles, so they are assigned to one agent class – *Designer*. The main activities executed by the *Task_manager* role are 1) revealing design artifacts, 2) specifying activities to be executed and the order of their execution as Pert chart, 3) assigning activities and 4) monitoring their execution. The main activities carried out by the *Executor* role are 1) scheduling assigned activities and 2) simulating their execution. Software tools are considered here as resources used for some activities execution and the task of the resource scheduling is solved by the *Tool_Provider* role. The tasks executed by the auxiliary *Time_simulator* role are 1) providing human actor with the interface for input description, and 2) synchronizing agents' operation.

---

[1] The mentioned entities of DEDP Ontology are **bold**.

Interaction model includes eight protocols. Initiator of each protocol is indicated by triangle. The *Initialization* protocol specifies interaction of the *Simulator* and *Designer* agent classes at the DEDP start up. In particular, when this protocol has been initialized the human actor assisted by the *Simulator* agent selects the task to execute, inputs the initial data, determines the settings of simulation parameters, etc. Then, according to the *Initialization protocol*, the above data are communicated to the agents of the *Designer* class. The simulation itself is then being performed in day-by-day mode under the control of the *Simulator* agent class. Three protocols, *Interruption, Negotiation* and *Simulation* may be performed in each work day. They are initialized by the *Simulator* agent one after another.

The *Interruption* protocol is started up if the human actor assisted by the *Simulator* agent class intends to view and analyze the workload and schedule of each designer via respective user interfaces and to modify the workload of designers for the remaining part of DEDP simulated. If the workload of a designer is modified the re-scheduling of the remaining activities is automatically executed.

During the *Negotiation* protocol execution, the *Task manager* role initiates the *Outsourcing* (nested) protocol (Fig. 2) based on the Contract Net Protocol (CNP) [13] to perform the assignment of the activities to the designers., If an agent performing the *Executor* role during the CNP–based negotiation intends to use a software tool it initiates negotiation with a *ST_provider* agent using the *Tool_usage_scheduling* (nested) protocol.

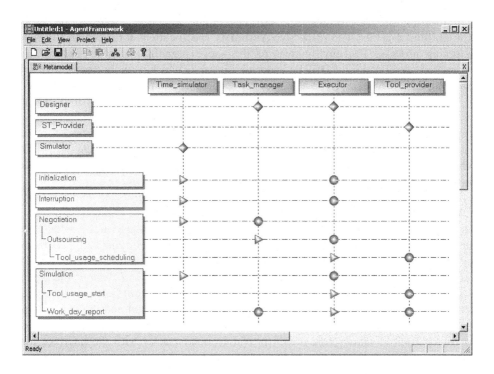

Fig. 1. Meta model of DEDP MAS prototype

After completion of the assignment and scheduling procedures (when all the above mentioned protocols are finished) the *Simulator* class agent initiates the *Simulation* protocol while simulating operation of the agents of the *Designer* class performing the *Executor* roles according to the schedule for the current day. If certain agents of the *Designer* class use software tools in simulation progress they initiate the *Tool_usage_start* (nested) protocol. After the work day activity simulation is completed the *Simulation* agent class reports the simulation results to the agents performing *Task_manager* and *Tool_provider* roles using *Work_day_report* (nested) protocol. Conceptual description of the above

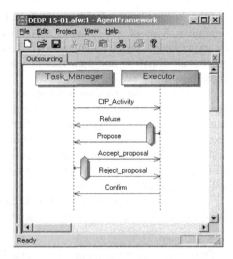

Fig. 2. Graphical specification of the Outsourcing protocol in MASDK

protocols is made using the *Protocol editor* of the MASDK platform in the standard style like depicted in Fig. 2 for *Outsourcing*.

At the design stage [23] a formal specification of (i) agent classes and (ii) their services (in terms of state machines) is developed. Specification of each agent class is reduced (i) to identifying its services associated with respective protocols in which agents of the class take part, and (ii) to specifying identified services. E.g. in the current version of DEDP-MAS the specification of *Designer* agent class comprises eighteen services, such as *Assignment management, Outsourcing, Activity scheduling, Proposal computing, Activity simulation,* etc. Detailed description of graphic editors used in MASDK for specifying agent classes and services (in terms of state machines) can be found in [14].

4 Application Scenarios and Experimental Settings

PSI simulator is used in two application modes: descriptive and predictive. In descriptive mode the simulation is used to assess the performance of the DEDPs which have been accomplished in the past.

The predictive mode supports project managers in planning of starting and re-planning of running design projects in case of emergent problems e.g. late changes to the design objective, sudden unavailability of the team members, the changes in the workload of the designers according to the influence of the other projects, etc.

Based on these usage modes PSI testbed comprises the following two parts. The first part (the initial testbed) contains the detailed records of 1 – 2 ongoing design projects and event log to extract the knowledge of the acting humans. DEDP model and the adequacy of the implemented interaction mechanisms are evaluated based on these "logs of DEDP execution". As the result the corrective factors are extracted to improve the quality of the simulation. The performance of the process can be accessed based on this improved simulation of a design process.

The second part of the testbed is under creation and covers the prediction capability. A set of 3 to 5 design artifacts will be used to create detailed project plans by experienced project managers (2-3 per artifact). As the part of this planning process all decisions and their reasons will be recorded in order to further extract the know-how of the project manager.

Initial set of experiments has been performed on the two simplified scenarios: the process of the design of a digital multimedia encoder [15] and the process of the design of an analog controlled amplifier [24]. These processes have been described according to the data collected by lead designers of Cadence Design Systems GmbH in their previous design projects. Execution logs have been created for the respective DEDPs through filling in the DEDP questionnaires [16]. These logs formed the initial testbed for DEDP-MAS prototype.

The scenarios were simplified to keep the complexity at a low to medium level. For example, the digital scenario is characterized by:

- 5 designers
- Design artifact comprising 4 functional blocks
- The process from RTL design up to tape-out in GDSII format resulted in 36 activities.

5   Experiments for Framework Prototype Checking

Experiments with the DEDP-MAS prototype are performed in frame of the real world project of low complexity and amount of work under some simplifications. It was assumed that the execution log does not exist at the beginning of the process, but is gradually developed in line with the DEDP flow. The objective of the experiments was to develop the so called prediction-correction methodology. The methodology should predict the development of the process up to the next checkpoint through the simulation based on the initial task and existing agents' mental models. General view of the experiments scenario is outlined in Fig. 3.

DEDP-MAS prototype configuration (the set of software agents with the accordingly prepared mental models) corresponds to the project design team. It is assumed in the experiments that only one agent of the *Designer* class performing the *Task manager* role in DEDP-MAS prototype assists the human *Project leader* and the rest of the agents of this class simulate the activities of the other design team members.

In the experiment along with the development of the DEDP the human expert repeatedly carries out the following activities:

- Gradually develops the execution log via specific event-based log editor, and
- Analyses the predictions of the further development of the process via interaction with the *Task manager* assistant agent.

Log editor allows to record all kinds of events that may occur in simulation: activity assignments, activity accomplishments etc. For example, activity assignment record includes: 1) assignment time, 2) list of designers possessing required capabilities and believed to be potential executors of the activity under assignment, 3) the log of negotiation with these designers, 4) the information about the winner of the accomplished CNP. The data associated with the events and which may be useful for computing different design process metrics is also recorded to the log.

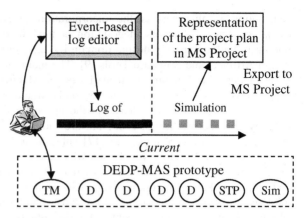

Simulation aiming at prediction of the future DEDP development is initiated after the playback of the log corresponding to the accomplished part of the process at the given point in time. During simulation the human *Project leader* may trim the available capacities

Fig. 3. General scenario of experiment supported by DEDP-MAS

of the designers and revise the assignments of the activities arranged by the assistant, *Designer* agent playing *Task_manager* role. Accordingly, the *Project leader* can evaluate the predicted path of DEDP in *What-if* mode. Simulation results are exported in Microsoft Project format. This facility allows the *Project leader* to compare the Gantt charts of DEDP paths executed in real life to that predicted by simulation. In DEDP-MAS prototype these checkpoints are allowed ones per simulated project day. Export to the Microsoft Project and the above comparison are done on daily basis. Therefore the *Project leader* can monitor and dynamically influence DEDP development in the mentioned checkpoints.

Thus, the experiments with the developed and implemented DEDP-MAS prototype support the solution of the following practically important problems:

1) Estimation of the adequacy of the world model representation in the DEDP-MAS prototype.
2) Estimation of adequacy of DEDP model used in the DEDP-MAS prototype. The adequacy is assessed through the comparison of actual processes with the ones simulated by the DEDP-MAS prototype in the predictive mode.

6 Discussion and Related Work

The constellation of projects pioneered R&D in agent-based engineering design support and automation began to appear about a decade ago, e.g. ([1], [3], [4]). These findings initially motivated PSI project. Some projects of the "second wave" ([5], [18]) helped to specify the focus of PSI in automating the near-optimal arrangement of DEDPs in terms of their productivity. Besides that PSI aims to provide the industrial strength solution in the mentioned niche.

DEDP modeling framework and simulator prototype implementation is based on research in: dynamic planning process modeling, methodologies and frameworks for the design and implementation of multi-agent systems.

DEDP modeling framework in the part of organizational and actor-related knowledge representation bases itself on the frameworks ([6], [7], [12], [21]). PSI contribution in this part is the incorporation of roles, actors with its specific subclasses, teams of actors, negotiation context in one coherent ontology and its binding to the engineering design domain by, e.g., introducing the sub-ontologies of Design Artifacts and Software Tools [9]. The main emphasis of PSI DEDP ontology is the model of a dynamic team of designers which is formed through contracting negotiations and performs dynamically orchestrated processes. In a part of process modeling, PSI borrows the ideas and the approach from ([2], [6], [11]). In DEDP ontology engineering design processes are modeled as tasks composed of subtasks and atomic activities. Similarly to [17] subtasks and activities may have weak and strong dependencies. However the knowledge on these dependencies is local in PSI and differs from actor to actor as specified in their partial local plans. Similarly to [11] activities have pre-conditions, post-conditions and post-effects. However PSI ontology constrains the semantics of pre-/post- conditions and effects by making them sub-classes of an event concept. Material inputs and outputs semantically and structurally belong to PSI Design Artifacts ontology. Some inspirations for the development of agent reasoning mechanisms in PSI were provided by RAPPID set based reasoning framework [18] and RACING negotiation framework [6]. PSI extends these initial percepts to the family of negotiation mechanisms: task allocation, design re-use, choice of a software tool to perform a design activity [10].

DEDP-MAS simulation prototype was designed and implemented using MASDK software tool [14]. This software tool implemented recently developed well grounded Gaia methodology [23] known as one of the most promising modern MAS design methodologies. MASDK software tool provides user-friendly GUI for analysis and design of multi-agent applications, exploits software reusability approach, supports the integrity of the development at different stages and uses basic standardization proposals resulting from joint efforts of FIPA and OMG, Agent UML Project. It supports the whole life cycle of a multi-agent application system including its modification if necessary.

7 Conclusions and Future Work

As reported in the paper the first outcomes of PSI are (i) the formal framework for modeling DEDPs, (ii) implemented simulation prototype of DEDP simulator software tool, (iii) initial PSI testbed comprising DEDP execution logs built for two mentioned application scenarios, (iv) results of the initial experiments which prove the feasibility of concept implementation.

The contribution of the modeling framework is the provision of the DEDP model in the form of the set of DEDP-full ontologies. These ontologies were simplified to DEDP-light version and used in the design of the meta-model of DEDP-MAS, in the implementation of PSI DEDP execution log questionnaire and editor as well as in the implementation of local knowledge models of DEDP-MAS agents. Another input of the modeling framework is the set of coordination and negotiation mechanisms. It provides CNP-based negotiation mechanisms for task or activity allocation, design artifact re-use and the choice of the proper software tool. Planned future work in this direction will develop the extensions for DEDP productivity assessment, process and result quality assessment and refine negotiation strategies and dynamic re-planning mechanisms.

The experiments with the DEDP-MAS prototype support solution of several practically important DEDP tasks e.g. the estimation of the adequacy of the world model and DEDP model itself represented in the DEDP-MAS prototype. It also provides a computational framework for development and evaluation of the reliable metrics concerning the design process productivity and to discover *sensitive parameters* of the design process influencing the mentioned metrics that is important for future design processes optimization. An important property of the DEDP-MAS prototype from the industrial viewpoint is the integration with Microsoft Project providing dynamic visualization of DEDP progress and the results of the *Project leader* intervention through it.

The development of the initial testbed allowed to adjust the requirements to the prototype as well as to prepare initial evaluation experiments. The initial set of experiments performed on the created prototype clearly showed the feasibility of this approach to model engineering design processes. For example, experiments with PSI application scenarios showed that DEDP-MAS simulator may be efficiently used for the planning and the adjustment of the design project plans according to the unexpected changes in design team members' capabilities. Planned experimental work will be to build the extension of the testbed by recording the execution log of currently running design project at Cadence Design Systems, GmbH and to develop the methodology for the evaluation of the initial design project plan through the usage of predictive simulation mode.

References

1. Balasubramanian, S., Norrie, D. H.: A multi-agent intelligent design system integrating manufacturing and shop-floor control. In: Proc. First International Conference on Multi-Agent Systems., San Francisco (1995) 3-9
2. Buhler, P., Vidal, J.M.: Enacting BPEL4WS specified workflows with multiagent systems. In Proc. of the Workshop on Web Services and Agent-Based Engineering, (2004)
3. Cutkosky, M.R., EngelMore, R. S., Fikes, R. E., Genereseth, M. R., Gruber, T. R., Mark, W. S., Tenenbaum, J. M. and Weber, J. C.: PACT: An Experiment in Integrating Concurrent Engineering Systems. IEEE Computer 26(1) (1993) 28-38
4. Darr, T. P., Birmingham, W. P.: An Attribute-Space Representation and Algorithm for Concurrent Engineering. CSE-TR-221-94, University of Michigan, Department of Electrical Engineering and Computer Science, Ann Arbor, Michigan 48109-2122 (1994)
5. Danesh, M. R., Jin, Y.: An Agent-Based Decision Network for Concurrent Engineering Design. CERA 9(1) (2001) 37-47
6. Ermolayev, V., Keberle, N., Kononenko, O., Plaksin, S. and Terziyan, V.: Towards a framework for agent-enabled semantic web service composition. Int. J. of Web Services Research, 1(3) (2004) 63-87
7. Ermolayev, V., Keberle, N., Tolok, V.: OIL Ontologies for Collaborative Task Performance in Coalitions of Self-Interested Actors. In: H. Arisawa, Y. Kambayashi, V. Kumar, H.C. Mayr, I. Hunt (Eds.): Conceptual Modeling for New Information Systems Technologies ER 2001 Workshops, Yokohama Japan, November 27-30, 2001. LNCS vol. 2465 (2001) 390-402
8. Ermolayev, V.: The State of the Art in Agent-Based Modeling and Simulation of Design Processes. TR-PSI-2-2004. Cadence Design Systems, GmbH (2004)

9. Ermolayev, V., Keberle, N.: DEDP-MAS Ontologies Specification v.1.0. TR-PSI-05-2004, VCAD EMEA Cadence Design Systems GmbH (2004)

10. Ermolayev, V. et al: Agent-Based Dynamic Engineering Design Process Modeling Framework. Technical Report. Cadence Design Systems, GmbH (2004)

11. Fensel, D., Bussler, C.: The Web Service Modeling Framework WSMF. Electronic Commerce Research and Applications 1(2) (2002) 113-137

12. Fox, M.C., Gruninger, M.: Enterprise Modelling. AI Magazine 19(3) (1998) 109–121

13. Foundation for Intelligent Physical Agents. FIPA Contract Net Interaction Protocol Specification. Ref. No XC00029E (2001)

14. Gorodetski, V., Karsaev, O., Samoilov, V., Konushy, V., Mankov, E., Malyshev, A.: Multi Agent System Development Kit: MAS software tool implementing GAIA Methodology. In: Z. Shi and Q. He (eds.) Int. Conf. on Intelligent Information Processing (IIP2004), Beijing, Springer (2004) 69-78

15. Jentzsch, E., Matzke, W.-E.: Case Study of a Digital Design Process. VCAD EMEA Cadence Design Systems GmbH (2004)

16. Keberle, N., Weber, S.: Questionnaire to create formal record of an Analog Design Process & A Walk-through Example. Cadence Design Systems GmbH, VCAD CIC2 (2004)

17. Nagendra Prasad, M. V., Lesser, V. R.: Learning situation-specific coordination in cooperative multi-agent systems. Autonomous Agents and Multi-Agent Systems. 2(2) (1999) 173-207

18. Parunak, H.V.D., Sauter, J. A., Fleischer, M. and Ward, A. C.: The RAPPID Project: Symbiosis between Industrial Requirements and MAS Research. Autonomous Agents and Multi-Agent Systems 2 (1999) 111-140

19. Shen, W. and Barthes J.-P.: An Experimental Multi-Agent Environment for Engineering Design, Int. J. of Cooperative Information Systems, 5(2-3) (1996) 131-151

20. Simon, H.: The Sciences of the Artificial. MIT Press, Cambridge, (1969)

21. Uschold, M. et al: The Enterprise Ontology. Knowledge Engineering Review, 13(1) (1998)

22. Vancza, J.: Artificial Intelligence Support in Design: A Survey. Keynote paper at the 1999 International CIRP Design Seminar, Kluwer (1999)

23. Wooldridge, M., Jennings, N. R. and Kinny, D.: The Gaia Methodology for Agent-Oriented Analysis and Design. Journal of Autonomous Agents and Multi-Agent Systems, 3(3) (2000) 285-312

24. Weber, S.: Case Study of an Analog Design Process. VCAD CIC2 Cadence Design Systems GmbH (2004)

Situated Agents and the Web: Supporting Site Adaptivity

Stefania Bandini, Sara Manzoni, and Giuseppe Vizzari

Department of Informatics, Systems and Communication,
University of Milano-Bicocca,
Via Bicocca degli Arcimboldi 8 20126 Milan - Italy
tel +39 02 64487835, fax + 39 02 64487839
{bandini, manzoni, vizzari}@disco.unimib.it

Abstract. A web site presents an intrinsic graph–like spatial structure defined by pages connected by hyperlinks. This structure may represent an environment on which reactive situated agents related to visitors of the web site are positioned and move in order to track their navigation. To consider this structure and to keep track of these movements allows the monitoring of the site and visitors, and supports the enhancement of the site itself through forms of adaptivity, by means of a specific interface agent. This paper presents an agent based model supporting the collection of information related to user's behaviour in a web site, and an application supporting the proposal of hyperlinks based on the history of user's movement in the web site environment.

1   Introduction

A web site presents an intrinsic graph–like spatial structure defined by pages connected by hyperlinks. However, this structure is generally not considered by web servers, which essentially act as a sort of extended and specific File Transfer Protocol servers, receiving requests for specific contents and supplying the related data. Several web–based applications instead exploit the structure of the sites itself to support users in their navigation, generating awareness of their position. For instance, many e–commerce sites emphasize the hierarchical structure linking pages related to categories (and possibly subcategories), included products and their specific views, and remind users' relative position (i.e. links to higher level nodes in the tree structure). Some specific web–based applications, mainly bulletin boards and forums (see, e.g., phpBB[1]), are also able to inform users about the presence of other visitors of the web site or even, more precisely, of the specific area of the site that they are currently viewing. Web site structure and users' context represent thus pieces of information that can be exploited to supply visitors a more effective presentation of site contents.

Different visitors, however, may have very different goals and needs, especially with reference to large web sites made up of several categories and subcategories.

---

[1] http://www.phpbb.com/

M. Pěchouček, P. Petta, and L.Z. Varga (Eds.): CEEMAS 2005, LNAI 3690, pp. 521–530, 2005.

This consideration is the main motivation for the research in the area of adaptive web sites [1]. The various forms of adaptation may provide a customization of site's presentation for an individual user or even an optimization of the site for all users. There are various approaches supporting these adaptation activities, but they are generally based on the analysis of log files which store low–level requests to the web server: this kind of file is generally made up of entries including the address of the machine that originated the request, the indication of the time and the resource associated to the request. In order to obtain meaningful information on users' activities these raw data must be processed (see, e.g., [2]), for instance in order to collapse requests related to various elements of a single web page (e.g. composing frames and images) into a single entry. Moreover this kind of information must be further processed to detect groups of requests that indicate the path (web pages connected by hyperlinks) that a user followed in the navigation.

This paper proposes to exploit the graph-like structure of a web site as an environment on which simple reactive agents representing visitors of the web site are positioned and move according to their navigation. This approach allows the gathering of a more structured information on user's activities, simplifying sub-sequent phases of analysis and adaptation of site contents. Furthermore, part of the adaptivity could be carried out without the need of an off-line analysis, but could be the result of a more dynamic monitoring of users' activities. In particu-lar, the paths that are followed by users are often related to recurrent patterns of navigation which may indicate that the user could benefit from the proposal of additional links providing shortcuts to the terminal web pages. Index pages may thus be enhanced by the inclusion of links representing shortcuts to the typical destinations of the user in the navigation of the web site. Users without a rele-vant history may instead exploit the paths that are most commonly followed by site visitors. Moreover such an information could also be communicated to the webmaster suggesting possible modifications to the static predefined structure of the site. This approach provides thus both a support for site optimization, but also for the customization to specific visitor's needs and preferences. This task is carried out by a specific interface agent provided with specific strategies guiding the choices on possible adaptation.

While the metaphor of a web site as an environment on which users move in search for information is not new (see, e.g., [3]), this proposal also allows the exploitation of this information to support a context-aware form of inter-action among users. In fact, by adopting of a supporting technology that goes beyond the request/response form (e.g. a Java applet), users may be informed of the presence of other site visitors' presence and may interact with them in a sort of hybrid between a common web site and an instant messenger (see, e.g., ICQ2Go![2]).

The following section describes the general framework of this approach, the mapping between the web site structure and agents' environment, while Sec-tion 3 describes the kind of gathered information on agents' movement in their

---

[2] http://go.icq.com/

environment. Section 4 describes an application providing the exploitation of this kind of information for the adaptation of web pages, both for customization and optimization; concluding remarks and future developments will end the paper.

2   Site Structure and Agents' Positions

A web site is made up of a set of HTML pages (generally including multimedia contents) connected by means of hyperlinks. It is possible to obtain a graph-like structure mapping pages to nodes and hyperlinks to edges interconnecting these nodes. This kind of spatial structure could be exploited as an *environment* on which agents related to site visitors are placed and move according to the related users' activities. This structure can be either static or dynamic, varying according to specific rules and information stored in a database (i.e. database driven web sites). However, this kind of structure (both for static and dynamic web sites) can be easily obtained by means of a crawler (see, e.g., Sphinx [4] and the related WebSphinx project[3]).

Given this spatial structure, a multi-agent model allowing an explicit representation of this aspect of agents' environment is needed to represent and exploit this kind of information. Environments for Multi Agent Systems [5] and situated agents represent promising topics in the context of MAS research, aimed at providing first class abstractions for agents environment (which can be more than just a message transport system), towards a clearer definition of concepts such as *locality* and *perception*. There are not many models for situated agents, which provide an explicit representation of agent's environment. Some of them are mainly focused on providing mechanisms for coordinating situated agent's actions [6], other provide the interaction among agents through a modification of the shared environment (see, e.g., [7,8]). An interesting approach that we adopted for this work is represented by the Multilayered Multi Agent Situated Systems (MMASS) [9] model. MMASS allows the explicit representation of agents' environment through a set of interconnected layers whose structure is an undirected graph of nodes (also referred to as sites in the model terminology; from now on we will use the term node to avoid confusion with web sites). The model was adopted given the similarity among the defined spatial structure of the environment and the structure underlying a web site. Moreover the model defines a set of allowed actions for agents' behavioural specification (including a primitive for agents' movement); for this specific application, however, the constraint which limits the number of agents positioned in a node was relaxed. In fact there is no limit to the number of users that are viewing the same web page.

Moreover a platform for the specification and execution of simulations based on the MMASS model [10] was exploited to implement the part of the system devoted to the management of agents in their environments. The definition of spatial structure of the environment was supplied by the previously introduced crawler, while agents' movement is guided by external inputs generated by the requests issued by the related web site visitor. The general architecture of the

---

[3] http://www-2.cs.cmu.edu/ rcm/websphinx/

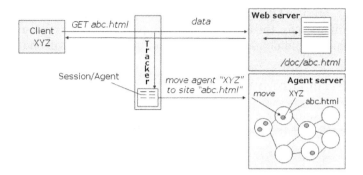

Fig. 1. A diagram showing how user actions influence the related agent through the capture of requests by the Tracker module

system is shown in Figure 1: the *Agent server* module is implemented through the MMASS platform, while the *Web server* is represented by SnipSnap[4], a Java-based weblog and wiki software. The highlighted *Tracker* module is a implemented through a Java Servlet, which is invoked by every page of the site but does not produce a visible effect on the related web page. It is responsible for the management of user authentication and requests, but it is also responsible for the creation of agents related to visitors and for the triggering of their movement in the environment related to the web site. The management of the mechanisms supporting this responsibility is not as simple as its intuitive description might indicate. In fact, the same user could be using different browser pages or tabs to simultaneously view distinct pages of the site. In other words, a user might be simultaneously following different trajectories in his/her web site navigation. In order to manage these situations, a user can be related to different agents, and his/her requests must be associated to the correct agent (possibly a new one). Finally, agents related to finished (or interrupted) user navigation should be eliminated by the system, storing the relevant part of their state in a persistent way, until the related user requires again a page of the site. In particular, remote users' requests may be divided into two main classes, according to their effects on the Tracker and Agent server:

• *creating a new agent*: whenever a new user requires a web page, the Tracker will invoke the Agent Server requiring the creation of an agent whose starting position is the node related to the required page; the same effect is generated by a request coming from an already registered user which was not present in the system, but in this case information related to previous user agents must be retrieved in order to determine the new agent's state; finally, when an already registered and active user requires a page that is not adjacent to its current one, a new agent related to the new browsing activity must also be created;

• *generating the movement of an agent*: when the viewer of a page follows one of the provided links, the related web browser will generate a request for a page

---

[4] http://snipsnap.org

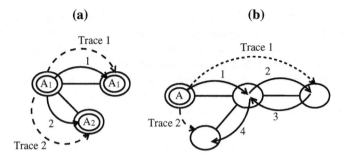

Fig. 2. A diagram describing two traces that are derived by a sequence of user requests

that is adjacent to one of the related agents which must be moved to the node related to the required page; whenever there are two or more agents in positions that are adjacent to the required page, in order to solve the ambiguity and choose the agent to be moved, the Tracker will invoke the Session object in which it stores the current URL related to the viewed page.

The following section will describe how the raw information that can be gathered thanks to the above described framework can be processed in order to obtain higher level indications on users' behaviours.

3   Gathered Information: Users' Traces

This system allows the gathering and exploitation of two kinds of information: first of all situated agents related to web site visitors have a perception of their local context, both in terms of relative position, adjacent nodes and presence of other visitors; second, agents may gather information related to the paths defined by the browsing activities or the related user in the site itself. There are inherent issues in determining in a precise way the actual users' activities on the web site, due to the underlying request/response model: the only available indications on these activities can be obtained by requests captured by the Tracker. In particular, we have an indication of the page that was required by a user and the time-stamp of the request. Starting from this raw information we can try to detect *emerging links*, which are hyperlinks that are not provided by the structure of the site but can be derived by the behaviour of specific visitors. To this purpose, the concept of *trace* was introduced as a higher level information describing the behaviour of a user. A trace synthesizes a path followed by a user, from the web page representing his/her entry point, to a different point of the environment (i.e. another web page) which may represent an interesting destination. Every agent related to a visiting user is associated to a *temporary* trace, and it may generate several actual traces (also called *closed* traces) in the course of its movement in the environment.

Formally a trace is a three-tuple $\langle A_{Id}, Start, Dest \rangle$, where A_{Id} represents the identifier of the agent to which the trace is related, while *Start* and *Dest* indicate the starting and destination node related to the browsing sequence which generated the trace. A new trace is generated when a user enters the site, triggering the creation of a related agent. The starting trace has a null value for the destination node. Subsequent requests by the user generated following hyperlinks will bring the related agent to an adjacent node, and the the *Dest* field of the corresponding trace will be modified in order to reflect user's current position. Non trivial traces provide *Start* and *Dest* nodes that are not directly connected by means of a hyperlink.

There are two relevant exceptions to the basic rule for trace update, that are related respectively to the *duplication* of a trace and to its *closing*. According to the previously introduced informal definition, a trace should be coherent in time and space. In fact, whenever the same user requires simultaneously two or more different pages he/she is probably following distinct search trajectories, possibly even related to different goals. In this case, as previously introduced, the Tracker will detect this situation and create additional agents that refer to the same user. Figure 2 shows two sample situations providing respectively trace duplication and closing: in (a) the user has chosen to open a hyperlink in a new browser page (request 1) and then has followed another link in the first browser page (request 2). According to the previously described Tracker behaviour, two agents are now associated to the user, and they are associated to different traces sharing the *Start* field.

In (b), instead, the user has followed links 1 and 2 from the starting page, then he/she made a step back (3) and eventually moved to the last known position (request 4). The step back causes the closure of the temporary trace associated to the agent (Trace 1 in the Figure), and the creation of a new temporary one with the same *Start* field (Trace 2). In this case the step back may have different interpretations: it could refer to a negative evaluation of the page contents but it could also indicate the fact that the user has found what he/she was searching for. An information that could be exploited to determine if the *Dest* field of the trace was interesting for the user is the time interval between request 2 and 3: for instance, given Δt_d a threshold indicating the minimum time required to reasonably inspect the content of a specific web page, if $timestamp(3) - timestamp(2) < \Delta t_d$ then Trace 1 could be ignored. However, the mere interval between the two requests is not a safe indicator of the fact that the page was actually viewed and considered interesting.

In fact, the time spent on a web page is also important in order to determine when a temporary trace must be closed. In fact, whenever a user does not issue requests for a certain time we could consider that his/her browsing activity has stopped, possibly because he/she is reading the page related to the *Dest* field of the trace associated to the related agent. In other words, every agent has a timer, set to the previously introduced threshold Δt_d, which is set when the agent is created and it is reset whenever it moves. The action associated to this timer specifies that its temporary trace becomes closed, and a new timer is set: the action associated to this second timer caused the disappearance of the agent from the system, and the storage of the related state.

The information generated by user agents, and in particular traces, can be used to influence the new pages that will be generated by the Web server, and more precisely by the SnipSnap based Content Management system. In fact the latter uses information stored in a database to compose the required web pages; agents store information related to closed traces into this database, and a specific dynamic user interface element exploits this information to propose links that are not included in the basic structure of the site that are considered interesting, according to the previous user's behaviour. The following section will more thoroughly discuss the application of this framework for web site adaptivity.

4   Web Site Adaptation

4.1   Proposed Approach

The adopted instrument for the dynamic generation of web pages based on the content of a database organizes the structure of pages in blocks. The implemented system provides a static header block, including relevant areas of the web site, a left column providing dynamic additional information, such as the current user position in the structure of the web site and relevant links, and a main central area in which the specific current content is shown in details. The area which is interested in the first experimentation of this approach to content adaptivity is included in the left column. It is aimed at showing a visitor emerging links, that are hyperlinks not included in the predefined structure of the site but are considered interesting according to the history of the related user. These emerging links have some kind of relationship with the previously introduced traces, which represent behaviours and movements of a user in a web site. The strategy which is adopted to select the most relevant traces to be presented to a given user in a given situation represents the behavior of an interface agent whose responsibility is the management of this adaptive sub-block of the user interface related to the web site. Figure 3 presents a screenshot of a sample adapted web page: the visitor is recognized and his/her movement are monitored by the Tracker. The lower part of the left column presents three links related to stored traces related to the same user.

A first element of this strategy is adopted when new users (or non authenticated ones) enter the site. In this case the user has no previous history (or it is not possible to correlate the user with his/her history), and the adopted strategy considers all stored traces, not considering the user which generated them. An additional information that is stored with traces is the number of times that the related trace was effectively selected and shown to a user and the number of times that the related link was effectively exploited by a user. This kind of information permits to obtain an indication of the success rate of the hyperlinks that were chosen by the interface agent, and can be exploited by this agent to select the traces to be shown in the adaptive block. Furthermore this success rate can be used by the web master to consider which traces should be considered as emerging links to be included in the predefined site structure. Summarizing, the interface agent, in order to select which traces must be proposed as emerging

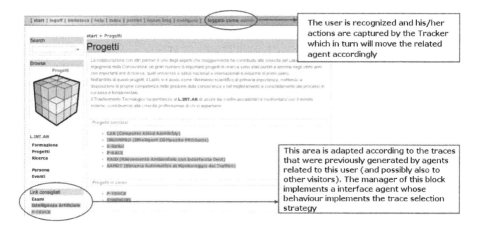

Fig. 3. A screenshot of a web page adapted according to gathered traces and interface agent selection strategy

links, considers two kinds of information: the occurrence of trace generation and the success rate of the traces that were proposed. When the interface agent has an indication of the user which issued the request, it may focus the selection activity to those traces that compose the history of user's activities in the web site, in a web customization framework. In fact traces include an indication of the agent which generated them, and in turn agents are related to registered users. As for the anonymous or new user case, also this strategy must consider both the occurrence of traces and their success rate. Moreover, in order to focus on a specific user's history but do not waste the chance to exploit other users' experiences, just two of the three available slots for emergent links are devoted to traces that were generated by that user and one is selected according to the strategy adopted for anonymous or new users.

These strategies for the exploitation of the gathered and stored traces, based on users' behaviours and movement in the web site environment, represent a very simple way of exploiting this kind of information without requiring an off-line analysis of the logs generated by the web server. The design, implementation and test of more complex strategies, for instanced based on details of the outcomes of emerging link proposals (e.g. which user effectively followed the suggested adaptive hyperlink) are object of future works.

4.2   Related Works

There are several approaches and relevant experiences in the area web site adaptation. The Avanti project [11] provides an automated customization of web site contents, basing on user modelling techniques and analysis of their behaviours. It also provided a specific attention to specific needs of elderly and partially disabled users. Footprints [3] instead provides a site optimization through the metaphor of site visitors leaving traces in their navigation. These signals accumulate in the environment, generating awareness information on the most frequently visited areas of the web site. No user profile is needed, as visitors are essentially provided this information which could represent an indicator of the most interesting pages to visit. The metaphor of the structure of the web site as an environment on which visitors move in their search for information is very similar to the one on which the proposed framework is based, but we also propose the exploitation of the gathered information on users' paths for user specific customization. Other approaches provide instead the generation of index pages [2], that are pages containing links to other pages covering a specific topic. These pages, resulting from an analysis of access logs aimed at finding clusters grouping together pages related to a topic, are proposed to web masters in a computer-assisted site optimization scheme.

A different approach provides the real-time generation of shortcut links [12], through a predictive model of web usage based on statistical techniques and the concept of expected saving of a shortcut, which considers both the probability that the generated link will be effectively used and the amount of effort saved (i.e. intermediate links to follow). In particular this framework is very similar to the one proposed here with reference to the aims of the overall system, but it incorporates a complex algorithm for off-line analysis of logs, while the proposed approach provides a light and dynamic generation of most probable useful links and the storage of these proposals and high level information on site usage for a possible further off-line analysis.

In the agent area, a relevant approach provides the adoption of information agents supporting users in their navigation [13], considering both his/her specific behaviour and the actions of other visitors and adopting multiple strategies for making recommendations (e.g. similarity, proximity, access frequency to specific documents).

5 Conclusions and Future Developments

This paper introduced a general framework providing the adoption of a web site as an environment on which agents related to visitors move and possibly interact. This approach allows to gather a more structured form of information on users' behaviours and activities in the web site. The concept of emerging links and traces have been introduced in order to support an application exploiting information on users' browsing history for sake of web pages adaptation. The introduced framework and the application to web site adaptation have been designed and implemented[5], exploiting a platform supporting systems based on the MMASS model. A campaign of tests aimed at evaluating the effectiveness of the adaptation approach, and also for sake of tuning the involved parameters (e.g. timings, number of presented possible emerging links) is under way, in the context of a collaboration with the Italian company Cosmovision Srl. This

---

[5] The adaptive web site is currently online at http://www.lintar.disco.unimib.it

evaluation will provide both forms for user interviews and the exploitation of the gathered information of the success rate of proposed adaptive hyperlinks.

The results of this evaluation might also lead to consider the modelling, design and implementation of more complex trace selection strategies, and thus a more complex behaviour for the interface agent. Moreover, the future application which will really exploit the full potential of the agent based architecture will provide the design and implementation of a context–aware form of interaction among visitors of the web site through the interaction mechanisms defined by the MMASS model (i.e. multicast diffusion of messages across the structure of the site and direct interaction among specific visitors of the same page).

References

1. Perkowitz, M., Etzioni, O.: Adaptive Web Sites: an AI Challenge. In: IJCAI (1). (1997) 16–23
2. Perkowitz, M., Etzioni, O.: Adaptive Web Sites. Communications of the ACM **43** (2000) 152–158
3. Wexelblat, A., Maes, P.: Footprints: History-Rich Tools for Information Foraging. In: Proceedings of the SIGCHI conference on Human factors in computing systems, ACM Press (1999) 270–277
4. Miller, R.C., Bharat, K.: Sphinx: a Framework for Creating Personal, Site-specific Web Crawlers. Computer Networks and ISDN Systems **30** (1998) 119–130
5. Weyns, D., Michel, F., Parunak, H.V.D., eds.: The First International Workshop on Environments for Multiagent Systems (E4MAS). Volume 3374 of LNAI, Springer (2004)
6. Weyns, D., Holvoet, T.: Model for Simultaneous Actions in Situated Multi-Agent Systems. In: First International German Conference on Multi-Agent System Technologies, MATES. Volume 2831 of LNCS, Springer (2003) 105–119
7. Mamei, M., Zambonelli, F., Leonardi, L.: Co-fields: Towards a Unifying Approach to the Engineering of Swarm Intelligent Systems. In: Engineering Societies in the Agents World III (ESAW2002). Volume 2577 of LNAI, Springer (2002) 68–81
8. Hadeli, K., Valckenaers, P., Zamfirescu, C., Brussel, H.V., Germain, B.S., Hoelvoet, T., Steegmans, E.: Self-organising in Multi-Agent Coordination and Control Using Stigmergy. In: Engineering Self-Organising Systems: Nature-Inspired Approaches to Software Engineering. Volume 2977 of LNCS, Springer (2004) 105–123
9. Bandini, S., Manzoni, S., Simone, C.: Dealing with Space in Multi–Agent Systems: a Model for Situated MAS. In: First International Joint Conference on Autonomous Agents and Multi-Agent Systems, ACM Press (2002) 1183–1190
10. Bandini, S., Manzoni, S., Vizzari, G.: Towards a Specification and Execution Environment for Simulations Based on MMASS: Managing at–a–distance Interaction. 17th European Meeting on Cybernetics and Systems Research (2004) 636–641
11. Fink, J., Kobsa, A., Nill, A.: User-oriented Adaptivity and Adaptability in the Avanti Project. Technical report, Microsoft Usability Group (1996)
12. Anderson, C.R., Domingos, P., Weld, D.S.: Adaptive Web Navigation for Wireless Devices. In: IJCAI. (2001) 879–884
13. Pazzani, M.J., Billsus, D.: Adaptive Web Site Agents. Autonomous Agents and Multi-Agent Systems **5** (2002) 205–218

An Operational Model for Mutual Awareness

Flavien Balbo[1,2], Julien Saunier[1], Suzanne Pinson[1], and Mahdi Zargayouna[1,2]

[1] LAMSADE, Université Paris-Dauphine,
Place du Maréchal de Lattre de Tassigny, Paris Cedex 16
[2] INRETS/GRETIA, 2, Avenue du Général Malleret-Joinville, F-94114 Arcueil
{balbo, pinson, saunier, zargayou}@lamsade.dauphine.fr

Abstract. Typical interaction models as addressed messages present several pitfalls. To overcome these limits, new interactional models close to the concept of mutual awareness have been proposed. These models enable the agents to share their interactions and to reason about them. However, the use of mutual awareness by these models is restrictive and presents several limits. To overcome them, we propose a generic and operational model for mutual awareness.

1 Introduction

Because of the sole use of dyadic interaction in cognitive MAS, a large part of potential interactions remain unexploited. Nevertheless, several recent works propose to use some kind of *mutual awareness*, such as *overhearing*, to deal with interaction. This is, for an agent, to be able to intercept messages which were not initially addressed to it. This paradigm enables agents to share their interaction and so to exploit them. In section 2, we describe what is called *mutual awareness*. In section 3, we propose EASI (Environment as Active Support of Interaction), a generic and operational model for mutual awareness.

2 Mutual Awareness

Interaction sharing is fundamental, as a big part of the solicitations in real-life situations come from other means than direct transmissions [3]. This fact has led simulation designers to simulate this means of communication [7]. In the context of teams of autonomous agents the coherence of the team increases significantly with the use of a protocol based on overhearing [5]. Overhearing has also been used in several works to monitor MASs, as in STEAM [4]. These three systems highlight the usefulness of the concept of overhearing, but their implementation using massive broadcast or subscription limits their usableness.

In order to limit the communication cost, channelled multicast [2] proposes a focused broadcast, by means of dedicated channels of communication where agents subscribe and/or emit. Nevertheless, two limits can be underlined: (1) the complexity of the system increases proportionally to the number of channels; (2) the sender still has to assume the emission of the messages to every agent.

M. Pěchouček, P. Petta, and L.Z. Varga (Eds.): CEEMAS 2005, LNAI 3690, pp. 531–534, 2005.
© Springer-Verlag Berlin Heidelberg 2005

However, we observe that proposing a solution for overhearing has also led to an improvement for the sender: it can choose to emit a message through a channel, which is the visible expression of the interests of the agents, instead of using addresses or capability (via middle-agents). This unified ability to emit and perceive via the accessible intentions of the agents is the major distinction we make between mutual awareness and overhearing – the latter only permitting the interception.

To facilitate its use in the multi-agent community, the mutual awareness paradigm must have a formal model. Tummolini [8] defines the concept of *Behavioral Implicit Communication* (BIC), within the framework of cooperative systems for task realization, as the set of every interaction that can be observed in an implicit way, i.e. information conveyed by actions or communications of the other agents. However, the properties that are required to fulfill BICs, like the ability for the agents to anticipate the effects of their own actions on the other agents, make this framework hardly useable. It needs very cooperative agents, that is why it is hard to model and implement in an heterogeneous and open system. Platon's model of overhearing [6] is the most generic to our knowledge, as it considers overhearing independently of the domain of the application. Nevertheless, their proposition has not already been implemented.

3   The EASI Model

As formal models can not be implemented directly, except in restricted domains, and as real applications are functionally limited by the use of inadequate technologies, there is a need for a more operational model. Our new communication model has to exhibit the following features: (1) The messages may be received by unpredicted agents. Therefore, it is not indiscreet listening, because private communications can be executed via other means of communication, more secure according to the needs. (2) The reception of the messages is not based on an explicit agreement of the sender. (3) The messages must not be broadcasted because it means that every agent has to process every messages, even the useless ones, and because it has a high cost in terms of pass band. (4) There is no subscription process, because it has a high message cost, and it limits the interactional autonomy of an agent. So, if it is not the agents which assure the message broadcast, we propose to use the environment as an active and intelligent entity which can send the right information to the right agent at the right time.

Mutual awareness is based on the sharing of interactions. To be efficient, this principle implies that agents share a common communication media. In the reactive agent community, the environment is already used as a common media of interaction. In the cognitive agent community, we have proposed the EASI model [1]. It enables cognitive agents to use the environment to exchange messages and, more precisely, it enables an agent to send messages to an other agent that is located by the environment and it enables agents to perceive every exchanged message. In our work, we consider that environment contains descriptions of

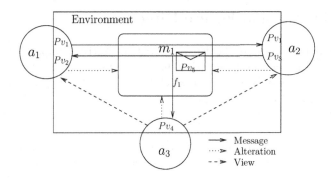

Fig. 1. Interaction for mutual awareness. The agents A1 and A2 exchange messages, and the second is intercepted by the agent A3. Each entity, agents and messages, has visible properties Pv_i. The message is broadcast via the set of filters f_i.

messages and agents. The interactional problem is to make possible for agents to use these descriptions to locate messages according to the environment state, that implies the matching between those properties and the needs of the agents.

We therefore propose to represent every component of the environment (e.g. the external properties of the environment itself as well as the agents and messages) as *entities*. Every entity has its *visible properties*, accessible via the environment, and the ability to put *filters* in the environment. These filters are logical expressions on properties, and determines, when a message is added to the environment, whether the agent is interested in it, in which case it will receive it, or not. In our EASI model, we have added this notation to formalize the knowledge about the description of interaction components (messages and agents). Because it enables to represent the agents, it makes possible for agents to create their interactional context as a set of filters. Each agent description is updated by the agent itself, modifying dynamically the value of its visible properties.

In Fig. 1, we represent graphically our model. The arrows that we called *alteration* show the agent capability to add, modify or remove its filters, and thus the way the environment will dynamically handle future messages. The arrows we called *view* show the capability of the agents to get the properties of the other entities, and so to refine their knowledge of the world by means of the environment. The new distribution of the messaging task via the environment permits us to extend the classical interactions to a property-based communication.

This model has been integrated in three different contexts. In a diagnosis transportation system, mutual awareness permits to reduce communication costs and improve faults detection thanks to the interception of every interesting message by the agents. In an agent server for a traveler information system, mutual awareness permits to add flexibility and personalization to the service, the attention of the agents headed toward its itinerary. Finally, in a classical multiagent platform, we have improved the interactions capabilities of the agent to the mutual awareness full extent, thus permitting its use in various domains.

4   Conclusions and Future Directions

We have shortly presented the Environment as Active Support of Interaction model, a new Interaction Model that has some useful characteristics, like the property-based communication and which helps to deal with the increasing complexity of interactional needs in MAS.

The distribution of the interaction between the agents and the environment leads to a new system design, which allows to decrease communication costs. The matching of the properties of the agents with those of the messages permits each agent to perceive all and only the interactions relevant to it.

In the near future some topics should be explored, one of them is the extension of our model to integrate the discovery and management of available interactions in the environment. Additional objectives are considered, such as to add multiple communication environments or to add heterogeneous agents.

References

1. Balbo, F., Pinson, S.: Toward a Multi-Agent Modelling Approach for Urban Public Transportation Systems. Omicini A., Petta P. et Tolksdorf R. (eds), Engineering Societies in the Agent World II, LNAI **2203**, Springer Verlag (2001) 160–174
2. Busetta, P., Don, A., Nori, M.: Channeled Multicast for group communications. Proceedings of the first international joint conference on Autonomous Agents and MultiAgent Systems AAMAS (2002) 1280–1287
3. Dugdale, J., Pavard, J., Soubie, B.: A Pragmatic Development of a Computer Simulation of an emergency Call Center. Designing Cooperative System, Frontiers in Artificial Intelligence and Applications, Rose Dieng et al, IOS Press' (2000)
4. Kaminka, G., Pynadath, C., Tambe, M.: Monitoring teams by overhearing: A mutliagent plan-recognition approach. Journal of Artificial Intelligence Research vol. **17** (2002) 83–135
5. Legras, F. Tessier, C.: Lotto: Group formation by overhearing in large teams. Proceedings of AAMAS, Melbourne Australia, Springer Verlag (2003) 425–432
6. Platon, E., Sabouret, N. Honiden,S.: T-compound: An Agent-Specific Design Pattern and its environment. Proceeding of the 3rd international workshop on Agent Oriented Methodologies at OOPSLA (2004) 63–74
7. Traum, D., Rickel, J.: Embodied agents for multi-party dialogue in immersive virtual worlds. Proceedings of the first international joint conference on Autonomous agents and multiagent systems, part 2 (2002) 766–773
8. Tummolini, L., Castelfranchi, C., Ricci, A., Viroli, M. Omicini, A.: "Exhibitionists" and "voyeurs" do it better: A shared environment approach for flexible coordination with tacit messages. Proceedings of Workshop on Environments for Multi-Agent Systems (E4MAS) LNAI **3374** Springer Verlag (2004) 215–231

Chomsky: A Content Language Translation Agent

António Lopes and Luís Botelho

"We, the Body and the Mind" Research Group, ADETTI - ISCTE,
Avenida das Forças Armadas, Edifício ISCTE,
1600-082 Lisboa, Portugal
{antonio.lopes, luis.botelho}@we-b-mind.org

Abstract. This paper describes Chomsky, a content language translation agent. This agent provides a service, which first translates the content expression from its original language into an abstract logic language (ALL). Then, the resulting ALL expression is translated to the desired target language. ALL has been designed as a superset of most known content languages to avoid loosing expressiveness during translation. For more than three supported languages, using an intermediate language approach involves fewer translators than a pair wise approach. Currently, Chomsky supports FIPA-SL, KIF, and Prolog Content Language. In one mode of operation, Chomsky returns the result of the translation request to the client agent. In the other mode, Chomsky receives a message from the intended sender whose content is expressed in language L1, it translates the content to the content language used by the intended receiver (L2), and it sends the message with the L2 content to the intended receiver.

1 Introduction

In open agent societies of heterogeneous agents it is likely to have agents using different languages to express the contents of their messages. Even if agents comply with current standardization specs [1], it is not mandatory to use a particular content language.

We have implemented Chomsky, an agent that translates content expressions from their original language into other desired content languages, enabling interoperability between heterogeneous agents. Currently, Chomsky does not require agent-level autonomy or intelligence. However, Chomsky was built as an agent (it communicates in FIPA-ACL) to facilitate its use by other agents and to facilitate its future sophistication to handle problems requiring more autonomy and intelligence.

This is a short version of the paper "Chomsky: a Content Language Translation Agent" which can be found in http://www.we-b-mind.org/publications/alopes-chomsky-ceemas05-final.pdf. More detailed explanations, examples, an overview of the literature and complete references are given in the larger version of the paper.

Section 2 presents the content language translation process and it describes Chomsky, the content language translation agent. In section 3, we conclude and present guidelines for future work.

M. Pěchouček, P. Petta, and L.Z. Varga (Eds.): CEEMAS 2005, LNAI 3690, pp. 535–538, 2005.
© Springer-Verlag Berlin Heidelberg 2005

2 Content Language Translation

This section describes the proposed content language translation process, it describes Chomsky, the agent providing the translation service, and it presents an example of an interaction with Chomsky. Chomsky is a working agent publicly available. For more information on the content language translation service as well as information on the agent can be found at http://clts.we-b-mind.org/

2.1 Translation Process and Supported Languages

The approach used in the development of the translation service was to create an internal content language to which all the object languages could be translated, and from which all the target languages could be generated. In our approach, any supported language can be object or target language.

In order to be possible to translate between any of the supported languages, it was decided that the internal content language should be a superset of the supported content languages. Notice that it is only necessary to have the adequate expressiveness. Inference mechanisms are not necessary since the internal content language is used only as an internal representation format. Certainly, this approach does not solve problems that are impossible to solve. The translation of expressions of a more expressive language into expressions of a less expressive language is not always possible. An alternative approach would be to create translators for each pair of object/target content languages. However, our approach requires only $2 \times N$ translators, in which N is the number of supported languages. The mentioned alternative requires $N!$ translators. Therefore, our approach is better when the number of supported languages is greater than 3.

Currently, the supported content languages are FIPA-SL [1], KIF [2] and PCL [3] (Prolog Content Language), each of which can be either an object or a target language. The internal content language is called ALL (Abstract Logic Language) [4]. FIPA-SL has been defined and used by FIPA to express the semantics of FIPA ACL. FIPA SL is a general-purpose representation formalism suitable for a number of different domains. SL is a quantified multi-modal logic with several referential (iota, any, all) and action (feasible, done) operators. Also, SL contains modal operators for beliefs, uncertain beliefs, persistent goals, and intentions.

The KIF parser used in the service is based on an extension of the KIF draft proposed to the American National Standards. However, not all of its features were covered by our current parser.

The PCL parser is based on the PCL draft definition proposed by the *"We, the Body and the Mind"* Research Group of ADETTI.

ALL is an abstract content language defined as a superset of the content languages FIPA-SL, KIF, and PCL. This way we ensure that it is possible to translate any content expression from any of these languages to ALL. Since FIPA-SL includes all the features of the two other languages, ALL closely mirrors SL. The addition of new languages may raise the need to further extend the expressive power of ALL. However, this would not interfere with the currently developed translators, since the added constructs would not be involved in the current translation process. ALL complete specification, including its abstract grammar, its class model, and a concrete S-Expression syntax is described in the longer paper.

2.2 Chomsky, the Agent

The initial idea was the development of a content language translation library that each agent in the network could integrate in its own program as a new component or package. However, not all the agents in an open agent society are built using the same implementation technology, therefore the library would have to be built for all implementation technologies used to create agents. Hence, the creation of a content language translation service deployed by an agent became the best solution.

Chomsky uses the translation process explained in section 2.1 and its interaction is governed by the FIPA request protocol, which is initiated by the reception of a FIPA-Request message. Chomsky can use any of the supported content languages. Chomsky provides two language translation services, corresponding to two operation modes: translator mode, and interpreter mode. In the translator mode, Chomsky translates received content expressions and sends them back to its client agents. In the interpreter mode, Chomsky acts as a gateway between two clients, translating the contents of messages from one of its clients and sending the resulting message to the other client.

The action that performs the translation, in the translation mode, is "*translate*". Its arguments are the object content language, the target content language, and the content expression to be translated. An example of this interaction is described in section 2.3. The action that performs the translation and forwards the result, in the interpreter mode, is "*forward_with_translated_content*". Its arguments are the *object content language*, the *target content language*, the *message to be translated and sent* and the *intended receiver* of the message.

Chomsky was implemented in JAVA, using the JADE agent platform, and some agent tools previously created by our research group. The parsers used in the translation process were implemented using JAVA Cup and JAVA Lex.

2.3 Example of Use

In this section we present the conversation in which the client agent (Dummy) requests Chomsky to translate a specific message from FIPA-SL to KIF (see Fig.1). According to the FIPA-Request interaction protocol [1], Chomsky sends a FIPA-agree message indicating that it agrees to perform the translation or a FIPA-refuse message indicating the reason for refusing to perform the translation.

```
(REQUEST
 :sender (agent-identifier :name dummy@somewhere)
 :receiver (set (agent-identifier
          :name chomsky@elsewhere))
 :content "((action (agent-identifier
            :name chomsky@elsewhere)
          (translate FIPA-SL KIF
            \"((all ?x (instance ?x Car)))\")))"
 :language FIPA-SL)
```

Fig. 1. Message requesting Chomsky to translate a message's content from FIPA-SL to KIF

In the case that Chomsky agrees to perform the translation, it sends a FIPA-Inform message containing the result of the translation to the Dummy agent.

3 Conclusions and Future Work

We presented Chomsky, a content language translation agent, performing a simple syntactic translation between any of the content languages FIPA-SL, KIF and PCL.

The next steps for future work will be to overcome some limitations of current parsers, to add support for additional content languages (e.g., FIPA-RDF), and to consider a more intensive use of semantics in the translation process, by considering the use of language ontologies.

Acknowledgments

The research described in this paper was partly supported by the EU project Agent-cities.RTD, reference IST-2000-28385. The opinions expressed in this paper are those of the authors and are not necessarily those of the Agentcities.RTD partners. We thank Nelson Antunes and Mohmed Ebrahim for having implemented part of the agent.

References

1. Foundation for Intelligent Physical Agents, 2002, "FIPA Specifications Grouped by Category", (http://www.fipa.org/repository /bysubject.html).
2. National Committee for Information Technology Standards, 1998, "Knowledge Interchange Format: Draft proposed American National Standards". *Technical Report* NCITS.T2/98-004, (http://logic.stanford.edu/kif/dpans.html).
3. "We, the Body and the Mind" Research Group of ADETTI, 2003, "Prolog Content Language Specification", (http://www.we-b-mind.org/clts/files/pcl.doc).
4. "We, the Body and the Mind" Research Group of ADETTI, 2003, "Abstract Logic Language Specification", (http://www.we-b-mind.org/clts/files/all.doc).

Roles and Hierarchy in Multi-agent Organizations

Emmanuel Adam and René Mandiau

LAMIH UMR CNRS 8530, University of Valenciennes,
Le Mont Houy, France, 59313 Valenciennes Cedex 9
{emmanuel.adam, rene.mandiau}@univ-valenciennes.fr

Abstract. Holonic Multi-Agent organisations are particular pyramidal organisations where agents of a layer (having the same coordinator) are able to communicate and to negotiate directly between them. Holonic agents are generally structured by services (for examples: to search information, to interact with the user). Some holonic agents, distributed in the system, can have same roles without being in a same layer. However, it is essential to interact with agents according to theirs roles: most of multi-agent methods and platforms are based on the roles management. In order to beneficiate of the two advantages which are the control allowed by the holonic architecture and the roles management, we propose a particular holonic architecture based on the workings mechanisms of human organisations. We have implemented this architecture by offering a role management capacity to a hierarchical multi-agent platform.

1 Introduction

Our researches aim at integrating multiagent organization into human organization, which are more and more based on data exchanges, in order to help actor these system to manage data, to communicate and cooperate between them. Admittedly, tools for aid in co-operative work have already been suggested, some with success, but they do not tackle the overall organization.

So, in order to take into account the human organization and the human factors, such as the human cooperation or even the human-machine co-operation, we have previously developed a method (AMOMCASYS, meaning the Adaptable Modelling Method for Complex Administrative Systems) that has helped us to design and to set-up some information multi-agent systems (IMAS). We have designed the different IMAS following a holonic architecture, and the resulting architecture is quite similar to architectures generally used to build the IMAS. Of course our architecture is not limited to IMAS design and is able to be used in other context (we have started some application in the area of house automation, intelligent vehicles).

In order to design an IMAS, we use both notion of role and hierarchy, and we propose the use of role managers, acting like Human Resources Agent in the human organisation (we call them HRA for Holonic Resource Agents). We have developed some functionalities on a platform dedicated to hierarchical multi-agent systems, that allows us to design and deploy our MAS by implementing the roles only and by describing the positions of the agents in a XML file.

This paper describes firstly the underlying concept of our works, which is the holonic concept; and then some details about the build of our platform.

M. Pěchouček, P. Petta, and L.Z. Varga (Eds.): CEEMAS 2005, LNAI 3690, pp. 539–542, 2005.
© Springer-Verlag Berlin Heidelberg 2005

2   Holonic Multi-agent Platform

We use holonic principles: in order to understand the workings mechanisms of the human organizations, in which we plan to set up information multi-agent systems; and to design the multi-agents organizations.

Agents of holonic system are organized following levels of responsibility. So, a holonic multi-agent system has a hierarchical structure where each agent is responsible of a holonic multi-agent sub-system.

We have used the social rules defined in the holonic concept in order to simplify and to accelerate the design of a multi-agent society (in the [1] sense), indeed, they provide a framework to build a fixed multi-agent society (which does not imply rigidity).

Applications of holonic MAS lead us to take into account the roles more explicitly. So our approach uses both the notion of role and notion of hierarchy in a same multi-agent system. Indeed, generally, like in the propositions of [2][3], the roles define links between agents; the interactions between agents depend of the roles. In our proposition, the interactions are defined by our MAS architecture. A holonic agent communicates with its coordinator, its neighbours (having the same coordinator) and its assistants, according to theirs roles or not.

We defined each agent by its name, its location, its acquaintances, its knowledge/or beliefs (sets of data relative to the environment, the acquaintances and the agent itself) and its role/s. Each role is defined by some knowledge (sets of resources that are necessary to play the role), and some behaviours (or skills). Finally each behaviour is composed of a set of methods that describe the interactions with the knowledge and with the other agents.

For example, we can define a seller role composed of an inventory management behaviour and a financial behaviour. The inventory management behaviour contains, for instance, the procedures 'inventory control', 'products order'. The financial behaviour contains procedures as the 'account management', 'price management'.

The buyer role could be composed of a call for proposals behaviour, which contains the procedures 'send proposals', 'wait responses', 'choose best proposal', ...

Each agent of the MAS is not limited to one role. So, we can find in the MAS, several seller agents, buyer agents and seller-buyer agents. Likewise, the behaviours are not used only in one role but can be used in other roles.

We have defined notion of essential behaviour and secondary behaviour for a role. Indeed, agents have to be able to modify the behaviours associated to their roles (by receiving a new version of these ones from the user or others agents for example, or by deleting one to free resources). However, an agent that deletes an essential behaviour of a role must be removed from the list of agents that play this role in the MAS. In our example, a secondary behaviour could be a complex display of the stock for the inventory agent, behaviour that could be updated or remove in run time.

Our architecture can be summarized by the following notation:

```
MAS = {role*, agent*}
agent = {name, location, coordinator:agent, assistant:agent*, knowledge*, role*}
role = {name, knowledge, essentialBehaviour:behaviour*, secondaryBehaviour:behaviour*}
behaviour = {name, attribute*, procedure*}
knowledge = {agentKnowledge|environmentalKnowledge|socialKnowledge}
```

To manage agents and roles of the system, we propose the use of a roles manager: the agent, which plays this role (called HRA for Holonic Resources Agent), owns the roles list, the tasks list linked to the roles, and the names of the agents (and their roles) that compose the multi-agent organization. In our architecture, we give this role to an agent located at the top of the system. Relatively to the FIPA multiagent platform architecture, this agent can be considered as an extended Directory Facilitator agent.

Each agent that appears in the multi-agent organization informs the RMA on its name, its location and on the roles that it wishes to play. If the RMA knows the roles, it sends it the behaviours linked to the requested roles and record the agent and its characteristics in its knowledge.

Each agent can modify its own behaviours (if they are not essential behaviours), and thus can have personal behaviours although it has same roles than other agents of the MAS. However, when a role is modified in a same way in a sufficient number of agents (number defined by a threshold relative to the number of agents playing the role in the whole organization), the role description is updated in the knowledge of the roles manager. Each agent, which asks for a role, receives the last version of this one.

We defined also the "*holonic role*" that describes the tasks relative to the management of the holonic acquaintances and the communication with them. Each agent of our organization owns this holonic role. It allows them to send messages to their acquaintances (the coordinator, the neighbours, the assistants) and the set of holonic agents whose they are the direct or indirect coordinators. The messages can be addressed to acquaintances having particular roles.

As the HRA is essential in our system, we have developed replication mechanisms for it, and we use in fact a hierarchy of sub-HRA, that are each dedicated to the roles management of an agents layer. These sub-HRA are not replicated but recreated by the main HRA if needed. These developments are currently under tests.

We do not have yet proposed particular communication protocols, all the "classical" protocols can be used, but we plan to propose adaptations of existing protocols to respect the holonic concepts.

The first prototype of this platform has been developed using the MAGIQUE [4] multi-agent platform and we have built an application that allows us to deploy into a network a holonic multi-agent system from its description (by a XML file).

3   Holonic Multi-agent Platform Implementation

We generally use the MAGIQUE [4] platform to build our prototypes. This platform provides libraries dedicated to hierarchical multi-agent systems development: a MAGIQUE agent is an empty shell having only communication capacities (with its supervisor and its team (agents under it)); an agent skill is a Java class, composed of functions or sub-processes; messages exchanged between agents consist in calls to functions or to sub-processes that are located in the skills[1].

---

[1] If a request cannot be satisfied, because the agent does not know how to answer (the function asked is not present in its skills), it is stored by the platform until the agent learns to answer to it.

In order to generate holonic multi-agent systems, we have defined two skills:

- HolonicOrganizationSkill, associated to the highest multi-agent organization supervisor. It owns the roles list, the skills list linked to the roles, and the names and the roles of the agents that compose the multi-agent organization.
- HolonSkill, linked to each agent. It defines the attribution of the neighbours and assistants, and the role oriented communication processes. A holonic agent is able to send a message to its neighbours or assistants having a particular role.

We have built an application that allows us to deploy into a network a holonic multi-agent system from an XML file that describes it. This XML file describes the roles, the agents, theirs hierarchic relations and the methods of the skills, associated to the roles linked to the agents, which are to be launched at the start of the multi-agent organization.

MAGIQUE platform allows us to easily create hierarchical multi-agent systems, but it is not yet FIPA compliant. We are currently developing our holonic platform as an extension to JADE [5], in order to have a FIPA compliant multi-agent platform. We hope that this will facilitate exchanges with MAS built on others FIPA compliant platform.

4   Conclusion

Our works use the holonic concept to understand and analyse human organizations and design multi-agent system particularly adapted to the studied human organizations. From this work, we propose a multi-agent organization using both notion of role and notion of hierarchy. The tools that we use to automatically deploy such an organization allow us to focus and to develop only on the role played by the agents and avoid us to have to develop the global organization. This platform allowed us to develop several IMAS, but need to be improved. So, currently we "consolidate" our platform by replication mechanisms and regeneration of essential agents.

References

1. Mandiau, R., Le Strugeon E. & Agimont G. Study of the influence of organizational structure on the efficiency of a multi-agent system. Networking and Information Systems Journal, 2(2) (1999) 153-179.
2. Mathieu, P., Routier, J-C., Secq, Y. RIO: Roles, Interactions and Organizations. CEEMAS 2003: Multi-Agent Systems and Applications III, Lecture Notes in Artificial Intelligence 2691. (2003)
3. Kendall, E. A. Role modeling for agent system analysis, design, and implementation. In First International Symposium on Agent Systems and Applications (ASA'99), Third International Symposium on Mobile Agents (MA'99), (1999).
4. Mathieu, P., Routier, J-C., Secq, Y. Dynamic skills learning: a support to agent evolution. Proceedings of AISB'01, York. ISBN 1 902956 17 0. (2001) 25-32.
5. Bellifemine F., Caire G., Poggi A., Rimassa G., "JADE - A White Paper", Sept. 2003,http://jade.tilab.com/papers/WhitePaperJADEEXP.pdf

Semantic and Virtual Agents Model in Adaptive Middleware Architecture for Smart Vehicle Space

Qing Wu and Zhaohui Wu

College of Computer Science, Zhejiang University,
Hangzhou, Zhejiang, China 310027
{wwwsin, wzh}@zju.edu.cn

Abstract. With the increasing prevalence of ubiquitous computing, various resources are constrained and run-time context is diverse, which poses many challenges in computer technologies. It specially requires software middleware architecture more adaptive to the changes in computing environments. This paper presents a semantic and virtual agents model for flexible structure-level and run-time adaptation. In addition, semantic interface protocol is put forward to implement multi-agent adaptation. We have applied this model to adaptive middleware and developed mobile music program. A large number of experiments are made to test the performance and reliability of our adaptive mechanism. The result shows our model and method are available and reliable for agent-level adaptation based on semantic information.

1 Introduction

In ubiquitous computing environments, multi-agent architectures and methodologies have been introduced for adaptive communication and cooperation [1,2]. The physical world and information space are integrated seamlessly and naturally. However, this environments demand plenty of computation resources for functional requests and performance requirements. In addition, changes of the heterogeneous context including people, smart devices, and environments are ubiquitous and pervasive. Therefore, it results in many problems in software middleware design and development technologies.

To deal with this complex dynamic environment, several solutions based on agent-level adaptation have been proposed [3,4,5,6]. Nevertheless, we focus on the agent model that enables flexible structure-level and run-time adaptation based on semantic information to meet the different computing environments and variant run-time context. This paper presents the SVA (*Semantic and Virtual Agent*) model and SIP (*Semantic Interface Protocol*) in adaptive middleware design and implementation in smart vehicle space for ubiquitous computing.

2 Semantic and Virtual Agents

With multi-agent technologies, we have developed ScudWare [7] platform, which is an adaptive middleware aiming at context-aware and adaptive aspects, applying to

M. Pĕchouček, P. Petta, and L.Z. Varga (Eds.): CEEMAS 2005, LNAI 3690, pp. 543–546, 2005.

mobile music program in smart vehicle space [8]. Furthermore, we have proposed SVA model and SIP including *sva discovery, join, lease,* and *self-updating* protocols for agent-level adaptation. One sva is a group of services, defined as an autonomous entity based on meta objects [8] and distributed components. SIP prescribes the principles of svas' communication. Next, we give following formal definitions.

Definition 1. *SVA=(CP, TASK, MO, KB, TB, SQ $\cup$ RQ). CP* is a set of svas' capabilities, defined as $CP=\{cp_1, cp_2, cp_3,..., cp_n\}$. cp_i is one minimal unit of sva's capability. Specially stated, each *sva* has abilities to change its cp_i according to the different context. $\Delta CP = OP(CP, CONTEXT)$ is the change of one sva's capability. $OP = \{append, modify, delete, find\}$ is a set of svas' operations. *CONTEXT* is a set of run-time environment information. *MO* is a set of meta objects. Each sva consists of some meta objects, defined as $\forall sva \in SVA \rightarrow \bigcup \exists mo_i \in MO$. *KB* is a knowledge base of *SVA*, defined as $KB=\{kb_1, kb_2, kb_3, ... , kb_n\}$. Each *kb* is a set of rules, defined as $kb = \bigcup rule(i)|_{i=1,...,n}$, and $rule = \bigcup (m_i, interface(m_i), key, lifetime, spi)|_{i=1,...,n}$, where m_i is a set of recently cooperating missions. Importantly, rules are dynamic and adaptive, self-updating when some relevant events come. *TB* is a trust policy base, defined as $TB = \bigcup (sva_i, TM(sva_i))|_{i=1,...,n}$, which includes trust security rules for cooperation of svas. $TM(x)$ is a trust evaluation function, defined as $TM(x)=(trustvalue, priority, prestige, history)$. *RQ* and *SQ* are two sets of message processing query, defined as $RQ = \bigcup Msg, SQ = \bigcup Msg$ and $Msg=\{req, accept, refuse,..., msg\}$, which are responsible for receiving and sending messages separately.

Definition 2. In run-time, one application maps to a set of missions. We define a mission set $M=\{m_1, m_2, m_3, ... , m_n\}$. To fulfill m_i, different svas cooperates, defined as $\forall m \in M \rightarrow \bigcup \exists sva_i, sva_j \in SVA \cdot R(sva_i.cp_x, sva_j.cp_y, c)|_{1<i,j<Q, 1<x,y<P}$. *P* is the max num of svas' capabilities and *Q* is the max num of svas. The prediction $R(a, b, c)$ is a cooperation relationship between *a* and *b* in terms of rule *c*.

Definition 3. *sva discovery protocol* is for one *sva* to find another *sva* without one fixed sva naming service. There are two discovery models: (a) peer-to-peer and (b) multicast model. If sav_1 demands capability c_1 and knows that sva_2 has c_1, sva_1 will use (a) model, sending request message to sva_2 for direct communication. On the other hand, if sva_1 does not know who has c_1, sva_1 will take (b) model. First, sva_1 send multicast request message *m* to other svas. Then if sva_n has c_1 and receives *m*, sav_n will send reply message to sva_1 after sva_1 is authentic to sav_n. Lastly, they begin to cooperate trustfully.

Definition 4. *sva join protocol* is for one *sva* to take part in one *sva* community. For example, there is one sva community sc_1, consisting of sva_4, sva_6, sva_8, where they cooperate directly, and trusty. If sva_2 comes and wants to attend sc_1, it will firstly get authentications from all members of sc_1, then it can act as one element of sc_1. *sva join protocol* also includes the rule of sva departs from one sva community.

Definition 5. *sva lease protocol* defines the rules of time and space principles in svas' cooperation. For example, if sva_1 requires sva_2's capability c_n and is authenticated to sva_2, sva_1 and sva_2 will negotiate about the usage restrictions of c_n. Let *time=10* and *space=Domain A*, which means sva_1 can use c_n for *10 seconds* and just *in Domain A*. If sva_1 want to continue using c_n after time expires, sva_1 will relet c_n with sva_2.

Definition 6. *sva self-update protocol* defines the rules of svas KB and CP updating. For instance, if sva_1 requires capability c_n to get one system parameter, sva_1 finds sva_2 has c_n based on its KB. Then sva_1 sends request message to sva_2. If sva_2 still has c_n currently, they will cooperate. However, if sva_2 has not c_n now, sva_2 will search other svas according to its KB and update this KB at the same time. This process will not stop until one sva has c_n or no one has. Specially, in one sva's lifecycle, it can acquire new knowledge from others. In addition, svas can obtain new capabilities and update its capability repository.

3 Experiments and Evaluations

To evaluate our method, we have made some preliminary experiments using the semantic and virtual agents model to develop the Mobile Music program. We have disposed many svas, which are distributed in smart vehicle space and interact with request-and-reply process. Because the context of this application is diverse, *SIP* set is used for better adaptation and efficiency. Our experiments are tested on ScudWare middleware platform. We used some PDAs (iPAQ) connected to the PC via the wireless LAN using 802.11b protocol to evaluate our model.

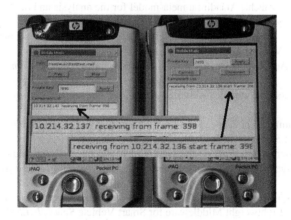

Fig. 1. One Screen Shot of Mobile Music Program

We placed many svas to PDAs and PCs randomly. The functions of these svas consist of (1) *acquiring the music source*, (2) *transmitting the music*, and (3) *playing the music*. As figure 1 shows: at first, sva_1 on the left PDA is playing the music with *stereo tune* and the current frame is No 398. If the run-time context changes (e.g. network bandwidth is not enough), the system then stops sva_1. Next, its brother sva_2 on the next PDA (right one) is discovered and sva_2 will start and play from No. 398 frame with *mono tune*. Therefore, the system can continue executing successfully without more delays and provide comparative satisfaction for users in terms of *SIP*.

4 Conclusions and Future Work

Multi-agent based adaptive method is playing a more important role in ubiquitous computing. This paper firstly analyzes the problems caused by dynamic characters of ubiquitous computing. Then we present a semantic and virtual agents model, considering both design-time aspects and run-time issues. Furthermore, semantic interface protocol set is proposed to implement *sva*'s adaptive mechanism. Next, we have made a large number of simulations to test SVA model. The experiment results show our method has efficiency and flexibility.

Our future work is to improve the adaptive agent model including the related algorithms. In addition, we will take other adaptive agent methods to realize more flexibility and reliability for ScudWare middleware design.

Acknowledgments

This research was supported by 863 National High Technology Program under Grant No. 2003AA1Z2080, 2003AA1Z2140 and 2002AA1Z2308.

References

1. J. Ferber, O. Gutknecht, Alaadin: a meta-model for the analysis and design of organizations in multi-agent systems. *ICMAS'98* (1998), 128-135
2. M. Wooldridge, N. Jennings, D. Kinny, The methodology Gaia for agent-oriented analysis and design. *AI*, Volume 10, No 2, (1999), 1-27
3. K. M. Carley, Adaptive organizations and emergent forms. *Organization Science*, V2, No 3, (1998)
4. J. Odell. Agents and complex systems. *Journal of Object Technology*, Volume 1, No 2, (2002),35-45
5. Zahia Guessoum, Mikal Ziane, Nora Faci, Monitoring and Organizational-level Adaptation of Multi-Agent Systems. *AAMAS'04*, (2004), 514-520
6. Victor R. Lesser. Reflections on the Nature of Multi-Agent Coordination and Its Implications for an Agent Architecture. *Autonomous Agents and Multi-Agent Systems'98* (1998), 89-111
7. Zhaohui Wu, Qing Wu, Jie Sun, Zhigang Gao, Bin Wu, Mingde Zhao, ScudWare: A Context-aware and Lightweight Middleware for Smart Vehicle Space. *ICESS'04*, (2004)
8. Qing Wu, Zhaohui Wu, Bin Wu, Zhou Jiang, Semantic and Adaptive Middleware for Data management in Smart Vehicle Space. *WAIM'04*, (2004) 107-116

Towards an Authority Sharing
Based on the Viewpoint Action Model

Abdenour Bouzouane

Université du Québec à Chicoutimi, Dép. Informatique et Mathématique,
555, blvd. Université, Chicoutimi (Québec), G7H2B1, Canada
abdenour_bouzouane@uqac.ca

Abstract. Within the human in the loop context, the realization of a task will not only be the accomplishment of human operator or the autonomous agent acting on his behalf, but rather of both entities, and in which they will have the same possibilities to propose, suspend, and refuse each other. However, this cohabitation is both rich and complex; owing to the fact that the human and the agent are bound to not only agree on the various levels of realization of the task, but also to manage the autonomy -*who controls who*-. The issue then is to work out a model of an agent authority sharing, for the purpose of safely transferring decision-making control to the human user and vice versa?

1   Introduction

The emergence of applications of the so-called new generation such as smarthomes, uninhabited aerial vehicles, etc, has gradually moved the autonomy's border of an agent, but the human remains in the loop. Within this forward-looking context, the realization of a task will not only be the work of the human or the agent, but also of the set within which they will have the same possibilities to propose, suspend, and refuse each other [4], [7]. However, this hybrid cohabitation feature is both rich and complex, owing to the fact that the human and the agent are bound not only to agree on the various levels of realization of the task, but also to manage the paradoxical problem of agent autonomy [5]. On the one hand, the agent autonomy is useful but risky because of misunderstanding, disagreements, and conflicts. On the other hand, the control of the decision-making by the human operator is also risky because he is not infallible. The problem is that the human can be submerged by the massive arrival of information inherent to the complex systems. Therefore, if one desires to maintain this autonomy property, its adjustment may provide a solution to this dilemma.

Scerri et al [11] view the adjustment of autonomy as determining whether and when transfer of decision-making control should occur, given an uncertain response of the human. Their approach is based on the markovian theory of the decision processes which they use to transform this problem into a choice of transfer-control strategy whose expected utility is the highest. This analytical approach is reductionistic in the sense that the world does not evolve in a finished number of states and apart from economic applications, the utility measurement can be subjective and difficult to

M. Pěchouček, P. Petta, and L.Z. Varga (Eds.): CEEMAS 2005, LNAI 3690, pp. 547–550, 2005.
© Springer-Verlag Berlin Heidelberg 2005

estimate. Conversely, the cognitive approach of Castelfranchi and Falcone [6], [8] considers the adjustment of autonomy according to the adjustment of the delegation which is a mental act that defines the autonomy level space. This solution which uses the trust measurement for delegation will be difficult to make operational because of the complexity of the trust analytical formulas. Moreover, there is no justification for the way the degrees of trust associated with the various beliefs are revised.

Our contribution is to rather consider the adjustment of autonomy as a non analytical process of sharing authority that can be reduced to bidirectional transfer-control of decision-making, by the interchangeability of the actions in a common task [3]. In this context, the user and his agent commutate from operating mode of control to the observer mode according to the convergence of their intentions. An agent in an observation mode is in a passive state, prohibited from making any decisions, but continues to construct viewpoints that synthesize the task process required for future activation. A viewpoint is a recognition function of actions observed in an environment where the result is an ontology of actions respecting a structure of lattice. For a given state of the world, if a viewpoint admits a nonempty lower bound, then the actions are interchangeable. Therefore, there is a possibility of relinquishing control to the entity in observation mode. We propose a formal approach of the actions classification permitting a safety transfer of control. Our approach follows the lines of the Description Logic (DL) [1] that, in our view, fits better to this problem of sharing authority.

2 A Viewpoint Action Model

An action a over a set of world states $W = \{w, s, e, ...,\}$ is a binary relation $a \subseteq W \times W$ such that $\langle w, e \rangle \in a$ if and only if $a(w) = \{e \mid \langle w, e \rangle \in W \times W \}$ where w and e are respectively the current and next states. The actions operate on the assertions formulas which are particular cases of first order logical formulas [2]. If the conceptual expressions and the assertions of the DL are used to describe facts about a state of the world, they can be satisfiable or unsatisfiable according to this state. Therefore, the states of the world can correspond to semantic structures. Let $w = \langle Dom(w), (.)^{I_w} \rangle$ a semantic structure such that $Dom(w)$ is the domain of interpretation, i.e., the non-empty set of objects called individuals that exist in the world when the world is in that state w at given time. The function $(.)^{I_w}$, referred to as interpretation function associated with w, assigns to each concept symbol, C, a subset of the domain $Dom(w)$, i.e., $C^{I_w} \subseteq Dom(w)$, and to each role a subset of the domain $Dom(w) \times Dom(w)$, such that the semantic equations of DL hold [1]. Let C and D designate concept names and r a name of a role in the sense of the DL. The subsumption relation among objects concept is given by C subsumes D, which is equivalent to $D^{I_w} \subseteq C^{I_w}$ in state w. The assertion of the form $C(i)$ stipulates that the individual i is an instance of concept C, and the assertion $r(i, j)$ indicate that the couple of individuals (i, j) is in the extension of r. In order to associate an interpretation to the assertions, the function $(.)^{I_w}$ is extended to individuals such that, e.g., $C(i)$ is satisfied by w, and we note $w \vDash C(i)$ if and only if $i \in C^{I_w}$. The action $a(w)$ is structured in a traditional formulation where each precondition $pre(a)$ is a conjunction of assertion formulas concerning the conceptual objects as well as the roles which bind these objects. The effects of actions can be expressed by the adding conditions of assertions described by the assertion formulas $pos^+(a)$, which means the addition to the interpretation of concept or role involved in an action $a(w)$ and the deletion from the interpretation of concept or role denoted by $pos^-(a)$. A point of view on action observed a in a state of the world w at time t, is expressed by the function $\rho v(a, w)$. The result of this function consists in proposing a set of possible actions A_w in this state w according to their precondition constraints, such that the set actions $\Pi_w^a = A_w \cup \{a\}$ forms a lattice ordered by the subsumption relation of these actions. Formally, $\rho v(a, w)$ defines a lattice structure $\langle \Pi_w^a, \prec_a \rangle$ such that the following constraints are satisfied:

- $\forall b \in \Pi_w^a$, b is subsumed by a if and only if

$$\forall \langle w, e \rangle \in b : w \vDash pre(b) \Rightarrow w \vDash pre(a)) \vee$$

$$(e \vDash pos^+(b) \Rightarrow e \vDash pos^+(a)) \vee (e \vDash pos^-(b) \Rightarrow e \vDash pos^-(a))$$

- $\forall b, c \in \Pi_w^a$, admits an upper bound $a \in \Pi_w^a$ which is the action observed. $a(w)$ forms the root of the lattice of the set of the possible actions in state w at time t because the agent in observation mode considers that this action has the highest expected quality according to the viewpoint of the entity in control.

- $\forall b, c \in \Pi_w^a$ admits a lower bound $b \wedge c \in \Pi_w^a$. This bound is represented by the symbol $\triangle$ that express a collection of actions (meta-action) subsumed by all member-actions of the lattice. This collection can be executed in any order guaranteeing the same state of the world obtained by $a(w)$ such that $b \triangle c(w) = b(c(w)) \cup c(b(w))$. Two actions $(b, c) \in \Pi_w^a \times \Pi_w^a$ are interchangeable if and only if $b \triangle c(w) \neq \emptyset$. The state $\emptyset$ is an empty state, i.e., a state of contradiction.

- $\forall b \in \Pi_w^a$, if $a \triangle b(w) = \emptyset$ where $a(w)$ is an observed action which is performed by the agent (or human) in control, then the agent observer must reduce its sharing of authority. In the case where $a \triangle b(w) \neq \emptyset$, the agent observer can extend its autonomy by requesting authority sharing owing to the fact that the intentions of the entity in control coincide with the observed action $a(w)$.

3 Conclusion

Our objective is to formally redefine the main issues surrounding the problem of adjustment of autonomy by relying on a formal approach of the action. It should be emphasized that this initial work is not meant to bring exhaustive answers to the questions raised by the multiple problems related to the human in the loop. However, it constitutes a first step towards a non analytical approach to the adjustment of autonomy. Our aim is to develop an action language based on the viewpoint paradigm, for the sharing of authority between two entities involved in a common task. Furthermore, this action language will give us an opportunity to introduce the dynamics into the description logic [9]. The actual case used as a validation is a smart home project aimed at providing cognitive assistance to people suffering from cognitive deficiencies [10].

References

1. Baader F., Calvanese D., McGuiness D., Nardi D. et Patel-Schneider P.: The Description Logic Handbook : Theories, implementation, and applications. Cambridge University Press, United Kingdom (2003)
2. Borgida A.: On the relative expressiveness of description logics and predicate logics. Artificial Intelligence Journal, Vol. 82. Elsevier, NewYork (1996) 353-367
3. Bouzouane A., Bouchard B., Giroux S.: Crédibilité de l'initiative usager-agent à base de la logique teminologique, In: Proc. JFSMA'04, Hermès (eds) (2004) 293-306
4. Bouzouane A., Demazeau Y., Drogoul A., Hélie P., Taillibert P. et Tessier C. : Table ronde: Des agents et des hommes, quels défis pour les nouveaux usagers, In: Proc. JFSMA'04, Hermès (eds) (2004) 323-329
5. Castelfranchi C., Falcone R.: Trust and Control: A Dialectic Link. Applied Artificial Intelligence Journal. Vol. 14. Taylor & Francis (eds) (2000) 799–823
6. Castelfranchi C., Falcone R.: From Automaticity to Autonomy: The Frontier of Artificial Agents. In: Hexmoor, H., Castelfranchi,C., Falcone, R., (eds): Agent Autonomy. Springer-Verlag (2003)
7. Dautenhahn K.: Socially Intelligent Agents: The Human in the loop. IEEE Trans. on Systems. Vol. 31:5 (2001) 345-348
8. Falcone R., Castelfranchi C.: The Human in the Loop of a Delegated Agent: The Theory of Adjustable Social Autonomy. IEEE Trans. on Systems. Vol. 33:5 (2001) 406-418
9. Gil Y.: Description Logics and Planning. To appear in AI Magazine. (2005) 1-22
10. Pigot H., Mayers A., Giroux S.: The intelligent habitat and everyday life activity support. In: 5th Conf. on Simulations in Biomedicine, Slovenia (2003) 507-516
11. Scerri P., Pynadath D.V, Tambe, M.: Towards Adjustable Autonomy for Real World. Journal of Artificial Intelligence Research. Vol. 17. Morgan Kauffman (eds) (2002) 171-228

Application of Multi-agent Systems and Social Network Theory to Petrol Pricing on UK Motorways

Alison J. Heppenstall, Olga E. McFarland, and Andrew J. Evans

School of Geography, University of Leeds, Leeds, UK, LS2 9JT
www.geog.leeds.ac.uk

Abstract. The work within this paper outlines ongoing research into the use of multi-agent systems and social network theory to examine the transmission of information within a dynamic geographical system. The system examined is the UK retail petrol market. Details of the model are provided and simple simulations run to test the robustness and behaviour of the model. The results of these basic simulations are presented alongside a discussion of the wider relevance of this work and future developments.

1 Introduction

Complex systems are characterised by containing many distributed subsystems, subsystem components, interactions and organisational relationships. These relationships are constantly changing in reaction to new information introduced or created within the system. This information can be transmitted around the system by networks established between subsystems or components. There are a variety of different networks [5], but this research will focus on the transmission of new information through *social* networks.

Determining what patterns emerge as a consequence of the introduction and emergence of new information within a network is an important area that affects many different applications. For example, in a rapidly changing economic environment such as retail markets, competitive advantage in an area becomes redundant with the advent of a new technology or social change.

The work within this paper is part of an ongoing project investigating the feasibility of using multi-agent systems (MAS) for modelling complex systems. Here the effects of transmitting pricing information through a complex system, in this case the UK motorway petrol station network are examined. This network is unusual in that it is explicitly geographical but contains a strong social network (petrol stations maintain a close check on their competitors price). A simple MAS model was created to simulate this network and initial idealised experiments are presented.

2 The Retail Petrol Market

Previous approaches to modelling the retail petrol market have comprised of empirical regression techniques that vary in complexity and focus on the rela-

M. Pěchouček, P. Petta, and L.Z. Varga (Eds.): CEEMAS 2005, LNAI 3690, pp. 551–554, 2005.

tionship between the petrol price and one or more variables [4]. These techniques are unable to model the numerous spatial and temporal influences evident within the retail petrol market [2].

The work of Heppenstall et al. [2] used agent-based systems to examine the transmission of information between petrol stations within a geographical region. However, due to the complexity of the system, this work did not study explicit geographical networks.

A simplified version of this market can be found by way of the UK motorway network. This consists of long stretches of linear roads with a small number of petrol stations located on them. This geographical network provides a convenient platform for the study of information diffusion and interactions between petrol retailers. Examining the behaviour of petrol stations within the retail petrol market is an area that is not heavily researched. Of the few studies, both Ning and Haining [3] and Heppenstall et al. [1] found that within the local competitive environment of a station, social networks were readily apparent. However, the nature of these networks are not easily determined. The work here represents a starting point to modelling such networks.

3   Model Overview

The model was a customised version of a small world application (created using Java) developed by the Multi-Agent Systems Simulation (MASS) group at the School of Geography, University of Leeds (the original model and source code can be found at http://www.geog.leeds.ac.uk/groups/mass/ resources/software/ smallworldagents/). The model was extended to incorporate application specific behaviour such as the ability to set prices and to calculate distance to neighbours (see §3.1 for further details). Conceptually, the model consists of two major components; the motorway network and the petrol agents that act upon it.

The network was designed to represent a real system of petrol stations connected via a transportation network. It is represented in graph space as in reality, i.e. petrol stations are sited at strategically located positions along a stretch of motorway. Representation in graph space enabled a convenient simplification of reality.

Individual petrol stations were created as agents and supplied with their location, their own price and the price of their neighbourhoods. Each petrol agent can be characterised as being *heterogeneous*, possessing both a fixed location and a petrol price; *communicative* and *cooperative* with pricing information shared between the agents for competition, and *reactive* making decisions and changing their prices based on information supplied to them. This construction follows the petrol agent developed by Heppenstall et al. [1].

3.1   Behaviour and Rules

The price of petrol that a station sells is decided via a set of rules. These rules can be assigned to an individual station, a group of stations or all the stations. The basis of these rules are derived from factors that the Competition Commission (1990) state as important in price variability between petrol stations, for example distance from, and price of a competitor. The effects of external factors, for example, crude oil prices and fuel tax were not incorporated within this research.

The parameters used to form the basis of the rules and an example rule by an agent are:

- **Minimum and maximum price**: the maximum and minimum price the stations can set. (This was only activated during development of the model. Once the model was stable, these parameters became redundant.)
- **Undercutting amount**: the amount by which one station can be cheaper than another.
- **Overpricing amount**: the amount by which one station can be more expensive than another.
- **Distance:** the distance between neighbouring stations. The impact of the price on a neighbours station was set by means of an exponential scale, i.e. the further away the neighbour, the small the impact of any price change.

Example.   Am I more expensive by Xp than my neighbours? If yes, drop my price by Xp.

4   Initial Experimentation: Fixed Price Drop

By standardising the geography and network through idealised data, the behaviour and sensitivity of the model can be easily understood. This is an essential step before application to the more complex real system.

Diffusion experiments provide a useful opportunity to examine the reaction of the system and in particular, give an understanding of how information is transmitted between stations. One of the simplest ways to test diffusion within the system is to drop the price of one station and examining if and how the cheaper price is transmitted through the network. A simple network with 9 stations located at 2km intervals was created. Each station was initialised with the same price, 68 pence (p) with the exception of station 5, the centre station which was set at 65p. The undercutting and overpricing parameters were both set to 1p and applied to all the stations.

Figure 1(a) shows the neighbours of station 5 quickly reacting to the lower price by dropping their prices in a symmetrical pattern. The transmission of the lower price can be clearly seen through the remainder of the network and by day 5, all the stations have been affected. Interestingly, station 5 increases its price by 1p on the first day as the other stations decrease their price. This is due to the underpricing and overpricing rules not allowing the stations to more than 1p cheaper or more expensive than their neighbours. This simulation shows that these rules are working sensibly.

To examine the effect of a price drop at a different position within the network, station 1 was initiated at 65p (all the other stations were set to 68p). Figure 1(b) shows the effects of the lower price being transmitted through the

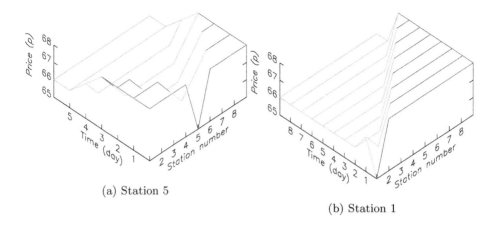

(a) Station 5

(b) Station 1

Fig. 1. Impact on the network of dropping the price by 3p at (a) station 5 and (b) station 1

network over the course of the simulation. The diffusion takes 8 days to reach all the stations, at this stage they each have a price of 66p.

5   Conclusions

The work within this paper has presented an agent-based system for modelling social and geographical networks. Although simplistic at this stage, this work represents the basis of two important strands of research. Firstly, the development of effective tools to model complex geographical systems and secondly, the further use of such tools to identify interesting patterns and behaviour within such systems. The model has been proved to work sensibly within the initial experiments performed. The next stage is to test the model using real world scenarios.

References

[1] A.J. Heppenstall, A.J. Evans, and M.H. Birkin. A hybrid multi-agent/spatial interaction model system for petrol price setting. *Transactions in GIS*, 9(1):35–51, 2005.

[2] A.J. Heppenstall, A.J. Evans, and M.H. Birkin. Application of hybrid multi-agent systems to a dynamic, locally interacting geographical system. *JASSS*, In review, 2005.

[3] X. Ning and R. Haining. Spatial pricing in interdependent markets: a case study of petrol retailing in Sheffield. *Environment and Planning A*, 35:2131 – 2159, 2003.

[4] B. Reilly and R. Witt. Petrol price asymmetries revisted. *Energy Economics*, 20: 297 – 308, 1998.

[5] R. Stocker, D. Green, and D. Newth. Consensus and cohesion in simulated social networks. *JASSS*, 4(4), 2001.

Combining Rule-Based and Plug-in Components in Agents for Flexible Dynamic Negotiations

Costin Bădică[1], Maria Ganzha[2], Marcin Paprzycki[3], and Amalia Pîrvănescu[1]

[1] University of Craiova, Software Engineering Department
Bvd.Decebal 107, Craiova, 200440, Romania
`badica_costin@software.ucv.ro`
[2] Gizycko Private Higher Educational Institute, Department of Informatics
Gizycko, Poland
`ganzha@pwsz.net`
[3] Oklahoma State University, Computer Science Department
Tulsa, OK, 74106, USA and
Computer Science, SWPS, 03-815 Warsaw, Poland
`marcin@cs.okstate.edu`

Abstract. For software agents to become part of e-commerce they have to be *flexible*—to engage in negotiations of forms which are not known in advance, and *mobile*—to migrate to remote locations. This note aims at combining flexibility with mobility by joining rule-based mechanism representation with modular mobile agents. Furthermore, we focus on a more complete e-commerce scenario and address questions like: what happens before negotiations start and after they are finished, where from the purchase is actually made etc. Description of agent interactions in such a complete e-commerce scenario is presented.

1 Introduction

Recent advances in auction theory have produced a general methodology of describing price negotiations [9]. To engage in negotiations, forms of which are unknown in advance, agents have to be appropriately flexible [3]. Furthermore, it is argued that they have to be mobile to be used in realistic applications [2]. However, mobile agents have to be lightweight to be able to swiftly move across the network. Unfortunately, *flexible agents cannot be lightweight* as they have to "carry" their intelligence with them [8].

In this note we describe architecture of a multi-agent e-commerce system that aims at combining flexibility and mobility. Our proposal builds on: (i) conceptual architecture of a multi-agent e-commerce system summarized in [3]; (ii) flexible framework that allows agents to participate in arbitrary negotiations described in [1], and (iii) lightweight modular agents that migrate to remote markets and engage in negotiations [3] (see also references quoted there). Furthermore, we extend the proposed approach beyond the "act" of negotiation. In [7] negotiations were extended to include matchmaking. In our work we consider: matchmaking, negotiating and purchasing. Interestingly, processes between completion of price negotiations and actual purchase, while involving a number of possibilities, are practically forgotten in literature.

M. Pěchouček, P. Petta, and L.Z. Varga (Eds.): CEEMAS 2005, LNAI 3690, pp. 555–558, 2005.

2   Rule-Based and Plug-in Components for Automated Negotiation

We start by summarizing the framework for automated negotiation introduced in [1] and the architecture of mobile agents capable of dynamic negotiations elaborated in [3]. Authors of [1] analyzed the existing approaches to agent negotiations (primarily the FIPA protocols) and argued that they do not provide enough structure for the development of portable agent-based e-commerce systems. They also sketched a framework for implementing agent negotiations involving a number of infrastructure providing sub-agents: *Gatekeeper*, *Proposal Validator*, *Protocol Enforcer*, *Information Updater*, *Negotiation Terminator* and *Agreement Maker*. Central point of this framework consisted of a generic negotiation protocol and a taxonomy of JESS rules ([5]) used for enforcing specific negotiation mechanisms.

In our earlier work we have implemented (using JADE [4]) agents capable of negotiation adaptation via dynamically loadable modules ([3]). These agents consisted of three main components: (i) *communication module*—responsible for agent-agent communication, ii) *protocol module*—responsible for enforcing protocols governing negotiations, and (iii) *strategy module*—responsible for producing protocol-compliant actions necessary to achieve agent goals. Advantages of this architecture were threefold: (i) separation between functionality of each module, (ii) separation of a "private" strategy and a protocol that is "public" to the market, (iii) support for lightweight mobility.

Let us now see how it is possible to combine these two approaches. (1) Work presented in [1] assumes implicitly that *Buyer* agents are intelligent and furthermore carry with them a "generic negotiation protocol" thus making them very heavy, while our approach can help avoid this problem. (2) The *Gatekeeper* sub-agent does not play any role in actual price negotiations and thus can be placed "in the system" as a full-fledged agent. (3) Analysis presented in [1] involves only *Buyer* agents entering a given host and becoming involved in price negotiations; actions of the system preceding and following negotiations are not considered; we have thus included them in our system.

3   Agents in an E-Commerce Environment

Let us now present details as to how the two approaches can be actually combined to balance flexibility and mobility. Fundamentally, our environment acts as a distributed marketplace that hosts e-stores and allows e-clients to visit them to purchase products. Buyers negotiate with sellers and choose where to make a purchase [3].

Figure 1 presents the complete UML activity diagram of the proposed system (illustrated from both *Client* and *Shop* "perspectives"). Note that box named *Negotiation Process* includes inside **all** processes conceptualized and illustrated by UML diagrams in [1]. Let us sketch functioning of the system depicted in figure 1 (further details can be found in [3] and [1]).

Client agent receives orders from customer, and attempts to make a purchase. In the system there exists a central repository (*yellow pages*), where all e-stores advertise information about products [7]. Therefore, *Client* queries the *yellow pages agent*, and then dispatches *Buyer* agents to each *Shop* selling the requested product. Hereafter, the *Client* agent enters a composite state, attempting to make purchase(s), as results of

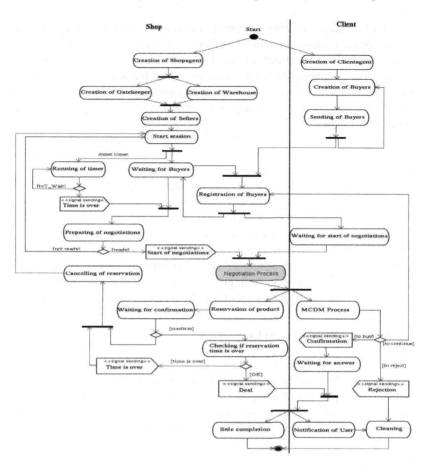

Fig. 1. UML activity diagram of the system operation

Buyer notifications. Whenever a *Buyer* agent reports a successful negotiation, the *Client* agent goes through a multi-criteria decision procedure (*MCDM Process*) that has three possible outcomes: (i) to complete the purchase, (ii) to cancel the purchase (awaiting better opportunity), or (iii) to declare the purchase impossible and notify the customer. The *Client* agent will terminate when all orders have been either honored or abandoned.

The *Shop* agent creates a *Gatekeeper*, a *Warehouse* and *Seller* agents (one *Seller*/one product)and then enters a complex state where it supervises negotiations. First, the *Shop* agent is waiting for finish of any negotiation. If it was successful, a given *Seller* informs the *Shop* which asks the *Warehouse* to reserve the product (for a specific amount of time). Then, if the winning *Buyer* confirms purchase, *Shop* asks the *Warehouse* to check reservation. If the reservation expired, then *Shop* hands rejection to the *Buyer*. Otherwise *Shop* informs *Buyer* about acceptance of transaction. This starts the final stage—named *Sale completion* which includes such actions as payment or delivery. If the *Client* rejects purchase (and informs the *Shop* about it through the *Buyer*), then *Shop* asks the *Warehouse* to cancel the reservation.

The *Gatekeeper* monitors incoming *Buyer*s and controls their admission to negotiations. When a minimum number of *Buyer*s have arrived or a timeout is triggered, the *Gatekeeper* passes identifiers of registered *Buyer*s to the *Seller* thus initiating negotiations. When negotiations are finished, the list of participating *Buyer*s is emptied and the admission/monitor process is restarted (assuming that the *Seller* is still alive). System allows loosing *Buyer*s to stay at the host and re-enter negotiations after updating protocol templates.

The *Warehouse* obtains from the *Shop* information about products and their quantities and saves them into a database. Then it waits for notifications or for timer events. The *Shop* notifies the *Warehouse* about: (1) registration of a new products for sale, (2) product reservations, (3) purchase confirmations and terminations. Time event triggers checking of existing reservations. All expired reservations are canceled, reserved products added to the pool of products for sale and the *Shop* is informed about a new amount of available goods. Note that the information about canceled reservation is provided to the *Shop* only when a purchase is requested by the *Buyer* and the *Shop* is checking if a transaction can be completed. Finally, if quantity of some product becomes 0 then *Warehouse* informs *Shop* accordingly and *Shop* terminates the corresponding *Seller* informing also the yellow pages agent that the product is not available anymore.

4   Concluding Remarks

In this paper we presented a multi-agent system that combines rule-based and mobile agent technologies for implementing flexible automated negotiations. Proposed system is being re-implemented using JADE and JESS (its earlier version, while fully functional, did not involve the general framework introduced in [1]). We are also working on agent strategies and decisions. We will report on our progress in subsequent papers.

References

1. Bartolini, C., Preist, C., Jennings, N.R.: A Software Framework for Automated Negotiation. In: *Proceedings of SELMAS'2004*, LNCS 3390, Springer Verlag (2005) 213–235.
2. Fuggetta, A., Picco, G.P., Vigna, G.: Understanding Code Mobility. In: *IEEE Transactions on Software Engineering*, vol.24, no.5, IEEE Computer Science Press (1998) 342–361.
3. Maria Ganzha, Marcin Paprzycki, Amalia Pîrvănescu, Costin Bădică, Ajith Abraham, JADE-based Multi-agent E-commerce Environment: Initial Implementation, In: *Analele Universității din Timişoara, Seria Matematică-Informatică* (2005) (to appear)
4. JADE: Java Agent Development Framework. See http://jade.cselt.it.
5. JESS: Java Expert System Shell. See http://herzberg.ca.sandia.gov/jess/.
6. Tamma, V., Wooldridge, M., Dickinson, I: An Ontology Based Approach to Automated Negotiation. In: *Proceedings AMEC'02: Agent Mediated Electronic Commerce*, LNAI 2531, Springer-Verlag (2002) 219–237.
7. Trastour, D., Bartolini, C., Preist, C.: Semantic Web Support for the Business-to-Business E-Commerce Lifecycle. In: *Proceedings of the WWW'02: International World Wide Web Conference*, Hawaii, USA, ACM Press, New York, USA (2002) 89–98.
8. Wooldridge, M.: *An Introduction to MultiAgent Systems*, John Wiley & Sons, (2002).
9. Wurman, P, Wellman, M., Walsh W.: A Parameterization of the Auction Design Space. In: *Games and Economic Behavior*, 35, Vol. 1/2 (2001), 271–303.

Group Interests of Agents Functioning in Changing Environments

Sarunas Raudys and Alvydas Pumputis

Mykolas Romeris University, Ateities 20, Vilnius-2057, Lithuania
raudys@ktl.mii.lt

Abstract. We consider agent populations with breeding split into groups with a naïve common goal to survive in changing environments. In order to grasp principal tendencies in cooperation, the agents are modeled as very simple systems, the single layer perceptron (SLP) based classifiers. They ought to learn how to train themselves rapidly, adapt to unexpected pattern recognition task changes, to comply the fitness function and survive. Failure to comply survivability condition will result in the agent being replaced by a newborn that inherits some upbringing information from one of successful agents in the group. We found that inherited fraction of incorrect training directives (a noise) which controls the agent's ability to adapt to changes is following environmental alterations. Restricted cooperation between agent groups is beneficial to overcome outsized changes.

1 Introduction

A great number of useful task-specific intelligent programs have been created using real world scenario [1, 2]. Important research directions are also development of formal and *ad-hoc* ways of knowledge representation allowing developers to simply "plug in" fully functional components into multi agent systems (MAS) design, to build rich, reliable and robust models [3]. Open environment in which agents can easily enter and interact with each other increases a speed and reduces a cost of developing MAS.

In the knowledge-based approach used to create first intelligent machines, scientists directly programmed the machines to perform the given tasks. In the learning-based approach, the machines were trained by task-specific learning programs utilizing human-edited sensory data. The complexities of decision making rules of the intellectual agents, however, often are beyond human programming, especially if environments are changing permanently. For that reason, traditional ways have been proved to be extremely difficult to develop robots running in a typical human environment. So presently in the "genetic search," many of intelligent machines are evolving through generations by the principle of survival of the fittest, mostly in a computer-simulated virtual world. In autonomous development paradigm, machines like humans should be designed to go through a long period of *self-directed mental development*, from "infancy" to "adulthood" [4]. "Learning styles" become very important elements which have to be learned by the machines themselves.

M. Pĕchouček, P. Petta, and L.Z. Varga (Eds.): CEEMAS 2005, LNAI 3690, pp. 559–563, 2005.
© Springer-Verlag Berlin Heidelberg 2005

Analysis of systems of complex intelligent agents capable to solve real-world problems takes huge computational resources. In such cases, many important aspects of the environment changeability remain to be uninvestigated. A necessity arises to perform exploration of some general learning principles while studying groups of simplified models of intelligent agents which require a smaller amount of computations. In our analysis we use non-linear SLP classifier as a simplified model of adaptive intelligent agent and take for granted: 1) A world is changing permanently. Designers do not know in which conditions the agents will work. 2) Agents have to learn how to teach themselves [4]. 3) During training, the weights (connection strengths) of the perceptron are increasing and we obtain a saturation of fitness (cost) function. Due to saturation gradient descent learning process slows down [5, 6]. 4) Re-adaptation to solve the changed pattern recognition (PR) task can be enlightened by a noise injection to training signals and the targets [6].

In paper [6] two different PR tasks model was suggested to analyze aging problems of the intellectual agents, individuals, groups of individuals or social groups. Aging was defined as inability to adapt rapidly to changed situation and survive. In [7] sequences of different PR tasks were considered each time starting training from previous weight vector. To help populations of almost identical agents to withstand lengthy series of strong environmental changes, populations with offspring and inheritance of regularization parameters have to be created. In this paradigm, different agents possess diverse values of the noise level. It was found that the optimal interval for the noise level follows variations of environmental changes.

A novelty of our analysis is *re-adaptation capabilities of agent populations* where they are organized into groups. Agents interact among themselves inside the groups and between them. The noise injection intensities characterize the "learning style".

2 Modeling of the Agent Survival in the Grouped Populations

The standard nonlinear SLP classifier with sigmoid activation function, *output*$=1/(1+\exp(-sum)$, targets: $t_1=0$ (first class) and $t_2=1$ (second class) and gradient descent training rule are selected to model adaptive intelligent agents. In training a sum of squares cost function is minimized. If the weights are small, the gradient used to update perceptron weights is large. When the weights are large, the gradient becomes small. During training, the magnitudes of the weighs are increasing and affect properties of the cost function [5, 6]. With an increase in the magnitude of the weights, the gradient is decreasing towards zero. It means that in situations when the perceptrons learned to solve their tasks properly, the weights are already large. *Due to the large weights, the perceptrons are unable to re-learn new PR tasks quickly.*

To elucidate factors affecting agent re-adaptation performance, we analyze sequences of different PR tasks that mimic environmental changes (EC). We consider two category classification problem of two dimensional (2D) Gaussian vectors with correlated features. We suppose that the agent has a limited time to adapt to changing situation and fulfill condition: $P_{generalization} < P_{goal}$. If the agent fails to fulfill this condition, it perishes, removes from the population and is replaced by an offspring.

In this paper we assume that *agents are modeling organizations accomplishing tasks and doing cognitive activities like learning*. Each agent possesses different fraction of incorrect training directives, parameter α_i that characterizes a noise injection intensity. The noise level, α_i, affects weights growth, the agent's re-training speed and its ability to survive the environmental changes [6, 7]. At the start of each experiment, for all m agents (we used $m=400$) that composed the population, we assigned different values of parameter α_i. A distribution of α_i values was obtained in preceding experiments (it was approximately Gaussian in interval [0.15 0.35]).

Random generated data sets (50 vectors from each class) were used to train each intelligent agent. Different values of α_i lead to the death of certain agents who fail to learn fast enough to satisfy survival condition after the t_{max} training epochs ($t_{max} = 180$). If the agent perishes, it is replaced with a new offspring that possesses its parent's noise intensity, α_i ($i=1, 2, ..., m$). Only best survived agents are given the right to produce offspring. Learning process of the offspring starts from zero initial weights. To have possibility to adapt to strengths of the PR tasks changes a small random variable $\varepsilon \sim N(0, 0.02^2)$ was added to α_i each time through the mutation process. In addition, small zero mean uniformly distributed noise was added to survival threshold, P_{goal}. Inheritance and noise injections result that during a sequence of environmental changes, parameters α_i follow variations of the changes' strength.

The m agents in the population were split into L equal sized groups. To reveal principal factors affecting the population survival, we considered simple cooperation model. The parameters of the model were tailored to situations where environmental changes are rare and especially large. The most successful agents in the group somewhat help less successful agents to survive. The agents' associations to the groups were fixed. We introduced restricted benevolent cooperation between the groups: if a quantity of agents that satisfy the survivability condition in one of the groups becomes less than *two*, a successful randomly chosen agent from other groups was allowed transfer its "genetic code", a_s, to the offspring.

In simulation experiments strengths, S, of the pattern recognition tasks alterations varied in a time. Changes were strongest between 70th and 130th alterations. Resulting distribution of the noise injection intensities followed S changes. In Fig. 1 we have survivability dynamics graphs obtained for two population models (two groups and 200 ones). We see that different mechanisms determine the number of agents that survived the strongest environmental changes: in two group situation, almost all agents died during the strongest PR task alterations. The populations without the split passed away after first ten strongest changes. The populations, split into 200 groups, however, become even more robust. It is the result of benevolent cooperation.

3   Discussion

Our study confirms that corrupted training signals and wrenched survivability conditions assist in faster adaptation of the agents to the PR tasks changes. It seems that in process of species and societies development, Nature's evolution selected only these populations of individuals which were split into groups and had controlled cooperation between them. Possibly these results will give stimulus and new ideas for creating *trainable MAS* with a noise injection and will encourage contemplations about usefulness of diversity of political systems, religions and economic alliances.

A novelty of our analysis is the noise injection to training signals used in agent populations with breeding, mutually cooperating in different ways. Striking conclusion derived from above analysis is that such simple element as single layer perceptron equipped with dynamic change of the pattern recognition tasks and the noise injections could explain several important aspects of MAS and society behavior.

Within the domain of social simulations, our study proposes a starting point and ideas how to create constructive methods for studying productive and destructive social phenomena affecting societies in transition from one political system to another one, sudden improvements of technologies, unexpected changes in human life conditions, enriching of some countries and depressing other ones. Our way of analysis can show and measure effects of environmental changes and organizing individuals into the groups as in contrast to mere verbal descriptions typically used in social sciences.

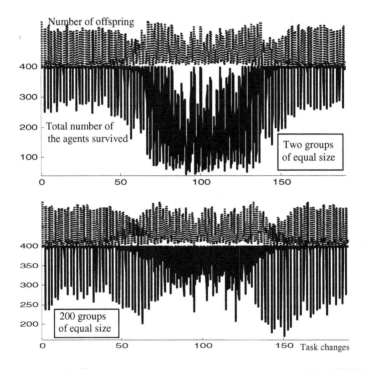

Fig. 1. A number of offspring and agents survived during sequences of the 190 PR tasks

References

[1] Sichman, J., Bousquet, F. and Davidsson, P., (eds). *Multi-agent-based simulation* II. *Lecture Notes in Artificial Intelligence.* Springer-Verlag, 2581, 2003.
[2] Prietula M., Carley K. and Gasser L. (eds). *Simulating Organizations: Computational Models of Institutions and Groups.* The MIT Press, Cambridge, MA, 1998.

[3] Boman M., Bubenko J., Johannesson P. and Wangler B. *Conceptual Modeling*. Prentice-Hall, Inc., Upper Saddle River, NJ, 1997.

[4] Weng J., McClelland J., A., Sporns O., Stockman I., Sur M., and Thelen E. Autonomous mental development by robots and animals. *Science*, Vol. 291, N.5504, Issue 26: 599-600.

[5] Raudys S. *Statistical and Neural Classifiers: An integrated approach to design*. Springer-Verlag, NY, 2001.

[6] Raudys S. An adaptation model for simulation of aging process. *Int. J. of Modern Physics, C.* 13(8): 1075-1086, 2002.

[7] Raudys S. Survival of intelligent agents in changing environments. *Lecture Notes in Artificial Intelligence*, Springer-Verlag, 3070: 109-117, 2004.

Policies for Common Awareness in Organized Settings*

Ioannis Partsakoulakis and George Vouros

Department of Information and Communication Systems Engineering
83200 Karlovassi, Samos, Greece
{jpar, georgev}@aegean.gr

Abstract. Groups of collaborative agents need to create group beliefs (*acceptances*) in order to act as a single entity. The notion of mutual or collective belief, which has been used extensively to cope with group belief, is not appropriate in organized settings where group members exploit shared policies to *accept* that certain states hold, even if some members of the group do not believe them. This paper distinguishes between beliefs and acceptances, introduces policies for acceptances, and investigates communication requirements towards forming acceptances.

1 Introduction

The objective of this research is to build multi-agent systems that form the digital analogues of human organizations and help humans to fulfil their responsibilities individually or in collaboration with other colleagues in well-organized settings [8, 6]. Investigating the capabilities of agents to fulfill collaborative responsibilities in organized settings, this paper focuses on the formation of acceptances. Acceptance is an important concept that is being studied in the context of philosophy [7, 10]; however, until now it has not been given much attention in the context of multi-agent systems.

Participating in a group, agents must reconcile their individual beliefs and reach group beliefs (*acceptances*) independently of their perceptual and cognitive abilities, permissions to access information sources, knowledge that they posses, preferences etc. Theoretical models of collaborative decision making [1, 2, 4, 9] adopt the notion of collective or mutual belief to cope with group belief. However, in settings where information is inherently distributed and access restrictions to information sources apply, the group belief cannot be based on the individual beliefs of all group members.

The above introduce the problem of representing and exploiting policies for building and maintaining group beliefs. For instance, in certain settings, group members must be able to exploit policies that state that the group shall accept something only if the majority of the group members believe it, although there may be group members with a different opinion. More than policies, the above example reveals the necessity for agents to clearly distinguish between their individual beliefs and their acceptances as group members.

---

* This research is supported by the Pythagoras grand no. 1349 under the Operational Program for Education and Initial Training.

M. Pěchouček, P. Petta, and L.Z. Varga (Eds.): CEEMAS 2005, LNAI 3690, pp. 564–567, 2005.

This paper distinguishes between acceptances and beliefs, and proposes state recognition recipes for the specification of group policies towards forming acceptances. Based on this distinction, we assume that group members form beliefs using *primitive* state recognition actions (r-actions) and acceptances using state recognition recipes (r-recipes).

Dealing with acceptances in organized settings, this paper deals with groups of agents that follow a pre-specified organizational model specified in terms of roles, as Fig. 1 shows. A role serves as a prototype that specifies the behavior of an individual or of a set of individuals that form a group. In this paper, we assume that each role comprises *responsibilities* and *recipes*, and that roles are interrelated via the transitive relation "*contains*". A position is a formally specified role-assignment [3]. Each role can be associated with one or more positions. We assume that agents under a composite role must act as a single entity by forming acceptances and by managing shared plans [2].

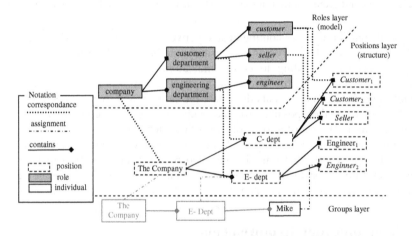

Fig. 1. Part of the organization that represents a company

A policy about a state s is a tree-like structure in which nodes are states and each arc is labelled with an element of the form ρ_{ind} where ρ is a role and *ind* an indicator that can take the value *all*, *most*, or *one*, indicating *all* the players of ρ, *most* of them, or at least *one* of them is required for the formation of an acceptance for the state s. A policy for the acceptance of a state is not represented explicitly, but it is constructed gradually by combining r-recipes towards the recognition of states.

For example, the policy in Fig. 2 has been constructed by the two recipes in the corresponding rectangles and specifies that a company shall accept that there is a pending order of a customer c about product p (i.e. pending-order(p,c)) when it is known that (a) all sellers believe the fact that the order is pending and (b) customer p wants product c. Sharing the above policy, each agent in a company is aware of the information needed towards accepting a state and proactively communicates this information.

Given a policy for a state s, a *potential* (or *required*) *contribution* of an agent to the state s is a path from s to a leaf node in the policy, if the edge leading to this node corresponds to an atomic role played by the agent. Each agent computes all its *personal contributions* by identifying its potential contributions and by unifying the leaf states with its beliefs. In other words, personal contributions are instantiated potential contributions identified by individuals.

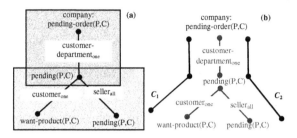

Fig. 2. A policy and group contributions C_1 and C_2 that match potential (required) contributions

Personal contributions are communicated between agents that play the same atomic role (e.g. between sellers). Personal contributions that are identified by a sufficient number of agents (according to policy indicators) are called *group contributions* because they can affect the acceptances of a group. Group contributions are communicated between the agents that share the same policy (e.g. between sellers and customers). This makes possible for the agents to check whether for each of the potential (required) contributions of a policy there is a corresponding group contribution (as Figure 3(b) shows). When this condition holds, then the state s is considered to be a state that must be accepted by all group members that share the policy. Therefore, the state s is communicated to all group members (including those not sharing the recipe) as an acceptance.

2   Communication Requirements

To study communication requirements for the formation of acceptances, let us assume that a group has n agents each playing one of m primitive roles and that each role has k players, therefore $n = k \cdot m$. Given a group policy with a required contribution for *each* primitive role we can distinguish between two extreme cases: (a) the policy requires the contribution of *all* the agents that play the corresponding primitive roles and (b) the policy requires the contribution of *one* of the agents that play the corresponding primitive roles.

In the first case, each agent must send its personal contribution to each of the $k-1$ agents that play the same role. This requires $n(k-1)$ messages. Then, each group contribution identified by each agent must be sent to the rest $n-1$ of the agents. In the worst case this requires $n(n-1)$ messages. The same number of messages is required for the formation of the acceptance. So, there is a total of $n(k-1)+2n(n-1)$ messages which results to $3n(n-1)$ messages, given that $k = n$. In the best case, only one agent for each primitive role will communicate the group contribution to the other agents (requiring $m(n-1)$ messages) and one agent will communicate the acceptance to the others (requiring $n-1$ messages). So, in the best case the formation of an acceptance requires $(k+m)n-m-1$ messages. Since the product $k \cdot m = n$ is constant, the quantity $k+m$ is minimized when $k = m = n^{1/2}$; therefore, the minimum total number of messages is of magnitude of $n^{3/2}$.

In the second case, agents do not need to communicate their personal contributions since each personal contribution is a group contribution. In this case, the worst case scenario requires $2n(n-1)$ messages while the best case scenario requires $2(n-1)$ messages for the formation of an acceptance.

To achieve the best-case in both of the above cases, agents may need to delay sending the recognition of group contributions. In this case, we can achieve lower communication overhead, although we cannot guarantee that we will always achieve the number of messages encountered in the best-cases.

Counting the number of messages required we have assumed a totally distributed setting: There is not a specific agent (e.g. a special seller or the manager of the selling department) that gathers all personal/group contributions, decides and communicates the formed acceptances. Given such a setting, then the required messages in the first case (where the contributions of all agents are needed), for the worst and the best scenario, drops to $2(n-1)$. In the second case (where only one agent is needed), the worst scenario (that results for $m = n$) requires $2(n-1)$ messages, while the best scenario (that results for $m = 1$) requires $n-1$ messages.

Currently, we have implemented a prototype system in which agents can reason about and pursue their responsibilities and we are also experimenting with different algorithms for creating acceptances and for pursuing responsibilities [5, 6].

References

[1] P. R. Cohen and H. J. Levesque. Teamwork. *Nous*, 25, 487 – 512, 1991.
[2] B. J. Grosz and S. Kraus. Collaborative Plans for Complex Group Action. *Artificial Intelligence*, 86(2), 269 – 367, 1996.
[3] James J. Odell, H. Van Dyke Parunak, and Mitchell Fleischer. The Role of Roles in Designing Effective Agent Organizations. In *Software Engineering for Large-Scale Multi-Agent Systems*, A. Garcia, C. Lucena, F. Zambonelli, A. Omicini, J. Castro (eds.), LNCS 2603, 2003.
[4] P. Panzarassa, N. R. Jennings, and T. J. Normal. Formalizing Collaborative Decision-making and Practical Reasoning in Multi-agent Systems. *Journal of Logic and Computation*, 11(6), 1 – 63, 2001.
[5] I. Partsakoulakis and G. Vouros. Building Common Awareness in Agent Organizations. In *Proc. of AMKM workshop (AAMAS conference)*, 2005.
[6] I. Partsakoulakis, V. Kourakos-Mavromichalis, and G. Vouros. Social Deliberating Agents for Human-Centered Knowledge Management. In *Proceedings of the IEEE International Conference on Systems, Man and Cybernetics*, The Hague, 2004.
[7] R. Tuomela. Group Knowledge Analyzed. *Episteme* 1(2), 2004.
[8] G. Vouros, I. Partsakoulakis and V. Kourakos-Mavromichalis. Realizing Human-Centred Systems via Socially Deliberating Agents. In *Proc. of the HCI International* 2003, vol. 4, pp. 1223 – 1227.
[9] M. Wooldridge and N. R. Jennings. Cooperative problem solving. *Journal of Logic and Computation*, 9, 563 – 592, 1999.
[10] K. Brad Wray. Collective Belief and Acceptance. *Synthese* 129, pp. 319 – 333, 2001.

Learning in a Multi-agent Approach to a Fish Bank Game

Bartłomiej Śnieżyński and Jarosław Koźlak

AGH University of Science and Technology,
Institute of Computer Science, Kraków, Poland
{sniezyn, kozlak}@agh.edu.pl

Abstract. In this paper application of symbolic, supervised learning in a multi-agent system is presented. As an environment Fish Bank game is used. Agents represent players that manage fishing companies. Rule induction algorithm is applied to generate ship allocation rules. In this article system architecture and learning process are described and preliminary experimental results are presented. Results show that learning agent performance increases significantly when new experience is taken into account.

1 Introduction

There are many cases, when it is impossible to predict all the circumstances that an agent faces. It can be caused by environment complexity, or difficulties with formulating appropriate strategy. As a consequence, it is very difficult to create an agent with fixed behavior in such cases.

Application of learning algorithms allows to overcome such problems. One can implement an agent that is not perfect, but it improves its performance. This is why machine learning term appears in a context of agent systems for several years. So far agent systems with learning capabilities were applied in many domains: to train agents playing in RoboCup Challenge [1], adapt user interfaces [2], take part in agent-based computational economics simulations (virtual markets) [3], analyze distributed data [4].

In this paper results of application of symbolic, supervised learning in multi-agent system are presented. As an environment Fish Bank game is used [5]. It is a simulation where agents run fishing companies that must decide how much, and where to fish.

2 System Description

Although Fish Banks game is designed for teaching people effective cooperation in using natural resources [6], it suits to using in multi-agent systems very well [5,7]. In this research the game is a dynamic environment providing all necessary resources, action execution procedures, and time flow (game rounds). Each round consists of the following steps: ships and money update, ship auctions, trading session, ship orders, ship allocation, fishing, and fish number update.

M. Pěchouček, P. Petta, and L.Z. Varga (Eds.): CEEMAS 2005, LNAI 3690, pp. 568–571, 2005.

Agents represent players that manage fishing companies. Each company aims at collecting maximum assets expressed by the amount of money deposited at a bank account and the number of ships. Company earn money by fishing at fish banks. Environment provides two fishing areas: coastal and a deep-sea. Agents can also keep their ships at the port. Cost of fishing at the deep-sea is the highest. Cost of staying at port is the lowest but such ship does not catch fish.

Initially it is assumed that the number of fish in both banks is close to the maximal capacity. During the game the number of fish in every bank changes because of birth and exploration. Usually exploration overcomes birth and after several rounds the number can decrease to zero. It is a standard case of "the tragedy of commons" [8]. It is more reasonable to keep ships at the harbor then, therefore companies should change theirs strategy.

Two types of agents are implemented: learning agent and random agent. The former uses experience to allocate ships, the latter allocates ships by random. Both types of agents observe the following aspects of the environment: new ships that they receive from a shipyard, money earned in the last round, ships allocations of all agents, fishing results for deep sea and inshore area. Both types of agents can execute the following two types of actions: order ships, allocate ships.

Order ships action is currently very simple. Ships allocation is more complex. It is based on the method used in [5]. Allocation strategy is represented by a triple (h, d, c), where h is the number of ships left in a harbor, d and c are numbers of ships sent to a deep sea, and a coastal area respectively. The random agent allocates ships using one of strategies chosen by random. Learning agent does the same in the first game, but in the following games it chooses strategy with the highest rating. Strategy rating is generated using rules that allow to classify allocation as *good* or *bad* taking into account allocation (h, d, c) and environment parameters (fish catch at the deep sea and at the coastal area in the previous round).

Every strategy gets a rate equal the number of rules with consequence *good* that match the strategy and current environment parameters minus the number of rules with consequence *bad* that match the strategy and current environment parameters. The rules are learned using agent experience (see section 3). If there are more then one strategy with the same rating, one occurring earlier in the list is chosen.

3   Learning

To support learning AQ21 program is used [9]. It is a machine learning software that allows to generate attributional calculus rules [10] for given examples. The main advantage of this program is that generated knowledge is easy to interpret for human what makes experimental results easier to check and can be useful in Fish Bank application to teach people.

The AQ21 program generates a classifier that is used to rate ship allocation strategies. Input attributes for the classifier are allocation and environment parameters. Target attribute is a rating of the allocation in a given environment state. It has two values: good and bad.

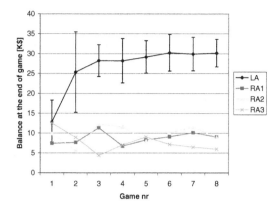

Fig. 1. Comparison of performance of learning agent (LA) and other agents using random strategy of ship allocation (RA1, RA2, RA3); values for LA are presented with the standard deviation

Training events are generated from agents observations. Every round the learning agent stores ship allocations of all agents, and fish catch in the previous round. The strategy of an agent with the highest income is classified as good, and the strategy of an agent with the lowest income is classified as bad. If in some round all agents get the same income, none strategy is classified, and as a consequence none of them is used in learning.

At the end of each game the learning agent uses events, which were generated during all games played so far, to learn a new classifier that is used in the next game.

4   Experimental Results

To test how learning changes agent performance, the following experiment was performed. Ten simulations were executed. Each simulation consisted of the sequence of 8 games. Four agents took part in every game. Three of them used random allocation strategy, one learned it from experience. Performance of agents measured as a balance at the end of every game is presented in Fig. 1. Average balance of the learning agent grows with the agent's experience, while performance of random agents generally doesn't change.

Experimental results show that the learning agent performance increases rapidly at the beginning of the learning process, when generated rules are used instead of a random choice. Next it increases slowly, because new examples do not contain any significant knowledge. The performance stabilizes at the end of the process, and the decreasing standard deviation suggests that performance does not depend on the specific case as much as at the beginning.

Experiments with two learning agents and some combinations of learning parameters were also performed, but because of the lack of space results are not described here.

5   Conclusion and Further Research

Results of research confirm that classical rule induction is useful in learning agent strategy in multi-agent systems. Fish Banks environment is complex enough to test supervised learning, if direct performance feedback is available (e.g. income at the end of the round), and, if there is no such information, and feedback is available at the end of game (reinforcement learning can be used in such situation).

Currently, we are working on cooperation learning. Future works will concern applying other learning algorithms, learning models of other agents, comparing with agents using more sophisticated strategies (see [5]), testing complex knowledge representation techniques such as logic of plausible reasoning, applying multistrategy inference and learning, and using reinforcement learning to generate ship order strategies.

Acknowledgments. The authors thank Arun Majumdar for providing prolog compiler Prologix used in implementation, and for help with using it.

References

1. Kitano, H., et al.: The RoboCup synthetic agent challenge 97. In: International Joint Conference on Artificial Intelligence (IJCAI97), Nagoya, Japan (1997) 24–29
2. Lashkari, Y., Metral, M., Maes, P.: Collaborative interface agents. In: AAAI. (1994) 444–449
3. Tesfatsion, L.: Agent-based computational economics: Growing economies from the bottom up. Artificial Life **8 (1)** (2001) 55–82
4. Stolfo, S.J., Prodromidis, A.L., Tselepis, S., Lee, W., Fan, D.W., Chan, P.K.: Jam: Java agents for meta-learning over distributed databases. In: KDD. (1997) 74–81
5. Kozlak, J., Demazeau, Y., Bousquet, F.: Multi-agent system to model the fishbanks game process. In: The First International Workshop of Central and Eastern Europe on Multi-Agent Systems (CEEMAS'99), St. Petersburg (1999)
6. Meadows, D., Iddman, T., Shannon, D.: Fish Banks, LTD: Game Administrator's Manual. Laboratory of Interactive Learning, University of New Hampshire, Durham, USA (1993)
7. Sniezynski, B.: Rule induction in a fish bank multiagent system. Technical Report 1, AGH University of Science and Technology, Institute of Computer Science (2005)
8. Hardin, G.: The tragedy of commons. Science **162** (1968) 1243–1248
9. Wojtusiak, J.: AQ21 User's Guide. Reports of the Machine Learning and Inference Laboratory, MLI 04-3. George Mason University, Fairfax, VA (2004)
10. Michalski, R.S.: Attributional Calculus: A Logic and Representation Language for Natural Induction. Reports of the Machine Learning and Inference Laboratory, MLI 04-2. George Mason University (2004)

Modelling of Agents' Behavior with Semi-collaborative Meta-agents

Jan Tožička, Filip Železný, and Michal Pěchouček

Czech Technical University,
Gerstner Laboratory, Prague, Czech Republic
{tozicka, zelezny, pechouc}@labe.felk.cvut.cz
http://gerstner.felk.cvut.cz

Abstract. An autonomous agent may largely benefit from its ability to reconstruct another agent's reasoning principles from records of past events and general knowledge about the world. In our approach, the meta-agent maintains a first-order logic theory, called the community model, yielding predictions about other agents' decisions. In this contribution we introduce a query-based collective reasoning process where the semi-collaborative meta-agents use active learning technique to improve their models. We provide empirical results that demonstrate the viability of the concept and show the benefits of collective meta-reasoning.

1 Introduction

We are working with a community of autonomous reasoning agents endowed by number of capabilities which allow them to form coalitions to solve complex tasks (e.g. logistics). Behavior of our agents is given by a permanent reasoning algorithm and a set of private knowledge describing e.g. agent's preferences concerning the tasks, cooperation with other agents, etc. Agent's private knowledge is permanent. Dynamics of agent's behavior is given by changing resources and their availability, by ever changing environment in which the agents operate, and by different behavior of the other members of the multi-agent community.

What can also change or evolve during the lifespan of an agent is agent's awareness about the private knowledge of other members of the community. An agent has no direct access to the private knowledge of any other agent, it only can try to estimate or reconstruct its content in order to e.g. influence complexity, quality and effectiveness of collaboration, as well as the response time of the system.

Meta-reasoning is a key concept in this article. Unlike in classical computer science literature [1], where the meta-reasoning process is strictly understood as a reasoning process about yet another reasoning process, we will refer to meta-reasoning as agent's capability to reason also about other agent's knowledge, preferences, etc. In this contribution we compare deductive vs. inductive approach to meta-reasoning and introduce collective meta-reasoning of semi-collaborative meta-agents.

In Section 2, we will firstly introduce used meta-reasoning architecture and then present possible approaches to collective meta-reasoning. Section 3 presents a logistic scenario and experiments evaluating presented methods. We summarize our contribution in Section 4.

M. Pěchouček, P. Petta, and L.Z. Varga (Eds.): CEEMAS 2005, LNAI 3690, pp. 572–575, 2005.

2   Meta-reasoning Architecture

In this section, we will briefly introduce meta-agents and collective meta-reasoning. More detailed description of architecture, knowledge, formal language and used logic can be found in [2]. The principal role of the meta-reasoning agent is to support meta-reasoning process through maintaining and exploiting a model of the agent community. Our meta-reasoning agent monitors the community and is completely independent from the functionality of the community of the 'ordinary' agents. In principle, the community model can be maintained in two ways: (i) **deductive reasoning** maintains the model to contain only knowledge that logically follow from the observations. It is implemented by resolution-principle-based automated prover; and (ii) **inductive reasoning** maintains an *approximative model* which also contains knowledge generalizing the monitored knowledge; this formula can prove to be in conflict with some future events. Inductive meta-reasoning has been implemented using inductive logic programming (ILP).

The meta-agent can use different AI methods in order to update assumed model to consider new incoming events, we will call this process **model revision** operation, and to query assumed model during **model inspection** operation, which has three possible outcomes for given query: *yes*, *no*, and *unsure*.

2.1   Collective Meta-reasoning

Our experimental configuration characterized by a set of agents observed by a set of deductive/inductive meta-agents naturally lends itself as a ground on which some interesting, recently emerged machine-learning approaches can be empirically evaluated. Specifically, we have taken inspiration from (i) the study [3] on distributed learning of first-order logic theories; (ii) the *active learning* framework, where the learner is allowed to actively pose queries to an oracle; and (iii) the paradigm of *closed-loop* learning [4], where the learner can initiate experiments determining the required answer to a query. Adapting these techniques in the agent environment, has the promise of achieving a favorable trade-off between the average quality of the models developed by the meta-agents, and the invested computational effort.

Indeed, pursuing the outlined efficiency motivation, the paper [3] demonstrates that the search for a first-order logic theory. Collaboration can take place in the query time: a query is answered by several agents and the collective answer may be obtained by voting – we call this approach **deductive collaboration**. However, we try to establish interaction in the inductive process itself. In active learning, the learner is able to actively pose queries to an oracle, whose answers guide the model formation. Our adaptation of this principle into an **inductive collaboration** scheme assumes that an inductive meta-agent, besides the ability to generalize provided learning examples, may query another meta-agent, whose answer follows from its current model (possibly only partially built). Query is created randomly even if several heuristic approaches have been identified.

In the collective meta-reasoning development we will also apply the ideas of *closed-loop* learning [4], where the learner actually triggers experiments determining the required answer to a query. In our scenario, a meta-agent, monitoring an agent A, collaborates with another agent B, from whom it asks to offer a coalition to A. The B's proposal along with the proposal outcome then form an new observations.

3 Experiments

We have experimented with our meta-reasoning ideas in the $\mathcal{A}$-**cross** multi-agent scenario that has been integrated in the $\mathcal{A}$-**globe** multi-agent platform [5]. For us, the most important part of $\mathcal{A}$-**cross** logistic scenario are **transport-agents** who organize the transport of commodities. They form coalitions in order to convey the cargo. Coalition formation of transport-agents is determined by (i) availability of resources and (ii) sets of collaboration restrictions. We have extended this scenario by **observer-agents** and **meta-agents** that implement our meta-reasoning architecture. The observer-agents watch the transport-agents in their neighborhoods, transform observations into formal language and send them to the meta-agents. The meta-agents build their models about the community and try to reconstruct collaboration restrictions of transport-agents.

The meta-reasoning in our scenario works with *events* and *queries*. Events are created based on messages sent during CNP communication protocol. Queries can be used by user to get some knowledge from created community model. Queries asked among the meta-agents (as described in the section 2.1), has similar form as events. The meta-agents are semi-collaborative as they can agree to cooperate with other meta-agents (depending on their private restrictions) and even if one decides to cooperate he will answer only limited number of other agents queries.

Our goal is to evaluate the quality of a meta-reasoning process in different *configurations* of the interactions between meta-agents. A configuration is described by a rooted directed graph, where vertices correspond to meta-agents and edges lead from a query-posing agent to the answering agent (an oracle). Each possible configuration is characterized by two parameters, called **distributedness** and **collaborativeness**. The distributedness of a configuration graph is defined as the average distance among all pairs of vertices in the graph. The collaborativeness is defined as the maximum number of agents querying the same oracle (i.e.. the maximum branching factor).

The *quality* of a meta-reasoning process is viewed as a trade-off between the total computational effort used in model developing and the average model quality achieved. We will proceed by fixing a total budget and measuring the average model quality. Here, the quality of a created model is its **predictive accuracy**, i.e.. the ration of correctly classified *test* observations containing observations that are not used for learning.

To postulate expense-consciousness among the meta-agents, we establish a form of information market in the community, with the following rules of trade: (i) a meta-agent has to pay for every *yes* or *no* answered query; (ii) adhering to a common understanding of *information value*, the price for a answered query should be low if so is the model quality used to answer the query; and (iii) the meta-reasoning process initiates by assigning a constant budget to each agent. Each agent adds to its budget any price it charges to another agent, and subtracts any price it is charged by another agent. The meta-reasoning process terminates when all agents' budgets have been consumed.

Results. Figure 1 shows the average model quality values in respect to the distributedness values for 35 randomly generated configurations. It is interesting to note that the trend-line fitting the average quality of the models grows with the value of distributedness. Similarly, Figure 2 shows that the average model quality grows with the collaborativeness, as could be expected, however the growth is remarkably slow.

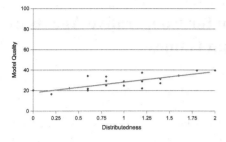

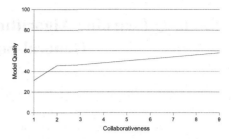

Fig. 1. X-Axis shows the distributedness of meta-agents and Y-Axis shows the average quality of the models

Fig. 2. X-Axis shows the collaborativeness among meta-agents and Y-Axis shows the average quality of their models

Both experiments suggest that distributed configurations, where only few meta-agents have direct or close access to the observations, allow a high average quality of the models created by the meta-agents, and, in the frame of a simple resource-conscious framework, they seem even superior to the centralized configurations.

4 Conclusions

In this paper, we focus on cooperation within a group of semi-collaborative meta-agents. Implemented technique in $\mathcal{A}$-**cross** scenario is evaluated in respect to the *distributedness* and the *collaborativeness* of meta-agents. The goal of meta-reasoning was to predict, based on the previous observations or using active learning technique, whether an agent will agree to join a coalition. Collective meta-reasoning proved to be useful when the meta-agents have to solve the trade-off between the average model quality and the total invested effort. We have shown, that under suitable settings, more distributed configuration can bring better model qualities than centralized case.

Acknowledgement. The presented research has been in parts supported by Office for Naval Research, project no.: N00014-03-1-0292 and European Office for Aerospace Research and Development, project no. F61775-99-WE099.

References

1. Maes, P.: Computational reflection. Tech. report 87-2, University of Brussels, AI Lab (1987)
2. Tožička, J., Bárta, J., Pěchouček, M.: Meta-reasoning for agents' private knowledge detection. In Klusch, M., Ossowski, S., Omicini, A., Laamanen, H., eds.: Cooperative Information Agent VII – Lecture Notes in Computer Science, LNAI 2782, Springer-Verlag, Heidelberg (2003)
3. Železný, F., Srinivasan, A., Page, D.: A monte carlo study of randomised restarted search in ilp. In: Inductive Logic Programming, 14th Int. Conf., Berlin, Springer (2004) 341–358
4. King, R., Whelan, K., Jones, F., Reiser, P.: Functional genomic hypothesis generation and experimentation by a robot scientist. Nature **427** (2004) 247–252
5. Šišlák, D., Rollo, M., Pěchouček, M.: A-globe: Agent platform with inaccessibility and mobility support. In Klusch, M., ed.: CIA VIII. Number 3191 in LNAI, Springer-Verlag (2004)

Pareto-Q Learning Algorithm for Cooperative Agents in General-Sum Games

Meiping Song, Guochang Gu, and Guoyin Zhang

College of Computer Science and Technology, Harbin Engineering University, China, 15001
songmeiping@hrbeu.edu.cn

Abstract. Rationality and convergence are two important criterions for multi-agent learning. A novel method called Pareto-Q learning is prompted for cooperative general-sum games, with the Pareto Optimum allowing rationality and social conventions benefiting the convergence. Experiments with the grid game suggest the efficiency of Pareto-Q. Compared with the single-agent Q-learning and Nash agent Q-learning, Pareto-Q learning performs best.

1 Introduction

With the development of multi-agent system, there have been many works focused on the learning of multi-agent. Most of them are under stochastic game framework[1], such as Minimax-Q for zero-sum games, and Nash-Q, FFQ and CEQ for general-sum games[2]. But only the Minimax-Q was proved to satisfy the convergence and rationality[3]. So that, a new method called Pareto-Q is prompted with the concept of Pareto optimum[4], which is more rational than Nash equilibrium[2] with regard to the cooperative system. At the same time, social conventions are also introduced to promise the convergence of learning. The performance is tested on the grid game.

2 Pareto-Q Algorithm

2.1 Formulation

Pareto-Q learning can be described as the followings.

$$Q_{t+1}^i(s,a^1,...,a^n) = (1-\alpha_t)Q_t^i(s,a^1,...,a^n) + \alpha_t[r_t^i + \gamma ParetoQ(s')] \tag{1}$$

$$ParetoQ_t^i(s) = \pi^1(s)\cdots\pi^n(s)\cdot Q_t^i(s) \tag{2}$$

where α_t is the learning rate decaying with t. $\pi^1(s)\cdots\pi^n(s)$ is the Pareto Optimum of the stage game $Q_t^1(s),...,Q_t^n(s)$.

2.2 Creating Lexicographic Convention

Occasionally, there are several Pareto optimums in a cooperative general-sum game, and agents may prefer to different ones. The issue is how to select the exact one for all

M. Pěchouček, P. Petta, and L.Z. Varga (Eds.): CEEMAS 2005, LNAI 3690, pp. 576–578, 2005.

agents, so as to guarantee the convergence. This problem can be solved by communicating or by imposing social conventions[5]. The former is not suitable for the learning process. Because too much communication will slow down the speed of decision, and the negotiated results could differ in time even for the same state, which will affect the convergence. The conventions are constraints on the possible action choices of the agents, and they form the common knowledge for all agents.

Jelle gave a lexicographic convention for simple cooperative multi-player games[5]. Here several general ones shown in figure1 are discussed to revise the conventions.

Game 1	Left	Right	Game 2	Left	Right	Game 3	Left	Right
Up	10, 9	0, 3	Up	5, 5	0, 6	Up	10, 9	0, 3
Down	3, 0	-1, 2	Down	6, 0	2, 2	Down	3, 0	2, 2
(1)			(2)			(3)		

Fig. 1. Three types of general-sum game

In each stage game, player 1 has two action choices: *Up* and *Down*. Player 2's action choices are *Left* and *Right*.

The first game has only one Nash equilibrium, with values (10,9), which is a global optimal point. The selection of both players will not be divergent.

The second game also has a unique Nash equilibrium, in this case a saddle point, valued at (2,2). But there still is a Pareto dominating solution, valued at (5,5), which will be better for the both players. In this case, we would impose the ordering '*Pareto optimum* ≻ *Saddle Nash*'.

The third game has two Nash equilibria: a global optimum which is also a Pareto optimum, (10,9), and a saddle, (2,2). In this case, we would impose the ordering '*Global Nash* ≻ *Saddle Nash*'.

Therefore, a series of conventions can be established as the following:

- The set of agents is ordered.
- The set of actions of each agent is ordered.
- The set of different types of solutions is ordered '*Global Nash* ≻ *Pareto optimum* ≻ *Saddle Nash*'
- These orderings are common knowledge among agents.

With these new conventions, the agents will achieve the same joint action without losing the optimal one. The choice for an optimal joint action proceeds as follows. The first agent in the agent ordering chooses an optimal action (that corresponds to a Pareto optimum) that appears first in its action ordering. The next agent then chooses its first optimal action in its action ordering given the first agent's choice. This procedure continues until all agents have chosen their actions.

3 Experiment Results and Conclusions

We test our Pareto Q-learning algorithm by applying it to the grid game which is also used in Nash-Q[2]. We implement three types of learning agents: single-agent

Q-learning, First Nash and First Pareto. One experiment uses 40,000 steps. The experimental results are shown in Table 1. For each case, we ran 100 trials and calculated the fraction that reaches an equilibrium joint path, that is, Nash path.

Table 1. Learning Performance

Learning Strategy		Results of Learning
Agent1	Agent2	Percent that reach a optimal Path
Single	Single	23%
First Nash	Single	45%
First Pareto	Single	54%
First Nash	First Nash	100%
First Pareto	First Pareto	100%

As we can see from the table, when both agent employ single-agent Q-learning, they reach a Nash equilibrium only 23% of the time. This is because the single-agent learner never models the other agent's strategic attitudes. When one agent is a First Nash agent and the other is a single-agent learner, the chance of reaching a Nash equilibrium increased to 45%. It approximates the result provided by Junling Hu[2] and is better than the first case. When one agent is a Pareto agent and the other one is a single-agent learner, the chance is increased to 54%, which is even better than Nash agent. Finally, when both agents are First Nash and First Pareto, they end up with a Nash equilibrium solution 100% of the time. But the problem of how to unify the selection of Nash agents is not discussed by Junling Hu.

The Pareto Q-learning algorithm introduces social conventions in cooperative multi-agent system to unify the choices of all agents, and replaces the Nash equilibrium with Pareto optimum to avoid losing the optimal solution. Compared with FFQ and CEQ, Pareto-Q makes agent more rational both for individual and group benefit. And it is more applicable than Nash-Q, because it doesn't need the strict conditions[2] any more. The experimental results also prove the efficiency of Pareto-Q.

References

1. Bowling M. and Veloso M.: Existence of Multiagent Equilibria with Limited Agents. Journal of Artificial Intelligence Research (2004(22)) 353-384
2. Junling Hu and Michael P. Wellman: Nash Q-Learning for General-sum Stochastic Games. Journal of Machine Learning Research (2003(4)) 1039-1069
3. Michael L. Littman and C. Szepesvari: A Generalized Reinforcement Learning Model: Convergence and Applications. Proceedings of the 13th International Conference on Machine Learning, Bari, Italy (1996) 310-318
4. K. Deb: Multi-Objective Evolutionary Algorithms: Introducing Bias among Pareto-Optimal Solutions. KanGAL report 99002, Indian Institute of Technology, Kanpur, India (1999)
5. Jelle R. Kok, Matthijs T. j. Spaan and Nikos Vlassis: An Approach to Noncommunicative Multiagent Coordination in Continuous Domains. Proceedings of the Twelfth Belgian-Dutch Conference on Machine Learning, Utrecht, Netherlands (2002) 46–52

Selection in Scale-Free Small World

Zsolt Palotai[1], Csilla Farkas[2], and András Lőrincz[1,*]

[1] Eötvös Loránd University, Department of Information Systems,
Pázmány Péter sétány 1/c, Budapest, H-1117, Hungary
andras.lorincz@elte.hu
[2] University of South Carolina, Department of Computer Sciences and Engineering,
Columbia, SC 29208, USA

Abstract. In this paper we compare our selection based learning algorithm with the reinforcement learning algorithm in Web crawlers. The task of the crawlers is to find new information on the Web. We performed simulations based on data collected from the Web. The collected portion of the Web is typical and exhibits scale-free small world (SFSW) structure. We have found that on this SFSW, the weblog update algorithm performs better than the reinforcement learning algorithm. It finds the new information faster than the reinforcement learning algorithm and has better new information/all submitted documents ratio.

1 Introduction

The largest source of information today is the World Wide Web. The ever-increasing growth of the Web presents a considerable challenge in finding novel information on the Web. In addition, properties of the Web, like scale-free small world (SFSW) structure [1,2] may create additional challenges. For example the direct consequence of the scale-free small world property is that there are numerous URLs or sets of interlinked URLs, which have a large number of incoming links. Intelligent web crawlers can be easily trapped at the neighborhood of such junctions as it has been shown previously [3,4].

In this paper we present a selection based algorithm and compare it to the well-known reinforcement learning algorithm in terms of their efficiency and behavior. The selection algorithm, called weblog update, modifies the starting URL lists of our crawlers based on the found relevant documents. The reinforcement learning algorithm modifies the URL orderings of the crawlers based on the received reinforcements for submitted documents. We have found that the weblog update selection algorithm performs better in this environment than the reinforcement learning algorithm, eventhough the reinforcement learning algorithm has been shown to be efficient in finding relevant information [4,5].

The paper is organized as follows. We overview the forager architecture in Section 2. After that in Section 3 we present our experiment on the Web and the conducted simulations with the results. Section 4 concludes our paper.

---

* Corresponding author.

M. Pěchouček, P. Petta, and L.Z. Varga (Eds.): CEEMAS 2005, LNAI 3690, pp. 579–582, 2005.
© Springer-Verlag Berlin Heidelberg 2005

2   Forager Architecture

There are two different kinds of agents: the foragers and the reinforcing agent (RA). The fleet of foragers crawl the web and send the URLs of the selected documents to the reinforcing agent. The RA determines which forager should work for the RA and how long a forager should work. The RA sends reinforcements to the foragers based on the received URLs.

Foragers may use two different kinds of algorithms to find relevant documents. The first algorithm, called weblog update algorithm selects the possibly good starting URLs and restarts periodically the forager from one of the possibly good starting URLs. The second algorithm is the reinforcement learning based URL ordering algorithm which selects the next document to be visited by the forager between two restarts. The documents found by a forager are represented as a 50 dimensional state vector. This algorithm updates the 50 dimensional weight vectors of the foragers in order to collect more rewards in the long run for sending relevant documents to the RA. The document to be visited next by the forager is the one with the highest value, where the value of a document is the scalar product of its state vector and the forager's weight vector. According to the weblog update algorithm the starting URL value of an URL is the sum of rewards collected during steps after visiting that URL and before the next restart. URLs with low starting URL values fall out from the weblog, while URLs of documents with high starting URL values go to the front of the weblog.

The algorithms and the architecture are detailed in [6].

3   Experiments

We conducted an 18 day long experiment on the Web to gather realistic data. We used the gathered data in simulations to compare the weblog update and reinforcement learning algorithms.

In the web experiment a fixed number of foragers were competing with each other to collect news at the CNN web site. The foragers were running in equal time intervals in a predefined order on one PC. We deployed 8 foragers using the weblog update and the reinforcement learning based URL ordering update algorithms. We also deployed 8 other foragers using the weblog update algorithm but without reinforcement learning. We used this heterogenous fleet of foragers to eliminate any biases on the gathered data. We investigated the link structure of the gathered Web pages. We have found that the links have a power-law distribution. That is the link structure has the scale-free property. We have also found that the links of gathered pages form small world structure.

We conducted simulations with two different kinds of foragers. The first case is when foragers used only the weblog update algorithm without URL ordering update (WL foragers). The second case is when foragers used only the reinforcement learning based URL ordering update algorithm without the weblog update algorithm (RL foragers). The simulation for each type of foragers were repeated 3 times with different initial weight vectors for each forager.

type	RL	std RL	WL	std WL
downloaded	540636	9840	669673	9580
sent	9747	98	6345	385
relevant	2419	45	3107	60
found URLs	31092	1050	33116	3370
download eff	0.0045	0.0001	0.0046	0.0001
sent eff	0.25	0.003	0.49	0.031
exploration	0.058	0.001	0.050	0.006
freshness	0.70	0.006	0.74	0.011
age (hours)	1.79	0.04	1.56	0.08

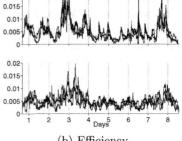

(a) Simulation results   (b) Efficiency

Fig. 1. Simulation results and Efficiency. (a): 2nd (3rd) and 4th (5th) columns show averages (standard deviations) of individual experiments. **(b):** Horizontal axis: time in days. Vertical axis: download efficiency, that is the number of found relevant documents divided by number of downloaded documents in 3 hour time intervals. Upper subfigure shows RL foragers' efficiencies, lower subfigure shows WL foragers' efficiencies. For all of the 3 simulation experiments there is a separate line.

Table 1(a) in Fig. 1 shows the measured parameter values averaged over the 3 runs of each type of foragers. From Table 1(a) we can conclude the followings. The efficiencies of RL and WL foragers from the point of view of the news site are about the same (download efficiency). From the point of view of the RA the efficiency of WL foragers is higher than RL foragers (sent efficiency). This shows that WL foragers divide the search area better among each other than RL foragers. Sent efficiency would be 1 if none of two foragers have sent the same document to the RA. RL foragers explore more than WL foragers: RL found more URLs per downloaded page than WL foragers did (exploration). WL foragers find faster the new relevant documents in the already found clusters. That is freshness is higher and age is lower than in the case of RL foragers.

Fig. 1(b) shows other aspects of the different behaviors of RL and WL foragers. Download efficiency of RL foragers has more, higher, and sharper peaks than the download efficiency of WL foragers has. That is WL foragers are more balanced in finding new relevant documents than RL foragers. The reason is that while the WL foragers remain in the found good clusters, the RL foragers continuously explore the new promising territories. The sharp peaks in the efficiency show that RL foragers *find and recognize* new good territories and then *quickly collect* the current relevant documents from there.

4   Conclusions

We presented and compared our selection algorithm to the well-known reinforcement learning algorithm. Our comparison was based on finding new relevant documents on the Web, that is in a dynamic scale-free small world environment. We have found that the weblog update selection algorithm performs better in this environment than the reinforcement learning algorithm, eventhough the reinforcement learning algorithm has been shown to be efficient in finding relevant information [4,5]. We explain our results based on the different behaviors of the algorithms. That is the weblog update algorithm finds the good relevant document sources and remains at these regions until better places are found by chance. Individuals using this selection algorithm are able to quickly collect the new relevant documents from the already known places because they monitor these places continuously. The reinforcement learning algorithm explores new territories for relevant documents and if it finds a good place then it collects the existing relevant documents from there by quickly adapting to the new neighborhood. Although RL is more flexible and has a fast tuning mechanims, nevertheless RL finds new relevant documents slower on the average than the more conservative weblog update algorithm. We conjecture that this conclusion may be restricted to highly clustered worlds, e.g., to scale-free small worlds.

Acknowledgement

This material is based upon work supported by the European Office of Aerospace Research and Development, Air Force Office of Scientific Research, Air Force Research Laboratory, under Contract No. FA8655-03-1-3036. This work is also supported by the National Science Foundation under grants No. INT-0304904 and No. IIS-0237782. Any opinions, findings and conclusions or recommendations expressed in this material are those of the author(s) and do not necessarily reflect the views of the European Office of Aerospace Research and Development, Air Force Office of Scientific Research, Air Force Research Laboratory.

References

1. Barabási, A., Albert, R., Jeong, H.: Scale-free characteristics of random networks: The topology of the world wide web. Physica A **281** (2000) 69–77
2. Kleinberg, J., Lawrence, S.: The structure of the web. Science **294** (2001) 1849–1850
3. Kókai, I., Lőrincz, A.: Fast adapting value estimation based hybrid architecture for searching the world-wide web. Applied Soft Computing **2** (2002) 11–23
4. Lőrincz, A., Kókai, I., Meretei, A.: Intelligent high-performance crawlers used to reveal topic-specific structure of the WWW. Int. J. Founds. Comp. Sci. **13** (2002) 477–495
5. Rennie, J., Nigam, K., McCallum, A.: Using reinforcement learning to spider the web efficiently. In: Proc. 16th Int. Conf. on Machine Learning (ICML), Morgan Kaufmann, San Francisco (1999) 335–343
6. Palotai, Z., Farkas, C., Lőrincz, A.: Selection in scale free small world. http://www.arxiv.org/pdf/cs.LG/0504063 (2005)

A Multi-agent System Architecture for the Adaptation of User Interfaces

Víctor López-Jaquero, Francisco Montero, José P. Molina, Pascual González, and Antonio Fernández-Caballero

Laboratory on User Interaction & Software Engineering (LoUISE),
University of Castilla-La Mancha, 02071 Albacete, Spain
{victor, fmontero, jpmolina, pgonzalez, caballer}@info-ab.uclm.es

Abstract. Nowadays the design of user interfaces has become a discipline of great importance in Software Engineering, mainly due to the increasing impact that a high quality user interface has in the success of a software product. However, the growing diversity in interaction devices and techniques has raised a big expectation for the design of both methods and architectures able to cope with context of use heterogeneity issues in an intelligent way. Multi-agent systems jump into scene as an alternative to design the adaptation capabilities required to cope with this problem in a natural manner.

1 Introduction

Nowadays the design of user interfaces has become a discipline of great importance in Software Engineering, mainly due to the increasing impact that a high quality user interface has in the success of a software product. To face the challenge of designing once and running in many different contexts of use (for instance, in different devices: PC, PDA, ...), model-driven architecture (MDA) appears as a solution, where the application is derived from a series of models describing both the dynamic and static aspects of an application. For the last decade, MDA has been a really active thread in UIs design research community, in the form of Model-Based User Interface Development Environments (MB-UIDE) [9]. In the design of a general technique that supports adaptivity [1] in a flexible manner, where knowledge can be reused and integrated with a UI design method that provides the required formalism to build UIs in a systematic way [7][6], a software architecture able to cope with all these requirements is needed. However, this software architecture needs to be able to make decisions about which adaptations should be applied, when they should be applied, etc. System decisions about adaptation should be grounded in the UI model developed at design time, along with the information about the context of use that the system gets from the environment. In this paper the use of the multi-agent paradigm in the design of a software architecture to support adaptative behaviour in UIs is proposed. A set of agents collaborate in a multi-agent system (MAS) to achieve the final goal of adaptation, by receiving through their sensors the changes in the environment (context of use) where they are involved.

---

[1] This work is partly supported the Spanish PBC-03-003 and CICYT TIN2004-08000-C03-01 grants.

M. Pěchouček, P. Petta, and L.Z. Varga (Eds.): CEEMAS 2005, LNAI 3690, pp. 583–586, 2005.
© Springer-Verlag Berlin Heidelberg 2005

2 The Adaptation Process

Within adaptivity there is a wide range of possibilities where several actors (usually the system and the user) can take the initiative in the different stages carried out in order to perform the adaptation. Thus, this adaptation is not preformed automatically, but semiautomatically. The stages needed to perform adaptation according to [3] are: (1) **initiative:** one of the actors involved in the interaction suggests its intention to perform an adaptation. The main actors are usually the user and the system, (2) **proposal:** if a need for adaptation is detected, it is necessary to make proposals of adaptations that could be applied successfully in the current context of use for that need for adaptation detected, (3) **decision:** as we may have different proposals from the previous stage we need to decide which adaptation proposals best fit the need for adaptation detected, and even if it is worth applying any of them, and (4) **execution:** finally, the adaptation chosen will be executed.

3 A Multi-agent Architecture for Adaptive User Interfaces

The multi-agent system perceives the changes in the context of use by means of sensors. Then, a set of adaptations will be chosen among the feasible adaptations taking into account the expected benefit evaluation that each feasible adaptation would produce to the user if it would be applied. Finally, the selected adaptations will be applied following a transformational approach.

At *Initiative stage* the adaptation process is fired. This can be achieved mainly in two different ways: (1) the user explicitly expresses his intention to perform an adaptation, (2) the system or a third-party agent detects that an adaptation might be helpful or needed. In this second case, this stage can be subdivided into two smaller sub-stages. On the one hand, the system needs to guess the current goal the user is pursuing, and on the other hand it should guess which needs the user has with respect to the detected current goal. In the multi-agent system proposed for the adaptation of the UI this stage is performed by means of *AgentContextPlatform*, *AgentContextEnvironment*, *AgentContextUser*, and the user itself. The three agents receive any change in the context of use perceived by the sensors and take advantage of the data collected during design and the data perceived to figure out whether the adaptation process should be fired or not.

Within agent design paradigm, just as in human reasoning model, the possible actions that an agent can use to face a situation (a change in the context of use in our case) are the plans. Thus, *AgentAdaptationProcess* agent has a plan for each possible adaptation that can be applied. Adaptations are represented as adaptivity rules at design time, which are translated later into agent's plans, following an approach based on *Prometheus* [8] method plan specification. The meta-model for an adaptivity rule is specified in terms of the context-of-use events that trigger the adaptivity rule, the sensors that produce those events, the data the rule accesses (read/write), the transformations of the UI needed in order to apply the rule, and the context precondition. The context precondition specifies the required conditions that the current context of use must meet in order for the adaptivity rule to be applicable. The transformation specifies the "real" adaptation of the UI. These transformations modify a graph representation of the usiXML [10] specification of the running UI. To modify the representation of the graph an attributed graph grammar engine is used.

Decision stage is performed by *AgentAdaptationProcess*. This agent will use the selected selection policy to choose the adaptations that should be applied. Notice that the user can also decide which adaptations to apply among the adaptations that match the current changes in context. We have two different policies available for the selection of the adaptations that best fit a context of use change. The first one is the simpler one. When this first adaptation selection policy is chosen, the first rule that could be applied to the current situation is selected. The selection order is the same as the order in which the rules were fired. Therefore, following this first policy no meta-planning method is required. However, it will yield unpredictable results in many cases, making adaptation a useless feature. The second policy is a little more sophisticated. It selects the rules taking into account usability criteria evaluation.

Execution stage is also performed by *AgentAdaptationProcess* agent. In this stage, there are three main sub-steps: (1) Get an up-to-date copy of the UI expressed in terms of usiXML language, (2) Apply the adaptations. The adaptations are applied performing the transformations specified for each chosen plan. And, (3) restore the UI out of the newly generated one. The adapted UI will be shown to the user, restoring interaction to the state it was before adaptation took place. An agent called *AgentStimuliGenerator* has been added to the architecture to make debugging and evaluation easier. This agent simulates the arrival of data from the sensors, following a pattern of events specified by the designer.

4 Implementing the Adaptive Architecture

In this section we will show an overview of the technologies used in the implementation of the architecture. For the MAS implementation we have used JACK Intelligent Agents[TM] [2]. To maximize platform independence we have wrapped the multi-agent java based system within an HTTP server interface. The HTTP server interface allows any platform capable of networking using TCP/IP protocol to access the adaptation engine. This HTTP server has been implemented as a servlet (server side applet) that runs on top of a TOMCAT server.

usiXML UI description language is able to describe a UI in a manner independent from the platform where it will run on. Therefore, a renderer is needed so the user can visualize the UI. For this purpose, a renderer for the concrete UI level of usiXML has been written for XUL language. This renderer translates a usiXML CUI specification into a XUL language specification that can be visualized by the user. XUL is an XML-based UI language that can be visualized in any Internet browser based on Mozilla engine (http://www.mozilla.org). At this moment, we have implemented the embedded sensors needed to capture the data from the interaction using JavaScript. JavaScript allows the implementation of the dynamic behaviour of the UI. The engine to execute the transformations associated to the adaptations uses the API from AGG [5] tool to perform the transformations. The engine transforms a usiXML specification expressed as an attributed graph into a new usiXML specification transformed according to the adaptation rules selected. In [5] a detailed description of the transformation process can be found.

5 Final Remarks

There have been many works related to the adaptation of UIs, especially in the field of intelligent tutoring systems. However, most of that research has led to solutions where the adaptations were hardcoded within the system, making it very difficult to modify the way adaptations are made, or to reuse the solution from one application to another. In this paper a MAS is proposed that is able to cope with the adaptation process in a flexible way, and where the same language is used for the specification of both the UI and the adaptation rules. Furthermore, the system detects the context of use by means of a set of sensors that modify the context model included inside the agents' beliefs, making the MAS react to accommodate the UI to the different situations produced by the changes in the context of use detected by sensors.

References

1. Benyon D., Murray D.. Developing adaptive systems to fit individual aptitudes. IUI 1993, pp. 115-121, Orlando, Florida, United States, ACM Press, 1993.
2. Busetta, P., Ronnquist, R., Hodgson, A. and Lucas, A. Jack intelligent agents - components for intelligent agents in java. AgentLink News Letter, January 1999. White paper.
3. Dieterich, H., Malinowski, U., Khme, T. and Schneider-Hufschmidt, M. "State of the Art in Adaptive User Interfaces". In: Schneider-Hufschmidt, M., Khme, T. and Malinowski, U., eds.: Adaptive User Interfaces: Principle and Practice. Amsterdam, Holland, 1993.
4. Fernández-Caballero, A., López-Jaquero, V., Montero, F., González, P. Adaptive Interaction Multi-agent Systems in E-learning/E-teaching on the Web. International Conference on Web Engineering, ICWE 2003. Springer Verlag, pp. 144-154. 2003.
5. Limbourg, Q., Vanderdonckt, J., Michotte, B., Bouillon, L., López-Jaquero, V. USIXML: a Language Supporting Multi-Path Development of User Interfaces. Proc. of 9th IFIP Working Conference on Engineering for HCI jointly with 11th Int. Workshop on Design, Specification, and Verification of Interactive Systems (Hamburg, July 11-13, 2004). LNCS, Vol. 3425, Springer-Verlag, Berlin, 2005, pp. 207-228.
6. López-Jaquero, V., Montero, F., Molina, J.P., Fernández-Caballero, A., González, P. Model-Based Design of Adaptive User Interfaces through Connectors Design, Specification and Verification of Interactive Systems 2003, DSV-IS 2003. Springer Verlag, 2003.
7. López-Jaquero, V., Montero, F., Molina, J.P., González, P., Fernández-Caballero, A. A Seamless Development Process of Adaptive User Interfaces Explicitly Based on Usability Properties. Proc. of 9th IFIP Working Conference on Engineering for HCI jointly with 11th Int. Workshop on Design, Specification, and Verification of Interactive Systems (Hamburg, July 11-13, 2004). LNCS, Vol. 3425, Springer-Verlag, Berlin, 2005.
8. Padgham, L., Winikoff, M. Prometheus: a methodology for developing intelligent agents. AAMAS 2002: 37-38
9. Paternò, F. Model-Based Design and Evaluation of Interactive Applications. Springer Verlag, 2000.
10. usiXML specification. Available at http://www.usixml.org
11. Wooldridge, M., Jennings, N.R. Agent Theories, Architectures, and Languages: A Survey, ECAI-Workshop on Agent Theories, Architectures and Languages. Wooldridge, M.J. and Jennings, N.R. (eds.), 1994.

ACE Agents – Mass Personalized Software Assistance

Jarogniew Rykowski

The Poznan University of Economics, Dept. of Information Technology,
Mansfelda 4, 60-854 Poznan, Poland
rykowski@kti.ae.poznan.pl

Abstract. In this paper we propose a new idea of developing personalized software assistants. We based our approach on the technology of software agents, and the Agent Computing Environment ACE. Rather than using a single, complicated, resident personal assistant of a fixed architecture and functionality, we use a distributed set of specialized, user-defined agents, working in parallel in an autonomous manner to fulfill given requests. The ACE agents may be imperatively programmed by their owners to achieve certain goals. The agents may be also orchestrated and self-adjusted to the environment, communication means, local hardware/software limitations, geographical location, etc.

1 Introduction

Nowadays we may observe a continuously growing trend in using computers and modern telecommunication technologies in many domains of our everyday life and work. This trend is especially visible in the scope of mobile technologies and computer-based personal assistance, usually combined with the software agents technology. A software agent is characterized by many features well-suited for personal assistance: autonomy, mobility, flexibility and self-adjustment to changes in the environment, etc. The main problem is that today's software agents cannot be fully personalized and thus effectively used in a mass environment. Typical "personal" agents, with a basic architecture common for all the users, and with similar functionality and behavior, are not flexible enough for mass environment with many users characterized by different requirements and expectations. As today's agents are specialized in certain tasks and services (e.g., shopping agents, schedulers), these agents are not well suited for modern application areas, with a need to differentiate an architecture and behavior of each individual agent, and a need to adjust agent structure to the requirements of the agent's owner, geographical zone, communication means, etc.

In this paper we present a new approach to mass, personalized, agent-based assistance. Instead of proposing a complicated, however fixed architecture of a new yet-another personal assistant, we propose a framework capable of creating, orchestrating, and executing small, personalized software agents. The remainder of the paper is organized as follows. In Section 2, current approaches to agent-based personal assistance are briefly presented, mainly monitors/informers and FIPA agents. In Section 3, ACE agents are presented, together with some basic features of the agent environment used. Section 4 concludes the paper.

M. Pĕchouček, P. Petta, and L.Z. Varga (Eds.): CEEMAS 2005, LNAI 3690, pp. 587–590, 2005.
© Springer-Verlag Berlin Heidelberg 2005

2 Current Approaches to Agent-Based Personal Assistance

There are three basic trends in today's agent-based personal assistance: information brokers and avatars, autonomous monitors, and complex "automatic secretaries". *Information brokers* are mainly implemented as resident agents of a fixed architecture and functionality. The main goal of such an agent is to provide an efficient access to certain information, in a certain manner. Broker-agents use WWW/WAP access channels, avatars with chatterbot support (e.g., Verbot and Microsoft Agent applications), and SMS/MMS messaging (e.g., SMS-B system). The broker-agents are usually equipped with a possibility of monitoring changes of selected information and notifying the users. Generic *agent-monitors* (e.g., SmartBookmarks, BargainFinder) are now being replaced by specialized agents used mainly for price comparison (Bizrate, Amazon, etc.), and change notification of given WWW pages (Mind-It by Pumatech), news servers (NewsPage), stocks and bank accounts, software releases, etc.

There are several reasons that all these systems do not cover the domain of our proposal. First, the "agents" are not software agents according to the classical definition. Second, a typical "agent" is not user-defined, usually it is fixed to perform some well-defined, repetitive tasks, and to contact a single service. Third, generic chatterbot avatars impose several restrictions while using external information sources.

FIPA agent is an example of a more complicated *personal assistant*. The main idea of this proposal is to provide a software assistance similar to a "human secretary", helping in everyday, tedious tasks. Each FIPA agent is build according to FIPA-PA reference model. The FIPA proposal lacks at least: (1) efficient and fast adaptation to changes in the environment, (2) distribution and mobility, including migration to mobile devices, and (3) unrestricted personalization of behaviour (agent code). The predefined (fixed) architecture and functionality of a FIPA personal agent seriously limits system flexibility and openness to new (not only communication) standards.

3 Agent Technology for Mass Personal Assistance

To solve the problem of mass personalized assistance, we propose to use imperative, distributed software agents and the Agent Computing Environment ACE. In our approach, we define software agents in classical way [5], as autonomous entities executed at a given place, able to communicate with the environment and other agents or humans. The ACE framework is based on a set of distributed Agent Servers, each of them capable of storing and executing software agents. The agents may be moved among Agent Servers. There are "light" Agent Servers with limited functionality to be executed in a "thin" hardware/software environment (e.g., mobile phones), and "thick", massively used Agent Servers located in stationary network hosts. The "light" servers are mainly used for executing individual agents of an owner of a mobile device, while the "thick" ones are used by many users in parallel, usually to access certain services, external software systems, and public communication channels.

There are two basic classes of ACE agents: public System Agents, and Private Agents. Public *System Agents* SAs are created by trusted users (usually system designers), to be used in a mass manner by many users, providing information in a standardized form and with optimum effort. As overall efficiency is of primary concern,

SAs are programmed in Java. A way of usage of a given SA cannot be changed by an ordinary user, however, it may be parameterized during the invocation.

The *Private Agents* PAs are created and controlled by their human owners. Unless directly ordered by its owner, the agent cannot be accessed by any other agent. For private agents, the main problem is to achieve a reasonable trade-off between overall system security and a need for remote (i.e., server-side) execution of user-defined, thus „untrusted" (from the local administrator point of view) code. Several restrictions and limitations must be applied to user-defined code, protecting the system from (intentional or accidental) damages. Thus, a specialized language is proposed to program agent behavior, based on XML and equipped with several non-standard mechanisms like run-time monitoring of CPU time and memory allocation. The language is of imperative type, thus allowing much wider personalization of the agent code in comparison with the classical declarative approach. XML-programmed private agents may invoke huge library of on-site, residential, Java-based system agents: communicators, services, brokers to external software systems, tools and utilities, etc. Usually, a small private agent, being a "light" mobile entity, is able to use (i.e., execute) several system agents, to achieve different goals. From the user point of view, the system is effective and powerful, and even small private agents are "intelligent" enough to fulfill complex requirements. From the system point of view, private agents executed at server-side do not pose a threat to local environment and other agents.

The interface for all the agents is reduced to a single-method with (hash)table of unique pairs of "name/text value" type as the input parameter. Similar to the input parameters, the output parameter (result) is also standardized as a single text value of unlimited type and length. This looks quite lean, however, as any result may be encoded as a flat text, such standardized interface improves a flexibility of the system. From a user point of view, private agents may use as complicated parameters as it is needed at the moment. Some agents/invocations may use flat text parameters, as for example an SMS message, while some of them are able to interpret such complex parameters, as XML documents (e.g., for intra-communication among agents). Moreover, different standards may be implemented for particular agents, supporting efficient knowledge representation and interchange (for example KQML, SOAP, etc.). Note that a way of interpretation of an input parameter depends on the agent owner, and different agents may use parameters of different purpose and complexity.

The standardization of both input parameters and the result does not limit internal agent logic. Despite parameters used and the returned result, an agent owner is able to define agent behavior according to any algorithm. Moreover, and agent may react in specific manner (i.e., according to different sub-algorithms) to specific sets of parameters, taking into account an internally stored history of previous invocations.

A typical Agent Server is equipped with several specialized system agents, so called input/output gateways, able to communicate with an external world (including other Agent Servers, local and remote software, and humans) via communication channels of different type and purpose. In general, two basic types of human-agent communication gateways are available: textual and Web-based. A *textual gateway* is able to exchange flat (unformatted) text messages, usually among humans and agents. Physically, textual gateways may use such means as an e-mail SMTP/POP3 connection, SMS (Short Message System)/MMS connection with a telecommunication network, a voice gateway, etc. Once sent by a textual message, an ACE agent may act as a chatterbot, analyzing the message via keyword extraction and analysis [4]. The chatterbot interface is especially useful for non-advanced users, and for users temporary handicapped due to limited hardware possibilities and communication costs.

Web-based gateways are used to access an agent via a WWW/WAP page, and from specialized ACE applications. For semi-automatic formatting of both contents and presentation of the data to be sent, XSL-T technology was adopted with XSL transformations defined in a personal manner and stored in private agent variables [3]. To improve data formatting and presentation, automatic detection of end-user device may be applied, allowing auto-adjustment to the availabilities and technical possibilities of both communication means and end-user devices.

Gateways to external data sources are mainly used for automatic monitoring of information changes. As a change is reported by an external data source, a gateway invokes a selected agent. The agent may next pass the notification about "interesting" changes to user(s), via certain tele-communication gateways. What is "interesting" for the user is programmed by him/her in the code of the private agents [1, 2]. Thus, a set of user's agents is an "intelligent", personalized filter of changes of monitored data.

The number and types of the gateways used (including some specific parameters, e.g., a phone number for an SMS center) is local-administrator dependent. Note that the gateways are implemented as system agents, thus one may easily extend a given Agent Server by some non-standard communication means.

4   Conclusions

ACE personal agents fulfill all the requirements for efficient software assistance. Each ACE agent may be individually programmed to achieve certain, user-specific goals. Agent's behavior may be settled to fulfill specific requirements of its owner. At the same time, the information propagated by the agent may be automatically adjusted to the environment the agent is executed in, current time, place, communication link, etc. ACE agents may be distributed across the network, including users' mobile devices. Several agents of the same user may be effectively orchestrated.

The ACE framework has been already tested as two industry applications: an "intelligent" assistant for clients of a bank, and notifying support for owners of mobile phones – generic information system using e-mail/SMS/MMS messaging.

References

1. Rykowski J., Agent Technology for Secure Personalized Web Services, 24th International Scientific School ISAT 2003, Szklarska Poreba, Poland, 2003, pp. 185-193
2. Rykowski J., Cellary W., Virtual Web Services - Application of Software Agents to Personalization of Web Services, 6th Int. Conf. ICEC 2004, Delft, Holland, 2004, pp. 409-418
3. Rykowski, J., Juszkiewicz, A., Personalization of Information Delivery by the Use of Agents, IADIS Int. Conf. WWW/Internet 2003, Algarve, Portugal, 2003, pp. 1056-1059
4. Rykowski, J., Using software agents to personalize natural-language access to Internet services in a chatterbot manner, 2nd Int. Conf. L&T'05, Poznan, Poland, 2005, pp. 269-273
5. Wooldridge, M., Jennings, N.R., Intelligent agents: theory and practice, Knowledge Engineering Review 10-1995-2, pp. 115-152

Assisting Robotic Personal Agent and Cooperating Alternative Input Devices for Severely Disabled Children

Gy. Hévízi, B. Gerőfi, B. Szendrő, and A. Lőrincz

Department of Information Systems, Eötvös Loránd University, Budapest, Hungary
http://nipg.inf.elte.hu

Abstract. A multi-component cooperating system have been designed for severely disabled children having various disabilities. Different input tools have been developed to exploit possible 'outputs', e.g., head motion or leg motion. Specific software tools serve to convert such 'outputs' in different computer aided tasks. Extendable software enables configurable networking. *Robotic personal agent* helps the communication.

1 Introduction

Recent technology provides a variety of hardware devices and software tools for people having only very limited control over their muscles, being restricted in speech or in other ways to communicate and to interact with their environment. They need sophisticated solutions. They cannot use typical devices so technology must adapt to them. These subjects need care and the most appropriate devices need to be utilized. In typical cases, adaptive devices are necessary, including adaptive filtering of signals and the recognition of behavioral patterns.

There are several commercial devices that were designed for severely handicapped people. For a survey on current state-of-the-art interfaces see [1]. Tools, however, are typically expensive. Thus, our goal is twofold: (i) use novel tools, such as wireless sensors and robots, and (ii) develop simple software that can be used by caretakers to select optimal feasible components.

We review our efforts on developing tools and personal agents for severely handicapped non-speaking but speech understanding children.

2 Cooperating Tools and Devices

We are to integrate different alternative input devices, hardware tools, software applications and personal robotic agents into a common framework. These means should cooperate both each other and with the user. We will briefly review some existing building blocks of this framework: *'input devices'*, that are responsible for capturing one or more of the *'outputs'* of the user, *'applications'*, i.e., software components designed to facilitate the user's interaction with the framework, *'software communication tools'* that connect the applications with the input

M. Pěchouček, P. Petta, and L.Z. Varga (Eds.): CEEMAS 2005, LNAI 3690, pp. 591–594, 2005.

tools, and *'learning algorithms'* that are designed to adapt the computer by detecting performance, mood, and non-typical states or behaviors of the user.

Input devices: *Head Mouse* is a head movement detector that translates head motions to cursor motions. It works with a webcam. *Voice Mouse* was developed for subjects who are able to control the pitch and volume of their voice. The user initializes the interaction by giving a reference voice and moves the cursor by altering its properties. Varying the pitch or the volume change the x or the y coordinates, respectively. *Tilt Mouse* is for children who are able to control certain parts of their body, e.g., one or more limbs. The rapid evolution of the RF-MEMS devices makes possible to measure and communicate, e.g., the acceleration in real-time and in a wireless manner. Tightening these devices to the subject we get alternative input devices. Present day RF-MEMS tools are inexpensive and some of them are already built into cloths like shoes and shirts, e.g., to measure the number of steps, heart rate, etc. [2]. *Utterance recognition* can be used by subjects being able to say recognizable utterances that can be translated to operations on the computer. *Eye Tracking:* For severely disabled people sometimes eye motion is one of the last possibilities. Despite the existence of reliable specific solutions there is still a need for a cheap and simple ones even at the price of reduced accuracy. Our system is equipped with a webcam and we have promising results in giving commands by 'eye gestures'.

Applications: Although alternative devices can give an input to the computer, disabled people usually need more support from the application side. A typical example is *Dasher*, the writing tool, which has been developed at Cambridge University[1]. Dasher is driven by pointing gestures, typing is achieved by choosing the appropriate letter. Dasher has a predictive language model. Probable pieces of text are made larger and can be selected [3]. We have provided Hungarian text for Dasher. *iConnTab* is our application designed for patients who cannot control the cursor accurately enough to keep it on the target icon and click on it. The idea is to execute leaky integration for each items on the screen. The value increases if the cursor is above an item and decreases towards zero if it is not. Irregular motion patterns can be integrated by this simple method: if the subject can ensure that the cursor spends the most time over the target item then proper selection can be made. *Aibo:* Sony has developed a robotic dog. It is ideal for disabled children to communicate with others. With our tools, the dog behaves as a personal agent, it can be controlled to move around in the flat. It has a camera and can send the image through WiFi. It also has a microphone and a speaker, so it can record, produce and transmit sound. *Dashboard* is a tiny application with user defined buttons to control running applications. Dashboard can be activated without clicking: The cursor should be moved to it. Dashboard contains iConnTab-like buttons so no click function is necessary. *TTS:* One of the most important function of technical assistance for non-speaking but speech understanding subjects who can produce texts is the text-to-speech tool. A standardized speech API interface under Windows

---

[1] http://www.inference.phy.cam.ac.uk/is/

XP is applied. Synthetic voice can be transmitted to the speakers of the user's computer, the partner's computer, or to the personal agent.

Communication: Practical configurations will be complex. Basic elements should be connected through platform independent extensible mechanisms. Standardized messages are necessary for modular construction. To each child, the optimal components need to be "plugged in". Communication between software components running on different machines is enabled by our TCP/IP based communication framework. Messages are transported through TCP/IP sockets. Interfaces that adapt by analyzing the user as well as adaptive communication layers are under development.

User Analysis: The users' interaction with the computer can be efficiently assisted if we can analyze the interaction and optimize performance, e.g., the typing speed. We have performed a series of Dasher experiments with healthy volunteers, who used different input devices. Traditional mouse was used for comparison. The trace of the cursor was analyzed [4]) by means of Hidden Markov Models ([5], [6]). We found that emergent behavioral patterns are similar for all input devices, can be interpreted and enable computer assistance.

3   Cooperating Tools and Personal Agent

A particular arrangement is detailed here. This arrangement is being implemented at the Alternative and Augmentative Communication (AAC) Center, Budapest. A framework of specific applications - including a personal message delivering and video transmitting personal agent - is outlined in Fig. 1. The child has a notebook mounted on his/her wheelchair. A webcam monitors his/her face. The notebook receives the camera stream. HeadMouse analyzes head motion and translates it to cursor movements. The motion of the cursor can be analyzed to assist and improve performance. The child can edit messages by using iConnTab

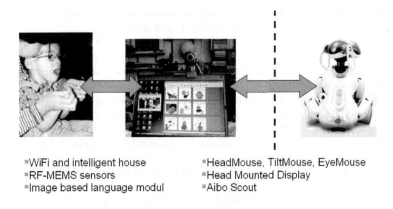

- WiFi and intelligent house   - HeadMouse, TiltMouse, EyeMouse
- RF-MEMS sensors   - Head Mounted Display
- Image based language modul   - Aibo Scout

Fig. 1. Schematics of alternative input devices and personal agent

or Dasher. Each message is converted to an acoustic stream via the Speech API and the utterances are produced by local, or remote notebook speakers, or, by Aibo, according to the user's intentions.

Present state of the implementation: Children at AAC Center are practising the use of Head Mouse. It was found, to our surprise, that many children could learn to use them, even that they seemed not to use their head before. Although it was typical that the first trials were disappointing for us, those delighted the children, because they could not control anything before. Suitable pointing precision was achieved in many cases. AAC is now equipped with laptops, webcams. RF-MEMS ultrasound distance measuring devices, acceleration meters, and the intelligent house will start to operate in the fall when the children return from their summer vacation. Collection of data will start afterwards.

3.1   Conclusion and Outlook

With the development of robotic technology and decrease of prices, personal robotic agents find their place in assisting disabled people. Our framework has been designed to enable flexible and standardized communication between components that can be configured for each individual differently. Technology should increase the choice of wireless sensors quickly. Components of the system shall become less and less expensive alike to trends we have witnessed over the years. We expect that intelligent motion analysis and motion prediction can assist severely handicapped people. This seems the main bottleneck now, because the quality of the sensors is satisfactory. Robotic personal agent should be part of the scheme. Communication is crucial for the cognitive development of the children at the AAC Center. It is expected that similar tools may be learned and used by elderly people. From this point of view, our project is a prototype project.

References

1. P. Ehlert, "Intelligent user interfaces: introduction and survey," 2003. [Online]. Available: citeseer.nj.nec.com/ehlert03intelligent.html
2. G. Yang, O. Wells, and B. Lo, Eds., *2nd Int. Workshop on Wearable and Implantable Body Sensor Networks.*   London, UK: Imperial College, April 2005.
3. D. J. Ward, "Adaptive computer interfaces," Ph.D. dissertation, Churchill College, Cambridge, 2001.
4. Gy. Hévízi, M. Biczó, B. Póczos, Z. Szabó, B. Takács, and A. Lőrincz, "Hidden Markov model finds behavioral patterns of users working with a headmouse driven writing tool," in *IJCNN 2004.*   Piscataway, NJ 08855-1331: IEEE Operations Center, July 2004, paper No. 1268. IJCNN2004 CD-ROM Conference Proceedings, IEEE Catalog Number: 04CH37541C.
5. L. R. Rabiner and B. H. Juang, "An introduction to hidden Markov models," *IEEE ASSP Magazine*, pp. 4–15, January 1986.
6. M. Welling, "Hidden Markov Models," http://www.cs.toronto.edu/ welling /class-notes/classnotes.html.

Building Agent-Based Systems in a Discrete-Event Simulation Environment

Botond Kádár[1], András Pfeiffer[1,2], and László Monostori[1,2]

[1] Computer and Automation Institute, Hungarian Academy of Sciences,
H-1111 Budapest Kende u. 13–17, Hungary
[2] Department of Production Informatics, Management and Control,
Budapest University of Technology and Economics,
H-1111 Budapest Müegyetem rkp. 3-9
{kadar, pfeiffer, monostor}@sztaki.hu

Abstract. The paper outlines a discrete-event simulation environment for modeling agent-based manufacturing systems. Exploiting the advantages of a general discrete-event simulation package, in the developed system agent-based features are directly included in the simulation environment providing the possibility to build agent-based models inside the simulation. The paper describes the agent-based functionalities of the system by presenting the communication mechanisms and predefined collaboration protocols. The modeling system implements the heterarchical control concept that is based on the contract net protocol.

1 Introduction

Research in *multi-agent systems (MAS)* considers the behavior of a collection of autonomous nodes aiming at solving a given problem. A MAS is defined as a loosely coupled network of problem solvers that work together to solve problems that are beyond their individual capabilities. The nodes of the system are called *agents* which are self-directed software objects with their own value system and capability to communicate with other agents. Advantages of multi-agent systems include: self-configuration, scalability, fault tolerance, emergent behavior, and massive parallelism [1]. Multi-agent systems are used for heterarchical control, where the complete decision process is performed without any form of hierarchy. A number of researchers attempted to apply agent technology - among other fields - in different segments of production systems. Examples exist for enterprise integration, supply chain management, manufacturing planning, scheduling and control, materials handling and holonic manufacturing [2].

In most of the cases, e.g. agent-based manufacturing control or material handling and manufacturing logistics the new approaches were tested in agent-based simulation environments where the simulation and the agent-based part of the system were separated. The simulation substituted the real manufacturing system and the heart of the agent-based mechanism was developed in a separate system [3], [4]. Today several different agent building frameworks, middleware are available providing basic functionalities for building distributed applications.

M. Pěchouček, P. Petta, and L.Z. Varga (Eds.): CEEMAS 2005, LNAI 3690, pp. 595–599, 2005.

However, none of these frameworks gives functionalities of objects suitable for modeling manufacturing systems. The paper outlines a discrete-event simulation environment which enables the modeling of agent-based manufacturing systems. Exploiting the advantages of a general discrete-event simulation package, in the developed system agent-based features are directly included in the simulation environment providing the possibility to build agent-based models inside the simulation.

2   The Agent-Based Manufacturing Simulation System

The proposed model is based on a general object-oriented simulation system consisting of material, personnel and information sub-systems. This environment provides an object library that contains a number of basic objects. Combining and customizing these basic elements user-defined objects can be created that enable the construction of application-specific libraries.

The agent-based manufacturing model applies a fully heterarchical architecture including two type of agents. Based on the physical decomposition approach resources are the basic active units of the system that can perform different tasks. They are represented by *Resource agents*. An *Order agent* (the other basic unit of the system), on the other hand, includes functions such as order management and task dispatching. The parts passing through the system are active information elements holding all the relevant information about themselves they assist the agents in their actions.

2.1   Communication Between Agents

The whole communication process between agents is modeled inside the simulation and the agents exchange only string based messages. For this purpose a specific communication protocol was developed. The protocol specifies the form of a message and the possible exchangeable amount of information. The template of a messages is as follows:

msg_ID|delivery_time|ack|sender|type|name|param1|param2|
param3|param4|param5|param6|receiver

- msg_ID: unique identification of the message,
- delivery_time: the point time when the message was sent,
- ack: flag indicating whether the sender needs acknowledgement of the reception,
- sender: the name of the sender agent,
- type: the type of the message, e.g. TASK_ANNOUNCEMENT, BID, etc.
- name: optional and type specific information for the identification of different messages belonging to the same type,
- param$n$: optional and type specific information, transporting the basic knowledge between agents,
- receiver: the name of the receiver agent.

The action flow in the discrete event simulation corresponds to discrete actions in the model that are mainly bounded with real physical parts. This means that the simulation controller continuously updates a list of points in time when part creation, part movements, starting of a process on a part, part deletion, method calls, etc. are occurred. A minor drawback of such a system is that changes in information blocks are not treated as discrete events. The message exchange between two agents is a typical information change that does not enter events automatically in the event list of the simulation controller. We overcame this drawback by applying *"active" message boxes* that are responsible for the management of the sending and the receiving processes. In this construction each message box sends and receives messages in predefined intervals. The intervals for incoming and outgoing messages are treated separately and can be adjusted by for each individual agent independently.

3   Resource Allocation by Using the Contract Net Protocol

The resource allocation process in the system is based on the well-known contract net protocol. Briefly, the order agent announces the tasks to be performed, the resource agents compete for the announced tasks by bidding and the order agent selects the resource to perform the task (Fig. 1).

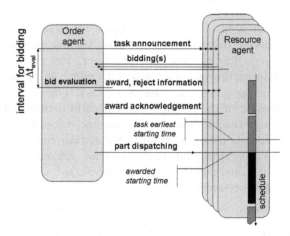

Fig. 1. Task announcement, bidding, awarding and dispatching cycle

Each task announcement message includes a bid evaluation interval (teval) after which the bids are not accepted (Fig. 1). During the determination of this interval the order agent has to take the communication replay delay of each agent into account. To have a smooth flow of task execution it is essential to adjust the communication parameters of the agents by setting the reading and sending intervals to be considerably smaller then the average task processing time.

Having received task announcements the resource agents construct and submit bids according to their local state variables. The resource checks the requirements of the operation and creates a bid only if it is capable to perform the operation. Each resource has an inner parameter indicating the bidding performance. This is a state variable of the resource through which the bidding behavior of the agent can be manipulated. The bid will include this earliest starting time, the processing time of the operation and the calculated cost.

The objective in the bid evaluation procedure can be the minimization of production costs, minimization of job tardiness, minimization of makespan or weighted combination of the above or similar factors. The weights of the objective functions can be dynamically adjusted on the basis of the system state and external conditions. Different weights and different rules will result in different control strategies and system performances. These can be regarded as parameters of the manufacturing system and they can be inspected from outside providing an exercising environment. All the bids submitted in the bidding period are evaluated and sorted according to the objectives. The task is offered for the resource that sent the most advantageous bid, while the others are informed about the rejection. The negotiation is completed when the awarded resource accepts and acknowledges the receiving of the announced task.

3.1   The Adaptive Behavior of Agents

In this concept, a purely local adaptation scheme was developed and included in the system. Considering the resource objectives, the resource agents can adjust their cost factors according to their local state variables and previous observations. Each agent incorporates a rule base with which it can locally decide on the cost factor to be applied for an announced task. The preconditions of these rules are the utilization of the resource and the ratio between the won and lost bids. The data about the bidding history are stored locally for each agent in the table of machine abilities and history. Simulation runs were performed to find and adjust the right thresholds in the rules for different manufacturing systems and loads. A detailed description of the developed adaptive algorithm and simulation results are presented in [5].

4   Conclusion

The paper presents a pioneer work to integrate agent-based mechanisms in a general discrete-event simulation environment by building templates that provide the well-known agent features directly in the simulation environment. The main aim of the work was to build a general and flexible modeling environment that enables the easy creation and evaluation of different agent-based manufacturing systems. Further work was initiated in order to integrate other collaboration templates in the system.

Acknowledgement

The research was supported, partially, by the projects "Real-time, cooperative enterprises" in the frame of the National Research and Development Programme by the Ministry of Education, Hungary (Grant Nos. 2/010/2004). A part of the work was covered by the National Research Fund, Hungary, Grant Nos. T043547, T046509 and T049486. Botond Kádár greatly acknowledges the support of Bolyai János Scholarship of the Hungarian Academy of Sciences significantly easing the contribution.

References

1. Baker, A. D.: A Survey of Factory Control Algorithms That Can Be Implemented in a Multi-Agent Heterarchy: Dispatching, Scheduling, and Pull. Journal of Manufacturing Systems, **17**/4, (1998) 297–320
2. Shen, W., Norrie, D.H.: Agent Based Systems for Intelligent Manufacturing: A state-of-the-art survey Knowledge and Information Systems, an International Journal, **1**/2, (1999), 129–156
3. Brennan, R. W., William, O.: A simulation test-bed to evaluatemulti-agent control of manufacturing systems. Proceedings of the 2000 Winter Simulation Conference, (2000) 1747–1756
4. Pěchouček, M., Vokřínek, J., Bečvář: ExPlanTech: Multiagent Support for Manufacturing Decision Making. IEEE Intelligent Systems **20**/1, (2005) 67–74
5. Kádár, B.; Monostori, L.; Csáji, B.: Adaptive approaches to increase the performance of production control systems, Proc. of the 36th CIRP Int. Seminar on Manufacturing Systems, June 3–5, 2003, Saarbrcken, Germany, pp. 305-312 and CIRP Journal of Manufacturing Systems, **34**/1, (2005) (in print).

Complexity of Task Coordination for Non Cooperative Planning Agents

Adriaan ter Mors, Jeroen Valk, and Cees Witteveen

Faculty of Electrical Engineering, Mathematics and Computer Science,
Delft University of Technology, P.O. Box 5031, 2600 GA Delft, The Netherlands
{a.w.termors, j.m.valk, c.witteveen}@ewi.tudelft.nl

Abstract. We discuss task planning problems where a number of agents have to work on a joint planning problem that consists of a set of interdependent, hierarchically ordered tasks. Each agent is assigned a subset of tasks to perform for which it has to construct a plan. The agents are non-cooperative in that they insist on planning autonomously and do not want to revise their individual plans when a joint plan has to be assembled. The aim of this paper is twofold: first of all to present a general formal framework to study some computational aspects of this *non-cooperative coordination* problem, and secondly to establish some complexity results and to identify some of the factors that contribute to the complexity of this problem.

1 Introduction

Coordination in multi-agent planning systems is a process ensuring that the plans of the participating agents do not conflict and the individual as well as the common goals of the agents can be achieved. In the multi-agent planning literature, one can distinguish three main approaches to coordination. In the first approach (c.f. [1,4]) coordination between the agents is established *after* the completion of the individual planning processes. It is assumed that agents independently work on their own part of the planning problem and achieve a solution for it. In an after-planning coordination phase, possible conflicts between independently generated individual plans are resolved and positive interactions between them are exploited by exchanging and revising parts of the individual plans. The second approach pushes the coordination process into the planning processes (c.f. [2,3]) by treating coordination and planning as *intertwined* processes where the agents continuously exchange planning information to arrive at a joint solution. In the third or *pre-planning* approach coordination takes place before the agents start to make plans. Examples of the latter approach are the use of *social laws* (cf. [6]), conventions (cf. [5]) and protocols as the Contract Net protocol [7].

We are focusing upon coordination between agents that are self-interested, do not want to be interfered *during* their individual planning process and do not want to revise their plans when a joint plan has to be composed. Examples are *multi-modal* planning tasks where several independent and competitive transportation companies have to coordinate in transporting goods or persons, manufacturing tasks and patient-centered health-care systems.

M. Pĕchouček, P. Petta, and L.Z. Varga (Eds.): CEEMAS 2005, LNAI 3690, pp. 600–603, 2005.

It can be easily seen that these autonomous planning and revision-free combination requirements exclude the first two coordination approaches from consideration. Therefore, we need to coordinate the agents *before* the planning phase. While existing pre-planning coordination research focuses on *implicit* coordination, i.e. constraints are imposed independently of the particular goals or tasks the agent has to solve, we are looking for an *explicit* coordination approach: based on the specific set of tasks to be achieved, the assignment policies and the (inter-agent) dependencies, we have to specify which constraints have to be imposed on the tasks. These constraints will enable the agents to make plans for their part of the complex task independently from each other and should guarantee that, once the plans have been constructed, these plans can always be combined in a revision-free manner into a joint plan solving the complex task. Our coordination problem then comes down to find a minimum set of such additional constraints.

2   A Framework for Coordination

To analyze this coordination problem, we use a task-based framework, where a set of non-cooperative agents $A = \{A_1, A_2, \ldots, A_n\}$, each having different capacities, have to solve a complex task $\mathcal{T}$. Such a complex task $\mathcal{T}$ consists of a set $T = \{t_1, t_2, \ldots t_k\}$ of (elementary) tasks t_i together with two relations ρ and $\prec$ whose transitive closures specify a partial order on T. The relation $\prec$ specifies a *precedence*[1] relation between tasks in T, $t \prec t'$ expressing that t' cannot start until t has been completed, i.e., in every plan t has to be planned to occur before t'. The *refinement* relation ρ consists of

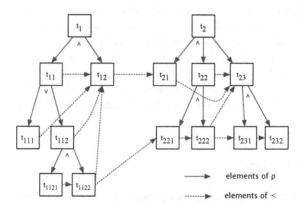

Fig. 1. A complex task with refinement (ρ) and precedence ($\prec$) relations between tasks. $T_0 = \{t_1, t_2\}$ is the set of initial tasks. Other tasks are refinements of these tasks.

two disjoint subsets: $\rho_\vee$, defining an OR-relation between the subtasks of a task, and $\rho_\wedge$, defining an AND-relation. Intuitively, if $\rho(t) \subseteq \rho_\wedge$, an agent that has to achieve t

---

[1] Note that such a precedence relation can be induced by various other dependency relations like resource dependencies, organizational regulations, etc.

might choose to complete t in its own way without taking notice to its set of subtasks, or might choose to complete every subtask $t' \in \rho(t)$; analogously, if $\rho(t) \subseteq \rho_\vee$, t can be completed by performing t (choosing the agent's own method to solve it) or by completing one of the subtasks $t' \in \rho(t)$. Finally, we require that for any pair of tasks t, t', $\rho(t) \cap \rho(t') = \emptyset$, i.e. refinements are unique.

A typical *free task instance* then is a tuple $(T, \rho, \prec, A, c(A), c(T))$. Here, $c(A)$ represents the agent capabilities and $c(T)$ the task capabilities required. Using these capabilities and the refinement relation we can define exactly what constitutes a suitable assignment of tasks to agents. Applying such an assignment to a free task instance $(T, \rho, \prec, A, c(A), c(T))$ results in a *fixed task instance* $([T_i]_{i=1}^n, \prec, A, c(A), c(T))$, where each T_i represents the non-overlapping subset of tasks assigned to agent A_i. Since now the refinement relation and the capabilities are no longer needed[2] and agents are characterized by the partition blocks of a ρ-independent set $T' \subseteq T$, we often abbreviate a fixed task instance by the tuple $([T_i]_{i=1}^n, \prec)$.

In such a fixed task instance $([T_i]_{i=1}^n, \prec)$ the set of precedence constraints $\prec$ is split up into two disjoint subsets: *(i)* the set $\prec_{intra} = \bigcup_{i=1}^n \prec_i$ of *intra-agent* constraints, where $\prec_i$ is the set of (inherited) precedence constraints between the tasks occurring in T_i and *(ii)* the set of *inter-agent* constraints, i.e., the set of constraints that hold between tasks assigned to different agents.

Each agent A_i then has to solve a subtask $(T_i, \prec_i)$ generated by the tasks T_i allocated to it. We assume that in order to complete T_i each agent has to construct a *plan* (or schedule) for it. Whatever plan/schedule representation the agents (internally) employ, we assume that the plan A_i develops for T_i can be represented as a structure $P_i = (T_i, \pi_i)$ *extending*[3] the dependency structure $(T_i, \prec_i)$, i.e., π_i^+ is a partial order containing (respecting) $\prec_i^+$.

Using this framework, the coordination problem can be easily stated: *how to guarantee that whatever individual extensions π_i are chosen, the resulting plans (T_i, π_i) can be simply combined into a joint plan.* It is not hard to see that such a joint plan respecting each of the individual plans, only exists if the relation $\prec \cup \bigcup_i^n \prec_i$ is acyclic.

Elsewhere, (see [8]) we have shown that coordination only can be guaranteed if it is allowed to add suitable dependency constraints Δ_i to each of the individual planning problems $(T_i, \prec_i)$. The coordination problem then consists in finding *minimum sets* of such constraints.

3   Complexity Results

We investigated the computational complexity of some aspects of this coordination problem and we showed that in general, even the easiest problems are intractable.

1. *checking coordination*: Given a *fixed* task instance, to *detect* whether or not additional dependency constraints need to be added in order to guarantee coordination, in general is a co-NP complete problem, even if each agent has to make a plan for

---

[2] Since it is assumed that each agent is able to complete the tasks assigned to it and no tasks assigned are ρ-related.

[3] Since a plan P_i at least has to satisfy all intra-agent constraints $\prec_i$.

achieving at most 4 tasks. Only if an agent has at most 3 tasks to plan, this problem can be solved efficiently.

For a *free* task instance the problem whether there exists a suitable assignment of tasks to agents such that no additional constraints need to be added, the coordination checking problem is Σ_2^p-complete.

2. *finding a minimal set of constraints*: Determining a minimal set of constraints has been proven to be even harder: the problem to decide whether k constraints suffice for a fixed task instance is a Σ_2^p-complete problem, even if agents have to plan for a small (8) number of tasks. Remarkably, it makes no essential difference in computational complexity whether the agents are already assigned to tasks or not. Only if we want to find out whether for all possible suitable assignements of tasks to agents adding k constraints suffices, the complexity increases: this problem is a Π_3^p-complete problem.

4   Conclusions

Note that ensuring coordination before planning even starts has many advantages: agents can plan independently of other agents, and there is no need for advanced multi-agent planning tools because an agent has only its own planning problem to solve. The drawback of pre-planning coordination is that it is either computationally very expensive. Approaches to practical application of pre-planning coordination therefore have to focus upon the construction of suitable approximation algorithms.

References

1. J.S. Cox and E. H. Durfee. Discovering and exploiting synergy between hierarchical planning agents. In *Second International Joint Conference On Autonomous Agents and Multiagent Systems (AAMAS '03)*, 2003.
2. E. Ephrati and J. S. Rosenschein. Multi-agent planning as the process of merging distributed sub-plans. In *Proceedings of the Twelfth International Workshop on Distributed Artificial Intelligence (DAI-93)*, pages 115–129, 1993.
3. V. Lesser, K. Decker, T. Wagner, N. Carver, A. Garvey, B. Horling, D. Neiman, R. Podorozhny, M. NagendraPrasad, A. Raja, R. Vincent, P. Xuan, and X.Q. Zhang. Evolution of the GPGP/TAEMS Domain-Independent Coordination Framework. *Autonomous Agents and Multi-Agent Systems*, 9(1):87–143, July 2004.
4. F. Von Martial. *Coordinating Plans of Autonomous Agents*, volume 610 of *Lecture Notes on Artificial Intelligence*. Springer Verlag, Berlin, 1992.
5. Y. Shoham and M. Tennenholtz. Emergent conventions in multi-agent systems: Initial experimental results and observations (preliminary report). In *Proceedings KR92*, pages 225–231, 1992.
6. Y. Shoham and M. Tennenholtz. On social laws for artificial agent societies: Off-line design. *Artificial Intelligence*, 73(1–2):231–252, 1995.
7. R. G. Smith. The contract net protocol: High-level communication and control in a distributed problem solver. *IEEE Transactions on Computers*, C-29(12):1104–1113, 1980.
8. A. W. ter Mors, J. Valk, and C. Witteveen. Complexity of coordinating autonomous planning agents. Technical Report PDS-2004-002, Delft University of Technology, 2004.

Resource Coordination on MAS Multi-plans Context[*]

Weihua Yi[1], C.H. Zhang[2], Z. Liu[3], and Xueguang Chen[1]

[1] Institute of Systems Eng., Huazhong University of Science and Technology, China
[2] Dept. of Electrical & Computer Eng., Kumamoto University, Japan
[3] Graduate School of Engineering, Nagasaki Institute of Applied Science, Japan

Abstract. Resource allocation is an important type of decision making activities. In distributed resource allocation, the privacies need to be considered, which is not easy for mathematical programming. Until now, the MAS method has been studied as it appeared to be a practical method for obtaining a collaborative solution to group decision-making. This paper proposes MAS multi-plans coordination to study distributed resource allocation, which considers both privacy and global goal. The numerical results obtained indicate the method is practical.

1 Introduction

Resource allocation is a crucial type of decision making activities. As Hazelrigg [4] pointed out, decision-making is resource assignment which will not be changed once made. Traditional method like mathematical programming needs super coordinator to compute centrally with global information, and neglects the privacy. However, in real world, privacy and dynamics are undeniable characteristics of distributed resource allocation problems. This emphasizes the strong need for making some breakthrough. This paper proposes a new method of multi-plans coordination to overcome above problems, which considers both privacy and global goal. It presents multi plans context and interdependencies amongst individuals with resource constraint. Then agent reasoning model is given to assure individual interests improvement and a multi agent negotiation protocol is presented to abate the differences among individuals.

2 Individual Reasoning Model

The decision variables here are plans. Some notations are given by Table 1.

Agent is to maximize its own interest indicated by preference. In this paper, the preference is denoted by utility function f_α, which is defined as a real number value of how agent α intends to perform a plan in certain environment. According to f_α, α prefers performing a plan π to another π':

$$\pi \succeq_\alpha \pi' \Leftrightarrow exec(\pi, s) \land f_\alpha(\pi, s) \geq f_\alpha(\pi', s) \tag{1}$$

[*] This research is funded by the NSFC(No. 60274065),http://www.nsfc.org.cn/

M. Pĕchouček, P. Petta, and L.Z. Varga (Eds.): CEEMAS 2005, LNAI 3690, pp. 604–607, 2005.
© Springer-Verlag Berlin Heidelberg 2005

Table 1. Notations of plans and agents

S	Set of environment status.
Σ	Set of activities.
T	Set of time period.
Π	Set of plans. $\pi = (\Sigma \times T)^*, \pi \in \Pi$.[4]
	Empty plan π_ε denotes a plan of no activity.
A	Finite set of agents, which denotes participant individuals.
$change(\pi, s)$	Function denotes the influence of plan π on environment s. $change : \Pi \times S \rightarrow S$.
$exec(\pi, s)$	Predicate indicates whether $change(\pi, s)$ is defined. Apparently $exec(\pi_\varepsilon, s)$ holds for everywhere, for in any cases, anyone could do nothing.
$capable(\alpha, \pi)$	Predicate indicates whether agent α is capable to enact plan π.
$goal(\alpha, s)$	Predicate indicates whether environment status is the goal of α.
S_α^{goal}	Set of environment status which agent α is intended to achieve.
$f_\alpha(\pi, s)$	Utility function denotes preference of agent α.

$f_\alpha(\pi, s)$ is related with the cost and benefit to perform π in s. In this paper we assume the benefit is constant, so we only need to consider the cost. Let $cost_\alpha : \Pi \times S \rightarrow \Re$, where $\Re$ is the set of all real numbers, denote the cost to enact a plan, and $dist_\alpha : S \times S_\alpha^{goal} \rightarrow \Re$ represent the distance between certain status and the goal status, then the utility may be the plan cost and the distance between $s' = change(\pi, s)$ and S_α^{goal} :

$$f_\alpha(\pi, s) = -cost_\alpha(\pi, s) - dist_\alpha(change(\pi, s), s_\alpha^{goal}) \qquad (2)$$

where $dist_\alpha(change(\pi, s), s_\alpha^{goal})$ is the estimation of the potential cost to achieve the goal.

3   Resource Constrained Multi-plans Context

In real world, the environment is not controlled by any single agent. This section assumes a close world, and then discusses the interaction among multi agents.

The set M of multi-plans comprises all multi-sets over the individual plans Π [6]. Multi-plans is a combination of multi simultaneous plans:

$$\mu = \pi_1 \circ \pi_2 \circ \cdots \pi_n, \pi_i \in \Pi, i = 1, 2, \cdots, n \qquad (3)$$

where operator $\circ$ expresses that its operands are executed together. Different with joint plans [2], multi-plans do not share goals.

The notions of previous section are extended to multi-plans as Table 2.

A group of agent $\gamma \in \Gamma$ is capable of executing a multi-plan μ, if there is an assignment such that every agent is to execute exactly one individual plan and this agent is capable of doing so, i.e. there is a bijective mapping Ψ from μ (a multi-set of individual plans) to γ (a set of agents), such that

$$capable(\gamma, \mu) \equiv \forall \pi \in \mu, \alpha = \Psi(\pi), capable(\alpha, \pi) \qquad (4)$$

Table 2. Notations of multi-plans

M	Set of multi-plans.
Γ	Power set of A, which denotes multi participants.
$change(\mu, s)$	Function denotes the influence of multi-plans μ on environment s. $change : M \times S \rightarrow S$.
$exec(\mu, s)$	Predicate indicates whether $change(\mu, s)$ is defined.
$capable(\gamma, \mu)$	Predicate indicates whether a group of agents γ is capable of enacting multi-plans μ.

In MAS, because of interdependencies between activities of each others, agents have to consider activities of acquaintances when planning their own behaviors. The dependency of an agent α performing a plan π on other agents $\gamma(\alpha \notin \gamma)$ performing multi-plans μ is one of the five as follows [6]:

$$DEP = \{enable_s, facilitate_s, indifferent_s, hinder_s, disable_s\} \qquad (5)$$

Then the MAS multi-plans context may be expressed as:

$$MASMP = \langle S, A, M, DEP, goal, exec, change, capable, f_\alpha \rangle \qquad (6)$$

In this paper, we concentrate on the dependencies mapped from resource constraint in resource limited contexts. Let $dep_\alpha(dep_\alpha \in DEP)$ be the set of all dependencies related with agent α, s_i be the environment status in the period τ_i, $\rho(\pi, \tau_i)$ be the resource requirement of the activity $[\sigma_i, \tau_i]$ in plan π, $\rho_\alpha(\tau_i)$ be the private resources of α in the period τ_i, and $\rho_{\overline{\alpha}}(\tau_i)$ be the resources available but out of α in the period τ_i.

From the local view of an agent, α can perform the plan π if and only if

$$\forall i \geq 0, \rho_\alpha(\tau_i) + \rho_{\overline{\alpha}}(\tau_i) \geq \rho(\pi, \tau_i) \wedge capable(\alpha, \pi) \qquad (7)$$

and from the global view, γ can perform the multi-plans μ if and only if

$$\forall i \geq 0, \sum_{\alpha \in \gamma} \rho_\alpha(\tau_i) + \rho_{\overline{\gamma}}(\tau_i) \geq \sum_{\pi \in \mu} \rho(\pi, \tau_i) \wedge capable(\gamma, \mu) \qquad (8)$$

Apparently, the resource information of agent will change while it performs a plan. Agent has to gather the information related with the resource required by its plan and reason based on the gathered information. Agents are presumed able to perceive only their local information, thus communicating and exchanging information may be necessary.

For example, there are only two agents $\alpha, \beta \in \gamma$, which will perform $\pi_\alpha \in \Pi_\alpha, \pi_\beta \in \Pi_\beta$ respectively, and $\rho_{\overline{\gamma}}(\tau_i)$ is the information of environment resources out of them. $\forall i \geq 0, \rho_\alpha(\tau_i) + \rho_{\overline{\gamma}}(\tau_i) \geq \rho(\pi_\alpha, \tau_i)$, but $\exists i, \rho_\alpha(\tau_i) + \rho_\beta(\tau_i) + \rho_{\overline{\gamma}}(\tau_i) < \rho(\pi_\alpha, \tau_i) + \rho(\pi_\beta, \tau_i)$. This is denoted by $disable(\alpha, \pi_\alpha, \beta, \pi_\beta)$ from the view of α, which means β executing π_β disables α executing π_β.

4   Resource Coordination in Multi-plans

Resource coordination is intelligent allocation of resources amongst different individuals and their goals [3]. Usually, the requirement of coordination comes from the distribution and interdependencies of resources, entities and information [5]. In resource coordination, individual plan is to be evaluated and refined, and it may be needed to acquire available resources from external environment.

In the MAS environment, agents will interact with each others. They affect each others negatively or positively, i.e. they may conflict or cooperate.

Firstly, if an agent gets no information of outside options, the agent will prefer the plan it is able to execute only with its private resources in current environment status. Risk dominance makes agent avoiding conflict.

Secondly, if agents cooperate on utilization of common resources, they would get more benefit. Even in MAS of self-interested agents, where local interests are aberrant from global goal, the difference may be abated through MAS negotiation [7] of social choice problems [1].

Lastly, with more information exchange, the private resources may be utilized to promote all the individual utilities and efficiency of the whole system, for it increases $\rho_{\overline{\alpha}}(\tau_i)$ for all $\alpha \in A$ who participate in the exchange.

5   Conclusion

Group decision-making is related with individual choices and the interdependencies among them, especially the interdependencies of resources. This paper proposes a new method combining MAS and Multi-plans. Under the assumptions of individual rationality, private information and collaboration, we give the solution based on negotiation of social choice.

References

1. Christopher P. Chambers. Multi-utilitarianism in two-agent quasilinear social choice. Technical report, California Institute of Technology, Division of the Humanities and Social Sciences, 2003. Working Papers 1177.
2. Philip R. Cohen and Hector J. Levesque. Intention is choice with commitment. *Artificial Intelligence*, 42(2-3):213–261, 1990.
3. Gifty Edwin and Michael T. Cox. Resource coordination in single agent and multi-agent systems. In *ICTAI*, pages 18–24, 2001.
4. G.A. Hazelrigg. *System Engineering: An Approach to Information-Based Design.* Prentice Hall, New Jersey, 1996.
5. Victor R. Lesser. Reflections on the nature of multi-agent coordination and its implications for an agent architecture. *Autonomous Agents and Multi-Agent Systems*, 1(1):89–111, 1998.
6. Sascha Ossowski. Co-ordination in artificial agent societies: social structures and its impli-cations for autonomous problem solving agents. LNAI 1535, 1999.
7. Naoki Yoshihara Yongsheng Xu. A new insight into three bargaining solutions in con-vex problems. Technical report, Institute of Economic Research, Hitotsubashi University, 2004. Discussion Paper Series a453.

Using Negotiation Techniques as Time-Restricted Scheduling Policies on Intelligent Agents

Patricia Maldonado[1,2], Carlos Carrascosa[1], and Vicente Botti[1]

[1] Universidad Politécnica de Valencia, Camino de Vera s/n, Valencia España
{pmaldonad, carrasco, vbotti}@dsic.upv.es
[2] Universidad de Magallanes, Av. Bulnes 01855, Punta Arenas Chile

Abstract. Tasks scheduling policies for real-time systems are generally not very flexible due to the time restrictions they have to fulfill. Nowadays, research lines to apply artificial intelligence techniques to real-time systems are becoming more relevant, because they can be used to soften tasks scheduling. In this work, we present a proposal in this line. That is, to apply negotiation techniques to optimize real-time systems decisions by increasing and improving the available information to schedule the tasks of an intelligent agent working in a real-time environment. To implement our proposal, we have used an agent working in a hard real-time environment such as $\mathcal{ARTIS}$ (*A Real-Time Intelligence System*). Finally, we show some results obtained of including such methods in an $\mathcal{ARTIS}$ agent.

1 Introduction

Real-Time Systems are trying to integrate artificial intelligence techniques into their scheduling methods as a way to soften their reasonings about a determined situation [1]. This kind of systems can be found in the literature as *Real-Time Artificial Intelligent System*, and their purpose is to develop intelligence in real-time. An example of this kind of systems is the $\mathcal{ARTIS}$ architecture [2,3].

In this paper we propose to include artificial techniques in the tasks scheduling of flexible real-time systems. Specifically, we use negotiation techniques to schedule a set of non-critical real-time tasks in the $\mathcal{ARTIS}$ architecture. We also present how these techniques have been implemented and the obtained results both in simulation and real execution tests.

2 $\mathcal{ARTIS}$ Agent Architecture

$\mathcal{ARTIS}$ agent ($\mathcal{AA}$) is an extension of the *Blackboard model* adapted to work in *Flexible Hard Real-Time* environments [2]. An $\mathcal{AA}$ consists of a set of in-agents [3], all of them cooperate to solve the agent problem. To do this, each *in-agent* is translated into a low-level task can have three parts [2]: *initial part*, it must always be executed and obtains a first low-quality reflex answer to the

M. Pěchouček, P. Petta, and L.Z. Varga (Eds.): CEEMAS 2005, LNAI 3690, pp. 608–611, 2005.

problem of the $\mathcal{AA}$; *optional part*, these optional components increase the quality of the answer calculated in the initial part; and *final part*, this part executes the answer which was generated in the previous parts of the in-agent. And, a *control module* which is responsible of the execution of the $\mathcal{AA}$'s in-agents. The Deliberative Server (DS) [3] is the specific module in charge of the agent's optional parts scheduling. The *Second-Level Scheduling (SLS)* of the (DS) is in charge of distributing the available slack time among the optional components of the in-agent. This improves the global quality of the agent's answer.

Previous to the work here presented, the scheduling policies used by the SLS (EDF, HSF, BIF)[4] are very strict. To be precise, this paper proposes to divide the responsibility of scheduling between all the entities directly involved in this process by improving the available information for these negotiations. So we propose to use negotiation methods as optional tasks scheduling policies.

As it has been explained above, the purpose of in-agents optional parts is to improve the $\mathcal{ARTIS}$ agent problem answers. This work pretends that the in-agents will become active part of their selection for execution taking into account their believes and desires (compatibles with the ones of the $\mathcal{ARTIS}$ agent they belong to).

3 $\mathcal{ARTIS}$ Agent Negotiations

Following the *"Real-Time Artificial Intelligence Systems"* idea, we are going to include the negotiation methods in $\mathcal{AA}$ architecture to increase its AI techniques. The purpose of this extension is to improve the usage of available processor time to execute optional parts [5]. These negotiation methods going to implement into the DS of $\mathcal{AA}$ architecture.

However, this process of awarding will have to be fast and advantageous for both parts. Considering all the exposed so far, the best option to this domain is to use auctions as negotiation techniques. Since the aim of auctions is to award the product to who gives the best offer based on the pre-determined conditions. Moreover, in this case, the time restrictions must be considered according to the $\mathcal{AA}$ characteristics.

We analyzed three kinds of auctions [5]: the English Auction (EA), the First Sealed-bid Auction (FSA) and the Dutch Auction (DA).

The auctions begin when the SLS sends a *"Call For Proposal"* (CFP) to the active in-agents in the system. When the active in-agents[1] receive this CFP, they evaluate it and decide if they participate or not in the auctions[2]. These in-agents' evaluations will be according to their believes. And, if the in-agents decide to participate in the auctions, they will send a final offer considering their limitations to generate the answer to $\mathcal{AA}$'s problem. In *Dutch Auction*,

---

[1] An active in-agent is such that its corresponding low-level task has executed completely its initial part, but its final part has not been executed. According to this, it can execute its optional parts to improve the answer to its problem.

[2] Also, if they don't understand the CFP of SLS, then they will have to wait till the next SLS' CFP .

the *SLS* makes an offer to the *participating in-agents* for available slack. The participant in-agents evaluate the offer sent by the *SLS*. If there are no in-agents interested in offering the required quality by the *SLS*, it decreases the quality (until minimum quality established by *SLS*). All auctions methods will repeat their process while there is negotiation time left.

In our previous work [5], we have shown these specifications and obtained some results. We will compare these results with real test results. For this tests, we implemented the same scenarios used in simulation tests directly in $\mathcal{AA}$ architecture.

Each test execution lasts until their tasks *hyper-period*[3]. For both kind of tests realized (simulated and real tests), we generate battery tests with the following common specifications: three, six, nine or twelve in-agents per $\mathcal{AA}$; tasks time restrictions obtained using probability functions proposed in [8]; and we have used two different situations regarding the in-agents time-features values: the one with deadlines[4] equal to periods[5] and the one which deadlines are minor than periods.

In order to compare the results obtained in the simulation tests with the results obtained in the real tests, we will use the final quality that was obtained in the answer to the problem of the $\mathcal{AA}$ which is called *Real Relative Quality* (*RRQ* that is detailed in [4])[6]

4   Conclusions and Future Works

As we can see at figure 1(a), when deadlines are equal to periods, the obtained *RRQ* for our auctions are equal to or better than the other $\mathcal{ARTIS}$'s policies. This behaviour is repeated when the deadlines are minor than periods (see figure 1(b)). However, in both cases, the *DA*'s *RRQ* obtained in all tests are better than other policies' *RRQ*.

On the other hand, figures 1(a) and (b), we can see that the obtained results in both cases are very similar. Nevertheless, when deadlines are equal to periods the percentage of executed in-agent's levels is major than when deadlines are minor than periods. On the other hand, when deadlines are equal to periods the percentage of executed in-agents's levels is 5% over than in the other case. Again, the *DA* method obtains better results than the other methods and policies of the *SLS*, with *EA* method in second place along with *HSF* policy.

Obtained experimental results prove not only the viability of the application of our methods, but that these results are similar or better the ones with current $\mathcal{AA}$'s policies.

---

[3] *"The tasks will be released together again at the least common multiple of the periods of the tasks."* [7]

[4] It indicates the maximum limit execution time so that the task gives an answer

[5] It is the frequency of the task's activation during the execution of the system.

[6] It is represented as the quotient between the *Obtained Real Quality* (*ORQ*) that is obtained by the in-agents of the $\mathcal{AA}$ and the *Ideal Quality* (*IQ*) that is offered by the same, $RRQ = \frac{ORQ}{IQ}$.

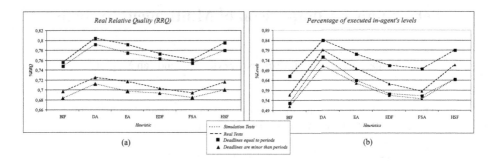

Fig. 1. Results of tests

Finally, based on the obtained results, the future tasks will be:

- To use the obtained simulation results to identify the most suitable situations (environment and internal state) for each scheduling policies, so that the $\mathcal{AA}$ can be programmed to adapt to this situation changing its current policy to the most suitable one [3].
- To orientate the auctions toward more deliberative methods that involve the planning of all the available slack in the whole application.
- To generalize these methods so that they can be applied to resource management in distributed systems.

References

1. Musliner, D.J., Hendler, J., Agrawala, A., Durfee, E., Strosnider, J., Paul, C.: The challenges of real-time ai. IEEE Computer 28 (1995)
2. Terrasa, A., García-Fornes, A., Botti, V.: Flexible real-time linux. Real-Time Systems Journal (2002) 149–170
3. Carrascosa, C., Fabregat, J., Terrasa, A., Botti, V.: Real-time agents: Reaction vs. deliberation. In: Second European Workshop on Multi-Agent Systems, EUMAS04, Barcelona – Espaa (2004)
4. Hernández, L., Botti, V., García-Fornes, A., Gonzalez, M.: A quality-based heuristic for real-time scheduling. Artificial Intelligence Research and Development.Frontiers in Artificial Intelligence Research and Development. 100 (2003) 462–473
5. Maldonado, P., Carrascosa, C., Botti, V.: Negotiation in real-time multi-agent systems. In: IADIS International Conference – Applied Computing 2005. Volume II., Algarve, Portugal (2005) 247–254 isbn: 972-99353-6-X.
6. FIPASpec: Fipa specifications. Foundation for Intelligence Phisycal Agents, 2000. http://www.fipa.org/specifications/index.html (FIPA)
7. Bernat, G., Burns, A., Llamosí, A.: Weakly hard real-time systems. IEEE Transaction on Computers 50 (2001) 308–321
8. Campos, A.M., García, D.: A real-time expert system architecture based on a novel dynamic task scheduling technique. In: IEEE Int. Conference on Industrial Electronics, Control and Instrumentation, IECON02. (2002) 1893–1898

Performance Comparison of Multi-agent Systems

Tomasz Babczyński, Zofia Kruczkiewicz, and Jan Magott

Abstract. Performance comparison of two information retrieval multiagent systems is carried over by simulation. The first system contains stationary agents only, while the second one contains one mobile agent. Performance models of these multiagent systems are expressed by performance statecharts. The performance statecharts are such a modification of UML statecharts that contain probability distributions for activity duration times and for transmission times, and probability distributions in order to solve non-determinism.

1 Introduction

In literature, performance evaluation of the following multi-agent systems (MASs): *ZEUS* [2], *JADE* [2], *Skeleton Agent* [2], *Aglets IBM* [3], *Concordia* [3], *Voyager* [3] is presented. When new MAS with performance requirements is designed then, according to software performance engineering [5], performance requirements have to be considered at each phase of life cycle. Performance analysis before implementation can be based on: performance models of agents and inter-agent communication.

Many MAS design methods are based on UML or its modifications [4]. Performance models are usually dynamics driven models. In the UML, the dynamics of components and inter-components communication can be expressed by statecharts. Performance statecharts have been presented in [1], and applied to performance analysis of multiagent industrial system.

In the paper, performance comparison of two multiagent systems using performance statechart simulator is carried over. In the first system, all agents are static, while the second system contains one mobile agent. The aggregated metric that takes into account the following metrics: probability and mean time of receiving of the good response, mean number of bytes transmitted through the communication network per second is used in comparison.

The paper is organized as follows. In Section 2, the compared MASs are presented. Then performance parameters and metrics of them are given. In Section 4, both systems are compared by simulation experiments. Finally, there are conclusions.

2 Compared Multi-agent Systems

The MAS with Static Agents

Manager agent sends the same queries Q of the size |Q| (in bytes) to *n Searcher Agents* that are in *n* sites S_{Bi} (*Data bases*), see Fig. 1. The *Searcher Agents* confirm the possibility of performing the searching task by sending the messages confirm C of the size |C| to the *Manager Agent*. The *Searcher Agent* searches an information in the *Data base*, and sends a response R of the size |R| to the *Manager agent*. The *Manager*

M. Pěchouček, P. Petta, and L.Z. Varga (Eds.): CEEMAS 2005, LNAI 3690, pp. 612–615, 2005.

agent is an intelligent agent, which is based on a decision tree. For each decision tree node, the response R is accepted with acceptance probability acc_p. The *Manager agent*, after receiving the responses from the *Searching agents*, can send next queries to all these agents or can stop the searching process provided a response has been accepted. Hence, during one searching process, the *Manager agent* can send a sequence of queries to the *Searching Agents* and receive a sequence of sets of responses. This sequence of queries is associated with a path in the decision tree. At each node of the tree the *Manager agent* waits for responses until the termination time _tm is elapsed. The time elapsing event is treated as negative response.

The MAS with one mobile agent

The *Manager Agent* (Fig. 2) sends the code CA of the *Mobile Agent* of the size |CA| to site S_{B1}. The *Mobile Agent* migrates through maximally n sites S_{Bi}. The *Mobile Agent* is based on similar decision tree and acceptance process as the *Manager agent* of the first system. At each site S_{Bi}, the *Mobile Agent* sends the sequence of queries, according to a path in its decision tree, to the *Data base* of this site and waits for the response. Next, the *Mobile Agent* migrates to the next site. When the required response R is found then the *Mobile Agent* completes the searching process, having the size |CA|+|R|, and returns to the site S_A.

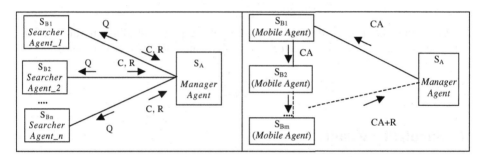

Fig. 1. System with static agents   **Fig. 2.** System with mobile agent

3 Performance Parameters and Metrics

The following performance parameters are used in simulation experiments.

In the MAS with static agents, the size of the messages |Q|=|C|=512 bytes.

In both systems, the size of the response is |R|=512+$RE(range(1,128))$·256 bytes, where 512 bytes is the size of constant part of the response, $RE(X)$ is a realisation of random variable X being the number of records, $range(1,128)$ is uniform random variable over the interval [1,127] of natural numbers, 256 bytes is the size of record.

Time of preparation of this response is a realisation of the uniform random variable over the interval $(60\mu s, 90\mu s)$.

In both systems, maximal length of path in the decision tree is equal to 4.

In the system with mobile agent, the size of the *Mobile agent* is |CA|=2048 for small one while |CA|=8192 for the large one.

The message transmission time is assumed to be linearly dependent of the size of the message. The (empirical) equation is taken as the result of measurements of the system having the following features: communication between two PC nodes with agent JADE 3.2 platform, there are 3 switches between the nodes. In simulation experiments, for given message size S, it is supposed that the message transmission time is expressed by such a random variable Z that: Z=min+V, where: min is the minimal transmission time of the message of the size S, V is exponential random variable with the mean E(V).

The following performance metrics are considered.

- bs_p_s– mean number of bytes transmitted through communication network per second (mean network load),
- p_g=s_g/s_t – probability of receiving of the good response, where s_g is the number of good responses received by the *Manager Agent* and s_t is the number of the searching processes initiated by the agent,
- mtg - the mean time of receiving of the good response. The metric is calculated as a mean value of all response times for cases when the *Manager Agent* received the first good response.

We would like to have the maximal value of the p_g, and minimal values of the mtg and the b_p_s. Therefore, the following aggregated quality metric is defined:

$$Q = \frac{p\_g}{mtg \cdot b\_p\_s}$$

4   Simulation Results

In simulation experiments, *Manager Agent, Searcher Agents, Databases, Mobile Agent* have been expressed by performance statecharts [1].

In the system with *Mobile Agent*, each response R from *Database* is accepted by the *Mobile Agent* with acceptance probability acc_p equal to 0.05, 0.1 or 0.2. In the system with static agents, each response from the *Searcher Agent* is accepted by the *Manager Agent* with the same acceptance probabilities. The comparison of MAS with small *Mobile Agent* (|CA|=2048 bytes) and MAS with static agents is shown at Fig. 3. The comparison of MAS with large *Mobile Agent* (|CA|=8192 bytes) and MAS with static agents is shown at Fig. 4. Each experiment was carried out for 1 to 15 *Databases* (and *Searcher Agents* in static model) – given at the X axe. All charts are also parameterised with the acceptance probability.

On the Fig. 3, the value of the aggregated quality metric Q is significantly greater for the system with the small *Mobile Agent* than for the MAS with static agents. The values of the calculated metric were very small for chosen units thus they have been multiplied by 10^9 before charting on Fig. 3 and 4. The Fig. 4 contains the metric Q for systems with the large *Mobile Agent* and static agents, respectively. Now, with respect to the metric Q, the system with static agents is better.

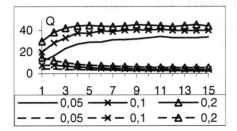

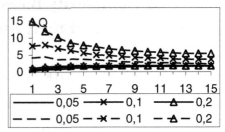

Fig. 3. The quality metrics Q for system with small mobile agent (continuous lines) vs. system with static agents (dashed lines)

Fig. 4. The quality metrics Q for system with large mobile agent (continuous lines) vs. system with static agents (dashed lines)

5   Conclusions

Performance comparison of the multiagent system which contains stationary agents with the multiagent system that contains one mobile agent has been carried over by simulation. The comparison has been executed with respect to the aggregated metric which takes into account the following metrics: probability and mean time of receiving of the good response, mean number of bytes transmitted through the communication network per second. The systems have been compared for two variants of *Mobile Agent*, i.e., small and large. We can draw the conclusion that the system with *Mobile Agent* is better than that with static agents, when the *Mobile Agent* is small. When the *Mobile Agent* becomes large, it is better to organize the system with static agents.

References

1. T.Babczyński, Z.Kruczkiewicz, J.Magott, Performance analysis of multiagent industrial system, in: Proc. 8th Int. Workshop Cooperative Information Agents - CIA, Erfurth, 2004, Lecture Notes in Computer Science / Lecture Notes in Artificial Intelligence, Springer-Verlag, Vol. 3191, 242-256
2. D.Camacho, R.Aler, C.Castro, J. M. Molina, Performance evaluation of ZEUS, JADE, and SkeletonAgent frameworks, in: Proc.IEEE Syst., Man, and Cybernetics Conference, 2002
3. M.Dikaiakos, M.Kyriakou, G.Samaras, Performance evaluation of mobile-agent middleware: A hierachical approach, In Proceedings of the 5th IEEE International Conference on Mobile Agents, J.P. Picco (ed.), Lecture Notes in Computer Science series, vol. 2240, pages 244-259, Springer, December 2001
4. James J.Odell, H.Van Dyke Parunak, Benhard Bauer, Representing Agent Interaction Protocols in UML, Agent-Oriented Soft. Engineering, Springer-Verlag, Berlin, pp.121-140,2001
5. C.U.Smith, Performance Engineering of Software Systems, Addison - Wesley, 1990.

A Complexity Based Feature to Support Emergence in MAS

Joris Deguet and Yves Demazeau

Laboratoire Leibniz, 46 avenue Félix Viallet Grenoble, France
{Joris.Deguet, Yves.Demazeau}@imag.fr

Abstract. *Emergence* is a widespread notion in complex systems, artificial life and multi-agent systems. In this paper, we try to clarify a specific emergence feature suggested by John Holland [1] : the "much from little" paradigm . Considering complexity measures, we exhibit some key issues for a precise definition of this feature. Seen from the VOWELS multi-agent perspective [2], our proposal might provide an indirect quantification of dynamic collective activity.

1 Introduction

Emergence is a widespread notion in complex systems, artificial life and multi-agent systems. It is often associated with the notion of complexity and suffers from the same profusion of definitions. In this paper, we try to clarify a specific "emergence feature" we can summarize as the "much from little" paradigm suggested by John Holland.

By explicitly considering complexity measures, we exhibit some key issues for a precise definition of this feature depending on both the complexity chosen and the distinction used to assert "much" and "little". This study tries to go deeper than the state of the art in the complexity issues provoked by some emergence definition.

Along the way from intuition to definition, we try to point out the choices we make, hoping this will allow fruitful discussion about alternate views on emergence.

First, we interpret the "much from little" idea as a *gap of complexity*. We show results of complexity on associated computational tasks. We compare our proposal to the one of Ronald and al. [3] showing a similar inspiration and a third one by Darley [4] using similar means.

2 An Emergence Feature

2.1 From Holland's Insight to a Complexity Gap

"The hallmark of emergence is this sense of much coming from little" [1]

Our first choice is to consider ourselves as designers who would like "little" to be the system S and "much" to be the phenomenon ϕ produced by S. We precise our framework by assuming that S is a system that outputs a tape of blank separated words over Σ, an alphabet of symbols. Then ϕ is a property of this tape.

Our second choice is to link the idea of "much" and "little" to the quantitative notion of complexity. "little" is a *simple* system and "much" is a *complex* phenomenon.

M. Pĕchouček, P. Petta, and L.Z. Varga (Eds.): CEEMAS 2005, LNAI 3690, pp. 616–619, 2005.

If we note C an abstract complexity measure, it corresponds to a positive value of our *emergence feature, eFeat*:

$$eFeat = C(\phi) - C(S) \geq 0$$

3   Complexity Measures

As we cannot apply the same complexity measurement on a machine S and a phenomenon ϕ, we associate a computational task to each of them. We define a phenomenon ϕ by a subset L_ϕ of the possible configurations so the associated computational task is deciding whether or not a configuration $w \in (\Sigma \cup \sqcup)^*$ belongs to the L_ϕ language. We associate the task "producing ϕ" to the system as it was our initial requirement.

Complexity measures such as algorithmic information and time complexity are usually defined within a model of machines, namely Turing machines. However, the definition over all Turing machines that achieve a given task might not be restrictive if the reader believes in the Church-Turing thesis that any machine of another kind might be efficiently and accurately simulated by a Turing machine.

Algorithmic information. Leibniz wrote that "God has chosen that which is the most simple in hypotheses and the most rich in phenomena"(translated from [5]). This fits in the "much from little" direction as well as the intuition of algorithmic complexity. Algorithmic information [6] of a finite string s (over the alphabet $(\Sigma \cup \sqcup)$) for a universal Turing machine U is defined as $H_U(s)$, with :

$$H_U(s) = min\{l(x)|U(x) = s\}$$

Usually x is a pair $< p, i >$ of two strings over $(\Sigma \cup \sqcup)$, program(p) and input(i). $l(x)$ is the length of the string x.

We define the complexity of the *production* task S as $H_U(S)$, with :

$$H_U(S) = min\{l(x)|U(x) \in L_\phi\}$$

and the complexity of the *detection* task ϕ as $H_U(\phi)$, with :

$$H_U(\phi) = min\{l(p)|\forall i \in (\Sigma \cup \sqcup)^*, U(< p, i >) = \begin{cases} 1 \text{ if } i \in L_\phi \\ 0 \text{ else} \end{cases}\}$$

For convenience, we define the $java$ machine that is an interpreter of the Java™ language, made Turing universal by the access to an infinite memory. Defined that way, we can exhibit a bound c thanks to a reduction between the two tasks :

$$\exists c \in \mathbb{N}, \text{ such that } \forall \phi, H_{java}(\phi) - H_{java}(S) \geq -c$$

Proof. Let e be a java method that associate to an integer n its representation in basis $Card(\Sigma \cup \sqcup)$ using $(\Sigma \cup \sqcup)$ as digits (Euclid's algorithm).

Let p be a java method such that $\forall s \in (\Sigma \cup \sqcup)^*, java(< p, i >) = \begin{cases} 1 \text{ if } i \in L_\phi \\ 0 \text{ else} \end{cases}$.

We define p', a java method (without input) as:

```
public String p'()
{int k = 0;
while (java(<p,java(<e,k>)>) == 0)   {k = k + 1;}
return java(<e,k>);}
```

This method will return the first string of L_ϕ. This holds for any p and in particular for the shortest one p_{min} of length $H_{java}(\phi)$. This reduction provides a specific solution for the production task with length $H_{java}(\phi) + c$ where c is the length of additional code. Then $H_{java}(S) \leq H_{java}(\phi) + c$ (as a minimum) and $-c \leq H_{java}(\phi) - H_{java}(S)$. $\square$

We now require the "production of ϕ" to be the enumeration of all of its elements :

$$H'_U(S) = min\{l(p)|U(<p,i>) = L_\phi(i)\}$$

where $L_\phi(i)$ is the ith element of L_ϕ sorted by represented integers. This time, instead of halting on the first k that gives a word of L_ϕ, we stop on the ith:

```
public String p'(int i)
{int k = 0; int j = 0;
while (j < i)
    {k = k + 1;
    if (java(<p,java(<e,k>)>) == 1)   {j = j + 1;} }
return java(<e,k>);}
```

Thus this alternate production task is reduced to the detection one. Here, we have been demanding enough to allow the reciprocal reduction : given a production method p, we have the following method for the detection task.

```
public String p'(String i)
{int k = 1;
    while (l(java(<p,k>) <= l(i)){
        if (java(<p,k>) == i)   {return 1;}
        k = k + 1;}
return 0;}
```

Whatever is ϕ we have two integer constants p and q such that $-p \leq H_{java}(\phi) - H'_{java}(S) \leq q$.

The two production tasks we define are extreme and allow different reductions. The main interest of these complexity results is to reveal a need to precise the meaning of producing a phenomenon for a multi-agent system.

Time Complexity. Reductions in time complexity must meet time constraints that are likely to depend on L_ϕ. Then, additionally to refinements on the meaning of production, further classification of phenomena might be necessary to assert reductions and complexity features, which are beyond the present work.

4 Situation

Ronald's emergence test [3] applies on systems where (1) a designer describes *local* interactions in a language L_1, (2) the *global* behavior is described using a language L_2

and (3) the link between L_1 and L_2 is *non-obvious* which makes the observer surprised. In our approach, the same distinction is made between the system and its behaviour, however we tried to give a further formalization of surprise as a complexity gap. Furthermore, the dependance on how we define our two tasks might extend to how L_1 and L_2 are defined.

Darley [4] asserts that "a true emergent phenomenon is one for which the optimal means of prediction is simulation". The other possibility is "a creative analysis" and a "deeper understanding" that allows this prediction with less computation. The phenomenon is emergent when $u(n) \geq s(n)$ where $u(n)$ and $s(n)$ are the amounts of computation of understanding or simulation (n is the size of the system). He compares two ways to accomplish the same task : deriving the macro-phenomenon from the micro-dynamics. This is disturbing from a computational complexity point of view as we might expect one computational task to have a single complexity. We think our distinction between a production task and a detection task is easier to import in traditional complexity theories. Out of the simulation domain, it seems more meaningful to distinguish what is designed and what is observed than two refinements of a prediction task.

Finally, VOWELS [2] is the perspective of **A**gents situated in their **E**nvironment constituting a system that produces a phenomenon through **I**nteraction and **O**rganisation. This suggests the pseudo equation $eFeat = C(\phi) - C(A, E) = C(I, O)$ and a link between our proposal and collective complexity.

5   Conclusion

We have tried to make a system and a phenomenon comparable through associated computational tasks. Therefore, the possibility of "much from little", possible reductions and complexity results depend on how we model production and detection as computations. Finally, within our VOWELS interpretation, it provides an alternate inspiration to direct collectivity measures.

References

1. Holland, J.: Emergence: From Chaos to Order. Perseus Books (1997)
2. Demazeau, Y.: Steps towards multi-agent oriented programming. In: 1st International Workshop on Multi Agent Systems. (1997)
3. Ronald, E., Sipper, M., Capcarrère, M.: Design, observation, surprise! a test of emergence. In: Artificial Life 5. (1999) 225–239
4. Darley, V.: Emergent phenomena and complexity. In Brooks, R., Maes, P., eds.: Artificial Life 4. (1994) 411–416
5. Leibniz, G.: Discours de métaphysique. Vrin (1686)
6. Chaitin, G.: A theory of program size formally identical to information theory. Journal of the ACM (1975)

Adaptive Document Analysis with Planning

Csaba Dezsényi, Tadeusz P. Dobrowiecki, and Tamás Mészáros

Budapest University of Technology and Economics,
Department of Measurement and Information Systems, Budapest, Hungary
{dezsenyi, dobrowiecki, meszaros}@mit.bme.hu

Abstract. Autonomous web information systems frequently have to answer queries by extracting information written in non-constrained natural language. This task is modeled as a planning problem. Elementary document processing modules are organized into query dependent information-processing graphs that are the tools of scheduling and controlling the execution and provide semantic fusion of heterogeneous information chunks.

1 Introduction

Planning proved fruitful in various information-gathering tasks on the Web. Automatic Web service composition works e.g. with wrapped services as operators and preconditions and effects built from relational data provided by the wrappers [1]. In this paper authors propose a different route on which planning could help in autonomous information extraction.

In a number of applications, queries are directed toward information hidden in larger natural language (NL) chunks in the surface Web sources or even in the deep Web (e.g. abstracts, news, papers). Such tasks pop up when one checks the background on trade partners or bank clients, attempts to classify and mine political and economical news or medical texts, or follows the company press image, scientific topics, etc. [2]. Albeit both information extraction problems are similar in the abstract setting, they are essentially different in details and call for different solutions:

(1) We allow for queries, for which the real answers lay not in the structured Web sources, but in sentences, paragraphs, documents, even whole electronic document collections referred by such sources.

(2) The search is practical at most at the keyword level, as service wrappers refer only to the documents containing the requested information somewhere within. A meaningful wrapper induction is generally not possible.

(3) The NL processing can range from simple recognizing regular expressions, to knowledge intensive procedures seeking "deep" information, hidden behind the facts.

Consequently, when the search is done and the hits collected, the task only begins. Our approach is based upon the library of elementary document processing modules (Document Analyzers – DAs) organized adaptively from query to query into an information-processing graph. Documents are treated uniformly as inputs and outputs to

M. Pěchouček, P. Petta, and L.Z. Varga (Eds.): CEEMAS 2005, LNAI 3690, pp. 620–623, 2005.

the processing modules. To this end "document views", essentially NL documents equipped with incrementally augmentable XML structure have been developed [3]. DAs annotate views according to their specific processing task (e.g. tokenization, stemming, sentence parsing) and also produce views as results. A complex framework system of handling these document views and processing has been developed [3]. The planning problem that our solution has to solve differs greatly from the automatic Web service composition due to:

(4) Document Analyzers vary greatly in abstraction (e.g. picking up regular expressions vs. checking the consistency of the client image in the whole news collection). Yet it is usually impossible to decompose a more abstract DA into a hierarchical sub-plan composed from DAs of smaller granularity.

(5) The majority of the plan operators (DAs) is application dependent and will be supplied by the end user, even as a part of system maintenance. Working with the Hungarian language means additional hardship. The sentence structure is variable, a formal grammar is missing, and parsing schemes are only partially developed.

(6) Multiple DAs can provide similar results, using different ideas, language and application knowledge. The identification of proper nouns e.g. can be achieved as a byproduct of the morphological analysis, or by a semantically oriented analysis.

These issues justify the idea of introduction into the plan more processing components of the same kind (worst-case planning), then giving up the execution of some of them during plan execution phase. Conversely, if more such components are executed, fusion of their effects may be required to yield a single precondition to go on with the plan. The focus further in the paper is on the planning problem.

2 Planning with Fusion Control

For planning the document processing standard STRIPS-based partially ordered planning was adopted. DAs that produce specific types of document views by analyzing and processing existing ones, are operators. Preconditions are made up from conditions on the required input views, while effects describe the resulting views. The initial state is a document with an initial XML structure, and the goal state is achieved when all of the views required for the information extraction are available.

The adaptation of the planner seems plausible; handling conflicts is however difficult, and namely when more than one DA is producing the required document view. Standard planner would handle this as a nondeterministic selection, since the effects coincide. Such DAs can yet produce views with significantly different quality of the content. Formal description of subtle differences may be impossible or impractical, thus it cannot be handled solely in the planning time. In our approach special operators are introduced to the planner, to control better the execution of the plan (Fig. 1a).

When conflict occurs, the planner first limits the number of conflicting DAs by evaluating available metadata (preselection). Decision about the remaining set can only be made during execution. The proposed solution is similar to the conditional planning [4].

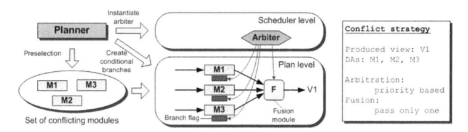

Fig. 1. (a) Main elements of the algorithm. (b) Strategy definition for the conflicting modules

The planner inserts all conflicting DAs into the plan, marking them with conditional branch flags, and linking their outputs to a *fusion module*. If the flag of a DA is true, it will be executed, when its preconditions are fulfilled. Flags are controlled by *arbiters*, instantiated by the planner for each conflicting set. An arbiter controls the conflicting modules by re-setting the corresponding flags. After some branches are executed and the results evaluated, arbiters can modify flags to rerun the modules in different configuration if necessary. Fusion modules merge the incoming views into a single view. Merging is based on the comparison of those XML elements that reference the same source information. Particular control strategy built-in into an arbiter and fusion module is associated with the particular set of the DAs (defined as a kind of macro operator, Fig 1b.). Typical choice can be the priority-based selection of the branches, or executing all branches together, merging the results (see below).

2.1   Example Scenario – Relevant Fact Extraction

Description of DAs and views for the example and the final plan can be seen in the Fig. 2. Fusion modules are rounded squares, and branch conditions are indicated below the DAs. There are three conflicting DA sets, each one connected to its fusion module (F_A, F_N, F_F). Each conditional branch is marked with proper flags (e.g. $A(w)$ and $A(ce)$ at the conflict of W and CE due to the common effect A). If a conditional branch has a preceding DA, the flag has to be propagated backward. See e.g. the CO module, which receives $F(fp)$ flag from FP and will be executed if the A_F arbiter decides to set the $F(fp)$ flag on. If a module forks out into more branches (see e.g. ST, or PO), it receives the disjunction of the corresponding branch flags. A module should run if at least one of the branches is selected. If however it receives flags of all of the following branches, the flags are redundant and can be deleted (indicated with crosses in the Fig 2.).

Arbiter mechanisms are different in all three cases. The A branches typically should run with a priority mechanism: if an HTML page has an associated wrapper definition, then W should run, otherwise CE tries to extract the textual content with a heuristic algorithm. Thus, arbiter A_A first tries to execute W by setting $A(w)$ true and $A(ce)$ false. If W doesn't yield result, $A(ce)$ will be set true, which enables the execution of CE. Arbiter A_N will execute each branch together, and F_N will merge the results, because that way the final document view will contain the most of the recognized named-entities. Arbiter A_F can also execute each branch in parallel.

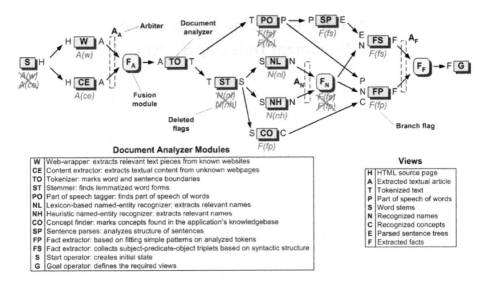

Document Analyzer Modules

W	Web-wrapper: extracts relevant text pieces from known websites
CE	Content extractor: extracts textual content from unknown webpages
TO	Tokenizer: marks word and sentence boundaries
ST	Stemmer: finds lemmatized word forms
PO	Part of speech tagger: finds part of speech of words
NL	Lexicon-based named-entity recognizer: extracts relevant names
NH	Heuristic named-entity recognizer: extracts relevant names
CO	Concept finder: marks concepts found in the application's knowledgebase
SP	Sentence parses: analyzes structure of sentences
FP	Fact extractor: based on fitting simple patterns on analyzed tokens
FS	Fact extractor: collects subject-predicate-object triplets based on syntactic structure
S	Start operator: creates initial state
G	Goal operator: defines the required views

Views

H	HTML source page
A	Extracted textual article
T	Tokenized text
P	Part of speech of words
S	Word stems
N	Recognized names
C	Recognized concepts
E	Parsed sentence trees
F	Extracted facts

Fig. 2. Description of the DAs and views for the example and the planned document processing schema for a particular task, defined by *S* and *G* operators

3 Conclusions and Further Work

The proposed approach shows two advantages. It fits into the standard planners. Its complex conditional branches can be handled effectively, due to the proper spreading of the flags, indicating the required execution paths. The method precisely separates the algorithmic steps of the decision-making and the result fusion. Currently the prototype version is being implemented, with a number of document processing modules, oriented toward short electronic news in Hungarian, although the architecture and the operation of the framework are language and context independent.

References

1. Kuter, U., Sirin, E., Nau, D., Parsia, B., Hendler, J.: Information Gathering During Planning for Web Service Composition. Lect. Notes in Comp. Sc., Vol. 3298, pp. 335–349, (2004)
2. Xu, F., Krieger, H.: Integrating Shallow and Deep NLP for Information Extraction. In Proceedings of RANLP 2003, Borovets, Bulgaria, September, (2003)
3. Dezsényi, Cs., Mészáros, T. Dobrowiecki, T.: Parser Framework for Information Extraction. Proc. of the EUROFUSE Workshop on Data and Knowledge Engineering, pp. 177-184, Sept 22-25, Warsaw, Poland (2004)
4. Russell, S., Norvig, P.: Artificial Intelligence. A Modern Approach. Prentice Hall Inc. (1997)

A Self-configuring Agent-Based Document Indexing System

L. Peng, R. Collier, A. Mur, D. Lillis, F. Toolan, and J. Dunnion

Department of Computer Science,
University College Dublin (UCD), Belfield, Dublin 4, Ireland
{peng.liu, rem.collier, mur.angel, david.lillis, fergus.toolan,
john.dunnion}@ucd.ie

Abstract. This paper describes an extensible and scalable approach to indexing documents that is utilized within the Highly Organised Team of Agents for Information Retrieval (HOTAIR) architecture.

1 Introduction

This paper describes the HOTAIR Search Engine architecture, an *extensible* and *scalable* architecture for the discovery, retrieval and indexing of documents from multiple heterogonous information sources. Within the HOTAIR architecture, extensibility is engendered through the design of an architecture that provides support for: (1) the plugging in of multiple retrieval strategies such as the Vector Space Model [5] and the Extended Boolean Model [6]; (2) the ability to rapidly and seamlessly integrate diverse sources of information. This requires the use of an open infrastructure that is able to dynamically adapt its configuration.

2 The HOTAIR Indexing System

The HOTAIR Document Indexing System has been implemented using Agent Factory [2], a cohesive framework that delivers structured support for the development and deployment of multi-agent systems, which are comprised of agents that are autonomous, situated, social, intentional, rational, and mobile [1].

A diagrammatical overview of the agents that make up the system architecture is presented in figure 1. The actual number of agents that exist at any time varies depending upon the demand on and the resources available to the system. In addition, these agents are deployed over a number of different agent platforms that reside on different physical machines.

The creation of agents is a service that is provided by the Platform Manager (PM) system agent. Each agent platform contains a PM, which is responsible for handling requests to create more agents. Upon receipt of a request, a PM negotiates with its counterparts to decide which on machine(s) the requested agent(s) should be created. If there are insufficient resources to create all of the requested agent(s), then the PM agents can either refuse or partially fulfil the request.

M. Pĕchouček, P. Petta, and L.Z. Varga (Eds.): CEEMAS 2005, LNAI 3690, pp. 624–627, 2005.

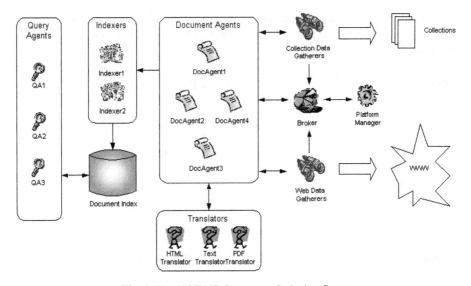

Fig. 1. The HOTAIR Document Indexing System

3 Experiments: Impact of Document Agents on Indexing Speed

The hypothesis for our experiment is that a specific number of Document Agents (DA) is anticipated for optimal indexing speed. The approach taken in the evaluation of this hypothesis was to configure the HOTAIR architecture to index four document collections with different features. (Figure 2)

To perform the experiment, a simplified version of the HOTAIR architecture was constructed, which consisted of: one *Data Gatherer* (DG), which is charged with the task of analyzing information sources; one *Indexer*, responsible for indexing documents and one *Broker,* which is responsible for monitoring the status of the DGs. The Broker can ask the local AMS (Agent Management Service) agent to create DAs. When significant disparities exist, the Broker re-assigns some existing DAs to different DGs. A fixed number of DAs encapsulate the workflow of the system, that is, they know how to get a document indexed.

Dataset	No. of documents	Average no. of terms per Doc	Coefficient of Variation
Cranfield	1400	95.18	50%
LISA	6003	46.58	45%
Med	1033	83.72	56%
Time	423	326.61	92%

Fig. 2. Table of the four collections used in the experiment

The figure 3 shows how the number of agents affects the indexing speed. Every graph plots the mean indexing speed for each document collection.

Cranfield, Lisa, and Med performance increases up to a point, and then slowly decreases after that point. Their optimal speed is approximately 170 milliseconds per document.

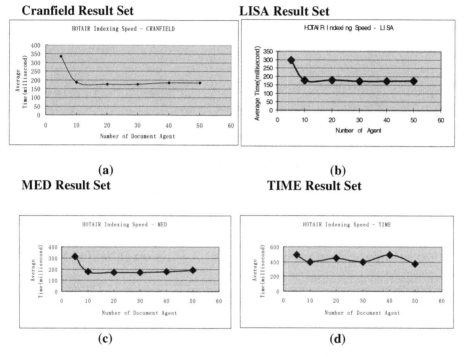

Fig. 3. Graphs illustrating the experimental result for the four collections

These results shows that increasing the number of DAs has the effect of improving performance up to a limit that corresponds to the speed at which the Indexer agent is able to index documents. Once this limit is reached, adding more DAs has the effect of degrading the indexing speed. The performance of the architecture is worse as it processes the first bundles of documents.

In contrast, the results generated for the TIME collection do not follow this pattern; the mean indexing speed of each document bundle fluctuates wildly, and there is no obvious correspondence between the number of DAs and the indexing speed. On closer inspection, it was felt that this incoherence resulted from a combination of the high level of variation in the number of terms in the documents of the collection (the coefficient of variation for this collection is 92% versus 45-55% for the other collections) and the relatively small number of documents, which makes this variation more marked.

In summary, the results for the Cranfield, Lisa, and Med collections support our hypothesis, namely that the number of DAs does have an impact on indexing speed. As indicated earlier, the optimal speed of the architecture is bounded by the speed at which the Indexer agent can index documents. This speed is proportional to the size of the document that it is indexing.

4   Conclusions and Future Work

This paper presents an agent-based document indexing system for the HOTAIR architecture. This architecture is able to dynamically reconfigure itself to reflect changes in demand through either the creation of additional DAs or through the cloning of Indexer or Translators agents.

It is our intention that, ultimately, this reconfiguration will be driven by built-in metrics for evaluating performance. However, in an effort to validate the architecture, we present the results of a set of experiments that seek to evaluate whether the number of Document Agents has an impact on the speed at which documents are indexed. These experiments have shown a general pattern of behaviour that supports this hypothesis.

It would seem sensible to assume that, once the optimal number of DAs has been reached for a given indexer, and then performance can only be improved by adding another indexer. Ultimately, we envisage that it will be possible to implement some form of mathematical model that can be used to estimate the number of DAs and Indexers required based on the available resources. The built-in metrics would then be used to make small adjustments to the community of agents based on the actual performance of the system.

References

1. Collier, R., Agent Factory: A Framework for the Engineering of Agent-Oriented Applications, PhD Thesis, Dept. Computer Science, University College Dublin, 2001.
2. Collier, R., O'Hare, G. M. P. Lowen, T. D., and Rooney, C. F. B., *Beyond Prototyping in the Factory of Agents*, In Proc. 3rd Int. Central and Eastern European Conference on Multi-Agent Systems (CEEMAS), Prague, Czech Republic, 2003.
3. Doorenbos, R. B., Etsioni, and Weld, D.S.: *A Scalable Comparison-Shopping Agent for the WWW*, in W.L. Johnson and B. Hayes –Roth (eds). Proc, Proceedings of the First International Conference on Autonomous Agents pp. 39-48, Marina del Rey, CA, USA. ACM Press, 1997
4. FIPA, The FIPA 2000 Specifications, FIPA Website URL: http://www.fipa.org
5. Salton, G. and Lesk, M.E.: *Computer evaluation of indexing and text processing*. Journal of the ACM, 15(1):8-36, January 1968
6. Salton, G., Fox, E. A., and Wu, H.. *Extended Boolean information retrieval*. Communications of the ACM, 26(11):1022-1036, 1983

Managing Trust for Secure Active Networks

Jian-Jun Qi and Zeng-Zhi Li

Institute of Computer Architecture and Network,
Xi'an Jiaotong University, Xi'an, 710049, PR China
qjjwv@nwu.edu.cn

Abstract. This paper proposes a security architecture that employs trust notion to address security issues in active networks. The subjectivity of trust is discussed, and the innovative idea is that how to compute trust should be decided subjectively by an entity. Then, a general framework for a trust system is described. Finally, a flexible trust management model, which employs the features of active networks, is presented. In this model, different entities can use different methods to compute trust, and an entity can change its computing method of trust over time.

1 Introduction

Active networks [1,2] represent a powerful new networking paradigm in which intermediate nodes become programmable. While they provide a much more flexible network infrastructure with increased capabilities than traditional networks, they also raise considerable security issues [2,3]. To achieve security in active networks, the trustworthiness of entities must be vouched for.

Current security schemes for active networks are based on "hard security" mechanisms [4] such as encryption, digital signatures, authentication protocols, etc. They are not sufficient. And we believe that "soft security" mechanisms such as trust systems are good complement. Some computational models of trust [5,6,7,8] have been developed, but none of them is applied to active networks, to the best of our knowledge. In this paper, we propose an active network security architecture in which computational trust models can be incorporated.

2 Trust and Its Subjectivity

Trust is a complex concept. It is subjective and computable [5,6,7,8]. When the trustor (the trusting entity) wants to interact with the trustee (the trusted entity), the trustor must judge subjectively according to attributes such as competence, honesty, security and dependability of the trustee. The trustor can not really know these attributes directly and thoroughly, but it can gather some information and evidence about the attributes. The two main sources of those are [5,6,7]: the trustor's direct experiences from interactions with the trustee, and recommendations provided by other entities (they are called recommenders) who have interacted with the trustee before (here, in order to avoid rumors and loops,

M. Pěchouček, P. Petta, and L.Z. Varga (Eds.): CEEMAS 2005, LNAI 3690, pp. 628–631, 2005.

recommendations must be based on first hand experiences only, and not on other recommendations). The trustor can derive a rating about the trustee from the direct experiences, and can also compute a reputation score of the trustee based on the received ratings from recommenders. Finally, the trustor's subjective trust judgement can be made according to personal experiences and recommendations as well as its own mental factors such as personality, emotion, etc.

Current computational trust models [5,6,7,8] assume implicitly that all of entities in a system use same method to compute trust (i.e., same computational trust model). This can not fully reflect the subjectivity of trust. We argue that how to compute trust, i.e. using which computational model of trust, should be decided subjectively by an entity. That is to say, different entities may use different methods to compute trust, while an entity may change its computing method over time.

3   General Framework for Computing Trust

From above discussion, three basic functions are needed to compute trust. One is to derive rating from personal experiences; one is to derive reputation based on recommendations; and one is to derive trust from a combination of rating and reputation as well as mental factors. These three functions constitute a computational trust model. It is illustrated in Figure 1. Additionally, some utilities are needed to maintain experiences, recommendations and so on in a trust model.

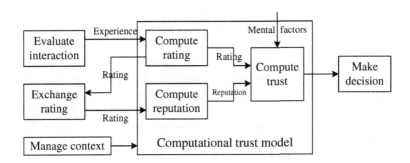

Fig. 1. General framework for a trust system

There are some auxiliary facilities to support a trust model. They are "Evaluate interaction", "Exchange rating" and "Manage context" in Figure 1. "Evaluate interaction" estimates a score of satisfaction for each interaction. It may simply judge whether the interaction is success or failure, or calculate a continuous value with a complex operation like the one in [6]. "Exchange rating" is in charge of exchanging recommendations between entities. It should be implemented as a protocol. "Manage context" administers the information about contexts, and it also provides a method to measure the distance between two contexts [6]. These facilities are very relevant to a specific application, so they should be implemented in the application.

We are trying to define standard API for computational trust models in order that each entity is able to use the method it needs to compute trust. In order to exchange recommendation among trust models, the syntax and the semantic of recommendation should be standardized.

4   Managing Trust in Active Networks

In our system, we do not use a specific computational trust model. Employing the features of active networks, we provide a flexible mechanism so that entities can use the computational trust models they need. Trust models are located at some code servers as a library of functions. The trust model for a node is specified by the administration, and downloaded from a code server. The trust model for an AA is specified by the user, and is used by all the active packets of the AA. When a packet arrives at a node, it checks if the required trust model is presented. If not, the trust model is downloaded from a code server. We define a group of common interfaces to trust models. With these interfaces, an entity can obtain the required trust values from its trust model, and it can also pass its experiences and recommendations from other entities to the trust model.

We consider two types of recommending. On the one hand, a node can get ratings about another from other nodes, this is performed through a simple protocol. On the other hand, an active packet can get ratings about other nodes from the node on which it executes, this is performed through a function call provided by the node. There are two contexts in our system, one is "IN" and the other is "OUT". In "IN" context, a node uses the trustworthiness of an active packet's source and previous hop to make decisions about the packet's executing when the packet arrives at the node. Executing the packet is the node's one interaction with the source and the previous hop. In "OUT" context, the packet itself or the node uses the trustworthiness of the node's neighbors to choose a next hop when the packet needs to be forwarded. Forwarding the packet is the node's or the AA's one interaction with the next hop.

5   Conclusion and Future Work

In this paper, we have applied the idea of computational trust models into security solutions for active networks. A novel trust management model based on the active networking technology has been outlined, that promises that each entity can use its own computing method of trust. This means that how to compute trust is subjective for an entity. While, at this stage, the proposed model is being developed, and we are not able to quantify potential performance gains. In the future we will evaluate the performance of our system. We will also work at applying our model into other environments (such as MANETs).

Acknowledgements

The authors gratefully acknowledge the suggestions of the reviewers and the hard work of the CEEMAS 2005 Program Committee. The authors also gratefully acknowledge the support of the National Natural Science Foundation of China (No.60173059).

References

1. Calvert, K.L.: Architectural Framework for Active Networks, version 1.0. University of Kentucky (1999)
2. Psounis, K.: Active Networks: Applications, Security, Safety, and Architectures. IEEE Communications Surveys. 2(1) (1999)
3. Murphy, S.: Security Architecture for Active Nets. A.N. Security Working Group, Network Associates Laboratories (2001)
4. Rasmusson, L., Janssen, S.: Simulated Social Control for Secure Internet Commerce. In: Meadows, C. (ed.): Proceedings of the 1996 workshop on New security paradigms. ACM Press, New York (1996) 18-25
5. Jøsang, A., Ismail, R., Boyd, C.: A Survey of Trust and Reputation Systems for Online Service Provision. Decision Support Systems. (2005) to appear
6. Liu, J.S., Issarny, V.: Enhanced Reputation Mechanism for Mobile Ad Hoc Networks. In: Jensen, C.D., Poslad, S., Dimitrakos, T. (eds.): Proceedings of the 2nd International Conference on Trust Management. Lecture Notes in Computer Science, Vol. 2995. Springer-Verlag, Berlin Heidelberg (2004) 48-62
7. Mui, L., Mohtashemi, M., Halberstadt, A.: A Computational Model of Trust and Reputation for E-businesses. In: King, D., Dennis, A.R. (eds.): Proceedings of the 35th Annual Hawaii International Conference on System Sciences - Volume 7. IEEE Computer Society, Washington, DC (2002) 188
8. Marsh, S.P.: Formalising Trust as a Computational Concept. PhD thesis, Department of Computing Sciece and Mathematics, University of Sterling (1994)

A Case Study of Agent-Based Virtual Enterprise Modelling

Mihaela Oprea

University Petroleum-Gas of Ploiesti, Department of Informatics,
Bd. Bucuresti Nr. 39, Ploiesti 100680, Romania

Abstract. The paper presents VIRT_CONSTRUCT, an agent-based virtual enterprise, dedicated to private houses construction, focusing on the specific ontology, and on the added value of learning capability inclusion.

1 Introduction

A virtual enterprise (VE) can be described as a network of cooperating enterprises that have common goals for a limited period of time. As a VE is composed by distributed, heterogeneous and autonomous entities, it can be modeled in a natural way as a multi-agent system (MAS). Several research projects have used intelligent agents in VE modelling (e.g. see [1], [2], [3], [4], [5]). The long-term goal of our research project is to develop an efficient real-world VE based on intelligent agents in the application domain of private houses construction. In this paper it is described the agent-based VE VIRT_CONSTRUCT, focusing on the architecture, on the specific ontology, and on the learning capability inclusion.

2 VIRT_CONSTRUCT: An Agent-Based VE

The virtual enterprise VIRT_CONSTRUCT has been modelled as a MAS. The client agent will delegate the VE Manager agent to create the VE. After selecting the partner enterprises a contract negotiation will be made. In order to motivate the agents to follow the strategy that the negotiation protocol designer wants to be followed we have used a leveled commitment contract similar with that given in [6]. During the settle of the VE, the rules of VE functioning, as well as norms specific to private houses construction has to be defined. For example, some norms are related to the construction legality: an official approval for the house construction, as well as a legal document proving that the client is the owner of the land where the house will be built. After the contract is signed the VE operation starts. Each worker of an enterprise is a human agent that has associated a software agent which simulates his work in the VE virtual environment, while he is doing his work in the real world. The VE operation will end when the VE goal is achieved (the finish of house construction), or when the client itself decide to stop it.

M. Pěchouček, P. Petta, and L.Z. Varga (Eds.): CEEMAS 2005, LNAI 3690, pp. 632–635, 2005.

2.1 The Architecture of `VIRT_CONSTRUCT`

The twelve main activities identified when building a house (see Figure 1), are performed by four partner enterprises: E1 (*House Design* 1), E2 (*Housing* 2÷8), E3 (*Installations* 9÷12), and E4 (*Suppliers*). The architecture of `VIRT_CONSTRUCT` (see Figure 1) is composed by a supervisor agent, SVA, which is the VE Initiator/VE Manager, and the partner enterprises. A monitoring service is used during the VE operation to supervise processes and provide to partners information about the state of partial processes. E1 has only one agent, HDA (House Designer Agent). Each of the other three enterprises has a monitoring agent, that could be the manager agent (MA).

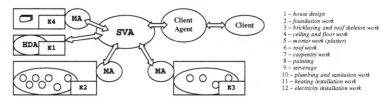

1 – *house design*
2 – *foundation work*
3 – *bricklaying and roof skeleton work*
4 – *ceiling and floor work*
5 – *mortar work (plaster)*
6 – *roof work*
7 – *carpentry work*
8 – *painting*
9 – *severage*
10 – *plumbing and sanitation work*
11 – *heating installation work*
12 – *electricity installation work*

Fig. 1. The architecture of `VIRT_CONSTRUCT`

2.2 The Ontology of `VIRT_CONSTRUCT`

In order to accomplish their goals, agents have to communicate between them, and thus, they need to share the same ontology. We have taken from the Enterprise Ontology described in [7] the basic concepts (e.g. VIRTUAL ENTERPRISE, RESOURCE, ACTIVITY), and we have extended it with the specialised concepts from the housing domain (e.g. WORKER, MATERIAL, HOUSE DESIGNER, PAINTING PUMP), and with the instantiated concepts (those effectively used during the `VIRT_CONSTRUCT` creation/operation as for example, HOUSE DESIGNER X) deriving the ontology *housing*. Figure 2 shows a small part of the *housing* ontology.

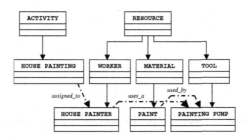

Fig. 2. Selection from the *housing* ontology - the house painting activity

2.3 The Learning Capability

In order to increase the performance of `VIRT_CONSTRUCT`, we have included a learning capability at the partner enterprise level, similar with the organizational learning model proposed in [8]. The purpose of the agent learning mechanism is to process the tasks within the shorter time. The knowledge of the other member's expected time to process a type of task is represented as $tt_i(a_j, t_k)$, i.e. task time. This value is evaluated by the manager (agent a_i) on the expected time of a worker (agent a_j) to process a specific task (task t_k) and is updated by relation (1).

$$tt_i(a_j, t_k) = (1.0 - \alpha)tt_i(a_j, t_k) + \alpha T \tag{1}$$

T is the time in which the worker perform a given task, α is the learning rate, $\alpha \in [0,1]$. The worker ability level, *wal*, is computed by relation (2).

$$wal(a_j) = \frac{1}{\exp\left(tt_i(a_j, t_k)/n\right)} \tag{2}$$

n is the exploration rate. If a new task t_k arrives at an agent a_i, the probability to choose agent a_j is given by relation (3).

$$P(a_j) = \frac{wal(a_j)}{\sum_{a \in Agents} wal(a)} \tag{3}$$

$P(a_j)$ is used by MA as a reinforcement parameter for the work of agent a_j when MA re-evaluates the ability of a_j.

2.4 Preliminary Experimental Results

We have implemented a preliminary version of VIRT_CONSTRUCT in JADE, and we have run it on several scenarios. In this paper we briefly present two types of experiments, related to the analysis of learning inclusion benefit, and VE scalability.

One of the experiments made analyses the evolution of the average processing time for a given task when learning / no learning is applied after the replacement of a worker. For example, consider the task of foundation construction, *task2*, which is divided in three subtasks: excavation and digging (*S1*), preparation of construction materials (*S2*), reinforce with concrete (*S3*). In the right part of Figure 3 it is given the past performance of the seven workers that might be involved in the three subtasks.

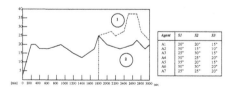

Fig. 3. The *task2* processing performance in the partner enterprise E2

We have made some simulations for the execution of the three subtasks in a time period of 3000 minutes. After the first three days (1800 minutes) a worker replacement was necessary, A3 being replaced with A4. Figure 3 shows the average of *task2* processing performance when learning is done (1), or not done (2) after the worker replacement. The performance of *task2* processing becomes worse after the worker replacement, and it will recover more quickly in case (1) than in case (2).

As stated in [9], scalability (i.e. the MAS performance when the number of agents increases) can be measured by several metrics as for example, the memory usage, the total number of messages transferred between agents or the response time between conversations. In the case of VIRT_CONSTRUCT we have analysed scalability at the stage of VE creation, and we have measured the duration of the contract negotiation as a function of the total number of selected partner enterprises. Figure 4 shows this relationship in two cases, when learning is used (1), and not used (2) in the partners selection process. As expected, when the number of selected partner enterprises is increased the learning mechanism maintain a better scalability of the system.

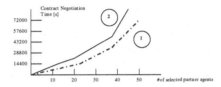

Fig. 4. Relationship of contract negotiation time and #of selected partner agents

3   Conclusion

The agent-based VE from the housing domain, that was briefly presented, uses a specific ontology, extended from the Enterprise Ontology, and a reinforcement learning mechanism for the selection of the best team at the partner enterprise level.

References

[1] Fischer, K., Müller, J.P., Heimig, I., Scheer, A.: Intelligent Agents in Virtual Enterprises, Proceedings of the 1st Int. Conf. and Exhibition on the Practical Applications of Intelligent Agents and Multi-Agent Technology, UK, (1996) 205-223.
[2] Petersen, S.A., and Matskin, M.: Agent Interaction Protocols for the Selection of Partners for Virtual Enterprises, Multi-Agent Systems and Applications III, V. Marík et al. (Eds): CEEMAS 2003, LNAI 2691, Springer, (2003) 605-615.
[3] Camarinho-Matos, L.M., and Afsarmanesh, H.: Virtual Enterprise Modeling and Support Infrastructures: Applying Multi-agent Systems Approaches, Multi-Agent Systems and Applications, M. Luck et al. (Eds): ACAI 2001, LNAI 2086, Springer, (2001) 335-364.
[4] Oliveira, E., Rocha, A. P. : Agents advanced features for Negotiation in Electronic Commerce and Virtual Organisations Formation Process, in Agent Mediated Electronic Commerce, F. Dignum and C. Sierra (Eds), LNAI 1991, Springer, (2001) 78-97.
[5] Oprea, M.: Applications of Multi-Agent Systems, Information Technology, R. Reis (Ed), Kluwer Academic Publishers, (2004) 239-270.
[6] Sandholm, T., Sikka, S., Norden, S.: Algorithms for Optimizing Leveled Commitment Contracts, Proceedings of IJCAI'99, vol. 1, (1999) 535-540.
[7] Uschold, M., King, M., Moralee, S., Zorgios, Y.: The Enterprise Ontology, The Knowledge Engineering Review, 13(1), (1998) 31-89.
[8] Terabe, M., Washio, T., Katai, O, Sawaragi, T.: A Study of Organizational Learning in Multiagent Systems, Proceedings of ECAI 1996 workshop W26, (1996) 110-119.
[9] Rana, O.F., Stout, K.: What is Scalability in Multi-Agent Systems?, Proceedings of the 4th Int. Conf. on Autonomous Agents AA2000, ACM Press, (2000) 56-63.

Agent-Based Support for Open Communities

Lorenzo Lazzari, Marco Mari, Alessandro Negri, and Agostino Poggi

Dipartimento di Ingegneria dell'Informazione,
Università degli Studi di Parma,
Parco Area delle Scienze 181/A, 43100 Parma, Italy
{lazzari, mari, negri, poggi}@ce.unipr.it
http://aot.ce.unipr.it/

Abstract. RAVE (Remote Assistance Virtual Environment) is a Web and multi-agent based system to support remote users during common projects or activities. A Personal Agent, associated with a specific user, helps her/him to solve problems proposing information and answers extracted from some information repositories. It's also able to forward answers received from other on-line users, recommended by their Personal Agents as experts in that specific topic. A profile is built and maintained for each user. A RAVE system is not a closed system, but it's based on a dynamic network of RAVE platforms managing groups of geographically localized users and documents. RAVE users and documents profile management subsystems provide a mechanism that dynamically adapts the relevance of each profile, according to the availability of experts and documents.

1 Introduction

Finding relevant information is a longstanding problem in computing. Conventional approaches such as databases, information retrieval systems and Web search engines partially address this problem. Nevertheless, the most valuable information is not widely available and cannot even be indexed or catalogued. Much of this information may only be accessed by asking the right people. The challenge of finding relevant information then reduces to finding the "expert" whom we may ask a specific question. However, people may easily get tired of receiving trivial questions or many times the same question, therefore, who needs help for solving a certain problem should look for documents related to it and then eventually look for a possible expert on that topic.

In this paper we present a multi-agent system, called RAVE (Remote Assistance Virtual Environment), that integrates information and expert searching facilities for communities of users working in similar topics. In the following sections we describe the multi-agent architecture and we talk about RAP (Remote Assistant for Programmers), an implementation of the RAVE system for communities of Java programmers.

2 System Architecture

RAVE associates a Personal Agent with each user which helps her/him to solve problems: the assistance is provided proposing information and answers extracted from

M. Pěchouček, P. Petta, and L.Z. Varga (Eds.): CEEMAS 2005, LNAI 3690, pp. 636–639, 2005.
© Springer-Verlag Berlin Heidelberg 2005

some information repositories and forwarding answers received by "experts" on the topic, selected on the basis of their profile. The system is based on seven different kinds of agents: Personal Agents, User Profile Managers, Answer Managers, Document Managers, E-mail Managers, Starter Agents and Directory Facilitators.

Personal Agents (PA) allow the interaction between the users and the different parts of the system and, in particular, between the users themselves. Moreover, a PA is responsible of building the user profile and maintaining it when its user is on-line. User-agent interaction can be performed in two different ways: through a Web-based interface when the user is active in the system, through e-mails when it is off-line. Usually there is a PA for each on-line user, but, when needed, PAs are created to interact with off-line users via e-mails.

User Profile Managers are responsible of maintaining and updating the profile of the system users. **Answer Managers** maintain the answers provided by users during the life of the system and they find the appropriate answers to the new queries of the users. Besides providing an answer, these agents update the score of the answer and forward the vote to the User Profile Manager for updating the user profile. **Document Managers** find the appropriate documents to answer the queries submitted by system users. **E-mail Managers** are responsible of the communication between the system and the off-line users. **Starter Agents** are responsible for activating a PA when either a user logs on or another agent requests it. **Directory Facilitators** are responsible to inform an agent about the address of the other agents active in the system (yellow pages service).

2.1   Profile Management and Open Communities

The management of user and document profiles is performed in two different phases: an initialization phase and an updating phase. In order to simplify and reduce the possibility of inaccuracy due to people's opinions of themselves and to incomplete information, we decided to build the initial profile of the users and documents in an automated way. Profiles are represented by vectors of weighted terms whose values are related to the frequency of the term itself in the user's documents. Document and user profiles are computed by using "term frequency inverse document frequency" (TF-IDF) [6] algorithm. Each user profile is built by user's PA through the analysis of the documents she/he produced or collected. This is only the initial user's profile, it will be updated when the user produces or collects new documents or when the user interacts with the system answering some queries.

An important requirement that has guided the design of RAVE has been the support for open and distributed users communities. RAVE structure is open, since new users can register and access the system, and a registered user can acquire new skills or produce new documents and therefore update his profile. The community beneath RAVE is distributed: the whole system can consist of a dynamic group of local communities. Each community can operate isolated, but can also decide to join a group of communities, sharing experts and documents repositories.

The open and distributed nature of the system entails some significant problems in the evaluation of information: the evaluation of both experts and documents is strongly dependent on the actual composition of the community group. For example, if a user is rated as the maximum expert to answer a query, he is rated considering only the users registered in the system at that moment. As a matter of fact, TF-IDF algorithm can be easily used in a centralized system where all the profiles and the data are managed, while our context is more complex. For these reasons, each profile component of RAVE is associated with two elements: an absolute element and a TF-IDF weighted element. The absolute one depends only on the user (or document) profile, instead the TF-IDF element is related to both the user profile and the whole community profiles. Moreover, while the absolute element is stored in a database, the weighted one is maintained in memory and it is recalculated when necessary.

3 RAP

RAP (Remote Assistant for Programmers) is an implementation of the RAVE system specialized to support communities of students and programmers during shared or personal projects based on the use of the Java programming language. User profiles are built on the basis of the software the users wrote.

A quite complete description of the system behaviour can be given showing the scenario where a user asks information to her/his PA about a particular problem. (1) First of all the user selects the types of answers she/he prefers to receive (e.g., documents, javadocs, answer repositories, on-line experts' answers). (2) The user submits the query through graphical interface. The query is composed of two parts: the first one identifies its context and contains keywords provided by a system glossary (we are using the "SUN Glossary of Java Related Terms"), the second part represent the textual content of the query. (3) The PA associated to the user performs different actions and interacts with the different agents of the system to collect the various types of answers; when the PA receives an answer, it immediately forwards it to the user. (4) The user, after the reception of all the answers or when she/he has already found a satisfying answer, has to rate the list of the answers. It's important to note that the rating cannot be known by the user that sent the answer and users that didn't send answers automatically receive a negative rating. Moreover, when an answer retrieved from the answer repository is rated, this value is also used to update the profile of the user that previously proposed that answer.

RAP has been developed using JADE (Java Agent DEvelopment framework) [3], a software framework that aids the realization of agent-based applications in compliance with the FIPA specifications [5]. JADE is an open source project and it can be downloaded from the JADE Web site [4]. Given the distributed nature of JADE-based agent systems, a RAP system can be distributed on a set of agent platforms connected usually via Internet and situated in different parts of the world.

In the next future, RAP will be tested in practical courses on JADE shared among students of some American Latin and European Universities inside the European Commission funded project "@lis Technology Net" [1]. Moreover, the system will be used by students and researchers involved in the ANEMONE project [2].

4 Conclusions

In this paper, we present a system called RAVE (Remote Assistance Virtual Environment) with the aim of supporting communities of users working or interested in common or similar topics. A first implementation of RAVE has been realized: RAP (Remote Assistant for Programmers) is a system to support communities of students and programmers during shared and personal projects based on the use of the Java programming language.

RAVE and RAP have similarities with WBT [7], I-MINDS [8] and, in particular, with the Expert Finder system [9]. All these systems provide agents that recommend possible "helpers", but none of them provides the integration of different sources of information (experts, answers archive and code documentation) and none of them integrates, in the user profile, information about user's day-to-day work products with information obtained from the answers the user provided to the other users of the system. Another original contribution of RAVE is the design of a recommendation system composed by an open and distributed group of communities; each community is independent and can dynamically join or leave a group.

In addition to complete the experimentation of the RAP system, future research activities will be related to the realization of a RAVE implementation allowing the concurrent management of different types of communities (i.e., centered on different topics).

References

1. @LIS Technet Home Page. Available from http://www.alis-technet.org.
2. ANEMONE Home Page. Available from http://aot.ce.unipr.it:8080/anemone.
3. Bellifemine, F., Poggi, A., Rimassa, G.: Developing multi-agent systems with a FIPA-compliant agent framework.. Software Practice and Experience, 31, (2001) 103-128.
4. JADE Home Page. Available from http://jade.tilab.com.
5. FIPA Home Page. Available from http://www.fipa.org.
6. Salton, G.: Automatic Text Processing. (1989), Addison-Wesley.
7. Ishikawa, T., Matsuda, H., Takase, H.: Agent Supported Collaborative Learning Using Community Web Software. In Proc. International Conference on Computers in Education, Auckland, New Zealand, (2002) 42-43.
8. Liu, X., Zhang, X. Soh, L., Al-Jaroodi, J., Jiang, H.: I-MINDS: An Application of Multi-agent System Intelligence to On-line Education. In Proc. IEEE International Conference on Systems, Man & Cybernetics, Washington, D.C., (2003) 4864-4871.
9. Vivacqua, A. and Lieberman, H.: Agents to Assist in Finding Help. in Proc. ACM Conference on Human Factors in Computing Systems, San Francisco, CA, (2000) 65-72.

Architecture-Centric Development of an AGV Transportation System

Danny Weyns[1], Kurt Schelfthout[1], Tom Holvoet[1], Tom Lefever[2], and Jan Wielemans[2]

[1] DistriNet, Department of Computer Science K.U.Leuven,
Celestijnenlaan 200 A, B-3001 Leuven, Belgium
{danny.weyns, kurt.schelfthout, tom.holvoet}@cs.kuleuven.be
[2] Egemin International n.v., Baarbeek 1, B-2070 Zwijndrecht, Belgium
{tom.lefever, jan.wielemans}@egemin.be

Abstract. Architectural design plays a key role in software engineering. The software architecture is the backbone of the designed solution, it has the functional requirements of the system and satisfies the quality requirements. In our research, we put forward situated multiagent systems (situated MAS) as an approach to build distributed applications with demanding quality requirements such as flexibility and openness. In this paper we illustrate how we apply situated MAS to an Automatic Guided Vehicle (AGV) transportation system. We discuss the high-level structure of the software architecture and explain how the architecture aims to meet important quality requirements.

1 Introduction

Software architecture is generally acknowledged as a crucial part of the design of a software system [1]. The software architecture has the functional requirements of the system and aims to satisfy the quality requirements. A common practice to document a software architecture is by using a set of related *views* [2]. A view is a representation of a set of system elements and the relationships associated with them. A module view enumerates principal implementation units and relationships among these units such as "is-part-of" or "uses". A process view focuses on dynamic aspects of the system such as synchronization between process elements. Other views can be part of the documentation of an architecture such as a deployment view that describes the allocation of system elements to available processors.

In the last three years, we have studied the engineering of distributed applications with demanding quality requirements such as flexibility and openness. Example domains we focus on are network management and decentralized control of logistic machines in a warehouse. In our research, we put forward situated MASs as an approach to build such distributed applications. A situated MAS consists of a distributed environment populated with a set of agents that cooperate to solve a complex problem in a decentralized way. Intelligence in a situated MAS originates from the interactions between the agents, rather than from their individual capabilities. Situated agents exploit the environment to coordinate their behavior, e.g. via digital pheromones or gradient fields [3]. We have developed a reference architecture for situated MASs that offers a

M. Pěchouček, P. Petta, and L.Z. Varga (Eds.): CEEMAS 2005, LNAI 3690, pp. 640–644, 2005.

blueprint for developing the intended applications. This reference generalizes and extracts common functions and structures from various experimental applications we have studied. For a detailed discussion of the reference architecture we refer to [4,5,6].

In this paper, we illustrate the architectural design of an AGV transportation system that is based on the reference architecture for situated MASs. The AGV transportation system is investigated in a R&D project in close cooperation with Egemin, a manufacturer of automated warehouse systems (http://www.egemin.com/). An AGV transportation system uses unmanned vehicles (AGVs) to handle *transports*, i.e. to move goods through a warehouse. Transports are generated by a *client system*, typically a business management program. An AGV uses a battery as energy source. AGVs can move through a warehouse guided by a laser navigation system, or by magnets or cables that are fixed in the floor. The low-level control of the AGVs such as staying on track on a segment, turning, picking a load or dropping it, determining the current position, etc., is handled by the AGV control software called E'nsor [R] (Egemin Navigation System On Robot).

Besides traditional qualities such as performance and robustness, the market for AGV transportation systems requests for more flexibility. AGVs should be able to exploit opportunities, e.g., when an AGV is assigned a transport and moves toward the load, it should be possible for this AGV to switch tasks on its way if a more interesting transport pops up. AGVs should also be able to anticipate possible difficulties, e.g., when the battery level of an AGV decreases, the AGV should anticipate this and prefer a zone near a charge station. Customers also expect that the system is able to deal with AGVs leaving the system, or new AGVs entering the system. One example is maintenance. Currently, maintenance of AGVs is based on fixed worst-case rules. This leaves room for improvement by allowing AGVs to decide themselves when to leave the system for service.

In the next section we discuss the main high-level views of the software architecture and we illustrate how the quality requirements are realized. Finally, Sect. 3 concludes the paper.

2   Architectural Design of an AGV Transportation System

Contrary to the traditional approach applied by Egemin, where vehicles are controlled by one central server, in this project, we explore the feasibility of applying the paradigm of situated MASs to decentralize the control of the AGVs. In [7], Ong compares decentralized with centralized control. According to Ong, decentralized control: (1) is more economical w.r.t. required processing power, and (2) is more reliable. Limitations of decentralization are: (1) performance of the system may be affected by the communication links between nodes, (2) there is a trade-off between its performance and the reactivity of the system to disturbances, and (3) myopic decision making may occur due to the lack of global information.

Besides the advantages of decentralization listed by Ong, we believe that in principle, a MAS-based AGV transportation system also becomes more flexible. Since each AGV acts locally, it can better exploit opportunities and adapt its behavior under changing circumstances. On the other hand, bandwidth must be considered carefully to en-

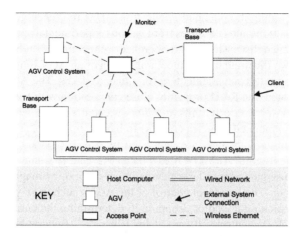

Fig. 1. Deployment view of the AGV transportation system

sure that the communication network does not become a bottleneck. The challenge in the project is to support the current functionality, while aiming to improve flexibility and openness.

Deployment View of the System. The decentralized architecture consists of two subsystems, *transport bases* and *AGV control systems.* Transport bases receive transport requests from the client system, and are responsible to assign the transports to AGVs. The AGV control software is responsible to ensure that the AGV completes the assigned transport. Fig. 1 depicts the deployment view of the software architecture. Transport bases are deployed on stationary hosts. The AGV control systems are deployed on the mobile AGV machines. The communication infrastructure provides a wired network that connects the client system with the transport bases and a wireless network that enables communication between AGVs and transport bases.

Module Decomposition View of the Subsystems. Fig. 2 depicts the module decomposition view of the AGV control system and the transport base. For each requested transport, the *transport base manager* creates a new *transport agent* at the transport base. A transport agent is responsible for assigning its transport to an *AGV agent.* the client system. AGV agents, that are located in the AGVs, are responsible for executing the assigned transports.

Since the physical environment of the AGVs restricts how agents can use their environment, we introduced a virtual environment for agents to live in. This virtual environment offers a medium that agents can use to exchange information and coordinate their behavior. For example, to avoid collisions, AGV agents coordinate with other agents through the virtual environment. AGV agents mark the path they are going to drive in their environment using *hulls.* The hull of an AGV is the physical area the AGV occupies. A series of hulls then describes the physical area an AGV occupies along a certain path. If the area is not marked by other hulls, the AGV can move along and actually drive over the reserved path. If the AGV's hull intersects with others, only the

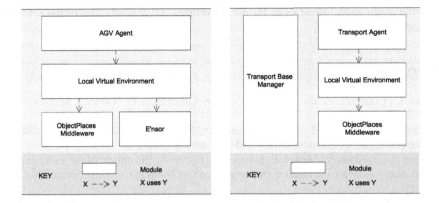

Fig. 2. Module view of the AGV control system on the left and the transport base on the right

AGV with the highest priority is allowed to move on. Afterwards, the AGV removes the markings in the virtual environment.

Since the only physical infrastructure available to the AGVs is a wireless network to communicate, the virtual environment is necessarily distributed over the AGVs. In effect, each AGV and each transport base maintains a *local virtual environment*, which is a local manifestation of the virtual environment. Synchronization of the state of the local virtual environment with neighboring machines is supported by the *ObjectPlaces middleware* [8].

Besides a medium for coordination, the virtual environment also serves as a suitable abstraction that shields the AGV agents form low-level issues, such as the physical control of the AGV. Therefore, we fully reused the E'nsor software.

Quality requirements. We have applied several architectural approaches to realize flexibility in the system. One example is transport assignment that is based on a flexible version of the Contract Net protocol. This protocol postpones final transport assignment until the load is picked. While the AGV is driving towards the load, the AGV agent and the transport agent are able to switch transport and AGV respectively. Openness in the system is basically realized by the virtual environment supported by the ObjectPlaces middleware. When an AGV leaves the system, or a new AGV enters, the ObjectPlaces middleware on neighboring machines will notice this and the local virtual environments will be updated accordingly.

3   Conclusion

In this paper, we illustrated how we have applied situated MASs as an approach to design an automated AGV transportation system. We discussed three high-level architectural views and illustrated how the architecture supports flexibility and openness. From the initial project phase we learned that the the reference architecture for situated MAS that underlies the software architecture of the AGV transportation system turned out to be an excellent guide for architectural design. On the other hand, the complexity of the application forced us to further decompose several modules of the reference architecture.

References

1. Bass, L., Clements, P., Kazman, R.: Software Architecture in Practice. Addison-Wesley (2003)
2. Clements, P., Bachman, F., Bass, L., Garlan, D., Ivers, J., Little, R., Nord, R., Stafford, J.: Documenting Software Architectures. Addison-Wesley (2003)
3. Weyns, D., Parunak, V., Michel, F., Holvoet, T., Ferber, J.: Environments for multiagent systems, state-of-the-art and research challenges. Lecture Notes in Computer Science, Vol. 3374 (2005)
4. Weyns, D., Holvoet, T.: Formal model for situated multi-agent systems. Fundamenta Informaticae, Vol. 63(1-2) (2004)
5. Weyns, D., Steegmans, E., Holvoet, T.: Protocol based communication for situated multiagent systems. 3th Joint Conference on Autonomous Agents and Multi-Agent Systems, New York (2004)
6. Weyns, D., Steegmans, E., Holvoet, T.: Towards active perception in situated multi-agent systems. Journal on Applied Artificial Intelligence, 18(8-9) (2004)
7. Ong, L.: An investigation of an agent-based scheduling in decentralised manufacturing control. Ph.D Disseration, University of Cambridge (2003)
8. Schelfthout, K., Holvoet, T., Berbers, Y.: Views: Customizable abstractions for context-aware applications in MANETs. Software Engineering for Large-Scale Multi-Agent Systems, St. Louis (2005)

Goodness and Lacks of MAS Methodologies for Manufacturing Domains

S. Valero, E. Argente, A. Giret, V. Julian, and V. Botti

Information Systems and Computation Dept., Polytechnic University of Valencia,
C/ Camino de Vera s/n, 46022 Valencia, Spain
{svalero, eargente, agiret, vinglada, vbotti}@dsic.upv.es

Abstract. Multi-agent system technology has achieved enough development level to be applied in complex problem domains, such as manufacturing systems. This work contributes to demonstrate this applicability,
evaluating its goodness and lacks. Thus we have employed a production
task scheduling problem in a ceramic tile factory as a real case study. This
complex problem requires robust and flexible software applications[1].

1 Introduction

The manufacturing industry is an interesting domain for applying multi-agent
technology, because on the one hand the high development level achieved by
this technology allows to tackle with complex problems fields; and on the other
hand these systems require software applications that need to be inherently distributed, robust and capable of adapting to the environment. The aim of our
work is to apply multi-agent system (MAS) technology to model a real scheduling problem in a Ceramic Tile factory using INGENIAS methodology [1], which
is based in MESSAGE [2] and integrates its meta-models in the Rational Unified Process (RUP) for developing software systems. INGENIAS incorporates
specific features that allow us to consider this methodology as the most appropriate option comparing with the other MAS methodology approaches. These
features are: (i) it covers the greatest number of aspects regarding the analysis
activity (for example, INGENIAS environment model allows us to specify the
environment in which the agent is located); (ii) it employs UML-based syntax
throughout the entire development process so INGENIAS is easier to be understood and managed, primarily due to the popularity and widespread use of UML;
(iii) it offers some complete examples in different application areas (and this is
not available in many methodologies); and (iv) it employs a visual development
toolkit during the whole process (Ingenias Development Kit, IDK). This toolkit
includes modules for automatic code generation.

Current problems of the ceramic tile sector and, more specifically, of the
production scheduling process are widely explained in [3]. Moreover, benefits

---

[1] This work has been partially funded by Polytechnic University of Valencia under
grant PII-UPV 5574. Financial support from Spanish government under grant FPU
AP2001-1516 and TIC2003-07369-C02-01 is also gratefully acknowledge.

M. Pěchouček, P. Petta, and L.Z. Varga (Eds.): CEEMAS 2005, LNAI 3690, pp. 645–648, 2005.

obtained when using a MAS approach to achieve integrated optimization of the dynamic production scheduling process are also related in [3].

In the following section the MAS approach is briefly described, presenting the agent-oriented models used in the development process of the scheduling problem of production tasks in a ceramic tile factory. Finally, conclusions are detailed.

2   Multi-agent Modelling Approach

In the scheduling problem of a ceramic tile factory we can identify four main scenarios, modelled as UML use cases: (i)*Schedule Creation* use-case, in which a feasible schedule to be carried out in the following weeks is created (this schedule is made based on the manufacture lots defined in the Master Plan[2]); (ii)*Schedule Modification* use-case, in which previous schedules that have arisen problems during their execution are modified, being reconfigured in order to adjust them to factory changes; (iii)*Schedule Execution Monitoring* use-case, where the current weekly schedule in execution is supervised, informing about the arisen problems; and (iv)*Master Plan Alteration Detection* use-case, in which problems that might alter the Master Plan are detected.

Once several use-cases have been noticed, INGENIAS methodology proposes to detail five different models: (i) organization, (ii) agent, (iii) interaction, (iv) environment and (v) tasks and goals models. Graphical representations of those models using the IDK tool are related in [3].

Regarding the organizational model, the scheduling process involves different activities: schedule creation and modification, execution monitoring and detection of possible alterations at the current Master Plan. Several roles are needed to carry out those tasks: (i) the *Manager*, that maintains the integrity of the system and regulates the cooperation among the different roles of the system; (ii) the *Schedule Creation Controller*, that oversees the information about a new schedule order; (iii) the *Schedule Modification Controller*, which maintains information about changes needed for adjusting the schedule because of failures in the manufacturing process; (iv) the *Scheduler*, who has the ability to schedule tasks and resources; (v) the *Production Plant Manager*, that maintains and provides information about all restrictions and features of each machine and plant element; (vi) the *Lot Planner*, that manages all information about task sequence needed to manufacture a given lot; (vii) the *Schedule Execution Monitor*, which supervises actual execution of a schedule in a specific plan; and (viii) the *Master Plan Monitor*, which controls possible changes in the Master Plan and informs the *Manager* role that an alteration has occurred and it must be propagated to the *Master Plan Generator* process.

In spite of the great number of modelling artifacts and notions provided by MAS methodologies in general, and by INGENIAS in particular, we have found some lacks applying MAS methodologies to the modelling of the manufacturing problem we are illustrating. Some of them are: (i) Due to the lack of domain

---

[2] Production plan for medium term orders.

specific guidelines, we used PROSA [4] guidelines in order to figure out the cooperating roles of the *Production Programming*. (ii) There is a lack of modelling artifacts to represent autonomous entities with recursive structures. This is a very important issue in manufacturing systems, since the only way to manage the complexity of these system is by considering higher level and complex entities as aggregation of lower level and simpler entities. Therefore, (iii) in order to manage the complexity of the development process itself there is a need to have a process guided by abstraction levels. In this way, at every design step, the designer can focus at the problem at hand, without worrying about other details.

Regarding the agent model, we have assigned a specific agent to each role identified in the system. Therefore, *Scheduler* agent is in charge of scheduling tasks and resources; *Production Plant Manager* agent provides information about actual plant configuration; *Lot Planner* agent provides the task sequence needed for a specific lot; *Schedule Creation Controller* agent creates new schedule orders, initializing the schedule and then building a final proposal; *Schedule Execution Monitor* agent supervises schedule execution; *Schedule Modification Controller* agent modifies schedules; *Master Plan Monitor* agent controls possible changes in Master Plan; and finally *Manager* agent controls cooperation between all other agents and tries to manage the production programming.

In our problem, the main goal of the system is *Manage production programming*. This goal is pursued by the *Manager* agent and can be decomposed through an implication diagram into five subgoals: *Generate lot schedule, Generate tasks, Modify lot schedule, Inform master plan alteration* and *Inform schedule problem*. Regarding the first subgoal, it must be generated and satisfied in the *Create Schedule* workflow. The process must start with the identification of the new lots to be scheduled, creating the *Generate Lot Schedule* goal. Then, it is necessary to initialize the new schedule which initiates the control of the schedule creation. Next, the process must obtain the task sequence which allows to obtain the sequence related to a specific lot. This sequence is generated by the *LotPlanner* agent. Previously to obtain the allocation task proposal, the process needs to get the current plant state. Finally, the *Generate Lot Schedule* goal will be satisfied when it is obtained the *Final Proposed Schedule*.

The MAS in charge of the scheduling process of the ceramic tile factory needs to interact and use external and/or internal applications, and resources in order to fulfill its goals. These entities are called environment elements. We have identified the following environment elements: (i) the *ExecutedScheduleDB* stores executed schedules created by the organization; (ii) the *ProductModelDB* stores the product definition specification in terms of production tasks; (iii) the *ProductModelDB* provides the task sequence needed to produce a given product; (iv) the *ProductDesignDB* stores the product definition specification in terms of materials and design patterns; (v) the *SuppliesDB* manages the warehouse of raw materials; (vi) the *MasterPlanDB* allows the Manager agent to figure out when the *ProductionProgramming* Group has to initiate a new schedule creation process; and (vii) the *PlantStateDB* maintains the plant status update and is used by the *PlantManager* to figure out whether a schedule modification is needed. Trying to specify the correct interaction with the environment, we have detected some cases where it is needed to express temporarily restricted and periodic behaviors related with perception and actuation processes (i.e. to maintain the production plant status updated). So, the methodology should allow expressing effective and timely routine-based behaviors.

3   Conclusions

This paper presents a methodological development, based on MAS technology, of an application for the production programming problem in a ceramic tile industry, using the IDK toolkit of the INGENIAS methodology, which has been successfully employed in other domains. From this modelling experience we have detected some manufacturing system modelling requirements or lacks which need to be taken into account by MAS methodologies to be able to tackle real industrial problems in a better and easier way. Some of these requirements are: (i) manufacturing control systems require autonomous entities to be organized in hierarchy and heterarchy structures [5]; (ii) manufacturing control units require a routine-based behavior that is both effective and timely [6]; (iii) a methodology for manufacturing systems should lead straight-forward from the control task on a factory resource or factory function to autonomous entities [6,5]; (iv) it should also define a development process guided by abstraction levels, and should also provide modelling artifacts, tools and guidelines to manage this process; (v) it should also describe a mixed top-down and bottom-up development process in order to produce flexible and reconfigurable organization structures; and (vi) it should also provide modelling guidelines to help the system designer to integrate the entire range of manufacturing activities (from order booking through design, production, and marketing) to model the agile manufacturing enterprise [5].

Currently, we are working on a MAS methodology and a toolkit based on these requirements and defined from the INGENIAS meta-models.

References

1. Pavon, J., Gomez, J.: Agent Oriented Software Engineering with INGENIAS. Multi-Agent Systems and Applications II, LNAI 2691 (2003) 394-403
2. EURESCOM.: MESSAGE: Methodology for engineering systems of software agents(Final), Technical Report P907-TI1, EURESCOM (2001)
3. Giret, A., Argente, E., Valero, S., Gomez, P., Julian, V.: Applying Multi-Agent Systems Modelling to the Scheduling Problem in a Ceramic Tile Factory. Proc. of International Mass Customization Meeting, (2005), 151-162.
4. Van Brussel, H., Wyns, J., Valckenaers, P., Bongaerts, L., Peeters, P.: Reference Architecture for Holonic Manufacturing Systems: PROSA, Computers In Industry, 37 (1998) 255-274
5. HMS, P.R.: HMS Requirements, http://hms.ifw.uni-hannover.de (1994)
6. Bussmann, S.:An Agent-Oriented Architecture for Holonic Manufacturing Control, Proc. of 1st Int. Workshop on Intelligent Manufacturing Systems, EPFL, (1998) 1-12

Multiagents Applied To Humanitarian Demining

Pedro Santana[1], José Barata[2], and Luís Flores[1]

[1] IntRoSys S.A., Quinta da Torre, Campus FCT-UNL, 2829-516 - Portugal
[2] New University of Lisbon, Quinta da Torre,
Campus FCT-UNL, 2829-516 - Portugal

Abstract. The complexity associated to Humanitarian Demining becomes very high due to its broad set of activities, which beyond the already complex of landmine removal, includes other socio-economic supporting activities. Hence, more complex computer based supporting systems are required. The main goal of this article is to describe potential applications of multi-agent systems to the Humanitarian Demining domain, covering areas such as: knowledge-based systems, collaborative networks, agent-based modelling and multi-agent robotic systems. This is the result of the work being carried out by the Portuguese company IntRoSys, whose main research objective is the development of tools and methods to support humanitarian demining.

1 Introduction

The complexity associated to Humanitarian Demining becomes very high due to its broad set of activities, which beyond the already complex of landmine removal, includes other socio-economic supporting activities. Hence, more complex computer based supporting systems are required, not only for the landmine removal itself, but for the socio-economic supporting activities. In addition to this these two different areas must be developed completely integrated, which just increases the complexity. Due to the involved complexity and the integration aspects that are required multiagents were considered as a suitable paradigm for supporting Humanitarian Demining.

The main goal of this article is to describe potential applications of multi-agent systems to the Humanitarian Demining domain.

Section 2 introduces the Humanitarian Demining domain. Then, section 3 proposes a set of potential applications of multi-agents systems to Humanitarian Demining. Finally the conclusions are described in section 4.

2 Humanitarian Demining Concepts

The estimated number for grounded anti-personal landmines all over the world is about 110 millions. Some consequences of using landmines are: unusable land (e.g. few landmines may hinder access to productive land), direct health consequences (e.g. amputation), indirect health consequences (e.g. victims' families

M. Pěchouček, P. Petta, and L.Z. Varga (Eds.): CEEMAS 2005, LNAI 3690, pp. 649–652, 2005.

are entirely affected), and development consequences (e.g. communication paths closed). These reasons make urgent the development of new techniques that speed up and enhance the demining process.

Humanitarian Demining is composed of two phases: the survey phase and the detection/clearance phase. Surveys are intended to rationalise the demining process, by analysing available resources, priorities, socio-economic impact, land end-use, etc. During the *Impact Survey* information to analyse priorities, social-economical impact, possible contaminated areas, etc. is gathered. Then, a *Technical Survey* is carried out to define the clearance requirements, the areas to be actually cleared, etc. Afterwards, the *detection and clearance* tasks are performed by following the requirements previously defined. Finally, a *Post-Clearance Survey* is performed to guarantee that the clearance requirements were met.

3   Multiagents Applied to Humanitarian Demining

As previously stated, Humanitarian Demining covers areas from detection and clearance to the socio-economic impacts of such operations. Thus, the problem can be analysed in two different branches, the support that Multi-Agents can provide to minefield operations and to the process itself.

3.1   Operations Support

It is well known the need for low-cost demining, so it can be afforded by local communities. Therefore, robotic systems must comply with such a requirement. Previous attempts to solve the problem of robotic demining as lead to high-cost solutions. Such attempts have tackled the problem with single robot systems, which carry all landmine detection sensors. Approaching the problem in a distributed perspective, where robots are simple and dispensable, allows to comply with the low-cost requirement. Hence, multi-agent systems, in particular multi-robot systems, are a suited approach to the problem. Nevertheless, must not be forgotten that each robot is itself an agent with all the challenges behind this.

We see with special interest Multi Unmanned Aerial Vehicles (UAV) that can be applied to assess the ground (e.g. using infra-red cameras) or just taking pictures faster and safer than ground vehicles. See for instance the ARC [4] project that makes use of airborne and satellite imaging to identify minefields.

Resource configuration and allocation Multi-Agent based configuration architectures, such as the CoBASA architecture [2], can be well applied to prepare robotic teams for the minefield.

It is important to integrate locals in the demining process, which are usually people with no formal education. Therefore, human-machine interfaces are both interesting and important to get closer high-tech and end-users. The user should interact with the system as it was actually in the minefield with its own methods. We envision a correct human-machine interface as the one capable of translating operational robotic semantics into operational end-user semantics, i.e. a correct *ontological commitment*.

3.2   Process Support

Information has been identified as a crucial aspect in Humanitarian Demining. Humanitarian Demining is mainly about decision making, which relies heavily on data, information and knowledge. In this sense, Knowledge Based Systems are extremely relevant to this domain, mainly to support the decision in the impact study and mission configuration.

The diversity of cultures and education level among the involved agents (e.g. locals, military, and governments) results in the need of intensive work on the area of Knowledge Engineering/Representation. To the problem of uncertain information is added the contradictions that may arise when merging different perspectives of the same problem. Hence, ontological commitments, belief revision and non-monotonic reasoning are certainly research opportunities for this domain.

A global minefield atlas that aggregates digital topographic maps, satellite image data, demining related information and equipment suitability is presented in [7]. A Decision Support System (DSS) based on Geographical Information Systems (GIS) information and multi criteria analysis is proposed in [9]. The DSS integrates multi-layer information covering strategic level (e.g. economic value of the areas) down to operational level (e.g. demining company selection).

Besides decision making intensive, Humanitarian Demining operations are highly distributed. Therefore, information sharing and collaborative tools are very important. Collaborative work tools may go from distributed devices that allow access to shared information sources (e.g. [6]) to autonomous mechanisms capable of managing the whole process.

Humanitarian Demining could be modelled as a business composed of several parties. Following such a model, Collaborative Networks [3] as well as coalition formation [10,1] and Multiagent Systems in general, may be interesting tools for the analysis and congregation of skills that are required to achieve the goal.

Modelling the Humanitarian Demining process would allow to reason more effectively about it. In this sense, every entity could be modelled as an agent and the process as an Multi-Agent System. These models are extremely important, since decision making can rely upon scientific assessments reducing lobbying opportunities (i.e. objectiveness). Some tasks where agent-modelling and simulation could be applied are: to analyse relationships between innovations and performance gains, to optimise the selection and configuration of the elements for a demining campaign, to perform risk assessment by integrating models of the involved aspects, such as environment and local human activities.

An approach for the economic modelling of cost-effective demining technologies is presented in ([11], pp. 19-26) and [5] presents a set of operational needs based on a demining model.

4   Conclusions

A brief overview on the Humanitarian Demining domain was presented. It has been shown that the Humanitarian Demining domain is much broader than just demining itself, which opens new horizons for the application of technology on it.

It has been proposed a set of scenarios where multi-agent system can be well applied, which includes: knowledge-based systems, collaborative networks, agent-based modelling and multiagent robotic systems.

The Humanitarian Demining domain is a network of many heterogeneous entities (e.g. robots, decision makers, operators) with highly intricate connections. Thus, the Multi-Agents paradigm is well suited to model this distributed, heterogeneous, and complex structure. First preliminary results support this.

References

1. Allsopp, D. N., Beautement, P., Kirton, M., Bradshaw, J. M., Suri, N., Knoblock, C. A., Tate, A. and Thompson, C. W.: Coalition Agents Experiment: Multiagent Cooperation in International Coalitions. IEEE Intelligent Systems, **173** (2002) 26–35
2. Barata, J.: Coalition Based Approach for Shop Floor Agility - A Multiagent Approach. PhD thesis, Universidade Nova de Lisboa, Faculdade de Cincias e Tecnologia, Monte Caparica (2004)
3. Camarinha-Matos, L. M., Afsarmanesh, H. and Ollus, M.: Virtual Organizations - Systems and Practices. Springer, New York (2005)
4. Eisl, M. and Khalili, M.: ARC – Airborne Minefield Area Reduction. In Proceedings of the International Conference Requirements and Technologies for the Detection, Removal and Neutralization of Landmines and UXO (2003)
5. GICHD/UNDP: Humanitarian Demining Equipment: Study of Global Operational Needs, Geneve (2002)
6. Horz, A. and Kunze, T.: MoMoSat – Collaborative Demining Information Management. In Proceedings of the Int. Conf. Requirements and Technologies for the Detection, Removal and Neutralization of Landmines and UXO (2003) 82–87
7. Littmann, F., Roux, S. and Sieber, A.: The global minefield atlas concept. In Proceedings of the Int. Conf. Requirements and Technologies for the Detection, Removal and Neutralization of Landmines and UXO (2003) 71–77
8. Long, M., Gage, A., Murphy, R. and Valavanis, K.: Application of the Distributed Field Robot Architecture to a Simulated Demining Task. In Proceedings of the IEEE International Conference on Robotics and Automation (2005)
9. Mladineo, N. and Knezic, S.: DSS for humanitarian Humanitarian Demining – case study Croatia. In Proceedings of the Int. Conf. Requirements and Technologies for the Detection, Removal and Neutralization of Landmines and UXO (2003) 93–98
10. Pechoucek, M., Marik, V. and Barata, J.: A Knowledge-based Approach to Coalition Formation. IEEE Intelligent Systems, **17** (2002) 17–25
11. Sahli, H., Bottoms, M. and Cornelis, J., eds: In Proceedings of the International Conference on Requirements and Technologies for the Detection, Removal and Neutralization of Landmines and UXO (2003)

Simulating Automatic High Bay Warehouses Using Agents

Cornelia Triebig[1], Tanja Credner[1], Franziska Klügl[1], Peter Fischer[2],
Titus Leskien[2], Andreas Deppisch[2], and Stefan Landvogt[2]

[1] University of Würzburg, Department of Artificial Intelligence
[2] SSI-Schäfer-Noell GmbH, Giebelstadt

Abstract. In this contribution we want to present a collaboration
project between the Department for Artificial Intelligence at the University of Würzburg and SSI Schäfer Noell GmbH (Giebelstadt) using
multi-agent systems for simulating high bay warehouses.

1 Motivation

In scientific and industrial applications simulation forms an important and well
established method. Comprehension as well as the quality of design and control of
complex systems is improved and increased. Particularly the reduction of time
and thus cost gained in industrial applications is a significant aspect for the
growing application of simulation methods. In the field of material flow systems,
including high bay warehouses, established simulation technology, like queuing
systems or object-oriented simulation is successfully used. Here simulation is
applied mostly to generate performance measures or to test layout design.

Nevertheless, additional scenarios exist for the use of simulation supporting
high bay warehouse construction:

- testing control software using a virtual version of the high bay warehouse
  before the real system is implemented and in use.
- generating reproducible error situations
- supporting design decisions in the beginning of the project
- simulation of the warehouse and control system for user training
- supporting requirement acquisition in discussion with the customer

Beyond appealing graphics specific requirements are posed on the simulation
software used for these application scenarios: The presentation of the warehouses
should be on a high level of detail. Changes in the warehouse configuration should
be easily and fast to perform. Because of high project pressure, it should be
possible to construct the model for simulation fast. Modeling should not require
simulation experts. It should be manageable by warehouse experts themselves.
These requirements are hardly fulfilled by standard simulation systems.

In the scope of our project we were able to show that the agent paradigm
allows highly flexible modeling on a sufficiently possible level of preciseness.
This level is accomplishable without costly training in modeling and simulation

M. Pĕchouček, P. Petta, and L.Z. Varga (Eds.): CEEMAS 2005, LNAI 3690, pp. 653–656, 2005.

techniques. In this collaboration project we use SeSAm (Shell for Simulated Agent Systems, *www.simsesam.de*) that allows high-level visual programming of multi-agent simulations.

2   SeSAm - A Simulation Environment

SeSAm is an open-source project developed by the Department for Artificial Intelligence (University of Würzburg). It offers an generic environment for modeling and analyzing with agent-based simulation. With SeSAm, a tool for easing the construction of complex models is provided.

SeSAm provides different categories of objects which can be implemented in simulations. These categories contain agent classes, resources and the so-called world. Resources cannot act themselves. They are objects without any behavior. The world represents the environment and is in fact an specialized agent. Each of these objects can handle a number of own variables. Variables are used to store the knowledge of the agent and to interact with other agents. An activity graph defines the behavior of an agent. The syntax therefor is abutted to UML. The actions which should be performed by an agent are defined by combining atomic activities that are offered by SeSAm. Actions are grouped into activities connected with directed edges that represent a condition. The agent will continue with the next activity as soon as the connected condition is evaluated as true during a simulation run.

For creating a real simulation run, a situation for the model needs to be built. Instances of the agent classes are placed on the map. The starting values of their variables can be edited. Thereafter the real simulation is ready to be started. The definition ordinary simulations as described above is implemented via the manipulation of graphical elements. If special requirements arise, e.g. the need for communication with external systems, SeSAm can easily be extended by Java-Plugins.

3   Simulation of High Bay Warehouses Using Agents

A high bay warehouse basically consists of transport routes for transport units, and high bay storage and retrieval. In particular, there are different modules like variable conveyor elements, scales and scanners, storage elements, but also human operators. Each of these elements may be treated as an agent, that is as an intelligent building block with local sensors and effectors. Beyond communication within the virtual high bay warehouse, i.e. with other agents, there has to be also communication with the warehouse control software.

Thus, reasonable arguments exist for using an agent-based approach for the simulation of high bay warehouses:

- facile mapping of the warehouse components on agents (modularity)
- easy modeling of specific projects because of layout independent agents
- generic agents reusable in all models of this domain

– detailed simulation with the integration of involved human beings, which can compensate errors or malfunctions with their natural intelligence

The construction of eight actual high bay warehouse projects were supported by agent-based simulation for testing the control software until now. The general procedure is that we start with the development of a multi-agent simulation of the high bay warehouse in SeSAm. The warehouse is concurrently build up. Thus, details of the realworld warehouse can be adapted almost synchronously.

At the beginning of the collaboration project an agent set with a fixed and also small number of agents were implemented. Therfore different kinds of modules as mentioned above were mapped to agents with a specific behavior. However, despite the reuseability of these agents, specific warehouse systems require an adpation of the agent set. Therefore the agents are constructed as generic as possible. The generic-ness of the agents supports the communication between control software and agents. This communication is datagram-based, much like some proprietary ACL-messages. The control software to test sends commands in reaction to notifications or alarms the agent. This is implemented using the plugin concept of SeSAm.

Agents may be grouped to higher-level components with some fixed organizational structure that again may be integrated into the overall virtual high bay warehouse in the same way as atomic agents. We developed aggregates partially with complex synchronization protocols, like storage-and-retrieval machines within their working environment, carousels for transport and delivery, bidirectional conveyor lines and vertical conveyors as well as shuttle vehicles.

4   Practical Example: A Simulated High Bay Warehouse

In this section we want to present a succesfully implemented project. Before the real system was implemented this high bay warehouse was simulated with SeSAm. Figure 1 shows the complete high bay warehouse with its storage and retrieval. For better understanding we added a legend showing the used agents. Additionally we divided the illustration into three sections: (1) the storage and retrieval area, (2) the part picking area and (3) the high rack storage area.

Section 1 shows Storage and Retrieval Points, conveyor line elements, Shuttle Vehicles and Displays. Conveyor lines consist of two different conveyor elements: Simple and Generic Conveyors. Simple Conveyors manage only one direction, Generic ones manage several directions in which TUs can be routed. Each of these agents is able to take only one TU at the same time. On Storage Points Transport Units (TUs) enter the warehouse system. On Retrieval Points TUs leave the system. In this project there is a Storage/Retrieval Point which offers the functionality of a Storage as well as of a Retrieval Point. However, this combined functionality causes difficulties: the connected conveyor line transports bidirectionally. If one and the same conveyor line is used by both, entering and leaving TUs, deadlocks can occur. To avoid this situation we implemented locked areas. If a TU enters an area of bidirectional conveyor lines the area is locked for other TUs. As soon as the TU has left the area, the area is unlocked and

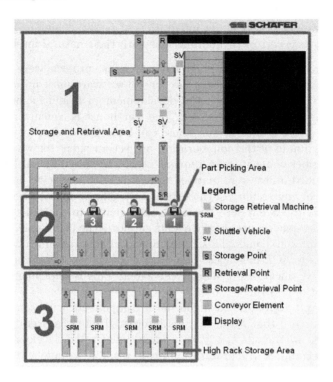

Fig. 1. Screenshot of a high bay warehouse simulated with SeSAm

can be used by the next TU. Locked areas are realized with the plugin function of SeSAm. In the right part of section 1 displays can be found which display informations when TUs leave the system. Also in section 1 there are three shuttle vehicles which connect or serve different conveyor lines.

Section 2 shows the part picking area where TUs are handled manually by human part pickers. In the High Rack Storage (section 3 of figure 1) you can additionally see the Storage Retrieval Machines serving the actual storage. The representation of the storage is facilitated because there is no need in this project to show in which way and on which place TUs are stored. If TUs enter the storage they will be destroyed. In case of a retrieval request of stored TUs Storage Points reproduce them.

5   Conclusion

Even with the first virtual warehouse we used, several errors in the control software could be found and fixed before the real-world warehouse was available. With every virtual warehouse the effort for its modeling was decreasing due to the improved set of agents. Thus, even considering the relatively high effort for modeling and designing the basic agent set in the beginning of the collaboration projects, several ten thousands of Euros were saved.

Strategies for Distributed Underwater Survey

Milan Rollo[1], Petr Novák[2], and Pavel Jisl[2]

[1] Center of Applied Cybernetics, Czech Technical University in Prague
[2] Gerstner Laboratory, Czech Technical University in Prague,
Technická 2, Prague 6, 166 27 Czech Republic
{rollo, novakpe, jisl}@labe.felk.cvut.cz

Abstract. Underwater survey by a team of autonomous robots brings couple of problems caused mainly by the communication restrictions due to the nature of environment. Communication range and bandwidth are very limited and individual robots can become temporarily inaccessible. To allow robots' efficient operation in such environment architecture of control part of autonomous robot and new algorithms for decentralized coordination within a group of such robots were developed. Besides these this paper describes experiments addressing different area search and video stream transmission path planning strategies.

1 Introduction

We decided to simulate the underwater survey problem [1] using a multi-agent system as it represents a natural choice to model distributed systems consisting of autonomous, self-interested entities like the teams of autonomous robots.

In such a type of scenario no dedicated central planning entity can be used: (i) because of the limited communication accessibility, robots can easy get out of the central entity's communication range and (ii) in case of malfunction of this entity robots without their own planning capabilities will fail to coordinate their activities. Unlike the other works where authors investigate mainly the team action planning activities e.g. [2,3], in this project we focused on communication and knowledge synchronization in environment with partial communication inaccessibility and transmission path establishment algorithms.

2 Scenario Implementation

In our scenario goal of the group of autonomous robots (unmanned underwater vehicles - UUVs) is to search a given coast area, detect and remove all mines located there. To allow an object analysis video transmission path must be established between the base (operated by human crew) and robot who found the suspicions object. Due to the specific scenario features (environment simulation, communication inaccessibility) we decided to use *A*-**globe** multi-agent platform [4,5] as a simulation environment.

Two types of communication accessibility are simulated – **high bandwidth** (very restrained, necessary for video transmissions) and **signaling** (higher than

M. Pěchouček, P. Petta, and L.Z. Varga (Eds.): CEEMAS 2005, LNAI 3690, pp. 657–660, 2005.

video but remains limited, used for coordination messages and position information). Each robot consists of following components:

- **Robot Pod** simulator, computes robot moves and updates its position with environment simulation server.
- **Mine Detector** simulator, provides the decision-making components with information about suspicions objects found.
- **Video** data acquisition and transmission element. This subsystem creates the video feed of suspicions object to the remote operator.
- **Robot Coordinator** implements search algorithm, transmission coalition establishment and negotiation.

3   Distributing the Coordination Process

The process of agents' coordination can be done centrally by a dedicated central coordination agent. This agent may however become a bottleneck in situations when several robots request new tasks at the same time or are out of the entity's communication range.

Coordination process can also be distributed among agents in several levels: (i) there is no central coordination agent, each robot can become a coordinator for a single feed planning process, (ii) coordination process is in parts distributed among the agents, but the participating robots are preselected, and (iii) coordination process is distributed completely among the agents. There is no central plan, robots negotiate in peer-to-peer manner.

The level-1 and level-2 distribution is desired for the increased efficiency, flexibility and survivability of the coordination process. The level-3 distribution of coordination makes sense only in the situations when it is impossible to bring all the planning information to the coordinator.

3.1   Transmission Collaborators Search Strategies

To transmit the video stream of suspicions object to human operator, relaying via several collaborators is usually required. If sufficient number of collaborators is not available, robot can search for other robots to help him to build the feed:

Central Planning Algorithm: Using this algorithm robots do not form the video feed immediately after the object is found, but store the object's position in memory and continue in search. Video stream of all objects is transmitted on their way back to base, after the whole area is searched.

Relayed Collaborator Search Algorithm: Robot who finds suspicions object becomes a coordinator of the transmission planning and asks other robots within its communication range for their actual status and position. Robots relay this information to their neighbors, etc. If sufficient number of collaborators is found, coordinator uses this information to plan the feed.

Elastic Collaborator Search Algorithm: In some cases robots can not find enough collaborators even when using the relayed communication. This algorithm allows robot to leave the suspicions object and look for the missing collaborators.

3.2   Transmission Path Planning Algorithms

We have developed three different algorithms to build the ad-hoc data transmission feed. The most straightforward are the approaches relying on a single agent mastering the planning process. Upon finding the suspicions object, it requests other visible robots to move to specific positions so that a high-bandwidth transmission link between the object and the base is established.

When we optimize the communication quality, minimal possible number of robots is used. On the other hand, when we try to minimize the impact on relay robots' own plans, relays are spread in the area between the transmission origin and target, in the proximity of their original areas. In the third approach, the control over the feed planning is not centralized, but rather passed along the communication link relays when the connection is constructed.

Direct Line Transmission Path Planner (DLTP): It achieves the level-1 coordination process distribution. Robot who finds the suspicions object has to select the best subset from all available robots. Positions of participants are placed on the join of base and object position in periodic distances. Length of this distance is equal to the video transmission range.

Minimal Time-To-Transmit Planner (M3TP): Using this planner more than the minimal required number of robots can participate in video transmission. Optimization criterion is to minimize the time the intermediate robots spend on transmission. Optimal placement of robots can form a general curve not only a line. It is computationally infeasible to search a whole state space, new algorithm based on modified Dijkstra's graph search algorithm was thus developed.

Decentralized Planner (DP): Robot that found a suspicions object only verifies accessibility of minimal required number of robots. If such a number is available, subset of all mutually accessible robots is selected to build a transmission path. All these robots are then informed about their order in the transmission path. Each of them then starts to move to the position where both the previous and next robot in the feed are accessible for video transmission and informs them about its new positions during the movement.

4   Experiments

A set of experiments was carried out, mainly to study the features of transmission collaborators search strategies. We were using two different environment setups, where the mines were placed: (i) in pattern and (ii) randomly with uniform distribution. As shown in fig. 1 use of the central planning algorithm ensures that all video streams will be transmitted online. For short transmission times this algorithm performs best also for the overall area search duration. Relayed search algorithm can be with advantages used in environments where each new detected object can bring additional tasks. This algorithm can be also interrupted at any moment and at least part of the area can be marked as searched. Use of elastic search algorithm increases the number of online transmissions compared to relayed search algorithm, but for the price of longer transmission times.

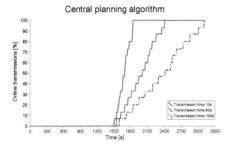

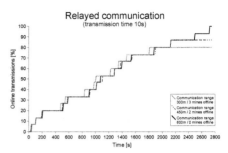

Fig. 1. Central planning algorithm - dependency of the number of online transmissions on length of transmission time

Fig. 2. Relayed communication - influence of communication range on the number of online transmissions

5 Conclusion and Future Work

Within this project we have developed a specific simulation environment using the 𝒜-**globe** multi-agent platform. Main reason to develop such environment was to enable a software simulation of real-life hardware robots where scalability experiments and efficient development and verification of embedded decision making algorithms can be carried out. The experiments conducted in the simulation environment with various environment settings (movement speed, number of mines, length of the transmission time) have proved that each collaborator search strategy is suitable for different area of tasks (hydrographic or geophysical surveys, minesweeping, etc.). Based on the actual task and environment features, operator can decide which algorithm will be used.

Acknowledgement

The presented research has been in parts supported by Office for Naval Research, project no.: N00014-03-1-0292 and by the Grants no.: 1M6840770004 and MSM6840770013 of the Ministry of Education, Youth and Sports of the Czech Republic.

References

1. Benthos Inc.: Transport of Underwater Images, Virtual Acquisition Showcase 2004. http://www.dawnbreaker.com/virtual2004/briefings/Benthos.pdf (2004)
2. Tambe, M.: Towards flexible teamwork. Journal of Artificial Intelligence Research **7** (1997) 83–124
3. Kaminka, G.A., Bowling, M.: Towards robust teams with many agents. Technical report, Carnegie Mellon University, Pittsburgh, PA 15213 (2001)
4. Šišlák, D., Rollo, M., Pěchouček, M.: A-globe: Agent platform with inaccessibility and mobility support. In Klusch, M., Ossowski, S., Kashyap, V., Unland, R., eds.: Cooperative Information Agents VIII, Springer-Verlag, Heidelberg (2004)
5. A-globe: A-globe Agent Platform. http://agents.felk.cvut.cz/aglobe (2005)

The Role of Ontologies in a Multi-agent Based Data Integration System

Rahee Ghurbhurn[1], Philippe Beaune[1], and Hugues Solignac[2]

[1] Génie Industriel et Informatique, Ecole des Mines de St Etienne,
158 cours Fauriel 42000 St Etienne, France
{ghurbhurn, beaune}@emse.Fr
[2] STMicroelectronics, zi Peynier Rousset 13790 Rousset
Hugues.solignac@st.com

Abstract. In this paper, we present a flexible architecture allowing applications to access heterogeneous distributed manufacturing data. The objective is to eliminate data duplication and therefore the need for their synchronization and complex update. We propose a multiagent architecture based on ontologies for integrating the different data sources and for retrieving desired data. Web services are also used for agent-application communication. This is still an on-going work.

1 Introduction

Let's consider an information system composed of ERPs, data-warehouses, data bases and applications exploiting data found in these repositories for statistical analysis, production planning etc. Due to changes in the technological or business environment, several changes taking the form of modifications in the data sources' physical or logical structure, replacement of a data source or replacement of an application may arise. These changes will impact the whole information system as the elements composing the system are tightly coupled, through the use of ERPs or hard coded queries.

Moreover, data may be organised into two layers. Second layer data sources being data sources that may collect, aggregate, transform data sub-sets from several first layer (master) data sources. The update of second layer data sources may be triggered manually, by the system administrator, or automatically at a regular interval of time. The applications, forming the information system, may sometimes either be linked to first layer or second layer data sources or both. The problem with second layer data sources is that they need some synchronization with the first layer data sources. This synchronization is rendered more complex by the fact that the repositories may have a different storage (relational schema, table names) and data structure (primary key, data type, data size), making it difficult to establish a mapping.

The dual objective of this paper is to firstly show how MAS and ontologies can help to achieve greater flexibility in the information system's architecture. That is reduce the impact, on the information system's architecture, of addition, removal or modification of applications or data sources. In other words loosen the links between the applications and the data sources while providing a single, knowledge base, point

M. Pěchouček, P. Petta, and L.Z. Varga (Eds.): CEEMAS 2005, LNAI 3690, pp. 661–664, 2005.

of entry for information retrieval from multiple heterogeneous data sources. Secondly how the use of a MAS and ontologies can help to achieve flexible semantic applications integration. The idea is to device web services representing business functions of applications we want to integrate, and use an ontology to convert the output of one application into an input format that can be understood by another.

We propose, in this paper, a Multi-agent system (MAS) [2] [3] [4] [7] that allows the application to directly retrieve data from the first layer data sources. Thus no update is needed and users can retrieve all the desired attributes. The knowledge contained in the data sources and the relationship existing between them is defined in an ontology [1][5]. The latter is used by an application to formulate user queries in terms of concepts. These queries are sent, by the application via messages, to the MAS, which finds its corresponding location(s) and retrieves the required data.

This paper is organized as follows. In section 2 we will briefly present a sub-set of an information system's architecture that will be used for our research. Section 3 describes the proposed architecture based on a data integration ontology [8] and MAS. In section 4 we will give a conclusion and some future works.

2 Information System's Context

Let us consider a maintenance-planning problem in an integrated circuit manufacturing company. To illustrate our problem, let us suppose that we have three data sources (Maintenance, Human Resource and Equipment) and an application.

The Human Resource data source (HRDS) stores personal and trainings data. The latter is frequently updated, due to a rapidly evolving environment. The manufacturing staff is regularly trained on new processes, new equipments and products to ensure a certain level of competence. These trainings are valid for a time period. Beyond this period, the concerned manufacturing staff members are no longer authorized to work on the machines.

The manufacturing data source (MDS) is fed with data coming from the different equipments, be it production, testing or control equipments. The stored data is aggregated before being dispatched to more specific applications for monitoring and production planning tasks.

The equipment data source (EDS) stores information about past maintenance actions but also documentations about the maintenance actions corresponding to each equipment.

The application is responsible for providing a list of machines to be serviced with the corresponding maintenance actions to be performed. It also provides a list of technicians authorized to perform these actions. To provide such an information, the application has to access the three data sources.

The critical point here is that the manufacturing and human resource data are manually fed into the EDS. Thus there is no access to the original MDS and HRDS. This poses the problem of data synchronization and data update between EDS and the other data sources. This synchronization is rendered more complex by the fact that the data stored in the EDS may have a different storage (relational schema, table names.) and data structure (primary key, data type, data size), making it difficult to establish a mapping.

We propose to use an ontology to model the knowledge contained in the data sources and relationships between them. This ontology is used by a MAS to retrieve the appropriate data before communicating it to the requesting application. Our proposal is explained in the following section.

3   Knowledge Retrieval and MAS

Our proposition consists in building an ontology, expressed in OWL, modelling the targeted users' domains' knowledge. For each property of the model, we define the location of the corresponding data in the data sources. This association, done manually by the user or the administrator, consists in associating the different data source attributes, retrieved by the resource agents, to the ontology's properties. This approach is less tedious than that followed by the Museum of Finland [6] as it requires less human intervention. Indeed, in our case, human intervention is limited ontology building and a simple concept/attribute association whereas in the case of the Museum of Finland the administrator has to build the ontology, the XML rules corresponding to the concepts' structure in the data sources, instantiate the rules with XQuery and choose the appropriate concept in case of multiple result.

To link the applications to the MAS web service connectors are defined for all the applications therefore providing a standard means to plug a new application to the MAS for data retrieval. During the initialisation, the application sends a SOAP message to a query database and retrieves the available predefined queries. These queries are proposed to users who compose and validate their queries. The latter is embodied into a SOAP message and is sent to the MAS for data retrieval.

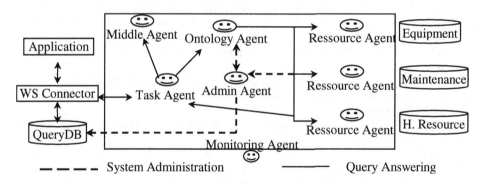

Fig. 1. The Proposed Architecture

For example in our context, one predefined query may be "Is employee having ID145 authorized to perform task number 158 on equipment xv156gt?" The task agent receives and decodes a SOAP message, locates the ontology agent, by means of the middle agent, and sends the query. The query is automatically converted, by the ontology agent, into appropriate SQL queries by means of the conversion matrix. The SQL queries are then dispatched to the appropriate resource agents who retrieve and send the data back to the task agent. The task agent sends the results, in a structured form, back to the web service via a SOAP message. A monitoring agent that computes performance indicators monitors all the agents.

A special agent allowing the systems administrator to build and maintain the ontology does the administration of the system. When ever a change in the data sources' data structures (removal/addition of an attribute or table) is made, a message is sent by the concerned resource agent to the ontology agent, via the admin agent, to evaluate the impact on the ontology. In case of simple changes (addition or removal of attributes), we may allow the ontology agent to update the ontology and in more complex cases the agent sends an alert message to the ontology administrator. Another task of the administration agents is to allow the testing of new queries before proposing them to the users via the query database (QueryDB). This function may prove to be useful when adding new data sources.

4 Conclusion

In this paper we presented a data retrieval architecture based on multi agents and ontologies. This architecture proposes an alternative to data duplication therefore avoiding the need of data synchronization and the necessary integrity controls. We are currently implementing our ontology-data source linking method. After this implementation phase performance tests will be performed and a comparison with the first method made.

References

[1] T.R.Gruber. "Towards Principles for the Design of Ontologies Used for Knowledge Sharing", International Workshop on Formal Ontology, N. Guarino & R. Poli, (Eds.), Padova, Italy, 1993

[2] P.M.Hatch 2001. Multiagent System Infrastructures for Information Integration on the Web.

[3] NR Jennings, K. Sycara, M. Wooldrige, "A Roadmap of Agent Research and development".International Journal of Autonomous Agents and Multi-agents Systems1(1),1998, 7-38.

[4] N.R.Jennings, M. Wooldrige. "Intelligent Agent: Theory and Practice".The Knowledge Engineering Review. 10(2), 1995, pp.115-152.

[5] N.F. Noy, D. L. McGuinness. "Ontology Development 101 : A guide to creating your first ontology." Stanford University, Stanford, CA, USA, 2001.

[6] V. Raatikka and E. Hyvonen. "Ontology-based semantic metadata validation." HIIT Publications number 2002-03, Helsinki Institute for InformationTechnology (HIIT), Helsinki, Finland, 2002.

[7] K. Sycara, K. Decker, A. Pannu, M. Williamson, and D. Zeng, "Distributed Intelligent Agents," IEEE Expert, 1996.

[8] H.Wache "Ontology-Based Integration of Information - A Survey of Existing Approaches".IJCAI-01 Ontologies and Information Sharing Workshop." 2001.

Author Index

Lecture Notes in Artificial Intelligence (LNAI)